경찰
대학

기출문제 정복하기

영어

Preface

경찰대학은 조국, 정의, 명예라는 학훈을 바탕으로, 국가
관과 봉사정신이 투철한 신념의 경찰인 · 전문인 · 지성인
의 양성을 위해 최선을 다하고 있습니다. 1979년 경찰대
학설치법이 제정되고 1981년 제1기생이 입학한 이래
2018년 제34기 졸업생까지 현재 약 4,054명(여자 240
명)의 졸업생이 경찰인으로서 사회에서 제 역할을 다하고
있습니다. 경찰대학은 전문성이 뒷받침된 창의적 능력과
인권을 존중하고 도덕성과 경찰정신으로 무장한 전인적
핵심리더 육성을 통해, 국민이 자랑하고 세계인들이 선망
하는 세계 최고수준의 경찰교육기관으로 발돋움하고 있습
니다.

경찰대학에 적합한 인재를 선발하기 위해 실시하는 1차시
험 문제의 형식은 수능시험의 형태를 유지하는 것을 기본
으로 합니다. 난도가 상당히 높은 편이므로 기출문제를
통해 출제경향을 파악하여 이에 따라 학습하는 것이 중요
합니다.

본서는 2011학년도부터 2020학년도까지 총 10개년 기출
문제와 상세한 해설을 수록하여 수험생들의 학습에 도움
이 되도록 하였습니다.

경찰대학 진학을 위해 지금 이 시간에도 열정과 노력을
아끼지 않고 있을 수험생 여러분의 합격을 기원합니다.

Information

1. 창학이념

① 국가관과 봉사정신에 투철한 신념의 경찰인을 양성한다. : 나라와 사회의 안녕질서를 지켜온 건국/구국/호국의 경찰정신을 계승하며, 민주주의 이념을 구현하는 국가수호의 견고한 보루로서 국민의 신뢰를 받는 봉사자로, 경찰조직의 정예간부로 역사적 소명을 다하는 경찰인을 양성한다.

② 치안업무 발전에 필요한 학술의 전문적 이론과 그 응용방법을 교수, 연구한다. : 인문/사회/자연과학등 일반학 및 경찰학 이론과 응용방법을 교수/연구하여 경찰업무에 대한 창의적이고 발전지향적인 치안시책을 개발한다.

③ 시대의 역사적 상황에 슬기롭고 기민하게 대처할 수 있는 역량을 갖춘 치안행정의 전문인을 양성한다. : 격변하는 사회의 변화발전에 대응할 수 있는 경찰지식과 그 실무능력을 갖춘 전문적인 인적자원을 육성한다.

④ 지도적 인격을 갖춘 지성인을 양성한다. : 국가와 민족을 위해 인할 수 있는 성실하고 유능한 인격체를 육성하기 위하여 지적/사회적/정서적/신체적 발달 및 도덕적 성장의 조화를 이룰 수 있는 전인교육을 실시한다.

2. 교육목표

① 법치질서를 확립하고 국민에 봉사하는 민주경찰 육성

② 올바른 가치관 확립과 지도적 인격도야

③ 체계적인 학습이론과 응용방법 습득

④ 창의적이고 전문적인 경찰 실무능력 배양

3. 학훈

① 조국 : 국가보위의 파수꾼이자 겨레의 선도자로서 자신보다 국가와 국민을 먼저 생각하고 사사로움 없는 충성심으로 자랑스러운 내 조국을 지켜나간다.

② 정의 : 올바르지 않은 것은 배척하고 바른 것은 굳건히 지키는 공명정대하고 청렴결백한 경찰인이 된다.

③ 명예 : 경찰과 자신의 명예를 목숨보다 소중히 여기며 이해를 초월하여 선악과 시비를 분명히 가릴 줄 아는 지도적 인격자가 된다.

4. 비전

① 사명(교육이념) : 경찰대학은 바른 인성과 전문 역량을 바탕으로 국민에 봉사하는 인재를 양성하고, 미래 치안을 선도하는 지식을 창출함으로써 국가와 인류사회 발전에 기여한다.

② 비전

구분		내용
비전		글로벌 치안 인재와 지식의 산실
4대 분야	교육	바른 인성과 전문역량을 갖춘 글로벌 인재 양성
	연구	미래 치안지식의 선도적 창출
	사회공헌	사회 나눔 활동을 통한 공유가치 실현
	인프라	세계 일류 치안중심대학 인프라 구축

5. 졸업 후 진로

① 의무복무
- 경찰대학을 졸업 후 6년간(병역기간 포함) 경찰에 의무적으로 복무
- 의무복무를 이행하지 못할 경우에는 소정의 학비를 상환해야 함

② 병역의무
- 졸업 전 군 훈련소에서 기초 군사훈련 이수(4주)
- 졸업 후 경찰교육원에서 전술지휘과정 이수(8주)
- 의경 기동대에서 총 2년간 지휘관 또는 참모 근무로 병역의무 이행
  →2019학년도 입학생부터 폐지

③ 인사관리
- 병역의무를 마친 후 경찰서에서 2년 6개월간 순환보직 실시(여학생은 졸업 후 전술지휘과정 이수 후 순환보직 실시)
- 지구대 또는 파출소 6개월, 경찰서 수사부서(경제팀) 2년의 순환보직을 마친 후 적성, 희망, 능력 등을 고려하여 인사배치 시행

④ 승진
- 경찰관의 승진은 시험승진과 심사승진으로 이루어지며, 일정한 기간 이상(병역의무기간을 제외하고 경감은 2년, 경정은 3년)의 승진소요연수 경과 후 승진 가능
- 경정까지는 시험승진과 심사승진이 병행되며, 총경부터는 심사에 의해서만 승진

전형일정

구분		일시	장소	내용
인터넷 원서접수 (11일간)		5~6월	인터넷	• 원서 접수 대행업체 홈페이지에 접속하여 원서접수(대학 홈페이지 상단 배너) • 접수 종료 전까지 24시간 접수 ※ 특별전형 지원자는 원서접수 후 지원자격 증빙 서류 기한 내 우편접수
1차 시험	시험	7~8월	응시지구 지방경찰청 지정장소	• 지구(14개) : 서울, 부산, 대구(경북), 인천, 광주(전남), 대전, 경기, 강원, 충북, 전북, 경남, 울산, 제주, 충남 ※ 지정장소는 원서접수 후 홈페이지 공지 • 수험표, 컴퓨터용 사인펜, 신분증(주민등록증, 학생증, 운전면허증, 여권 등 사진대조 가능) 휴대
	시험문제 이의제기		인터넷	• 홈페이지 1차시험 이의 제기 코너에서 이의 접수
	합격자 발표		인터넷	• 대학 홈페이지 발표(SMS 발송) • 원서접수 홈페이지 성적 개별 확인
2차 시험	구비서류제출	8월	인편 또는 우편(등기)	• 지정일 지정시까지 도착분만 유효함 • 미제출자 불합격 처리
	체력, 인적성, 신체검사, 면접시험	8~10월	경찰대학 경찰병원	• 세부일정은 1차시험 후 홈페이지 공지 ※ 신체검사 수수료, 식비 수험생 부담
최종 합격자 발표		12월	인터넷	• 대학 홈페이지 발표(SMS 발송) ※ 최종 사정 진행에 따라 조기발표 가능
합격자 등록		다음해 1월	인터넷	• 대학 홈페이지에서 합격증 출력 및 등록표 작성 입력
1차 추가합격자 발표		1월	인터넷	• 대학 홈페이지 개별 확인, 합격증 출력
1차 추가합격자 등록			인터넷	• 대학 홈페이지에서 합격증 출력 및 등록표 작성 입력 ※ 이후 등록포기자 발생 시 개별 통지
청람교육 입교		별도 계획에 의거 홈페이지 공지	경찰대학	• 본인이 직접 입교(2주 간 합숙) ※ 미입교(퇴교)자 발생 시 추가합격 개별 통지

※ 2020학년도 모집요강을 바탕으로 작성되었습니다.

1. 모집정원

① 50명(법학과 25명, 행정학과 25명), 학과는 2학년 진학 시 결정

2. 수업연한 : 4년

3. 지원자격

① 일반 · 특별전형 공통(연령, 국적, 학력)

- 2021학년도부터 신입생 입학연령 상한 41세
- 고등학교 졸업자, 입학년도 2월 졸업예정자 또는 법령에 따라 이와 같은 수준 이상의 학력이 있다고 인정된 자

  ※ 인문 · 자연계열 구분 없이 응시 가능

② 특별전형 지원자격 : 세부사항 경찰대학 홈페이지 참조(http://www.police.ac.kr/)

4. 결격사유

① 지원자격으로 제시된 학력, 연령, 국적에 해당되지 않는 사람

② 경찰공무원법 제7조 제2항의 결격사유에 해당하는 자

  ※ 「국적법」 제11조의2 제1항에 따른 복수국적자는 청람교육 입교 전에 타국적 포기절차가 완료되어야 함

③ 학장이 정한 신체기준 또는 체력기준에 미달하는 자

5. 구비서류

① 원서접수 구비서류(대상 : 응시자 전원)

- 홈페이지에서 응시원서 접수(수수료 : 원서접수 시 고지)
- 인터넷에 게시된 양식에 따라 응시원서 작성
- 칼라사진 3.5×4.5㎝ (온라인 응시원서 작성 시 첨부파일로 첨부)

  ※ 특별전형 지원자격 증빙 서류는 경찰대학 홈페이지 참조

② 2차시험 구비서류(대상 : 1차시험 합격자)

- 신원진술서 2부(수험생 본인이 자필로 작성하고 사진 부착, 양식은 홈페이지 다운로드)
- 개인정보제공동의서 2부
- 기본증명서 1부
- 가족관계증명서 1부
- 고등학교 개인별 출결 현황 1부
- 고등학교 학교생활기록부 2부(비적용 대상자는 졸업증서나 합격증 사본을 제출하되 원본은 2차 시험 시 지참)

6. 시험내용

구분		내용			비고
1차 시험	과목	국어	수학	영어	·모집정원의 400% 선발 ·최종사정에 반영
	문항 수	45문항	25문항	45문항	
	시험시간	60분	80분	60분	
	출제형태	객관식(5지선다형) ※ 수학은 단답형 주관식 5문항 포함			
	배점 전체	100점	100점	100점	
	점 문항	2점, 3점	3점, 4점, 5점	2점, 3점	
	출제범위	대학수학능력시험과 동일			
		화법과 작문, 독서와 문법, 문학	수학Ⅱ, 미적분Ⅰ, 확률과 통계	영어Ⅰ, 영어Ⅱ	
2차 시험	신체검사, 체력시험, 인적성검사, 면접시험				·신체검사는 합격, 불합격만 결정 ·체력시험·면접시험은 합격, 불합격 결정 후 최종 사정에 반영 ·인적성검사 결과는 면접 자료로 활용
최종 사정 (1,000점)	·제1차시험 성적 : 20%(200점) ·체력시험 성적 : 5%(50점) ·면접시험 성적 : 10%(100점) ·학교생활기록부 성적 : 15%(150점) ·대학수학능력시험성적 : 50%(500점)				·학생부 3학년 1학기까지 반영 ·수능시험 표준점수 적용, 영역별 가산점 없음 ·복수지원 제한규정 미적용 ※ 최종사정 방법 참조

7. 최종사정 방법(1,000점)

① 1차시험 성적(20%) : 총점 300점을 200점으로 환산

② 체력검사 성적(5%) : 50점 만점, 20+[(평가 원점수)×3/5]로 환산

　　※ 체력조건 및 평가기준은 경찰대학 홈페이지 참조

③ 면접시험 성적(10%) : 100점 만점

항목	점수(100)	비고
인성·적격성 면접	40	·평가점수는 100점 만점으로 60점 미만 불합격 ·최종사정 성적환산 : 평가점수÷2+50
창의성·논리성 면접	30	
집단토론 면접	30	
생활태도 평가	감점제	

④ 학교생활기록부 성적(15%) : 교과 성적 135점, 출석성적 15점 만점

　　㉠ 교과성적 산출방법 : 이수단위와 석차등급(9등급)이 기재된 전과목 반영

　　　·산출공식＝135점－(5－환산평균)×5

- 환산평균＝환산총점÷이수단위 합계
- 환산총점＝과목별 단위 수×석차등급 환산점수의 합계
- 학교생활기록부 석차등급 환산점수

석차등급	1등급	2등급	3등급	4등급	5등급	6등급	7등급	8등급	9등급
점수	5점	4.5점	4점	3.5점	3점	2.5점	2점	1.5점	1점

※ 예체능 교과(우수, 보통, 미흡 3등급 평가) 제외

ⓛ 출석성적 산출방법
- 1·2학년 및 3학년 1학기까지의 결석일수를 5개 등급으로 구분

결석일수	1일 미만	1~2일	3~5일	6~9일	10일 이상
점수	15점	14점	13점	12점	11점

- 지각, 조퇴, 결과는 합산하여 3회를 결석 1일로 계산
- 질병 및 천재지변 등으로 인한 결석, 지각, 조퇴, 결과는 결석일수 계산에서 제외
- 학교생활기록부 출결사항에서 사고(무단)의 경우만 산정

ⓒ 학교생활기록부 비적용대상자의 성적 산출 방법
- 검정고시, 외국고등학교 일부 또는 전 과정 이수자, 조기졸업(예정)자, 입학년도 2월 기준 3년 전 졸업자 등에 한하여 적용
- 수능성적에 의한 비교내신으로 산출

⑤ 대학수학능력시험 성적(50%) : 국어 · 영어 · 수학 및 탐구 2과목 필수, 한국사 필수

영역	국어 · 수학 · 영어	한국사	탐구	합계
점수	각 140점	등급별 감점 여부	80점	500점

※ 제2외국어, 직업탐구는 제외

8. 남 · 여 공통 신체조건

구분	내용
체격	경찰공무원채용신체감사 및 약물검사 결과 건강상태가 양호하고 사지가 완전하며 가슴, 배, 입, 구강, 내장의 질환이 없어야 함
시력	시력(교정시력을 포함한다)은 좌우 각각 0.8 이상이어야 함
색신	색신 이상이 아니어야 함(약도색신 이상(異常)은 제외한다)
청력	정상(좌우 각각 40데시벨(db) 이하의 소리를 들을 수 있는 경우)이어야 함
혈압	고혈압(수축기 혈압이 145mmHg을 초과하거나 확장기 혈압이 90mmHg 초과) 또는 저혈압(수축기 혈압이 90mmHg을 미만이거나 확장기 혈압이 60mmHg 미만)이 아니어야 함
사시 (斜視)	검안기 측정 결과 수평사위 20프리즘 이상이거나 수직사위 10프리즘 이상이 아니어야 함(안과전문의의 정상 판단을 받은 경우는 제외한다)
문신	시술동기, 의미 및 크기가 경찰공무원의 명예를 훼손할 수 있다고 판단되는 문신이 없어야 함

Information

Q 1차 시험의 시험시간, 출제형태, 난이도 등은 어떻게 되나요?

A 시험시간은 국어 60분, 수학 80분, 영어 60분이며, 문항수는 국어 45문항, 수학 25문항, 영어 45문항입니다. 또한 각각 5지선다형이며 말하기, 듣기평가는 제외이고, 수학은 단답형 주관식 5문항이 포함됩니다. 문제의 난이도는 응시자의 수준을 고려하여 출제하므로 일반적인 시험보다 어렵다고 느끼는 학생들이 있으며, 문제형식은 가급적 수능시험형태를 유지하는 것을 기본으로 합니다.

Q 1차 시험은 어디에서 보나요?

A 1차 시험은 수험생 응시지구의 관할 지방경찰청이 지정하는 장소에서 실시되며 보통 해당 지방경찰청 소재지 내 지정학교에서 시행됩니다. 예를 들어 경기도의 경우 보통 수원에서 실시합니다. 장소는 원서접수 후 별도로 대학 홈페이지에 공지합니다.

Q 경쟁률은 어떤가요?

A 2015학년도 신입생 경쟁률은 남학생 59 : 1, 여학생 160.5 : 1입니다.

Q 경찰대학의 학과는 무엇이 있나요?

A 법학과, 행정학과 등 총 2개의 학과가 있습니다.

Q 법학과, 행정학과 구분은 어떻게 하나요?

A 신입생 모집은 학과 구분 없이 50명을 모집하며, 그 후 희망에 따라 학과지원을 받고 한쪽이 과원일 경우 성적순으로 재배분합니다. 예를 들어 행정학과 지원자 60명일 경우 초과지원자 10명은 법학과로 재배분하는데 그 기준은 입학성적순으로 하게 됩니다. 학과별 정원은 각각 25명입니다.

Q 계열별(인문계, 자연계)로 모집하거나 특혜 또는 차별이 있나요?

A 응시생의 계열과 상관없이 최종성적순에 따라 50명을 모집하며 계열에 따른 특혜나 차별은 전혀 없습니다.

Q 이과생, 실업계, 검정고시 합격자도 지원할 수 있나요?

A 문과, 이과, 실업계 고등학교 학생 모두 아무 제한 없이 지원할 수 있습니다. 물론 검정고시 합격자도 지원 가능합니다. 다만, 우리대학에서 요구하는 대학수학능력시험의 영역을 응시해야 합니다.

Q 수시모집, 편입학제도가 있는가요?, 타 대학 수시합격자도 지원가능한가요?

A 수시모집, 편입학제도는 없습니다. 따라서 모집요강에 나와 있는 절차에 따라 응시해야 합니다. 경찰대학은 특별법에 의해 설립된 대학으로 복수지원 금지규정에 해당되지 않습니다. → 2023학년도부터 편입학 도입 예정

Q 재외교포 특례입학 등 수능을 보지 않고도 입학할 수 있는 방법이 있나요?

A 경찰대학 입학을 위해서는 반드시 수학능력시험에 응시하셔야 합니다.

Q 외국어 특기, 경시대회 입상, 학생회 활동, 봉사활동, 무도단증 등에 대한 어떠한 가산점이 있나요?

A 어떤 종류에 대해서도 가산점을 부여하지 않고 있으며, 아울러 차별이나 감점도 없습니다.

Q 내신반영 과목중 비중이 더 높은 과목이 있나요?

A 전 과목 모두 반영하되 과목의 단위수가 높은 경우 그만큼 비중이 크다고 생각하면 되겠습니다. 만약 국어가 4단위이고, 생물이 2단위라고 하면 단위수가 높은 국어과목이 전체에서 더 큰 비중을 차지하게 됩니다.

Q 비교내신제는 구체적으로 어떻게 하나요?

A 수험생의 수학능력시험성적을 기준으로 상위자와 하위자, 차차상위자와 차차하위자의 점수를 표준으로 비교하여 평균된 내신성적을 산출합니다.

Contents

01 경찰대학 기출문제

02 경찰대학 정답 및 해설

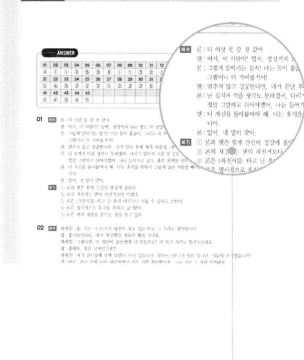

기출문제

2011학년도부터 2020학년도까지
10개년의 경찰대학 기출문제를
수록하여 실전에 완벽하게 대비할
수 있습니다

정답 및 해설

상세하고 꼼꼼한 해설을
함께 수록하여 학습효율을
확실하게 높였습니다.

기출문제 정복하기

▶ 해설은 p. 2에 있습니다.

※ 글의 흐름으로 보아, 밑줄 친 단어의 뜻으로 가장 적절한 것을 고르시오. 【01-05】

01 The colt was terrified, Separated from the group, he was vulnerable to predators. Anxiously, he walked back and forth, his head close to the ground. It looked like a sign of <u>deference</u>, almost a bow.

① hilarity   ② kindness

③ submission   ④ aggression

⑤ uncertainty

02 From that day on he specialized in the reptiles. His course included both theory and practice. In the morning there were long lectures on each aspect of the reptiles. He did not distinguish himself in these studies. He had a marvelously <u>versatile</u> gift for forgetting things.

① adaptable   ② upright

③ vested   ④ visible

⑤ dizzy

03 When the streets are slippery, every nerve and muscle of our bodies is straining to keep our balance, and the fear of falling is the most <u>exhausting</u> of all.

① fatiguing   ② inciting

③ raging   ④ invigorating

⑤ intriguing

04　By his own admission, Phillip Johnson plays "a lot of <u>obsolete</u> games." So when Johnson, supervisor of historic house restoration for the Chicago Parks and Recreation Department, walked into the cellar of the city—owned Hurst House, he had no trouble identifying a pattern of lines that someone once carved into a rock there.

① destructive   ② elaborate

③ entertaining   ④ antiquated

⑤ annoying

05　The <u>cleavage</u> between the city and the countryside is not a uniquely American idea. The great European social theorists of the nineteenth century described the social changes taking place in terms of a shift from a supportive community based on kinship to a larger, more impersonal society in which ties are based on socioeconomic interests.

① discord   ② separation

③ unison   ④ resemblance

⑤ integration

※ 글의 흐름으로 보아, 밑줄 친 부분 중 어법상 틀린 것을 고르시오. [06-11]

06　With most men the knowledge that they must ultimately die ①<u>does not weaken</u> the pleasure in being at present alive. To the poet the world ②<u>is appeared</u> still more beautiful as he gazes at flowers that ③<u>are doomed to</u> wither. The loveliness of May moves him ④<u>the more deeply</u> because he knows that it is fading even as he looks at it. It is not that the thought of universal mortality gives him pleasure, but that he cherishes the pleasure all the more dearly because he knows it cannot be ⑤<u>his</u> for long.

07 No matter what road is chosen the travelers who started from different valleys will all meet on the top of the mountain, ① provided they keep on ascending. No one must pride himself on having chosen the best route nor force his neighbor ② to follow him. Everyone takes the path which suits him best, ③ imposed by the structure of the brain, by heredity, by traditions. One can offer support, enlightenment, help. But ④ what succeeds with one may fail with others. Every man must wage his own fight ⑤ without that he cannot progress. There is no short cut to truth.

08 Of course people ① hunger for the strange and wonderful. And they can find it. And they can find it. We can sense what people thousands of miles away ② are thinking by calling them on the phone. And psychic healers ③ relieve people of despair by offering them the false hope of a better life. Authors of innumerable occult books make fortunes by peddling nonsense to ④ the gullible. even clever people ⑤ are taking in if the rational, practical alternatives are not presented.

09 Another barrier to peasant migrants to Beijing in China is city workers ① standing at the gate. Although most urban residents now enjoy services provided by migrants, urbanites ② could soon feel the cut of their competitive edge. In tough times city workers would want to reclaim ③ as their own the dirty jobs that urban administrators turn over to newcomers—road pavement, ditch digging, etc. Urban unemployment, grossly under-calculated by the government at just 2.9 percent, could soar once huge ④ state-run enterprises are privatized. Peasants will be their natural competition, and the coming conflict ⑤ hasn't been addressing.

10 In response to the wave of mergers and the ① <u>growing</u> concentration of industry in the late nineteenth century, Congress passed a bill ② <u>commonly knowing</u> as the Sherman Act. "Every contract, combination in the form of a trust or otherwise, or conspiracy in restraint of trade" ③ <u>was</u> declared illegal. It was likewise illegal to monopolize or ④ <u>attempt to monopolize trade</u>. The surge of legal activity initiated during the presidency of Teddy Roosevelt ⑤ <u>led to</u> the breakup of Standard Oil and American Tobacco Company in 1911.

11 Trevor and Patricia Janz were walking through a light snowfall in Waterton Lakes Park, Canada, when they experienced a hiker's worst nightmare—a grizzly bear mother with cubs, ① <u>feeding on</u> an animal's body. What happens next ② <u>is captured</u> in the TV program, "Deadly Encounters." The segment shows how humans con protect ③ <u>themselves</u> in the domain of the grizzly. ④ <u>Says</u> Stephen Herrero, a bear behavior expert : "If you surprise a grizzly bear and contact seems inevitable, you've got to protect your face and neck. Lie face down, put your hands behind your neck, and pretend ⑤ <u>being dead</u>."

12 밑줄 친 "these"가 가리키는 것으로 가장 적절한 것은?

One of the questions which interested the ancient Greeks was "what is the ultimate structure of matter?" Let us imagine ourselves doing what they pictured, taking a piece of matter and cutting it into smaller pieces, and then each piece into smaller pieces still. Could one go on for ever, or would one in the end arrive at bits which could not be divided any more and were the final bricks of which all matter is built? The final bits which could not be cut are called <u>these</u>. Scientists are very prone to give graphic illustrations of very small size of <u>these</u>, such as the well-known one that if a drop of water were magnified to the size of the world, <u>these</u> in it would be about as large as cricket balls.

① cells   ② units

③ atoms   ④ bacteria

⑤ essences

13 밑줄 친 "It"이 가리키는 것으로 가장 적절한 것은?

> It is a major part of administration and is concerned with helping staff use their knowledge and skill in getting the job done efficiently and well. It has been defined by Dr. Towle as "an administrative process which has as one of its purposes to contribute to staff development." Towle further explains that staff members responsible for the work of other staff have the obligation of giving leadership that results in the development of worker competence. It focuses upon helping others acquire knowledge and apply it to practice. It is a teaching-learning situation, educational as well as administrative.

① selection   ② supervision

③ promotion   ④ distribution

⑤ introduction

※ 다음 글을 읽고, 빈칸에 들어갈 말로 가장 적절한 것을 고르시오. 【14-21】

14 Chemical wastes have sometimes been dumped into a stream, put into drums and then buried, or simply abandoned in a huge chemical "graveyard." Sometimes they have been spread over deserted country roads by speeding "outlaw trucks" that simply open their valves and let the chemicals slowly spill out. Often this dumping is done by a small firm hired by the large company that has produced the chemical waste. No questions asked; the less the large firm's executives know, the better. But ignorance will no longer be a defense: Congress is now acting to make all parties _____, and to ensure that chemical wastes will be tracked from "the cradle to the grave."

① responsible   ② independent

③ innocent   ④ ready

⑤ divided

15   It is said that a first novel is usually autobiographical, in the sense that the writer puts what he knows of life and people into it. But even a twentieth novel is also to some extent a personal document. For the novelist is still writing from his personal experience. The novelist will assert that his characters are purely imaginary, but this only means that they have come out of his own imagination, his own way of thinking about people, his own understanding of them. No novelist remains completely _____.

① hidden   ② beautified

③ unrivalled   ④ under control

⑤ beyond criticism

16   To truly understand a country and its culture, you have to be part of it. That's why, at KAB, we have local banks in more countries than anyone else. all of our offices around the world are staffed by local people. It's their insight that allows us to recognize financial opportunities invisible to outsiders. But these opportunities don't just benefit our local customers. Innovations and ideas are shared throughout the KAB network, so that everyone who banks with us can benefit. Think of it as local knowledge that just happens to _____.

① aim at metropolitan areas   ② enter the next decade

③ stop being universal   ④ cover the world

⑤ return home

17   There was a gray—eyed man that I at once hoped would buy me. I knew by the way he handled me that he was used to horses. He offered to buy me, but the sum was too low, and he was refused. A very hard, loud—voiced man came after him, and I was dreadfully afraid he would have me, for he offered a better price. But the gray—eyed man stroked me, saying "Well, I think we should suit each other," and _____. "Done," said the dealer.

① he raised his bid   ② he lowered his voice

③ he cancelled his offer   ④ I roared for mercy

⑤ I suggested another deal

18 The extension of ethics, so far studied only by philosophers, is actually a process in ecological evolution. Its sequences may be described in ecological as well as in philosophical terms. An ethic, ecologically, is a limitation on freedom of action in the struggle of existence. An ethic, philosophically, is a differentiation of social form from anti-social conduct. These are two definitions of one thing. The thing has its origin in the tendency of interdependent individuals or groups to evolve modes of co-operation. The ecologist calls these symbioses. Politics and economics are advanced symbioses in which the original free-for-all competition has been replaced, in part, by _____.

① a new version of competitive activities

② recent trends in the survival of the fittest

③ co-operative mechanisms with an ethical content

④ independence of individual members from the whole groups

⑤ striking similarities between ecological ethic and philosophical one

19 Suburbia today is remarkably divers. Affluent commuter suburbs have been joined by working-class suburbs, suburbs of condominiums, and industrial-park suburbs. Historically suburbs were considered "sub" because _____. Suburban residents had to commute to the central city in order to earn their livelihood. That no longer holds ; suburbs are increasingly becoming major centers of employment. Census figures reveal that as of 1970, in the fifteen largest metropolitan areas, a full of 72 percent of workers who lived in the suburbs also worked in suburban areas. Our image of the suburbs, obviously, has not caught up with reality.

① they consisted of working-class neighbors

② they were not economically self-supporting

③ they did not have sufficient facilities for leisure

④ most people did not want to spend money in them

⑤ their landscape was different from that of the central city

20 History seeks to link the past with the future in a continuous line along which the historian himself is constantly moving. It is clear that we should not expect to extract from history any absolute judgment, either on the past or on the future. Such judgments it is not in its nature to give. All human judgment, like all human action, is involved in the logical dilemma of determinism and free will. The human being is indissolubly bound, in both his actions and his judgment, by a chain of causation reaching far back into the past; yet _____ at a given point—the present—and so alter the future.

① he is expected to refasten the chain

② he has a qualified power to break the chain

③ it is beyond his natural ability to mould a new chain

④ it is virtually impossible to lift the restrictions of the chain

⑤ he has a moral responsibility to keep away from a stronger chain

21 A close inspection of our countryside would reveal, thrown away over it, thousands of worthless refrigerator, "disposable" containers, broken toaster, mixers, microwave ovens, as well as unregulated food waste. Much of our waste problem is to be accounted for by the intentional waste problem is to be accounted for by the intentional unrepairability of the labor-savers and gadgets that we have become addicted to. This amounts to saying that much of the litter that now defaces our country is fairly directly caused by _____. We have made a social ideal of minimal involvement in the growing and cooking of food. Nevertheless, the more dependent we become on the industries of food and cooking appliances, the more waste we are going to produce. The mess the surrounds us, then, must be understood as a symptom of a greater and graver problem: the centralization of our economy, the gathering of the productive property and power into fewer and fewer hand, and the consequent destruction of the local economies of household, neighborhood, and community.

① the food industry's attempt to recycle its own products

② the excessive consumption that devours natural resources

③ the innumerable local kitchens involved in the food economy

④ the careless behavior of most people who throw away usable products

⑤ the exclusion of most of us from active participation in the food economy

22 빈칸 (A)와 (B)에 들어갈 말로 가장 적절한 것끼리 짝지은 것은?

Black women whose ancestors were brought to the United States beginning in 1619 have lived through conditions of cruelties so horrible that the women had to reinvent themselves. They had to find safety and sanctity inside themselves or they would not have been able to tolerate those tortuous lives. They had to learn to be tolerate those tortuous lives. They had to learn to be self-forgiving quickly, for often their exterior exploits were at odds with their interior beliefs. _____(A)_____ they had to survive as wholly and healthily as possible in an infectious and sick climate. Lives lived in such environment are either obliterated or forged into impenetrable alloys, _____(B)_____, early on and consciously, black women as reality became possibilities only to themselves. To others they were mostly seen and described in the abstract, concrete in their labor but surreal in their humanness.

	(A)	(B)
①	Similarly	However
②	Still	Moreover
③	Still	Thus
④	Further	Moreover
⑤	Further	However

※ 다음 (A), (B), (C)의 각 밑줄 안에서 가장 문맥에 맞는 표현을 골라 짝지은 것을 고르시오. 【23-25】

23 Rituals may serve the social function of creating temporary or permanent (A) solicitation / solidarity between people—forming a social community. We see this also in religious practices known as totemism. Totemism was particularly important in the religions of the Native Australians. Totems could be animals, plants, or geographical features. In each tribe, groups of people had particular totems. Member of each totemic group believed themselves to be (B) descendants / dissidents of their totem. They customarily neither killed nor ate it, but this taboo was lifted once a year, when people (C) assented / assembled for ceremonies dedicated to the totem.

	(A)	(B)	(C)
①	solicitation	descendants	assented
②	solicitation	descendants	assembled
③	solidarity	descendants	assembled
④	solidarity	dissidents	assembled
⑤	solicitation	dissidents	assented

24 Contrast the features of renewable energy sources with nonrenewable. Coal and oil are lifeless—thus nonrenewable—quantities. They can be divided and redivided and still the individual parts will contain the same attributes as the whole. A speck of coal is (A) little / very different in composition from a chung of coal. Nonrenewable resources represent a fixed stock. They can be easily (B) quantified / qualified. They are prone to precise measurement. They can be ordered. Renewable resources, on the other hand, are forever changing and flowing. With the solar energy, the concept of order and decay was an ever-present reminder of the ways the world unfolds. The cycles of birth, life, death, and rebirth were qualitative processes, and renewable resources are (C) hard / easy to subject to precise measurement.

(A)	(B)	(C)		(A)	(B)	(C)
① little	qualified	hard	② little	quantified	easy
③ little	quantified	hard	④ very	quantified	easy
⑤ very	qualified	easy				

25 In the black community, almost no one is complaining about the resegregation of Leland's schools. In recent months, black activists have been more focused on keeping alive the tradition of the old all-black high school. Last fall, the building's white principal wanted to replace some athletic trophies from the days before (A) integration / segregation in a display case with the work of current students. The black community was outraged. This acute nostalgia reflects a growing sense among some blacks that the cost of giving up schools that they controlled may have been greater than the benefits of integration. Before (B) resegregation / desegregation, black children's schools were woven into the fabric of the community and were a sanctuary from the racial denigration that marks life outside. (C) Resegregation / Integration changed all that, removing blacks from top policy-making positions in the schools and raising racial questions about every faculty promotion and every student disciplinary action.

	(A)	(B)	(C)
①	integration	desegregation	Integration
②	integration	resegregation	Resegregation
③	segregation	resegregation	resegregation
④	segregation	desegregation	Integration
⑤	segregation	desegregation	resegregation

26 다음 글의 밑줄 친 부분 중, 문맥상 낱말의 쓰임이 적절하지 않은 것은?

It is a ① paradox that the greatest gifts of man, the unique faculties of conceptual thought and verbal speech which have raised him to a level high above all other creatures and given him mastery over the globe, are not altogether blessings, or at least are blessings that have to be paid for very ② dearly indeed. All the great dangers threatening humanity with extinction are direct consequences of conceptual thought and verbal speech. They drove man out of the paradise in which he could follow his instincts with ③ impunity and do or not do whatever he pleased. Knowledge springing from conceptual thought robbed man of the ④ insecurity provided by his well-adapted instincts long, long before it was sufficient to provide him with an equally safe adaptation. Man is, as Amold Gehlen has so truly said, by nature a ⑤ jeopardized creature.

27 다음 글의 내용을 한 문장으로 나타낼 때, 빈칸에 들어갈 말로 가장 적절한 것은?

E-mail deepened my friendship with Ralph. Though his office was next to mine, we rarely had extended conversations because he is shy. Face to face he mumbled so, I could barely tell he was speaking. But when we both got on e-mail, I started receiving long, self-revealing messages ; we poured our hearts out to each other. A friend discovered that e-mail opened up that kind of communication with her father. He would never talk much on the phone, but they have become close since they both got online. Why, I wondered, would some men find it easier to open up on e-mail? It's a combination of the technology and the obliqueness of the written word, just as many men will reveal feeling in drabs and drabs while riding in the car or doing something, which they could never talk about sitting face to face.

*in dribs and drabs : 조금씩

In e-mail communications, people feel freer to talk because it guarantees _____.

① the freedom of selecting topics

② lengthy and informal encounters

③ a smaller amount of responsibility

④ indirect contacts with the people one writes to

⑤ manifest identities of those who send messages

28 밑줄 친 "a morality play"가 의미하는 것으로 가장 적절한 것은?

In the bullfighting, the bull is often honored and the man falls into despair. The bull is never left to die, but killed in the open, in hairsbreadth contact with a man on foot who has nothing to defend himself with except his courage and only a piece of red cloth. Yet the bullfighting tells us something. It tells us much about the love of contradiction in a race of intense individualists. It aims at an ideal of bravery and style, and falls into dullness and squalor. It is in miniature one image of life as Latin people tend to see it, a challenge to high romance always defeated by the rich and fatuous disorder of life itself. It is a morality play, that isolates, and sets against each other, the qualities which this courteous, passionate, and chivalrous people value most : which I take to be—courage, manners, pride of self cautioned by its opposite reminder that nothing is more helpful to humanity than the immediate prospect of a violent death.

① 자만과 수치를 분간하는 척도

② 윤리적 삶의 추구와 예절의 실천

③ 영웅적 삶의 품격과 이미지의 재현

④ 개인주의적 가치관에 내재된 득실의 재인식

⑤ 삶의 높은 가치 추구와 그것의 붕괴 사이의 긴장

29 다음 글의 내용을 한 문장으로 나타낼 때, 빈칸 (A)와 (B)에 들어갈 말로 가장 적절한 것끼리 짝지은 것은?

For more than a thousand years the Japanese have written the tancho, a red-crowned crane, into poems and folktales. They have painted it and made sculptures of it. They have revered it as a symbol of long life, happiness, and good luck. From its life habits they have drawn phrases and metaphors to describe their own behaviors. They imitated it and tried to dance as it dances. Most of all, they have made it into an icon and put its image everywhere, so that this extremely rare bird is, ironically, seen throughout Japan—on teacups and trays and fans, on lampposts, on wedding cards, on the back of thousand—yen notes, and the tail fins of jets.

Japanese people have a long tradition of _____(A)_____ the tancho, a red-crowned crane, and their attitude toward it is widely reflected in their _____(B)_____ lives.

	(A)	(B)
①	rearing	everyday
②	rearing	religious
③	cherishing	everyday
④	cherishing	traditional
⑤	admiring	traditional

30 다음 도표의 내용과 일치하지 않는 것은?

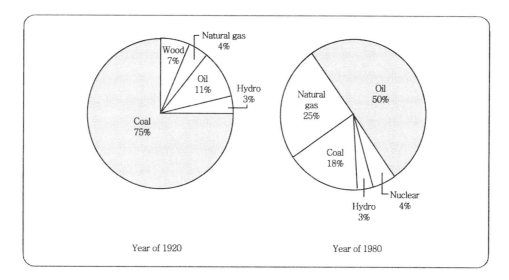

Year of 1920   Year of 1980

It is worth studying how energy sources changed during the twentieth century for finding a solution to possible energy shortage in the near future. The above graphs show how energy sources changed in America between 1920 and 1980. ①Coal was the king in the picture of energy supply, and exactly consisted of three quarters of the total energy supply in 1920. ②However, it constituted only 18 percent of the supply in 1980 and dropped to the third place from the first. ③The percentage of oil use had been more than quadrupled between 1920 and 1980 and it became the greatest energy source in 1980. ④Natural gas stepped up from the fifth to the second in 1980 and consisted exactly of a quarter of the total energy supply. ⑤In 1980, wood was dropped out of the picture, while hydropower maintained the same percentage and nuclear power was newly included.

31 Unlike its avian peers, the ostrich spawns a variety of luxury products. Start with the meat, which aficionados liken in taste to beef tenderloin. At about $20 per lb., there's a wealth of cuts to be had from the average 400-lb. bird. Ostrich meat is healthful as well : half the calories of beef, one-seventh the fat and considerably less cholesterol, and it even bests chicken and turkey in those categories. "Our customers thought we were kidding at first. Ostrich?" says a restaurant manager. "But then they became fascinated by it." One out of four diners orders the lean meat in the restaurant. Even if ostriches don't become high class cuisine, investors are hoping the big birds achieve greater fame than a spot on Sesame Street. Ostrich eyelashes are used as paintbrush bristles, feathers for dusting and hats and coats, and the thick, tough hide is prized for everything from cowboy boots to sofas.

* aficionado : 애호가

① 타조 고기는 육질이 떨어져 상품화 가능성이 낮은 편이다.
② 타조 고기는 칼로리 함유량이 쇠고기의 절반이다.
③ 타조 고기는 닭이나 칠면조 고기에 비해 콜레스테롤 함유량은 낮지만 칼로리 함유량은 높다.
④ 타조 요리는 초창기에는 식당에서 인기가 많았으나 점차 열기가 식어갔다.
⑤ 타조 깃털은 카우보이 부츠와 소파에 사용된다.

32 Long ago on the little island of Nauru, far away in the western Pacific, a happy people lived and had everything they needed there : coconut trees for food and drink, abundant bird life and an ocean full of fish. And the natives of Nauru were living on one of the richest piles of phosphate rock on the globe. Then it happened one hundred years ago that a piece of fossilized wood, carried off from Nauru to Australia as a souvenir, caught the eye of a chemist. He examined it and found it was quite valuable. for most of the 20th century, millions of tons of the phosphate were shipped to Australia and New Zealand, where they fertilized fields and farms. Following the island's independence in 1968, the phosphate mines were nationalized, and the citizens of the smallest republic in the world joined the ranks of the wealthiest. Today, however, these once self-sufficient people are caught up in a grim fairy tale. The phosphate is almost gone, and most of the money, too. The heart is dug out of four-fifths of the island.

* phosphate : 인산염, 인산 광물

① 나우루 사람들은 조상 대대로 인산염을 생계 수단으로 삼았다.
② 오스트레일리아 화학자가 검사한 인산염은 별로 가치가 없었다.
③ 오스트레일리아와 뉴질랜드로 선적된 인산염은 비료로 사용되었다.
④ 인산염이 국유화한 직후부터 나우루 사람들은 가난해졌다.
⑤ 나우루 섬에서 인산염을 채굴한 면적은 절반 정도이다.

※ 다음 글의 내용과 일치하지 않는 것을 고르시오. [33-34]

33

The first humans to give up the hunter-gatherer way of life settled down on the eastern Mediterranean coast to grow wheat and barley, then tamed sheep and goats for meat and milk, most archaeologists believe. But excavations at a 10,000-year-old village in Turkey paint a different picture. Residents of round stone houses hunted wild sheep and goats and ate nuts and legumes but also raised pigs, perhaps 500 years before the earliest known Rosenberg of the University of the University of Delaware, reveals a community that lasted several hundred years. Evidence that villagers raised pigs includes teeth that are generally smaller than those of wild pigs. Most of the pig bones came from males; females were likely spared for breeding. Methods learned in raising pigs were later applied to wild sheep and goats, Rosenberg believes.

① 대부분의 고고학자들은 Rosenberg의 발굴 결과와 다른 의견을 가지고 있다.
② Rosenberg가 발굴한 돌집에 거주했던 사람들은 양과 염소를 사냥했었다.
③ Rosenberg가 발굴한 마을은 수백 년 동안 지속되었던 것으로 밝혀졌다.
④ 돼지를 길렀다는 증거는 발견된 뼈가 야생 돼지 뼈보다 크다는 점이다.
⑤ Rosenberg는 돼지를 기르는 방법이 양과 염소에 적용되었다고 믿는다.

34 In coming years, NASA and other space agencies will intensify the search for life in the solar system. But the search is complicated by a fundamental mystery : What is life, anyway? NASA has been using a simple working definition : "Life is a self–sustained chemical system capable of undergoing Darwinian evolution." Other scientists have circulated their own definition, such as, "Life is a chemical system able to replicate itself through autocatalysis and to make mistakes that gradually increase the efficiency of the autocatalysis" Life tends to elude capture by any single definition. Maybe life, for example, doesn't have to evolve. Imagine creatures that have no information–bearing molecules like DNA. They might reproduce but not replicate. The parent would be no more biologically related to the child than to a complete stranger.

* autocatalysis : 자가 촉매작용

① Definitions of life complicate the search for life in the solar system.
② The concept of Darwinian evolution is reflected in NASA's definition of life.
③ Many scientists have their own definition of life different from that of NASA.
④ It is very difficult for a single definition to capture the nature of life.
⑤ If an organism replicates, its child is not biologically related to its parent.

35 다음 글의 주제로 가장 적절한 것은?

Some will say, so far so good. "We are mammal primates. But we have language, and the animals don't." By some definitions perhaps they don't. But they do communicate extensively, and by call systems we are just beginning to grasp. It would be a mistake to think first language and then society. Language and culture emerge from our biological–social natural existence, animals that we were / are. Language is a mind–body system that co–evolved with our needs and nerves. Like imagination and the body, language rises unbidden. It is of a complexity that eludes our rational intellectual capacities. All attempts at scientific description of natural languages have fallen short of completeness, as the descriptive linguists readily confess, yet the child leans the mother tongue early and has virtually mastered it by six.

① 인간과 동물의 언어적 차이
② 인류의 정신문화가 반영된 언어
③ 동물 언어의 신경학적 접근 가능성
④ 언어 습득 과정에 대한 분석적 접근의 유용성
⑤ 생물학적 자연 상태와 연관된 인간 언어의 이해

36 다음 글의 요지로 가장 적절한 것은?

Scholars have often wondered exactly why the notion of unlimited progress by human beings took hold. The answer is to be found in their development of skill to secure the energy base. A gigantic, seemingly endless stock of solar energy—3 billion years' worth, to be precise—was there from the beginning. But we gradually have had all the energy we needed to replace the sun and would never again have to wait for nature to take its course. The concept of time, then, was changed : It became equivalent to a function of how fast we could harness the stored energy that lay deep in the coal seams and oil reservoirs. We could make the sun stay out twice as long if we chose, because we were dealing with the "stored sun"—sun that we could take out of the ground and manipulate at will. With these energy resources people became increasingly convinced that they were no longer dependent upon nature, and that they could reorder the world to their own making.

① 대체에너지 개발이 시급하다.
② 태양에너지는 언젠가 소멸할 것이다.
③ 문명의 발달은 무한히 지속될 수 있다.
④ 태양열 발전을 통해 환경 친화적 문명 발전을 이룰 수 있다.
⑤ 에너지 개발을 통하여 인간은 자연의 지배로부터 점차로 벗어났다.

※ 다음 글에서 전체의 흐름과 관계가 없는 것을 고르시오. 【37-38】

37

If the moon can stir the oceans, why not the blood of humans? We are, after all, more than 60 per cent water ourselves. Perhaps tides within our blood cause an ebb and flow in our emotions and self-control. ① Shakespeare sensed some truth in this, charging tat the moon "makes men mad." ② And, in fact, that was the claim of the man who served as a model for Mr. Hyde in Robert Louis Stevenson's Strange Case of Dr Jekyll and Mr Hyde—he blamed his crimes on moon-induced lunacy. ③ Some observations also support the notion, suggesting that violent crime increases under a full moon : as the moon waxes, ice hockey players were said to spend more time in the penalty box, while casualty departments gear up for busier times. ④ and the moon's regular appearance through our skies—29 days, 12 hours and 44 minutes from one new moon to the next—is a comforting constant. ⑤ Still, there's no denying the restlessness some of us feel beneath the moon—the sudden desire to climb mountains, cower in the shadows or just rear up and howl.

38 All intentional actions which we perform enjoy a certain latitude. ① Our intention applies as a rule only to the what and not so much to th how. ② Whether I want to lift the receiver of the telephone or put the key into the lock, I always gratefully rely on my eyes, which guide the hand to its target and save me the effort of groping, because any false movement is immediately corrected by visual control. ③ In the language of engineers this kind of interaction is known as feedback. ④ Engineers' words are always concise and precise in order to communicate ideas without any confusion. ⑤ On the whole we may say that the intention determines the what and the feedback the how. It is the character of this interaction which enables humans to deal with the environment effectively.

39 다음 글에서 추론할 수 있는 것으로 가장 적절한 것은?

You are sharpest in your 20's, around 30, memory begins to decline, particularly your ability to perform mathematical computations. But our I.Q. for other tasks climbs. Your vocabulary at age 45, for example, is three times as great as when you graduated from college. At 60, your brain possesses almost four times as much information as it did at age 21. Though the peak in most fields comes early—most Nobel prize winners did their top research in their late 20's and 30's, and most of the great music was written by men between 33 and 39—some people continue to produce quality work throughout their lives. At 71, Tolstoi completed Resurrection ; Voltaire wrote his marvelous satire Candide at 64. Will Durant began to write five volumes of the monumental History of a Civilization when he was 69.

① Memory loss does not affect the well-conditioned body.

② Aged women tend to be better at figures than aged men.

③ Life has certain achievement patterns, but it has some exceptions.

④ People can have only one prime period in their lives, so don't miss it.

⑤ There are times in which the balance between loss and gain is broken.

40 While the students can decode and even become fluent oral readers, they do not truly comprehend the materials; they cannot read between the lines, infer meaning, or detect the author's bias, among other things. Reading is much more complex than simply mastering phonemic awareness and alphabet recognition. It is an incredibly complex psycholinguistic activity involving not only letter sounds, but also comprehension in all its facets, adjusting reading for varying purposes, literary appreciation, and most importantly, authentic and lifelong application. Plus, reading requires having a purpose for applying the skills. Am I reading this for pleasure or to prepare for a test, for example? Finally little of this complete knowledge will be engaged if the student is not interested, motivated, or enjoying the experience. Learning to read is hard work and takes energy and concentration. If it does not seem fun to children, it is difficult to sustain their interest.

① Reading as a Complex Activity Rather Than Just Decoding
② Keeping a Delicate Balance Between Coding and Decoding
③ Caught in a Trap While Reading Between the Lines
④ Experiential Approach to Teaching Reading Skills
⑤ Pleasure and Hardship of Learning Experience

41 Gardens are short-lived in the chill of Flin Flon, a small mining town in Canada. But now residents of this mining town enjoy fresh fruits and roses year-round. The bounty grows 1,170 feet beneath the surface in what was a vacant chamber of a copper and zinc mine. The experiment was conceived by Wayne Fraser and Brent Zettle of Prairie Plant Systems Inc. to test the quality, yield, and cost of subterranean gardening. "The chamber is totally isolated from the surface, so the environment can be controlled cheaply and accurately," Zettle says. The mine installed high-intensity lights, a drip irrigation system, and computers. "Woody plants grow at a phenomenal rate," notes Zettle. Three months after planting, 80 rose plants produced 1,100 flowers, instead of the normal 700. The results are sold in local markets. Miners take great pride in their garden.

① A Shady Side of Mines
② Roses Bloom Deep in a Mine
③ A heart Warmed in the Chill
④ A Miner's Love of Wild Flowers
⑤ A Prosperous Local Market for Miners

42 주어진 글 다음에 이어질 글의 순서로 가장 적절한 것은?

Spend a day among elephants, and you will come away mystified. Sudden, silent, synchronous activities—a herd taking a flight for no apparent or audible reason, a mass of scattered animals simultaneously raising ears and freezing in the track—such events demand explanation, but none is forthcoming.

(A) It turned out that the elephants, like the organ pipe, were the source of the throbbing. Elephants communicate with one another by means of calls too low pitched for human beings to hear.

(B) Some unknown capacity beyond memory and the five senses seems to inform elephants, silently and from a distance, of the whereabouts and activities of other elephants.

(C) Only later did a thought occur to me : As a young choir girl in New York, I used to stand next largest deepest organ pipe in the church. When the organ blasted out the bass line in a Bach chorale, the whole chapel would throb, just as the elephant room did at the zoo.

(D) I stumbled on a possible clue to these mysteries during a visit to a zoo in Portland, Oregon. While observing three Asian elephant mothers and their new calves, I repeatedly noticed a palpable throbbing in the air like distant thunder, yet all around me was silent.

① (A)−(C)−(B)−(D)

② (B)−(A)−(D)−(C)

③ (B)−(D)−(C)−(A)

④ (C)−(B)−(A)−(D)

⑤ (C)−(D)−(B)−(A)

The majority of persons, if asked what were the uses of dust, would reply that they did not know it had any, but they were sure it was a great nuisance. It is true that dust, in our towns and in our houses, is often not only a nuisance, but a serious source of disease, sometimes resulting in total blindness. Dust, however, is only matter in the wrong place, and whatever injurious or disagreeable effects it produces are largely due to our own dealing with nature. If we adopt purely mechanical means of conveyance, we can almost wholly abolish disease-bearing dust from our streets ; while another kind of dust, that is caused by the imperfect burning of coal, may be got rid of with equal facility if we consider pure air and sunlight to be of more importance to the population as a whole than are the prejudices or the interests of those who produce the smoke. But though we can minimize the dangers and the inconveniences arising from dust, we cannot wholly abolish it, and _____, since it has now been discovered that it is to the presence of dust we owe much of the beauty, and perhaps even the very habitability, of the earth we live upon. Were it not for dust, we could not admire the blue sky or the gorgeous tints seen at sunset and sunrise not only in the atmosphere but on the clouds near the horizon.

43 위 글의 빈칸에 들어갈 말로 가장 적절한 것은?

① we are very busy searching for the ways to do so

② we will be easily forgetful of having done so

③ it is one of our greatest missions to do so

④ it is indeed fortunate we cannot do so

⑤ no one knows how to avoid doing so

44 위 글의 내용과 일치하는 것은?

① 먼지가 쓸모 있다는 점이 널리 알려져 있다.

② 먼지는 질병과 실명의 원인이 될 수 있다.

③ 석탄의 불완전 연소에 의한 먼지는 제거될 수 없다.

④ 질병을 옮기는 먼지는 제거될 수 없다.

⑤ 먼지 때문에 지구의 아름다움을 음미할 수 없다.

(A) Government programs such as Comprehensive Employment and Training Act (CETA), which provide jobs for the unemployed might be made more ambitious. The government might act as the employer of _____. That is, the government might stand ready to provide jobs to all those who want work but are unable to find it in the private sector.

(B) On the other side, opponents object that such a program would be expensive. Just how expensive was indicated during 1977–1978, when the new Carter administration more than doubled the size of Public Service Employment Programs to 725,000 jobs, at a cost of $8.4 billion. That works out to more than $11,500 per job. The average worker got considerably less than that–about $7,200 Part went into administration and supporting services.

(C) Proposals to make the government _____ are controversial. (Because of opposition, those provisions were dropped from later versions of the Humphrey–Hawkins bill. And President Reagan suggested that CETA be eliminated by the end of 1983.) On the positive side, government projects might give the unemployed something useful to do. For example, the unemployed might do maintenance jobs in the cities and carry out public works projects similar to those of Roosevelt's recovery program in the 1930s.

(D) Although the government has no such commitment to provide jobs for those who are rejected by private companies, a closely related proposal was included in the original 1976 draft of the Humphrey–Hawkins bill. That bill would have committed the government to offer whatever jobs were needed to get the unemployment rate down to a target of 3 percent per year.

45 위 글에서 (A)에 이어질 내용을 순서에 맞게 배열한 것으로 가장 적절한 것은?

① (B)－(D)－(D)　　　　　② (C)－(B)－(D)

③ (C)－(D)－(B)　　　　　④ (D)－(B)－(C)

⑤ (D)－(C)－(B)

46 빈칸에 공통으로 들어갈 말로 가장 적절한 것은?

① public loan　　　　　② last resort

③ optimal condition　　　④ short supply

⑤ security check

47 위 글의 제목으로 가장 적절한 것은?

① Today's Tough Job Market Situations
② Necessary Conditions for Full Employment
③ Controversial Government Employment
④ Official Guidelines for Government Employment
⑤ History of Employment-related Legislation

48 다음 글에서 필자가 주장하는 바로 가장 적절한 것은?

> Citizens ought to begin a movement, one that will take years, to inject the public trust notion into federal and state land and wildlife statutes. The responsible agencies are trustees, and the law ought to say so in forceful terms. What matters about the public trust doctrine is not just whether the courts will enforce it, but whether the trust can become a working part of federal and state policy. We must press the agencies to acknowledge the trusteeship and its high duties as a matter of administrative policy. Officials in the federal land agencies ought to say, with force and pride, "Yes, we are trustees of the nation's wonders." Those kinds of pronouncements will help set higher standards and create a climate for principled actions.

① 민간 기업에 야생지역 보호를 위탁해야 한다.
② 공공 기관의 야생지역 관리 정책은 재검토 되어야 한다.
③ 시민들이 직접 관리해야 야생지역이 효과적으로 보존될 수 있다.
④ 야생보호 시민운동이 제대로 진행될 수 있도록 공공기관이 지도해야 한다.
⑤ 야생지역 관리 임무가 자신에게 위탁된 것임을 관리기관이 자각하게 해야 한다.

I was eight years old and a tomboy. I had a cowboy hat, cowboy boots, checkered shirt and pants, all red. My playmates were my brothers, two and four years older than I. My parents decided to buy my brothers guns. These were not "real" guns. They shot "BBs," copper pellets that my brother said would kill birds. Because I was a girl, I did not get a gun. Instantly I was relegated to the position of Indian. Now there appeared a great distance between us. They shot at everything with their new guns. I tried to keep up with my bow and arrows. Then I felt an incredible blow in my right eye. I looked out just in time to see my brother lower his gun. I remember the accident now : I confront for the first time, consciously, the meaning of the doctor's words years ago : "Eyes are sympathetic. If one is blind, the other will likely become blind too." I realize I have dashed about the world madly, looking at this, looking at that, storing up images against the fading of the light. Then, the gratitude that I have still maintained my sight for over twenty-five years sends me literally to my knees. Word after word comes—which is perhaps how one prays.

*pellet : 작은 총알

49 위 글의 내용과 일치하지 않는 것은?

① 여덟 살 때 나는 카우보이 복장을 한 말괄량이 소녀였다.
② 오빠들이 BB총알을 사용하는 총을 갖게 된 후에 나는 인디언 역할을 했다.
③ 내가 눈에 상처를 입은 것을 보고나서 오빠들은 가해자를 찾아 나섰다.
④ 한 쪽 눈을 실명한 이후 나는 많은 것들을 보고 기억에 저장하려 했다.
⑤ 한 쪽 눈의 시력을 상실하면 다른 쪽 눈도 실명할 수 있다고 의사가 말했다.

50 위 글에 나타난 필자의 현재 심경으로 가장 적절한 것은?

① apologetic   ② regretful
③ reserved   ④ appreciative
⑤ absent-minded

02 | 2012학년도 기출문제

▶ 해설은 p. 20에 있습니다.

※ 글의 흐름으로 보아 밑줄 친 단어의 뜻으로 가장 적절한 것을 고르시오. 【01-06】

01 For years, concerns about the health effects of cellphones have been largely dismissed because the radio frequency waves emitted from the devices are believed to be <u>benign</u>. Cellphones emit non-ionizing radiation, waves of energy that are too weak to break chemical bonds or to set off the DNA damage known to cause cancers.

① harmless   ② vibrating

③ potent   ④ transmitting

⑤ cancerous

02 The Gods had condemned Sisyphus to ceaselessly rolling a rock to the top of a mountain, whence the stone would fall back of its own weight. They had thought with some reason that there is no more dreadful punishment than <u>futile</u> and hopeless labor.

① repetitive   ② fruitless

③ detestable   ④ toilsome

⑤ disciplinary

03 Artists past and present understand that manual facility is <u>inextricably</u> bound to observational prowess, and vice versa. In fact, many believe that what the hand cannot draw, the eye cannot see.

① unduly   ② inescapably

③ undeservedly   ④ incompetently

⑤ incomprehensively

04 The government is working on a plan for a limited form of <u>mandatory</u> identification. Under a law being prepared, identification would have to be carried in certain situations, such as when applying for a job.

① portable   ② impeccable
③ makeshift   ④ simplified
⑤ obligatory

05 There are no potholes in the streets of Tucson, Arizona, just "pavement deficiencies." There are no more poor people, just "<u>fiscal</u> underachievers." There was no robbery of an automatic teller machine, just an "unauthorized withdrawal." And the doublespeak goes on. Doublespeak is language that makes the negative appear positive, the unpleasant appear attractive or at least tolerable.

① financial   ② actual
③ academic   ④ physical
⑤ modest

06 Smells can lift our spirits, calm us, and maybe even help us lose weight. Some odors can <u>repulse</u> us, too, and for good reason: They can tell us that gas is leaking, the milk is sour or the meat is spoiled.

① attract   ② invigorate
③ repel   ④ replenish
⑤ rebuke

07 One of the most peculiar public health hazards—epidemic fainting at pop-music concerts—is a phenomenon familiar to ① legions of adolescents. Their parents may ② be less aware of the threat, which has barely engaged the attention of modern science despite decades of documentation that many a fan ③ are prone to unconsciousness. ④ Concerned that the mechanism of mass fainting had been neglected in the medical literature, two German physicians recently braved a concert by New Kids on the Block and worked with first-aid staff at a Red Cross infirmary where ⑤ the stricken were treated. According to the doctors' report in the Thursday issue of The New England Journal of Medicine, some 400 concertgoers fainted, all of them girls aged 11 to 17.

08 Families are the people ① whom it matters if you have a cold, are feuding with your mate or training a new puppy. Family members use magnets ② to fasten the newspaper clipping about your bowling team on the refrigerator door. They save your drawings and homemade pottery. They like to hear stories ③ about when you were young. They'll help you can tomatoes or change the oil in your car. They're the people who will come and visit you in the hospital, will talk to you when you call with a "dark night of the soul" and will ④ loan you money to pay the rent if you lose your job. ⑤ Whether or not they are biologically related to each other, the people who do these things are family.

09 When the mammals ① evolved out of the reptiles, their brains began to change. First, they developed a new package of instincts, related to the reptilian instincts for sex and procreation, but ② modifying for the special needs of a mammalian lifestyle. Chief among these was the instinct for parental care of the young. Here was ③ a revolutionary advance over the behavior of reptile parents, for whom ④ the newly hatched young provided a tasty snack if they could catch them. But the reptile young were prepared to fight for their lives; they came into the world with all the needed programs of action ⑤ wired into their brain. These hatchlings were miniature adults from the moment of birth. On the other hand, the young mammals arrived in a helpless and vulnerable state, and parental affection was essential for their survival. That is why mammals developed the new instincts for parental care.

10 Still no one knows who he was. But scientists are now certain of one thing about the naturally mummified Alpine Iceman, ① whom hikers discovered in September 1991 in the melting ice on the Austrian-Italian border at an elevation of 10,530 feet. In the first genetic analysis of the body, they determined that he was European born and bred, closely ② related to modern northern and alpine Europeans. Scientists said this finding should lay to rest lingering suspicions of a hoax. An international research team, writing in the journal Science, said the genetic findings made the possibility of fraud ③ highly unlikely. Among the most recent results of their research ④ is a descriptive inventory of alpine fashions in those remote times. Scientists may not be able to account for the man's presence on the mountain crest, but they know ⑤ that he was wearing, down to his underwear.

11 Grandmother and I lived beside the plaza in a one-room house. It was composed of a traditional fireplace, a makeshift cabinet, and a wooden crate that held our two buckets of all-purpose water. At the far end of the room ① were two rolls of bedding we used as comfortable sitting "couches." ② Consisted of thick quilts, sheepskin, and assorted blankets, these bed rolls were undone each night. A wooden pole, the length of one side of the room, ③ was suspended about 10 inches from the ceiling beams. A dresser, which was traded for some of grandmother's pottery, held the few articles of clothing we owned. Grandmother always had a flour sack filled with candy and store-bought cookies. ④ Tucked securely in my blankets, I listened to one of her stories or accounts of how it was when she was a little girl. These accounts ⑤ seemed so old-fashioned compared to the way we lived.

12

밑줄 친 it이 의미하는 것으로 가장 적절한 것은?

Closely related to the societal customs of touching are those of spatial relationships. Anthropologists tell us that each of us walks around inside "bubbles of personal space." The size of the bubble represents our personal territory, territorial imperatives, or "personal buffer zones." We neither like nor tolerate it when someone invades our bubbles. We become distinctly uncomfortable. But as we travel to different places around the world, we learn that some cultural bubbles are larger or smaller than others.

① feeling uncomfortable   ② walking inside the bubble

③ the size of the bubble   ④ someone's invasion of our bubbles

⑤ our personal territory

13

밑줄 친 this가 의미하는 것으로 가장 적절한 것은?

People often show this—even when doing so means contradicting their own perceptions of the world. A major reason for this is to gain the approval or avoid the disapproval of other people. We often want others to accept us, like us, and treat us well. In growing up, people often learn that one way to get along with a group is to go along with group standards. In deciding how to dress for the senior prom, we may try to wear the right clothes so that we will fit in, give a good impression, and avoid disapproval. We may not really like wearing formal clothes, but do it anyway because it's socially appropriate for the occasion. When we're with our weight-conscious friends, we may eat salads and health foods even though we don't especially like them; when we're alone, we're more likely to follow our personal preferences by eating hamburgers and fries. In such situations, this leads to an outward change in public behavior, but not necessarily to a change in the individual's private opinions.

① authority   ② conformity

③ obstinacy   ④ independence

⑤ dominance

14 Most men think of themselves as average-looking. Being average does not bother them ; average is fine, for men. This is why men never ask anybody how they look. Their primary form of beauty care is to shave themselves, which is essentially the same form of beauty care that they give to their lawns. Women do not look at themselves this way. If I had to express, in three words, what I believe most women think about their appearance, those words would be : "not good enough." No matter how attractive a woman may appear to be to others, when she looks at herself in the mirror, she thinks : woof. Why do women have such _____? There are many complex psychological and societal reasons, by which I mean Barbie. Girls grow up playing with a doll proportioned such that, if it were human, it would be seven feet tall and weigh 81 pounds.

① low self-esteem
② femininity
③ high pride
④ reflection
⑤ appearance

15 If we accept that we cannot prevent science and technology from changing our world, we can at least try to ensure that the changes they make are in the right directions. In a democratic society, this means that the public needs to have a basic understanding of science, so that it can make informed decisions and not leave them in the hands of experts. At the moment, the public has a rather _____ attitude toward science. It has come to expect the steady increase in the standard of living that new developments in science and technology have brought to continue, but it also distrusts science because it has no clear understanding of science.

① ambivalent
② hostile
③ sympathetic
④ amphibious
⑤ amorphous

16 My father vehemently opposed my decision to work part-time during the school year at a local grocery store. He wanted me to stop pushing myself and to save work for later life. I agreed with him that quitting my job would have obvious advantages, but I also knew that there were other advantages to working that _____. For example, I enjoy the independence that comes with having my own income, small as it is. His lack of approval has made me angry, but I have listened to his objections, and we have again been able to reach a compromise. I have agreed to quit work at the first sign that I am pushing myself too hard or that my schoolwork is suffering. As a result, both his anger and mine have been effectively dissolved.

① interfered with my independence

② significantly contributed to my schoolwork

③ initially consolidated our relationship

④ eventually opposed my views

⑤ outweighed the disadvantages

17 The theory of Multiple Intelligences(MI) challenges traditional ideas about intelligence. It also questions the value of intelligence tests. MI researchers point out that traditional teaching and testing focus only on two of the seven kinds of intelligences that people possess – language and logic skills. So children who don't learn in a style that depends on language and logic are called inadequate. However, according to Thomas Armstrong, author of Seven Kinds of Smart, the children are fine but the teaching methods are inadequate. "In traditional education, we try to get students to learn in our way. On the contrary, we need to remake the way we teach so that _____," he explains. "We need to recognize that different children learn in different ways and that all ways of learning are okay. Then we will really be in the business of education," he adds.

① it can fit students

② they can answer questions better

③ we can choose our own teaching methods

④ they can develop language and logic skills

⑤ learning theories can contribute to education

18 To begin with, it was not the hapless victims of the Nazis who named their incomprehensible and totally unmasterable fate the "holocaust." It was the Americans who applied this artificial and highly technical term to the Nazi extermination of the European Jews. But while the event when named as mass murder most foul evokes the most immediate, most powerful revulsion, when it is designated by a rare technical term, we must first in our minds translate it back into emotionally meaningful language. Using technical or specially created terms instead of words from our common vocabulary is one of the best-known and most widely used distancing devices, _____. Talking about the "holocaust" permits us to manage it intellectually where the raw facts, when given their ordinary names, would overwhelm us emotionally — because it was catastrophe beyond comprehension, beyond the limits of our imagination.

① separating the technical from the intellectual terms
② separating the technical from the incomprehensible terms
③ separating the common from the comprehensible terms
④ separating the ordinary from the intellectual experience
⑤ separating the intellectual from the emotional experience

※ 빈칸 (A)와 (B)에 들어갈 말로 가장 적절한 것을 고르시오. 〔19-22〕

19 Because reading demands complex mental manipulations, a reader is required to concentrate far more than a television viewer. An audio expert notes that "with the electronic media it is openness that counts. Openness permits auditory and visual stimuli more direct access to the brain." It may be that a predisposition toward (A) _____, acquired, perhaps, through one's reading experience, makes one an inadequate television watcher. But it seems far more likely that the reverse situation obtains : that a predisposition toward (B) _____, acquired through years and years of television viewing, has influenced adversely viewers' ability to concentrate, to read, to write clearly.

(A)	(B)
① concentration	involvement
② concentration	openness
③ manipulation	involvement
④ manipulation	closeness
⑤ stimulation	openness

20 Many people, both teens and adults, think that multitasking is the best way to accomplish a lot in a small amount of time. But scientific evidence says this isn't true. "When people try to perform two or more related tasks, either at the same time or quickly switching back and forth between them, they do a worse job on both of them," says David E. Meyer, director of the Brain, Cognition, and Action Laboratory at the University of Michigan. "They make more errors and it takes them much longer than if they worked on the tasks (A) _____." He says it can take up to 400 percent longer to do a homework assignment if you're trying to do something else at the same time. Why is this? The human brain is simply not wired to process more than one complex task at a time. What your brain does instead is (B) _____ tasks. So if you're listening to music and reading a book, your brain will concentrate on the music, and when that's finished, it will focus on taking in the information from the book. "But it takes a lot of mental energy for your brain to keep reorienting itself back to each task," Meyer says. The result is that neither task is done efficiently.

(A)	(B)
① simultaneously	prioritize
② sequentially	prioritize
③ sequentially	perform
④ randomly	alienate
⑤ randomly	perform

21 Television's contribution to family life has been an equivocal one. For while it has, indeed, kept the members of the family from (A)_____, it has not served to bring them together. By its domination of the time families spend together, it destroys the special quality that distinguishes one family from another, a quality that depends to a great extent on what a family does, what special rituals, game, recurrent jokes, familiar songs, and shared activities it accumulates. Yet parents have accepted a television-dominated family life so completely that they cannot see how the medium is involved in whatever problems they might be having. Even when families make efforts to control television, too often its very presence (B)_____ the positive features of family life.

	(A)	(B)
①	gathering	maintains
②	gathering	counterbalances
③	dispersing	enhances
④	dispersing	counterbalances
⑤	wavering	enhances

22 The nineteenth-century American philosopher Henry David Thoreau was famous for saying, "Simplify, simplify." Unfortunately, the trend these days seems to be "complicate, complicate" instead. Many people are working longer hours, spending more money, and getting in more debt than ever before. They are also relaxing less and spending less time with family and friends. (A)_____, there is also a trend toward voluntary simplicity. People in the voluntary simplicity movement take various steps to make their lives both simpler and more enjoyable. Some people work fewer hours each week. Others plant a vegetable garden; this gives them fresh air, exercise, and time with their families —not to mention organic produce. Still others try to buy less; they stop buying unnecessary items. (B)_____, the priority for people in the voluntary movement is to follow Thoreau's suggestion : simplify.

	(A)	(B)
①	Furthermore	Besides
②	Furthermore	In short
③	Therefore	Besides
④	However	Similarly
⑤	However	In short

※ (A), (B), (C)에 들어갈 말로 가장 적절한 것을 고르시오. 【23-25】

23 If ignorance about the nature of pain is widespread, ignorance about the way pain-killing drugs work is even more so. What is not generally understood is that many of the vaunted pain-killing drugs (A) conceal/reveal the pain without correcting the underlying condition. They (B) awaken/deaden the mechanism in the body that alerts the brain to the fact that something may be wrong. The body can pay a high price for (C) suppression/release of pain without regard to its basic cause.

(A)	(B)	(C)
① conceal	awaken	suppression
② reveal	deaden	release
③ conceal	awaken	release
④ reveal	awaken	release
⑤ conceal	deaden	suppression

24 How do geniuses come up with ideas? What links the thinking style that produced Mona Lisa with the one that (A) spawned/followed the theory of relativity? What can we learn from the thinking strategies of the Galileos, Edisons, and Mozarts of history? For years, scholars tried to study genius by analyzing statistics. In 1904, Havelock Ellis noted that most geniuses were fathered by men older than 30, had mothers younger than 25, and usually were sickly children. However, other researchers reported that many were celibate (Descartes), fatherless (Dickens), or motherless (Darwin). In the end, the data illuminated (B) something/nothing. Academics also tried to measure the links between intelligence and genius. But they found that run-of-the-mill* physicists had IQs much higher than Nobel Prize winner and extraordinary genius Richard Feynman, whose IQ was a merely (C) respectable/respectful 122. Genius is not about mastering 14 languages at the age of seven or being especially smart. Creativity is not the same as intelligence.

*run-of-the-mill : 평범한

(A)	(B)	(C)
① spawned	something	respectful
② spawned	nothing	respectable
③ spawned	nothing	respectful
④ followed	something	respectable
⑤ followed	nothing	respectful

25 Scientists are beginning to uncover evidence that meditation has a (A) negligible/tangible effect on the brain. Skeptics argue that it is not a practical way to try to deal with the stresses of modern life. But the long years when adherents were unable to point to hard science to support their belief in the technique may finally be coming to an end. When Carol Cattley's husband died, it (B) tackled/triggered a relapse of the depression which had not plagued her since she was a teenager. Carol sought medical help and managed to control her depression with a combination of medication and a psychological treatment called Cognitive Behavioral Therapy (CBT) which primarily consists of meditation. One of the (C) opponents/pioneers of CBT, Professor Mark Williams from the Department of Psychiatry at the University of Oxford, describes CBT as 80% meditation and 20% cognitive therapy.

(A)	(B)	(C)
① negligible	tackled	pioneers
② negligible	triggered	opponents
③ negligible	triggered	pioneers
④ tangible	triggered	pioneers
⑤ tangible	tackled	pponents

26 다음 글의 밑줄 친 부분 중, 문맥상 낱말의 쓰임이 적절하지 않은 것은?

Experts disagree about how serious our population and environmental problems are and what we should do about them. Some suggest that ① human ingenuity and technological advances will allow us to clean up pollution to acceptable levels and find substitutes for any scarce resources. They are called technological optimists, who argue that technological innovations can preserve the earth's natural resources. Many leading ② environmental scientists disagree. They appreciate and applaud the significant environmental and social progress that we have made, but they also cite evidence that we are ③ upgrading the earth's life-support systems in many parts of the world at an exponentially accelerating rate. They call for much more action to protect ④ the natural capital that supports our economies and all life. They are called environmental pessimists, who argue that our environmental situations are getting worse and global economy is ⑤ outgrowing the capacity of the earth to support it.

27 다음 글의 주제로 가장 적절한 것은?

The enormous outpouring of concern over juvenile delinquency in the 50's presented the movie industry with dangerous but lucrative possibilities. An aroused public of parents, youth-serving agencies, teachers, adolescents, and law enforcers constituted a huge potential audience for delinquency films at a time when general audiences for all films had declined. Yet this was a perilous subject to exploit, for public pressure on the film industry to set a wholesome example for youth remained unremitting. Moreover the accusation that mass culture caused delinquency was the focus of much contemporary attention. If the film industry approached the issue of delinquency, it had to proceed cautiously. It could not present delinquency favorably; hence all stories would have to be set in the moral firmament of the movie Code. Yet to be successful, films had to evoke sympathy from young people who were increasingly intrigued by the growing youth culture of which delinquency seemed to be one variant.

① the filming environments in the 50's
② challenges for the juvenile delinquency films in the 50's
③ the moral principles of juvenile delinquency films in the 50's
④ the rise and demise of juvenile delinquency films in the 50's
⑤ juvenile delinquency films as a lucrative business in the 50's

28 밑줄 친 "demon"이 의미하는 것으로 가장 적절한 것은?

In late October, I began rehearsal for a play. The rehearsal schedule was not rigorous at first, and did not rule my life. But it was there and the demon assured me I had nothing to worry about. I was persuaded because the January deadline was still a long way off. It was not long into rehearsal when the other, smaller deadlines began to creep up and rear their ugly heads, and paper after paper after test struck me unmercifully. It was almost Christmas and the responsibilities of shopping allied themselves with my academic obligations and thrashed me mercilessly while the demon chuckled, knowing that the real deadline would be painful to meet. I began the ordeal that would increase my misery daily until when the real deadline was met. I cursed the demon, loudly at first. However, I think I learned from this experience that all I need to do is seize the deadline in the distance and never shall the demon haunt me again.

① competitiveness
② obsession
③ procrastination
④ agitation
⑤ fastidiousness

29 다음 글의 내용을 한 문장으로 나타낼 때, 빈칸에 들어갈 말로 가장 적절한 것은?

If the language of literary work is quite straightforward and simple, this may be helpful but is not in itself the most crucial yardstick in choosing literary works for foreign language learning. Interest, appeal, and relevance are all more important. In order for us to justify the additional time and effort which will undoubtedly be needed for readers to come to grips with a work of literature in a language not their own, there must be some special incentives involved: enjoyment, suspense, and a fresh insight into issues which are felt to be close to the heart of people's concerns. All these are incentives which can lead readers to overcome enthusiastically the linguistic obstacles that might be considered too great in less involving material.

⇓

The crucial factor in choosing literary works for foreign language learning is not just the level of language but whether the works _____.

① help the readers learn to overcome linguistic obstacles

② tell the readers something about fundamental human issues

③ justify the readers' time and effort spent reading them

④ provide a fresh insight into foreign language learning

⑤ stimulate the readers' involvement by providing incentives

30 다음 도표의 내용과 일치하지 않는 것은?

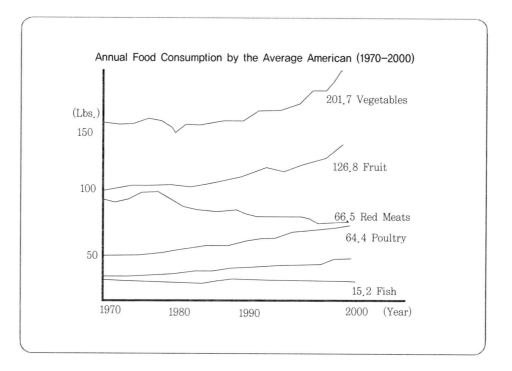

Annual Food Consumption by the Average American (1970-2000)

The graph above shows the changes in the amount of the consumption of different foods during the period ranging from 1970 to 2000. ① The consumption of vegetables and fruits increased more than 20 percent during the 30 year span. ② The difference between red meats and poultry consumption was minimized in the year 2000. ③ The consumption of cheese had increased continuously while that of fish had stayed almost still throughout these three decades. ④ No food showed any decrease in the consumption rate during the same period. ⑤ The total amount of fruits and vegetables consumed by the average American in the year 2000 exceeded that of all other foods in the same year.

31 The Whistling Swan is an all-white bird of amazing grace and beauty, except its bill and feet which are black. Its name does not refer to the call of the bird which is a low, melodic sound, but refers to the sound the bird's powerful wings make in flight. The migration of this swan is an incredible 3,725 miles round trip. While these animals flock together during migration, they are solitary nesters, choosing a site near a pond or slow-moving river. An excellent nesting site may be used year after year by the same birds. The female usually lays four to five eggs and incubates them for about a month with some help from the male. After the eggs hatch, both parents tend to the young swans and lead them to food source. Although the young can fly at two to three months of age, they usually stay with the parents through the first winter.

① Whistling Swan의 부리는 하얀색이다.
② Whistling Swan의 이름은 울음소리에서 유래되었다.
③ Whistling Swan은 둥지를 숲에 짓는다.
④ Whistling Swan의 수컷은 새끼를 돌보지 않는다.
⑤ Whistling Swan은 부화 후 2~3달이 지나면 날 수 있다.

32 It is not enough to say, "We must not wage war." It is necessary to love peace and sacrifice for it. We must concentrate not merely on the eradication of war but on the affirmation of peace. A fascinating story about Ulysses and the Sirens is preserved for us in Greek literature. The Sirens had the ability to sing so sweetly that sailors could not resist steering toward their island. Many ships were lured upon the rocks, and men forgot home, duty and honor as they flung themselves into the sea to be embraced by arms that drew them down to death. Ulysses, determined not to succumb to the Sirens, first decided to tie himself tightly to the mast of his boat and his crew stuffed their ears with wax. But finally he and his crew learned a better way to save themselves: They took on board the beautiful singer Orpheus, whose melodies were sweeter than the music of the Sirens. When Orpheus sang, who would bother to listen to the Sirens? So we must see that peace represents a sweeter music, a cosmic melody that is far superior to the discords of war. Somehow we must transform the dynamics of the world power struggle from the nuclear arms race, which no one can win, to a creative contest to harness man's genius for the purpose of making peace and prosperity a reality for all the nations of the world.

① 평화를 위해 노력하는 것보다 전쟁을 억제하는 것이 더 중요하다.

② 사이렌의 유혹에서 벗어나기 위해 선원들은 돛대에 몸을 묶었다.

③ 선원들은 사이렌의 노래보다 달콤한 오르페우스의 노래에 귀를 기울였다.

④ 오르페우스의 노래는 전쟁의 승리를 상징한다.

⑤ 핵무기 경쟁을 피하기 위해 인간의 천재성을 발휘해야 한다.

※ 다음 글의 내용과 일치하지 않는 것을 고르시오. 【33~34】

33 The Pleiades, also known as Messier 45, are among those objects which are known since the earliest times. According to Kenneth Glyn Jones, the earliest known references to this cluster are mentionings by Homer in his Iliad (about 750 B.C.) and his Odyssey (about 720 B.C.). The stars in the Pleiades are thought to have formed together around 100 million years ago, making them 1/50 the age of our sun. Even though they lie some 425 light years away, at least 6 member stars are visible to the naked eye, while under clear dark skies this number jumps up to more than a dozen. Modern observing methods have revealed that at least about 500 mostly faint stars belong to the Pleiades star cluster, spread over a 2 degree (four times the diameter of the Moon) field. Their density is pretty low, compared to other open clusters. This is one reason why the life expectation of the Pleiades cluster is also pretty low.

① Homer는 그의 저서에서 Pleiades에 대해 언급하였다.

② Pleiades는 태양보다 훨씬 오래 전에 생성되었다.

③ Pleiades는 약 425광년 떨어져 있다.

④ Pleiades에는 적어도 약 500개의 별들이 무리를 이루고 있다.

⑤ Pleiades에 속하는 일부의 별은 육안으로 관찰할 수 있다.

34 After I realized the extent to which men work from a base of unacknowledged privilege, I understood that much of their oppressiveness was unconscious. Then I remembered the frequent charges from women of color that white women whom they encounter are oppressive. I began to understand why we are justly seen as oppressive, even when we don't see ourselves that way. I began to count the ways in which I enjoy unearned skin privilege and have been conditioned into oblivion about its existence. My schooling gave me no training in seeing myself as an oppressor, as an unfairly advantaged person, or as a participant in a damaged culture. I was taught to see myself as an individual whose moral state depended on her individual moral will. My schooling followed the pattern my colleague Elisabeth Minnich has pointed out : whites are taught to think of their lives as morally neutral, normative, and average, and also ideal, so that when we work to benefit others, this is seen as work which will allow "them" to be more like "us".

① 화자는 남성들이 대개 무의식적으로 억압자의 역할을 한다고 믿는다.
② 유색인 여성들은 종종 백인여성들이 억압적이라고 비난한다.
③ 학생시절 화자는 백인여성들이 억압적이라고 생각하지 않았다.
④ 화자는 개인의 윤리가 집단윤리에 근거한다고 배웠다.
⑤ 화자는 백인들의 삶이 도덕적으로 중립적이고 이상적이라고 학교에서 배웠다.

35 이민자들에 대한 필자의 태도로 가장 적절한 것은?

Ten years ago, Jefferson Boulevard in south Dallas was a dying inner-city business district filled with vacant storefronts. Today, there are almost 800 businesses there and on neighboring streets, and about three-quarters of them are owned by Hispanics, many of them first- and second-generation immigrants. "They were hungry enough to start their own businesses." says Leonel Ramos, president of the Jefferson Area Association. And sociologist Kasarda adds, "There is a whole multiplier effect throughout the community." Immigrants provide a hardworking labor force to fill the low-paid jobs that make a modern service economy run. In many cities, industries such as hotels, restaurants, and child care would be hardpressed without immigrant labor.

① appreciating   ② cynical
③ indifferent   ④ arrogant
⑤ shunning

※ 다음 글에서 전체의 흐름과 관계가 없는 것을 고르시오. 【36-37】

36 On May 18, at 8 : 32 in the morning, Mount St. Helens blew its top, literally. Suddenly, it was 1,300 feet shorter than before. At the same moment, an earthquake with an intensity of 5 on the Richter scale was recorded. ① It triggered an avalanche of snow and ice, mixed with hot rock. ② A wave of scorching volcanic gas and rock fragments shot horizontally from the volcano's flank, at 200 miles per hour. ③ There is no doubt that the activity of Mount St. Helens has influenced our climate. ④ As the sliding ice and snow melted, it touched off devastating torrents of mud and debris, which destroyed all life in their path. ⑤ Pulverized rock climbed as a dust cloud into the atmosphere. Finally, lava, accompanied by burning clouds of ash and gas welled out of the volcano's new crater and cracks in its flanks.

37 Since skeletal remains of Giganotosaurus do not include skin, scientists must theorize as to their coloring. ① They tried to make educated guesses about the dinosaurs' skin colors. ② Since a Giganotosaurus hunted smaller prey, it is likely that the appearance of its skin allowed it to blend into its surroundings for camouflage. ③ The Giganotosaurus lived in the grassy wetlands of what is now Argentina, an environment similar to the African savanna. ④ It had big teeth which were much larger than those of other dinosaurs eating grass. ⑤ Therefore, this dinosaur probably had skin that closely matched the colors of the vegetation around it.

38 다음 글에서 추론할 수 있는 내용으로 적절하지 않은 것은?

> Taking turns attempts to build consensus while recognizing political or social differences, and it encourages everyone to play. The taking-turns approach gives those with the most support more turns, but it also legitimates the outcome from each individual's perspective, including those whose views are shared only by a minority. I do not believe that democracy should encourage rule by the powerful — even a powerful majority. Instead, the idea of democracy promises a fair discussion among self-defined equals about how to achieve our common aspirations. To redeem that promise, we need to put the idea of taking turns at the center of our conception of representation. Particularly as we move into the twenty-first century as a more highly diversified citizenry, it is essential that we consider the ways in which voting and representational systems succeed or fail at encouraging the system in which majority rules but is not tyrannical.

① The idea of monolithic majority should not be encouraged.

② The majority that rules, but is not overbearing is desirable.

③ The majority should not be shifting, but fixed for effectiveness.

④ The minority will show active participation under the taking turns system.

⑤ Despotism comes not just from kings or lords, but from the majority of people as well.

※ 다음 글의 제목으로 가장 적절한 것을 고르시오. [39-40]

39 In India, the new year celebrations at the end of October focus on no one food but rather a balance of flavors, according to Julie Sahni, author of Classic Indian Cooking. Appam, a traditional cake made with rice flour, coconut, milk, and a kind of palm sap, is served along with a fudge called barifi. Both symbolize the wish for life to be lucky. But Sahni said other dishes, like mulligatawny soup (said to be good for a hangover) and green mango chutney, which is both sweet and hot, are served as well because a new year's feast must include tastes that are at once sweet, savory, sour, and hot. "The idea is to serve something that brings many flavors in your mouth, with the hope that life is going to bring many elements of pleasure and pain and you should take it all in good spirit," Sahni said.

① The Recipe of Traditional Indian Foods

② New Year Ceremonies in India

③ The Relation of Food to Health

④ The Elements of Pleasure and Pain in India

⑤ Food for Luck and Wisdom in India

40 Mr. Halle acknowledged that it was difficult to get people to dig into their pockets to save some of life's more unpleasant varmints. "There are all sorts of species that we have a hard time finding arguments for," he said. "And one of the things that does environmentalists poor credit is to insist overly for any particular individual species. The millions that went into saving the California Condor, for example, as far as I'm concerned could have been better spent." Nevertheless, Mr. Halle said, genetic diversity is important and man ought to think carefully about the wider consequences before allowing any species to be endangered and die out. Everything, no matter how disgusting, is something else's lunch. As Jonathan Swift put it, "A flea hath smaller fleas that on him prey; and these have smaller still to bite them, and so proceed ad infinitum." Thus losing any plant or creature from what used to be called the Great Chain of Being can have all kinds of unforseen effects.

① Various Kinds of Endangered Species

② How to Preserve the California Condor

③ Maintenance of Biological Diversity

④ Problems of Environmentalists' Approach

⑤ How to Save Unpleasant Animals

41 주어진 글 다음에 이어질 글의 순서로 가장 적절한 것은?

The sense of sight has been served and illuminated by the visual arts for as long, almost, as we have been human. For a little over a hundred years, it has also been served by the camera.

(A) Since relatively few of its operators are notably well endowed in any of these respects, save perhaps in technical skill, the results are, generally, disheartening. It is now probably well on the conservative side to estimate that during the past ten to fifteen years, the camera has corrupted thousands of pairs of eyes.

(B) Well used, the camera is unique in its power to develop and to delight our ability to see. Ill or indifferently used, it is unique in its power to defile and destroy that ability. It is clear enough by now to most people that "the camera never lies" is a foolish saying.

(C) Yet it is doubtful whether most people realize how extraordinarily slippery a liar the camera is. The camera is just a machine, which records with impressive and as a rule very cruel faithfulness what is in the eye, mind, spirit, and skill of its operator.

① (A)−(B)−(C)
② (B)−(A)−(C)
③ (B)−(C)−(A)
④ (C)−(A)−(B)
⑤ (C)−(B)−(A)

In the past few decades, the term The Other has become an increasingly common one in discussions about difference, diversity, prejudice, and racism. It is even sometimes used as an odd-sounding verb: You can be "othered" – That is, you can be categorized as "other" than something, which usually means less than that something. Most often, people belonging to minority groups or non-mainstream cultures are "othered" in this way, but the idea can apply to any person or group treated in a way that reflects prejudice or bias. All of us have probably been in circumstances in which we have been The Other, but it's clear that some groups have long been categorized as Other in systematic ways that are damaging and disturbing. It's worth thinking about what this idea of The Other says about how we respond to each other's identities. In discussions of injustices based on such things as race, gender, ethnicity, religion, and culture, this term has acquired a particular kind of meaning. It suggests something more than prejudice. To have prejudice is to dislike or have negative feelings about someone or something; conversely, we can have a prejudice in favor of something – for example, a sports fan can be prejudiced toward a favorite team. But to consider someone as an Other is to place that person in a category that is separate from ourselves and, importantly, somehow _____ ourselves. It is to consider that person's identity undesirable in some way.

42 위 글의 빈칸에 들어갈 말로 가장 적절한 것은?

① specific to　　　　　　② different from

③ tantamount to　　　　　④ inferior to

⑤ more than

43 위 글의 내용과 일치하지 않는 것은?

① 타자(Other)라는 용어는 명사뿐 아니라 동사로도 활용될 수 있다.
② 소수집단이나 비주류집단이 종종 타자화의 대상이 된다.
③ 어떤 집단은 체계적인 방식으로 오랜 기간 타자로 분류되었다.
④ 편견을 갖는다는 말은 무엇을 선호하는 경우에도 쓰인다.
⑤ 타자화는 긍정적 또는 부정적 의미로 사용될 수 있다.

(A) Researchers who have spent thousands of hours observing the behavior of bottlenose dolphins off the coast of Australia have discovered that the males form _____ with one another that are far more sophisticated than any seen in animals apart from human beings.

(B) Should the female be so unimpressed as to attempt to flee, the males will chase after her, bite her, slap her with their fins or slam into her with their bodies. The scientists call this effort to control females "herding" but they acknowledge that the word does not convey the aggressiveness of the act.

(C) And after they have succeeded in spiriting a female away, the males remain in their tight-knit group to assure that the female stays in line, performing a series of feats that are spectacular and threatening. Two or three males will surround the female, leaping, bellyflopping, and somersaulting, all in perfect synchrony with one another.

(D) They have found that one team of male dolphins will recruit the help of another team of males to gang up against a third group. According to scientists, this sort of battleplan requires considerable mental calculus to work out. But the purpose of these complex _____ is not exactly sportive. Males collude with their peers as a way of stealing fertile females from competing dolphin bands.

44 주어진 글 (A)에 이어질 내용을 순서에 맞게 배열한 것으로 가장 적절한 것은?

① (B)-(C)-(D)　　　　　② (C)-(B)-(D)

③ (C)-(D)-(B)　　　　　④ (D)-(B)-(C)

⑤ (D)-(C)-(B)

45 위 글의 제목으로 가장 적절한 것은?

① Symbiosis Between Male and Female Dolphins

② Dolphins Display Cunning in Courtship

③ Gender Differences of Dolphins

④ Male Dolphins Threaten Their Female Counterparts

⑤ Spectacular Behaviors of Endangered Species

46 위 글의 빈 칸에 공통으로 들어갈 말로 가장 적절한 것은?

① altruistic coalitions　　　② attractive skills

③ age groups　　　④ interfering relations

⑤ social alliances

※ 다음 글을 읽고 물음에 답하시오. 【47-48】

Whatever (A) they may be in theory, in the workplace, biological incapacity and natural preference are the counters used to defend against accusations of discrimination. Larry Summers, President of Harvard University, argues that competition makes discrimination irrational; that wouldn't hold, though, if an entire field is pervaded with discrimination, if there's a consensus that women don't belong there and if female candidates are judged more harshly by all potential employers. It also doesn't work if the threat of competition isn't so credible; it will be a long time before Ivies* feel the heat from Northwestern, which has improved its profile by hiring the first-rate women (B) they foolishly let go. The history of women and minorities in the workplace shows that vigorous enforcement of antidiscrimination law is what drives progress. Moreover, the competition argument can be turned against Summers; after all, given its prestige and wealth, Harvard could compete for women with any university on the planet. So why doesn't it?

*Ivies : 미국 동부의 유명 사립대학들

47 다음 중 필자의 의견으로 적절하지 않은 것은?

① Summers는 여성의 기회 균등을 경쟁이라는 논리로 부정한다.

② Harvard 대학은 여성에게 동등한 기회를 부여하는데 앞장서지 않고 있다.

③ 생물학적 능력의 결핍, 자연적 선호가 모두 여성을 차별하는 수단으로 이용된다.

④ Ivies와 Northwestern대학은 여성에 대해 차별적이다.

⑤ 반차별 정책을 강력하게 적용해야 여성과 소수자의 권리가 신장된다.

48 위 (A)와 (B)의 they가 각각 가리키는 것은?

	(A)	(B)
①	biological incapacity and natural preference	Ivies and Northwestern
②	biological incapacity and natural preference	Ivies
③	counters	Ivies and Northwestern
④	accusations	Ivies
⑤	accusations	Ivies and Northwestern

※ 다음 글을 읽고 물음에 답하시오. 【49~50】

(A) In their recent report, "One Nation, Many Peoples: A Declaration of Cultural Interdependence," a committee of scholars and teachers recommends that public schools provide a multicultural education. What that means, according to the report, is recognizing that America was shaped and continues to be shaped by people of diverse ethnic backgrounds and its history is an ongoing process of discovery and interpretation of the past, and that there is more than one way of viewing the world.

(B) Several dissenting committee members publicly worry that America will splinter into ethnic fragments if this multicultural curriculum is adopted. They argue that the committee's report puts the focus on ethnicity at the expense of national unity.

(C) In particular, according to the report, the curriculum should help children "to assess critically the reasons for the inconsistencies between the ideals of the U.S. and social realities. It should provide information and intellectual tools that can permit them to contribute to bringing reality closer to the ideals." In other words, show children what really happened, and give them the skills to help improve their country. What could be more patriotic?

(D) Downplaying ethnicity, however, will not bolster national unity. The history of America is the story of how and why people from all over the world came to the United States, and how in struggling to make a better life for themselves, they changed each other, they changed the country, and they all came to call themselves Americans.

(E) Thus, the westward migration of white Americans is not just a heroic settling of an untamed wild, but also the conquest of indigenous peoples. Immigrants were not just white, but Asian as well. Blacks were not merely passive slaves freed by northern whites, but active fighters for their own liberation.

49 주어진 글 (A)에 이어질 내용을 순서에 맞게 배열한 것으로 가장 적절한 것은?

① (E)-(C)-(B)-(D)
② (C)-(D)-(E)-(B)
③ (E)-(C)-(D)-(B)
④ (C)-(E)-(B)-(D)
⑤ (B)-(D)-(E)-(C)

50 위 글의 내용과 일치하는 것은?

① 위원회의 모든 구성원들이 다문화교육과정의 도입에 동의했다.
② 미국은 이상과 실제가 일치하는 국가이다.
③ 민족성을 부각시키지 않을 때 비로소 미국의 국가적 통합이 가능하다.
④ 백인의 영웅적인 서부이주와 정착의 이면에는 원주민에 대한 정복이 있었다.
⑤ 흑인노예는 남부 백인에 의해 해방되었을 뿐 아니라 스스로 해방을 위해 싸웠다.

▶ 해설은 p. 39에 있습니다.

※ 글의 흐름으로 보아, 밑줄 친 단어의 뜻으로 가장 적절한 것을 고르시오. [01-06]

01 Wagner's The Ring of the Nibelungs is distinctive in that it is almost entirely operatic; also unusual is the fact that the libretti for his operas were written by the composer himself — a task normally <u>reserved</u> for a poet or literary notable.

① retained   ② booked

③ modified   ④ substituted

⑤ suspended

02 The original garbage crisis occurred when people first settled down to farm and could no longer leave their campsites after their garbage grew too deep. Since then, every society has had problems with discards that are usually <u>odoriferous</u>.

① harmful   ② futile

③ biodegradable   ④ invaluable

⑤ stinky

03 Michael was a very capable salesman. He could sell a refrigerator to an Eskimo. However, Michael's <u>belligerent</u> attitude during team projects had his boss at his wits' end.

① hostile   ② arrogant

③ apathetic   ④ gregarious

⑤ unscrupulous

04 The prime minister wants to strengthen the <u>rickety</u> alliance with the United States and stress economic growth over redistribution.

① social

② dominant

③ clandestine

④ sturdy

⑤ precarious

05 The modern version of Shakespeare's "Romeo and Juliet" was met with mixed reviews. One <u>sardonic</u> review of the play called it a "true masterpiece for the uneducated sophist."

① fallible

② cynical

③ obsequious

④ charismatic

⑤ overindulgent

06 One of your main competitors offers you a <u>lucrative</u> position, more than commensurate with your present duties and at almost double the salary.

① leisurely

② propitious

③ charitable

④ classy

⑤ well-paying

※ (A), (B), (C)에 들어갈 말로 가장 적절한 것을 고르시오. [07-08]

07 Once hunted for their pelts, beavers are back in demand, not for their bodies but for their minds — specifically, for their engineering skills. As changing climate leaves streams short on water in the summer, researchers are (A) betting/refuting that the industrious rodents could provide a natural solution. Based on a survey of how dams store water, the Lands Council in Washington State predicts that (B) prohibiting/reintroducing beavers to 10,000 miles of suitable habitat in the state could help retain more than 650 trillion gallons of spring runoff, which would slowly be released by the animals' naturally leaky dams. The council began (C) investigating/terminating the beaver option after learning that the state was considering artificial dam projects that might cost billions of dollars. It argues that beavers can do the job at a small fraction of the expense.

(A)	(B)	(C)
① betting	prohibiting	investigating
② betting	reintroducing	investigating
③ betting	reintroducing	terminating
④ refuting	reintroducing	terminating
⑤ refuting	prohibiting	investigating

08 The need for presidents to travel is (A) obscure/obvious, but it can be asked whether motion is replacing substance. Nixon's cross-country swing was an engineered spectacle that started with his speech in the Oval Office, sped south to Florida, then on to New Orleans, and came to rest by the Pacific. It was supposed to be a triumphal march from coast to coast, but it failed because it was a hollow concept. Ever since John F. Kennedy, there has been the (B) compulsion/abhorrence to fly off some place. There is something about being at 35,000 feet that increases President's sense of omnipotence. Kennedy's spirits lifted when he got on his magic carpet. Even when Nixon is earthbound in California, he often sets out for a spin along the roaring California freeways. The amateur psychologists who travel with Nixon insist that in part he is running from his problems, seeking some (C) vignette/vista where solutions will appear. They may never do.

	(A)	(B)	(C)
①	obscure	compulsion	vista
②	obscure	abhorrence	vignette
③	obvious	compulsion	vista
④	obvious	abhorrence	vista
⑤	obvious	compulsion	vignette

※ 다음 글의 밑줄 친 부분 중, 문맥상 낱말의 쓰임이 적절하지 않은 것을 고르시오. [9-10]

09
The buyers and sellers at the happiness-market seem too often to have lost their sense of the pleasure of difficulty. Heaven knows what they are playing, but it seems a ① dull game. And the Indian holy man, whose idea of happiness is in needing nothing from outside himself, seems boring to us, I suppose, because he seems to be refusing to play anything at all. The Western weakness may be in the ② illusion that happiness can be bought. Perhaps the Eastern weakness is in the idea that there is such a thing as perfect (and therefore static) happiness. Happiness is never more than ③ partial. There are no pure states of mankind. Whatever else happiness may be, it is neither in having nor in being, but in becoming. What the Founding Fathers declared for us as an inherent right, we should do well to remember, was not happiness but the ④ acceptance of happiness. What they might have underlined, could they have foreseen the happiness-market, is the ⑤ cardinal fact that happiness is in the pursuit itself, in the meaningful pursuit of what is life-engaging and life-revealing, which is to say, in the idea of becoming.

10
The world does not much like curiosity. The world says that curiosity killed the cat. The world dismisses curiosity by calling it idle, or mere idle curiosity — even though curious persons are ① seldom idle. Parents do their best to ② foster curiosity in their children, because it makes life difficult to be faced every day with a string of unanswerable questions about what makes fire hot or why grass grows. They have to ③ halt junior's investigations before they end in explosion and sudden death. Children whose curiosity survives parental ④ discipline and who manage to grow up before they blow up are invited to join the college faculty. Within the university they go on asking their questions and trying to find the answers. In the eyes of a scholar, that is mainly what a university is for. It is a place where the world's hostility to curiosity can be ⑤ defied.

11
Julie's main goals for freshmen year were to do well academically and to figure out ① about what kind of engineering she'd major in. But she knew that engineering was tough and that to do well, she'd have to shorten the long list of extracurricular activities she'd participated in for the past ② few years. She'd been a cheerleader and a member of the student government through high school. She'd taken piano lessons and she'd spent the past year as Elkhart's Junior Miss, ③ which had earned her a college scholarship. That's not to say Julie wanted to bury her face in her books for the next four years. She did want to make time ④ to swim and do aerobics for exercise. She knew she'd check out the Purdue social scene, especially weekend fraternity parties. And then there was her boyfriend. "I know I'll go out ⑤ whenever I feel like it," she said. "But homework will be my priority."

12
The chickens that saved Western civilization were discovered, according to legend, by the side of a road in Greece in the first decade of the fifth century B.C. The Athenian general Themistocles, on his way to confront the invading Persian forces, stopped ① to watch two cocks fighting. He summoned his troops, saying: "Behold, these do not fight for their household gods, for the monuments of their ancestors, for glory, for liberty or the safety of their children, but only because one will not give way to ② another." The tale does not describe what happened to the loser, nor ③ does it explain why the soldiers found this display of instinctive aggression inspirational rather than pointless and depressing. But history records that the Greeks, thus heartened, went on to repel the invaders, ④ preserving the civilization that today honors those same creatures by breading, frying, and dipping them into one's choice of sauce. The descendants of those roosters might well think — if they ⑤ were capable of such profound thought — that their ancient forebears have a lot to answer for.

13
Some people today think of work ① as a four-letter word. But when I was an undergraduate during the Depression, work was a very popular word. Those who had it gloried in it, and those who did not ② speak of it with longing. After I completed my university years in Canada I went to Oxford, and there I found a

different state of affairs. Work was not mentioned. Sometimes students would leave a party ③ saying, "Well, I have to be getting along now." Everybody knew they were sneaking away to work, but we were all too polite to mention it. Professors were never seen ④ to work. Part of the charm of Oxford was that nobody seemed to work at all. There was an Oxford secret, however, which I soon uncovered: everybody worked like hell, but they thought it bad form ⑤ to admit any such thing. One was supposed to take in one's learning from the air.

14 At least 20 million people have worked in a McDonald's since Ray Kroc opened his first McDonald's hamburger stand 40 years ago. Behind that number ① is several corporate strategies including using armies of part-time workers. In addition, ② hourly pay for McDonald's crew members is typically only a bit higher than the $5.25 minimum wage, and fringe benefits are meager. Employees leave ③ so frequently that this year McDonald's and its franchisees, which employ more than 500,000 workers in the United States and Canada, will have to hire well over that number of new employees to ④ stay fully staffed. But there is an upside to this upheaval. The fast-food chains have been forced to concentrate more than other businesses on training programs with an eye toward ⑤ adapting large numbers of raw recruits.

15 밑줄 친 It[it]이 가리키는 대상이 다른 것은?

Many of us have an item of endearment that we cannot dare part with. Perhaps ① it is an old tattered T-shirt with an autograph from your favorite movie star. ② It could also be a lucky pen that is out of ink, but has been your trusty sidekick through countless exams. For others, ③ it may be a tarnished silver ring that has long lost its shine. Although the ring no longer serves its purpose as an item of adornment, ④ it can conjure up a memory of a loved one, such as a grandmother who passed away. Whatever the item, the real reason for keeping it is not for its face value, but because ⑤ it represents part of our past, a memory we hold dear to our hearts.

16 밑줄 친 This[this]가 의미하는 것으로 가장 적절한 것은?

This not only affects expectations for success or failure; it also influences motivation through goal setting. If we have a high sense of <u>this</u> in a given area such as foreign language learning, we will set higher goals, be less afraid of failure, and persist longer when we encounter difficulties. If our sense of <u>this</u> is low, however, we may avoid a task altogether or give up easily when problems arise. <u>This</u> also seems to be related to attributions. People with a strong sense of <u>this</u> for a given task attribute their failures to lack of effort. But people with a low sense of <u>this</u> tend to attribute their failures to lack of ability. You can see that motivation would be destroyed when failures were attributed to lack of ability.

① self-efficacy
② proportion
③ empathy
④ self-consciousness
⑤ interest

17 Hollywood sign에 관한 다음 글의 내용과 일치하는 것은?

The Hollywood sign in the hills that line the northern border of Los Angeles is a famous landmark recognized the world over. The white-painted, 50-foot-high sheet metal letters can be seen from great distances across the Los Angeles basin. The sign was not constructed, as one might suppose, by the movie business as a means of celebrating the importance of Hollywood to this industry; instead, it was first constructed in 1923 as a means of advertising homes for sale in a 500-acre housing subdivision in a part of Los Angeles called "Hollywoodland." The sign that was constructed at the time, of course, said "Hollywoodland." Over the years, people began referring to the area by the shortened version "Hollywood," and after the sign and its site were donated to Los Angeles in 1945, the last four letters were removed. The sign suffered from years of disrepair, and in 1973 it was completely replaced, at a cost of $27,000 per letter. Various celebrities including Alice Cooper were instrumental in helping to raise needed funds.

① Los Angeles 북쪽 경계인 평야지대에 있다.
② Hollywood의 영화 산업을 홍보하기 위해 제작되었다.
③ 1945년에 부지와 함께 Hollywoodland에 기부되었다.
④ 1973년에 총 $27,000의 비용을 들여 교체되었다.
⑤ 유명 인사들이 교체 비용을 모금하는 데에 기여했다.

18 India is part of the Asian subcontinent and is home to over 1 billion people. Only China has a larger population. A little over half of India's land is suited to agriculture, but about 65 percent of Indians are farmers or farm laborers. They raise rice, wheat, cotton, cattle, sheep and water buffalo. To increase output, the government instituted irrigation and land reclamation projects. Newer types of crops and fertilizers have also been tried. India is one of the nations benefiting from the Green Revolution. Unfortunately, India's initial high hopes for the Green Revolution have proven to be illusory because of the high costs for the seeds and fertilizer and the environmental issues arising from the massive use of pesticides.

① India의 인구는 10억이 넘는다.
② India에서 농업에 적합한 토지는 전 국토의 절반을 조금 넘는다.
③ India의 농부들은 물소를 숭배한다.
④ India 정부는 관개 사업과 토지 개간 사업을 실시했다.
⑤ Green Revolution에 대한 India의 기대치가 처음에는 높았다.

19 Thoreau noted that "many a traveler came out of his way to see me," including his friends, schoolchildren, aimless tourists, and the down and out from local almshouses who were far more interesting than some of his more affluent drop-ins. Thoreau had no tolerance for babble but was responsive to children who brought him flowers, weeds, and dead animals. On the whole, they entertained themselves, unlike some of his adult "unreckoned guests." Some of the more shameless, Thoreau suspected, came when he was out walking in the woods and rooted through his drawers and cabinets. Most of the guests came from nearby Concord and Lincoln, or from Boston. "Girls and boys and young women generally seemed glad to be here in the woods," Thoreau wrote. "They looked in the pond and at the flowers, and improved their time. Men of business, even farmers, thought only of solitude and employment, and of the great distance at which I dwelt from something or other; and though they said they loved a ramble in the woods occasionally, it was evident that they did not."

① Thoreau의 방문객 중에는 부유층뿐만 아니라 빈민층도 있었다.
② Thoreau는 죽은 동물을 가져오는 어린이들에게 화를 내기도 했다.
③ Thoreau는 일부 방문객들이 그의 서랍을 뒤진다고 의심했다.
④ Thoreau를 찾는 대부분의 방문객은 Concord, Lincoln, Boston에서 왔다.
⑤ Thoreau는 사업가나 농부가 숲속 산책을 즐기지 않는다고 생각했다.

20 If forgiveness feels so good, why do so many people lug around so much resentment? One reason is that it may compensate for the _____ they experienced when they were hurt. "People may feel more in charge when they're filled with anger," points out Mart Grunte, author of How to Forgive When You Don't Know How. "But forgiving instills a much greater sense of power. When you forgive, you reclaim your power to choose. It doesn't matter whether someone deserves forgiveness; you deserve to be free."

① vengefulness   ② unforgetfulness

③ powerlessness   ④ indebtedness

⑤ guiltlessness

21 A train ticket buys a front-row seat to the greatest show on earth : the human condition. Without suffering jet lag or driver fatigue, the passenger is a privileged pilgrim upon whom no demands are made and for whom time is suspended for a while in the rocking of the rail car. He is a witness to life, which passes in vivid pictures outside the window; he glides through the small moments that make a day. Backyards, beautiful trees, city squares—nothing _____. If he chooses, he can step down at any stop along the way to enter what he is observing. There is no adventure quite like that promised by arriving in the middle of the night at a brightly lit station in a foreign country, where a customs officer is smoking a cigarette and a wagon stacked with milk cans rolls by.

① hurts scenic beauty

② adds to driver fatigue

③ reminds him of the past

④ improves quality amenities

⑤ escapes the view

22 "At least 80 percent of our statues and sculptures are in bad shape from assaults ranging from acid rain to mechanical damage," said the director of conservation at the Culture Ministry. "Our roads were planned for horse carriages and now we have cars backing into statues." The Culture Ministry has increased the money for restoration in the belief that better-kept statues will reap an economic return from visitors. For Mr. Branda and his fellow restorers, however, the work is _____ than a passion to preserve the soul of the city. Sometimes the passion led them to go to extraordinary lengths. Many nights past midnight Mr. Branda and his colleagues clambered onto the windswept roof of St. Salvator Church at the foot of Charles Bridge to wrap and tie up seven 17th-century stone statues of the disciples. In the dark, a crane then plucked the statues for safekeeping and repair in a workshop.

① more repairs for making money

② less a desire to become famous

③ more research on architecture

④ less cosmetics for tourists

⑤ less a labor of love

23 Ben Jonson, a well-known playwright and seventeenth-century contemporary of John Donne, wrote that while "the first poet in the world in some things," Donne nevertheless "for not keeping of an accent, deserved hanging." Donne's generation admired the depth of his feeling, but was puzzled by his often irregular rhythm and obscure references. It was not until the twentieth century and modern movements that celebrated emotion and allusion that _____. Writers such as T.S. Eliot and W.B. Yeats admired the psychological intricacies of a poet who could one moment flaunt his earthly dalliances with his mistress and the next, wretched, implore God to "bend your force, to break, blow, burn, and make me new."

① Donne really began to be appreciated

② the forgotten works of Donne were rewritten

③ Jonson admitted that he had misjudged Donne

④ Donne's unclear references became more obscure

⑤ rhythm in poetry became more commonly practiced

24   One may ask : Why does the great fame of classical authors continue? The answer is that the fame of classical authors is entirely independent of the majority. Do you suppose that if the fame of Shakespeare depended on the man in the street, it would survive a fortnight? The fame of classical authors is originally made, and it is maintained, by a passionate few. Even when a first-class author has enjoyed immense success during his lifetime, the majority have never appreciated him so sincerely as they have appreciated second-rate men. He has always been _____. And in the case of an author who has emerged into glory after his death, the happy sequel has been due to the obstinate perseverance of the few.

① made equal to less-able authors by the elite reader

② indebted to the man in the street for his fame

③ reinforced by the ardour of the passionate few

④ distinguished naturally from second-rate men

⑤ inspired by the immense admiration from the public

25   If you could take a picture of the soul, it might look something like the black and white photos of certain slaves and soldiers during the Civil War. They are men and women who didn't have time to look at themselves or worry about their appearance, and it shows. Their faces transmit their passions and experiences and never betray their character. One photo shows a large man with a hard stare and a spiky beard that conveys fierceness. In another, a mother's wisdom can be seen in the dark circles under her eyes. A child's skepticism is visible in his small, taut mouth. Somehow, their situations allowed their spirits to develop in their faces, _____.

① mirroring one another's agony and despair

② complemented by their warm souls

③ forever seeking an inner peace

④ unlike in the bodies of modern men

⑤ untainted by luxury and self-examination

26 In the last movie you saw, did you notice the soda the hero was drinking? How about the car the female star was driving? Actors in TV shows and in movies have always drunk sodas and driven cars, but now the name on the soda can and the emblem on the car are more (A) _____. Advertisers have figured out that they can get exposure for their products by having them featured on TV and in movies. Movie studios have figured out that they can be paid for these so-called "embeds." So what? The next time you order soda X over Y, think about whether the last movie you saw featured X or Y. Have you been (B) _____ by an advertiser and a movie producer?

(A)	(B)
① covert	dissuaded
② covert	tricked
③ subliminal	manipulated
④ prominent	dissuaded
⑤ prominent	manipulated

27 Chain reactions are occurring all the time on Earth. Chain reactions occur in chemical plants when a single excited molecule prompts its neighbors into a cascade of combination to create plastics. (A) _____, they are commonplace in nuclear reactors, where a speeding subatomic particle slams into a heavy atom and splits it apart, releasing more particles that repeat and amplify the process in bursts of energy. Now, experts say, a dangerous new kind of chain reaction is getting under way in space, where it threatens to limit mankind's endeavors beyond the planet. (B) _____, it could put billions of dollars worth of advanced communications and weather satellites at risk of destruction. The problem is that some orbits near Earth have become junkyards of dead and active satellites, spent rocket stages and billions of bits of whirling debris.

(A)	(B)
① In consequence	However
② In addition	However
③ By contrast	For instance
④ In addition	For instance
⑤ By contrast	Unfortunately

28 The amount of sunshine that reaches the Earth dropped by 10 percent between the early 1950s and the early 1990s. Scientists have found that the problem is not the sun. No instruments have recorded any dimming of the sun's rays. The problem appears to be between the Earth and the Sun. Pollution has gotten in the way. Particulates in pollution reflect sun back into outer space. Pollution also causes increased condensation in the air. This condensation forms thicker, darker clouds. To verify their theory, scientists point to areas with little or no pollution. Instruments in those places have shown sunshine as bright as ever.

① Let's Give the Sun a Vacation

② Sunshine : The More the Better

③ Pollution : An Unnatural Sunshade

④ How Can We Stop the Sun's Dimming?

⑤ Look for a Silver Lining in Every Cloud

29 Walter Benjamin identifies traditional storytelling not only with the traveller, who returns from his wanderings with something to tell, but also with the preserver of local traditions, rooted in his native place. In the Middle Ages, these two types of storytelling interpenetrated because of the craft structure, whereby the resident master craftsman and the travelling journeyman came together in the workplace. But through the workings of "the secular productive forces of history," narrative has been taken from the realm of living speech. What stands in opposition to storytelling, what is in the process of replacing it entirely, is of course the novel, inseparably linked to the invention of printing and the notion of the book. The novelist is necessarily isolated, invisible, a hidden god who does not have the capacity to enter into colloquy with his fellow man, and thus cannot communicate that wisdom that is good counsel.

① Two Times, One Narrative

② Storytelling : Living Speech vs Dead Letters

③ A Solitary Hero in the Modern Narrative

④ The Decline of Storytelling, the Rise of the Novel

⑤ Craftsman and Journeyman : Two Sides of the Coin

30 Modern psychology has been called "the science of the behavior of the college sophomore." During the 1960s and 1970s, several psychologists analyzed four journals in the field and found that 58 percent to 96 percent of the articles were based on studies with college students. More recently, I analyzed the articles in two of those journals in 1991 and found that 77 percent reported on research done with college students. Melvin Manis, a University of Michigan psychologist, who is also an editor of one of the journals studied, explains that convenience dictates the choice of subjects in other fields as well. "There's very little genetic research going on with elephants," he says. "Most of it is done with fruit flies, not only because they have short life spans but because they're much cheaper." That's fine if elephants and fruit flies have comparable genetic mechanisms. But do college students think, behave, and feel as their non-college peers do? Or, for that matter, as older adults do? The answer to both questions is "no."

① College Students : Now and Then
② Genetic Research : Smaller is Better?
③ Sampling Error in the Study of Psychology
④ College Students in Psychology : Too Many?
⑤ Thought Patterns of College Students and Older Adults

※ 다음 글의 주제로 가장 적절한 것을 고르시오. [31~32]

31 There is consideration to which some advocates of freedom attach too little importance. In a community of children which is left without adult interference there is a tyranny of the stronger, which is likely to be far more brutal than most adult tyrannies. If two children, two or three years old, are left to play together, they will, after a few fights, discover which is bound to be the victor, and the other will then become a slave. Where the number of children is larger, one or two acquire complete mastery, and the others have far less liberty than they would have if the adults interfered to protect the weaker and less pugnacious. Consideration for others does not, with most children, arise spontaneously, but has to be taught, and can hardly be taught except by the exercise of authority. This is perhaps the most important argument against the abdication of the adults.

① the importance of freedom in child care

② understanding children's behaviors in various learning contexts

③ the relation of victors to slaves in a community of children

④ the necessity for adult interference in child care

⑤ various factors affecting children's leadership

32 The place of secondhand smoke in causing disease has been under study for years. A mid-sized city in a western state unexpectedly added to the data. Smoking in public and in workplaces was banned and six months later the ban was lifted. During the time that smoking was prohibited in public places, the rate of hospital admissions for heart attacks was 24. During the typical six-month period, the rate is 40 admissions. The researchers believed that the drop was evidence of the negative effects of secondhand smoke. Secondhand smoke contributes to heart attacks by elevating heart rate and decreasing the ability of blood vessels to dilate.

① effects of smoking in the workplace

② causes of heart attacks in mid-sized cities

③ the importance of a stress-free working environment

④ the relationship of secondhand smoke and heart attacks

⑤ the necessity of banning smoking in public and workplaces

33 다음 글의 주장으로 가장 적절한 것은?

If there is a garbage crisis, it is that we are treating garbage as an environmental threat and not as what it is : a manageable — though admittedly complex — civic issue. Although many old urban landfills are reaching their capacity, the reality is that there is — and always will be — plenty of room in this country for safe landfill. We've chosen to look at garbage not as a management issue, however, but as a moral crisis. The result is that recycling is now seen as an irreproachable virtue, beyond the scrutiny of cost-benefit analysis. But in the real world, the money municipalities spend on recycling is money that can't be spent on schools, libraries, health clinics, and police. In the real world, the sort of gigantic recycling programs that many cities and towns have embarked upon may not be the best use of scarce government funds.

① 쓰레기 매립지의 확대는 바람직하지 않다.
② 쓰레기 재활용은 도덕적 관점에서 접근해야 한다.
③ 쓰레기 재활용에는 충분한 사전 홍보가 선행되어야 한다.
④ 쓰레기 재활용에 쓰이는 과다한 정부 기금은 재고되어야 한다.
⑤ 쓰레기 재활용 프로그램은 공공기관부터 참여해야 한다.

34 다음 글의 분위기로 가장 적절한 것은?

The sun was just far enough in the west to send inviting shadows. In the center of a small field, and in the shade of a haystack which was there, a girl lay sleeping. She had slept long and soundly when she was awoken by a gentle breeze. She opened her eyes and stared a moment up in the sky of blue and white. She yawned and stretched her long brown legs and arms, lazily. Then she arose, never minding the bits of straw that clung to her black hair, to her red sweater, and to the blue cotton skirt that did not reach her ankles. The girl absentmindedly watched a cloud that floated lazily overhead, trying to decide what kind of animal it most looked like.

① calm and relaxing   ② lively and exciting
③ funny and amusing   ④ sad and frightening
⑤ urgent and desperate

※ 다음 글에서 전체 흐름과 관계 없는 문장을 고르시오. [35-36]

35 Some of the men working nearby would watch me and laugh. ① Two or three of the older men took the trouble to teach me the right way to shovel. "You're doing it wrong," one man scolded. ② Beginning around seven each morning, I would feel my body resist the first thrust of the shovel. "Don't make your back do so much work," he instructed. ③ I stood impatiently listening, vaguely watching, then noticed his work-thickened fingers clutching the shovel. I was annoyed and wanted to tell him that I enjoyed shoveling the wrong way. I was about to, but, as it turned out, I didn't say a thing. ④ Rather it was at that moment I realized that I was fooling myself if I expected a few weeks of labor to gain me admission to the world of laborer. I would not learn in three months what my parents had meant by "real work." For me the sensations of exertion and fatigue could be savored. ⑤ For my parents, working at comparable jobs when they were my age, such sensations were to be feared. Fatigue took a different toll on their bodies and minds.

36 "What is your blood type?" is an unusual question from the Western point of view. From the Korean and Japanese perspective, such a question is quite normal. ① People of these cultures believe that specific personality traits are related to blood type. ② These days, however, more and more Westerners are buying into the idea of a connection between these two seemingly distinct features. ③ This belief is very similar to Western notions of astrology and signs of the zodiac. ④ Most Westerners are surprised by such a question because they are unaware of the concept of a relationship between blood type and personality. ⑤ I n fact, many Westerners do not even know their own blood type.

37 글의 흐름으로 보아, 주어진 문장이 들어가기에 가장 적절한 곳은?

If, instead, an enlightened course is pursued, allowing workers to benefit from increases in productivity with shorter workweeks and adequate income, more leisure time will exist than in any other period of modern history.

In the future, a growing number of people around the world will be spending less time on the job and have more time on their hands. (①) Whether their "free" time will be coerced, involuntary, and the result of forced part-time work, layoffs, and unemployment, or leisure made possible by productivity gains, shorter workweeks, and better income remains to be worked out in the political arena. (②) If massive unemployment of a kind unknown in history were to occur as a result of the sweeping replacement of machines for human labor, then the chances of developing a compassionate and caring society are unlikely. (③) The more likely course would be widespread social upheaval, violence on an unprecedented scale, and open warfare, with the poor lashing out at each other as well as at the rich elites who control the global economy. (④) That free time could be used to renew the bonds of community and rejuvenate the democratic legacy. (⑤) A new generation might transcend the narrow limits of nationalism and begin to think and act as common members of the human race, with shared commitments to each other, the community, and the larger biosphere.

38 다음 글의 내용을 한 문장으로 나타낼 때, 빈칸 (A)와 (B)에 들어갈 말로 가장 적절한 것은?

Perhaps you are one of millions of people who depend on the television to keep you company, or you may have caught yourself actually talking to your computer. But all of your relationships with machines may not be love relationships. You may also hate certain machines — the computer that has a mind of its own, the car that won't start, the toaster that always burns your toast, the vending machine that robs you of your money. Although machines are usually designed to make your life easier, they may also, on occasion, make your life frustrating if not miserable. Machines certainly contribute to much that is bad in our lives: Guns contribute to the high crime rate; automobiles increase air pollution and cause accidents; and machines in general often put people out of work. Yet no one is eager to do without machines. Having become used to them, to the convenience and entertainment and stimulation they provide, people cannot imagine a life in which machines do not play a major role.

Machines may sometimes be troublesome, frustrating, and even (A)_____ once accustomed to the advantages they provide, however, you would feel that they are almost (B)_____ to your daily life.

	(A)	(B)
①	addictive	superfluous
②	disappointing	inessential
③	harmful	superfluous
④	addictive	indispensable
⑤	harmful	indispensable

39 주어진 글 다음에 이어질 글의 순서로 가장 적절한 것은?

> Logic promotes truth; yet we can go far in logic without knowing or caring much whether a particular statement is true or false, in the ordinary acceptation of those words. By true in ordinary speech we mean true to fact, and by false we mean the opposite. Now a statement, true to fact, may in its context infringe a rule of logic; and a statement, false in fact, may in its context conform to the rules of logic.

> (A) The logician, as such, is not directly concerned with fact, but is much more concerned with the observance of the rules of logic, and therefore he uses a pair of technical terms, valid and invalid, to express, respectively, what conforms to the rules of logic and what does not conform thereto.
>
> (B) A valid passport may make mistakes in fact, but if duly signed and not out of date, it may do its work and get you through the barrier. On the other hand, it may give the color of the eyes and all the other facts correctly, but if it is out of date, it will not do its work; it is invalid.
>
> (C) By the aid of these terms he can set out the rules of reasoning without committing himself as to whether a particular statement is true to fact, or not. Valid comes from the Latin, validus, or strong.

① (A)−(B)−(C)　　　　　　② (A)−(C)−(B)

③ (B)−(A)−(C)　　　　　　④ (B)−(C)−(A)

⑤ (C)−(A)−(B)

※ 다음 글을 읽고, 물음에 답하시오. 【40~41】

This much is known. Neuron No. 28, say, fires an electrical signal, and in the synapse where one of 28's connectors touches a receiver of neuron No. 29, a chemical change triggers an electrical signal in 29. That signal gets passed on to neuron No. 30, and on and on. If the connection between 28 and 29 is made often enough, the bond between the two neurons grows stronger. This crucial marriage seems to be the stuff that memory is made of. Unlike cells elsewhere in the body, neurons don't divide. By the time someone reaches 65 or 70, neuron No. 28 and some of its neighbors may be dead, or so feeble they no longer transmit electrical charges efficiently.

Still, there are billions more neurons remaining. And even though the brain cannot grow new ones, the neurons can probably sprout new synapses and thereby form new connections with one another.

A researcher supplied certain lab rats with new toys daily and changed the chutes and tunnels in their cages. When he cut open their brains, he counted many more synapses than in rats that got no toys and no new decor. It's a good guess that the human brain, too, grows more synapses when stimulated and challenged. So the brain—even while shrinking—may be able to blaze ever more trails for laying down memory. If neuron No. 28's path is no longer easily passable, _____. The trick is to force the brain to make them.

*synapse : 신경세포의 자극 전달부

40 윗글의 주제로 가장 적절한 것은?

① the vital role of neurons in creating new memory
② the mechanism of neurons for overcoming weakening memory
③ the similarity in memory function between human and rat brains
④ the function of brain cells in triggering and transmitting electrical signals
⑤ the brain cell's demand of stimulation and challenge for its reproduction

41 윗글의 빈칸에 들어갈 말로 가장 적절한 것은?

① the number of alternate routes may be virtually limitless
② the memory functions in one's brain stop temporarily
③ the neuron can probably make its channel even stronger
④ the brain still tries to bring it back to life by lengthening it
⑤ the brain creates new neurons to deliver electrical signals

※ 다음 글을 읽고, 물음에 답하시오. 【42~44】

(A) When ordinary young adults realize how little they learned in school, they usually assume there was something wrong with the school they attended or with the way they spent their time there. But the fact is that the best possible graduate of the best possible school needs to continue learning in the days to come.

(B) However, never just read, for reading without discussion with others who have read the same book is not nearly as profitable. And as reading without discussion can fail to yield the full measure of understanding that should be sought, so discussion without the substance that good and great books afford is likely to degenerate into little more than an exchange of _____.

(C) How should they go about doing this? In a book published last year, I tried to answer the question, "How should persons proceed who wish to conduct for themselves the continuation of learning after all schooling has been finished?" The brief and simple answer to this crucial question is: Read and discuss.

(D) Those who take this prescription seriously would, of course, be better off if their schooling had given them the intellectual discipline and skill they need to carry it out. But even the individual who is fortunate enough to leave school or college after extensive reading followed by insightful discussions, would still have a long road to travel before he or she became an educated person.

42 주어진 글 (A)에 이어질 내용을 순서에 맞게 배열한 것으로 가장 적절한 것은?

① (B)–(D)–(C) ② (C)–(B)–(D)
③ (C)–(D)–(B) ④ (D)–(B)–(C)
⑤ (D)–(C)–(B)

43 윗글의 주제로 가장 적절한 것은?

① the importance of reading and discussion in continuing learning
② the contribution of schooling to lifelong education
③ problems of schooling for young adults
④ the necessity for extensive reading for young adults
⑤ factors affecting reading and discussion throughout schooling

44 윗글의 빈칸에 들어갈 말로 가장 적절한 것은?

① critical questions
② profound schooling
③ superficial opinions
④ insightful understanding
⑤ intellectual discipline

(A) It happened one day that a fisherman putting out to sea in a boat was just about to cast a net, when right in front of him he saw a man on the point of drowning. Being a stout-hearted and at the same time an agile man, he jumped up and, seizing a boathook, thrust it toward the man's face. It caught him right in the eye and pierced it. The fisherman hauled the man into the boat and made for shore without casting any of his nets. He had the man carried to his house and given the best possible attention and treatment, until he had got over his ordeal.

(B) The other promptly spoke up and said, "Gentlemen, I cannot deny that I knocked his eye out, but if what I did was wrong, I'd like to explain how it all happened. This man was in mortal danger in the sea, in fact he was on the point of drowning. I went to his aid. I won't deny I struck him with my boathook, but I did it for his own good. I saved his life on that occasion. I don't know what more I can say. For God's sake, give me justice!"

(C) The court was quite at a loss when it came to deciding the rights of the case, but a fool who was present at the time said to them, "Why this hesitation? Let the first speaker be thrown back into the sea on the spot where the other man hit him in the face, and if he can get out again, the defendant shall compensate him for the loss of his eye. That I think, is a fair judgment." Then they all cried out as one man, "You're absolutely right! That's exactly what we'll do!" Judgment was then pronounced to that effect. When the man heard that he was to be thrown back into the sea, just where he had endured all that cold water before, he wouldn't have gone back there for all the world. He released the goodman from any liability, and his earlier attitude came in for much criticism.

(D) For a long time, that man thought about the loss of his eye, considering it a great misfortune. "That wretched fellow put my eye out, but I didn't do him any harm. I'll go and lodge a complaint against him — why, I'll make things really hot for him." Accordingly he went and complained to the magistrate, who fixed a day for the hearing. They both waited till the day came round, and then went to the court. The one who had lost an eye spoke first, as was appropriate. "Gentlemen," he said, "I'm bringing a complaint against this worthy, who, only the other day, savagely struck me with a boathook and knocked my eye out. Now, I'm handicapped. Give me justice, that's all I ask. I've nothing more to say."

45 주어진 글 (A)에 이어질 내용을 순서에 맞게 배열한 것으로 가장 적절한 것은?

① (B)-(D)-(C) ② (C)-(B)-(D)
③ (C)-(D)-(B) ④ (D)-(B)-(C)
⑤ (D)-(C)-(B)

46 윗글이 시사 하는 바로 가장 적절한 것은?

① It's All Water under the Bridge.

② Don't Bite the Hand That Feeds You.

③ Beauty is in the Eye of the Beholder.

④ You Can't Judge a Book by Its Cover.

⑤ The Grass is Always Greener on the Other Side.

47 밑줄 친 as one man이 의미하는 것으로 가장 적절한 것은?

① uniquely   ② humanely

③ unanimously   ④ as he believed

⑤ one after another

※ 다음 글을 읽고, 물음에 답하시오. 【48~50】

I am not by nature a country person. But once, long ago, the country was forced upon me. It was 1942, and we were evacuated to a farmhouse about 15 miles out of Cardiff, my home town. We'd watch the bombers comb the country sky on their way to Cardiff docks. We stuck it out in that farmhouse for almost six months and during that time I underwent a radical change. It all started one morning when I was leaving for school. My mother was standing at the window, watching a lone cow ambling across a distant field. "I wonder where that cow is going," she said, "and when it will get there." My mother was a woman with a practical head on her shoulders, and I thought for a frightening moment that the countryside had finally sent her round the bend.

That morning I did miss the train for school, because I dawdled on my way to the station. My mother's wonderings had unnerved me. I caught a later train. But all day I couldn't concentrate, and after school, on my way back from the station, I found myself studying the hedgerow flowers and finding pleasure in their discovery. When I got home to the farm, I said, "I saw some pretty flowers in the hedges today. I wish I knew their names."

Thereafter we took walks every day, my mother and I. At first we said little to each other, as was our wont in the city. Because city subjects — homework neglected, drawers untidied, piano unpractised — were beyond discussion, best covered with (A) _____. As the days passed, we identified each hedgerow flower. We also watched birds and savoured their newly discovered names. Moreover, at night when the bombers had quit the skies, we looked at the stars and whispered, Orion, the Plough and the Bear.

When we returned to Cardiff, we slipped back into our urban (B) _____, into the sham priorities of exams and tidy drawers. But often we would smile at each other as we recalled that rural magic, that sane wand that tapped everything into its right and proper place. And even now, so many years later, and urban-riddled, I can still watch a dog wandering in a crowded street, and wonder where it is going.

*round the bend: 정신이 나간

48 윗글의 'I'에 관한 내용과 일치하는 것은?

① 전쟁 때문에 Cardiff에서 15마일 떨어진 농장을 비우고 떠났다.
② 어머니는 원래 감성적인 성격의 소유자였다.
③ hedgerow flowers를 본 이후 어머니와 함께 산책을 매일 했다.
④ 시골생활 중에 꽃, 새, 별들의 이름을 새로 지어주었다.
⑤ 도시로 돌아와서는 시골생활을 회상할 겨를이 없었다.

49 윗글의 제목으로 가장 적절한 것은?

① Disenchanted from the Rural Beauty
② A Dangerous Pastime Amidst the War
③ Rural Magic : Opening Our Eyes to a New World
④ An Unexpected Exodus from Rural Imprisonment
⑤ Surviving the War : The Unwithering Hedgerow Flower

50 윗글의 빈칸 (A), (B)에 공통으로 들어갈 말로 가장 적절한 것은?

① eloquence　　　　② rush
③ melody　　　　　④ riddle
⑤ silence

▶ 해설은 p. 58에 있습니다.

※ 글의 흐름으로 보아, 밑줄 친 단어의 뜻으로 가장 적절한 것을 고르시오. 【1-5】

01 An experimental method that would be <u>deemed</u> inappropriate for one kind of research may be the method of choice for another kind of research.

① proven   ② coined

③ considered   ④ classified

⑤ pronounced

02 The World Heritage site has been threatened by the country's civil war. Experts are <u>wielding</u> satellite technology to monitor and protect endangered museums, monuments and other places of historical importance.

① legalizing   ② employing

③ developing   ④ avoiding

⑤ clarifying

03 Unable to cope with the fact that he was diagnosed with colon cancer, Michael suspected his doctor of being a <u>quack</u> and decided to seek out a second opinion.

① clown   ② demagogue

③ professional   ④ charlatan

⑤ benefactor

04 Aristotle does not <u>hector</u> students with some piety against the desire for material goods. To him, concern for money is a good thing, and one of the good things is that people with money can exercise generosity.

① associate   ② incite

③ criticize   ④ appease

⑤ address

05 The boxing commentator remarked of the heavyweight champion, "His left hook is a real <u>sockdolager</u>. It would take a tank to withstand such impact."

① decisive blow   ② powerful defense

③ sneaky attack   ④ elusive punch

⑤ fragile delivery

06 (A), (B), (C)에 들어갈 말로 가장 적절한 것은?

> There has been growing awareness in recent years of the inadequacy of GDP as a measure of true wealth, with its exclusive focus on economic capital formation but with no reference to other forms of capital — the health and biodiversity of the natural environs, the (A)[strength/weakness] of communities, and the well-being and happiness of people. A society should consciously develop its various forms of capital in a (B)[less/more] balanced and integrated way. Societies have to substitute other forms of capital for economic wealth, demonstrating how quality of life could be maintained or even enhanced while significantly (C)[maximizing/reducing] consumption and material throughput.

       (A)   (B)   (C)

① strength － more － maximizing

② strength － less － reducing

③ strength － more － reducing

④ weakness － less － reducing

⑤ weakness － less － maximizing

07 There is a constant demand for writers who can create good stories, especially for the big screen. However, there is an even greater ① supply of stories and screenplays that don't work and will never make it to the screen. In fact, there are over 100,000 scripts written every year, and only a few hundred actually make it. Even then, most of these movies do not ② succeed. Usually the script is the ③ culprit, and the most common script problem is lack of story. Believe it or not, ④ enormous attention is given to the process of developing good stories and screenplays for the big screen. But these statistics are startling proof of just how ⑤ easy it is to create a good story.

08 To different forms of rule ① corresponded different kinds of military organization. In medieval times, independent cities commonly created their own militias and ② obliged citizens to serve. Citizens never included all of the urban population, and often ③ narrowed to elected members of self-renewing councils. In the case of Venice and many other maritime cities, military duties ④ consisted of not only militia but also naval service. In manorial systems, landlords often ⑤ disbanded military units of their own vassals, tenants, and serfs, sometimes carrying on their own private wars, at other times joining an overlord's armies for a season of combat before returning to the country.

*manorial: 장원의, 영지의

09 Last year, American car buyers named fuel economy the most important consideration when shopping for a car, ① outranking even quality and safety. The change coincides nicely with the ② flood of hybrid and high-efficiency internal-combustion engines on the market. But as efficient as engines may be, they can't compensate for one glaring ③ efficiency : us. Poor driving habits can ④ slash fuel economy by as much as one-third. To ⑤ maximize it, engineers need to not only remake the cars; they need to remake the drivers.

※ 밑줄 친 부분 중 어법상 틀린 것을 고르시오. 【10-12】

10 Insensitivity to pain is dangerous. People with a gene that ① inactivates pain axons suffer repeated injuries and generally fail to learn ② to avoid dangers. One boy with this condition performed street theater in Pakistan by thrusting a knife through his arm or ③ walking on burning coals. He ④ has died at age 14 by falling off a roof. Nevertheless, although we wouldn't want to eliminate pain, it ⑤ would be good to hold it under control.

11 Menno Aden is fascinated by the influence of architecture and design on spaces and the people who inhabit ① them. The 41-year-old artist has ② explored both the exteriors of residential developments and interiors of corporate buildings in his home city of Berlin, rearranging images of each into grids and panel mosaics, ③ occasionally transposing them into video works. But the inspiration for his recent project came from a photographic food diary, ④ which he shot his meals by standing on a chair and aiming his camera downward. This view put more emphasis on the space than the food, and he wondered ⑤ if he could capture an overhead view of an entire room.

12 One of the ① most contesting issues in using local land-use controls for environmental protection purposes is the "takings" problem. The Fifth Amendment to the U.S. Constitution contains the following language: "No person shall ② be deprived of life, liberty, or property, without due process of law; ③ nor shall private property be taken for a public use, without just compensation." This authorizes the government ④ to "take" private property, but only if it is for a public purpose and only if the owners receive just compensation. Land may be taken physically (e.g., for a public park or highway), and the main question will revolve around ⑤ how much the compensation should be.

13 밑줄 친 it이 가리키는 대상이 다른 것은?

It started off like just any other winter day on the farm. But in the afternoon, all hell broke loose. The snow that had accumulated on the roof of the pig pen proved to be too much for it. The roof caved in and a heavy wooden beam trapped one of the baby pigs. The beam pinned ①it down and it couldn't move. When I arrived at the scene, ②it was squealing in pain. I tried to lift the beam off of ③it but faced an unexpected obstacle. The mother pig was protecting the baby pig. It would not let anyone get near its offspring. Little did ④it understand that I was just trying to help. Only when another farm hand restrained the mother with a rope was I able to reach the baby and set ⑤it free.

14 Kevin Han에 관한 다음 글의 내용과 일치하는 것은?

Twenty-seven-year-old lawyer Kevin Han is frugal. Breakfast is 5 yuan (82 cents) for a cup of soybean milk and a hard-boiled egg. He has a 20-yuan lunch of white rice with small portions of meat and vegetables in the cafeteria at his workplace in Beijing. He spends the same for dinner. Han gets deals buying clothes online, lives in a cheap rental apartment, and takes the subway to work (4yuan round-trip). Scrimping is a must if he's to buy his own place. He makes 13,000 yuan per month and saves about half. "My parents are not rich. So I have to save everything by myself."

① 저축하기 위해 아침을 거른다.
② 점심보다 비싼 저녁식사를 한다.
③ 온라인 의류 사업을 한다.
④ 매달 약 6,500 yuan을 저축한다.
⑤ 부유한 부모 밑에서 자랐다.

15 Ed Sheeran에 관한 다음 글의 내용과 일치하는 것은?

"I'm going to go home and watch TV," says Ed Sheeran after serenading a sold-out crowd at his Radio City Music Hall show. The 22-year-old Grammy-nominated singer-songwriter isn't concerned with being anything other than who he really is : the folk-pop rapper your parents might actually listen to. And so far, this refreshing approach seems to be getting him places. Don't believe us? Ask his 6.5-plus million Twitter followers and the thousands of screaming girls who show up at countless concerts simply to see him. Some think Ed is an overnight music sensation, but the Halifax, England native grew up in an artistic home where his love of music was nurtured at a young age.

① 관중들에게 노래하기 전에 TV를 시청할 거라고 말했다.
② Grammy상 후보가 되는 것 말고는 관심이 없다.
③ 6천 5백 만 명 이상의 Twitter follower가 있다.
④ 아무도 그가 하루 밤 사이에 성공했다고 믿지 않는다.
⑤ England 출신으로 예술적 가정 분위기에서 자랐다.

16 Pete Bodharamik에 관한 다음 글의 내용과 일치하지 않는 것은?

Five years ago Pete Bodharamik was a 35-year-old with a big challenge. He had just taken over Jasmine International, the telecom holding company his father had started back in 1982. It was going through rough times, emerging from years in bankruptcy court after his father had diversified on borrowed money in the 1990s. And expectations weren't high that Pete was the one to turn things around. But Pete had spent his time delving into content for new forms of media and pursuing his love of pop culture and entertainment. He invested heavily in expanding Jasmine's limited broadband network in the provinces far from Bangkok, where there was little competition. He fed those big pipes with movies, television shows, music videos, games and other rich content, sometimes produced by the media company he had started.

① 부친이 시작한 회사를 인수했다.
② 부친은 돈을 빌려 사업을 다양화했다.
③ 대중문화에 대한 애정을 버리지 않았다.
④ Bangkok 시내 지역에 투자를 집중했다.
⑤ 자기가 시작한 회사가 콘텐츠를 생산하기도 했다.

17 Sousa에 관한 다음 글의 내용과 일치하지 않는 것은?

> John Philip Sousa started his music education by playing the violin at the age of six. At the age of thirteen, his father, a trombonist in the Marine Band, enlisted Sousa in the U.S. Marine Corps as an apprentice. Several years after serving his apprenticeship, Sousa joined a theatrical orchestra where he learned to conduct. The marching brass bass, or sousaphone, was created in 1893 by J. W. Pepper, a Philadelphia instrument maker, with several of Sousa's suggestions in its design. He organized the Sousa Band the year he left the Marine Band. The band played both in America and around the world, including at the World Exposition in Paris. Sousa passed away from a heart attack at the age of 77 in Pennsylvania. He had conducted a rehearsal of "The Stars and Stripes Forever" the previous day with the Ringgold Band. He was posthumously enshrined in the Hall of Fame for Great Americans in 1976.

① 어릴 때 바이올린을 연주하였으며, 아버지는 미 해병대 밴드의 트롬본 연주자였다.
② 미 해병대 실습생 생활을 마치고, 극장 오케스트라 단원이 되었고, 거기서 지휘를 배웠다.
③ 필라델피아 악기제작자 J. W. Pepper의 제안으로 sousaphone을 만들었다.
④ 그의 Sousa Band는 파리 세계 엑스포에서도 연주하였다.
⑤ 심장 마비로 갑자기 죽은 후, 명예의 전당의 일원이 되었다.

※ 다음 글을 읽고, 빈칸에 들어갈 말로 가장 적절한 것을 고르시오. 【18-22】

18 Perhaps the greatest trap ever set for the human race was the coining of the phrase, "Having it all." Bandied about in speeches, headlines, and articles, these three words are intended to be aspirational but instead make all of us feel like we have fallen short. I have never met a person who has stated emphatically, "Yes, I have it all." Because no matter what any of us has, no one has it all. The antiquated rhetoric of "having it all" disregards the basis of every economic relationship : _____. All of us are dealing with the constrained optimization that is life, attempting to maximize our utility based on parameters like career, kids, and relationships, doing our best to allocate the resource of time. Due to the scarcity of this resource, therefore, none of us can "have it all," and those who claim to are most likely lying.

① the idea of trade-offs
② the pursuit of happiness
③ the notion of absolute wealth
④ the belief of equal distribution
⑤ the law of supply and demand

19 Discussions of ecological sustainability typically focus on greenhouse gas emissions, bio-diversity, and other measurements of the natural world. They include economic and social trends in production or population. But they rarely feature time use. Yet patterns of human time use are key drivers of ecological outcomes. People combine time, money, and natural resources to carry out their daily lives and activities. Firms combine time, physical capital, and natural capital to create production. To a great extent, time and natural resources are substitutes for each other: doing things faster usually takes a greater toll on Earth. So _____ tend to have heavier ecological footprints and greater per capita energy use.

① misconceptions about time and money

② time-stressed households and societies

③ temporal constraints on resource development

④ time-honored notions of sustainable environments

⑤ cases where recycling resources takes greater time

20 Plato in his *Republic* criticizes the poets for corrupting the young. Also, he says that an ideal republic controls music even more tightly than it controls poetry and plays. Musical rhythms, Plato remarks, have great capacity to "insinuate themselves into the inmost part of the soul." Sometimes this is for the good, as when music softens the disposition of a citizen made too rough by time in the gymnasium. But at other times, taste in music threatens the moderation we seek in spirit and sets ferocity on fire. _____ if the republic is to train its young citizens well.

*insinuate: (사상 등을) 은근히 심어 주다

① Aesthetics must defer to politics

② Gymnastics must accompany poetics

③ Moderation must yield to military ferocity

④ Individual taste must prevail over common good

⑤ Citizens must not be indulged in one kind of music

21 I adore riding fast. I love descending in the drops and turns as if I've escaped the bounds of gravity. Though in pictures I might resemble a bike racer, I am the proud owner of ordinary mitochondria, although that does not stop me from occasionally trying to go as quickly as I can. I discover something significant about myself when I push myself that hard. I equally adore riding slow. When I sit upright and spin, I see the world and feel energized and connected to my community. I feel more complete as a cyclist when I pedal to the farmer's market in jeans or meander through the countryside. I am truly _____.

① on track to be a racer

② moved by my own body

③ in love with my saddle

④ convinced of my territory

⑤ at ease with my storytelling

22 Exactly how a gene increases the probability of a given behavior is a complex issue. Some genes control brain chemicals, but others affect behavior indirectly. Suppose your genes make you unusually attractive. As a result, strangers smile at you and many people want to get to know you. Their reactions to your appearance may change your personality, and if so, the genes altered your behavior by altering your environment. For another example, imagine a child born with genes promoting greater than average height, running speed, and coordination. The child shows early success at basketball, and soon spends more and more time playing basketball. Soon the child spends less time on other pursuits — watching television, playing chess, or collecting stamps. Thus the measured heritability of many behaviors might depend partly on genes that affect leg muscles. This is a hypothetical example, but it illustrates the point : _____.

① Success depends heavily on genetic formulas

② Genes influence behavior in roundabout ways

③ Personality is a matter of genes and behavior

④ Environmental adaptation is the key to evolution

⑤ Natural selection is stimulated by behavioral cues

23 빈칸 (A)와 (B)에 들어갈 말로 가장 적절한 것은?

Earth's upper atmosphere — below freezing, nearly without oxygen, flooded by UV radiation — is no place to live. But last winter, scientists from the Georgia Institute of Technology discovered that billions of bacteria actually __(A)__ up there. Expecting only a smattering of microorganisms, the researchers flew six miles above Earth's surface in a NASA jet plane. There, they pumped outside air through a filter to collect particles. Back on the ground, they tallied the organisms, and the count was staggering: 20 percent of what they had assumed to be just __(B)__ or other particles was alive. Earth, it seems, is surrounded by a bubble of bacteria.

	(A)	(B)
①	thrive	— dust
②	thrive	— cells
③	thrive	— germs
④	disintegrate	— radiation
⑤	disintegrate	— microorganisms

※ 다음 글의 제목으로 가장 적절한 것을 고르시오. [24-25]

24

When billionaires turn to philanthropy after making their fortune, they often fund scholarships for poor students, work to improve health care, or contribute to the arts. Chang Yung-Fa's mission is nothing less than to "reorganize" social values. Five years ago he started a cartoon-illustrated magazine, Morals, that each month seeks to uplift people's sense of morality in Taiwan and around the world. Whether he's making money or giving away money, morality underpins much of what the 85-year-old Chang does. He believes that his Evergreen Group — which includes the world's fourth-largest container shipping company, hotels, EVA Airways and long-distance buses to the island's main airport — prospers largely because of congenial staff relations backed by the company culture of morality.

① Bothered Philanthropist in Taiwan

② Higher Morality, Greater Happiness

③ Instilling Morality in Taiwanese Companies

④ Entrepreneur Turned Morality Missionary

⑤ Business and Morality: Like Oil and Water

25 Perhaps the scientists most excited about reigniting the lunar program are not lunar specialists, but astronomers studying a wide range of subjects. Such scientists would like new missions to install a huge telescope with a diameter of 30 meters on the far side of the moon. Two things that a telescope needs for optimum operation are extreme cold and very little vibration. Temperatures on the moon can be as frigid as 200 degrees Celsius below zero in craters on the dark side. Because there is no seismic activity, the moon is a steady base. Permanent darkness means the telescope can be in constant use. Proponents claim that under these conditions a lunar-based telescope could accomplish as much in seventeen days as the replacement for the Hubble telescope will in ten years.

*seismic : 진동의

① Lunar Program: Once in a Blue Moon

② The Case for a Lunar Space Observatory

③ Moon Exploration: One Small Step for Mankind

④ The New Hubble Telescope: Is It Worth It?

⑤ Lunar Specialists vs. General Astronomers

※ 다음 글의 주제로 가장 적절한 것을 고르시오. [26-27]

26 The belief that optimism can keep you alive − or at least stave off cancer − gained traction after the release of a study on recovering breast-cancer patients in the Lancet medical journal in 1979. Since then, it has become a household idea that patients with a "fighting spirit" fare better than those with feelings of hopelessness. However, a few recent large-scale meta-analyses have found a lack of convincing evidence that optimism really extends the lives of cancer patients. Despite the lack of definitive data, the belief in the power of positive thinking has become so widespread that it might actually be doing harm. Cancer patients may feel inclined to act upbeat even when they are distraught, hide their despair instead of seeking solace or treatment, or blame themselves if their disease progresses.

① the dangers of hopelessness for cancer recovery

② the necessity of optimism for recovering patients

③ the downfalls of positive thinking for cancer patients

④ the importance of a sound doctor-patient relationship

⑤ the discovery of new preventative measures for cancer

27 Aristarchus of the Aegean island of Samos first suggested that the earth and the other planets moved about the sun — an idea that was rejected by astronomers until Copernicus proposed it again 2,000 years later. After Copernicus, the Danish astronomer Tycho Brahe watched the motions of the planet Mars from his observatory on the Baltic island of Hveen; as a result Johannes Kepler was able to show that Mars and the earth and the other planets move in ellipses about the sun. Then Isaac Newton proposed his universal law of gravitation and laws of motion, and from these it was possible to derive an exact description of the entire solar system. This occupied the minds of some of the greatest scientists and mathematicians in the centuries that followed.

*ellipse : 타원

① human endeavors to understand the solar system

② distortions of the solar system by ancient scientists

③ superstitions about the solar system in ancient times

④ history of pre-Newtonian physical laws and principles

⑤ some newly discovered information about planet movements

28 다음 글의 요지로 가장 적절한 것은?

In commercial society based upon exchange, every man "becomes in some measure a merchant." The pursuit of self-interest in the market, with its division of labor and his resulting dependence on others, leads him to adapt his behavior to the expectations of others. The market itself is therefore a disciplining institution. "The real and effectual discipline which is exercised over a workman, is not that of his corporation," Adam Smith wrote, "but that of his customers. It is the fear of losing their employment which restrains his frauds and corrects his negligence." In order to become successful in his economic exchanges with others, the individual is led to develop the moderate level of self-command which Smith calls "propriety." The character that the market promotes includes prudence and the ability to defer short-term gratification for long-term benefits.

① 시장에서의 개인의 경제 활동은 자기훈육을 가져오게 된다.

② 개인의 이득추구는 자기조절에 의해 절제되어야 한다.

③ 노동자는 동료 노동자보다 고객에게 더 관심을 가져야 한다.

④ 개인은 지속적인 이득을 위해 즉각적인 만족을 희생해야 한다.

⑤ 시장에서의 개인 활동은 분업과 타인에의 의존을 바탕으로 한다.

29 다음 글의 주장으로 가장 적절한 것은?

Purported to treat a variety of ailments, from fevers to measles to epilepsy, rhinoceros horns have been prized ingredients in Chinese medicines for thousands of years. Sought after for their horns, white rhinos saw their population fall to 100 animals in South Africa by 1910. Today, despite a 1977 ban on the selling of rhino parts, Africa's rhinos once again are facing extinction. Since the ban has not been able to protect the rhinos from illegal poaching, ironically, legalizing a highly regulated trade in rhino horns can end up saving the animals. Rhino horns can be cut or shaved without injuring the animals, and they grow back. If tightly controlled by a single centralized organization, the current demand can be satisfied through legal horn cuttings, along with stockpiles of confiscated black-market horns and those collected from rhinos that die naturally.

① Rhino horns should be considered as an alternative to conventional medicine.
② Legalizing and regulating the trade of rhino horns can save the rhinos.
③ The government must strictly enforce the penalties of illegal poaching.
④ Confiscated black-market rhino horns need to be put to better use.
⑤ Cutting the horns of rhinos is inhumane and should be abolished.

30 다음 글의 상황에 나타난 분위기로 가장 적절한 것은?

It was just another dog day of summer. The sun was shining down brightly but Jake was in the comfort of the shade in his backyard. He had a glass of iced tea in his right hand and a good read in his left. Jake was without a single care in the world. Today, he was just going to sit around and vegetate until dusk. His playful puppy was playing with a ball. She looked at Jake as if to invite him to a game of fetch. But he would not oblige her today. Only an earthquake of 10 points on the Richter scale could drive him from his snug nest.

① bored   ② relaxed
③ nervous   ④ surprised
⑤ playful

※ 다음 글에서 전체 흐름과 관계 없는 문장을 고르시오. [31-32]

31 Thanks to advances in cell cultivation, researchers are closer than ever to growing real, edible meat in labs. Beyond the ethics of raising some 9 billion animals to be killed for food each year in the U.S., factory farms produce vast amounts of waste. ① Scientists are working to come up with efficient ways to recycle this waste. ② The 2 trillion pounds of animal waste pollutes the air and water. ③ Besides the pollution problem, the global demand for meat is expected to grow 60% by 2050, and the amount of farmland and grain needed to feed those chickens, pigs, and cows may be unsustainable. ④ But producing in vitro meat — muscle tissue that is cultured from animal cells and grown in a laboratory — has none of those hang-ups. ⑤ In fact, it's mouthwateringly efficient compared with existing methods of meat production, using 45% less energy and 99% less land.

*hang-up : 고민, 곤란

32 An infant's lack of sparkling dialogue may obscure the fact that we are all born with an ability to communicate. ① A capacity for language exists in our tiny, screaming bodies in the delivery room, along with our eyes, ears, arms, legs, and vital organs. ② The capacity must be stimulated — we need to hear people talk in order to form words — but we are born eager to speak. ③ The newborn baby is patiently waiting for answers to questions: "What will I call the objects that surround me? How will I form positive and negative sentences? How can I express feelings about objects and people?" ④ Only when the baby is able to clearly articulate such questions, do the parents initiate communication. ⑤ The child's brain instinctively searches for answers to these questions and then, like a sponge, soaks them up.

33 글의 흐름으로 보아, 주어진 문장이 들어가기에 가장 적절한 곳은?

Who's going to take care of all of those people?

For a country that has managed to outspend every other developed nation in the world on health care, the U.S. is oddly short on doctors. (①) We have about 30 primary-care physicians per 100,000 people. (②) That is far fewer than any other industrialized country. (③) You may have seen the headlines about U.S. physician shortages and how they're posed to get even worse, with baby boomers entering retirement. (④) This is only worsened by the millions of previously uninsured people about to enter the health care system. (⑤) The most viable solution is a growing population of nurses and other clinicians who have obtained advanced and academic training and are licensed to do many of the same things as physicians.

34 다음 글의 내용을 한 문장으로 나타낼 때, 빈칸 (A)와 (B)에 들어갈 말로 가장 적절한 것은?

For hundreds of years in Europe, religious art was almost the only type of art that existed. Churches and other religious buildings were filled with paintings that depicted people and stories from the Bible. Although most people couldn't read, they could still understand biblical stories in the pictures on church walls. By contrast, one of the main characteristics of art in the Middle East was its absence of human and animal images. By Islamic law, artists are not allowed to copy human or animal figures except on small items for daily use such as rugs and bowls. Thus, on palaces, mosques, and other buildings, Islamic artists have created exclusive arabesques — decoration of great beauty with shapes such as circles, squares, and triangles.

European art differed from Middle Eastern art in that the former contained __(A)__ images, whereas the latter used __(B)__ patterns.

	(A)	(B)		(A)	(B)
①	sacred	animal	②	secular	non-secular
③	religious	circular	④	plain	exquisite
⑤	biblical	geometric			

35 주어진 글 다음에 이어질 글의 순서로 가장 적절한 것은?

Judging by the moon, I knew it was almost four weeks since I had been trapped by the snowstorm. I had stopped counting days on January 6, because on that day my prospects had suddenly taken a turn for the worse.

(A) Blustering clouds engulfed my mountainside in snow, quickly undoing all the good works of the sun. Still, I hadmade some progress during the sunny spell.

(B) The sensation of cool water trickling down my throat felt so good that I almost became addicted to it. I anticipated the small pleasure for hours beforehand.

(C) I discovered that if I compacted snow into balls of ice and set them in the sun, water would drip off the bottom for drinking. This was much easier than melting snow or ice in my mouth. Melting snowballs became a part of my daily ritual.

① (A)−(B)−(C)　　　　　　　　② (A)−(C)−(B)

③ (B)−(A)−(C)　　　　　　　　④ (B)−(C)−(A)

⑤ (C)−(A)−(B)

※ 다음 글을 읽고, 물음에 답하시오. 【36-37】

Near−Earth Objects (NEOs) is a contemporary term for massive objects that periodically cross Earth's orbit, and in doing so come close to our planet. They include asteroids, meteoroids, and comets. (A) Almost all asteroids are confined to the asteroid belt, situated between Mars and Jupiter. It is estimated that more than a thousand asteroids are at least a mile wide. (B) Perhaps a dozen are three or more miles wide. There is no lower limit to asteroid size because they grade down to tiny rocks and particles of dust, but no asteroid is big enough to hold an atmosphere. What produced the asteroids? Isaac Asimov posed the once popular science fiction idea that asteroids are remnants of a small planet whose inhabitants discovered nuclear energy and blew their world to tiny pieces of fragments. (C) But not even a nuclear explosion would be great enough to form the asteroid belt. The prevailing scientific view is that asteroids are material that failed to combine into a planet. (D) One of the recent appearances of the massive NEO was its 1908 crash in Siberia. (E) Earth is spotted with dozens of visible craters that testify to similar impacts. It is widely believed that the impact of a giant NEO caused a mass extinction of life that included the dinosaurs, 65 million years ago.

36 다음 문장이 들어가기에 가장 적절한 곳은?

> It flattened trees for many miles around and killed a herd of reindeer.

① (A) ② (B)
③ (C) ④ (D)
⑤ (E)

37 asteroids에 관한 위 글의 내용과 일치하는 것은?

① 대기권을 형성할 수 있을 만큼 큰 것도 있다.
② 핵폭발로 인해 발생했다는 생각이 한때 유행했다.
③ 행성으로 만들어지기 쉬운 물질로 이루어져 있다.
④ 일반적으로 지구에 떨어지면 높은 언덕을 만든다.
⑤ 1908년에 처음 발생한 것으로 알려져 있다.

※ 다음 글을 읽고, 물음에 답하시오. 【38~39】

Two historical facts highlight a fundamental problem that needs to be addressed in the area of computer security. First, all complex software systems have eventually revealed flaws or bugs that subsequently needed to be fixed. Second, it is extraordinarily difficult to build a computer hardware/software system that is not vulnerable to a variety of security attacks. An illustration of this difficulty is the Windows NT operating system (OS), introduced by Microsoft in the early 1990s. Windows NT was promised to have a high degree of security. Sadly, Windows NT did not deliver on this promise. This OS and its successor Windows versions have been _____.

Problems to do with providing strong computer security involved both design and implementation. It is difficult, in designing any hardware or software module, to be assured that the design does in fact provide the level of security that was intended. This difficulty results in many unanticipated security vulnerabilities. Even if the design is in some sense correct, it is difficult, if not impossible, to implement the design without errors or bugs, providing yet another host of vulnerabilities.

38 위 글의 주제로 가장 적절한 것은?

① finding solutions to design and implementation problems

② building secure computer programming companies

③ difficulty of building secure computer systems

④ responsibilities of bug-free software developers

⑤ requirements for installing a new hardware system

39 위 글의 빈칸에 들어가기에 가장 적절한 것은?

① recently stabilized after numerous trial and error

② constantly updated to outperform their predecessors

③ unduly promoted and sold to over ten million consumers

④ erroneously recognized by software developers as the strongest

⑤ chronically plagued with a wide range of security vulnerabilities

※ 다음 글을 읽고, 물음에 답하시오. 【40-42】

Like many stories, certain details of who or what the Bell Witch was vary from version to version. The prevailing account is that it was (A) the ghost of a woman named Kate Batts, a mean old neighbor of John Bell. Batts believed Bell cheated her in a land purchase and on her deathbed she swore that she would haunt John Bell and his family. This version appears in a Tennessee guidebook published in 1933:

"Sure enough, the Bells were tormented for years by the malicious spirit of Old Kate Batts. John Bell and his daughter Betsy were the principal targets. Toward the other members of the family the witch was either indifferent or, as in the case of Mrs. Bell, friendly.

No one ever saw (B) her, but every visitor to the Bell home heard her all too well. The spirit of Old Kate led John and Betsy Bell on a merry chase. She threw furniture and dishes at them. She pulled their noses, yanked their hair, poked needles into them. She yelled all night to keep them from sleeping, and snatched food from their mouths at mealtimes."

News of the Bell Witch spread quickly. When word of the haunting reached Nashville, one of its most famous citizens, General Andrew Jackson, decided to gather a group of friends to investigate it. The future president of the U.S. wanted to either expose it as a hoax or send (C) the spirit away. Jackson and his men were traveling when suddenly the wagon stopped. The men pushed and pushed, but the wagon could not be moved. Then came the sound of a voice from the bushes saying, "All right general, let the wagon move on. I will see you tonight." The astonished men could not find the source of the voice. The horses then unexpectedly started walking on their own and the wagon moved along again. Jackson indeed encountered (D) the witch that night and left early the next morning, claiming he would rather fight the British than the Bell Witch.

A few explanations of the Bell Witch phenomena have been offered over the years. One is that the haunting was a hoax created by Richard Powell, the schoolteacher of Betsy Bell and Joshua Gardner, the boy with whom Betsy was in love. It seems Powell was deeply in love with Betsy and would do anything to destroy (E) her relationship with Gardner. Through a variety of tricks, it is believed that Powell created all of the ghostly effects to scare Gardner away. In fact, Gardner eventually did break up with Betsy and left the area. It has never been satisfactorily explained, however, how Powell achieved all the effects. But Powell did come out the winner. In the end, he married Betsy Bell.

40 위 글의 제목으로 가장 적절한 것은?

① Story Behind the Bell Witch
② Watch Out for a Witch's Tricks
③ Don't Fall in Love with a Witch
④ General Jackson's Unsuccessful Witch Hunt
⑤ Invention of Witchcraft in the American South

41 밑줄 친 부분 중 가리키는 대상이 다른 것은?

① (A) ② (B)
③ (C) ④ (D)
⑤ (E)

42 위 글의 내용과 일치하지 않는 것은?

① Bell Witch는 Mrs. Bell에게는 우호적이었다.
② Bell Witch는 가구를 던지고 머리카락을 잡아당기기도 했다.
③ Andrew Jackson 장군은 후에 대통령이 되었다.
④ Andrew Jackson은 영국과 싸우기 위해 남부에서의 전투를 중지하였다.
⑤ Powell은 Betsy와 결혼하는 데 성공했다.

※ 다음 글을 읽고, 물음에 답하시오. 【43-45】

(가) I first heard about Veranda Beach on my grandparents' porch the summer I was 13. It was a lazy night that left the hills a smoky blue and the air heavy with the smell of rain. The last shadows were melting into dusk as conversation turned to the summer ahead.

(나) Well, summer passed, and with age came wisdom. I realized the front porch was no enemy to adventure. It was a window on the world and a lesson in how that world works. What's more, the love affair continues to this day — with new lessons adding to the old. On my family's porch, I learned about life and love, hopes and dreams, and promises and trust. One day it was the front door to Tara, as my sister and I assumed awful Southern accents and scouted the horizon for Rhett Butler. The next day it was a castle fortress or a ship at sea. For the adults, lighthearted bantering and games of checkers were __(A)__; talk about taxes and checkbooks was not. The veranda was a place to enjoy the little things. Life was slower there.

(다) Now, more than a few verandas later, I have become a connoisseur of the porch. This summer I am spending time perched on a porch rail, trading stories with my children. As I watch a new generation write their names in the sweat of a lemonade pitcher, I hope they, too, are learning the lessons of Veranda Beach. Be strong against the wind. Be colorful and imaginative — grow in unexpected ways. Watch for the shooting stars. Above all, know that sometimes it's better to have a place to be yourself than to have a place to go.

(라) "Any plans?" my grandfather asked. Tipping his chair back, my father answered, "Just Veranda Beach." They all chuckled. My heart pounded. Veranda Beach? Where was it? When would we go? "Why, you're there already," my father teased. There was a gentle chorus of laughter as they told me the awful truth. Veranda Beach was the front porch. We were going nowhere. My adolescent spirits __(B)__. What did they see in that boring porch? Didn't they know the grass was surely greener in some distant place?

*connoisseur: 감식가, 전문가

43 주어진 글 (가)에 이어질 내용을 순서에 맞게 배열한 것으로 가장 적절한 것은?

① (나)-(다)-(라)
② (나)-(라)-(다)
③ (다)-(나)-(라)
④ (다)-(라)-(나)
⑤ (라)-(나)-(다)

44 위 글의 제목으로 가장 적절한 것은?

① The Gentle Chorus in the Front Porch

② The Greener Grass in My Front Yard

③ Veranda Beach: The Place to Be Yourself

④ The Memory Never Gone with the Wind

⑤ Life's Lesson: Getting Older, but Wiser

45 위 글의 빈칸 (A), (B)에 들어갈 말로 가장 적절한 것은?

	(A)	(B)		(A)	(B)
①	encouraged	– plunged	②	discredited	– plunged
③	explored	– arose	④	favored	– arose
⑤	altered	– drooped			

▶ 해설은 p. 71에 있습니다.

※ 글의 흐름으로 보아, 밑줄 친 단어의 뜻으로 가장 적절한 것을 고르시오. [01-05]

01 Silver dollars <u>doled out</u> by my grandfather were kept by my parents, who did not trust us with them.

① distributed   ② incurred

③ invested   ④ withdrawn

⑤ deposited

02 Magazine titles play a large part in shaping the reader's expectations. They are always written in large letters <u>conjuring up</u> particular associations in the reader's mind.

① customizing   ② invoking

③ traversing   ④ stripping

⑤ circumventing

03 Though the twentieth century saw horrific genocides inspired by Nazi pseudoscience about genetics and race, it also saw horrific genocides inspired by Marxist pseudoscience about the <u>malleability</u> of human nature.

① duality   ② fallibility

③ obscurity   ④ plasticity

⑤ viciousness

04 The oligarchical power of the aristocracy was <u>coveted</u> by the other class of Roman citizens, the plebeians, who included farmers, laborers, and tradesmen.

① deprived   ② strengthened

③ granted   ④ criticized

⑤ envied

05 "Will you take my little brother to New York?" Having lived as a foreigner for a decade, I was accustomed to <u>non sequitur</u> conversations, but that opener left me speechless.

① personal   ② frank

③ elongated   ④ irrelevant

⑤ practical

※ 밑줄 친 부분 중 어법상 틀린 것을 고르시오. 【06-08】

06

Bowling was very popular in the colonies. At first it was called ninepins. Ninepins was ①<u>actually</u> one of several bowling games played by the colonists. Another kind of bowling involved players rolling a larger ball and ②<u>attempted to</u> stop it as close as possible to a smaller ball resting on the green. The player ③<u>closest</u> to the target ball was declared the winner. This type of bowling was similar to the modern game of pitching pennies at a line ④<u>drawn</u> in the dirt. In pitching pennies, the player ⑤<u>whose</u> penny is nearest the line wins the game.

07

The next time you step into a retail store — ① whether it sells consumer electronics, hardware or high fashion — stop and carefully consider your surroundings. Think about the store's layout and displays. Listen to the background sounds. Smell the smells. Chances are everything in the store from the layout and lighting to the music and even the smells ② has orchestrated to help shape your shopping experience — and to open your wallet. In most cases, you're probably being affected in ways so subtle that you don't even realize ③ what is happening to you. Thus, once inside a store, ④ how you as a shopper move in and around the store is not, really, up to you. The next time you visit a store, see if you can spot the subtle things ⑤ that retailers do to affect your shopping behavior.

08

The No. 1 recommendation for great pots is: Think big! Small containers hold too little soil for good root growth and are too much work ① to keep watered. So the larger the container, ② the better. Glazed, fiberglass, and molded-plastic containers hold moisture better than unglazed terra-cotta. Regardless of the type, ③ be sure pots to have drainage holes, and use pot feet or shims to raise them about a half-inch off the ground to allow water to drain away. Fiberglass and plastic pots are less likely to degrade ④ in weather extremes and are easier to move. But heavy containers can give tall plants the foundation needed to prevent toppling in the wind. Lighter pots should ⑤ be secured to prevent tipping.

09 (A), (B), (C)에 들어갈 말로 가장 적절한 것은?

Marketing's impact on individual consumer welfare has been criticized for its high prices, deceptive practices, and poor service to disadvantaged consumers. Marketing's impact on society has been criticized for creating false wants and too much materialism, too (A)[many/few] social goods, and cultural pollution. Critics have also criticized marketing's impact on other businesses for harming competitors and reducing competitions through acquisitions, practices that (B)[create/lift] barriers to entry. Some of these (C)[concerns/suggestions] are justified; some are not.

	(A)	(B)	(C)
①	many	— create	— concerns
②	many	— lift	— suggestions
③	few	— create	— concerns
④	few	— lift	— suggestions
⑤	few	— lift	— concerns

※ 다음 글의 밑줄 친 부분 중, 문맥상 낱말의 쓰임이 적절하지 않은 것을 고르시오. 【10-12】

10

The backstage area, between the stage wall and the rear of the building, was known as the 'tiring house.' Here costumes and props were ① stored and the players got themselves ready. In the early days, tiring houses had been ② free-standing structures, but now they were built into the framework. Immediately behind the stage was a packed and jumbled room where everyone and everything ③ inessential for the day's play were gathered in readiness. Costumes hung everywhere. Players who had several changes in the play would be dressing or undressing, while 'tiremen' tried to keep the clothes in ④ order. Tables and benches were ⑤ covered with players' gear, false beards and wigs, and make-up.

11

As a rule, law enforcement officials can conduct searches upon consent. To be considered valid, consent searches must satisfy two criteria. First, permission must be freely and voluntarily granted. Second, the individual granting consent must have the authority to do so. Once permission is obtained the police may ① legitimately search, but the search may not extend beyond the limits imposed by the person giving consent. The required voluntary nature of the consent means that permission cannot be granted as a result of ② intimidation. If the police extract consent by actual or threatened physical force or by means of trickery, the permission is ③ invalid and so is the resulting search. The second requirement is that only an ④ authorized person can give permission to search. Normally such permission can be granted only by an adult who owns, occupies, or otherwise ⑤ partially controls the house, automobile, office, or whatever other area the police desire to search.

12

A medical system that deploys social support and caring to help boost patients' quality of life may well enhance their very ability to heal. For example, a patient lying in her hospital bed, awaiting major surgery the next day, can't help but ① worry. In any situation, what one person feels strongly tends to pass to ② others: The more stressed and vulnerable someone feels, the more ③ sensitive they are, and the more likely to catch those feelings. If the worried patient shares a room with another patient who also faces surgery, the two of them may well make each other more ④ anxious. But if she shares a room with a patient who has just come out of surgery successfully — and so feels relatively relieved and calm — the emotional effect on her will be more ⑤ aggravating.

13 밑줄 친 ①~⑤ 중에서 의미하는 바가 나머지와 다른 것은?

There used to be ① a tradition at Eton, known as 'capping' — when boys would salute the beaks in the street by pointing a finger at their heads, as an abbreviated doffing of the hat (like a naval or military salute); this would be reciprocated by the beaks. Recently, despite government drives for the promotion of what ② it is pleased to call 'respect,' ③ this tradition has died out: I suppose it takes too much time and effort and shows too much deference — so, like many similar customs, ④ it is doomed in modern Britain. In fairness, soon after having written the above, I was cheered to note that many of the golfers on TV are still following ⑤ the old custom to salute the crowd.

* beak: (영국학생속어) 교사, 교장

14 Garth Brooks에 관한 다음 글의 내용과 일치하는 것은?

Garth Brooks has had a nice, long retirement. Now, it appears to be over. During a news conference Thursday in Nashville, Brooks, 52, is expected to announce details of his comeback, most likely including plans for a world tour. The country superstar, who ranks behind only The Beatles and Elvis Presley in U.S. album sales, walked away from the music business in 2001 to raise his three daughters. Since then, he has only sporadically performed and released music. With Brooks' youngest daughter, Allie, entering college in the fall, the stage is set for his return. He's a master at building anticipation: Last week, his website teased an announcement about the day he'd make his real announcement. It's entirely possible he'll reveal only a portion of his big plan at the event. Or a tour could be only part of what he announces. What else might Brooks be ready to talk about?

① 2001년 은퇴에 대한 이유가 밝혀지지 않았다.
② 은퇴 이후에는 음악 활동을 하지 않았다.
③ 미국내 앨범 판매량에서 2위를 차지한다.
④ 자신의 행보에 대한 궁금증을 잘 유발시킨다.
⑤ 세계 순회공연의 세부계획을 발표하였다.

15 Youth Ambassadors campaign에 관한 다음 글의 내용과 일치하는 것은?

Starting this summer the Hong Kong government plans to have 200,000 youths search Internet discussion sites for illegal copies of copyrighted songs and movies, and report them to the authorities. The campaign has delighted the entertainment industry, but prompted misgivings among some civil liberties advocates. The so-called Youth Ambassadors campaign will start on Wednesday with 1,600 youths pledging their participation at a stadium in front of leading Hong Kong film and singing stars and several Hong Kong government ministers. The Youth Ambassadors represent a new reliance on youths to keep order on the Internet. All members of the Boy Scouts, Girl Guides, and nine other uniformed youth groups, ranging in age from 9 to 25, will be expected to participate.

① 홍콩 젊은이들이 노래와 영화에 대해 토론하는 장이다.
② 연예계뿐만 아니라 모든 계층의 환영을 받았다.
③ 참가선서는 체육계 인사들 앞에서 할 예정이다.
④ 비슷한 캠페인이 예전에도 시도된 적이 있다.
⑤ 열 개 이상의 단체가 참여할 예정이다.

16 Interconnect Adventure Tour에 관한 다음 글의 내용과 일치하지 않는 것은?

> Utah offers the advanced skier the opportunity to ski up to five world-class resorts in a single day with the Interconnect Adventure Tour. The tours, operated by Ski Utah under a special-use permit granted by the U.S. National Forest Service, are conducted by experienced backcountry guides trained in avalanche safety and control. Skiers registering for the tour must be in good physical condition with ski experience in various snow conditions. Each participant's ability is tested prior to the tour's departure. Tours operating on Sunday, Monday, Wednesday and Friday begin at Park City and take in Park City, Brighton, Solitude, Alta and Snowbird; it takes eight hours to complete, with a rest stop for lunch. Tours operating on Tuesday, Thursday and Saturday begin at Snowbird and include Snowbird, Alta, Brighton and Solitude.

① 하루 동안 여러 개의 리조트에서 스키를 즐길 기회를 제공한다.
② 참가자는 눈사태 발생에 대비한 안전 교육을 받아야 한다.
③ 다양한 조건의 눈에서 스키를 탄 경험이 있어야 등록할 수 있다.
④ 출발 전에 모든 참가자의 스키 실력을 테스트한다.
⑤ 토요일에 진행되는 투어는 Park City를 이용할 수 없다.

17 Gersenson에 관한 다음 글의 내용과 일치하지 않는 것은?

Even as he was disassembling cardboard boxes in a garage that served as the warehouse for his just-launched organic produce home-delivery venture, David Gersenson's gut told him Door to Door Organics was destined for big things. "While I was breaking down the boxes, I knew this thing was going to take off," he recalls of that moment in 1997 when he foresaw the future of his company. Started for about $700 in Upper Bucks County, Pa., the business was based on an idea he hatched in his early 20s after eating organic produce on a trip to India. While Gersenson's vision proved prophetic, he could hardly have predicted the outcome of the strategic decisions he made along the way to turn Door to Door Organics into the bustling multistate company it is today. The online grocer of natural and organic produce employs more than 200 people in five metro markets around the country, posted $26 million in revenue in 2013 and is projected to grow to more than $40 million this year.

① 사업을 시작한 초창기에는 차고를 창고로 활용하였다.
② 사업에 대한 구상은 20대 때 인도 여행을 준비하면서 착안하였다.
③ 그의 회사는 유기농 식품을 온라인으로 주문받아 집으로 배달 해준다.
④ 회사 성장과정에서 내린 결정들이 가져올 결과를 거의 예측할 수 없었다.
⑤ 올해 회사의 수익은 2013년 대비 50% 이상 성장할 것으로 추정된다.

※ 다음 글을 읽고, 빈칸에 들어갈 말로 가장 적절한 것을 고르시오. 【18-23】

18 A pay increase is a public good in that workers who are not union members, or who choose not to strike in furtherance of the pay claim, are treated equally with union members and those who did strike. This creates opportunities for individuals to become free riders, reaping benefits without incurring the various costs that group membership may entail. This analysis is significant because it implies that there is no guarantee that the existence of a common interest will lead to the formation of an organization to advance or defend that interest. The pluralist assumption that all groups have some kind of political voice therefore _____. It is also argued that group politics may often empower small groups at the expense of large ones. A larger membership encourages free riding because individuals may calculate that the group's effectiveness will be little impaired by their failure to participate.

① is to be developed into a theory

② will not be on the critic's table

③ will face a loose competition

④ becomes highly questionable

⑤ gains more solid grounds

19 Not surprisingly, many contend that America was born with _____. American stories came from Europe. American myths weren't unique. It took Europeans to tell Americans who they were. The American form of government was borrowed from Europe. Until the great capitalists took their stand, Americans had no kings and queens and castles. No amount of wealth and power have erased this sense of voidness, hence millions of Americans travel to Europe each summer to catch and taste a touch of class. (Perversely the obverse is true, for millions of Europeans travel to America each summer to see the last frontier and see what Americans have done with the heritage Europeans gave them.) America is a mirror that Americans and Europeans continually look into, hoping to find 'that which, for whatever reasons, they have been conditioned to see.'

① an inferiority complex   ② frontier ethics

③ a perfectionist spirit   ④ a pragmatist mind

⑤ a silver spoon

20 With practice in meditation, the whole cognitive system is trained to build models which are less centered on a 'me,' on an imagined self who controls the body's actions and decides what to do. As this illusory self is gently let go, the world appears clearer and less distorted by its needs. Emotions arise and fall away. Ideas form and are let go. To be such a model is to feel free and flowing and able to laugh with the follies of our self-made illusions. It is quite unlike being a closely bound and defended model of self as most of us _____.

① succeed in doing so   ② try to be

③ are allowed to go   ④ are most of the time

⑤ depend on each other

21 Art, like most things, is more enjoyable when you know something about it. You can walk for hours through the Louvre admiring paintings, but the experience becomes much more interesting when someone knowledgeable is walking with you. A multimedia document can play the role of guide whether you're at home or in a museum. It can let you hear part of a preeminent scholar's lecture on a work. It can refer you to other works by the same artist or from the same period. You can even zoom in for a closer look. If multimedia reproductions and presentations make art more accessible and approachable, people who see the reproductions will _____. Exposure to the reproductions is likely to increase rather than diminish reverence for the real art and encourage more people to get out to museums and galleries.

① become more creative

② want to see the originals

③ depreciate the delicacy of art

④ elaborate on the multimedia works

⑤ deplete their crave for quality artworks

22 _____ he might have lived longer. According to legend, many evil portents preceded his death, among them, according to Plutarch, "the lights in the heavens, the noises heard in the night, and the wild birds which perched in the forum." And, famously, the dictator had been warned by a fortuneteller to "Beware the Ides of March." The morning of his last day, his wife, Calpurnia, told him she'd had terrible dreams during the night; weeping, she begged him not to go to the Senate. Caesar was alarmed, says Plutarch, "for he never before discovered any womanish superstition in Calpurnia." He decided to heed her warning, but changed his mind when one of the conspirators against him, Decimus Brutus, hinted that the Senate planned that day to declare him king of all the Roman provinces outside Italy.

① Had Caesar believed in signs and omens

② Unless Calpurnia had gone to hear the prophecy

③ Had Caesar ignored Calpurnia's womanish superstition

④ As long as Caesar had not listened to the fortunetellers

⑤ Had the Senate declared Caesar king of all the Roman provinces

23
One of the things that distinguishes television news (and other so-called 'informational' shows) is that unlike drama, the news never attempts to _____. We are always acknowledged by being directly, openly addressed ; when we look at television anchors, they look directly back at us, in a kind of staring contest that one might have with one's cat. In this contest, though, it is always we who blink or look away, out of boredom or, more likely, because any television presentation, even the news, is little more than part of an ongoing electronic and informational 'flow' that is only intermittently heeded. We look away, but the anchors never do, for this is the focus of their day, of their existence. We think we watch them, but they watch us, or a virtual us, even harder.

① fix its gaze on us, the viewers   ② divert viewers' attention to trivialities
③ disguise our presence, our looking   ④ presuppose our being, our watching
⑤ garner information on viewing figures

24 빈 칸 (A)와 (B)에 들어갈 말로 가장 적절한 것은?

In retrospect, it looks as if Massachusetts made (A) in 1994 when it let its two most prestigious and costly hospitals — Massachusetts General Hospital and Brigham & Women's Hospital, both affiliated with Harvard — merge into a single system known as Partners HealthCare. Investigations have documented that the merger gave the hospitals enormous market leverage to drive up health care costs in the Boston area by demanding high reimbursements from insurers that were unrelated to the quality or complexity of care delivered. Now, belatedly, Attorney General Martha Coakley is trying to (B) the hospitals with a negotiated agreement that would at least slow the increases in Partners' prices and limit the number of physician practices it can gobble up, albeit only temporarily. The experience in Massachusetts offers a cautionary tale to other states about the risks of merging big hospitals.

       (A)   (B)
① a serious mistake − rein in
② a serious mistake − shut down
③ a big contribution − rein in
④ a big contribution − choke up
⑤ remarkable progress − shut down

25 You must follow Cross-Continent Enterprise's (CCE) processes and adhere to the system of internal controls around supplier selection. Supplier selection should never be based on receipt of a gift, hospitality or payment. When supplier selection is a formal, structured invitation for the supply of products or services (often called a ' tender'), it is most important we maintain documentation supporting our internal controls. In the public sector, such a tender process may be required and determined in detail by law to ensure that such competition for the use of public money is open, fair and free from corruption. A tender process includes an invitation for other parties to make a proposal, on the understanding that any competition for the relevant contract must be conducted in response to the tender, no parties having the unfair advantage of separate, prior, closed-door negotiations for the contract where a bidding process is open to all qualified bidders and where the sealed bids are in the open for scrutiny and are chosen on the basis of price and quality.

① CCE's Regulations of the Supplier Selection Process
② Why Is Supplier Selection Important at CCE?
③ How to Boost Employee Morale of the Company
④ Legal Issues Surrounding the Tender Competition Process
⑤ Documentation Requirements in the Bidder Selection Process

26 As light hits the Earth's atmosphere, the different colors react in different ways. Some of them get absorbed by the gas molecules while others do not. Most of the longer-wavelength colors (such as red and orange) pass straight through the atmosphere and are unaffected, while many of the shorter-wavelength colors (such as violet and blue) get absorbed by the gas molecules, because the wavelengths (i.e., the distance between the peaks of each wave) of these colors are similar in size to the diameter of an atom of oxygen. The gas molecules then radiate these colors and scatter them across the sky, causing the sky to appear blue.

① The Fate of Colors Destined by Wavelengths
② Science Behind the Science of Gas Molecules
③ The Nature of Light: The Longer, the Brighter
④ Gas Molecules vs. Wavelengths: Who Wins?
⑤ How Do Our Naked Eyes Perceive Colors?

※ 다음 글의 주제로 가장 적절한 것을 고르시오. 【27-28】

27 Observational studies provide information as to some of the things mothers do around children, but little about their feelings, ideas and beliefs concerning children, child care and themselves. Mothers hold a range of views about children and parenting which are not necessarily in agreement with those of formal psychology and these may influence how they interact with their children. Some mothers find that being sensitive to their children does not come easily. This may be because they cannot relate easily to their children, because they are depressed or isolated, or because they do not believe that sensitivity is an important part of their relationship with the child. For some mothers there may be a mismatch between their behavior and feelings and those prescribed by psychological theories; and there may be conflict between their own needs and those of their children.

① reasons for mothers' negligence in child-rearing
② necessity to establish a philosophy of mothers' parenting
③ gaps between what mothers want and what their children want
④ psychological underpinnings of conflict between mothers and children
⑤ discrepancy in the concept of parenting between mothers and psychologists

28 Alexander the Great launched Egypt's Greco-Roman period in 332 B.C. After conquering parts of western Asia, the Macedonian general was welcomed in Egypt by a people politically weary after several hundred years of unrest and occupation by outsiders. The mixing of Greek (and later Roman) influences with a still rich Egyptian culture helped set social and religious change spinning around the Mediterranean. In this newest period of vibrancy the Egyptians' styles of dress and sculpture worked their way to Greece and Rome, while Egyptian gods and demigods mingled with their counterparts in Greek and Roman mythology. The mother goddess Isis would eventually have temples built to her in the land of the Caesars, while many Greco-Roman gods and heroes would be honored in temples throughout Egypt.

① Egypt's social reform efforts during the Greco-Roman period
② political unrest in Egypt caused by Alexander the Great
③ cultural interchanges between Egypt and Greece/Rome
④ penetration of Egyptian lifestyles into the Greco-Roman world
⑤ Greek and Roman influences on Egyptian peasants' daily lives

29 다음 글의 주장으로 가장 적절한 것은?

A lapse is a single event during which you take up an old behavior you've been trying to change. The key to overcoming lapses is to expect them on occasion just as traffic tie-ups and road construction may delay you on the highway. Think about the last time you embarked on a long road trip. Chances are you encountered something along the way that slowed you down — but you did not give up, turn the car around, and head home. You still reached your intended destination, though it may have taken you a little longer than expected. It's the same with personal change. Let's say you've been balancing your plate, adding more fruits and vegetables, but suddenly give in to the urge to eat a fast — food hamburger. You've just had a lapse.

① You should remind yourself of the direction you'd like to be headed in.

② When you have an urge to resume an old habit, try to resist the urge.

③ Take a shortcut when your plan for change meets unforeseen delays.

④ Occasional deviations encountered on your way to change are not abnormal.

⑤ Seek support from those who are trying to change the same behavior as you are.

30 다음 글에 나타난 "I"의 심정으로 가장 적절한 것은?

During the day the air was hot and dry, and filled with fine particles of dust. At night, when it was cooler, gnats and mosquitoes made me appreciate all the more their absence in the forest. My hut, ten times the size of my home in the hunting camp, seemed close and stuffy, and as I lay in bed I could hear the huge spiders, some several inches across, crawling about in the leaves of the roof. Occasionally one dropped onto the bed with a dull thud and lay there for a while before stalking away. At first I carried out an active campaign to get rid of them, but it was useless — and a mosquito net would have been unbearably hot. The familiar night sounds of the forest were replaced by the cries of drunks coming home from a dance at the nearby hotel.

① gloomy and detached   ② depressed but curious

③ daunted but anticipating   ④ exhilarated and energized

⑤ reminiscent and displeased

31

To conclusively set new safety standards for CT radiation, researchers are beginning to directly investigate the number of cancers among people who have received CT scans. ① About a dozen such studies from different countries will be published in the next few years. ② In the meantime, some researchers have started testing whether good images can be produced with radiation doses lower than those generated in typical CT scans. ③ Radiologists at Mass General Hospital have an unusual way of conducting such investigations. ④ A single CT scan subjects the human body to between 150 and 1,100 times the radiation of a conventional X-ray. ⑤ In that way, they scan bodies many times without worrying about making people sick and perform an autopsy to check whether the scan has correctly identified a medical problem. Rather than recruiting living, breathing human volunteers for their studies, they work with cadavers.

32

Foreign language learners may perform different speech acts than native speakers in the same contexts, or, alternatively, they may elect not to perform any speech act at all. The best examples of this come from authentic conversations and role-plays where speakers have some flexibility in determining what they will say or do. In academic advising sessions, native speakers and learners favor different speech acts. ① Native speakers produce more suggestions than learners per advising session, whereas learners produce more rejections per advising session than native speakers do. ② In addition, the absence of the speech act of advice was salient for academic advisers. ③ The two speech acts of suggestion and rejection seem to serve the same function, that of control. ④ Native speakers exert control over their course schedules by making suggestions ; in contrast, the learners do so through rejections, by blocking the suggestions of the advisers. ⑤ Although both groups of students participate in determining what courses they ultimately take, the resulting feeling of harmony in the interview is perceived by the advisers to be noticeably different.

33 글의 흐름으로 보아, 주어진 문장이 들어가기에 가장 적절한 곳은?

> Other promising leads come from a major source virtually untapped by both traditional and modern medicine systems — the ocean.

All frogs and toads secrete defensive fluids, many of which possess antibiotic properties. (①) That's why Chinese folk healers have treated wounds such as sores and dog bites with toad secretions, sometimes obtained by surrounding the toads with mirrors to scare them. (②) While such methods may sound strange, a large percentage of medicines used in Western countries come from nature or from chemical formulas found in nature. (③) Steroids, penicillin, digitalis, morphine, and aspirin are only a few examples. (④) One of the most exciting discoveries in medicine is Taxol, which fights breast and ovarian cancer and is derived from the bark of the yew tree. (⑤) Candidates include an anticancer drug from the Antarctic seabed and a painkiller from the venom of a tropical cone snail.

34 다음 글의 내용을 한 문장으로 나타낼 때, 빈칸 (A)와 (B)에 들어갈 말로 가장 적절한 것은?

Cinema's status as a spatiotemporal medium owed as much to its historical context as to its technologically granted abilities. Debuting at the end of the nineteenth century, the moving picture stood as the culmination of a series of inventions that emphasized the capacities of technology to collapse conventional boundaries of time and space. The cinema operated as part of a continuum that stretched from the telegraph and the telephone (which had enabled communication to take place between two locations separated by considerable distance), through to the locomotive and automobile (which allowed their passengers to traverse substantial areas with previously unequalled speed, thereby collapsing travel time), and the phonograph and photograph (which had frozen time through the capturing of sound and image, respectively, from reality via a photoelectric process). Cinema was the latest of inventions expanding the traditional sense of how to represent and conceptualize space and time.

The (A) of cinema in history represents the culmination of technological achievements that helped (B) the boundaries of time and space.

	(A)	(B)			(A)	(B)
①	advent	condense		②	advent	surpass
③	waning	condense		④	waning	surpass
⑤	revival	collapse				

35 주어진 글 다음에 이어질 글의 순서로 가장 적절한 것은?

Imagine that you are feeling a bit down because you have just moved to a new neighborhood and are finding it difficult to meet people.

(A) After a few weeks you find that you are indeed surrounded by a close circle of friends. In fact, it is quite possible that the fortuneteller did not actually see into the future but instead actually helped to create it.

(B) Just for fun, you decide to go along to the local fortuneteller to find out what the future holds for you. The fortuneteller gazes into her crystal ball, smiles and says that the future looks bright. She says that within a few months you will be surrounded by many close and loyal friends.

(C) You are reassured by her comments and walk away feeling much happier than when you arrived. Because you now feel happy and confident about the future, you smile more, go out more and chat to more people.

① (A) − (B) − (C)　　　　② (A) − (C) − (B)

③ (B) − (A) − (C)　　　　④ (B) − (C) − (A)

⑤ (C) − (A) − (B)

※ 다음 글을 읽고 물음에 답하시오. 【36~37】

Professor Balak at the Indian Institute of Technology (IIT) in Delhi heads a team behind the Smartcane™, a new device using ultrasound to guide the visually impaired through the busy streets of India by building upon the widely used white cane. "A white cane is an excellent device, providing a lot of information to users," he says. (A) "But it is poor at detecting obstacles that are above waist height and do not have a touch-point on the ground, such as a tree branch sticking out into your path." (B) The smart technology version instead sends out ultrasound waves via a device attached to a standard white cane; it detects them on their return, and uses vibrations to inform users of any obstacles in their way. (C) The real benefit comes from the ultrasound scanning a 45 degree span above the knee, providing information a regular cane simply can't provide. (D) As people move the cane from left to right when they walk, vibrations detected on one side mean they should move towards the other. (E) Differing patterns and intensities of vibration tell users the distance of the object obstructing their path, as far as three meters away.

36 다음 문장이 들어가기에 가장 적절한 곳은?

> The team at Smartcane™ took on this challenge by copying the skills of animals such as bats, which emit sonar calls into their surroundings and use the echoes bouncing back from nearby objects to divert around them.

① (A)   ② (B)
③ (C)   ④ (D)
⑤ (E)

37 Smartcane™에 관한 위 글의 내용과 일치하지 않는 것은?

① IIT의 한 교수가 이끄는 팀에 의해 개발되었다.
② 기존에 사용되던 제품을 토대로 만들었다.
③ 이용자의 무릎 위 45도 범위를 감지한다.
④ 이용자는 진동이 탐지된 방향과 반대로 이동한다.
⑤ 진동의 패턴으로 장애물의 높이를 식별한다.

※ 다음 글을 읽고 물음에 답하시오. 【38-39】

Once, a long time ago, I was a young lieutenant in the 82nd Airborne Division, trying to orient myself on a field problem at Fort Bragg, North Carolina. As I stood studying a map, my platoon sergeant, a veteran of many junior officers, approached. "You figure out where we are, lieutenant?" he asked. "Well, the map says there should be a hill over there, but I don't see it," I replied. "Sir," he said, "if the map doesn't agree with the ground, then the map is wrong." Even at the time, I knew I had just heard a profound truth.

Over the many years I have spent listening to people's stories, especially all the ways in which things can go awry. I have learned that our passage through life consists of an effort to get the maps in our heads to conform to the ground on which we walk. Ideally, this process takes place as we grow. Our parents teach us, primarily by example, what they have learned. Unfortunately, we are seldom wholly _____ to these lessons. And often, our parents' lives suggest to us that they have little useful to

convey, so that much of what we know comes to us through the frequently painful process of trial and error.

38 위 글의 주제로 가장 적절한 것은?

① reasons for teaching students how to read maps
② difficulties of transferring leadership to subordinates
③ value of maps drawn on our mind
④ importance of personal experience in life
⑤ ways to expose children to direct experiences

39 위 글의 빈칸에 들어가기에 가장 적절한 것은?

① receptive   ② inappropriate
③ restricted   ④ addicted
⑤ conducive

Hunter-gatherers reached Australia about 50,000 years ago. Armed with fire and primitive tools they were able to have a significant impact on the environments they colonized. The fossil record shows a sudden extinction of many large mammals in Australia, which appears to coincide with human colonization, but the evidence for cause and effect is (A)<u>equivocal</u>. There is some debate as to whether the extinctions were caused by human activity or by a period of rapid climate change to which many species were (B)<u>able to</u> adapt. During the late Pleistocene, humans arrived in Australia and more than 85% of large (body mass exceeding 44kg) marsupials and birds were extinct. Was this just coincidence? Dr. David Miller examined evidence for the cause of extinction of the mihirung (a large flightless bird) related to the emu. The time of extinction corresponds to a period of only moderate climate change and he concludes that human impact on this bird's habitat is the most likely (C)<u>cause</u>. However, Dr. Susan Bowman argues that there is no convincing evidence that human predation was the direct cause of the extinction of such a large amount of the Australian megafauna unless the aboriginal population was considerably (D)<u>denser</u> than today. A more likely scenario is that the impact of the use of fire by early aboriginal populations changed the landscape so radically that many species were unable to survive. Aboriginal landscape burning played a crucial role in the (E)<u>formation</u> of typical Australian grassland plant communities before the arrival of Europeans. This has created habitats suitable for some species that are adapted to grazing, but hostile to many browsing animals reliant on scrubby vegetation: browsing is a characteristic of many of the extinct species.

40 위 글의 제목으로 가장 적절한 것은?

① What the Burning Brought to the Landscape

② Magnitude of Human Activity on Climate Change

③ Footprints of Humans' Arrival in Australia

④ How Australians Colonized the Environment

⑤ The Effects of Disappearance of Habitats for Animals

41 밑줄 친 단어 중에서, 글의 흐름에 적절하지 않은 것은?

① (A)   ② (B)

③ (C)   ④ (D)

⑤ (E)

42 위 글의 내용과 일치하지 않는 것은?

① A sudden disappearance of a number of large mammals in Australia can be substantiated by fossils.

② Dr. Miller believes that people's arrival in Australia and the extinction of many birds during the late Pleistocene is not coincidental.

③ Dr. Bowman says human predation cannot be blamed for the extinction of large Australian animals on a massive scale.

④ The mihirung got extinct in a period of moderate climate change.

⑤ Grassland plant communities created habitats for both grazing and browsing species.

※ 다음 글을 읽고 물음에 답하시오. 【43 – 45】

(가) When you slap some meat inside two slices of bread, you have a sandwich, at least according to the U.S. Department of Agriculture, which enforces the safety and labeling of meat and poultry. "We're talking about a traditional closed-face sandwich," says Mark Wheeler, who works in food safety at the USDA. "A sandwich is a meat or poultry filling between two slices of bread, a bun or a biscuit." That excludes items like burritos, wraps or hot dogs.

(나) The debate got so heated that in 2006, a contract dispute over whether Qdoba Mexican Grill's burritos qualify as sandwiches went to trial. Expert witnesses including chefs and food critics testified, much deliberation took place, and in the end, Superior Court Judge Jeffrey Locke ruled burritos are not sandwiches. That settled it in Massachusetts. But for every solid definition in every place, you can find __(A)__. An ice cream sandwich isn't really a sandwich, according to the feds. But we call it that. A taco is not a sandwich in New York. But a burrito somehow is. But New York hasn't explained why — at least not yet.

(다) What do all these say? Sliced bread brought us sandwiches. But they keep changing. Food trends flash in and out. And keeping up with all the innovation is a losing game for __(B)__. Whether it's sandwiches or smartphones, the government tries to classify these things to protect the public. But innovation moves faster than the standards can change — a tension Veltman sees again and again. "The people that write these memos are in the business of trying to classify the unclassifiable. Human behavior is kind of infinitely varied. You can never come up with a scheme for it that actually fits everything," Veltman says.

(라) But the USDA isn't the only place that must define a sandwich. It matters to jurisdictions across the country, mainly for inspection and tax purposes. Noah Veltman, a computer developer, has a weird hobby, which is reading obscure government memos. He says, "My new home state of New

York has a special tax category for sandwiches. So they publish this memo that explains that a sandwich includes club sandwiches, BLTs, hot dogs and burritos. And then you wonder, are burritos really a sandwich?" New York says yes, the USDA says no, and it makes a difference when it's inspection time.

43 주어진 글 (가)에 이어질 내용을 순서에 맞게 배열한 것으로 가장 적절한 것은?

① (나) — (다) — (라)
② (다) — (나) — (라)
③ (다) — (라) — (나)
④ (라) — (나) — (다)
⑤ (라) — (다) — (나)

44 위 글의 제목으로 가장 적절한 것은?

① Superior Courts Sandwiched between Two Forces
② When Is the Right Time to Call Burritos Sandwiches?
③ Tension between New York vs. USDA : A Story Behind
④ Defining Sandwiches : A Lesson on Regulations and Innovation
⑤ Local Food Always Wins : The Case of Burritos and Sandwiches

45 위 글의 빈 칸 (A), (B)에 들어갈 말로 가장 적절한 것은?

	(A)	(B)
①	an edge case	— regulators
②	an edge case	— chefs and food critics
③	a lucid case	— software developers
④	a lucid case	— chefs and food critics
⑤	a lucid case	— regulators

06 2016학년도 기출문제

▶ 해설은 p. 84에 있습니다.

※ 밑줄 친 단어의 뜻으로 가장 적절한 것을 고르시오. 〔01 – 05〕

01 Who would have guessed that the movie star's fame would be <u>ephemeral</u>?

① fleeting
② residual
③ perpetual
④ legendary
⑤ credulous

02 Karen tried to <u>cajole</u> his friend into driving her to the mall, but to no avail.

① coax
② bully
③ slander
④ provoke
⑤ hypnotize

03 She is extremely <u>fastidious</u> about keeping the premises spotless, almost to a fault.

① perilous
② insidious
③ insolvent
④ vindictive
⑤ meticulous

04 Dreams help people work through the day's emotional <u>quandaries</u>. It is like having a built-in therapist.

① bonds   ② dilemmas

③ failures   ④ ecstasies

⑤ irritations

05 He's going to promote me to Clare's level, and he's telling me <u>discreetly</u> so she won't get jealous.

① rashly   ② mildly

③ enviously   ④ cautiously

⑤ impartially

※ 밑줄 친 부분 중, 어법상 틀린 것을 고르시오. 【06-08】

06 I once lived in a coastal village of Papua New Guinea. Children there did not live with their own parents but moved from house to house ①<u>as</u> they wished. Ten-year-olds could ②<u>be seen</u> carrying babies or tending cooking fires. By fourteen they were doing adult work with confidence and pride. As the newest and most interesting thing in the village, I had a dozen or so kids ③<u>sleeping</u> on my veranda. When tropical diarrhea struck in the small hours of the night, I had to pick my way out through a carpet of small brown bodies. It occurred to me ④<u>what</u> this would be an easy place to be a parent, since the work and pleasure of parenting was shared by the whole village. In fact, any adult ⑤<u>who</u> was present was a parent.

07 Born into great wealth but plunged into poverty as a teen, I grew up knowing more about the perils of losing success than the secrets of ①<u>attaining</u> it. Although my parents recovered after ②<u>being stripped</u> of everything in midlife, they never regained a prosperous mind-set. And I absorbed their fears ③<u>more fully</u> than their successes. Those fears fueled my desire to be financially successful and ④<u>was</u>, in part, what drove me to make a living out of teaching people how to achieve. I grew up to be a motivational speaker who inspired thousands of business executives and professional athletes ⑤<u>to achieve</u> their goals using valuable principles of success.

08 There are numerous myths and legends associated with gems. Some tell of cursed stones; ①others of stones with special powers of healing, or that protect or give good luck to the wearer. Some of ②the largest known diamonds have legends associated with them that have been told and retold over centuries, and ③many now lost are surrounded by tales of intrigue and murder. Some mines ④are thought to be cursed—probably rumors spread by the mine owners to keep unwanted prospectors away. In Myanmar, for instance, where all gemstones belonged to the monarch, the belief that anyone who took a stone from a mine would be cursed ⑤ may have deliberately cultivated to curb losses of a valuable national asset. [3점]

09 (A), (B), (C)에 들어갈 말로 가장 적절한 것은?

Last summer, a 26-year-old woman in California called 911 to report an emergency. Had she placed her emergency call on a landline, first responders would have been able to (A) [pinpoint/overlook] her location in a matter of seconds. But because the current 911 system has gone largely unchanged since it was designed in the 1960s, police were forced to use (B) [precise/imprecise] information provided by her wireless carrier to determine where she might be. When an emergency call is made on a mobile device, telecommunications companies use (C) [triangulation/circulation]—comparing the signal strength and time the signal takes to reach a number of cell towers—to approximate the phone's position. This technique placed the woman within a one-block radius, and it took over 20 minutes to find her.

	(A)	(B)	(C)
①	pinpoint	··· imprecise	··· triangulation
②	pinpoint	··· imprecise	··· circulation
③	overlook	··· precise	··· circulation
④	overlook	··· precise	··· triangulation
⑤	overlook	··· imprecise	··· circulation

※ 다음 글의 밑줄 친 부분 중, 문맥상 낱말의 쓰임이 적절하지 않은 것을 고르시오. 【10-12】

10 In all history, nothing is so surprising or so difficult to account for as the sudden rise of civilization in Greece. Much of what makes civilization had already existed for thousands of years in Egypt and in Mesopotamia, and had ①spread thence to neighbouring countries. But certain elements had been ②lacking until the Greeks supplied them. What they achieved in art and literature is familiar to everybody, but what they did in the purely intellectual realm is even more ③ordinary. They invented mathematics and science and philosophy; they first wrote history as ④ opposed to mere annals; they speculated freely about the nature of the world and the ends of life, without being ⑤bound in the fetters of any inherited orthodoxy. [3점]

11 For ordinary citizens the electric lights that dispelled the gloom of the city at night offered the most dramatic evidence that times had changed. Gaslight—① illuminating gas produced from coal—had been in use since the early nineteenth century, but its 12 candlepower lamps lighted the city's public spaces only ②dimly. The first commercial use of electricity was for ③better city lighting. Charles F. Brush's electric arc lamps, installed in Wanamaker's department store in Philadelphia in 1878, threw a brilliant light and soon ④established gaslight on city streets and public buildings across the country. ⑤Electric lighting then entered the American home, thanks to Thomas Edison's invention of a serviceable incandescent bulb in 1879. Edison's motto—"Let there be light!"—truly described the experience of the modern city.

12 What else, besides love, gets passed on during a kiss? Dutch researchers tracked how kissing affected the ①oral bacteria of 21 couples. They asked one person in each pair to ②consume a probiotic yogurt drink with specific bacterial strains to track the spread of germs. Then that person was asked to ③share a ten-second kiss with his or her partner. The average kiss ④extinguished as many as 80 million bacteria. Although this doesn't sound very hygienic, experts say exposure to someone else's bacteria could actually help ⑤strengthen your immunity.

13 밑줄 친 ①~⑤ 중에서 의미하는 바가 나머지와 다른 것은?

It's really not that hard to build a flying car—the first working model got up in 1947. The real challenge turns out to be building ①<u>a flying car</u> that makes sense. Elon Musk, CEO of both Tesla and SpaceX, keeps getting asked why he can't mate his two companies and give birth to ②<u>a rocket car</u>. He answered in a series of recent tweets, including: "③ <u>Airborne auto</u> pros: travel in 3D fast. Cons: risk of car falling on head much greater than ④<u>one moving in two vectors</u>." And Peter Thiel, the famous investor, goes around saying, "We wanted ⑤<u>real sky cars</u>; instead we got junk."

14 Temple Grandin에 관한 다음 글의 내용과 일치하는 것은?

What do neurologists, cattle and fast-food restaurants have in common? They all owe a great deal to one woman, a renowned animal scientist born with autism, Temple Grandin. Though she did not utter a word until her fourth birthday, she splashed onto the stage of public awareness in 1995, thanks to the famed neurologist Oliver Sacks. But as with many psychological disorders, autism is a spectrum, and Temple is on one edge. Living on this edge has allowed her to be an extraordinary source of inspiration for autistic children. She is also a source of hope for another mammal: the cow. Using her unique window into the minds of animals, she has developed housing for cattle that improves their quality of life by reducing stress. And though the fast-food industry continues to use cattle in its patties, it has come to appreciate the ethics and compassion of a Grandin burger.

① 자폐증을 갖고 태어난 동물 과학자다.
② 1995년 한 사회 비평가에 의해서 알려지게 되었다.
③ 모든 어린이들에게 영감의 원천이었다.
④ 소의 스트레스를 줄이는 사료를 개발했다.
⑤ Grandin 버거의 비윤리성을 비난했다.

15 filefish에 관한 다음 글의 내용과 일치하는 것은?

Now you see it, now you don't. The slender filefish has a neat way to avoid its predators. It has evolved the ability to become almost invisible. Justine Allen of Brown University was amazed by how fast the fish camouflaged themselves when she saw them in the Caribbean. It took them just two seconds to match the colors of the sea fans, or gorgonians, they swam past. How does it work? To see an object for what it is, you need to be able to perceive its edges, which mark it out as being separate from the background. Allen found that the filefish changes its coloration to create "false edges." For example, it can make a dark, longitudinal stripe appear on its body that looks like a real edge. The eye sees this false edge, and so can miss the true outline of the fish.

① 천적을 피하는 기술이 없다.
② 눈에 안 띄게 하는 능력을 상실했다.
③ 2초 만에 몸의 색을 바꿀 수 있다.
④ 몸의 크기를 늘려서 가짜 윤곽을 만든다.
⑤ 몸에 가로 줄무늬를 만든다.

16 다음 글의 내용과 일치하지 않는 것은?

A source of confusion and misunderstanding that leads to disappointment is the often complex and ambiguous language in insurance contracts. Much of the billions of dollars of damage wrought by Hurricane Katrina on the Gulf Coast of Mississippi occurred when Katrina's huge storm surge damaged or destroyed thousands of homes and businesses. Homeowners, infuriated when they realized that their policies covered wind—not water— damage, teamed with their state governments to sue insurance carriers. They argued that, even if their insurance did not cover water damage, it still should pay because Katrina's screaming winds drove a wall of water that damaged their property. The homeowners lost the suit, but the insurance industry lost much credibility and people became more concerned that their coverage was much less than it appeared to be on paper.

① 보험 계약서 상의 언어로 인해 오해가 일어나기도 한다.

② Hurricane Katrina로 수십억 달러의 피해가 발생했다.

③ 주택소유자들은 보험회사를 상대로 소송했다.

④ 주택소유자들은 물로 인한 피해도 보상하라고 요구했다.

⑤ 주택소유자들은 보험회사를 상대로 한 소송에서 승소했다.

17 Candace Hill에 관한 다음 글의 내용과 일치하지 않는 것은?

Eleven seconds is the benchmark that separates the women from the girls in the 100 meters. Last Saturday, at the Brooks PR Invitational in Seattle, 16-year-old Candace Hill joined the elite group with a scorching win in 10.98 seconds, becoming the first U.S. high school girl to break the 11-second barrier, smashing the American junior and world youth records. Candace, who finished her second year at Rockdale County High in Georgia last month, is a five-time national champion, and already held Georgia state records in the 100- and 200-meter dash. Her record-setting race would have earned third place at this year's NCAA championships and tied for 10th best in the world this season.

① Seattle에서 개최된 대회에 참가했다.

② 11초 벽을 깬 최초의 미국 여고생이다.

③ 지난달에 고등학교 2학년을 마쳤다.

④ Georgia주 200미터 경주 기록 보유자이다.

⑤ 올해 NCAA 대회에서 3등을 차지했다.

※ 다음 글을 읽고, 빈칸에 들어갈 말로 가장 적절한 것을 고르시오. [18-23]

18 People's relationship with animals is fraught with _____. They express love and appreciation for them and have enacted laws to forbid cruelty to them. The United States is a pet-keeping society, with more dogs, cats, parrots, hamsters, and other pets combined than people and a $60-billion-a-year industry for their care. Millions of Americans are engaged with wildlife in some way, and some of their happiest moments are spent in unspoiled settings. And yet at the same time, they exploit animals on a massive scale, with billions of creatures killed or abused every year for food, clothing, research, and other purposes.

① gratitude   ② hostility

③ protectiveness   ④ responsibilities

⑤ contradictions

19 We are such social animals that we are completely preoccupied with what others think about us. The social pressure to conform involves being valued by the group because, after all, most success is really defined by what others think. This preoccupation is all too evident in our modern celebrity culture, and especially with the rise of social networking, where normal individuals spend considerable amounts of time and effort _____. Over 1.7 billion people on this planet use social networking on the Internet to share and seek validation from others. When Rachel Berry, a character in a hit musical series about a performing-arts school, said " Nowadays being anonymous is worse than being poor," she was simply echoing our modern obsession with fame and our desire to be liked by many people—even if they are mostly anonymous or casual acquaintances.

① in pursuit of recognition from others

② to extend their domain of friendship

③ despite massive criticism by experts

④ prompting misgivings among the public

⑤ beyond the limits imposed by authorities

20 Let us unite profound knowledge of the art with the happiest talent for inventing lovely melodies, and then link both with the greatest possible originality, in order to obtain the most faithful picture of Mozart's musical genius. Nowhere in his work does one ever find an idea one had heard before: Even his accompaniments are always novel. One is, as it were, incessantly pulled along from one notion to another, without rest, so that admiration of the latest constantly swallows up admiration for what has gonebefore, and even by straining all one's forces one is scarcely able to absorb all the beauties that present themselves to the soul. If any fault had to be found with Mozart, it could surely be only this: That such _____ almost tires the soul and the effect of the whole is sometimes obscured thereby. But happy is the artist whose only fault lies in an all too great perfection.

① plethora of faith   ② desolation of spirit

③ command of words   ④ redundancy of melodies

⑤ abundance of beauty

21 A picture may be worth a thousand words, but for centuries words ruled the legal domain. Rhetoric, the art of using language, has always been the trademark of lawyers, and trials, especially in Common Law, have been widely understood as battles by words. Alas, all glory is doomed to pass and the second half of the nineteenth century saw a new mode of persuasion rising to dominance, driven by a new class of machine—made testimonies that threatened to turn words into an inferior mode of communicating facts. Ever alert and never involved, machines such as microscopes, telescopes, high—speed cameras and x—ray tubes purported to communicate richer, better, and truer evidence, often inaccessible otherwise to human beings. The emblem for this new type of mechanical objectivity was _____. "Let nature speak for itself," became the watchword, and nature's language seemed to be that ofphotographs and mechanically generated curves. [3점]

① visual evidence   ② verbal testimony

③ legal terminology   ④ linguistic eloquence

⑤ subjective expression

22 A study in the J ournal of Consumer Psychology explored the power of repetition by comparing all No. 1 songs on Billboard's Hot 100 list from 1958 to 2012 with tracks that never broke past No. 90. Researchers observed that the simpler and more repetitive a song's lyrics were, the better its chance of reaching the top spot. Such songs also climbed the chart faster than less repetitive ones. This finding supports the theory of processing fluency, which suggests that the easier a message is to digest, _____. Musicians aren't the only ones in on the secret: Similar strategies are used in advertising, through slogans that saturate commercials, and even in comedy; stand-ups often loop to the same punch line throughout a set. [3점]

① the more effort the brain has to exert

② the more positively people will react to it

③ the higher the likelihood of tuning out the message

④ the less the chances of people singing after the song

⑤ the less likely people will decode the hidden message

23 In modern Western society, religion's original explanatory role _____. The origins of the universe as we know it are now attributed to the Big Bang and the subsequent operation of the laws of physics. Modern language diversity is no longer explained by origin myths, such as the Tower of Babel or the snapping of the lianas holding the New Guinea ironwood tree, but is instead considered as adequately explained by observed historical processes of language change. Explanations of sunrises, sunsets, and tides are now left to astronomers, and explanations of winds and rain are left to meteorologists. Bird songs are explained by ethology, and the origin of each plant and animal species, including the human species, is left to evolutionary biologists to interpret.

① provides the basis for scientific theories

② has increasingly become usurped by science

③ has risen to give the best account of nature

④ evokes controversy on the adequacy of science

⑤ is reinforced by creationists and evolutionists alike

24 빈 칸 (A)와 (B)에 들어갈 말로 가장 적절한 것은?

The use of tobacco illustrates what happened to what was almost an element of religion in Maya eyes when it became part of Spanish or, for that matter, all Western culture. Tobacco among the Maya had a very important role in religious life; it was an important element in the prevention and cure of disease, and in some parts was deified. Its pleasure-giving qualities seem in Maya eyes to have been quite (A) to its other functions. Yet when tobacco was taken over by the Spaniards it was only as a commodity which gave pleasure to the individual; all the Maya ritualistic and community associations were shed. This process was in line with Spanish (B) of those cultural elements of the conquered natives which they absorbed. Maize was no longer the beloved and sacred staff of life; it became for the conqueror an item of tribute and commercial transactions. Cacao suffered the same degradation. [3점]

	(A)		(B)
①	relevant	⋯	authorization
②	relevant	⋯	enlightenment
③	identical	⋯	destruction
④	subordinate	⋯	inquisition
⑤	subordinate	⋯	secularization

※ 다음 글의 제목으로 가장 적절한 것을 고르시오. 【25-26】

25 The earliest Robin Hood ballad was printed in 1450, and it does not portray the dashing hero that we have come to know in popular culture. He was a yeoman, rough and cruel at times. The legend was more than likely based on a robber who kept the money he stole from the rich and occasionally helped the poor. He did not want to set up an ideal society in the forest. He and his men sought mainly to rectify social injustices and to live well. Robin Hood became so popular by the seventeenth century that people named places and ships after him. By the nineteenth century, many stories and songs had brought about major changes in the Robin Hood legend. His yeoman origins disappeared, and he increasingly became the heroic outlaw of Sherwood Forest who defended the rights of the poor.

① Robin Hood as a Robber
② Origins of Medieval Yeomen
③ Earlier Struggles of Robin Hood
④ Ideal Society in Sherwood Forest
⑤ Transformations in the Robin Hood Character

26 In one study a hundred men and women wore devices that took readings of their blood pressure whenever they interacted with someone. When they were with family or enjoyable friends, their blood pressure fell; these interactions were pleasant and soothing. When they were with someone who was troublesome, there was a rise. But the biggest jump came while they were with people they felt ambivalent about: an overbearing parent, a volatile romantic partner, or a competitive friend. A mercurial boss looms as the archetype, but this dynamic operates in all our relationships.

① High Blood Pressure : The Silent Assassin

② Uneasy Relationships : Your Body Doesn't Lie

③ Don't Be Bossed Around by Your Biorhythm

④ Can Health Monitoring Devices Save Your Life?

⑤ How Can You Deal with Uncomfortable Interactions?

※ 다음 글의 주제로 가장 적절한 것을 고르시오. 【27-28】

27 Music that was exciting to the contemporaries of Bach and Beethoven is still exciting, although we do not share their culture. The early Beatles' songs are still exciting although the Beatles have unfortunately broken up. Similarly, some Venda songs that must have been composed hundreds of years ago still excite me. Many of us are thrilled by Koto music from Japan, sitar music from India, Chopi xylophone music, and so on. I do not say that we receive music in exactly the same way as the players, but our own experiences suggest that there are some possibilities of cross-cultural communication. I am convinced that the explanation for this is to be found in the fact that at the level of deep structures in music there are elements that are common to the human psyche, although they may not appear in the surface structures.

① the potential of music to enrich culture

② the gradual divergence of music from culture

③ the ability of music to nourish the human psyche

④ the advantages of cross-cultural transmission of music

⑤ the universality of music that transcends time and culture

28 We often see stories of inspiring people and wonderful successes. Some of us put their pictures on our walls or clip notable quotes from them. But what does that do for us if the inspiring person has done things we will never or could never do? For many of us, the choice of a role model invites comparison, and if our abilities and outcomes do not measure up, the role model serves not as an inspiration but as a source of frustration and defeat. Choose as your role model someone who has accomplished something you can accomplish and something you want to accomplish. There is tremendous value in using co-workers or family members who you admire rather than famous athletes, leaders, or historical figures, who have experienced great successes but whose experience has less in common with yours.

① the success stories of a realistic role model

② the source of frustration in emulating a role model

③ the importance of selecting a reachable role model

④ the necessity for having an inspiring person around

⑤ the positive effects of imitating a person of high status

29 다음 글의 요지로 가장 적절한 것은?

Recently I was reading about the endangered grizzly bears on the coast of British Columbia. The authors emphasized how the cubs were keen observers of their mothers' skills in searching for and consuming food. What the cubs learned by the mothers' modeling was a matter of life and death; without that knowledge the cubs probably would not survive. The same principle applies to us. How can we believe that when we live life like a rat race, our children somehow will not? That as we mindlessly acquire and consume, our children will somehow know moderation and meaning in their relationship to things? If I regularly cheat on little things—like not returning the extra change I receive at the counter, or pocketing found money without trying to find its owner—I am teaching that behavior to children. [3점]

① Parents are spending more time reading books on wildlife.

② Mindful consumption lies at the center of being good parents.

③ Good parenting begins and ends with setting a good example.

④ Teaching good behavior to children outweighs earning money.

⑤ Children's behavior is subconsciously mirrored by their parents.

30 다음 글에 나타난 Dave의 심경으로 가장 적절한 것은?

> Dave was never quite sure how it happened. He only knew that he awoke as he was being hurled from his bed and, mingled with the startled awakening, there was a terrific explosion. For a moment or more he lay absent-mindedly on the deck of his room, struggling to regain his senses. Then slowly he realized the steady throb of the engines, to which he had grown so accustomed in the week since boarding the ship, had abruptly ceased. What happened? He got up and, feeling his way to the light switch, gave it a turn with a trembling hand. Nothing happened, and he tried it again. The lights did not come on.

① distracted and angry   ② confused and nervous

③ overjoyed and proud   ④ indifferent and bored

⑤ irritated and stimulated

※ 다음 글에서 전체 흐름과 관계 없는 문장을 고르시오. 【31-32】

31 On the face of it, industrialized agriculture promised to be a most welcome solution to the timeless problem of world hunger. ① But some so-called solutions, as writer and farmer Wendell Berry observed, led to ramifying sets of new problems. ② And during the past several decades, it has become increasingly clear that industrial agriculture has indeed created a host of new problems impacting the health of people and the planet. ③ So corporations and governments, recognizing the opportunity presented by the new technologies, fostered the rapid spread of industrialized agriculture. ④ The use of fertilizers and pesticides, for example, has led to higher rates of cancer and the contamination of soil, streams, and groundwater. ⑤ Monoculture farming has led to the loss of biodiversity, undermining the productivity and stability of ecosystems.

32 From the artfully styled grain bowls to the popular slow-simmered bone broth, the message is clear: The beauty-and-wellness set has become obsessed with nutrition. ① Today, eating virtuously isn't just a means to stay trim; it's a crucial step in fortifying the body for an increasingly fit, and busy, life. ② But in this multitasking age, where lunch comes with a side of email, everyone's got a lot on their plate except, too often, a square meal. ③ This lack of proper nutrition from local foods is only worsened by a sedentary lifestyle. ④ Answering the call across the country is a wave of enterprising young chefs and tech pioneers who are marrying wholesome meals with door-to-door convenience. ⑤ If last year was dominated by the juice cleanse, this is shaping up to be the year of the designer meal delivery. [3점]

33 글의 흐름으로 보아, 주어진 문장이 들어가기에 가장 적절한 곳은?

> At one point, he clapped me on the back and said: "Son, make sure you talk with everyone here tonight and see that each one feels better about himself when he leaves than he did when he walked in the door."

One of my daughters was married recently, and I spent the evening celebrating with 200 people of all ages. (①) They ranged from my 3-year-old granddaughters to my 85-year-old uncle, who fought in World War II and ran successful law and accounting practices for 5 decades. (②) The advice made me consider what it means to be mentally sharp. (③) Although our ability to learn and remember gradually declines throughout adulthood, there's mounting evidence that our skill at making sense of important information and experiences increases. (④) This is what's known as wisdom, and it's something that scientists are just beginning to study. (⑤) Its classic elements include sound judgment, psychological insight, long and diverse life experience, emotional control, empathetic understanding, and, of course, knowledge.

34 다음 글의 내용을 한 문장으로 나타낼 때, 빈칸 (A)와 (B)에 들어갈 말로 가장 적절한 것은?

Average life expectancy has risen steadily for decades and except for cancers caused by smoking and exposure to the sun, cancer death rates have dropped or remained relatively stable. Yet surveys have repeatedly shown that people have never been more fretful about their health. "People just seem to see the apocalypse everywhere they turn," said Bruce Ames, who was among the first to point out that natural pesticides are at least 10,000 times more common than those made by man. "There are some important risks, of course. But everyone should just relax a bit and have some fun." At times that seems hard to do. Provocative warnings about too much cholesterol, not enough vitamin A and what can happen to people who do not exercise enough have become part of the tapestry of American life. To some, cancer seems hidden in every meal.

Although Americans have become ___(A)___ than ever, they seem to be experiencing high levels of ___(B)___ about their health.

	(A)		(B)
①	healthier	⋯	anxiety
②	trendier	⋯	anxiety
③	healthier	⋯	hope
④	trendier	⋯	concern
⑤	slimmer	⋯	concern

35 주어진 글 다음에 이어질 글의 순서로 가장 적절한 것은?

Many people don't want to be travelers. They would rather be tourists, flitting over the surface of other people's lives while never really leaving their own. [A] To be a real traveler, however, you must be willing to give yourself over to the moment and take yourself out of the center of your universe. You must believe totally in the lives of the people and the places where you find yourself. [B] Become part of the fabric of their everyday lives. You will realize that the possibilities of life in this world are endless, and that beneath our differences of language and culture we all share the same dream of loving and being loved, of having a life with more joy than sorrow. [C] They try to bring their world with them wherever they go, or try to recreate the world they left. They do not want to risk the security of their own understanding and see how small and limited their experiences really are.

① [A] − [C] − [B]
② [B] − [A] − [C]
③ [B] − [C] − [A]
④ [C] − [A] − [B]
⑤ [C] − [B] − [A]

Since 2008 Zsofia Viranyi and her colleagues at the Wolf Science Center in Austria have been raising dogs and wolves to figure out what makes a dog a dog—and a wolf a wolf. "You can leave a piece of meat on a table and tell one of our dogs, 'No!' and he will not take it," Viranyi says. "But the wolves ignore you. They'll look you in the eye and grab the meat." And when this happens, she wonders yet again how the wolf ever became (A) the domesticated dog. "You can't have an animal—a large carnivore—living with you and behaving like that," she says. "You want an animal that's like a dog: one that accepts 'No!'"

Dogs' understanding of the absolute no may be connected to the structure of (B) their packs, which are not egalitarian like those of the wolves but dictatorial, the center's researchers have discovered. Wolves can eat together, Viranyi notes. Even if a dominant wolf flashes its teeth and growls at a subordinate, (C) the lower-ranked member does not move away. The same is not true in dog packs, however. "Subordinate dogs will rarely eat at the same time as the dominant one," she observes. "They don't even try." Their studies also suggest that rather than expecting to cooperate on tasks with humans, dogs simply want to be told what to do.

How the independent-minded, egalitarian wolf changed into (D) the obedient, waiting-for-orders pet and what role ancient humans played in achieving this feat baffle Viranyi. She is not alone in her bafflement. Although researchers have successfully determined the time, location and ancestry of nearly every other domesticated species, from sheep to cattle to chickens to guinea pigs, they continue to debate these questions for (E) our best friend, Canis familiaris.

36 위 글의 밑줄 친 부분 중 그 의미하는 바가 나머지와 다른 하나는?

① (A) ② (B)

③ (C) ④ (D)

⑤ (E)

37 위 글의 내용과 일치하지 않는 것은?

① Viranyi는 개와 늑대를 키우며 그들의 본질에 대해 연구한다.

② 늑대는 고기를 먹지 말라는 사람의 명령을 무시하고 먹는다.

③ 무리 중 강한 늑대가 약한 늑대에게 으르렁대면 약한 늑대는 먹이로부터 물러난다.

④ 무리 중 약한 개와 강한 개가 먹이를 동시에 먹는 일은 없다.

⑤ 양, 소, 닭이 가축화된 시간이나 장소는 알려져 있다.

Why do people try to make their expectations their best possible guess of the future, using all available information? The simplest explanation is that it is costly for people not to do so. Joe Commuter has a strong incentive to make his expectation of the time it takes him to drive to work as accurate as possible. If he underpredicts his driving time, he will often be late to work and risk being fired. If he overpredicts, he will, on average, get to work too early and will have given up sleep or leisure time unnecessarily. Accurate expectations are desirable, and the incentives are strong for people to try to make them equal to optimal forecasts by using all available information.

The same principle applies to businesses. Suppose that an appliance manufacturer knows that interest-rate movements are important to the sales of appliances. If the company makes poor forecasts of interest rates, it will earn less profit, because it might produce either too many appliances or too few. The incentives are strong for the company to acquire all available information to help it forecast interest rates and use the information to make the best possible guess of future interest-rate movements. The incentives for equating expectations with optimal forecasts are especially strong in financial markets. In these markets, people with better forecasts of the future get rich.

38 위 글의 제목으로 가장 적절한 것은?

① Set Your Goals As High As Possible

② Reap the Rewards of Optimal Predictions

③ Maximize Profit by Manipulating Interest Rates

④ The Gap Between Theory and Practice in Business

⑤ How Does Commuting Distance Affect Productivity?

39 위 글의 빈칸에 들어갈 말로 가장 적절한 것은? [3점]

① match ② exceed

③ negate ④ transform

⑤ underestimate

Motivation gains refer to circumstances that increase the effort expended by group members in a collective task. Motivational gains in which the less capable member works harder is known as the Kohler effect. In some investigations, athletes curled a bar attached to a pulley system until exhaustion. They did this first individually and then in groups of two. Motivation gains happened when the athlete pairs had moderately different abilities. ____(A)____, motivation gains did not emerge when athletes had equal or very unequal abilities. It was the weaker member of the group who was responsible for the motivation gain. The psychological mechanisms underlying the Kohler effect are social comparison (particularly when someone thinks that their teammate is more capable) and the feeling that one's effort is indispensible to the group. Group members are willing to exert effort on a collective task when they expect their efforts to be instrumental in obtaining outcomes that they value personally. Moreover, in particular, the weakest member of a team is more likely to work harder when everyone is given feedback about people's performance in a timely fashion.

A more common observation in groups is motivation losses, also known as social loafing. A French agricultural engineer named Max Ringelmann was interested in the relative efficiency of farm labor supplied by horses, oxen, machines, and men. In particular, he was curious about their relative abilities to pull a load horizontally, such as in a tug-of-war. In one of his experiments, groups of 14 men pulled a load, and the amount of force they generated was measured. The force that each man could pull independently was also measured. There was a steady decline in the average pull-per-member as the size of the rope-pulling team increased. One person pulling on a rope alone exerted an average of 63 kilograms of force. ____(B)____, in groups of three, the per-person force dropped to 53 kilograms, and in groups of eight, it plummeted to only 31 kilograms—less than half of the effort exerted by people working alone. This revealed a fundamental principle of teamwork: People in groups often do not work as hard as they do when alone.

40 위 글의 제목으로 적절한 것은?

① Mechanisms of a Tug of War

② Motivational Effects in Teamwork

③ How to Measure Work Efficiency

④ Boosting Motivation in Individual Tasks

⑤ Psychology Behind the Ringelmann Effect

41 위 글의 내용과 일치하지 않는 것은? [3점]

① The Kohler effect occurs when the less capable person works harder in a group.

② Motivation gains are likely to happen when working with people of the same ability.

③ The weakest member tends to work harder when timely feedback is provided.

④ Max Ringelmann studied the efficiency of labor between different groups.

⑤ Max Ringelmann found that people tend to expend less effort when working collectively.

42 위 글의 빈칸 (A)와 (B)에 들어갈 말로 가장 적절한 것은?

	(A)		(B)
①	Likewise	⋯	However
②	Instead	⋯	Meanwhile
③	Conversely	⋯	However
④	Conversely	⋯	As a result
⑤	Likewise	⋯	Meanwhile

Sheldon Cohen, a psychologist at Carnegie Mellon University, has intentionally given colds to hundreds of people. Under carefully controlled conditions, he systematically exposes volunteers to a rhinovirus that causes the common cold. About a third of people exposed to the virus develop the full panoply of symptoms, while the rest walk away with nary a sniffle.

On the first day, Cohen's experimental volunteers are quarantined for twenty-four hours before they are exposed, to be sure they have not picked up a cold elsewhere. For the next five days the volunteers are housed in a special unit with other volunteers, all of whom are kept at least three feet from one another, lest they reinfect someone. During those five days their nasal secretions are tested for technical indicators of colds (like the total weight of their mucus) as well as the presence of the specific rhinovirus, and their blood samples are tested for antibodies.

We know that low levels of vitamin C, smoking and sleeping poorly all increase the likelihood of infection. The question is, can a stressful relationship be added to that list? Cohen's answer: definitely. Cohen assigns precise numerical values to the factors that make one person come down with a cold while another stays healthy. Those with an ongoing personal conflict were 2.5 times as likely as the others to get a cold, putting rocky relationships in the same causal range as vitamin C deficiency and poor sleep. Conflicts that lasted a month or longer boosted susceptibility, but an occasional argument presented no health hazard. While perpetual arguments are bad for our health, isolating ourselves is worse. Compared to those with a rich web of social connections, those with the fewest close relationships were 4.2 times more likely to come down with the cold.

The more we socialize, the less susceptible to colds we become. This idea seems counterintuitive: Don't we increase the likelihood of being exposed to a cold virus the more people we interact with? Sure. But vibrant social connections boost our good moods and limit our negative ones, suppressing cortisol and enhancing immune function under stress. Relationships themselves seem to _____ the risk of exposure to the very cold virus they pose.

43 위 글의 제목으로 가장 적절한 것은?

① The Nature of Antibiotic Metabolism in the Human Body

② Rhinovirus Exposure: A Methodology of Utmost Precision

③ The More Social Interactions, the More Severe the Cold

④ Uncommon Findings from the Common Cold Experiment

⑤ New Health Hazards Discovered in Cyberspace

44 빈칸에 들어가기에 가장 적절한 것은? [3점]

① be modified by

② push them to

③ be weakened by

④ protect us from

⑤ gradually increase

45 Cohen의 실험과 일치하는 것은?

① 첫날 피험자를 감기 바이러스에 노출시킨다.

② 총 5일 동안 진행된다.

③ 피험자간 신체적 접촉을 허용한다.

④ 코 분비물을 검사한다.

⑤ 혈액 샘플 검사는 생략한다.

▶ 해설은 p. 101에 있습니다.

※ 밑줄 친 단어의 뜻으로 가장 적절한 것을 고르시오. 【01 – 05】

01 It was time to devise a new plan of action as the attorneys <u>categorically</u> rejected our offer.

① unequivocally
② typically
③ impolitely
④ reluctantly
⑤ maliciously

02 After emerging victorious in his long–fought bout against cancer, the media tycoon tried to turn over a new leaf by denouncing his <u>opulent</u> way of life.

① immoral
② proud
③ luxurious
④ unhealthy
⑤ incompetent

03 Sanctions against the country are expected to be among the most <u>contentious</u> issues.

① controversial
② complex
③ elusive
④ secretive
⑤ fruitless

04 That the days of capitalism were <u>numbered</u>, and that the capitalist era must now give way to socialism: these were assumptions widely held by intellectuals on both sides of the Atlantic.

① limited
② prolonged
③ preserved
④ accelerated
⑤ overlapped

05 Many politicians viewed that nation's economic hegemony as <u>presumptuous</u>.

① attentive and alert
② accurate and precise
③ assiduous and diligent
④ achievable and pragmatic
⑤ arrogant and disrespectful

※ 밑줄 친 부분 중, 어법상 틀린 것을 고르시오. [06-08]

06 An important interruption in the usual flow of energy apparently occurred millions of years ago when the growth of land plants and marine organisms ①<u>exceeded</u> the ability of decomposers to recycle them. The ②<u>accumulating</u> layers of energy–rich organic material were gradually turned into coal and oil by the pressure of the overlying earth. The energy stored in their molecular structure we can now ③ <u>release</u> by burning. And our modern civilization depends on immense amounts of energy from such fossil fuels ④<u>recovering</u> from the earth. By burning fossil fuels, we are finally passing most of the stored energy on to the environment as heat. We are also passing back to the atmosphere—{in a relatively very short time—}large amounts of carbon dioxide that ⑤<u>had been</u> removed from it slowly over millions of years.

07 The earth has many resources of great importance to human life. Some are ① readily renewable, some are renewable only at great cost, and some are not renewable at all. The earth comprises a great variety of minerals, whose properties depend on the history of how they were formed as well as on the elements ② which they are composed. Their abundance ranges from rare to almost unlimited. But the difficulty of ③ extracting them from the environment is as important an issue as their abundance. A wide variety of minerals ④ are sources for essential industrial materials, such as iron, aluminum, magnesium, and copper. Many of the best sources are being depleted, making it more and more difficult and expensive ⑤ to obtain those minerals.

08 On the European continent, Kant rejected the utilitarian defense of liberalism but put forward a compatible case for the autonomy that comes only to the person ① free to choose his own conception of the good life. J.S. Mill himself took inspiration from other German liberals, ② being noted in the frontispiece to On Liberty the work of a contemporary, Wilhelm von Humboldt. But this moment of convergence of German and Anglo–American liberalism was soon ③ to pass. With Hegel, and then Marx, German intellectual thought centrally explored the deficiencies in the ethic of individualism ④ held to characterize liberal societies. The transmission of ideas from Kant to Hegel to Marx is so dramatic as ⑤ to rival the initial flow of thought from Plato to Aristotle to Augustine. [3점]

※ (A), (B), (C)에 들어갈 말로 가장 적절한 것을 고르시오. [09-10]

09 Many of us take broadband Internet for granted, but nearly 1 in 5 Americans lacks access to it, says the Federal Communications Commission (FCC). In rural areas, telecom companies balk at the cost of wiring far-flung homes, while low-income families can find the fees (A) [prohibitive/affordable]. Closing the broadband gap is about more than being able to stream the latest TV dramas. High-speed Internet is a critical tool of modern life, (B) [constraining/enabling] kids to learn digitally and adults to work via the cloud. The FCC recently approved a small broadband subsidy, but the real solution may lie in (C) [increased/decreased] competition for a notoriously consolidated industry. [3점]

10 As evolutionary scholar Henry Plotkin says, gaining knowledge of the world across countless generations of organisms, evolution conserves knowledge selectively relative to criteria of need, and that collective knowledge is then held within the gene pool of species. Such collective knowledge is doled out to individuals, who come into the world with (A) [innate/acquired] ideas and predispositions to learn only certain things in specific ways. In other words, whether you're hunting on the savannah or choosing between millions of videos on YouTube, your brain is programmed to (B) [adopt/ignore] almost everything and home in only on what is most important or interesting. Otherwise, you'd be pointing your spear at every tree and rock or, just as annoyingly, you'd be lost in an infinite trail of video links, hoping in vain to find something worthwhile. With an understanding of the (C) [discriminating/integrating] nature of our genes, we can begin to construct the basis for stories that grab our attention and stay in our memory.

※ 다음 글의 밑줄 친 부분 중, 문맥상 낱말의 쓰임이 적절하지 않은 것을 고르시오. [11-13]

11 Sea level rise along any given stretch of coast depends on how far away it is from the globe's two big ice buckets: Greenland and Antarctica. While it's easy to think the closest countries will see the biggest rise as the ice melts, it's not so ① simple. Greenland and Antarctica's massive ice sheets ② exert a strong gravitational pull on the waters around them, but as they melt, the attraction weakens, causing nearby sea levels to fall. In addition, without the burden of weight from the ice, the land uplifts, ③ rising slightly more above the water. The effect diminishes with distance, so it's actually the places farther away from the melting ice that will see the biggest ④ drop in sea level. Ocean currents help push the meltwater around the globe. "It's really an amazing and somewhat ⑤ counterintuitive result, but that's the reality," says Jerry Mitrovica, a geophysicist at Harvard University. [3점]

12 Four little heads pop up simultaneously in a pool of blue–black water surrounded by ice as far as the eye can see. They seem to hesitate, reluctant to leave the watery world through which they swim as ① <u>effortlessly</u> as fish. They are Adelie penguins, and the ice ② <u>endangers</u> their existence. The birds leap about excitedly in tight circles, going in and out of the water, perfectly at ease in this ③ <u>frigid</u> sea that surrounds the shores of Antarctica. Their food is tied, literally, to the frozen ocean. Within layers of sea ice, microscopic algae bloom in profusion as sunlight floods in from above. When the sea ice melts with the beginning of summer, the ice algae escape into the water, where they are ④ <u>grazed</u> on by dense swarms of krill—a type of shrimplike crustacean. The krill, ⑤ <u>in turn</u>, are the Adelie penguins' primary food source.

13 The human genome contains an ① <u>enormous</u> amount of information to guide the construction of a complex organism. In a growing number of cases, particular genes can be tied to aspects of cognition, language, and personality. When psychological traits vary, much of the variation comes from ② <u>differences</u> in genes: identical twins are more similar than fraternal twins, and biological siblings are more similar than adoptive siblings, whether ③ <u>raised</u> together or apart. A person's temperament and personality emerge early in life and remain fairly ④ <u>unpredictable</u> throughout the lifespan. And both personality and intelligence show few or no effects of children's particular home environments within their culture: children reared in the same family are similar mainly because of their ⑤ <u>shared</u> genes. Furthermore, neuroscience is showing that the brain's basic architecture develops under genetic control. [3점]

14 Walter Reed에 관한 다음 글의 내용과 일치하는 것은?

Walter Reed, medical doctor, was a U.S. Army physician who in 1901 found that yellow fever is transmitted by a particular mosquito species. He was born in Virginia and completed the M.D. degree in 1869 at the University of Virginia. Reed obtained his second M.D. in 1870 at New York University's Bellevue Hospital Medical College. Reed joined the U.S. Army as a medical doctor. Then, he got married in 1876. The couple had a son and a daughter, and they adopted a Native American girl later. He also served as the curator of the Army Medical Museum, which later became the National Museum of Health and Medicine. He was stationed to Cuba to study yellow fever, which killed thousands of soldiers. With the help of other doctors, Reed confirmed that the disease is transmitted by mosquitoes. This finding saved countless lives. To commemorate his achievements, many U.S. hospitals were named after Reed.

① yellow fever의 백신을 개발했다.
② medical doctor 학위를 두 번 취득했다.
③ 두 아이의 아버지가 된 후에 중국 아이를 입양했다.
④ 버지니아 의대 박물관 curator를 역임했다.
⑤ 쿠바에 자신의 이름을 딴 병원을 설립했다.

15 Lewis와 Clark의 탐사에 관한 다음 글의 내용과 일치하는 것은?

In 1803, the U.S. government purchased the entire area of Louisiana from France. The territory stretched from the Mississippi River to the middle of the Rocky Mountains, but no one was really sure where the Mississippi River started or where exactly the Rocky Mountains were located. President Thomas Jefferson commissioned an expedition in this area. It comprised a selected group of U.S. Army volunteers under the command of Captain Meriwether Lewis and Second Lieutenant William Clark. Their perilous journey lasted from May 1804 to September 1806. Their primary objective was to explore and to map the newly acquired territory, and to find a practical route across the western half of the continent. Lewis and Clark departed with forty-three men and supplies for two years. They became acquainted with a sixteen-year-old Native American woman named Sacajawea, which means Bird Woman. With her help, Lewis and Clark obtained horses from the Indians and passed the Indian territory without much trouble.

① 미국은 영국으로부터 Louisiana 지역을 매입했다.
② 탐사는 이미 알려진 Mississippi 강의 시작점에서 출발했다.
③ 탐사 대원들은 육군의 추천을 통해 선발됐다.
④ 모든 탐사를 마치기까지 4년 이상의 기간이 걸렸다.
⑤ 탐사 중에 원주민 여성의 도움을 받았다.

16 halibut에 관한 다음 글의 내용과 일치하지 않는 것은?

Halibut is a common name principally applied to the two flatfish from the family of right-eye flounders in the North Atlantic and the North Pacific. Halibut is dark brown on the top side with an off-white underbelly and has very small scales invisible to the naked eye embedded in its skin. At birth, it has an eye on each side of the head. After six months, one eye migrates to the other side. Halibut is often boiled, deep-fried or grilled while fresh. Smoking is more difficult with halibut meat than it is with salmon, due to its ultra-low fat content. Currently, the Atlantic population is so depleted through overfishing that it may be declared an endangered species.

① 북대서양과 북태평양에 서식하는 넙치과 생선이다.

② 육안으로 볼 수 없는 비늘을 가지고 있다.

③ 부화 후 6개월까지는 눈이 머리 양쪽에 있다.

④ 지방 함유량이 낮기 때문에, 연어보다 훈제하기가 어렵다

⑤ 태평양 지역에서 멸종위기 종으로 공표되었다.

17 alien species에 관한 다음 글의 내용과 일치하지 않는 것은?

Ecologists generally define an alien species as one that people, inadvertently or deliberately, carried to its new location. "Only a small percentage of alien species cause problems in their new habitats," says a professor of ecology and evolutionary biology. Yet appearances can deceive, ecologists caution, and many of these exotics may be considered acceptable only because no one has documented their harmful effects. What is more, non-native species can appear innocuous for decades, then turn invasive. Faced with such uncertainty, many ecologists argue for strong steps to be taken. Their approach is to remove exotics from natural ecosystems. But a number of experts question the scientific wisdom of trying to roll back ecosystems to a time when they were more natural. Even many ecologists who would like to rid ecosystems of all exotics admit that this goal is impractical. Further, Professor Rosenzweig at the University of Arizona challenges the prevailing view that invasive alien species reduce biodiversity. The exotics increase the number of species in the environment. Even if alien species cause extinctions, the extinction phase will eventually end, and new species may then begin to evolve, he explains.

① 새 환경에서 거의 문제를 일으키지 않는다고 생각하는 것은 잘못된 관측일 수 있다.
② 새 환경에서 수 십 년간 무해했으나, 그 이후 환경을 해치는 경우도 있다.
③ alien species가 제거된 생태계를 선호하는 생태학자들이 있다.
④ Rosenzweig 교수는 alien species가 생태 다양성을 저해한다는 견해를 반박한다.
⑤ 다른 species의 멸종을 초래하기 시작하면 그 현상은 멈추지 않는다.

※ 다음 글의 빈칸에 들어갈 말로 가장 적절한 것을 고르시오. [18-23]

18 Judges read statutes and the Constitution for help in devising or refining a rule of conduct that may have a significant impact on the welfare of the community. The community is not always willing to allow its choices to be controlled by what people who lived two centuries ago wrote into the Constitution. The procedure for amending the Constitution is, however, so cumbersome that the judges are under great pressure to use the interpretive process to keep the original document _____.

① obsolete   ② translated

③ concise   ④ flexible

⑤ judgmental

19 I go to the Grand Canyon, for instance. I take great pleasure in the views, and I write to you, my good friend, a postcard with the simple message "Wish you were here." What do I mean by this familiar saying? I mean that my pleasure in seeing the Grand Canyon would be greater if I could share it with you. I sense that, as good as it is to be at the Grand Canyon even by myself, it would be that much better if I could share the experience with you. In other words, my postcard is saying that friends share a common good in the special sense that our pleasure in seeing the Grand Canyon together _____ my pleasure and your pleasure in seeing the canyon on separate days.

① can be divided into

② is more than the sum of

③ equals the combined amount of

④ can last in memory longer than

⑤ does not have to take into consideration

20 The coyote is a long, slim, sick and sorry-looking skeleton, with a gray wolf-skin stretched over it, a tolerably bushy tail that forever sags down, a furtive and evil eye, and a long, sharp face, with slightly lifted lip and exposed teeth. He has a general slinking expression all over. The coyote is a living, breathing _____. He is always hungry. He is always poor, out of luck, and friendless. The meanest creatures despise him, and even the fleas would desert him in a blink of an eye. [3점]

① epitome of wrath   ② analogy of sadism

③ allegory of want   ④ symbol of efficiency

⑤ metaphor of dominance

21 When I was young I was very impressed by how food producers could fill jars with whole walnuts. Somehow they could crack the shells while leaving the nuts intact. Most of the times I tried it, I ended up with mixed pieces of shell and nut, managing to get the nut out whole only once every ten times or so. Later, however, I learned that although the manufacturers had a better success rate than I did, they often ended up with mixed shell and nut pieces, too. But I also learned that they did something else: they _____. On those occasions when they were successful, they'd take the whole nuts and stick them in a jar labeled "Whole Walnuts." And on the other occasions, they'd separate the nut pieces from the shell and stick them in a jar labeled "Walnut Pieces."

① selected their results

② bred special kinds of nuts

③ used brand new equipment

④ mixed up their nuts for sale

⑤ learned the lesson the hard way

22 In Hobbes's special vocabulary, "natural rights" are what we have already in the state of nature: a right to do anything that protects our vital motions. Hobbes derives the first law of nature from the fear of death in the state of nature. He derives the second law from the first: I should be willing to surrender my natural right to wage war against you, to the extent that you are reciprocally willing to surrender your natural right to wage war against me. _____. Each individually seeks "some Good to himself" in agreeing to surrender the rights of war, and this Good is "nothing else but the security of a man's person." [3점]

① This mutual disarming is in each person's self-interest
② This shared indifference promotes the peace of the society
③ This reciprocal surrender of rights means fostering animosity
④ This social compromise is conducive to reinforcing the law of nature
⑤ This restraint of waging wars does do good to the weaker of the parties

23 Social learning in the form of stimulus or local enhancement plays an indispensable role in human development, as it does in the cognitive development of many social species. In some cases, however, human beings learn from one another in a qualitatively different way. Human beings sometimes engage in what we call cultural learning. In cultural learning, learners do not just direct their attention to the location of another individual's activity; rather, _____. It is learning in which the learner is attempting to learn not from another, but through another.

① they rely on their own insight to understand others
② they extensively enhance the overall cultural flexibility
③ they attempt to see a situation the way the other sees it
④ they learn to second-guess the hidden agenda of others
⑤ they empower themselves to engage in autonomous learning

24 빈칸 (A)와 (B)에 들어갈 말로 가장 적절한 것은?

One basic criterion for comparing countries is their levels of economic development. The most common tool that economists use to measure economic development is gross domestic product (GDP). GDP provides a basic benchmark for the average per capita income in a country.   (A) , GDP statistics can be quite misleading. For one thing, people may earn far more in some countries than they do in others, but those raw figures do not take into account the relative costs of living in those countries.   (B) , as exchange rates between national currencies rise or fall, countries can look richer or poorer than they are.

(A) (B)

① In contrast ⋯ However

② In contrast ⋯ For example

③ Moreover ⋯ Therefore

④ However ⋯ Moreover

⑤ However ⋯ In contrast

※ 다음 글의 제목으로 가장 적절한 것을 고르시오. [25-26]

25 When you're carrying extra pounds, the extra expenses add up, starting with health care. In a 2013 Duke study, researchers tracked health care spending by body mass index (BMI) levels. The average annual cost for a person with a low BMI of 19 was $2,541. With a BMI of 25─{ considered overweight─{it was $2,893. At a BMI of 33, what's deemed obese, the costs topped $3,439. "The risk of illness starts increasing already from the lower end of 'normal weight,'" says lead researcher Truls Ostbye. The add-ons don't end at the doctor's office. A 2010 McKinsey study estimated that obese Americans spend an aggregate of $30 billion extra on clothes. It is also estimated that a 40-year-old obese man will pay twice as much for life insurance.

① Increasing Costs of Health Care

② Lose Weight, Lower Risk of Illness

③ The Price You Pay for Extra Pounds

④ Do Obese People Spend More on Clothes?

⑤ BMI: Not an Accurate Indicator of Weight

26 Climbing the automobile ladder was hard work, and staying on top was even harder. Each year, employing the practice of perceived obsolescence, Chevrolet would roll out an entirely redesigned, and usually larger, model. A car that had been the height of fashion yesterday would look small, embarrassing, and worn-out tomorrow. As you would imagine, all of this provoked a good deal of anxiety from the bottom to the top of American society. Then in 1959, seemingly out of nowhere, simple full-page newspaper ads began to appear with an unadorned image of the Volkswagen Beetle and the headline "Think Small." The ad didn't say much more, except that the car was modest and efficient—it even called the Beetle a "flivver," contemporary slang for a piece of junk. People found the ads shockingly honest and hilarious, allowing them to publicly express an unnamed anxiety that marketers had been instilling in them for years. Will I make it to the top of the ladder? Who Cares? [3점]

① Hard Economic Times: Think Small
② At the Top of the Automobile Ladder
③ New Ad: Step Down From Your Ladders
④ Does Your Car Represent Your Social Status?
⑤ International Automobile Warfare: Size Matters

※ 다음 글의 주제로 가장 적절한 것을 고르시오. [27-28]

27 The emotional reaction of disgust is often associated with the obdurate refusal of young children to consume certain vegetables. While such disgust may seem absurd to parents determined to supply their children with nutritious foods, scientists interested in hygienic behavior have a rational explanation. This theory contends that people have developed disgust as a protective mechanism against unfamiliar and possibly harmful objects. A recent study shows that disgust not only deters the ingestion of dangerous substances, but also dissuades people from entering potentially contagious situations. For instance, subjects of the study declared crowded railcars to be more disgusting than empty ones and lice more disgusting than wasps.

① the role of disgust in keeping people safe
② the advantages of getting proper nutrition
③ the difference between danger and contagion
④ the importance of avoiding harmful substances
⑤ the necessity of practicing good hygienic behavior

28 Success as a scientist is not simply a function of the quality of the ideas we hold in our heads, or of the data we hold in our hands, but also of the language we use to describe them. We all understand that "publish or perish" is real and dominates our professional lives. But "publish or perish" is about surviving, not succeeding. You don't succeed as a scientist by getting papers published. You succeed as a scientist by getting them cited. Having your work matter, matters. Success is defined not by the number of pages you have in print but by their influence. You succeed when your peers understand your work and use it to motivate their own.

① the enduring belief of 'the more writing, the better'

② the importance of influencing others in scientific writing

③ the necessity for pursuing research in unexplored areas

④ the favorable peer reviews needed for journal acceptance

⑤ the working ethics and strict quality control in publications

29 다음 글의 요지로 가장 적절한 것은?

You don't have to go vegan, pledge allegiance to an exercise cult or become a full-time meditator to get the longevity benefits of healthy habits. The latest science is showing quite the opposite, in fact: that extending healthy life is attainable for many of us with just a few small changes that aren't especially hard to do—{and won't make you miserable. Researchers have learned that logging hours at the gym cannot counteract the negative effects of sitting for long periods, for instance—{but something as simple as fidgeting can. They've also discovered that cutting down on how much you eat doesn't have to be excruciating—{and it can improve your chance for a longer life.

① Living a healthy lifestyle is easier said than done.

② Key changes in your diet can help you live longer.

③ Exercising is important for people with sedentary lifestyles.

④ Physical and mental well-being can be achieved with hard work.

⑤ Achieving longevity is not as difficult as one might imagine.

30 다음 글에 나타난 David의 심경으로 가장 적절한 것은?

When the elevator began its descent, a broad smile began to form on David's face. The spinning and nausea were gone. The pressure on his chest vanished. He was doing it. He was leaving the job and saying farewell to a nightmare. He found the spine to walk away that gloomy morning. He was standing in the empty elevator, watching with a wide grin as the floor numbers went down in bright red digital numbers. The elevator rocked gently as it fell through the center of the building. When it stopped, David got off and darted to the descending escalators. Somebody called out, "Hey, David, where are you going?" David smiled and waved in the general direction of the voice, as if everything was under control. He went outside, and the air that had seemed so wet and dreary earlier now held the promise of a new beginning.

① sad and agitated

② relieved and hopeful

③ bored and indifferent

④ nervous and confused

⑤ empty and abandoned

※ 다음 글에서 전체 흐름과 관계없는 문장을 고르시오. 〔31-32〕

31 Pasta's ethnic roots have been long debated. ① Many theories have been put forward, some notably far-fetched. ② An enduring myth, based on the writings of the 13th-century explorer Marco Polo, that pasta was brought to Italy from China, rose from a misinterpretation of a famous passage in Polo's Travels. ③ In it, Polo mentions a tree from which something like pasta was made. ④ It was probably the sago palm, which produces a starchy food that resembles, but is not pasta. ⑤ This tree, native to Asia, provided undeniable evidence that Pasta originated in China.

32 Another difference in the concept of justice lies in various societies' ideas of what laws are. In the West, people consider "laws" quite different from "customs." There is also a great contrast between "sins" (breaking religious laws) and "crimes" (breaking laws of the government). ① In many non-Western cultures, however, there is little separation of customs, laws, and religious beliefs; in other cultures, these three may be quite separate from one another, but still very much different from those in the West. ② For these reasons, an action may be considered a crime in one country but be socially acceptable in others. ③ For instance, although a thief is viewed as a criminal in much of the world, in a small village where there is considerable communal living and sharing of objects, the word thief may have little meaning. ④ In small villages, everyone, in a sense, becomes a judge; in such societies, social disapproval of people's activities can serve both as powerful punishment for and as strong deterrent to crime. ⑤ Someone who has taken something without asking is simply considered an impolite person. [3점]

33 글의 흐름으로 보아, 주어진 문장이 들어가기에 가장 적절한 곳은? [3점]

Humans also automatically adjust their behavior to blend with the people around them. When you interact with other people, you are quite likely to find yourself mimicking them in certain ways. (①) You may, for example, unconsciously match your friends' speech patterns and accents. (②) Social psychologists labeled this type of mimicry the chameleon effect. (③) Chameleons automatically change their color to blend in with their environment. (④) It is speculated that this form of mimicry functions as a type of "social glue." (⑤) By producing identical motor gestures, people make themselves more similar to the other individuals around them.

34 다음 글의 내용을 한 문장으로 나타낼 때, 빈칸 (A)와 (B)에 들어갈 말로 가장 적절한 것은?

Just thinking that a particular brand's products are especially effective may have a kind of placebo effect, researchers have found. In a series of studies, participants received nearly identical tools for skill tests in golf and math. The only difference: Half of the putters bore Nike labels, while half of the earplug sets given to test takers were said to have been made by 3M. Those who thought they were using a Nike putter indeed needed fewer putts, on average, to sink a ball, and participants who thought they had 3M earplugs during the math test answered more questions correctly. It was also found that those with the lowest initial confidence in their abilities seemed to gain the most from the subtle upgrade.

Studies showed that, on average, the performance of participants on tests was ____(A)____ when they believed they were using more ____(B)____ brands.

	(A)		(B)
①	enhanced	⋯	generic
②	enhanced	⋯	athletic
③	enhanced	⋯	prominent
④	diminished	⋯	popular
⑤	diminished	⋯	ordinary

35 주어진 글 다음에 이어질 글의 순서로 가장 적절한 것은?

From all the meals you've shared with family and friends, you are probably aware that people have very different taste preferences. [A] The group of individuals who have considerably more than an average number of taste buds are called supertasters. The variations in the density of taste buds on different people's tongues appear to be genetic. Women are much more likely than men to be supertasters. [B] In fact, the foods mothers eat change the flavor of amniotic fluid, so some food preferences may be shaped in utero. However, people also show remarkable differences in the numbers of taste buds they possess. [C] Some people love spicy food, for example, whereas others shudder at the thought of a hot pepper. Some preferences are explained by differences in the flavors people experience quite early in life.

*in utero: 자궁 내에

① [A] − [C] − [B]
② [B] − [A] − [C]
③ [B] − [C] − [A]
④ [C] − [A] − [B]
⑤ [C] − [B] − [A]

※ 다음 글을 읽고 물음에 답하시오. 【36 – 37】

So effective was the mass conversion to the new engineering values that even when the depression hit in 1929, Americans continued to defend the technological vision. (①) They chose instead to vent their anger and fear against greedy businessmen who, in their mind, had undermined and thwarted the lofty aims and goals of the nation's new heroes—the engineers. (②) Quite a few Americans agreed with the earlier criticism of economist and social theorist Thorstein Veblen. He contended in 1921 that only by entrusting the nation's economy to the professional engineers—whose noble standards stood above pecuniary and parochial concerns—could the economy be saved and the country transformed into a new Eden. (③) Internal bickering among its leaders led to a splintering of the movement into warring factions. (④) Then too, Hitler's meteoric rise to power and the Third Reich's fanatical obsession with technological efficiency gave many social thinkers second thoughts about the Technocrats' call for a technological dictatorship in the United States. (⑤) The technological world view suffered an even more critical setback in 1945 when U.S. airplanes dropped atomic bombs on Japanese cities: the entire world was abruptly forced to look at the dark side of the techno-utopian vision. The postwar generation was the first to live with the constant reminder of modern technology's awesome power to destroy as well as create the future.

36 윗글의 흐름으로 보아, 주어진 문장이 들어가기에 가장 적절한 곳은?

> But the success of technocracy was to be short-lived.

37 윗글의 주제로 가장 적절한 것을 고르시오.

① the technocratic vision and its downfall

② the brief honeymoon for democracy and technology

③ the inevitable arrival of the technological world view

④ the belligerent approach of Technocrats for a better society

⑤ the imbalance between the bright and dark sides of technocracy

Even before there is a nation or other organized community to take over from the victims of aggression and their families the responsibility for catching and punishing aggressors, customs evolve that alleviate some of the problems of revenge practices. Among these is the principle of retribution, that is, exact retaliation for a wrong—an eye for an eye. Rather than being bloodthirsty, which is the modern connotation of the word, retribution reduces the likelihood of overreactions (your life for my eye) that are likely to engender feuds. Another ____(A)____ principle is "composition" (blood money), whereby the victim or the victim's family is required, or at least encouraged, to accept payment in compensation for an injury, discharging the injurer's liability. A transfer of money or goods is less costly to society as a whole than an act of violence, which besides inflicting a net social loss rather than merely transferring wealth from one person to another may provoke further violence. Another ____(B)____ institution is bilateral kinship. Icelanders reckoned kinship through both the father and the mother (many societies reckon it only through the father and some only through the mother). This not only increased the credibility of revenge as a deterrent to aggression by strengthening the family; it made it more likely that a disputant would have kin on both sides of the dispute. The Iliad hints at the further possibility that pity and empathy might limit the savagery of revenge.

38 윗글의 빈칸 (A)와 (B)에 공통으로 들어갈 말로 가장 적절한 것은? [3점]

① modifying　　　　　　② penalizing

③ conflicting　　　　　　④ moderating

⑤ captivating

39 윗글의 내용과 일치하는 것은?

① 국가가 가해자를 처벌할 책임을 맡기 전 보복은 주로 폭력으로 이루어졌다.
② '눈에는 눈' 원칙은 피해자의 과잉대응 가능성을 줄였다.
③ 피해자에 대한 물질적인 보상은 공동체가 담당했다.
④ 부모는 가족 구성원의 폭력에 대한 책임을 질 필요가 없었다.
⑤ 연민이나 공감은 보복의 가능성을 줄이는 데 도움이 되지 않았다.

[A] Many states have laws requiring individuals to wear a helmet while riding a motorcycle. These laws are frequently challenged, on the grounds that their sole purpose is to protect cyclists from injuring themselves.

[B] In college I had a motorcycle-riding friend who steadfastly refused to wear a helmet. He had been ridiculed so often by the rest of us for his foolishness that (a) he developed a rather eloquent defense that went something like this: "Look, I'm tired of this bourgeois life; I'm out for a little adventure, that's why I ride a bike in the first place. I want it to be dangerous; the thrill is the risk. And the more I risk, the bigger the thrill."

[C] It would seem from the episode that the helmet-free motorcyclist is engaged in other-regarding conduct after all. It is not that the public cares much about what happens to the motorcyclist; we care about the costs to the rest of us that flow from daredevil behavior. Not everyone's lifestyle is equal in terms of the burden or tax (b) he places on public resources. My reckless pal seems a particularly extreme example of an egoist asking the public to support his choice, not just leave (c) him alone.

[D] Was my friend's decision to ride without a helmet a decision that affected only himself? Stones or other objects might fly up from the road, causing (d) him to swerve into others. Even were he to injure only himself, that injury might involve head trauma that could have been avoided by wearing a helmet. My friend would then expect not to be left alone but to be ministered to by ambulance drivers, medics, and EMTs. Valuable time and money would be expended to subsidize his thrill seeking. The medics might not get to another victim in time because they were busy working to stuff brain tissue back inside (e) his cracked skull. Hospital space and resources would also be taxed, doctors called upon, and medical and auto insurance rates pushed upward for all of us.

40 윗글의 [A]에 이어질 내용을 순서에 맞게 배열한 것으로 가장 적절한 것은?

① [B] - [C] - [D]
② [B] - [D] - [C]
③ [C] - [B] - [D]
④ [C] - [D] - [B]
⑤ [D] - [C] - [B]

41 윗글의 주제로 가장 적절한 것은?

① the psyche of a helmetless biker

② a recipe for an accident−free society

③ lifestyles of risk and non−risk takers

④ personal freedom at the expense of others

⑤ a controversial regulation for traffic violators

42 밑줄 친 (a)~(e) 중에서 지칭하는 대상이 나머지와 다른 것은?

① (a)　　　　　　　　② (b)

③ (c)　　　　　　　　④ (d)

⑤ (e)

※ 다음 글을 읽고 물음에 답하시오. 【43−45】

I have always had an interest in the art of magic. By the time I was ten, I could make handkerchiefs vanish and shuffle a deck of cards thoroughly without altering their order. In my early teens I joined one of the world's best−known magic societies in London. By my early twenties I had been invited to the U.S. to perform several times at prestigious shows. My love for the world of fascinating tricks and illusion had started with a chance encounter. When I was eight I was asked to complete a school project on the history of chess. Being a diligent young student, I decided to pay a visit to my local library to find books on the topic. I was directed to the wrong shelf and came across some books on magic. I was curious, and started to read all about the secrets that magicians use to achieve the impossible. I have no idea what might have happened if I had been directed to the correct shelf and found the chess books. Many people have reported how chance meetings and unplanned encounters with strangers frequently led to a significant shift in career directions. Each one of us could tell stories of how crucial, unplanned events have had a major career impact and how untold thousands of minor unplanned events have had at least a small impact. Influential unplanned events _____; they are everyday occurrences. Serendipity is not serendipitous. Serendipity is ubiquitous. Take Joseph Pulitzer as an example. He was born in Hungary. As a young man Pulitzer suffered from both poor health and extremely bad eyesight. When he was seventeen, he came to America for a better life.

However, he could not find a job there. Pulitzer spent a great deal of time playing chess in his local library. On one such visit he happened to meet an editor of a local newspaper. This unexpected meeting resulted in Pulitzer being offered a job as a junior reporter. He was quite successful in his newspaper career, and became an editor, and eventually owner of two of the best-known newspapers of his day.

43 윗글의 제목으로 가장 적절할 것은?

① Diligence Always Pays Off
② Chances Are It's a Great Chance
③ Joseph Pulitzer : Untold Anecdotes
④ Prestige and Your Career Choices
⑤ Magical Moments Long Remembered

44 윗글의 빈칸에 들어가기에 가장 적절한 것은?

① are preconceived
② are not welcome
③ are not uncommon
④ can predict the future
⑤ can lose their influence

45 윗글에서 Joseph Pulitzer에 관한 내용과 일치하지 않는 것은?

① Hungary에서 출생했다.
② 시력이 나빠서 고생했다.
③ 열일곱 살 때 미국에 갔다.
④ 프로 chess 기사가 됐다.
⑤ 두 개의 신문사를 소유했다.

08 | 2018학년도 기출문제

▶ 해설은 p. 118에 있습니다.

※ 밑줄 친 단어의 뜻으로 가장 적절한 것을 고르시오. [01 – 05]

01 The students in the movement were deceived into thinking they were in the vanguard of a revolution.

① turmoil   ② forefront

③ protection   ④ opposition

⑤ preparation

02 The government concluded that the manufacturers colluded to sell their products to minors.

① collaborated   ② proposed

③ pretended   ④ intended

⑤ intervened

03 His penchant for the finer things in life led to the demise of his family fortune.

① obsession   ② aptitude

③ reproach   ④ inclination

⑤ extravagance

04 Rawls's sternest critics often tried to cabin him as "relevant only for American or at most Anglo–American audiences."

① confine   ② rebuke

③ introduce   ④ safeguard

⑤ exemplify

05 Questions about the pending lawsuit were met with <u>circumlocutory</u> replies by the pharmaceutical company representative.

① unequivocal   ② succinct

③ unfounded   ④ roundabout

⑤ conciliatory

※ 밑줄 친 부분 중, 어법상 틀린 것을 고르시오. [06-08]

06 I was greeted immediately by a member of the White House's legislative staff and led into the Gold Room, ① <u>where</u> most of the incoming House and Senate members had already gathered. At sixteen hundred hours on the dot, President Bush ② <u>announced</u> and walked to the podium, looking vigorous and fit, with that jaunty, determined walk ③ <u>that</u> suggests he's on a schedule and wants to keep detours to a minimum. For ten or so minutes he spoke to the room, ④ <u>making</u> a few jokes, calling for the country to come together, before inviting us to ⑤ <u>the other</u> end of the White House for refreshments and a picture with him and the First Lady.

07 San Francisco Giants pitcher Ryan Vogelsong and his wife, Nicole, watched the Fourth of July fireworks from their apartment's rooftop deck, which ① <u>offers</u> breathtaking views of landmarks such as the Bay Bridge, Alcatraz Island and Coit Tower. It was also there ② <u>where</u> they toasted with champagne his selection to the National League's All-Star team, the improbable high point—at least so far—of an itinerant career. The San Francisco Chronicle recently named him ③ <u>as</u> a candidate for the Cy Young Award. It ④ <u>has been</u> that kind of fairy-tale season for Vogelsong, 34, who has an 8-1 record and a 2.23 ERA for the defending World Series champs. Though his accomplishments this year overshadow anything Vogelsong has done before in baseball, they would not ⑤ <u>be</u> possible without the toils of an odyssey that has included stops in 10 minor league cities, plus San Francisco, Pittsburgh, Japan and Venezuela.

08 The absence of comparisons from the state of nature is crucial to Rousseau. By insisting that creatures who lived apart from sustained relationships could not yet ① have evolved the mind it takes to rank persons, Rousseau draws two great conclusions. First, natural inequalities—greater physical strength, better singing voice, or higher intelligence—come to matter only when a quality we happen to possess ② wins us respect, praise, worth, or value in the eyes of others. The second conclusion is ③ that natural man—and natural man alone—is honest. In society we are always concerned with ④ what others think of us ; we are motivated to do what will win us honor and the respect of others. It gets to the point where my sense of myself is derived from the impressions other people ⑤ have me.

※ (A), (B), (C)에 들어갈 말로 가장 적절한 것을 고르시오. [09-10]

09 The realization that the universe consists of atoms and void and nothing else, that the world was not made for us by a providential creator, that we are not the center of the universe, that our emotional lives are no more (A) [distinct / indistinct] than our physical lives from those of all other creatures, that our souls are as material and as mortal as our bodies—all these things are not the cause for (B) [despair / hope]. On the contrary, grasping the way things really are is the crucial step toward the possibility of happiness. It is possible for human beings to live happy lives, but not because they think that they are the center of the universe. Unappeasable desire and the fear of death are the principal (C) [paths / obstacles] to human happiness, but they can be surmounted through the exercise of reason.

	(A)		(B)		(C)
①	distinct	–	despair	–	paths
②	distinct	–	despair	–	obstacles
③	distinct	–	hope	–	obstacles
④	indistinct	–	hope	–	obstacles
⑤	indistinct	–	despair	–	paths

10 Music therapy as an explicit set of practices first developed in the West during the twentieth century — especially during the First World War, when doctors and nurses witnessed the effect that music had on the psychological, physiological, cognitive and emotional states of the wounded. The first major academic study of music's (A) [aesthetic / medicinal] properties was published in 1948, partly as a response to the continued use of music therapy in military hospitals and in factories during the Second World War. Music therapy is now (B) [rarely / widely] used for those with mental and/or physical disabilities or illnesses. One of its most significant functions is to relax patients who are preparing for, undergoing or recovering from surgery, notably dental, burns and coronary treatments. It is now well attested that music with slow, steady tempos, legato passages, gentle rhythms, predictable change, and simple sustained melodies is (C) [detrimental / conducive] to relaxation.

	(A)		(B)		(C)
①	aesthetic	−	rarely	−	detrimental
②	aesthetic	−	widely	−	detrimental
③	medicinal	−	widely	−	detrimental
④	medicinal	−	widely	−	conducive
⑤	medicinal	−	rarely	−	conducive

※ 밑줄 친 부분 중, 문맥상 낱말의 쓰임이 적절하지 않은 것을 고르시오. [11−13]

11 The spiritual dimension is a complex, and controversial area, and is often overlooked within holistic approaches, although it is increasingly being identified as a ① vital element which can have a large influence on the physical, mental and emotional aspects of work. Unfortunately the majority of studies that explore spirituality and resilience treat spirituality as a single entity which is ② easily measured and controlled. Spirituality is in reality a complex, ③ multi-dimensional phenomenon. Hence research which ④ excludes a broad interpretation of spirituality is important in order to expand our understanding. There are some who interpret spirituality using just a religious definition. This ⑤ narrow religious interpretation of spirituality, often seen in America and the UK as a Christian interpretation, is not appropriate for the government agencies that pride themselves on their anti-discriminatory practices.

12 According to one theory, within certain limits the more similar the communicators are, the more effective their communication will be. One limiting condition is that if the similarities between people are so ① pervasive that they have the same attitudes and beliefs about every subject, there is no need for communication. For example, the conversation might be ② lively at a party in which every person was in agreement about every subject from movies to politics. On the other hand, people who are ③ dissimilar in almost every respect lack a common ground, a base from which to share experiences and exchange ideas. According to this theory, the ideal situation is one in which people have many similarities but are dissimilar enough in their attitudes about the subject at hand to interact and perhaps to influence one another's attitudes. Similarity clearly ④ prevails, however. After all, the goal of attitude influence is to change the other person's attitude so that it more closely ⑤ resembles your own.

13 The fourth industrial revolution will affect the scale of conflict as well as its character. The distinctions between war and peace and who is a combatant and noncombatant are becoming uncomfortably ① clarified. Similarly, the battlefield is increasingly both local and global. Organizations such as ISIS operate ② principally in defined areas in the Middle East but they also recruit fighters from more than a hundred countries, largely through social media, while related terrorist attacks can occur anywhere on the planet. Modern conflicts are increasingly ③ hybrid in nature, combining traditional battlefield techniques with elements that were previously mostly associated with armed non-state actors. However, with technologies ④ fusing in increasingly unpredictable ways and with state and armed non-state actors learning from each other, the potential magnitude of change is not yet widely ⑤ appreciated. [3점]

14 ger에 관한 다음 글의 내용과 일치하는 것은?

The large, white felt tent, known as a *ger* and seen all over Mongolia, is probably the most identifiable symbol of the country. (The word "yurt" is a Turkic word introduced to the west by the Russians. If you don't want to offend the nationalistic sensibilities of the Mongolians, use the word "ger.") Most Mongolians still live in gers, even in the suburbs of Ulaan Baatar. And it's not hard to understand why: wood and bricks are scarce and expensive, especially out on the steppes, and animal hides are cheap and readily available. Nomadic people obviously have to be flexible and mobile and gers can be moved easily — depending on the size, a ger can be assembled in one to three hours. If the opportunity arises, an invitation to visit or stay in a ger is one that should not be missed.

① Most Mongolians prefer to call it a "yurt."
② You can only find it in urban areas of Ulaan Baatar.
③ It is made of wood and bricks.
④ It can be built in three hours or less.
⑤ It is not recommended for the modern traveler.

15 Yellowstone National Park에 관한 다음 글의 내용과 일치하지 않는 것은?

Yellowstone National Park was created in 1872 to protect its geyser basins. But the 2-million-acre park put the government in the wildlife business, and unfortunately scientific wildlife management did not begin until more than half a century later. No detailed records exist of the area's animal population and feeding behavior at the time the park was established. Early rangers fed elk and bison as one would feed cattle and began killing wolves. By 1926, following a federal directive, the last wolves had been eliminated. Then elk overpopulated the park, eating through grass, brush, and any part of a tree they could reach. So in 1934 the rangers began shooting them, too; records show that in 1962 alone, 4,619 were killed. In 1967 public distaste forced the Park Service to stop the shooting. But the park did not recover.

① The wildlife began to be managed scientifically in the 1900s.
② The exact animal population in 1872 is not known.
③ Elks flourished after the elimination of their natural predator.
④ A total of 4,619 elks were killed in 1962.
⑤ Public opinion halted the shooting of wolves.

16 A good rocket launch site has a few important characteristics. An unpopulated patch of land near an ocean is preferable, so no one gets showered with wayward bits of flaming metal. It's also nice if it's on the equator—like all spheres rotating on an axis, the Earth spins fastest in the middle, which provides rocket boosters with extra oomph. In other words, the best sites tend to be in remote, tropical locations. That such places are also often among the world's poorest gives many launches a _____ feel: billions of dollars in futuristic machinery rising up over rainforests and shantytowns. [3점]

① majestic
② fleeting
③ catastrophic
④ universal
⑤ counterintuitive

17 _____. It is not uncommon to find analysts failing to distinguish between facts and inferences or operating on the assumption that an inference was a fact. It is not unusual to hear an analyst state that his conclusions followed "logically" from the evidence, even though generalizations arrived at inductively are not subject to logical proof. That different types of inquiry are subject to different types of "proof" is an alien concept to many researchers. And the common misuse of *infer* and *imply* reflects not only a lack of knowledge of terminology but also an unfamiliarity with underlying concepts of logic as well. [3점]

① Terminological confusion further aggravates flawed logic
② Logical thinking is a precursor to scientific research
③ Examples of the inability to reason well abound
④ Generalizations are subject to rigorous testing
⑤ Inductive logic prevails in academia

18 The doublespeak flows in the government, whether people in government are talking to the public or to each other. The Bureau of Land Management issued a press release in 1986 which began, "In a move to add administrative procedures regarding compliance with statutory requirements, the Department of the Interior's Bureau of Land Management (BLM) today published a rulemaking concerning federal coal leasee qualifications." This doublespeak simply means that the BLM intends to crack down on coal leases. An official in the Department of Commerce who had requested an increase in salary was told that "Because of the fluctuational predisposition of your position's productive capacity as juxtaposed to government standards, it would be monetarily injudicious to advocate an increment." In other words, _____.

① the pink slip   ② all petitions suspended

③ no pay raise   ④ no new openings

⑤ an early retirement

19 _____. We've found a hormone that can rejuvenate the muscles of elderly mice. Osteocalcin—a hormone secreted by bone—boosts the ability of muscles to burn fuel and generate energy, researchers at Columbia University discovered. When the team injected the hormone into old mice, the animals were able to run just as far as their younger counterparts, despite being up to a year older—a long time in mouse years. Old mice that did not receive the hormone ran about half as far. Osteocalcin levels decline with age in both mice and humans, and the team now plans to test whether the hormone can improve muscle function in people too. [3점]

① Wind back the clock   ② A stitch in time saves nine

③ Time waits for no man   ④ Give the elderly their due

⑤ Speed up the sands of time

20 Like the iron cage of capitalism in which human needs are sacrificed to the exigencies of production, there is a sense in which science in the modern world has also become _____ : Within the domain of institutionalized science and academic scholarship, creativity and innovation must be accommodated to the specialized criteria of achievement that govern the various professional disciplines.

① a torchlight shining on intellectual avenues

② emancipated from bureaucratic demands

③ a fortress impregnable to any attack

④ vulnerable to moral issues at hand

⑤ the prison house of the mind

21 During the late nineteenth and early twentieth century, the Frenchman Joseph Pujol was famous for his ability to fart _____ by drawing air into his anus. He put on a stage show, calling himself Le Petomane, which is French for "The Fartiste." Dressed formally, he would open with a rumble of cannon-fire farting. Various routines followed, most spectacularly an imitation of the 1906 San Francisco earthquake. He could rectally project a jet of water a distance of 15 feet (4.5 m) and to close, he sang a rhyme about a farm, punctuated with farts that sounded like different animal noises.

① at will
② silently
③ intermittently
④ to no avail
⑤ inadvertently

22 For most of your past life experiences, you would probably agree that you need to reconstruct the memories. For example, if someone asked you how you celebrated your birthday three years ago, you'd likely count backwards and try to reconstruct the context. _____(A)_____, there are some circumstances in which people believe that their memories remain completely faithful to the original events. These types of memories—which are called flashbulb memories—arise when people experience emotionally charged events: People's memories are so vivid that they seem almost to be photographs of the original incident. The first research on flashbulb memories focused on people's recollections of public events. _____(B)_____, the researchers asked participants if they had specific memories of how they first learned about the assassination of President John F. Kennedy. All but one of the 80 participants reported vivid recollections.

	(A)		(B)
①	As a result	—	Consequently
②	As a result	—	For example
③	Moreover	—	However
④	Moreover	—	Consequently
⑤	However	—	For example

23 In order to promote social engagements among my students, I began encouraging them to bring food and drinks, as well as mats and cushions, to class. With these items, the classroom space is ____(A)____ in terms of form and function as it gains a "social" aspect. During the reflection exercises, I observed how some students brought not just mats and cushions, but also pillows and stuffed toys as though they were attending a slumber party! When mats and cushions are not in use, students are seated in chairs strategically arranged around the tables, eating and drinking, as they discuss or review each other's drafts. As food and drinks are vital to any sociocultural discourse, they help enhance the social atmosphere, ____(B)____ communal bonds, and heighten the students' shared identity.

	(A)		(B)
①	altered	—	cement
②	preserved	—	dissolve
③	altered	—	weaken
④	preserved	—	solidify
⑤	modified	—	loosen

※ 다음 글의 제목으로 가장 적절한 것을 고르시오. 【24-25】

24 The center of mining and armor technology was Augsburg, in Germany, and that was no coincidence. Augsburg was near one of Europe's major deposits of iron ore, and the demand for metal from feudal states building forces of armored knights soon created a booming mining industry and an equally flourishing armorer business. To the annoyance of their customers throughout feudal Europe, the Germans charged sky-high prices, aware that those customers had no alternative: German armor was the best in the world, and if a customer didn't like the prices, he could sally forth on his next war with sticks and stones. Underwritten by these lavish profits, the German armorers could afford an extensive research and development effort. It resulted in stronger armor, for example, steel helmets with movable visors that covered the entire head.

① Farewell to Arms and Armors
② Past and Future of Armor Business
③ Stones vs. Steel: The Obvious Choice
④ Germany, the Hub of Armor Technology
⑤ High Quality and Low Prices: A Double-Edged Sword

25 Hate to haggle? You're not alone. A national survey found that just 48 percent of shoppers tried bargaining for a better deal on everyday goods and services in the past three years, down from 61 percent in 2007. But if you're chicken, you lose. Eighty-nine percent of those who haggled were rewarded at least once. Successful furniture hagglers saved $300 on average, as did those who questioned a health-related charge. Those who challenged their cell-phone plans saved $80. Clearly, people who don't haggle are leaving money on the table. [3점]

① Can't Hurt to Ask
② ABCs of Haggling Better
③ Furniture Haggling Made Easy
④ Shopping Around: Reap the Rewards
⑤ Does Haggling Actually Inflate Prices?

※ 다음 글의 주제로 가장 적절한 것을 고르시오. [26-27]

26 Catholicism held that the only God-given vocation was priesthood, but Protestants thought that people could be called to any of the secular crafts and trades. The belief that they were serving God encouraged them to work with religious fervor, leading them to produce more goods and make more money. Weber believed that the Protestant faith led inevitably to a capitalist economic society because it gave believers the chance to view the pursuit of profit as evidence of devotion, rather than of morally suspect motives such as greed and ambition. The idea of predestination also meant that believers need not worry about social inequalities and poverty, because material wealth was a sign of spiritual wealth.

① role of religion in creating social equality
② reasons for the rise of the Protestant faith
③ influence of Protestantism on economic ideals
④ importance of morality in economic activities
⑤ differences between Protestants and Catholics

27 Whether out of curiosity, vanity, or a motive as yet unexplored, people throughout the ages have wanted to see their own reflection. As early as 2500 B.C. the Egyptians had mirrors of highly polished metal, usually of bronze, occasionally of silver or gold. The first commercial glass mirrors were made in Venice in 1564; these were made of blown glass that was flattened and coated with an amalgam of mercury and tin. The Venetians proceeded to supply Europe with mirrors for centuries. It wasn't until 1840 that a German chemist named Justus Liebig came up with the method of silvering that we use today. By this technique, silver-ammonia compounds are subjected to the chemical action of a reducing agent, such as invert sugar, Rochelle salt, or formaldehyde, and the resulting metallic silver is spread evenly over the back of a smooth pane of plate glass.

① economic motivations behind the invention of the mirror

② outstanding achievements of German chemists

③ development of commercial glass mirror technology

④ human desires hidden in commercial glass mirrors

⑤ commonalities of ancient mirror technology in Europe

28 다음 글의 목적으로 가장 적절한 것은?

What could be more comforting than seeing your dog or cat curled up in blissful sleep? Both species spend almost half their day engaged in some form of sleep. But not all find it restful: older animals, those with muscular or joint issues, or very active dogs will often pace or relocate frequently. If your companion fits into one of these categories, he might benefit from a therapeutic bed. These specialized products offer support and comfort unlike regular beds or an impromptu sleeping spot. Regardless of age and health, a good bed promotes muscular-skeletal health and offers additional rejuvenating and healing benefits.

① to prevent domestic animal abuse

② to promote specialized pet furniture

③ to explain the benefits of good sleep

④ to inform pet owners of furniture hazards

⑤ to warn pet owners of poor pet sleep habits

29 다음 글의 요지로 가장 적절한 것은? [3점]

You cannot buy happiness. You cannot go to the nearest grocery store and order a pound of happiness as you would a pound of butter. But, since happiness comes from within, you can secure a measure of happiness by your own acts. You can find that feeling of contentment by helping your less fortunate fellowmen. You can help those who, because of ill-fate, will not have a happy Christmas unless we share with them. During this season of peace and good will, let us not force those in need to look at happiness through our eyes. Rather, let us help them to see and find happiness through their own eyes. Let us not fail the less fortunate of the community.

① Measure your true happiness level by acts of good will.
② Catch the happiness virus in your local community.
③ Do not force your happy ways on your neighbors.
④ Exercise self-contentment to achieve mental well-being.
⑤ Find happiness by helping the needy around you.

30 다음 글에 나타난 "I"의 심경으로 가장 적절한 것은?

Taking a deep breath, I began sprinting again, counting my strokes, telling myself that I wouldn't look up again until I'd swum one thousand strokes. Slowly I gained a foot, then a few hundred yards. Now I realized why the English Channel was the Mount Everest of swimming: though everyone's goal is to get to the top, the summit is where the air grows thinner, where everything becomes challenging. *Don't look up for five hundred strokes. Go as fast as you can go. Push it. Pull your arms with everything you have. Kick. Yes. Kick those legs. Pull deeper. Faster. Come on. Pull.*

① frustrated but resilient   ② determined and persistent
③ daunted and disappointed   ④ surprised but exhilarated
⑤ overwhelmed and discouraged

31 As a rule, physicians should not be considered altruistic when acting in their patients' best interests because they do not have the choices in acting that we ordinarily associate with altruism. Doctors have professional duties to patients that they cannot discharge as a matter of choice. To be sure, becoming a doctor and thereby entering into a professional relationship with patients is an optional act. ① Once a doctor enters into this relationship, however, he or she cannot choose obligations. ② A doctor can choose not to treat a particular patient in a particular situation if doing so would compromise personal and professional integrity. ③ Thus there arises a potential conflict for a physician who sees patients as individuals needing therapeutic treatments. ④ But the doctor must ensure that the patient's care is transferred to another physician. ⑤ Once one becomes a physician, one promises to promote the best medical interests of one's patients. This is not optional, but obligatory. [3점]

32 Unlike other climate issues, the science of sea level rise is fairly simple. ① Ocean levels are increasing mostly because of what heat does to water, in all its various states. ② To combat the rise in ocean levels, it is of utmost importance to understand the molecular structure of water. ③ As global temperature rises, most of the extra heat in the atmosphere — about 90 percent — sinks into the ocean. ④ As the water warms, it expands like mercury in a thermometer. ⑤ This thermal expansion accounts for one-third of sea level rise. The other two-thirds comes from melting mountain glaciers and ice sheets in Greenland and Antarctica.

33 다음 글의 내용을 한 문장으로 나타낼 때, 빈칸 (A)와 (B)에 들어갈 말로 가장 적절한 것은?

In some cases, researchers simply observe animals in nature as a function of different times of day, different seasons of the year, changes in diet, and so forth. These procedures raise no ethical problems. In other studies, however, animals have been subjected to brain damage, electrode implantation, injections of drugs or hormones, and other procedures that are clearly not for their own benefit. Anyone with a conscience (including scientists) is bothered by this fact. Nevertheless, experimentation with animals has been critical to the medical research that led to methods for the prevention or treatment of polio, diabetes, measles, smallpox, massive burns, heart disease, and other serious conditions. Most Nobel prizes in physiology or medicine have been awarded for research conducted on nonhuman animals. The hope of finding methods to treat or prevent AIDS, Alzheimer's disease, stroke, and many other disorders depends largely on animal research. In many areas of medicine and biological psychology, research would progress slowly or not at all without animals.

Though some _____(A)_____ studies conducted on animals, unlike simple observational research, raise ethical issues, they are _____(B)_____ in making progress in various medical fields.

	(A)		(B)
①	experimental	–	instrumental
②	statistical	–	successful
③	field	–	critical
④	developmental	–	plausible
⑤	laboratory	–	negligible

34 글의 흐름으로 보아, 주어진 문장이 들어가기에 가장 적절한 곳은?

It preserves, and sometimes further simplifies, the relevant information.

Generally speaking, a model is a simplified representation of reality created to serve a purpose. (①) It is simplified based on some assumptions about what is and is not important for the specific purpose, or sometimes based on constraints on information or tractability. (②) For example, a map is a model of the physical world. (③) It abstracts away a tremendous amount of information that the mapmaker deemed irrelevant for its purpose. (④) For example, a road map keeps and highlights the roads, their basic topology, their relationships to places one would want to travel, and other relevant information. (⑤) Various professions have well-known model types: an architectural blueprint, an engineering prototype, and so on. Each of these abstracts away details that are not relevant to their main purpose and keeps those that are.

※ 주어진 글 다음에 이어질 글의 순서로 가장 적절한 것을 고르시오. 【35-36】

35 Common law is otherwise known as case law, which is the law developed by the judges in their judgments (or rulings) on particular cases. The judges are guided by the theory and rules of precedent, which means they are bound by previous rulings that set "precedents."

(A) Equally, judges must sometimes interpret laws that Parliament has passed. One such example involved the Abortion Act 1967. A secretary declined to type a referral letter for a termination, claiming that the right to conscientiously object to participation in an abortion protected her refusal.

(B) This essentially means that they must take into account similar cases decided in the past, particularly those decided in the highest courts. This area of judge-made law is important because there will be situations where Parliament has not enacted a law and it falls to the judges to plug the gap.

(C) The judges looked at the word "participation" and decided that the secretary was not covered, as she was not sufficiently involved in the procedure. [3점]

① (A)-(C)-(B)　　　　　② (B)-(A)-(C)

③ (B)-(C)-(A)　　　　　④ (C)-(A)-(B)

⑤ (C)-(B)-(A)

36 As robotics starts to spread, the degree to which countries can succeed in the robot era will depend in part on culture — on how readily people accept robots into their lives.

(A) As a result, Japanese culture tends to be more accepting of robot companions as actual companions than is Western culture, which views robots as soulless machines.

(B) The ancient Shinto religion, practiced by 80 percent of Japanese, includes a belief in animism, which holds that both objects and human beings have spirits.

(C) Western and Eastern cultures are highly differentiated in how they view robots. Not only does Japan have an economic need and the technological know-how for robots, but it also has a cultural predisposition.

① (A) – (C) – (B) ② (B) – (A) – (C)

③ (B) – (C) – (A) ④ (C) – (A) – (B)

⑤ (C) – (B) – (A)

We've come back to the United States, but Julie's mind is still in Italy. She's yearning for some more of that pizza. She decides to make it herself, with me as her sous chef.

I chop my eggplant and zucchini. We're both quiet, focused on our chores. Next up, the onion chopping. I peel my onion, take it to the sink, turn on the faucet, and start slicing it under the flow.

"What are you doing?"

"I'm cutting the onion underwater."

"Why?"

"It says in the Britannica it stops you from crying."

This was an Heloise-style hint from the Britannica—one of those rare useful ones—and I was quite excited to be putting it into practice.

"Nope, too dangerous."

"But it's in the Britannica."

"Nope, I'm the executive chef. You're the sous chef."

Here I'm confronted with an unfortunate situation: the Britannica versus my wife. Two big sources of authority. Which do I choose? Well, the Britannica is pretty trustworthy. However, as far as I know, it can't carry my child or ignore me for several days or throw out the T-shirts that it hates.

So I decide Julie wins this one. _____.

37 윗글의 제목으로 가장 적절한 것은?

① Peel Onions Underwater to Avoid Tears

② Battle of Genders Ending in a Draw

③ Aftermath of an Italian Cooking Tip

④ Real Boss in My Home

⑤ Sous Chefs in the Britannica

38 윗글의 빈칸에 들어가기에 가장 적절한 것은?

① Which attests to how strong working women are

② I might have to call the Britannica for corrections

③ The onion will be cut without water and I will cry

④ I will ignore her for the next few days

⑤ But I'll be the executive chef tomorrow

We have long known that ravens are no birdbrains. They have been spotted caching food for later, gathering string to pull up hanging food and even trying to deceive one another. A study published today in Science adds an especially impressive twist: Ravens can ＿＿＿＿＿ that they never encounter in nature.

The new study was led by cognitive zoologists in Sweden, who replicated a series of experiments previously used to (a) testing apes' planning abilities, this time using ravens. The ravens were first taught to use a stone to knock a food pellet out of a puzzle box. The next day, without the box present, the birds were (b) offered a choice between the stone tool and "distracter" objects—toys too light or bulky to use as tools. The box (c) would then be brought back 15 minutes after the selection. Despite the delay, the ravens chose the correct tool nearly 80 percent of the time, and successfully used the tools they selected 86 percent of the time. The birds performed almost (d) as well when they had to give an experimenter a bottle cap in exchange for a piece of food. The birds almost always selected the bottle cap over distracters, even though they would have (e) to wait 15 minutes to barter with it. The preference for soon-to-be-useful items persisted when the ravens had to pass up a smaller treat in favor of either the tool or the bartering token—and even when they could use each item only after a 17-hour delay.

39 윗글의 밑줄 친 부분 중 어법상 틀린 것은?

① (a)　　　　　　　② (b)

③ (c)　　　　　　　④ (d)

⑤ (e)

40 윗글의 빈칸에 들어가기에 가장 적절한 것은? [3점]

① preserve tools for emergencies

② work in groups for situations

③ predict events yet to happen

④ trick potential competitors

⑤ plan for future needs

I had decided to go and I would go, and I had to be there by my mother's birthday. This was extremely important. I believed that if there was any chance to bring my mother back home it would happen on her birthday. If I had said this aloud to my father or to my grandparents, they would have said that I might as well try to catch a fish in the air, so I did not say it aloud. But I believed it. (①) My father says I lean on broken reeds and will get a face full of swamp mud one day.

When at last Gram and Gramps Hiddle and I set out that first day of the trip, I prayed for the first thirty minutes solid. I prayed that we would not be in an accident (I was terrified of cars and buses) and that we would get there by my mother's birthday — seven days away — and that we would bring her home. Over and over, I prayed the same thing. I prayed to trees. This was easier than praying directly to God. There was nearly always a tree nearby. As we pulled onto the Ohio Turnpike, which is the flattest, straightest piece of road in God's whole creation, Gram interrupted my prayers. "Salamanca —" (②)

I should explain right off that my real name is Salamanca Tree Hiddle. Salamanca, my parents thought, was the name of the Indian tribe to which my great-great-grandmother belonged. (③) My parents were mistaken. The name of the tribe was Seneca, but since my parents did not discover their error until after I was born and they were, by then, used to my name, it remained Salamanca. (④) My middle name, Tree, comes from your basic tree, a thing of such beauty to my mother that she made it part of my name. She wanted to be more specific and use Sugar Maple Tree, her very favorite, but Salamanca Sugar Maple Tree Hiddle was a bit much even for her. (⑤) My mother used to call me Salamanca, but after she left, only my grandparents Hiddle called me Salamanca (when they were not calling me chickabiddy). To most other people, I was Sal, and to a few boys who thought they were especially amusing, I was Salamander.

41 윗글의 'I'에 관한 내용과 일치하지 않는 것은?

① The purpose of her trip was to bring her mother home.

② Her grandparents accompanied her on the trip.

③ She found it easier to pray to trees than to God.

④ Her parents had a misunderstanding when they named her.

⑤ Most people called her Salamanca or Salamander.

42 다음 문장이 들어가기에 가장 적절한 곳은?

> Sometimes I am as ornery and stubborn as an old donkey.

※ 다음 글을 읽고 물음에 답하시오. 【43-45】

On disembarking at Amsterdam's Schipol Airport, I am struck, only a few steps inside the terminal, by the appearance of a sign hanging from the ceiling, which shows the way to the arrivals hall, the exit and the transfer desks. It is a bright-yellow sign, one meter high and two meters across, simple in design, a plastic fascia in an illuminated aluminum box suspended on steel struts from a ceiling webbed with cables and air-conditioning ducts. Despite its simplicity, even its mundanity, the sign delights me, a delight for which the adjective exotic, though unusual, seems apt. The exoticism is located in particular areas: in the double *a* of *Aankomst*, in the neighborliness of the *u* and the *i* in *Uitgang*, in the use of English subtitles, in the word for "desk," *balies*, and in the choice of practical, modernist fonts, Frutiger or Univers.

If the sign provokes in me genuine pleasure, it is in part because it offers the first conclusive evidence of my having arrived elsewhere. It is a symbol of being abroad. Although it may not seem distinctive to the casual eye, such a sign would never exist in precisely this form in my own country. There it would be less yellow, the typeface would be softer and more nostalgic, there would — out of greater indifference to the _____ of foreigners — be no subtitles, and the language would contain no double as, a repetition in which I sense, confusedly, the presence of another history and mind-set.

That a sign could be different in different places is evidence of a simple but pleasing idea: countries are diverse, and practices variable across borders. Yet difference alone would not be enough to elicit pleasure, or not for long. The difference has to seem like an improvement on what my own country is capable of. If I call the Schipol sign exotic, it is because it succeeds in suggesting, vaguely but intensely, that the country that made it and that lies beyond the uitgang may in critical ways prove more congenial than my own to my temperament and concerns. The sign is a promise of happiness.

43 윗글의 제목으로 가장 적절한 것은?

① At Once Exotic and Nostalgic

② Too Esoteric a Sign Kills Curiosity

③ Sweet Bewilderment: Am I Elsewhere?

④ Various Languages on the Same Platter

⑤ Across the Border: The Pioneering Traveler

44 윗글의 빈칸에 들어가기에 가장 적절한 것은?

① talent   ② excitement

③ confusion   ④ intimacy

⑤ number

45 Schipol Airport의 표지판에 관한 윗글의 내용과 일치하지 않는 것은? [3점]

① Its length is twice its height.

② It is written in two languages.

③ Its simplicity is the main reason for its exoticism.

④ It gives proof of arriving in another country.

⑤ The writer could not find a sign like it back home.

09 | 2019학년도 기출문제

▶ 해설은 p. 131에 있습니다.

※ 밑줄 친 단어의 뜻으로 가장 적절한 것을 고르시오. [01~03]

01 Nothing could be firmer than the tone of this letter, in spite of its <u>pensive</u> gentleness.

① overt   ② excessive
③ pervasive   ④ thoughtful
⑤ optimistic

02 The doctor asserted that his lifelong research on the human genome was by no means <u>exhaustive</u>.

① rewarding   ② revolutionary
③ lenient   ④ independent
⑤ thorough

03 This <u>conundrum</u> was like no other that the police officers had faced before.

① instrument   ② robbery
③ criminal   ④ puzzle
⑤ demonstration

04
A : How did the meeting go yesterday?

B : It couldn't have been worse.

A : What happened?

B : I said something I shouldn't have and now Jack won't talk to me.

A : _____.

B : Now I need to gather every ounce of courage to do so.

① It's never too late to apologize

② You can't please everyone all the time

③ Sometimes a quarrel is good for the team

④ Just like everything else, time heals all wounds

⑤ That's why you have to think before you speak

05
A : Detective Mills, I think this is the guy we are looking for.

B : Do his prints match the ones from the scene of the crime, Officer Flaherty?

A : The results haven't come in yet, but two witnesses say they saw someone with his descriptions.

B : That won't be enough for an arrest warrant.

A : But, I'm sure this is the perpetrator.

B : _____.

A : Okay. Then we'll just have to wait for the results from the lab.

① I'll ask for a warrant right away

② We move on evidence, not feelings

③ I think we already have all the proof we need

④ Let's concentrate on the statements of the witnesses

⑤ Our main duty is to ensure the safety of the civilians

※ 밑줄 친 부분 중, 어법상 틀린 것을 고르시오. 【06-07】

06 A recurrent issue for courts is whose viewpoint to adopt in deciding how much should be disclosed to patients about ① their medical treatment. The majority of states favor the experts, holding that physicians are responsible for disclosing only as much as ② would be considered reasonable by a "reasonable medical practitioner" in the same community and the same specialty. This approach is grounded in the so-called therapeutic privilege, ③ which recognizes the physician's preeminent right to withhold any information that might harm the patient. The less deferential minority rule holds that the adequacy of disclosure should be judged from the standpoint of the "reasonable patient," not from ④ those of the "reasonable physician." Although these general rules are well settled, questions about the adequacy of disclosure still ⑤ arise.

07 Raku is a popular low-temperature, fast-firing process that yields exciting, ① chance surface effects on ceramic ware. From a simple white crackle glaze to a surprising spectrum of color, from humble tea bowls to sculptural forms abstract or figurative, the range of possibility and innovation ② that resides in raku practice keeps it always young and vibrant. The modern Western practice of this ancient process, as well as ③ its purpose, differs from its Eastern roots, but the results of raku are still infinite in their variety, energy, and beauty. Japanese and Western raku offer the ceramist the possibility ④ of experiencing the final results of the firing in a relatively short time, and it is this very quality that makes the practice of raku ⑤ so satisfied. [3점]

08 Crabs, birds, and manta rays regularly try to crush sea horses for dinner, but a sea horse has some unusual protective armor. Its tail can be (A) [compressed/expanded] to half its normal size without lasting damage, researchers at the University of California, San Diego, recently found. The tail's (B) [resilience/rigidity] comes from its structure: approximately 36 square segments, each made of four bony plates. The plates connect to the spinal column's vertebrae with collagen and can glide past one another, keeping the spine (C) [safe/vulnerable]. Ultimately, the researchers would like to build a robotic arm out of 3-D-printed plates that mimic the seahorse's flexible and tough tail and use it for underwater excursions or to detonate bombs.

	(A)	(B)	(C)
①	compressed	resilience	vulnerable
②	compressed	rigidity	safe
③	compressed	resilience	safe
④	expanded	rigidity	safe
⑤	expanded	resilience	vulnerable

09 Studies of priming effects have yielded discoveries that (A) [confirm/threaten] our self-image as conscious and autonomous authors of our judgments and our choices. For instance, most of us think of voting as a deliberate act that reflects our values and our assessments of policies and is not influenced by (B) [consensus/irrelevancies]. Our vote should not be affected by the location of the polling station, for example, but it is. A study of voting patterns in precincts of Arizona in 2000 showed that the support for propositions to increase the funding of schools was significantly greater when the polling station was in a school than when it was in a nearby location. A separate experiment showed that exposing people to images of classrooms and school lockers also (C) [increased/minimized] the tendency of participants to support a school initiative. The effect of the images was larger than the difference between parents and other voters. [3점]

	(A)	(B)	(C)
①	confirm	consensus	minimized
②	confirm	consensus	increased
③	confirm	irrelevancies	minimized
④	threaten	irrelevancies	increased
⑤	threaten	irrelevancies	minimized

10 Think of a "discovery" as an act that moves the arrival of information from a later point in time to an earlier time. The discovery's value does not ① <u>equal</u> the value of the information discovered but rather the value of having the information available earlier than it otherwise would have been. A scientist or a mathematician may show great skill by being the first to find a solution that has ② <u>eluded</u> many others; yet if the problem would soon have been solved anyway, then the work probably has not much ③ <u>benefited</u> the world. There are cases in which having a solution even slightly sooner is immensely valuable, but this is most plausible when the solution is immediately put to use, either being ④ <u>deployed</u> for some practical end or serving as a foundation to further theoretical work. And in the latter case, where a solution is immediately used only in the sense of serving as a building block for further theorizing, there is great value in obtaining a solution slightly ⑤ <u>later</u> only if the further work it enables is itself both important and urgent.

11 We are committed to reason. If we are asking a question, evaluating possible answers, and trying to persuade others of the value of those answers, then we are reasoning, and therefore have tacitly signed on to the ① <u>validity</u> of reason. We are also committed to whatever conclusions follow from the careful application of reason, such as the theorems of mathematics and logic. Though we cannot logically ② <u>prove</u> anything about the physical world, we are entitled to have confidence in certain beliefs about it. The application of reason and observation to discover ③ <u>steadfast</u> generalizations about the world is what we call science. The progress of science, with its dazzling success at explaining and manipulating the world, shows that knowledge of the universe is ④ <u>possible</u>, albeit always probabilistic and subject to revision. Science is thus a paradigm for how we ought to gain knowledge—not the particular methods or institutions of science but its value system, namely to seek to explain the world, to evaluate candidate explanations ⑤ <u>objectively</u>, and to be cognizant of the tentativeness and uncertainty of our understanding at any time.

12 On a boat off Costa Rica, a biologist uses pliers from a Swiss army knife to try to extract a plastic straw from a sea turtle's nostril. The turtle ① <u>writhes</u> in agony, bleeding profusely. For eight painful minutes the YouTube video ticks on; it has ② <u>logged</u> more than 20 million views, even though it's so hard to watch. At the end the increasingly desperate biologists finally manage to ③ <u>dislodge</u> a four-inch-long straw from the creature's nose. Raw scenes like this, which lay ④ <u>bare</u> the toll of plastic on wildlife, have become familiar: The dead albatross, its stomach bursting with refuse. The turtle stuck in a six-pack ring, its shell ⑤ <u>unscathed</u> from years of straining against the tough plastic. The seal snared in a discarded fishing net. Who is to blame? Take a good look in the mirror. [3점]

13 다음 글의 제목으로 가장 적절한 것은?

Do we live on a rare earth? One so exceptional that it is pretty much alone in hosting a rich diversity of life, with almost all other planets being home to simple microbes at best? Or are we in a universe teeming with living things as complex as those here, meaning that we exist as part of a vast, cosmic zoo? Debate on this rages on, but we say it is time to accept that the latter is very likely. To date we know of at least 3,700 exoplanets and there are likely to be trillions of other potentially habitable exoplanets and exomoons in our galaxy and beyond. We do not know how commonly life arises on them, but many scientists think that it may well emerge from the chemical and physical properties of any suitable planet.

① Earth, the Extraordinary Home
② The Intergalactic Superhighway
③ Are Microbes Our True Ancestors?
④ The Cosmic Zoo: The Big Hoax
⑤ Is Anybody Out There?

14 Frank O'Connor에 관한 다음 글의 내용과 일치하는 것은?

Frank O'Connor was born in Cork, Ireland, of a family too poor to give him a university education. During Ireland's struggle for independence he was briefly a member of the Irish Republican Army. Then he worked as a librarian in Cork and Dublin and for a time was director of the Abbey Theatre before he was established as a writer of short stories. From 1931 on he published regularly in American magazines and taught for some years at Harvard and Northwestern Universities. His declared objective was to find the natural rhythms and stresses of the storyteller's voice in shaping his material. He was indeed a prolifichistorian of Irish manners and the Irish character.

① He is an Irish playwright holding a Harvard degree.

② He was a member of the stage crew at the Abbey Theatre.

③ His writing career in the US took off in the early 1930s.

④ He tried to blur the rhythms of the storyteller's voice.

⑤ His stories are concerned with early American manners.

15 baiji에 관한 다음 글의 내용과 일치하지 <u>않는</u> 것은?

The baiji is a functionally extinct species of freshwater dolphin formerly found only in the Yangtze River in China. It is also called the Chinese river dolphin. It is not to be confused with the Chinese white dolphin. The baiji population declined drastically in decades as China industrialized and made heavy use of the river for fishing, transportation, and hydroelectricity. The baiji could be the first dolphin species in history that humans have driven to extinction. Efforts were made to conserve the species, but a late 2006 expedition failed to find any baiji in the river. In August 2007, a Chinese man reportedly videotaped a large white animal swimming in the Yangtze, believed to be a baiji. The World Wildlife Fund is calling for the preservation of any possible baiji habitat, in case the species is located and can be revived.

① Its sole habitat was the Yangtze River.

② It should not be mistaken for the Chinese white dolphin.

③ Industrialization played a role in its decline in population.

④ It did not turn up during the 2006 expedition.

⑤ The World Wildlife Fund has given up all hope in reviving the species.

16 다음 글의 목적으로 가장 적절한 것은?

Please let me take this opportunity to introduce myself and to welcome you to the neighborhood. My wife, Monica, and I live at #19, just up the road from your new home. We have lived on Meadow Street for the past twenty years. Most likely because I'm older than everyone else around here, I am often addressed as the unofficial "mayor" of the neighborhood.

I have been asked by several of our neighbors to communicate their wishes about a problem that has arisen since you moved in. We all love music, and most of us have had, or will have, teenagers. We would, though, appreciate it if you would ask your teens to turn down the volume.

We all look forward to meeting and greeting you properly after you have the chance to settle in.

① to solicit donations for needy neighbors
② to invite a neighbor to a block party
③ to offer best wishes to a leaving family
④ to request an exchange for a better stereo
⑤ to complain about a neighbor's loud music

17 다음 글의 요지로 가장 적절한 것은?

Laughter is one clue to compatibility. It tells you how much you will enjoy each other's company over the long term. If your laughter together is good and healthy, and not at the expense of others, then you have a healthy relationship to the world. Laughter is the child of surprise. If you can make each other laugh, you can always surprise each other. If you can always surprise each other, you can always keep the world around you new. Beware of a relationship in which there is no laughter. Even the most intimate relationships based only on seriousness have a tendency to turn dour. Over time, sharing a common serious viewpoint on the world tends to turn you against those who do not share the same viewpoint, and your relationship can become based on being critical together.

① A key to a healthy relationship is laughing together.
② "No action, talk only" is the seed of relationship failures.

③ Serious talk leads to endless criticism of one another.

④ The element of surprise brings laughter into your relationship.

⑤ Laugh a lot, and you will end up with new relationships.

※ 다음 글의 빈칸에 들어갈 말로 가장 적절한 것을 고르시오. [18~24]

18 Good reductionism consists not of replacing one field of knowledge with another but of connecting or unifying them. The building blocks used by one field are put under a microscope by another. A geographer might explain why the coastline of Africa fits into the coastline of the Americas by saying that the landmasses were once adjacent but sat on different plates, which drifted apart.

The question of why the plates move gets passed on to the geologists, who appeal to an upwelling of magma that pushes them apart. As for how the magma got so hot, they call in the physicists to explain the reactions in the Earth's core and mantle. None of the scientists is _____.

① innocent   ② dispensable

③ meticulous   ④ qualified

⑤ connected

19 Even small differences in annual economic growth rates, if sustained for decades or centuries, eventually lead to huge differences in the levels of economic well-being. The per capita gross national product of the United States, for example, grew at an annual rate of around 1.7 percent per year during the period 1820 to 1998. This led to a twenty-five-fold increase in living standards, with per capita incomes rising from around $1,200 per person in 1820 to around $30,000 today (in 1990 dollars). The key for the United States to become the world's richest major economy was not spectacularly fast growth, such as China's recent achievement of 8 percent growth per year. The key was _____, the fact that the United States maintained that income growth rate for almost two centuries.

① velocity   ② originality

③ transparency   ④ liquidity

⑤ consistency

20 Believing-for-a-reason _____. I may believe that my neighbor has few friends because no one ever visits him. I may never have made this reasoning explicit, either to myself or to anyone else. Still, if asked the question "Why do you think he has few friends?" I can reply, without any introspection or self-observation: "Because no one ever visits him." That a subject is in the relevant state does not necessarily manifest itself in conscious review of the reasoning but does necessarily include the ability to express it both in the form of a demonstration and an expressive self-explanation, i.e., a rational explanation of one's own belief that one can just give. [3점]

① often results from the state of mutual contradictions

② need not be the result of any conscious process at all

③ may lie in the subject's ability to review a conclusion

④ seldom denies the existence of premise and conclusion

⑤ ought to be constantly mediated by connecting principles

21 We know that blind evolutionary processes can produce human-level general intelligence, since they have already done so at least once. Evolutionary processes with foresight —that is, genetic programs designed and guided by an intelligent human programmer—should be able to achieve a similar outcome with far greater efficiency. This observation has been used by some philosophers and scientists to argue that human-level AI is not only theoretically possible but feasible within this century. The idea is that we can estimate the relative capabilities of evolution and human engineering to produce intelligence, and find that human engineering is already vastly superior to evolution in some areas and is likely to become superior in the remaining areas before too long. The fact that evolution produced intelligence therefore indicates that human engineering will _____.

① compete against superintelligence

② lag far behind evolutionary processes

③ disguise itself as human-level AI

④ soon be able to do the same

⑤ repeat similar mistakes

22 The number of electric cars in the world passed the 2 million mark last year and the International Energy Agency estimates there will be 140 million electric cars globally by 2030 if countries meet Paris climate agreement targets. This electric vehicle boom could leave 11 million tons of spent lithium-ion batteries in need of recycling between now and 2030. However, in the EU as few as 5% of lithium-ion batteries are recycled. _____. Not only do the batteries carry a risk of giving off toxic gases if damaged, but core ingredients such as lithium and cobalt are finite and extraction can lead to water pollution and depletion among other environmental consequences.

① This has an environmental cost

② It is prohibited to take further steps

③ It has identified the cause

④ This ratifies the Paris climate agreement

⑤ This supports current energy policies

23 The electromagnetic field is everywhere, and every single electron that exists in the universe not only belongs to it, but also is exactly identical to any other electron, anywhere and anywhen. Interchange two of them, and the universe won't notice. Because of that, because of the quantum field they are an expression of, electrons cannot be described as one would describe a macroscopic object. They belong to the field. They are part of it, like a drop of water in the vast ocean, or a gust of wind in the night air, a drop or a gust you cannot localize. As long as one does not look, drops and gusts are just like the ocean itself, like the wind. Mingled into an entity much vaster than themselves, _____. [3점]

① they provide vectors to the core of the universe

② they create a ripple effect in the quantum field

③ they have no identity of their own

④ they fail to achieve their full potential

⑤ they serve as catalysts for many reactions

24   Cost of production concepts are not very useful to the understanding of the economics of agriculture, just as cost of production of pizza is not very useful to understanding the pizza industry. A more appropriate comparison, given the nature of joint production in agriculture, is the relation of cost of production of pizza to the structural understanding of the restaurant industry. Too great a reliance on cost of production is a danger because of the inherent weaknesses of analyses that follow, the resources devoted to cost of production which would be better used elsewhere, and the limited focus of issues which can result from its emphasis. Cost of production seems, on the surface, to be a useful and basic element to economic analysis. Further, noneconomists relate well to the concept of cost of production, while supply functions, input demand functions, length-of-run and other important issues are less obvious concepts. As a result, cost of production often becomes considered as _____.

① an instrumental source of agricultural investment decision

② an end rather than a tool with limited analytic capability

③ one of the weakest indices of long-term market growth

④ a test of inter-industry collaboration assessment

⑤ an obscure measurement of market assets

25 In the U.S. the proportion of infants who were nursed at all by their mothers, and the age at which those nursed infants were weaned, decreased through much of the 20th century. For example, by the 1970s only 5% of American children were being nursed at the age of six months. In contrast, among hunter−gatherers not in contact with farmers and without access to farmed foods, infants are nursed far beyond six months, because the only suitable infant food available to them is mother's milk: they have no access to cow's milk, baby formula, or soft food replacements. The age of weaning averaged over seven hunter−gatherer groups is about three years old, an age at which children finally become capable of fully nourishing themselves by chewing enough firm food.

① relationship between the age of weaning and available food

② necessity of early weaning in hunter−gatherer societies

③ controversy over the role of weaning in children's health

④ agricultural motivations for early weaning in children

⑤ demographic contrasts between farmers and hunter−gatherers

26 Never has China's bond market had such a stormy spring. It has already set a record for defaults in the second quarter. The cost of credit for firms has shot up. Even the state−owned companies that invest in infrastructure, previously sacrosanct, are seen as risks. What has gone wrong? The answer is nothing at all. Defaults are progress for China, which needs to clear a backlog of accumulated debt. This year's casualties amount to a mere 0.1% of the bond market. But that is still an improvement on the recent past, when investors assumed that the government would rescue any big firm in trouble. [3점]

① the hidden pitfalls of China's economy

② the risky investments on China's infrastructure

③ the critical need for governmental intervention in China

④ the unwarranted concern about China's bond market

⑤ the doomed future of China's accumulating debt

※ 다음 글의 빈칸 (A), (B)에 들어갈 말로 가장 적절한 것을 고르시오. [27-28]

27 Deficiencies of innate ability may be compensated for through persistent hard work and concentration. One might say that work substitutes for talent, or better yet that it __(A)__ talent. He who firmly determines to improve his capacity will do so, provided that education does not begin too late, during a period when the plasticity of nerve cells is greatly reduced. Do not forget that reading and thinking about masterpieces allows one to assimilate much of the skill that created them, providing of course that one extends beyond conclusions to the author's insights, guiding principles, and even style. What we refer to as a great and special talent usually implies superiority that is expeditious rather than qualitative. In scientific undertakings, however, the slow prove to be as useful as the fast because scientists like artists are judged by the quality of what they produce, not by the __(B)__ of production.

	(A)	(B)		(A)	(B)
①	creates	power	②	creates	speed
③	suppresses	quantity	④	suppresses	speed
⑤	encourages	power			

28 Professions embody expertise, prestige, autonomy, dignity, and formal learning, values that often are incompatible with politics. The historic struggles of public professions to purge themselves of politics—for example, the city manager versus party hacks; the librarian versus ignorant censors; the environmental scientist versus political ideologues—all reflect this __(A)__. Nor do professionals like bureaucracy, which they often view as an impediment to the free exercise of their specializations. Certain kinds of specialized professionals, such as scientists and engineers, working for the federal government express much less satisfaction with their work than federal executives. Put bluntly, professionals who choose the public service often must overcome their __(B)__ for its two major features: politics and bureaucracy. [3점]

	(A)	(B)		(A)	(B)
①	resistance	antipathy	②	congruence	affinity
③	resistance	affinity	④	congruence	antipathy
⑤	incompatibility	aspiration			

29

For most of Western history, curiosity has been regarded as at best a distraction, at worst a poison, corrosive to the soul and to society. There's a reason for this. Curiosity is unruly.

(A) In short, curiosity is deviant. Pursuing it is liable to bring you into conflict with authority at some point, as everyone from Galileo to Charles Darwin to Steve Jobs could have attested. A society that values order above all else will seek to suppress curiosity.

(B) It doesn't like rules, or, at least, it assumes that all rules are provisional, subject to the laceration of a smart question nobody has yet thought to ask. It disdains the approved pathways, preferring diversions, unplanned excursions, impulsive left turns.

(C) But a society that believes in progress, innovation, and creativity will cultivate it, recognizing that the inquiring minds of its people constitute its most valuable asset. By the time of the Enlightenment, European societies started to see that their future lay with the curious and encouraged probing questions rather than stamping on them.

① (A)-(C)-(B)
② (B)-(A)-(C)
③ (B)-(C)-(A)
④ (C)-(A)-(B)
⑤ (C)-(B)-(A)

30

Most existing drones need to be flown by an experienced operator. Indeed, the law often requires this. Drones also need technical support and maintenance.

(A) The drone may fly autonomously, according to a preprogrammed schedule, find its way automatically to a point it is ordered to visit, or be piloted remotely by an operative of the company that supplies the system, from a control centre anywhere on the planet.

(B) This is a term being applied to the offerings of several firms that aspire to sell the advantages of drones without the associated worries. The box in question is a base station that houses the drone, recharges it and transfers the data it has collected to the customer.

(C) And the people operating them would be well advised to have an understanding of the legal and safety implications of what they are up to. Hence the appeal of the " drone-in-a-box."

① (A)-(C)-(B)　　　　　　② (B)-(A)-(C)
③ (B)-(C)-(A)　　　　　　④ (C)-(A)-(B)
⑤ (C)-(B)-(A)

31　다음 글에서 전체 흐름과 관계 <u>없는</u> 문장은?

Many animals cooperate effectively, and a few even give loans. The most famous lenders in nature are vampire bats.

These bats congregate in their thousands inside caves and every night fly out to look for prey. When they find a sleeping bird or careless mammal, they make a small incision in its skin, and suck its blood. ① But not all vampire bats find a victim every night. ② In order to cope with the uncertainty of their life, the vampires loan blood to each other. ③ Vampires, however, don't give loans in order to alleviate their evolutionary pressure. ④ A vampire that fails to find prey will come home and ask a more fortunate friend to regurgitate some stolen blood. ⑤ Vampires remember very well to whom they loaned blood, so at a later date if the friend returns home hungry, he will approach his debtor, who will reciprocate the favour.

32 글의 흐름으로 보아 주어진 문장이 들어가기에 가장 적절한 곳은? [3점]

> When you see grass as green, the green is no more a property of grass than rustish is a property of water.

Imagine that you are a piece of iron. So there you are, sitting around doing nothing, as usual, when along comes a drop of water. What will be your perception of the water? Yes, of course, a bar of iron doesn't have a brain, and it wouldn't have any perception at all. But let's ignore that inconvenient fact and imagine what it would be like if a bar of iron could perceive the water. From the standpoint of a piece of iron, water is above all rustish. (①) Now return to your perspective as a human. (②) You know that rustishness is not really a property of water itself but of how it reacts with iron. (③) The same is true of human perception. (④) Green is the experience that results when the light bouncing off grass reacts with the neurons in your brain. (⑤) Greenness is in us—just as rust is in the piece of iron.

33 다음 글에 나타난 "I"의 심경 변화로 가장 적절한 것은?

I left for Brussels by train in April 1939. Leaving my parents behind when I was only nine years old was deeply distressing. As I reached the border between Germany and Belgium, the train stopped for a brief time and German customs officials came on board. They demanded to see any jewelry or other valuables I might have. I had been forewarned of this request by a young woman who was traveling with me. I had therefore hidden in my pocket a small gold ring with my initials on it, which I had been given as a present on my seventh birthday. My anxiety in the presence of Nazi officers reached almost unbearable heights as they boarded the train, and I feared that they would discover the ring. Fortunately, they paid little attention to me and allowed me to go undisturbed. As their footsteps grew fainter, a quiet sigh escaped my lips.

① nervous → relieved
② joyous → discouraged
③ indifferent → outraged
④ irritated → terrified
⑤ surprised → disappointed

People who learn to extract the key ideas from new material and organize them into a mental model and connect that model to _____ show an advantage in learning complex mastery. A mental model is a mental representation of some external reality. Think of a baseball batter waiting for a pitch. He has less than an instant to decipher whether it's a curveball, a changeup, or something else. How does he do it? There are a few subtle signals that help: the way the pitcher winds up, the way he throws, the spin of the ball's seams. A great batter winnows out all the extraneous perceptual distractions, seeing only these variations in pitches, and through practice he forms distinct mental models based on a different set of cues for each kind of pitch. He connects these models to what he knows about batting stance, strike zone, and swinging so as to stay on top of the ball. These he connects to mental models of player positions: if he's got guys on first and second, maybe he'll sacrifice to move the runners ahead. Because he has culled out all but the most important elements for identifying and responding to each kind of pitch, constructed mental models out of that learning, and connected those models to his mastery of the other essential elements of this complex game, an expert player has a better chance of scoring runs than a less experienced one who cannot make sense of the vast and changeable information he faces every time he steps up to the plate.

34 위 글의 제목으로 가장 적절한 것은?

① Split-Second Decisions Made Easy
② When Baseball Players Go Wild
③ Baseball 101: Choose the Right Bat
④ The Anatomy of a Baseball Pitcher
⑤ How Far Can a Batter Hit the Ball?

35 위 글의 빈칸에 들어갈 말로 가장 적절한 것은? [3점]

① future course of events   ② athletic endowment
③ prior knowledge   ④ de facto principles
⑤ controlled motivation

In the region of western New York State in which I was brought up, as indeed in a huge part of the English-speaking regions of the world, the form *doesn't* (a) <u>scarcely</u> exists in vernacular speech. Where I come from, almost everyone says *It don't matter* and *He don't need that*.

Naturally, my high school English teacher, Mrs. Breck, took strong exception to this usage, and she relentlessly (b) <u>waged</u> her own little war upon it. I well remember sitting in class one day when her campaign was in full swing. Having heard my classmate Norman say, for the seven hundredth time that day, something like "He *don't* know that," she decided to strike: "He *doesn't* know that, Norman." "Yeah, that's right," replied Norman, "he don't." "Not *don't*, Norman," reiterated Mrs. Breck, her face turning an interesting colour, "say 'He DOESN'T know that.'" "But… but…" A look of (c) <u>contentment</u> appeared on Norman's face. "But it don't *sound* right!"

This little episode encapsulates very neatly the (d) <u>contrast</u> between the very special position of one particular form of English, which we call standard English, and all the other varieties of English that there are, which we may collectively term non-standard English. The great majority of English-speakers grow up learning and speaking the (e) <u>local</u> vernacular form of English, which is almost always significantly different from standard English, and is sometimes spectacularly different.

36 위 글의 제목으로 가장 적절한 것은?

① Good Old Days: Reflections on My English Teacher
② Avoid Dialect Extinction for Diversity's Sake
③ Sounding Right: A Dilemma for Policy-Makers
④ Standard vs. Non-standard English: Don't It Matter?
⑤ Vernacular vs. Prestige English: End the War

37 위 글의 밑줄 친 부분 중, 문맥상 낱말의 쓰임이 적절하지 <u>않은</u> 것은?

① (a) ② (b)
③ (c) ④ (d)
⑤ (e)

That music can increase cooperation and helpfulness by inducing good moods has been demonstrated experimentally.

Rona Fried and Leonard Berkowitz undertook a study with their students at the University of Wisconsin. They divided them into four groups and induced different moods in three of them by playing them different pieces of music. Two selections from Mendelssohn's 'Songs Without Words' were chosen to instill a soothing mood in one group; Duke Ellington's 'One O'Clock Jump' was played to create feelings of excitement in another; and John Coltrane's 'Meditations' was used to instill negative emotions, of sadness and despondency, in the third group. The fourth, control group simply sat in silence for the seven-minute duration of the musical recordings. The students had to complete a mood questionnaire both before and after listening to the music, and this confirmed that the music had made a significant difference to their feelings.

Just before they were dismissed, the experimenter asked for volunteers to help with another, quite unrelated experiment which would require anywhere between fifteen minutes and two hours of their time. They were requested to complete a form to specify whether they were prepared to help, and if so for what amount of time. This, of course, was the test of helpfulness—the experimenter wanted to discover whether the four groups varied in their willingness to help according to the type of music to which they had been listening.

This _____. Those who had listened to the Mendelssohn pieces turned out to be the most helpful, as measured by their willingness to help with the second experiment and the length of time they were prepared to offer. On both measures, the students who had listened to Coltrane's music, leading to adverse moods, were the least willing to be helpful.

38 위 글의 요지로 가장 적절한 것은?

① Cooperative groups tended to prefer Mendelssohn's music.
② Classical music instilled soothing moods in people.
③ Cooperation and helpfulness were affected by musical talents.
④ Types of music influenced people's willingness to help.
⑤ Excited moods led people to offer more assistance.

39 위 글의 빈칸에 들어갈 말로 가장 적절한 것은?

① had been tested before ② proved to be the case
③ was challenged by many ④ contradicted earlier findings
⑤ needed further support

According to most definitions of intelligence, a million years ago humans were already the most intelligent animals around, as well as the world's champion toolmakers, yet they remained insignificant creatures with little impact on the surrounding ecosystem. They were obviously lacking some key feature other than intelligence and toolmaking.

Perhaps humankind eventually came to dominate the planet not because of some elusive third key ingredient, but due simply to the evolution of even higher intelligence and even better toolmaking abilities? It doesn't seem so, because when we examine the historical record, we don't see a direct correlation between the intelligence and toolmaking abilities of individual humans and the power of our species as a whole. Twenty thousand years ago, the average Sapiens probably had higher intelligence and better toolmaking skills than the average Sapiens of today. Modern schools and employers may test our aptitudes from time to time but, no matter how badly we do, the welfare state always guarantees our basic needs. In the Stone Age natural selection tested you every single moment of every single day, and if you flunked any of its numerous tests you (A) <u>were pushing up the daisies in no time</u>. Yet despite the superior toolmaking abilities of our Stone Age ancestors, and despite their sharper minds and far more acute senses, 20,000 years ago humankind was much weaker than it is today.

Over those 20,000 years humankind moved from hunting mammoth with stone-tipped spears to exploring the solar system with spaceships not thanks to the evolution of more dexterous hands or bigger brains. Instead, the crucial factor in our conquest of the world was our ability to connect many humans to one another. Humans nowadays completely dominate the planet not because the individual human is far smarter and more nimble-fingered than the individual chimp or wolf, but because *Homo sapiens* is the only species on earth capable of cooperating flexibly in large numbers. Intelligence and toolmaking were obviously very important as well. But if humans had not learned to cooperate flexibly in large numbers, our crafty brains and deft hands would still be _____ (B) _____.

40 위 글의 밑줄 친 (A)가 의미하는 바로 가장 적절한 것은?

① might prosper eternally ② would die soon

③ sharpened tools slowly ④ could pick flowers quickly

⑤ became a farmer eventually

41 위 글의 빈칸 (B)에 들어갈 말로 가장 적절한 것은? [3점]

① developing far more acute senses

② significantly impacting the ecosystem

③ overcoming numerous hurdles in the wild

④ searching for easy prey in groups

⑤ splitting flint stones rather than uranium atoms

42 위 글의 내용을 한 문장으로 나타낼 때, 빈칸 (C)와 (D)에 들어갈 말로 가장 적절한 것은?

> It is not higher intelligence or better ___(C)___, but large-scale, flexible cooperation abilities which played a key role in Homo sapiens' ___(D)___ of the world.

　　　　　(C)　　　　(D)

① dexterity − domination

② dexterity − exploration

③ evolution − cultivation

④ welfare − domination

⑤ welfare − exploration

(A) Do you know a childlike view of the world can frequently put adult life in perspective? The innocent view of children can help adults to not be so weighed down by their problems. Nancy Craver, director of a day-care center, relates the following story of how a child's perspective helped (a) her turn a big problem into a small one. It was the center's annual multicultural dinner, created as a chance for parents, children, and staff to celebrate both their diversity and their ability to work well together.

(B) As (b) she instinctively reached out her arms, she not only caught the little one but also caught her laughter and excitement. Immediately, those first terrible images melted away. Swinging (c) her around, Nancy was reminded by the child's enthusiasm that this was a celebration. Her laughter and play did not fix things, but it did change Nancy's perspective. And the evening continued better for her and for those around her.

(C) The previous year's celebration had been quite challenging for Nancy, as she had just been hired as the new director. This year (d) she planned things out early so that she could relax and participate in the dinner—or so she thought. At first just minor things went wrong. Then, someone dropped the slide projector that was to be used for an after-dinner presentation. When the dinner itself was over, the woman who had been hired to take the children to another place to play did not show up. The kids became restless and began running about.

(D) In the midst of all this commotion, an elderly man insisted on someone moving the car that was blocking his in the parking lot. With her tension— and temperature— rising, Nancy went to help him get out of the lot. Just as (e) she started back into the building, one of the young children came charging down the stairs and threw herself at her. The images that flashed across Nancy's mind as the child was flying through the air included an injured child, shocked parents, and people saying, "You see, she cannot control or even protect our children!"

43 주어진 글 (A)에 이어질 내용을 순서에 맞게 배열한 것으로 가장 적절한 것은?

① (B)-(D)-(C)
② (C)-(B)-(D)
③ (C)-(D)-(B)
④ (D)-(B)-(C)
⑤ (D)-(C)-(B)

44

밑줄 친 (a)-(e) 중에서 가리키는 대상이 나머지와 <u>다른</u> 것은?

① (a)　　　　　　　　　② (b)

③ (c)　　　　　　　　　④ (d)

⑤ (e)

45

위 글의 Nancy에 관한 내용과 일치하지 <u>않는</u> 것은?

① She was in charge of a day-care center.

② She caught a child in mid-air.

③ She became the director three years ago.

④ She planned for this year's dinner in advance.

⑤ She helped out with a parking problem.

10 | 2020학년도 기출문제

▶ 해설은 p. 147에 있습니다.

※ 밑줄 친 단어의 뜻으로 가장 적절한 것을 고르시오. 【1~6】

01 Procrastination becomes a major problem in your work life when important tasks or responsibilities are left undone or are completed in a slipshod manner because inadequate time was left to complete the task properly.

① hastiness
② postponement
③ spontaneity
④ concern
⑤ exaggeration

02 A worldwide financial crisis began in the last half of 1997, when the currencies of several Asian economies plummeted in value.

① boomed suddenly
② bounced back
③ got stuck
④ made a difference
⑤ dropped sharply

03 If you can't weave quotations deftly into the fabric of your prose, abjure them altogether and paraphrase instead.

① abandon
② compose
③ revise
④ brainstorm
⑤ elaborate

04 The increasing power of the personal computer is making it possible to develop applications that are smarter and more responsive to the user. Anyone who has used a spelling or a grammar checker has experienced this type of application at a very <u>rudimentary</u> level.

① basic   ② deep
③ optimal   ④ conscious
⑤ abstract

05 One reason to think that written languages will look more or less like they do now is the fact that so far they have proved extremely <u>tenacious.</u> The Chinese system has changed little in more than 3,000 years, and Modern Greek is written with an alphabet that has been used for almost as long.

① arbitrary   ② reliable
③ useful   ④ graphic
⑤ persistent

06 Lacking a clear formula for making decisions, we get reactive and fall back on familiar, comfortable ways to decide what to do. As a result, we <u>haphazardly</u> select approaches that don't support our goals.

① covertly   ② invariably
③ explicitly   ④ randomly
⑤ precisely

07 As with the question of the date ①at which European antiquarianism was superseded by archaeology, it is not easy to suggest a specific date when the writings of 'early travellers' and the collecting of Egyptian antiquities ②became transformed into something approaching the modern discipline of Egyptology. Most histories of Egyptian archaeology, however, see the Napoleonic expedition at the beginning of the 19th century as the first systematic attempt to record and describe the standing remains of pharaonic Egypt. The importance of the Description del' Egyptek, which was the multi-volume publication that ③resulted from the expedition, lay not only in its high standards of accuracy but also in the fact that ④they constituted a continuous and internally consistent appraisal by a group of scholars, thus ⑤providing the first real assessment of ancient Egypt in its entirety.

*antiquarianism : 골동품 연구

08 Fire destroys about 350 ①million ha (1,350 mi^2) of forest every year. Some fires are set by humans to cover up illegal logging or land clearing. Others are started by natural causes. The greatest fire hazard in the world is in sub-Saharan Africa, which accounts for about ②half the global total. Uncontrolled fires tend to be ③worst in countries with corrupt or ineffective governments and high levels of poverty, civil unrest, and internal refugees. ④As global climate change brings drought and insect infestations to many parts of the world, there's a worry ⑤which forest fires may increase catastrophically.

09 If contemporary experience ① has taught us anything, surely it is the need for a president to hit the ground running. The difference between Reagan's quick start and Clinton's stumble put one on the path toward ② a succession of legislative triumphs and the other on the road to a debacle in health care and a loss of Congress. Had Clinton not been as agile as he was in recovering in late 1993 and then again in 1995, he ③ would be a one-term president. As it was, he never became the transformational figure he had hoped. In most institutions, the power of a leader grows over time. A CEO, a university president, the head of a union, acquire stature through the quality of their long-term performance. The presidency is ④ just the opposite : power tends to evaporate quickly. It's not that a president must rival Franklin Roosevelt in his First Hundred Days, but his first months in office are usually the widest window of opportunity he will have, ⑤ even if he serves two full terms. That's why he has to move fast.

※ 다음 글의 밑줄 친 부분 중, 문맥상 낱말의 쓰임이 가장 적절하지 <u>않은</u> 것을 고르시오. 【10-11】

10 The book, "Superforecasting : Arts and Science of Prediction," opens with a discussion of Archie Cochrane, a Scottish doctor born in 1909, who did more than perhaps anyone else to transform medicine from a black art into a ① fully fledged science. His insight—deeply controversial half a century ago—was that a doctor's qualifications, eminence and confidence are ② irrelevant and that the only test of a treatment's effectiveness was whether it could be shown, statistically and rigorously, to work. Mr. Tetlock, the author of the book, hopes to bring about a similar rigor to how people ③ analyze forecasts of the future. That will be an ④ easy struggle. Prediction, like medicine in the early 20th century, is still mostly based on ⑤ eminence rather than evidence. [3점]

11 Polling is like Internet dating. There is a little wiggle room in the ① veracity of information provided. We know that people ② shade the truth, particularly when the question asked are embarrassing or sensitive. Respondents may overstate their income. They may not ③ deny that they do not vote. They may hesitate to express views that are unpopular or socially unacceptable. For all these reasons, even the most carefully designed poll is dependent on the ④ integrity of the respondents' answers. Election polls depend crucially on ⑤ sorting those who will vote on Election Day from those who will not. Individuals often say they are going to vote because they think that is what pollsters want to hear. Studies that have compared self-reported voting behavior to election records consistently find that one-quarter to one-third of respondents say they voted when in fact they did not.

※ (A), (B), (C)의 각 네모 안에서 문맥에 맞는 낱말로 가장 적절한 것을 고르시오. [12~13]

12 Biologists classify organisms into species. Animals are said to belong to the same species if they tend to mate with each other, giving birth to (A) fertile/sterile offspring. Horses and donkeys have a recent common ancestor and share many physical traits. But they show little sexual interest in one another. They will mate if induced to do so—but their offspring are (B) fertile/sterile . Mutations in donkey DNA can therefore never cross over to horses, or vice versa. The two types of animals are consequently considered two distinct species, moving along (C) separate/similar evolutionary paths. By contrast, a bulldog and a spaniel may look very different, but they are members of the same species, sharing the same DNA pool. They will happily mate and their puppies will grow up to pair off with other dogs and produce more puppies.

(A)	(B)	(C)
① fertile	sterile	similar
② fertile	fertile	similar
③ fertile	sterile	separate
④ sterile	fertile	separate
⑤ sterile	fertile	similar

13 Big data has its drawbacks. The flood of information—some of it useful, some not—can (A) overwhelm/maximize one's ability to quickly and efficiently process data and take appropriate action. If we fail to create and utilize methodologies and tools for effectively using big data, we may continue to (B) evolve/drown in it. In the context of national security, lacking adequate big data tools could have profound, even deadly, consequences. However, there are steps that we can take now—steps that are already being taken in many cases—to ensure that we successfully (C) harness/renounce the power of big data. [3점]

(A)	(B)	(C)
① overwhelm	drown	harness
② overwhelm	evolve	renounce
③ overwhelm	drown	renounce
④ maximize	evolve	harness
⑤ maximize	drown	renounce

※ 다음 글에서 전체 흐름과 관계 <u>없는</u> 문장을 고르시오. 【14-15】

14 America is not actually a "melting pot" in the sense that people from different backgrounds somehow all become the same. America has always included a great diversity of ideas, attitudes, and behaviors. ① For example, the constitutional separation of church and state, a fundamental principle present since early days in the United States, guarantees that people of all religion have the same freedoms and rights for worship and religious behavior. ② People of diverse religious backgrounds are not expected to "melt" together into one religion. ③ Conflicts simply occur among people, whether of the same or different background. ④ Other laws guarantee the equal rights of all people regardless of skin color, gender, and age. ⑤ The United States does not even have an official national language—and many government and other publications in various geographical areas are offered in a variety of languages as well. In short, America as a nation has always recognized the realities and benefits of diversity.

15 No one questions that machines displace individual workers from certain jobs and that in the short run this often creates difficult problems. ① For example, the use of diesel engines and electric power by railroads has made obsolete the position of fireman—the employee who shoveled coal into the locomotive boiler that produced the steam for the train's steam engine—but because of union support, railroads had to fill this position for many years after steam power ceased being used by trains. ② However, such problems are temporary. ③ Ultimately, advances in machine technology tend to reduce costs and prices or to hold them down, and by enabling people to buy more goods, they create new employment opportunities. ④ Machines reduce the need for human skills. ⑤ If some industries employ fewer workers, others employ more. At the same time, new products are introduced and new industries are established. [3점]

※ 다음 글의 빈칸에 들어갈 말로 가장 적절한 것을 고르시오. [16~23]

16 It is a principle in many legal systems that a competent adult has a right to refuse any, even lifesaving, treatment. This principle applies to the treatment of physical illness. It does not apply however in many countries to those with mental illness. Take the case of England, where it is the Mental Health Act that governs the _____ treatment of patients with mental disorder.

① alternative　　　　　② compulsory
③ adjunctive　　　　　④ incremental
⑤ preventive

17 A social-conflict analysis begins by pointing out that sports are closely linked to social inequality. Some sports—including tennis, swimming, golf, and skiing—are expensive, so participation is largely limited to the well-to-do. Football, baseball, and basketball, however, are accessible to people of all income levels. In short, the games people play are not simply a matter of choice but also reflect social

_____.

① bonds　　　　　② needs
③ trends　　　　　④ standing
⑤ preference

18 What should the effect of success on motivation be? Should it necessarily increase motivation? The argument earlier suggests that if learners realize that successful performance in some activity leads toward their goal, then expectancies are likely to rise. This would appear to say that success will tend to increase motivation, but matters are not that simple. This argument considers potential motivation and ignores motivational arousal. Motivational arousal is based on a person's assumption of how much effort is needed to perform an activity correctly. Studies indicate that motivational arousal is greatest for tasks that are assumed to be of moderate difficulty. If success rate is considered very high or very low, motivational arousal is _____. In other words, we try hardest for things we consider challenging but not nearly impossible.

① weakened   ② mobilized

③ fluctuated   ④ stabilized

⑤ alternated

19 For historians of Africa identity can be a tricky intellectual issue. Africans are, like people everywhere, compilations of numerous identities, some of which are personally or collectively claimed, others of which are imposed by outsiders. If people are asked who the most famous living African is, the usual answer is 'Nelson Mandela.' But as we write this in the aftermath of the 2006 World Cup, there is a good case for saying that the most famous living African is Zinédene Zidane. Let's consider this one individual. Who, or what, is Zidane? He's a Frenchman, born and raised in Marseilles. But he's also a North African, whose parents emigrated from Algeria; and a Berber, with family roots in the Kabyle mountains and reportedly fiercely proud of his ancestral village. He also describes himself as a Muslim. And he is, of course, a footballer. Whichever of these labels Zidane himself chooses to use would depend both on where he is and how he's thinking at the time. Identity, in other words, is as _____ as it is multifaceted. [3점]

① unique   ② ethnic

③ political   ④ indigenous

⑤ fluid

20 Picasso's oeuvre includes more than 1,800 paintings, 1,200 sculptures, 2,800 ceramics, and 12,000 drawings, not to mention prints, rugs, and tapestries—only a fraction of which have garnered acclaim. In poetry, when we recite Maya Angelou's classic poem "Still I Rise," we tend to forget that she wrote 165 others; we remember her moving memoir I Know Why the Caged Bird Sings and pay less attention to her other 6 autobiographies. In science, Einstein wrote papers on general and special relativity that transformed physics, but many of his 248 publications had minimal impact. If you want to be original, "the most important possible thing you could do," says Ira Glass, the producer of This American Life and the podcast Serial, "is _____."

*oeuvre : 일생의 작품

① do a lot of work
② reject the default
③ take radical risks
④ gain new insights
⑤ explore better options

21 Lightner Witmer received his doctorate in psychology in 1892 in Germany under Wilhelm Wundt, who many view as the founder of experimental psychology. He also studied under James McKeen Cattell, another pioneer of experimental psychology. At the time Witmer received his doctorate, psychology was essentially an academic discipline, a field of research. It had almost none of the applied functions that characterize the field today. In short, in the late 1800s, _____.

① the field of experimental psychology was not popular
② psychologists didn't practice psychology, but studied it
③ Lightner Witmer was a leading psychologist in Germany
④ it took much effort to receive a doctoral degree in psychology
⑤ Wilhelm Wundt set the stage for the birth of clinical psychology

22 When Adam Smith lectured at the University of Glasgow in the 1760s, he introduced the study of demand by posing a puzzle. Common sense, he said, suggests that the price of a commodity must somehow depend on what that good is worth to consumers—on the amount of utility that the commodity offers. Yet, Smith pointed out, some cases suggest that _____. Smith cited diamonds and water as examples. He noted that water has enormous value to most consumers; indeed, its availability can be a matter of life and death. Yet water generally either is free or sells at a very low price, whereas diamonds sell for very high prices even though few people would consider them necessities.

① a good's price may depend on its availability

② a good's price may be intertwined with its value

③ a good's utility may have little influence on its price

④ a good's utility may depend on its supply and demand

⑤ a good's quantity demanded may not depend on its price

23 While to-do lists serve as a useful collection of our best intentions, they also tyrannize us with trivial, unimportant stuff that we feel obligated to get done—because it's on our list. Which is why most of us have a love-hate relationship with our to-do lists. If allowed, they set our priorities the same way an inbox can dictate our day. Most inboxes overflow with unimportant e-mails masquerading as priorities. Tackling these tasks in the order we receive them is behaving as if the squeaky wheel immediately deserves the grease. But, as Australian prime minister Bob Hawke duly noted, "The things which are most important _____." [3점]

① can easily lead you astray

② don't always scream the loudest

③ sometimes undermine our success

④ are just first things we thought of

⑤ must be at the mercy of things which matter least

24 다음 글의 빈칸에 공통으로 들어갈 말로 가장 적절한 것은?

A blockchain is used in bitcoin to prevent the double-spend problem. Before bitcoin, the issue with a digital currency was that someone could spend the same unit of digital currency in multiple places at the same time. A blockchain solves this problem by providing a shared ledger, which ensures that everyone knows and agrees on how much of the digital currency has transacted among users at any point in time. It is thought that blockchains might provide an effective tool in detecting and preventing corrupt or fraudulent activities. This thinking is premised on the _____ of a blockchain. The _____ prevents any one party from altering past entries, as one might be able to do with paper or digital records.

① availability   ② innovation

③ multiplicity   ④ flexibility

⑤ immutability

25 다음 글의 빈칸 (A), (B)에 들어갈 말로 가장 적절한 것은? [3점]

Former Congresswoman Patricia Schroeder pinpointed one of the most important reasons for women to enter the workforce when she argued that the primary reason they do so in such unprecedented numbers is that they have to maintain their families. Many family women work because they must work. For others, although families have become smaller, wants have become larger. __(A)__, for these family women, work is not an actual necessity but it is a social need: It is the only way the family can meet its desires. __(B)__, for black and other minority females, work has been a necessity for much longer than for white females. Women in the workforce as a percentage of total women of working age rose from 32 percent in 1972 to over 70 percent in the early 2000s. Analysts who study such trends say that the percentage of working women with children is expected to continue to grow even through some very high-income women may choose to stop working and stay home with their children.

	(A)		(B)
①	Therefore	......	However
②	Otherwise	......	In addition
③	Thus	......	Nevertheless
④	Moreover	......	Therefore
⑤	For example	......	On the other hand

※ 다음 글을 읽고 물음에 답하시오. 【26-27】

Convinced that human actions derived their emotional energy from the 'heart', which could only be addressed and activated by judiciously selected symbols, Gandhi evolved a powerful cluster of culturally (1)evocative symbols including the spinning wheel, the cow, and the 'Gandhi cap' (a white cotton cap popularized by him). The spinning wheel, for example, which Gandhi asked everyone to ply, served several symbolic purposes. It was a way of gently (2)rebelling against modern technological civilization and (3)denouncing the dignity of India's rural way of life. (a)It united the cities and the villages and the Westernized elite and the masses, and was an 'emblem of their fellowship.' The spinning wheel also established the dignity of manual labor and those engaged in (b)it and (4)challenged the traditional Indian culture which despised both. (c)It symbolized social compassion, for those who did not need the proceeds of (d)its products were urged to give away those products to the needy, an infinitely superior moral act to the (5)patronizing donation of money. And (e)it also forced the individual to be alone with himself and observe silence for at least some time. Gandhi not only evolved countless symbols of this kind but also became one himself.

*ply : 연장을 부지런히 쓰다
**proceeds : 수입, 매상

26 밑줄 친 (1)~(5) 중에서 문맥상 낱말의 쓰임이 가장 적절하지 <u>않은</u> 것은? [3점]

① (1) ② (2)

③ (3) ④ (4)

⑤ (5)

27 밑줄 친 (a)~(e) 중에서 의미하는 바가 나머지 넷과 <u>다른</u> 것은?

① (a) ② (b)
③ (c) ④ (d)
⑤ (e)

28 다음 글에 나타난 Annemarie의 심경 변화로 가장 적절한 것은?

The train started again. The door at the end of their car opened and two German soldiers appeared. Annemarie tensed. Not here, on the train, too? They were everywhere. Together the soldiers strolled through the car, glancing at passengers, stopping here and there to ask a question. One of them had something stuck in his teeth; he probed with his tongue and distorted his own face. Annemarie watched with a kind of frightened fascination as the pair approached. One of the soldiers looked down with a bored expression on his face. "Where are you going?" he asked. "Gilleleje," Mama replied calmly. "My brother lives there. We are going to visit him." The soldier turned away and Annemarie relaxed. Then, without warning, he turned back. "Are you visiting your brother for the New Year?" he asked suddenly. Mama stared at him with a puzzled look. "New Year?" she asked "It is only October." "And guess what!" Kirsti exclaimed suddenly, in a loud voice, looking at the soldier. Annemarie's heart sank and she looked at her mother. Mama's eyes were frightened. "Shhh, Kirsti," Mama said. "Don't chatter so." But Kirsti paid no attention to Mama, as usual. She looked cheerfully at the soldier, and Annemarie knew what she was about to say: This is our friend Ellen and it's her New Year! But she didn't. Instead, Kirsti pointed at her feet. "I'm going to visit my Uncle Henrik," she chirped, "and I'm wearing my brand-new shiny black shoes!" The soldier chuckled and moved on. Annemarie gazed through the window again. The trees, the Baltic Sea, and the cloudy October sky passed in a blur as they continued north along the coast.

① hopeful → disappointed
② terrified → relieved
③ excited → offended
④ surprised → upset
⑤ miserable → ashamed

다음 글의 내용과 일치하지 <u>않는</u> 것은?

Millions of years ago, a dozen or so genetic changes took place in the ancestor of all of today's felids, which have locked them into eating meat ever since. All cats require a large amount of animal protein in their diet—protein from plants lacks certain amino acids such as taurine that cats need but other mammals (including ourselves) do not. Cats can't make their own prostaglandins—hormones essential to reproduction—and so need to get these from meat. Compared to other mammals, all cats need large amounts of several vitamins, such as niacin, thiamine and retinol, which are more easily extracted from meat than from plants. And because they don't need to tell the difference between ripe and unripe fruit, they've lost the ability to taste sugars. They have adapted their 'sweet' taste buds for distinguishing between different flavors in meat—which is why pet cats sometimes walk away from food that seems fine to their owners. This knowledge has only come to light in the past 40 years, benefiting not only pet cats but also the captive breeding of endangered felids such as the clouded leopard.

*felids : 고양이과 동물

① 고양이의 조상은 수백만 년 전에 유전적 변이를 겪었다.
② 고양이는 많은 양의 동물성 단백질을 필요로 한다.
③ 고양이는 번식에 필수적인 호르몬을 만들 수 없다.
④ 고양이는 설탕 맛을 느끼지 못한다.
⑤ 고양이는 고기의 다른 맛을 구별하지 못한다.

30 Philip에 관한 다음 글의 내용과 일치하지 <u>않는</u> 것은?

As soon as he came to the throne, Philip began transforming the Macedonian military into a more successful image of what he had seen at Thebes. Philip further lengthened the already longer spears used by the Thebans, creating the Macedonian sarissa, a spear of about eighteen feet in length, double that of the traditional Greek hoplite spear. He retained the Theban wedge formation but also added heavy cavalry to the line, thus incorporating the Macedonians' strongest element into the phalanx. The results spoke for themselves, as over the next twenty years, Philip systematically conquered all of mainland Greece, with the exception of Sparta, which he chose to leave alone. Philip's final great victory was at the Battle of Chaeronea (338 B.C.), in which the Macedonian armies defeated the combined forces of Athens and Thebes. Philip's conquest of the entire mainland was the end of an era, as for the first time, the entire territory was united under the rule of a king.

*phalanx : (고대 그리스의) 방진(方陣)

① 창의 길이를 약 18피트로 늘렸다.
② 기병을 전선에 추가하였다.
③ Sparta를 정복했다.
④ Athens와 Thebes의 연합군을 격퇴했다.
⑤ 그리스 본토를 통합했다.

31 The Code of Hammurabi에 관한 다음 글의 내용과 일치하지 <u>않는</u> 것은?

The Babylonian emperor Hammurabi, who ruled Mesopotamia from about 1792 to about 1750 B.C., is best known for the code of laws that bears his name, one of the earliest law codes yet discovered. His main concern was to maintain order in his empire through authority, which answered the needs of his people. To that effect, he gave his subjects a complex law code. Its 282 decrees, collectively termed the Code of Hammurabi, were inscribed on stone stelae or columns and erected in many places. One was discovered in Persian Susa in the nineteenth century and is now in the Louvre in Paris.

The code dealt primarily civil affairs such as marriage and inheritance, family relations, property rights, and business practices. Criminal offenses were punished with varying degrees of severity, depending on the social status of the offender and the victim. There were clear distinctions between the rights of the upper classes and those of commoners. Payments are generally allowed as restitution for damage done to commoners by nobles. A commoner who causes damage to a noble, however, might have to pay with his head. Trial by ordeal, retribution by retaliatory action, and capital punishment were common practices. But judges distinguished between intentional and unintentional injuries, and monetary fines were normally used as punishment where no malicious intent was manifested. The "eye for an eye" morality often associated with Hammurabi's code was relatively restricted in application and applied only to crimes committed by and against social equals.

① 법전이 새겨진 비석이 19세기에 발견되었다.
② 법전은 형법을 주로 다루었다.
③ 신분에 따라 동일 범죄에 대한 처벌이 달랐다.
④ 사형제도가 포함되었다.
⑤ 재판관들은 상해의 고의성 여부를 구별하였다.

32 다음 글의 제목으로 가장 적절한 것은?

People can actually do two or more things at once, such as walk and talk, or chew gum and read a map; but, like computers, what we can't do is focus on two things at once. Our attention bounces back and forth. This is fine for computers, but it has serious repercussions in humans. Two airliners are cleared to land on the same runway. A patient is given the wrong medicine. A toddler is left unattended in the bathtub. What all these potential tragedies share is that people are trying to do too many things at once and forget to do something they should do. When you try to do two things at once, you either can't or won't do either well. If you think multitasking is an effective way to get more done, you've got it backward. It's an effective way to get less done.

① Fallacy of Multitasking
② The ABCs of Multitasking
③ Multitasking : Why and How
④ Coping Strategies for Multitasking Demands
⑤ Simple Truth behind Great Results: Multitasking

33 다음 글의 주제로 가장 적절한 것은?

Divorce statistics are often used as a measure of family disorganization, and the present high divorce rate is cited as proof that the U.S. family is in serious trouble. However, higher divorce rates today than in the past are not entirely the result of more family unhappiness. In earlier generations, many couples avoided divorce even though their married life was unhappy. They avoided it because it meant social ostracism or, in the case of women, poverty because there were few opportunities for them to earn a good living. As the possibilities for divorced people increased and it became easier to get divorces, more unhappy couples have chosen this route.

① uses of divorce statistics
② collection of divorce statistics
③ reasons why people get divorced
④ cautious interpretation of divorce statistics
⑤ coping with divorce and family breakdown

34 다음 글의 요지로 가장 적절한 것은?

When infant mortality rates are high, as they are in much of the developing world, parents tend to have high numbers of children to ensure that some will survive to adulthood. There has never been a sustained drop in birth rates that was not first preceded by a sustained drop in infant mortality. One of the most important distinctions in our demographically divided world is the high infant mortality rates in the less-developed countries. Better nutrition, improved health care, simple oral rehydration therapy, and immunization against infectious diseases have brought about dramatic reductions in infant mortality rates, which have been accompanied in most regions by falling birth rates. It has been estimated that saving 5 million children each year from easily preventable communicable diseases would avoid 20 or 30 million extra births.

① Infant mortality rates affect birth rates.
② Infant mortality around the world is declining very rapidly.
③ Disparities of wealth are reflected in infant mortality rates.
④ A primary cause of infant mortality is poor quality of water.
⑤ Good prenatal care has been linked to reduced infant mortality.

※ 글의 흐름으로 보아 주어진 문장이 들어가기에 가장 적절한 곳을 고르시오. 【35-36】

35

Yet, despite its ubiquity, astronomers have no real idea what constitutes dark matter.

Dark matter is measurable; it is just not visible. (①) It is invisible because it is 'dark.' (②) Astronomers infer the presence of dark matter because it explains how galaxies manage to hold themselves together, how gravitational lenses work and the observed temperature distribution of hot gas seen in galaxy clusters. (③) The conclusion is that over 80 per cent of the mass of the Universe is in a form we simply can't see. (④) It may include subatomic particles such as heavy neutrinos or other hypothetical particles like axions. (⑤) Some of it may be locked up in objects that simply elude detection. Currently, astronomers believe most dark matter consists of new elementary particles called weakly interacting massive particles (WIMPs), which apparently do not interact with electromagnetic radiation or atoms. They are therefore invisible to conventional means of detection. [3점]

36

Burned—out workers sometimes depersonalize the people they need to help, thinking about them as objects or things rather than as feeling human beings.

Burnout is a special kind of psychological consequence of stress that afflicts some employees who experience high levels of work stress day in and day out for an extended period of time. It is especially likely to occur when employees are responsible for helping, protecting, or taking care of other people. Nurses, doctors, social workers, teachers, lawyers, and police officers are at risk for developing burnout due to the nature of their jobs. (①) Three key signs of burnout are feelings of low personal accomplishment, emotional exhaustion, and depersonalization. (②) Burned—out workers often feel that they are not helping others or accomplishing as much as they should be. (③) Emotionally they are worn out from the constant stress of dealing with people who are sometimes in desperate need of assistance. (④) A burned—out social worker, for example, may think about a foster child in need of a new one as a case number rather than as a very scared 12—year—old. (⑤) This psychological consequence may lead to a behavioral consequence when the burned—out social worker treats the child in a cold and distant manner.

※ 주어진 글 다음에 이어질 글의 순서로 가장 적절한 것을 고르시오. 【37-38】

37

Historically, rational analytic approaches are often seen as providing superior outcomes compared with intuition, although this decision-making process is much slower.

(A) These types of tasks are common in human resource management, strategic, aesthetic, and investment decisions. In short, intuition is most effective when experts are performing judgmental and holistic tasks.

(B) Hence, some talk about a speed versus effectiveness trade-off in decision making. Intuitions, however, can yield better outcomes than rational models depending on the level of the experience of the decision maker and the nature of the task at hand.

(C) Put simply, individuals who have a lot of experience (i.e., experts) in a particular area are primed to be more effective with intuition than rational decision making depending on the type of task they face. Experts, in general, are most effective in their use of intuitive decision making when the task at hand is one where there is more than one right answer or where the task cannot easily be subdivided into smaller chunks.

① (A) – (B) – (C)　　　　　② (B) – (A) – (C)

③ (B) – (C) – (A)　　　　　④ (C) – (B) – (A)

⑤ (C) – (A) – (B)

38

Today, we are all aware that the ability of airline cabin crew, pilots, flight attendants, and so on to communicate effectively with each other and with passengers is vital to prevent crises.

(A) Because of this, and other dangerous incidents that resulted from poor communication, Federal Aviation Administration made assertiveness and sensitivity training for all airline crew members mandatory to ensure they have the ability to communicate effectively.

(B) Federal Aviation Administration investigators determined that the crash resulted in part because the copilot failed to tell the pilot about problems with engine power readings that were caused by ice on the engine sensors.

(C) A tragic example that demonstrated the way effective communication is so important on an airliner occurred when an Air Florida 737 plane crashed into a bridge over the Potomac River after taking off from National Airport in Washington, D.C.

① (A) − (C) − (B)　　　　② (B) − (C) − (A)

③ (B) − (A) − (C)　　　　④ (C) − (A) − (B)

⑤ (C) − (B) − (A)

From childhood on, social interactions, whether within the family or with other groups, provide the context within which the majority of food experiences occur, and hence by which learning of food likes is (a)facilitated. The pleasure associated with such interactions—the festivity of a meal shared with friends, for example—may represent just as positive a conditioning stimulus for a new food flavor as sweetness. Thus, it may be that our estimation of the food at a restaurant has as much to do with the (b)social environment as it does with the chef's skills. In children, pairing foods with the presence of friends, a liked celebrity, or attention by adults all increase liking for those foods, no doubt reflecting the positive value of each of these groups to the child. This process is strongly evident in the (c)relative impact of different social interactions on the food preferences of children. Surprisingly, despite the enormous opportunities in a family for exposing children to the foods eaten by the parents, parental preferences are (d)strong predictors of child food preferences; in fact, they are no better predictors than the preferences of other adults. This suggests that the extent to which these sets of preferences are related has more to do with the wider culture than with any specific food habits within the family. A child's food likes and dislikes are much more likely to be associated with those of peers, especially specific friends, than those of its parents. The ultimate impact of social facilitation of food choice is that the liking eventually becomes (e)internalized. That is, foods chosen because others do so become liked for their own sensory properties.

39 윗글의 제목으로 가장 적절한 것은?

① Cravings for Sweets
② Yum! : Innate Reponses to Food
③ Conditioning Stimulus for New Flavors
④ Judicious Food Choice for Child Rearing
⑤ How is Food Preference Socially Constructed?

40 밑줄 친 (a)~(e) 중에서 문맥상 낱말의 쓰임이 가장 적절하지 <u>않은</u> 것은? [3점]

① (a) ② (b)
③ (c) ④ (d)
⑤ (e)

(A) Meerkats might not be the biggest animals on the African plains, nor appear to boast any particularly formidable weapons, like the rhino's horn, or impressive skills, like the cheetah's speed.

(B) Some of these subterranean networks can play host to up to 50 or so individuals, though an average colony is about half this size, with two or three families living together communally. A type of mongoose, they are equipped with sharp, curved claws used for digging and self-defence, as well as acute vision, which comes in very handy for spotting danger. In fact, when they do venture out of their burrows to search for food, there will always be at least one meerkat that stands sentry—often on a rock or in a bush—primarily looking to the skies for their number-one enemy: birds of prey.

(C) As soon as any threat is detected, the lookout will give a shrill warning bark and the others will immediately make a dash for a nearby bolthole or other cover. It's thought that meerkats have dozens of different calls to signify a range of threats. As well as hunting together over a territorial range, meerkats also share childcare duties. Typically, only the colony's alpha pair will mate, but all the others pitch in to babysit, rooming and feeding the pups, as well as demonstrating valuable life skills, like where to find food, play-fighting and which parts of a scorpion to eat.

(D) Nevertheless, through a combination of hardy biology, smart tricks and a unique community spirit, these mammals have adapted perfectly to their harsh environment. They escape the most extreme temperatures of southern Africa—as well as the vast majority of predators who'd like to make a meal of them—by living in underground burrows.

*sentry : 보초, 감시자

41 주어진 글 (A)에 이어질 내용을 순서에 맞게 배열한 것으로 가장 적절한 것은?

① (B) – (C) – (D)
② (C) – (D) – (B)
③ (C) – (B) – (D)
④ (D) – (C) – (B)
⑤ (D) – (B) – (C)

42 윗글의 내용과 일치하지 <u>않는</u> 것은?

① 미어캣은 몽구스의 한 종류이다.
② 미어캣은 일반적으로 독립적인 생활을 한다.
③ 미어캣은 땅을 파거나 자기방어를 위한 뾰족한 발톱이 있다.
④ 미어캣은 우두머리만 짝짓기를 한다.
⑤ 미어캣은 위협이 있을 경우 보초가 즉시 동료에게 알린다.

※ 다음 글을 읽고 물음에 답하시오. 【43-45】

[가] Two researchers reported that after college students listened to a Mozart piano sonata they scored higher on a spacial reasoning test. Soon after this observation made the news, doting parents were playing Mozart for their babies around the clock. Obviously, they hoped that, like the college students, their babies would become smarter. However, parents should be suspicious of any practice that claims to offer such magical benefits.

[나] What does the evidence suggest? A few studies have found small increases in spatial intelligence following exposure to Mozart's music. However, most researchers have been unable to ___(A)___ the effect.

[다] A major ___(B)___ with the "Mozart effect" is that the original experiment was done with adults; it tells us nothing about infants. Also, the study didn't test other styles of music. Why not use the music of Bach or Schubert for that matter? An even more important question is, Does the Mozart effect actually exist?

[라] Why do some studies support the effect and others disconfirm it? Most studies have compared students who heard music to students who rested in silence. However, two psychologists found that listening to a narrated story also improves test scores. This is especially true for students who like listening to stories. Thus, students who scored higher after listening to Mozart were just more alert or in a better mood.

43 주어진 글 [가]에 이어질 내용을 순서에 맞게 배열한 것으로 가장 적절한 것은? [3점]

① [나] – [라] – [다]   ② [다] – [나] – [라]

③ [다] – [라] – [나]   ④ [라] – [나] – [다]

⑤ [라] – [다] – [나]

44 윗글의 제목으로 가장 적절한 것은?

① Mozart Effect : Nothing Magical

② Mozart : The Making of a Prodigy

③ Why is Classical Music Good for Babies?

④ Mozart's Sonatas : The Highest Musical Fidelity

⑤ Mozart's Music and Its Pedagogical Implications

45 윗글의 빈칸 (A), (B)에 들어갈 말로 가장 적절한 것은?

(A)		(B)
① support	……	concern
② duplicate	……	benefit
③ duplicate	……	problem
④ disconfirm	……	benefit
⑤ disconfirm	……	problem

정답 및 해설

01 ③

colt : 수망아지   vulnerable : 공격당하기 쉬운   predator : 포식자   deference : 복종, 경의

☞ deference는 지문 상에서 복종 내지 항복이라는 의미로 쓰였다. 이와 유사한 단어인 보기 ③의 submission이 정답이다.

① 유쾌함   ② 친절   ③ 복종   ④ 공격   ⑤ 불확실성

「수망아지는 무서웠다. 그는 자신의 무리에서 떨어져 포식자에게 위협받았다. 걱정스럽게 왔다 갔다 하였고, 머리는 땅에 닿을 듯 늘어져 있었다. 마치 절하는 것처럼, 항복의 표시처럼 보였다.」

02 ①

specialize : ~을 전공하다   course : 교과과정   reptile : 파충류   distinguish : 돋보이게 하다   marvelously : 놀라울 만큼   versatile : 다재다능한

☞ 지문의 문맥상 versatile은 융통성이 있다는 의미로 쓰이고 있음을 알 수 있다. 이와 가장 유사한 단어는 보기 ①의 adaptable이다.

① 적응하는   ② 정직한   ③ 확립된   ④ 보이는   ⑤ 어지러운

「그날부터 그는 파충류를 전공했다. 교과과정은 이론과 실습을 모두 포함하였다. 아침에 파충류 각각의 외관에 대한 긴 수업이 있었다. 그는 이 수업에서는 돋보이지 않았다. 그는 배운 것을 잊어버리는 데에는 놀라울 만큼 다재다능한 재능이 있었다.」

03 ①

slippery : 미끄러운   strain : 애쓰다, 노력하다   exhausting : 기진맥진하게 하는

☞ exhausting과 fatiguing은 매우 피곤함을 나타내는 말이다.

① 피곤한   ② 선동하는   ③ 격렬한   ④ 활력을 불어넣는   ⑤ 재미있는

「길이 미끄러우면, 우리 몸의 모든 신경과 근육은 균형을 잡기 위해 애쓰고, 넘어짐에 대한 공포는 무엇보다도 우리를 가장 지치게 한다.」

04 ④

by one's admission : 자백에 의하여   obsolete : 구식의, 쓸모없는   restoration : 복원   cellar : 지하저장고

☞ obsolete와 antiquated는 '오래된, 구식의'라는 뜻을 가지고 있다.

① 파괴적인   ② 정교한   ③ 즐거운   ④ 구식인   ⑤ 짜증나는

「필립 존슨은 그의 고백에서, 자신은 "많은 구식 일"을 했다고 한다. 그래서 존슨이 시카고 공원 관리소의 역사관 복원 담당자였을 때, 시 소유의 허스트 하우스의 지하저장고에 들어가서 지난날 그곳의 바위에 누군가가 새겨놓은 선의 형태를 확인하는 데 어려움이 없었다.」

05 ②

cleavage : 분리, 균열   countryside : 시골   kinship : 친족   impersonal : 비인간적인   ties : 유대관계
socioeconomic : 사회경제적   interests : 이해관계

☞ cleavage는 분리 내지는 집단 간의 분열을 의미하는 단어인데, 지문에서는 도시와 시골을 나눈다는 의미로 쓰였으므로 전자의 개념에 가깝다. 따라서 ①의 discord보다는 ②의 separation이 적절하다.

① 불화 ② 분리 ③ 화합 ④ 닮음 ⑤ 통합

「도시와 시골 사이의 균열은 특별히 미국인의 생각은 아니다. 19세기 유럽의 위대한 사회 이론가들은 그것이 친족에 바탕을 둔 협력 공동체에서 유대관계를 사회경제적인 이해관계에 두는 더 커지고 더 비인간화된 사회로의 이동에 의해 발생하는 사회적 변화라고 설명했다.」

06 ②

ultimately : 궁극적으로   at present : 현재   gaze : 응시하다   doom : 불행한 결말을 맞게 하다   wither :
시들어가다   fade : 바래다, 사라지다   mortality : 죽을 운명   cherish : 아끼다

☞ appear는 자동사이므로 is appeared와 같이 수동태로 사용될 수 없다. 따라서 appears로 고쳐 써야 한다.

「대부분의 사람들에게, 인간은 결국 죽는다는 인식이 현재 살아있는 삶에서의 기쁨을 약화시키지는 않는다. 시인에게는 시들 것이 분명한 꽃을 바라볼 때 세상이 여전히 더 아름답게 보인다. 5월의 사랑스러움은 그것이 이미 사라지고 있다는 것을 알기 때문에 그를 더 깊게 감동시킨다. 모든 것이 죽을 운명이라는 생각이 그에게 기쁨을 가져다주는 것은 아니지만, 그가 이것들을 오래 가질 수 없다는 것을 알기 때문에 그만큼 더 애정을 가지고 아낀다.」

07 ⑤

provided : (만약) ~라면   ascend : 오르다   pride : 자랑하다   impose : 강제하다   heredity : 유전   wage :
(전쟁을) 벌이다

☞ 관계대명사 that은 전치사와 같이 쓰일 수 없다. 따라서 관계대명사절을 이끌기 위해서는 that 대신 which로 바꾸어주어야 한다.

「어떤 길을 선택하든지 다른 골짜기에서 시작한 여행자들은 계속 오르는 한, 산 정상에서 만날 것이다. 누구도 최선의 길을 선택했다고 자만해서는 안 되고, 이웃에게 그를 따르라고 강요해서도 안 된다. 모든 사람은 자신의 뇌 구조, 유전, 전통에 의해 주어진, 자신에게 적합한 최선의 길을 선택해야 한다. 사람들은 지원, 알림, 도움을 줄 수 있다. 그러나 한 사람에게 성공인 것이 다른 사람에게는 실패일 수 있다. 모든 사람은 스스로와 싸우지 않고서는 앞으로 나아갈 수 없다. 진리로 가는 길에 지름길은 없는 것이다.」

08 ⑤

hunger : 열망하다   psychic healer : 심령술사   relieve : 덜다, 완화하다   innumerable : 셀 수 없을 정도로
많은   occult : 초자연적인   make fortunes : 재산을 모으다   peddle : 퍼뜨리다   gullible : 속기 쉬운

☞ 똑똑한 사람들이 속이는 것이 아니라 속임을 당하는 것이므로 수동태가 와야 한다. ⑤번의 are taking in을 are taken in으로 고쳐야 한다.

「물론 사람들은 신기하고 놀라운 것에 목말라한다. 그리고 그들은 그런 것을 찾을 수 있다. 우리는 사람들에게 전화하면서 수 천 마일이나 떨어진 사람들이 무엇을 생각하는지를 느낀다. 그리고 심령술사는 삶이 나아질 것이라는 헛된 희망을 제공함으로써 사람들의 절망을 덜어준다. 수많은 주술서 작가들이 비상식적인 이야기를 속기 쉬운 사람들에게 유포하여 돈을 번다. 심지어 똑똑한 사람들조차 이성적이고 실질적인 대안이 나타나지 않으면 속는다.」

09 ⑤

peasant : 소작농 migrant : 이주자 urbanite : 도시인 reclaim : 되찾다 pavement : 포장지역 ditch : 도랑
grossly : 지독히 soar : 급증하다 privatize : 민영화하다

☞ 스스로 처리하는 것이 아니라 처리되는 것이므로, ⑤번은 수동태인 hasn't been addressed가 되어야 한다.

「중국의 베이징으로 간 소작농 이주민에게 또 다른 장벽은 해고 상태의 도시 노동자이다. 대부분의 도시인들은 이제 이주민들에 의해 제공되는 서비스를 누리고 있지만, 도시인들은 그들의 경쟁력이 깎이는 느낌이 들 것이다. 어려운 시기에 도시 노동자들은 도시 행정가들이 이주민에게 넘기는 도시의 도로 포장, 땅파기 등 원래 그들의 일이었던 힘든 직업을 되찾기 원한다. 정부에 의해 과소 측정되어 겨우 2.9퍼센트를 차지하는 도시의 실업률은 공기업이 민영화 되면서 치솟을 수 있다. 소작농들은 자연스럽게 그들과 경쟁을 하게 되고, 이로부터 예상되는 갈등은 다루어지지 않고 있다.」

10 ②

bill : 법안 conspiracy : 공모, 모의 declare : 선언하다 monopolize : 독점하다 surge : 급증 presidency : 대통령임기 breakup : 붕괴

☞ 셔먼법이라고 "알려진" 법안이므로 ②번은 수동태인 commonly known이 되어야 한다.

「19세기 말의 산업 집중화 증가와 합병의 물결에 대응하여, 국회는 흔히 셔먼법이라고 알려진 법안을 통과시켰다. "신용 형식인지 여부를 떠나 모든 담합에 의한 계약, 혹은 무역 규제에 있어서의 모의"는 불법으로 선언되었다. 무역을 독점하거나 독점을 시도하는 것도 마찬가지로 불법이었다. 테디 루즈벨트 대통령 재임 시기 시작된 합법적인 활동의 급증은 1911년 스탠다드 오일과 아메리칸 타바코 컴퍼니의 붕괴를 가져왔다.」

11 ⑤

snowfall : 강설량 grizzly bear : 회색곰 cub : (동물의) 새끼 deadly : 치명적인 segment : 부분 domain : 영역 inevitable : 불가피한

☞ pretend는 동명사가 아니라 to부정사를 목적어로 취한다. 따라서 ⑤번의 being dead는 to be dead로 고쳐야 한다.

「트레보와 패트리사 잔즈는 캐나다의 워터톤 호수 공원에서 약하게 내리는 눈 속을 걷고 있었다. 그 때 그들은 도보여행자로서의 최악의 악몽을 경험했다. 회색곰 어미가 새끼와 함께 죽은 동물을 먹고 있는 것이었다. 그 다음에 일어난 일은 "치명적 만남"이라는 TV 프로그램에 포착되었다. 여기에서는 어떻게 인간이 회색곰 영역에서 자신을 보호할 수 있는지를 보여줬다. 곰 행동 전문가인 스테펜 헤레로는 "만약 당신이 회색곰을 놀라게 하거나 마주칠 수밖에 없다면 당신은 얼굴과 목을 보호해야 합니다. 엎드리고, 손을 목 뒤로 올리고, 죽은 척해야 합니다."라고 말한다.」

12 ③

picture : 마음에 그리다 prone : ~하기 쉬운 magnify : 확대하다

☞ 더 이상 쪼개지지 않는 물질의 기본 단위로서의 최소입자를 atom이라 한다.
① 세포 ② 조각 ③ 원자 ④ 박테리아 ⑤ 본질

「고대 그리스인들이 궁금해 했던 문제 중 하나는 "물질의 본질적인 구조는 무엇인가?"라는 것이다. 그들이 무엇을 그려봤는지 상상해보자. 물질의 한 조각을 떼어내서 이를 작은 조각으로 부수고, 각각의 조각들을 더 작은 조각으로 부순다고 하자. 이 작업을 끝까지 계속해 보면 마침내 더 이상 쪼갤 수 없는 조각이 되는데, 이것으로 모든 물질을 구성할 수 있을까? 자를 수 없는 최종적인 조각을 이것이라고 부른다. 과학자들은 매우 작은 크기의 이것에 대해, 물방울을 지구 크기로 확대한다면 그 물방울 안의 이것은 크리켓 공 만할 것이라는 잘 알려진 비유처럼, 시각적인 비교 설명을 하는 경향이 있다.」

13 ②

administration : 행정, 관리 obligation : 의무 result in : ~을 야기하다 competence : 능숙도, 권한
apply : 적용하다 supervision : 감독, 관리

☞ 관리의 주요한 부분으로, 직원들의 능력을 향상시키려는 노력에 해당하는 단어는 보기 ②의 supervision
이다.

① 선택 ② 감독 ③ 승진 ④ 분배 ⑤ 도입

「이것은 관리의 주요 부분이고, 직원들이 일을 효율적으로 잘 해내도록 지식과 기술을 사용하는 것을 도와주는데 관계된 것이
다. 이것은 토울 박사가 "직원의 발전에 기여하는 목적으로써 관리 과정"이라고 정의한 것이다. 토울 박사는 더 나아가 직원들
이 일을 잘 수행하도록 할 책임이 있는 직원들은 직원의 역량 개발을 유도하는 리더십을 발휘해야 한다고 설명했다. 이것은
다른 직원들이 지식을 습득하고 이를 실전에 적용하는 것을 돕는데 초점을 맞추고 있다. 이것은 관리적일 뿐만 아니라 교육적
이기도 한, 가르치고 배우는 상황이다.」

14 ①

dump : 내다버리다 abandon : 버리다 graveyard : 폐기장 deserted : 인적이 끊긴 outlaw : 금지하다
spill out : 쏟아지다 cradle : 요람

☞ 화학 폐기물이 잘못 버려지는 것은 큰 회사의 방관과 하청업체의 도덕성 결여가 결합되어 나타나는 것이
다. 화학폐기물에 대해 강력하게 추적하는 내용의 조치는 모든 이해 관계자를 책임감 있게 만들 것이
다. 따라서 정답은 ①번이다.

① 책임감 있는 ② 독립적인 ③ 무죄의 ④ 준비된 ⑤ 나누어진

「화학 폐기물은 때로는 개천에 버려지고, 드럼통에 담아 묻히거나, 단순히 거대한 화학적 "폐기장"에 내버려진다. 가끔, 화학
폐기물은 빨리 달리는 "불법 트럭"에 의해 버려진 시골길에 뿌려지는데, 그 트럭들은 밸브를 열어놓고 달려서 폐기물이 천천
히 흘러내리게 한다. 종종 이러한 폐기는 화학 폐기물이 발생하는 큰 회사에 고용된 작은 회사에 의해 이루어진다. 큰 회사의
간부들이 모르면 모를수록 좋은 것이다. 그러나 무지는 더 이상 변명이 되지 않는다. 국회는 이제 모든 관련자가 책임을 지도
록, 화학폐기물이 "요람에서 무덤까지" 추적될 수 있도록 조치를 취할 것이다.」

15 ①

autobiographical : 자서전의 extent : 정도, 범위 assert : 주장하다 beautified : 미화된

☞ 제시문은 모든 소설이 자서전적인, 개인적인 성격을 어느 정도 가지고 있다고 주장하고 있으므로, ①의
hidden이 가장 적절하다.

① 숨겨진 ② 미화된 ③ 비할 데 없는 ④ 통제된 ⑤ 비난을 넘어선

「작가가 그의 인생과 사람에 대해 아는 것을 글에 녹인다는 점에서 최초의 소설은 보통 자서전적이라고 말한다. 그러나 심지어
스무 번째의 소설도 어떤 정도까지는 개인적인 글이다. 왜냐하면 소설가는 여전히 자신의 경험을 통해 글을 쓰기 때문이다.
소설가는 소설 속 등장인물이 순전히 상상의 인물이라 주장하지만, 이는 작가의 상상 속에서 나왔고 그 나름의 방식으로 사람
을 생각하고 이해했다는 점을 의미할 뿐이다. 어떠한 소설가도 완전히 감춰질 수 없다.」

16 ④

staff : ~에 직원을 두다 insight : 통찰력 invisible : 보이지 않는 throughout : 도처에

☞ 혁신과 아이디어가 KAB 네트워크를 통해 공유되어야 한다는 것이 요지이므로, 그 지식에 대해서 "세계를 포함하는" 것이라고 표현하는 것이 자연스럽다.

① 대도시 지역을 목표로 하는
② 앞으로의 십 년에 들어서는
③ 보편적이기를 거부하는
④ 세계를 포함하는
⑤ 집으로 돌아가는

「완벽하게 한 나라와 그 나라의 문화를 이해하려면, 당신은 그들의 일부가 되어야 한다. KAB에서 타 은행보다 더 많은 나라에 현지 은행을 가지고 있는 것은 이러한 이유가 있기 때문이다. 전 세계의 KAB 지점은 현지 사람들을 고용하고 있다. 외부인에게 잘 보이지 않는 금융 기회를 인식할 수 있게 만드는 것이 바로 그들의 통찰력이다. 그러나 그 기회들이 우리의 현지 고객에게만 도움이 되는 것은 아니다. 혁신과 아이디어가 KAB 네트워크를 통해 공유되어야 우리와 함께하는 모두가 이익이 될 수 있다. 그것을 세계를 포함하는 현지 지식이라고 생각해 보라.」

17 ①

at once : 즉시, 당장 dreadfully : 몹시 stroke : 어루만지다

☞ 빈칸 전까지는 낙찰이 이루어지지 않다가 마지막 문장에서는 낙찰을 부른 것으로 보아 그가 입찰가를 높여 불렀을 것이라 예상할 수 있다.

① 그가 입찰 가격을 올렸다.
② 그가 목소리를 낮추었다.
③ 그가 제안을 취소했다.
④ 나는 자비를 간청했다.
⑤ 나는 다른 거래를 제안했다.

「바로 나를 사려고 하는 회색 눈의 남자가 있었다. 나는 그가 나를 다루는 방식으로 보아 그가 말에 익숙하다는 것을 알았다. 그는 나를 사려고 했지만, 그 액수가 너무 적어서 거절당했다. 매우 거칠고 큰 목소리의 남자가 그 다음에 와서, 더 나은 액수를 제시하였기 때문에 그가 나를 가지게 될까 매우 무서웠다. 그러나 회색 눈의 남자는 나를 쓰다듬으면서 "흠, 내 생각에 우린 잘 맞을 거야."라고 말했고, 그는 입찰 가격을 올렸으며, 파는 사람은 "낙찰"이라고 말했다.」

18 ③

philosopher : 철학자 sequence : 연속적인 사건 differentiation : 차별, 구별 mode : 방법, 양식 co-operation : 협력 symbiosis : 공생관계 free-for-all : 무한경쟁

☞ 정치학과 경제학은 진보한 공생관계라는 것을 지지하는 내용이 들어가야 한다. 이에 해당하는 보기는 ③번이다.

① 경쟁 행위의 새로운 단계
② 적자생존의 최근 경향
③ 윤리적 개념의 협력기제
④ 전체 집단으로부터 개인들의 독립성
⑤ 생태윤리와 철학윤리의 놀라운 공통점

「지금까지 철학자들에 의해서만 연구된 윤리학의 확장은 사실상 생태학적 진화의 과정이다. 이 과정은 철학 용어뿐만이 아니라 생태학 용어로 설명될 수 있다. 생태학적으로 윤리는 생존 경쟁에서의 행동의 자유에 제한을 가하는 것이다. 철학적으로 윤리는 반사회적 행위로부터 사회적 형태를 구별하는 것이다. 한 가지 단어에 두 개의 정의가 있는 것이다. 윤리는 상호의존적인 개인이나 그룹이 협력의 형태로 진화하려는 성향에 기초하고 있다. 생태학자는 이것을 공생이라고 한다. 정치학과 경제학은 진보한 공생관계로, 본래의 무한 자유경쟁이 부분적으로 윤리적 개념의 협력 기제로 대체되었다.」

19   ②

suburbia : 교외의 생활양식 remarkably : 매우, 몹시 affluent : 부유한 commuter : 통근자 industrial-park : 산업단지 livelihood : 생계, 살림 census : 인구조사

☞ 빈칸 이후 바로 이어지는 문장은 교외 거주자는 시내까지 생계를 위해 통근해야 했다는 내용이다. 그러므로 빈칸은 교외가 경제적으로 자족적이지 않았다는 내용이 나와야 자연스럽다. 따라서 정답은 ②번이다.

① 교외는 노동 계층의 이웃들로 구성되어 있다.
② 교외는 경제적으로 자족적이지 않다.
③ 교외는 여가를 위한 충분한 시설이 없다.
④ 대부분 사람들은 교외에서 돈 쓰기를 원하지 않는다.
⑤ 교외의 풍경은 도심의 풍경과 다르다.

「오늘날 교외의 생활양식은 매우 다양하다. 부유한 통근자가 사는 동네는 노동계층, 아파트, 산업단지와 함께 있다. 역사적으로 교외 지역은 "부수적"으로 여겨졌는데, 이는 경제적으로 자립되지 않았기 때문이다. 교외 거주자는 생계를 위해 시내까지 통근해야 했다. 그러나 이러한 해석은 더 이상 통하지 않는다. 교외 지역은 점차 고용의 주요 중심지가 되고 있다. 인구조사 수치는 15개 대도시 지역에서 1970년에 교외 지역에 거주하는 노동자의 72퍼센트가 교외지역에서 근무한다고 밝혔다. 분명히, 우리의 교외에 대한 이미지는 현실을 반영하지 못한다.」

20   ②

extract : 추출하다 determinism : 결정론 indissolubly : 분리될 수 없게 causation : 인과관계 refasten : 재고정하다 mould : 주조하다 virtually : 사실상

☞ 빈칸 바로 앞 문장에서는 인과관계의 연쇄가 매우 밀접하다고 하였으나 마지막 문장에서는 미래를 바꿀 수 있다고 하였다. 따라서 연쇄성을 끊을 수 있다는 내용이 들어가면 문장의 연결이 자연스러워진다.

① 그는 연쇄성을 더 단단하게 하려고 한다.
② 그는 연쇄성을 깨기에 충분한 힘을 가지고 있다.
③ 새 연쇄성을 만드는 자연적인 능력을 넘어선다.
④ 연쇄성의 제한을 푸는 것은 사실상 불가능하다.
⑤ 인간은 더 강해진 연쇄작용을 피하도록 도덕적 책임을 갖는다.

「역사는 역사가 자신이 끊임없이 연구하는 흐름의 선상에서 과거와 미래를 연결시키려고 한다. 우리가 과거나 미래에 대해 역사적으로 어떤 절대적인 판단을 기대할 수 없다는 것은 명백하다. 그러한 판단은 역사의 본질이 아니다. 모든 인간의 판단은 모든 인간의 행위처럼 결정론과 자유의지 간의 논리적 딜레마와 연관되어 있다. 인간은 아주 먼 옛날 과거에서 이어지는 인과관계의 연쇄에 의해 행동과 판단 모두에서 불가분의 관계를 지닌다. 그러나 현재 주어진 시점에서, 인간은 연쇄성을 깰 수 있는 적절한 힘을 가지고 있어서 미래를 바꾸어나간다.」

21 ④

reveal : 드러내다 inspection : 검사, 점검 disposable : 일회용의 account for : ~의 이유가 되다 litter : 쓰레기 deface : 외관을 훼손하다 excessive : 지나친 devour : 집어삼키다

☞ 바로 앞의 문장에서 쓰레기의 원인이 노동 절약 기계를 의도적으로 수리하지 않았기 때문이라고 말하고 있다. 이와 같은 맥락의 문장을 완성하려면 ④번이 자연스럽다.

① 상품 재활용을 향한 식품 산업계의 노력
② 천연자원을 낭비하는 과소비
③ 식량 경제에 관련한 수많은 지역 주방
④ 사용가능한 제품을 버리는 대다수 사람들의 부주의한 행동
⑤ 식량 경제에의 적극적인 참여로부터 우리 대다수의 배제

「시골을 면밀히 살펴보면, 규제되지 않은 음식물 쓰레기만큼이나 수천의 쓸모없는 냉장고, "일회용" 용기, 고장난 토스터, 믹서기, 전자레인지를 드러낸다. 쓰레기 문제의 많은 부분은 의도적으로 고치지 않은, 우리가 이미 중독되어버린 노동 절약 기계로 설명된다. 현재 우리나라가 직면한 쓰레기의 많은 직접적인 부분은 쓸 수 있는 제품을 버리는 대다수 사람들의 부주의한 행동에서 비롯된다. 우리는 음식을 재배하고 조리하는데 최소한의 개입을 한다는 사회적 이상을 만들어냈다. 그럼에도 불구하고, 우리는 식품 산업과 조리 기구에 더 의존적이 되고, 이럴수록 더 많은 쓰레기를 만들어낸다. 따라서 우리를 둘러싼 쓰레기는 더 크고 무거운 문제의 징후로 이해되어야 한다. 경제의 중앙집권화, 생산적인 자원과 힘의 소수에게로의 집중, 가정, 이웃, 공동체 지역 경제의 파괴가 바로 그 문제들이다.」

22 ③

cruelty : 잔학행위 reinvent : 다른 모습을 보여주다 sanctity : 존엄성 tortuous : 우여곡절의 exploit : 위업, 공적 be at odds with : ~와 마찰을 빚다 obliterate : 없애다 forge : (금속을) 벼리다 impenetrable : 불가해한 alloy : 합금 concrete : 구체적인 surreal : 비현실적인

☞ (A) 전후 문장을 살펴보면, 어려운 환경에서 자신에게 너그러워지는 것을 배웠다는 내용과 건강하게 생존해야 했다는 내용으로 서로 반대된다. 따라서 still이 적절하다. (B)가 속한 문장의 경우 이전 문장의 결과에 해당하므로 thus가 적절하다.

「1619년 초에 선조가 미국으로 건너온 흑인 여성들은 잔혹하고 참담하게 살았기 때문에 그들 스스로가 다른 모습을 보여주어야 했다. 그들은 자신의 내부에서 안전과 존엄성을 찾아야 했는데, 그렇지 않았으면 자신의 우여곡절인 삶을 견딜 수 없었을 것이다. 그들은 종종 외부적 위업이 마음속의 신념과 충돌하기 때문에, 자신에게 너그러워지는 법을 빠르게 배워야 했다. 그럼에도 불구하고, 감염되기 쉽고 불건전한 환경에서 그들은 전적으로 건강하게 살아남아야만 했다. 이러한 환경 속에 살았던 삶은 지워지거나, 뚫을 수 없는 합금으로 벼려진다. 따라서 일찍부터 의식적으로 흑인 여성들은 현실적으로 그들 자신에게만 가능성을 만들었다. 다른 사람들에게, 그들은 대부분 노동에 대해서는 구체적이지만 인간성 측면에서는 비현실적으로, 추상적으로 제시되고 묘사되었다.」

23 ③

ritual : 의식 solicitation : 간청 solidarity : 연대, 결속 descendant : 후예 dissident : 반체제 인사 taboo : 금기 assent : 찬성하다 dedicate : 헌납하다

☞ 사람들 사이의 "연대"가 자연스러우므로 (A)에는 solidarity가 적절하다. 토템을 죽거나 먹지 않는다는 것은 그들이 토템의 dissidents(반대자)가 아니라 descendants(후손)이라고 여김을 알 수 있으므로, (B)에는 descendants가 들어간다. 사람들은 의식을 "모여서" 행하므로 (C)에는 assembled가 들어간다.

「의식은 사회 공동체를 형성하는 사람들이 일시적 또는 영구적인 유대관계를 만드는 사회적 기능을 할지도 모른다. 우리는 이를 토테미즘으로 알려진 종교적 예식에서 본다. 토테미즘은 호주 원주민의 종교에서 특히 중요하다. 토템은 동물, 식물, 또는 지리적 특징이 될 수 있다. 각 부족의 사람들은 저마다의 독특한 토템을 가졌다. 각 토템 집단의 구성원들은 자신들이 토템의 후손이라고 믿었다. 그들은 관습적으로 토템을 죽이거나 먹지 않았지만, 이러한 금기는 일 년에 한 번 사람들이 토템에 바치는 의식을 위해 모였을 때 풀렸다.」

24 ③

speck : 작은 입자   composition : 구성요소   chunk : 덩어리   quantify : 수량화하다   qualify : ~에게 자격을 주다   decay : 쇠퇴   qualitative : 질적인

☞ 석탄과 석유의 독립적인 부분들은 전체적으로 하나의 동일한 특질을 가지고 있으므로 (A)에는 거의 다르지 않다는 의미인 little이 들어간다. qualify는 자격을 부여한다는 의미이고 quantify는 수량화한다는 의미로, (B)에는 quantify가 자연스럽다. (C)에는 hard를 넣어서 재생 가능한 자원이 정확하게 측정되기 어렵다는 의미를 전달해야 적절하다.

「재생 가능한 에너지와 재생이 불가능한 에너지원의 특징을 비교해 보라. 석탄과 석유는 생명이 없어서 재생할 수 없다. 석탄과 석유는 분리되고, 또 분리되지만, 여전히 개별적인 부분들은 전체적으로 하나의 동일한 성질을 포함할 것이다. 하나의 석탄 조각은 석탄 한 덩어리와 구성에 있어 조금 다르다. 재생이 불가능한 자원은 고정된 보유량을 나타낸다. 이것들은 쉽게 수량화될 수 있다. 정확하게 잴 수 있다. 주문될 수도 있다. 반면에, 재생 가능한 자원은 언제나 변하고 흘러간다. 태양에너지에 대해 주문하고 없애는 개념은 항상 세상이 전개되는 방식을 생각나게 하는 것이었다. 이러한 탄생, 삶, 죽음, 부활의 주기는 질적 과정이고, 재생 가능한 자원은 정확하게 측정되기 어렵다.」

25 ①

segregation : 인종차별   activist : 사회운동가   outrage : 격분하게 하다   acute : 극심한   nostalgia : 향수   weave : 엮어서 만들다   fabric : 구조, 조직   sanctuary : 안식처   denigration : 명예훼손   faculty : 능력   disciplinary : 징계의

☞ (A)에는 문맥상 인종 차별이 아니라 인종 통합이 자연스러우므로 integration이 와야 하고, (B)가 속한 문장은 인종차별 폐지 이전을 설명하므로 desegregation이 알맞다. 마지막 문장은 인종통합 이후를 설명하므로 (C)에는 integration이 들어가야 한다.

「흑인 공동체에서, 르랜드 학교의 인종차별 부활에 관해 거의 아무도 불평하지 않았다. 최근 몇 달간, 흑인 사회운동가들은 오래된 흑인 고등학교가 전통을 유지시키는데 더 초점을 두어 왔다. 지난 가을, 학교의 백인 교장이 인종통합 정책 시행 이전에 받았던 운동 경기 트로피 일부를 최근 학생들의 것으로 교체하려고 하였다. 흑인 공동체는 매우 분개했다. 이 극심한 향수는 일부 흑인들 간에 그들이 통제했던 학교를 포기하는 대가가 인종통합의 혜택보다 더 클 것이라는 인식이 증가한다는 것을 반영한다. 인종차별 폐지 전, 흑인 아이들의 학교는 공동체 구조를 바탕으로 짜여 있었고, 삶을 밖으로 내모는 인종 차별로부터의 피난처였다. 인종통합 정책은 흑인들을 학교에서 최고 정책을 수립하는 위치에서 쫓아내고 모든 교직원의 승진과 학생의 훈육 조치에 대한 인종 문제를 제기하며 모든 것을 바꾸었다.」

26 ④

paradox : 역설   gift : 재능   mastery : 지배력   impunity : (처벌의) 면제   spring : 발생하다, 일어나다
jeopardize : 위태롭게 하다

☞ 지문은 개념적인 생각과 언어능력이 초래한 부정적인 결과를 말하고 있으므로, insecurity가 아니라 security가 되어야 한다.

「인간을 다른 어떤 생명체보다 높은 위치로 격상시켰고 전 세계에 대한 지배력을 부여한 인간의 가장 위대한 자질인 개념적 사고와 언어 능력이 축복이 아니고, 최소한 매우 비싼 대가를 치러야 한다는 것은 역설이다. 인간을 멸종으로 위협하는 모든 큰 위험들은 개념적 사고와 언어 능력의 직접적인 결과이다. 그것은 인간이 편안하게 본성을 따를 수 있고 즐거워하는 것은 무엇이든 하거나 하지 않도록 하는 낙원에서 벗어나게 했다. 개념적 사고로부터 얻어진 지식은 인간에게 똑같이 안전한 적응력을 주기에 충분하였던 매우 오래전의 인간에게서 자신의 잘 적응된 본성이 가져다주는 안정감을 빼앗았다. 아놀드 게렌이 말했듯 사람은 본질적으로 위태로운 존재이다.」

27 ④

mumble : 중얼거리다   barely : 겨우   obliqueness : 간접성   feel free to : 마음대로 ~하다

☞ 전자우편을 통해 사람들이 더 자유롭게 이야기하는 것은, 얼굴을 마주보지 않고 기술과 글의 간접성의 조합이 긍정적인 영향을 끼치기 때문이다. 따라서 ④번이 정답이다.

① 주제 선택의 자유
② 장황하고 비정형적인 만남
③ 약간의 책임감
④ 글을 쓰는 사람과의 간접적인 교제
⑤ 메시지를 보낸 사람의 명확한 정체성

「전자우편은 랄프와 나의 우정을 깊게 해주었다. 그의 사무실은 내 옆이지만, 그는 부끄러움이 많아서 우리는 긴 대화를 거의 나누지 못했다. 그는 얼굴을 맞대고 있으면 중얼거리므로 나는 그의 말을 겨우 알아들을 수 있었다. 그러나 우리 둘이 전자우편을 하게 되었을 때, 나는 길고 자신이 드러나는 메시지를 받기 시작했다. 우리는 서로 마음을 터놓았다. 한 친구는 전자우편이 자신의 아버지와 일종의 대화창을 열어주었음을 알게 되었다. 아버지는 전화로는 말을 많이 하지 않았지만, 온라인으로 연락하며 더 가까워졌다. 왜 어떤 사람은 전자우편으로 마음을 여는 것을 더 쉽게 생각할까? 나는 궁금했다. 그것은 많은 사람들이 차를 타고 있거나 어떤 일을 하는 동안 얼굴을 맞대고 앉아서는 결코 말할 수 없는 감정을 조금씩 드러내는 것처럼, 기술과 글의 간접성의 조합이다.
전자우편을 통한 의사소통에서, 이것이 글을 쓰는 사람과의 간접적인 교제를 보장하기 때문에 사람들은 거리낌 없이 이야기 한다.」

28 ⑤

bullfighting : 투우   hairsbreadth : 아슬아슬한   contradiction : 모순   intense : 강렬한   squalor : 더러움
fatuous : 어리석은   morality : 도덕(성)   chivalrous : 예의바른

☞ 이 글에서 a morality play는 삶의 고귀함과 코앞까지 닥친 죽음의 가능성이 혼재하는 상황을 빗대어 표현하였다. 따라서 정답은 ⑤번이다.

「투우에서 황소는 종종 영예롭지만 사람은 절망에 빠진다. 황소는 죽게 내버려두지는 않지만 공개된 장소에서 붉은 천과 용기만으로 자신을 방어하는 사람과의 아슬아슬한 접촉으로 죽게 된다. 그러나 투우는 우리에게 어떤 것을 말해준다. 우리에게 경쟁 속에서 모순의 사랑에 대해 많은 이야기를 해준다. 이것의 목적은 용맹함과 품위라는 이상을 지향하지만, 지루함과 비열함에 빠져버린다. 라틴 사람들은 투우를 어이없고 어리석은 삶 그 자체의 혼란으로서 항상 패배하는 고귀한 사랑에 대한 도전으로 보는 경향이 있기 때문에, 투우는 인생의 작은 축소판이다. 투우는 예의바르고 열정적이고 정중한 사람들이 중요하게 여기는 가치를 고립시키고 서로 대항시키는 도덕극이다. 격렬한 죽음을 맞을 수 있다는 가능성보다 인간에게 더 도움이 되는 것은 없다는 그것의 반대 의미를 생각나게 하는 용기, 예의, 자부심을 투우로부터 생각해볼 수 있다.」

29 ③

red-crowned crane : 붉은관두루미 folktale : 설화 revere : 숭배하다 metaphor : 은유

☞ 일본인들은 탄조를 그림으로 그리고 조각으로 만들었으며, 현재에도 그 이미지를 곳곳에 넣고 있다. 따라서 (A)에는 탄조를 귀하게 여긴다는 뜻의 cherishing이, (B)에는 일상에서 널리 반영된다는 의미로 everyday가 들어가는 것이 자연스럽다.

「일본인들은 탄조라고 하는 붉은관두루미에 대해 천 년 이상 시와 민담에 기록했다. 일본인들은 탄조를 그림으로 그리고 이를 조각으로 만들었다. 그들은 탄조를 장수, 행복, 행운의 상징으로 숭배해왔다. 그들은 탄조의 생활 습관을 빗대어 자신의 행동을 묘사하는 문구와 은유를 끌어냈다. 탄조를 모방하고, 탄조처럼 춤추려고 하였다. 무엇보다도, 그들은 탄조를 상징으로 만들고 그 이미지를 찻잔, 쟁반, 선풍기, 가로등의 기둥 위, 청첩장, 천 엔짜리 지폐 뒷면, 제트기의 꼬리 등 곳곳에 넣어서, 매우 희귀한 새가 역설적으로 일본 전역에서 보인다.
일본인들은 붉은관두루미인 탄조를 귀하게 여기는 오랜 전통을 가지고 있고, 이것에 대한 그들의 태도는 일상생활에서 널리 반영되고 있다.」

30 ④

constitute : 구성하다 quadruple : 4배가 되다 hydropower : 수력 nuclear power : 원자력

☞ 천연가스의 이용은 4위(1920년)에서 2위(1980년)로 상승하였으므로 도표의 내용과 일치하지 않는 것은 ④번이다.

「1920년 / 1980년
coal 석탄, oil 석유, wood 목재, hydro 수력, nuclear 원자력, natural gas 천연가스
가까운 미래에 가능한 에너지 부족에 대하여 실현 가능한 해결책을 찾기 위해 20세기에 에너지원이 어떻게 변화했는지 연구할 가치가 있다. 위의 그래프는 1920년부터 1980년까지 미국의 에너지원 변화를 보여준다. 석탄은 1920년에 가장 중요한 에너지원으로, 전체 에너지 공급량의 4분의 3을 차지한다. 하지만 1980년에는 공급의 18퍼센트로, 가장 중요한 에너지원에서 3위로 떨어졌다. 석유 사용비율은 1920년과 1980년 사이에 4배 이상 증가하여 1980년에는 가장 큰 비중의 에너지원이 되었다. 천연가스는 1980년에 5위에서 2위로 증가했고, 전체 에너지 공급의 4분의 1을 차지하였다. 1980년에 목재는 그래프상에 나타나지 않으나, 수력은 같은 비율을 유지했고 원자력이 새롭게 추가되었다.」

31 ②

avian : 조류의 peer : 동료 ostrich : 타조 spawn : 낳다 aficionado : 애호가 tenderloin : (고기의) 안심
lean meat : 살코기 eyelash : 속눈썹 bristle : (솔 등의) 털 hide : 가죽

☞ 네 번째 줄에 'half the calories of beef'라고 나오므로 정답은 ②번이다.

「같은 조류들과는 달리, 타조는 다양한 사치품을 낳는다. 우선 고기는 맛이 좋아 애호가들이 쇠고기 안심에 비유한다. 파운드당 20달러이고, 평균 400파운드(lb)의 새로부터 얻을 수 있는 고기는 풍부하다. 타조 고기는 건강에도 좋다. 쇠고기의 절반 정도인 칼로리, 7분의 1의 지방, 상대적으로 적은 콜레스테롤 등 심지어 같은 조류인 닭과 칠면조보다 건강에 좋다. "저희 고객들은 처음에는 저희가 농담을 한다고 생각했어요. 타조라고요?"라고 한 식당 지배인이 말한다. "그러나 그들은 곧 타조에 곧 매혹되었지요." 식당 고객의 4명 중 1명은 식당에서 기름기 적은 타조 고기를 주문한다. 만약 타조가 최고급 요리가 되지 못한다고 하더라도, 투자자들은 커다란 타조들이 세사미 스트리트의 스팟보다 더 큰 명성을 얻을 것이라고 기대하고 있다. 타조 속눈썹은 화장용 붓털로 이용되고, 깃털은 먼지떨이, 모자, 외투에 이용되며, 두껍고 질긴 가죽은 카우보이 부츠에서부터 소파까지 모두 이용되어 귀하게 여겨진다.」

32 ③

abundant : 풍부한 phosphate : 인산염 globe : 지구, 세계 fossilize : 화석화하다 fertilize : 비옥하게 하다
mine : 광산 nationalize : 국유화하다 dug out : ~을 파내다

☞ 여덟 번째 줄의 'where they fertilized fields and farms'로부터 ③번이 지문과 일치함을 알 수 있다.

「옛날, 서태평양에서 멀리 떨어진 나우루라는 작은 섬에서 사람들은 행복하게 살았고, 그 섬에서 식량과 음료수로 이용되는 코코넛 나무, 풍부한 새와 물고기가 가득한 바다를 통해 필요한 모든 것들을 얻었다. 그리고 나우루의 원주민들은 지구에서 가장 풍부한 인산염 퇴적암 위에서 살고 있었다. 백여 년 전 나우루에서 호주로 기념품으로 옮겨진 화석화된 목재 조각이 한 화학자의 눈길을 사로잡았다. 그는 이것을 조사했고, 매우 가치 있다는 것을 알아냈다. 20세기 대부분동안, 수백만 톤의 인산염 퇴적암이 호주와 뉴질랜드로 선적되었고, 밭과 농장의 비료로 이용되었다. 1968년 이 섬이 독립한 이후 이 인산염 광산은 국유화되었고, 세계에서 가장 작은 공화국의 주민들은 최고의 부자가 되었다. 그러나 오늘날 이 자족적인 사람들은 동화에서나 볼 수 있다. 인산염 퇴적암은 거의 없어졌고, 대부분의 돈 또한 없어졌다. 섬 중심부의 5분의 4는 파헤쳐졌다.」

33 ④

settle down : 정착하다 Mediterranean : 지중해의 wheat : 밀 barley : 보리 tame : 길들이다 excavation
발굴 legume : (콩과의) 식물 domesticate : 사육하다 spare : 할애하다

☞ 여덟 번째 줄에서, 마을에서 기른 돼지의 이빨보다 야생 돼지의 이빨이 두 배 정도 크다는 것을 알 수 있다. 따라서 정답은 ④번이다.

「최초의 인류는 수렵채집이라는 삶의 방식을 포기하고 동부 지중해 연안에 정착하여 밀과 보리를 재배하였고, 양과 염소를 길들여 고기와 우유를 얻었다고 대부분의 고고학자들은 믿고 있다. 하지만 터키의 만 년 된 마을의 유적은 다른 모습을 보여 주었다. 둥근 돌로 된 주택의 거주민들은 야생 양과 염소를 사냥했고, 견과류와 콩류를 먹었다. 또한 최초로 가축화된 동물인 양과 염소보다 약 오백여년 정도 먼저 돼지를 키웠다. 델라웨어 대학의 마이클 로젠버그가 지휘한 이 발굴은 수백 년간 존재했던 한 공동체를 보여주었다. 마을 사람들이 돼지를 길렀다는 증거에는 야생돼지보다 일반적으로 더 작은 이빨이 포함되어 있다. 돼지 뼈의 대부분은 수퇘지이고, 암퇘지들은 교배를 위해 살려 두었을 것이다. 로젠버그는 돼지를 기르면서 배운 방법이 이후에 야생 양과 염소에 적용되었을 것이라고 믿는다.」

34 ⑤

intensify : 강화하다 self-sustained : 자립한 undergo : 겪다, 경험하다 circulate : 퍼뜨리다 replicate : 자기 복제를 하다 autocatalysis : 자체촉매작용 elude : 이해할 수가 없다

☞ 지문에 따르면, DNA 같은 정보를 포함하지 않는 생명체들은 생식하지만 복제되지 않고, 따라서 부모와 자식 사이에 생물학적으로 매우 다를 수 있다. ⑤는 이를 잘못 표현하였다.

① 생명체의 정의는 태양계의 생명체에 대한 탐사를 복잡하게 만든다.

② 다윈적 진화의 개념은 NASA의 생명에 대한 정의를 반영한다.

③ 많은 과학자들은 생명체의 정의에 대해 NASA와 다른 그들만의 정의를 가진다.

④ 하나의 정의로 생명체의 본질을 잡아내기란 어렵다.

⑤ 생명체가 복제한다면, 그들의 자식은 부모와 생물학적으로 연결되어 있지 않다.

「미 항공우주국과 다른 우주관련 기구들은 수년 내에 태양계의 생명 탐사를 강화할 것이다. 그러나 이 탐사는 근본적인 신비감으로 인하여 복잡하다. 무엇이 생명체란 말인가? 미 항공우주국은 간단한 실제 정의로 "생명체는 다윈적 진화가 가능한 자립된 화학 체계이다."를 사용한다. 다른 과학자들은 "생명체는 자체 촉매 작용을 통해 자가 복제가 가능하거나 자체 촉매작용의 효율성을 점진적으로 증가시키는 실수를 할 수 있는 화학 체계이다."와 같은 자체 정의를 사용한다. 생명체는 어떤 하나의 정의로 이해하기 어렵다. 예를 들면, 생명체는 아마도 진화할 필요가 없을지도 모른다. DNA 같은 정보를 포함하지 않은 생명체를 상상해 보라. 그러한 생명체들은 생식은 하지만 복제되지는 않을 것이다. 부모는 생물학적으로 완벽하게 낯선 사람처럼 더 이상 생물학적으로 아이와 무관할 것이다.」

35 ⑤

mammal : 포유동물 primates : 영장류 grasp : 이해하다, 파악하다 linguist : 언어학자 readily : 손쉽게 confess : 고백하다 master : 숙달시키다

☞ 이 글의 요지는 인간의 언어가 자연적으로 발생하였고 이를 과학적으로 설명하기 어렵다는 것이므로, ⑤번이 정답이다.

「어떤 사람들은 지금까지는 매우 좋았다고 말할 것이다. "우리는 포유류이다. 그러나 우리는 언어를 가지고 있고, 다른 동물들은 그렇지 않다." 일부 정의에 의하면, 동물들은 언어가 없을지도 모른다. 하지만 동물들은 광범위하게 의사소통하고, 우리는 호출 체계에 의해 단지 이해하기 시작한다. 먼저 언어가 생기고 사회가 생긴다는 생각은 실수일 것이다. 언어와 문화는 우리가 예나 지금이나 동물인 생물학적, 사회적, 자연적 실존을 통해 형성된다. 언어는 우리의 욕구와 신경과 함께 진화한 정신과 육체 사이의 체계이다. 상상력과 육체처럼, 언어는 스스로 발생한다. 이는 우리의 합리적이고 이성적인 능력을 피해가는 어떤 복잡성을 가진다. 기술적 언어학자들이 쉬이 고백하는 것처럼, 모든 자연 언어에 대한 과학적 설명을 하려는 모든 시도는 완전함과는 거리가 멀다. 그러나 아이들은 일찍 모국어를 배우고 6살이면 이를 거의 모두 습득한다.」

36 ⑤

notion : 개념 secure : 확보하다 gigantic : 거대한 harness : (동력으로) 이용하다 seam : (광물질의) 층 manipulate : 처리하다 convince : 확신시키다

☞ 지문은 인간이 지속적으로 대체에너지를 개발해 나가면서 자연에 대한 의존에서 벗어나고 있다는 내용이다. 이를 잘 나타내주는 보기는 ⑤번이다.

「학자들은 종종 인류에 의한 무한한 진보라는 개념이 왜 성립했는지 궁금해 한다. 이에 대한 정답은 에너지 기반을 확보하려는 기술의 발전에서 찾아야 한다. 겉보기에 거대하고 끝없는, 정확히 30억 년간 이용할 수 있는 가치를 지닌 태양 에너지는 처음부터 그대로였다. 하지만 우리는 점차적으로 태양 에너지로 대체하기 위해 필요로 했던 모든 에너지를 가지게 되었고, 또 다시 이를 확보하기 위해 자연에 맡기지 않아도 된다. 그리고 시간의 개념은 바뀌었다. 이는 석탄층과 석유매장지에 깊숙이 묻혀있는 에너지를 얼마나 빨리 이용할 수 있는지의 기능에 상응한다. 우리는 지상으로 꺼내서 마음껏 처리할 수 있는 "저장된 태양"을 다룰 수 있으므로 태양을 우리가 선택하면 두 배나 오래 안 보이게 할 수 있다. 이러한 에너지원을 가지고, 사람들은 점차적으로 더 이상 자연에 의존할 필요가 없다고 믿게 되었고, 세상을 원하는 대로 다시 재정립할 수 있다고 확신하게 되었다.」

37 ④

stir : 휘젓다, 뒤섞다   tide : 조류, 흐름   ebb and flow : 밀려왔다갔다하다   charge : ~라고 설명하다
induced 유도된 lunacy : 정신병 wax : (달이) 차오르다 casualty department : 응급실 gear up : 준비를 갖추다 beneath : 아래에 cower : 웅크리다 rear up : 자리를 박차다

☞ ④번에서 달의 평범한 모습이 위안이 된다는 내용은 보름달이 사람을 흥분하게 만든다는 지문의 요지에서 벗어난다.

「달이 바다를 움직일 수 있다면, 왜 인간의 혈액은 안 되는가? 우리는 어찌됐든 60퍼센트 이상의 물로 구성되어 있다. 아마도 혈액의 흐름은 우리의 감정과 자제력에 흐름과 변화를 만들 것이다. 셰익스피어는 달의 이러한 작용에서 몇 가지 사실을 느끼고는 달이 "사람을 미치게 한다."고 설명했다. 그리고 사실상 이는 로버트 루이스 스티븐슨의 '지킬박사와 하이드에 대한 이상한 사건 보고서'에서 하이드의 모델이 되었던 남자가 했던 주장이었다. 그는 그의 범죄를 달이 이끌어낸 광기 때문이라고 했다. 일부 논평은 이를 뒷받침해주는데, 보름달이 뜰 때 강력 범죄가 늘어난다는 주장을 지지한다. 달이 차면, 아이스하키 선수들은 페널티 박스에서 더 많은 시간을 보낸다. 반면 병원의 응급실은 바쁠 때를 대비해 준비를 한다. (그리고 하나의 달이 차오르고 지는 29일 12시간 44분 동안 달의 평범한 모습은 위로가 된다.) 그럼에도 불구하고 우리 중 어떤 사람들은 달 아래서, 갑자기 산을 오르고 싶거나, 어둠 속에서 웅크리거나, 자리를 박차고 일어나 울부짖고 싶은 욕구가 있다는 사실을 부인하기 힘들다.」

38 ④

latitude : (선택ㆍ행동의) 자유 gratefully : 기꺼이 groping : 손으로 더듬는 in the language of : ~의 말을 빌리면 concise : 간결한 on the whole : 전반적으로

☞ 이 글의 요지는 첫 번째 문장에 잘 나타난다. 보기 ④는 공학자들의 용어에 대해 부연설명하고 있는데, 이 글의 요지와 벗어나는 내용이다.

「우리가 행하는 모든 의도적인 행동은 특정한 허용범위가 있다. 우리의 의도는 하나의 규칙으로서 어떻게 할 것인가 보다는 무엇을 할 것인가에 대해 적용된다. 내가 전화기의 수화기를 들고 싶은지 열쇠를 자물쇠에 넣고 싶은지 관계없이 항상 기꺼이 내 눈에 의존하고, 내 손으로 하여금 목표로 이끌며, 나로 하여금 손으로 더듬는 수고를 줄여준다. 왜냐하면 어떤 잘못된 움직임은 시각적 통제에 의해서 바로 수정되기 때문이다. 공학자들의 말을 빌리면, 이런 종류의 상호작용은 환류작용으로 알려져 있다. (공학자들의 용어는 특정한 혼란이 없도록 생각을 교환할 수 있도록 항상 간결하고 정확하다.) 전반적으로, 우리는 의도가 무엇을 할 것인지, 피드백이 어떻게 할 것인지를 결정한다고 말할지 모른다. 그것은 사람들이 환경을 효율적으로 다룰 수 있도록 가능하게 하는 상호작용의 특성이다.」

39 ③

computation : 계산   marvelous : 훌륭한   satire : 풍자

☞ 대부분은 이른 나이에 중요한 성과를 달성하지만, 몇몇 저서의 경우에서 보듯 인생 후반기에 최고의 작품
을 만들기도 한다. 이와 일치하는 보기는 ③번이다.

① 몸 상태가 좋으면 기억력 상실이 일어나지 않는다.

② 나이든 여성은 나이든 남성보다 수치에 강하다.

③ 인생에서 특정한 업적 유형이 있으나, 약간의 예외가 있다.

④ 인생에 있어 단 한 번의 전성기가 있으므로, 놓쳐서는 안 된다.

⑤ 얻고 잃는 것 사이에 균형이 깨지는 때가 있다.

「당신은 20대에 가장 똑똑하다. 30대에 이르면 기억력, 특히 수학 계산 능력이 떨어진다. 그러나 다른 업무에 대한 지능지수
는 오른다. 예를 들면, 45세 때 당신의 어휘력은 대학을 졸업했을 때의 3배 정도로 증가한다. 60세에, 당신의 뇌는 21세
때보다 거의 4배에 달하는 정보를 가진다. 대부분의 노벨상 수상자들은 최고의 업적을 20대 후반이나 30대에 이루었고 위대
한 음악의 대부분은 33세에서 39세 사이에 만들어졌듯 거의 모든 분야에서 전성기가 빨리 오지만, 어떤 사람들은 계속해서
평생 동안 우수한 작품을 만들어 낸다. 톨스토이는 71세에 '부활'을 완성했고, 볼테르는 훌륭한 풍자 작품인 '캉디드'를 64세
에 썼다. 윌 듀란트는 '문명사회의 역사'라는 5권짜리 기념비적인 작품을 69세에 쓰기 시작했다.」

40 ①

decode : 해독하다   oral : 구두의   comprehend : 이해하다   detect : 알아내다   bias : 성향, 경향   phonemic
: 음소의   psycholinguistic : 심리언어학   facet : 측면, 양상   authentic : 정확한   sustain : 지속시키다

☞ 독서는 단순한 해독을 넘어 모든 측면에서 이해가 수반되어야 하는 복잡한 심리언어학적 활동이라는 것
이 지문의 요지이다. 따라서 ①번이 제목으로 가장 적절하다.

① 단순히 해독하는 것이 아닌 복잡한 행위로서의 독서

② 쓰는 것과 독해 사이의 미묘한 균형을 지키기

③ 행간을 읽다가 함정에 빠짐

④ 독서 기술을 가르치는 실험적인 접근법

⑤ 학습 경험에 있어 즐거움과 고충

「학생들은 글자를 해독할 수 있고, 심지어 이를 유창하게 소리 내어 읽게 되지만, 진정으로 내용을 이해하지는 못한다. 그들은
여러 가지 중에 행간의 의미, 유추된 의미를 알지 못하고, 작가의 성향을 찾아내지 못한다. 독서는 단순히 음소를 인식하고
문자를 인지하는 것 에 능숙해지는 것보다 훨씬 더 복잡하다. 이는 놀라울 정도로 복잡한 심리언어학적 활동으로서, 철자
발음뿐만 아니라 문학적 감상, 무엇보다도 중요하게 진정 평생에 걸쳐 전념하고 다양한 목적을 위해 읽기를 조절하면서 모든
측면에서 이해해야한다. 게다가, 독서는 이 기술을 적용하기 위한 목적을 가지는 것이 필요하다. 예를 들면, '나는 즐거움을
위해, 아니면 시험을 준비하기 위해 책을 읽고 있는 것인가?'와 같은 질문이다. 마지막으로, 만약 학생이 관심이 없거나, 흥미
가 없거나, 독서가 즐겁다고 느끼지 않았다면 이러한 완전한 지식을 거의 얻지 못할 것이다. 독서를 배우는 것은 어려운 일이
고 많은 에너지와 집중이 요구된다. 만약 이것이 아이들에게 재미있어 보이지 않는다면, 관심을 지속시키기는 어렵다.」

41 ③

bounty : 풍부함 vacant : 텅 빈 chamber : 공간, 방 copper : 구리 zinc : 아연 conceive : (계획 등을) 생각해내다 subterranean : 지하의 irrigation : (농업에서의) 관개 phenomenal : 경이적인 note : 언급하다 miner : 광부 prosperous : 번영한

☞ 지문은 버려진 광산에 꽃과 과일을 재배하여 수확하고 있다는 내용으로, 이에 적합한 제목은 ③번이다.

① 광산의 어두운 면
② 광산 깊은 곳에서 피는 장미
③ 추위 속에서 따뜻해지는 마음
④ 야생 꽃에 대한 광부의 사랑
⑤ 광부를 대상으로 번창하는 지역 시장

「캐나다의 작은 광산 마을인 플린 플런의 추위 때문에 정원은 오래가지 못한다. 그러나 이제 이 마을의 주민들은 신선한 채소와 꽃을 일 년 내내 즐긴다. 이 풍요로움은 지표의 1170 피트 아래에 있는 구리와 아연 광산의 텅 빈 방에서 자란다. 이 시도는 지하 재배의 질, 수확량, 비용을 시험하기 위해 프레리 플랜트 시스템스사의 웨인 프레이저와 브렌트 제틀이 생각해냈다. "이 방은 지표에서 완전히 동떨어져서, 저렴하고 정확하게 환경을 통제할 수 있습니다."라고 제틀이 말한다. 광산에는 고광도 점등, 세류 관개 시스템, 컴퓨터를 설치했다. "목본류 식물은 놀라운 속도로 성장합니다."라고 제틀이 언급한다. 심은 지 3개월 후, 보통 700송이의 장미를 생산하는 80그루의 장미 묘목은 1,100송이의 꽃을 생산했다. 광부들은 이 정원에 큰 자부심을 가진다.」

42 ③

mystify : 어리둥절하게 하다 synchronous : 동시에 발생하는 herd : 가축 무리 audible : 들리는 simultaneously : 동시에 forthcoming : 기꺼이 말하는 throb : 진동하다 whereabouts : 행방 choir : 성가대 blast : (음악이) 울리다 chorale : 합창곡 chapel : 예배당 stumble : 우연히 발견하다 palpable : 감지 가능한

☞ 주어진 글에서 코끼리의 행동에 대해 설명이 필요하다고 말하고 있고, (B)부분에서 이를 설명할 수 있을 내용에 대해 언급하고 있다. (D)부분에서 '나'는 미스터리를 풀 수 있는 실마리를 발견하였고, (C)부분에서 구체적으로 코끼리의 행동과 나의 성가대 경험을 연결했다. 마지막으로, (A)부분에서 파이프 오르간에서 코끼리의 행동을 설명하는 내용의 결론을 제시한다.

「코끼리 틈에서 하루를 보낸다면, 당신은 어리둥절해서 돌아올 것이다. 갑자기, 조용하게 동시에 일어나 움직임을 보이는데, 한 무리가 명백히 혹은 소리에 기인하지 않고 도망을 가거나, 흩어져 있던 코끼리 무리가 동시에 귀를 세우고 그 자리에 가만히 있는 행동을 보인다. 이러한 사건에는 설명이 필요하지만, 아무도 밝히지 못한다.

(B) 기억력과 오감을 넘어선 어떤 알려지지 않은 능력이 코끼리에게 다른 코끼리들의 거리와 근황에 대해 알려주는 듯하다.

(D) 나는 오레건주 포틀랜드의 동물원 관람 중에 이러한 신비에 대한 실마리를 발견하여 움찔했다. 아시아 코끼리 어미 3마리와 어린 새끼들을 보는 동안, 나는 공기 중에서 감지할 수 있는 진동이 멀리서 울리는 천둥소리처럼 반복되는 것을 알아차렸지만, 아직 내 주변은 조용했다.

(C) 나중에서야 생각이 떠올랐다. 내가 어릴 적 뉴욕의 성가대에 있을 때, 가장 크고 묵직한 소리를 내는 교회의 파이프 오르간 옆에 서 있곤 했다. 그 오르간이 바흐 합창곡의 저음을 울릴 때, 동물원의 코끼리 구역이 그랬던 것처럼 교회 전체가 진동했다.

(A) 파이프 오르간처럼, 코끼리가 진동하는 것의 원인이었다. 코끼리들은 사람이 듣기에 매우 낮은 조정된 울음소리를 통해서 서로 의사소통한다.」

43 44

nuisance : 골칫거리   disagreeable : 불쾌한   conveyance : 수송   abolish : 폐지하다, 파괴하다   arise : 생기다
habitability : 살기에 알맞음   tint : 색조

「먼지의 기능이 무엇인지 대부분의 사람들이 질문을 받는다면, 그들은 어떤 기능이 있는지는 모르겠지만 먼지가 매우 성가신 것은 분명하다고 말할 것이다. 마을이나 집의 먼지는 종종 성가신 것뿐만이 아니라 질병의 근원이며, 때때로 완전히 실명하게 만드는 것이 사실이다. 그러나 먼지는 부적절한 장소에서만 문제일 뿐이고, 먼지가 일으키는 해롭거나 불쾌한 효과는 우리가 자연을 다루는 방식에 기인한 것이다. 만약 우리가 완전히 순수한 기계 운송 수단을 받아들인다면, 길거리에서 완벽하게 질병을 포함한 먼지를 폐기시킬 수 있다. 반면, 석탄의 불완전 연소로부터 야기되는 다른 종류의 먼지들은, 먼지를 발생시키는 사람들의 편견이나 이익보다 깨끗한 공기와 햇빛이 전반적으로 주민 전체적으로 중요하다는 사실을 고려한다면, 똑같이 쉽게 제거될 수 있을 것이다. 그러나 우리는 먼지로부터 야기되는 위험과 불편함을 최소화한다고 할지라도 이를 완전히 없앨 수는 없다. 그리고 우리가 그렇게 할 수 없는 것이 정말 다행스러운 일이다. 왜냐하면 이제 우리는 이 지구의 아름다움의 대부분과 살기에 매우 알맞은 것이 먼지의 존재 덕분이라는 것을 발견하고 있기 때문이다. 먼지 없이는 푸른 하늘과 수평선 가까이의 구름 위에서 일출과 일몰 때 보이는 아름다운 색깔에 감탄할 수 없다.」

43 ④

☞ 지문의 빈칸 이후에는 먼지가 가져다주는 좋은 점이 제시된다. 따라서 먼지를 없앨 수 없다는 사실을 다행이라고 생각한다는 내용인 ④번이 적절하다.
① 우리는 그렇기 하기 위한 방법을 찾기 위해 매우 바쁘다.
② 우리는 우리가 그렇게 했던 것들을 쉽게 잊을 것이다.
③ 이는 우리가 해야 할 큰 과제 중 하나이다.
④ 우리가 그것을 할 수 없다는 것이 다행이다.
⑤ 아무도 그 일들을 어떻게 막는지 모른다.

44 ②

☞ 네 번째 줄에서 먼지가 질병과 실명의 원인이 될 수 있다고 말하고 있으므로 정답은 ②번이다.

45 47

comprehensive : 포괄적인   opponent : 반대자   administration : 행정부   considerably : 상당히   proposal : 법안, 계획   controversial : 논란의   provision : 조항, 규정   eliminate : 없애다   commitment : 약속   draft : 원고, 초안

「(A) 실업자를 위해 일자리를 제공하는 "직업훈련종합계획"과 같은 정부 정책은 더 의욕적으로 만들어질지도 모른다. 정부는 최후의 수단으로서 고용주로 활동해야 한다. 즉, 정부는 일을 하고 싶으나 민간 부분에서 일자리를 찾을 수 없는 모든 사람들에게 일자리를 제공할 준비가 되어 있어야 할지 모른다.
(D) 정부가 민간 기업에서 내쫓긴 사람들을 위해 일자리를 제공해야 할 의무는 없지만, 밀접하게 관련된 법안인 험프리-호킨스 법안의 1976년 원안에 삽입되었다. 이 법안은 정부가 연간 3%를 목표로 실업률을 낮추기 위해 어떤 일자리든지 제공할 의무가 있다는 내용을 포함한 것이다.

(C) 정부를 최후의 수단으로 만들려는 법안은 논란의 여지가 많다. (반대 때문에, 이러한 조항들은 험프리-호킨스 법에서 나중에 삭제되었다. 그리고 레이건 대통령은 "직업훈련종합계획"을 1983년 말까지 없앨 것을 제안했다.) 긍정적인 측면에서, 정부 계획은 실업자들에게 유용한 할 일을 제공한다. 예를 들면, 실업자들은 1930년대 루즈벨트의 경제회복 프로그램에서 시행하였던 것처럼 공공 근로를 수행하거나 도시 보수 관리 일을 할지도 모른다.

(B) 반면에, 반대하는 사람들은 이러한 계획이 너무 비싸다고 주장한다. 카터 행정부는 84억 달러의 비용을 들여 공공 서비스 고용 프로그램을 2배 이상 늘려 725,000의 일자리를 제공하였는데, 1977~1978년 동안 이 프로그램이 얼마나 비싼 것인지 발표되었다. 일자리 하나당 11,500달러 이상의 비용이 산출되는데, 평균적인 노동자는 이보다 꽤 적은 금액인 7,200달러로 상당히 적게 받았다. 반대편은 행정부와 지원 부서를 지지했다.」

45　⑤

☞ (A)에서 정부가 일자리를 제공할 의무에 대해 언급하고 있는데 다음에 이어질 내용은 이에 대한 법안을 언급한 (D)이다. 이어서, 이 법안이 논쟁적이라는 내용을 (C)가 밝혀주고 있고, 마지막으로 (B)에서 이 법안의 비효율성에 대해 언급하고 있다.

46　②

☞ 정부는 "최후의 수단"으로서의 고용자이고 지원자이다. 따라서 정답은 ②번이다.
① 국공채　② 최후의 수단　③ 최적 조건　④ 과소공급　⑤ 안전 점검

47　③

☞ 제시문은 정부가 일자리를 제공할 의무가 있는지에 대한 찬반논쟁을 담고 있다. 따라서 이 글의 제목으로 ③번이 가장 알맞다.
① 오늘날의 힘든 고용시장 상황
② 완전 고용을 위한 필요조건
③ 정부고용에 관한 논쟁
④ 정부고용에 대한 공식 권장사항
⑤ 고용 관련 법안의 역사

48　⑤

statute : 법령　trustee : 수탁자　matter : 중요하다　doctrine : 정책　court : 법정　enforce : 집행하다
acknowledge : 인정하다　trusteeship : 신탁 관리 업무　administrative : 관리상의　wonder : 경이
pronouncement : 공표　climate : 분위기, 풍조

☞ 필자는 관리 기관이 야생 지역 관리 임무를 인지하고 노력을 다하도록 압력을 가해야 한다고 주장한다. 이를 나타내는 보기는 ⑤번이다.

「시민들은 시간이 좀 걸리겠지만, 연방과 주 지역과 야생동물법에 대중의 신뢰를 담은 생각을 도입하기 위한 운동을 시작해야 한다. 책임 있는 기관들이 수탁자이고, 해당 법은 강제적으로 말해야 한다. 대중의 신뢰주의에 대하여 중요한 것은 단지 법정에서 시행할 것인지의 여부가 아니고, 그러한 신뢰가 연방과 주의 정책에 작용하는 부분이 되는가의 여부다. 우리는 그 기관들이 위탁 업무를 인지하고, 시정 방침으로서 그에 따른 엄중한 임무를 다해주도록 압력을 가해야 한다. 연방 지역 기관의 관리들이 힘 있고 자신감 있게 "네, 우리는 국가의 경이로운 것을 맡고 있습니다."라고 말하게 해야 한다. 이러한 공표는 더 높은 기준을 만들고, 원칙 있는 행동에 알맞은 풍토를 만들어내도록 도울 것이다.」

tomboy : 말괄량이 playmate : 놀이친구 pellet : 탄알 relegate : 격하시키다 blow : 강타, 타격 confront : 직면하다 madly : 미친 듯이 literally : 문자 그대로

「나는 8세 때 말괄량이였다. 나는 모두 빨간색인 카우보이 모자, 부츠, 체크무늬 스커트와 바지를 가지고 있었다. 내 놀이 친구는 나보다 2살, 4살 위인 내 오빠들이었다. 부모님은 오빠들에게 총을 사주기로 결정하셨다. 그것들은 "진짜" 총은 아니었다. 그것은 새를 죽일 수 있는 구리 총알인 "BB탄"을 발사했다. 나는 총이 없었는데, 여자아이이기 때문이었다. 나는 즉시 인디언 위치로 전락했다. 이제 우리 사이에는 확연한 차이가 있었다. 오빠들은 새 총으로 무엇이든지 쏘았다. 나는 활과 화살로 지지 않으려고 했다. 그러다 나는 내 눈에 믿을 수 없는 타격을 느꼈다. 나는 그 순간 오빠가 총을 내리는 것을 보았다. 나는 그 사고를 아직도 기억한다. 나는 처음으로, 의식적으로 몇 년 전 의사가 한 말의 의미를 마주한다. "눈은 함께 움직여요. 한쪽이 실명하면, 다른 한쪽도 멀어버리죠." 나는 여기저기 바라보며 빛이 사라져가는 것에 대한 이미지를 저장하면서, 미친 듯 세상에 충돌했다는 것을 느낀다. 그러고는, 내가 여전히 25년간 시력을 유지하고 있다는 고마움이 나를 말 그대로 무릎 꿇게 한다. 감사의 기도가 나온다.」

49 ③

☞ 나의 가해자는 오빠이다.

50 ④

☞ 필자는 어린 시절 사고로 눈을 실명할 위기를 겪었으나 현재까지 시력을 계속 유지하고 있다는 사실에 감사하고 있다.

① 용서하는 ② 후회하는 ③ 소심한 ④ 감사하는 ⑤ 정신없는

01 ①

dismiss : 떠나게 하다, 깨끗이 처리하다   ionize : 이온화하다   radiation : (빛, 열의)방사, 복사
☞ benign은 '친절한, 양성의, 무해한'이라는 뜻으로 보기 중에서는 ① harmless와 가장 가깝다.
② 진동하는   ③ 세력 있는   ④ 전달하는   ⑤ 암(癌)의

「최근 몇 년 동안, 핸드폰이 건강에 미치는 영향에 대한 걱정이 사라지게 되었다. 핸드폰 장치들로부터 방출되는 고주파가 무해한 것으로 판명되었기 때문이다. 핸드폰은 비전리 방사선을 내뿜는데, 이는 화학결합을 파괴하거나 암을 야기하는 것으로 알려진 DNA 손상을 유발하기에는 너무 약한 파동이다.」

02 ②

condemn : 비난하다, 형을 선고하다   whence : 어디서, (~하는) 거기서부터   dreadful : 무서운, 두려운
☞ futile은 '무익한, 쓸데없는'의 의미로 보기 중에서는 ② fruitless와 가장 가깝다.
① 반복적인   ③ 혐오하는   ④ 고된   ⑤ 훈련의, 규율의

「신들은 시지프스에게 돌을 산 정상까지 계속해서 굴려 올리는 형벌을 내렸다. 정상에서 돌은 무게로 인해 다시 굴러 떨어졌다. 그들은 무익하고 희망 없는 노력보다 더 무서운 형벌은 없다고 생각했다.」

03 ②

manual : 손의   bound to : 반드시 ~하는   prowess : 기량   vice versa : 역으로
☞ inextricably는 '헤어날 수 없는'의 의미로 보기 중에서는 ② inescapably와 가장 가깝다.
① 과도하게   ③ 부당한   ④ 무능한   ⑤ 이해할 수 없는

「현재와 과거의 예술가들은 손으로 그릴 수 있는 능력이 반박의 여지없이 실현화하는 기량으로 연결된다고 믿었고, 또한 역으로 실측될 수 있는 재능은 손재주라고 믿었다. 사실, 대부분의 예술가들은 손으로 그릴 수 없는 것은 눈으로 본 것이 아니라고 믿는다.」

04 ⑤

work on : (어떤 일, 주제에 대해) 일하다, 작업 중이다   identification : 신원 확인   prepare : 준비하다
☞ mandatory는 '의무적인, 필수의'의 의미를 지닌 단어는 ⑤ obligatory와 가장 가깝다
① 휴대용의   ② 흠이 없는   ③ 미봉책   ④ 단순화된

「정부는 제한된 형식의 '의무적 신원확인' 제도를 진행하고 있다. 현재 준비되고 있는 법안에는 구직 시와 같은 특정 상황에서 신원확인이 반드시 수행되어야 한다는 내용이 포함되어 있다.」

05 ①

pavement : 도로 포장 withdrawal : (예금 등의) 회수, 인출 doublespeak : 이중화법

☞ fiscal은 '재정상의'의 의미로 이와 유사한 단어는 ① financial이다.

② 실제로 ③ 학원의 ④ 육체의 ⑤ 겸손한

「Arizona의 Tucson에는 도로에 움푹 파인 곳이 없다. 다만 '도로 포장상의 부족'만 있을 뿐이다. 더 이상 가난한 사람들은 없다. 다만 '재정상의 목표 미달성자'만 있을 뿐이다. ATM(현금자동입출금기)에 대한 도둑질은 없다. 다만, '허가받지 않은 인출'만 있을 뿐이다. 이중화법은 계속된다. 이중화법이란 부정적인 것을 긍정적인 것으로, 불쾌한 것을 매력적인, 적어도 견딜만한 것으로 보이게 하는 언어이다.」

06 ③

leak : 새다 spoil : 상하다, 부패하다

☞ repulse는 '되쫓아버리다, 격퇴하다'의 의미와 가장 유사한 단어는 ③ repel이다.

① 매혹하다 ② 활기를 돋우다 ④ 채우다, 공급하다 ⑤ 비난하다

「냄새는 우리의 기분을 향상시킬 수도, 가라앉힐 수도, 심지어는 몸무게를 줄이는 것을 도울 수도 있다. 어떤 악취는 우리를 내쫓기도 하는데, 이에는 충분한 이유가 있다. 그 악취가 우리에게 가스가 샌다는 것, 우유가 상했다는 것, 고기가 부패했다는 것을 알려주는 것이다.」

07 ③

peculiar : 기이한, 독특한 epidemic : 유행성의 neglect : 무시하다 first-aid : 응급의

☞ ③ '~하는 경향이 있는'의 의미로, 'is prone to'로 쓰여야 한다. many a fan을 단수 취급하여 are가 아닌 is가 필요한 것이다.

　① '수많은'이라는 의미로, 뒤에 복수형 명사가 붙는다.

　② '잘 알지 못하다'라는 의미로, 조동사 may의 영향으로 are가 아닌 be 원형태로 쓰였다. 'many a 단수 명사'도 many fans 형태처럼 '많은'의 의미이나 단수동사를 쓴다

　④ '~을 염려하는'의 의미로, 본래 'two German physicians are concerned that the mechanism of mass fainting had been neglected in the medical literature.'의 문장이 분사구문으로 쓰이며 be동사가 생략되었다.

　⑤ '피해자들, 사상자들'의 의미로, 'the+형용사'는 '~하는 사람들'로 해석한다.

「팝음악 콘서트에서의 유행성 기절은 수많은 청소년들에게서 관찰되는 가장 기이한 대중 건강 위기 중 하나이다. 대부분의 부모들은 이러한 위협에 대해 잘 알지 못할 것이다. 많은 팬들이 의식을 잃기 쉽다는 수십 년간의 자료에도 불구하고 이 문제가 현대 과학의 주목을 끌지 못했기 때문이다. 대량 기절 사태가 의학 조사에서는 무시되었음을 염려하여 최근 독일의 두 내과의는 'New Kids on the Block'의 콘서트에 참여했다. 여기에는 기절 피해자들이 치료받던 적십자사에서 파견된 응급 치료원들도 함께했다. 'The New England Journal of Medicine'의 목요일 기사에 보도된 이 의사들에 보고서에 따르면, 콘서트 관람객 400명이 기절했고 이들은 모두 11살에서 17살 사이의 소녀들이었다고 한다.」

08 ①

feud : 반목하다   biologically : 생물학적으로

☞ ① 'Families are the people'와 'It matters to them if you have a cold ~' 두 문장의 합성이므로 'to whom'이 옳다.

　② to 부정사의 부사적 용법 중 목적의 의미로 쓰였다.

　③ 'They like to hear stories'와 'Stories are about when you were young' 두 문장의 합성이다.

　④ 'loan+사람+사물'의 형태로 쓰인다.

　⑤ '~이든 아니든'의 의미로 양보의 부사절에 쓰인다.

「가족은 당신이 감기에 걸린 것, 친구와 불화를 겪는 것, 애완견을 훈련시키는 것 따위를 중요한 문제로 생각하는 사람들이다. 가족들은 당신의 볼링 팀에 대한 기사를 자석으로 냉장고 문에 붙여두고 당신의 그림들과 집에서 만든 도자기들을 보관할 것이다. 그들은 당신이 어렸을 적의 이야기를 듣는 것을 좋아한다. 당신이 토마토 통조림을 만드는 것을 도와주고 자동차 오일을 교체하는 것을 도와준다. 그들은 당신이 입원해있을 때 찾아주고 '영혼의 어두운 밤에 당신과 이야기를 나눠주며 당신이 직업을 잃었을 때 임대료를 내기 위한 돈을 빌려줄 사람들이다. 생물학적인 연관 여부와는 상관없이 이런 일을 해주는 사람들이 가족이다.」

09 ②

procreation : 출산하다, 생식하다   modify : 변경하다   hatchling : 부화한 (조류, 파충류, 어류 따위의) 유생

☞ ② 'they developed a new package of instincts'와 'Instincts are modified for the special needs' 두 문장의 합성이므로 'modified'가 옳다

　① '~에서 진화하다'의 의미로 맞게 쓰였다.

　③ '혁명적인 진보'의 의미로, 'advance'는 '셀 수 없는 명사'이므로 단수 취급하여 'a'를 붙이는 것이 맞다.

　④ '갓 부화한 새끼'의 의미로, 'the+형용사'는 '~하는 사람들'로 해석한다.

　⑤ 'They came into the world with all the needed programs of action'와 'The needed programs of action are wired into their brain' 두 문장의 합성으로 옳게 쓰였다.

「포유류가 파충류에서부터 진화할 때, 그들의 뇌는 변화하기 시작했다. 먼저, 그들은 새로운 본능들을 발달시켰는데, 이는 성과 번식에 대한 파충류의 본능과 비슷하지만 포유류의 새로운 생활양식의 특별한 요구사항에 따라 변형된 것이었다. 그 중 가장 중요한 변화는 새끼에 대한 부모의 돌봄이었다. 이것은 파충류의 행동에 대항하는 혁명적인 진보였다. 파충류에게 막 부화한 새끼들은 잡을 수만 있다면 충분히 맛있는 식사를 제공해주는 대상이었다. 파충류 새끼들은 그들의 생존을 위한 싸움의 준비를 모두 갖춘 채로 태어난다. 그들은 날 때부터 필요한 모든 프로그램들을 뇌에 가진 채 낳아진다. 새끼들은 출생의 순간에 이미 작은 어른 파충류이다. 이와는 반대로, 포유류의 새끼들은 힘없고 취약한 상태로 출생하기에 부모의 보호가 그들의 생존에 있어서 필수적이다. 이것이 바로 포유류가 '부모의 돌봄'이라는 새로운 본능을 발달시킨 이유이다.」

10 ⑤

mummify : 미라로 만들다 born and bred : ~에서 나고 자란 fraud : 사기, 협잡 crest : 산꼭대기

☞ ⑤ 'that'으로 이어진 뒤 문장에는 목적어가 없다. 즉, 'what'으로 연결사를 넣어 '그가 무엇을 입었는지를 안다'로 표현하는 것이 옳다.

　① 'Scientists are certain of one thing about Iceman'와 'Hikers discovered him' 두 문장의 합성이므로 목적격 'whom'이 맞다.

　② 'He was European born and bred'와 'He is closely related to modern northern and alpine Europeans' 두 문장의 합성으로 'is → being'이 되면서 생략되었다.

　③ 'make+목적어+목적보어'의 형태로, 'unlikely' 형용사로 쓰였다.

　④ '여러 연구 중에 가장 최근의 것'이 주어로 단수동사 'is'가 맞다.

「여전히 우리는 그가 누구인지 알지 못한다. 그러나 과학자들은 그 알프스의 냉동 미라에 대해 한 가지는 자신할 수 있다. 이 미라는 1991년 9월 오스트리아와 이탈리아의 경계에 있는 10,530 피트 산맥의 해빙되는 빙하 사이에서 발견되었다. 유전학적 조사에서, 과학자들은 이 미라가 유럽에서 나고 자란 사람이라고 결론 내렸다. 특히 현재의 북부 알프스 지방의 유럽인과 유전상의 연관이 깊은 것으로 보인다. 이 미라에 대한 국제 조사단은 미라의 조작 가능성이 매우 낮다고 Science 저널에 밝혔다. 이 조사단의 가장 최근 연구는 미라가 살던 먼 과거의 알프스 일대의 의생활에 대한 연구였다. 과학자들은 어째서 이 남자가 산꼭대기에서 발견되었는가는 알 수 없겠지만, 적어도 그가 무엇을 입었는지는, 속옷까지도 확인할 수 있다.」

11 ②

makeshift : 임시의 suspend : 매달다 tuck : 숨기다, 밀어넣다 old-fashioned : 구식의

☞ ② 'consist'는 자동사가 그 자체로 '이미 ~로 구성되어 있다'의 의미를 가진다. 'be consisted of'와 같은 수동형으로 쓰일 수 없다.

　① 도치된 문장이다. 주어는 'two rolls of bedding'이므로 복수동사 'are'가 맞다.

　③ 'suspend'는 '매달다'의 의미이고, 여기서 나무 막대기는 매달려 있어야하기 때문에 수동형으로 쓰는 것이 맞다.

　④ 'I was tucked in blankets'와 'I listened to one of her stories' 두 문장의 합성으로, 'was → being'으로 바뀌며 생략되었다.

　⑤ 'seem +형용사'의 형태로, 해석하면 '구식처럼 보였다'가 되어 수동형이지만 자동사 'seem'을 수동으로 바꾸지는 않으므로 'old-fashioned'로 쓰는 것이 맞다.

「할머니와 나는 광장 뒤에 있는 방 하나짜리 집에서 살았다. 그 집에는 전통양식의 벽난로, 임시 보관장, 생활에 필요한 물을 담은 상자가 있었고 방의 끝에는 소파만큼이나 편안한 두 개의 침낭이 있었다. 우리는 매일 밤 솜과 양가죽, 분류된 피복으로 이뤄진 이 침낭을 이용했다. 방 길이만큼 기다란 나무 막대기가 천장 들보에서 10인치 정도 매달려있었다. 할머니의 도자기와 맞바꾼 서랍에는 우리가 가지고 있던 의류 몇 벌이 들어 있었다. 할머니는 사탕과 슈퍼에서 산 쿠키가 가득 찬 밀가루 포대를 가지고 있었다. 담요 속에 몸을 숨긴 채로, 나는 할머니의 이야기나 할머니 어릴 적 세상에 대한 이야기를 듣곤 했다. 할머니가 설명해주는 세상은 내가 살았던 세상에는 너무도 먼 옛날의 이야기였다.」

12 ④

anthropologist : 인류학자   territorial imperative : 세력권   buffer : 완충
☞ ④ 'when someone invades our bubbles'을 가리키는 것으로 'someone's invasion of our bubbles'이
  옳다.
  ① 불편하게 느끼는
  ② 방울(영역)을 드나드는
  ③ 방울(영역)의 크기
  ⑤ 우리의 개인 공간

「공간 관계는 접촉에 대한 사회 관습과 밀접하게 관련된다. 인류학자들은 인간이 서로 '사적공간의 영역(방울)' 사이를 드나든
다고 말한다. 그 영역의 크기는 개인적 공간, 세력권 또는 '개인의 완충 지대'를 나타낸다. 타인이 우리의 영역을 침범할 때,
우리는 이를 좋아하지도 관대히 봐주지도 않는다. 우리는 분명히 불편함을 느낄 것이다. 그러나 우리가 세상 곳곳을 경험하게
된다면, 우리는 어떤 사회는 개인 영역이 우리의 사회보다 작거나 클 수 있다는 것을 배우게 될 것이다.」

13 ②

contradict : 반대하다, 모순되다   approval : 승인, 인정   standard : 기준
☞ ② 이 글은 '개인이 사회 관습과 기준에 순응하는 것의 이유와 그 의미'에 대한 글이다. 보기 중에서
  'conformity'가 가장 옳다.
  ① 권위   ③ 완고함   ④ 독립   ⑤ 지배

「사람들은 규범과 관습에 순응한다. 비록 그들이 세상을 바라보는 관점이 관습과는 충돌하더라도 대부분의 사람들은 순응을
택하는데, 사회의 인정을 받고 다른 이들의 비난을 피하기 위해서이다. 우리는 다른 사람들이 우리를 인정하고, 좋아하고,
잘 대우해주기를 원한다. 성장하면서, 사람들은 집단 내에서 잘 지내는 방법이 집단의 기준에 따르는 것임을 배운다. 당신은
정장과 같은 공식적 복장을 싫어할 수도 있지만, 특별한 일에는 그러한 옷을 입는 것이 사회적 관습이므로 어쩔 수 없이 따른
다. 체중 관리 중인 친구와 만날 때, 당신은 그 친구를 좋아하지 않더라도 샐러드와 같은 건강식을 먹을 것이다. 그러나 당신
이 혼자 있다면 당신은 자신의 취향에 따라 햄버거와 감자튀김과 같은 음식을 먹는다. 사회 관습에 순응하는 것은 당신에게
외적인 행동의 변화를 요구하는 것이지, 당신 스스로의 의견을 바꾸라고 강요하지는 않는다.」

14 ①

lawn : 잔디   psychological : 심리학적인   proportion : 비율
☞ ① 이 글은 자신의 외모에 만족하는 남성과 달리 여성은 외모에 만족하지 못하고 스스로의 외모를 못났다
  고 자조한다고 이야기한다. 따라서 여성의 '낮은 자존감'을 뜻하는 'low self-esteem'이 가장 옳다.
  ② 여성성   ③ 높은 자부심   ④ 반영   ⑤ 외모

「대부분의 남자들은 자신이 평균 정도의 외모라고 생각한다. 남자에게 있어서 '보통 정도'라는 것은 괴로운 일이 아니다. 남자
들은 보통에 만족한다. 이것이 바로 남자들이 다른 사람들에게 자신이 어떻게 보이는 지를 묻지 않는 이유다. 남자들의 주요
미용은 면도인데, 그들이 마당의 잔디를 손보는 것과 본질적으로 동등한 관리다. 여자는 남자와 다르다. 단 세 단어로 여자의
생각을 표현해 본다면 아마도 '만족하기엔 조금 부족하다' 정도가 될 것이다. 남들이 보기에 얼마나 매력적인 사람이든, 그녀
스스로는 거울을 보며 이렇게 생각할 것이다. "으으, 세상에! 왜 여자들은 이렇게 낮은 자존감을 가질까? 여기에는 복잡한
심리적, 사회적 이유들이 있다. 바로 바비 인형이다! 여자 아이들은 바비 인형을 가지고 놀며 이 인형처럼 되기를 꿈꾸며
자란다. 그런데 바비 인형은 사람이라면 키는 7피트에 몸무게는 81 파운드인 비현실적 비율로 제작된다.」

15 ①

informed decision : 정보가 제공된 결절   distrust : 불신하다

☞ ① 대중들이 과학이 우리의 삶을 향상시킬 수 있다고 믿으면서도 다른 한편으로는 과학을 불신한다고
　　했으므로 이러한 태도는 양면적이다.
　　② 적개심있는　　③ 동정적인　　④ 양서류의　　⑤ 무정형의

「과학과 기술이 세상을 변화시키는 것을 막을 수 없다면, 적어도 그 변화가 옳은 방향으로 이뤄질 수 있게 노력해야 한다.
민주사회에서, 이는 곧 대중이 과학에 대해서 기초적 이해는 할 수 있어야 함을 의미한다. 대중이 충분한 정보를 가진 상태에
서 전문가에 휘둘리지 않고 결정을 내리는 것을 보장하기 위해서이다. 현재 대중들은 과학에 대해 다소 양면적인 태도를 취한
다. 과학과 기술이 진보가 계속되면서 인류의 생활수준을 향상시킬 것이라 믿으면서도 또 한편으로는 과학에 대한 명확한
이해가 부족하기 때문에 과학을 불신하는 것이다.」

16 ⑤

vehemently : 격렬히   compromise : 타협, 양보   dissolve : 풀다, 해산하다

☞ ⑤ 글쓴이는 일을 하지 않는 것의 장점도 인정하지만, 일을 하는 것이 더 장점이 많다고 생각했으므로
　　일을 하겠다고 주장한다. 따라서 '단점보다 더 가치있는'의 뜻인 'outweighed the disadvantages'가
　　적절하다.
　　① 독립심을 방해하는
　　② 학교생활에 큰 기여를 하는
　　③ 우리의 관계를 돈독하게 하는
　　④ 결국 내 관점과 상충하는

「아버지는 학교를 다니면서 지역 식료품점에서 아르바이트를 하겠다는 내 결정을 격렬히 반대하셨다. 아버지는 내가 스스로를
지나치게 혹사시키는 것을 우려하셨고 조금 더 자란 후에 일하기를 원하셨다. 나는 아르바이트를 그만 두는 것의 장점을 충분
히 인정했지만, 일하는 것이 가져다 줄 혜택이 손해보다 크다고 생각했다. 예를 들어, 비록 월급이 적다고 해도 나는 스스로
돈을 벌어 독립적인 삶을 즐길 수 있는 것이다. 아버지가 허락을 하지 않으셔서 화가 나기는 했지만, 그래도 나는 아버지의
반대 의견을 끝까지 경청했다. 결국 긴 대화 끝에 우리는 합의점에 도달할 수 있었다. 내가 나를 지나치게 힘들게 한다거나
학교생활에 지장을 주면 바로 일을 그만두기로 약속한 것이다. 결과적으로는 아버지도 나도 모두 언짢은 기분을 풀 수 있었다.」

17 ①

multiple intelligence : 다중지능   point out : 지적하다   inadequate : 부적합한

☞ ① 글쓴이는 교육이 다양한 지능을 가진 아이들을 언어와 논리라는 틀에만 맞추려 한다고 비판한다. 따라서 글쓴이가 지향하는 교육방식은 아이들을 교육에 맞추는 것이 아닌, 교육을 아이들에게 맞추는 방식일 것이고, 이는 'it can fit students'와 가장 가깝다.
② 그들은 질문에 더 잘 답변할 수 있다.
③ 교육 방식을 우리 스스로 결정한다.
④ 그것들이 언어와 논리 기술을 발달시킬 수 있다
⑤ 배움은 교육에 기여할 수 있다.

「다중 지능 이론은 지능에 대한 종래의 인식을 뒤흔들었으며 기존 지능검사의 실효성에 대해서도 의문을 제기했다. 다중 지능 연구가들은 이전까지의 교육과 지능검사가 인간이 가진 일곱 가지의 지능 중 단 두 가지, 언어와 논리 지능에만 초점을 맞춰 이뤄졌다고 지적한다. 따라서 언어와 논리 지능의 방식을 배우지 않은 아이들은 부적합하고 모자란 아이들로 치부되었다. 그러나 Seven Kinds of Smart의 저자 Thomas Armstrong은 아이들이 문제가 아니라 교육 방식이 적합하지 않았던 것이라 주장한다. "전통적인 교육은 어른들의 방식에 아이들을 맞춰 넣으려고 노력했다. 그러나 이제는 교육을 아이들에 맞춰 바꿀 필요가 있다. 우리는 제각기 다른 아이들이기에 각기 다른 방식으로 배운다는 것을 이해해야 한다. 그리고 이런 다양한 방식의 배움이 모두 문제없다는 것을 인정해야 한다. 그렇게 하는 것이 진정한 교육이다."」

18 ⑤

hapless : 불운한   unmaster : 대적불가능하다   technical term : 특수용어, 전문용어
extermination : 근절, 박해   revulsion : 혐오, 불쾌감   overwhelm : 압도하다

☞ ⑤ 홀로코스트라는 용어를 통해 사건에 대한 보다 이성적인 판단을 가능케 한다는 것이 글의 핵심 내용이다. 따라서 '감정적 경험과 이성을 분리시킨다.'는 의미의 'separating the intellectual from the emotional experience'가 맞다.
① 지적 용어와 기술적 언어를 분리시키는
② 이해할 수 없는 언어와 기술적 언어를 분리시키는
③ 이해할 수 있는 언어와 일상용어를 분리시키는
④ 지적 용어와 일반 언어를 분리시키는

「우선 말해둘 것은, 홀로코스트라는 대항불가능하고 이해할 수 없던 운명에 대해 이름붙인 것이 불운했던 나치 희생자들이 아니었다는 사실이다. 나치의 유대인 박해에 대해 홀로코스트라는 대단히 인위적이고 전문적인 이름을 붙인 것은 바로 미국인들이었다. 대량 학살이라고 이름붙일 때 우리가 가장 즉각적이고 강렬한 혐오를 느끼는 것과 달리, 생소한 특수용어로 이름 정해진다면 우리는 이를 감정적으로 와 닿는 언어로 바꾸는 과정을 거쳐야 한다. 일상용어 대신에 전문적이고 특수한 용어들을 사용하는 것은 가장 잘 알려지고 가장 잘 이용되는 분리 장치인데, 이를 통해 이성과 감성을 분리시키는 것이다. 이 사건이 우리의 이해 가능 범위를 넘어서는 상상조차 불가능한 비극이었기 때문에, 대량 학살이라는 일반적인 단어를 사용하는 것은 우리를 감정적으로 압도할 것이다. '홀로코스트'의 채택은 그 사건의 본질에 대해 우리가 이성적으로 대처하는 것을 가능케 한다.」

19 ②

manipulation : 조작, 속임수   predisposition : 경향, 성질   inadequate : 부적합한

☞ ② 읽기를 통한 집중력이 텔레비전 시청에 방해되는 것이 아니라, 오히려 텔레비전 시청을 통해 얻은 감지능력이 독서를 힘들게 한다는 것이 글의 내용이다. 따라서 (A)에는 concentration에는, (B)에는 openness가 맞다.

① 집중력, 연루, 연관
③ 조작, 연루, 연관
④ 조작, 밀폐, 접근
⑤ 자극, 개방성

「읽기는 복잡한 정신 조작을 요구하기 때문에 독자는 텔레비전 시청자보다 더 높은 집중력을 가져야 한다. 청각 전문가들은 "자극에 대한 개방성(감지능력)이 전자매체의 가장 큰 특징이다. 개방성은 청각과 시각적 자극이 곧바로 뇌로 받아들여지도록 한다."라고 말한다. 독서를 통해 향상된 집중력은 텔레비전을 시청하기에는 부적합한 것처럼 보이는 경향이 있다. 그러나 실은 그 반대이다. 오히려, 텔레비전 시청을 통해서 획득된 다양한 자극에 대한 개방성(감지 능력)이 그 사람의 기질로 굳어져서 독서를 하고 글을 쓰는 데에 방해가 된다.」

20 ②

switch : 재빨리 바꾸다   cognition : 인지   reorient : 새로 순응시키다, 재교육하다

☞ ② (A) 멀티태스킹의 반대가 되어야 하므로 일을 하나씩 순차적으로 처리하는 것의 의미인 'sequentially' 이 적당하며, (B) 일을 한꺼번에 묶어서 처리하는 것의 반대가 되어야 하므로 우선순위를 매겨 처리하는 것의 의미인 'prioritize'이 적당하다.

① 동시에, 우선순위를 매기다
③ 순차적으로, 수행하다
④ 무작위로, 소외시키다
⑤ 무작위로, 수행하다

「청소년은 물론 대다수의 성인들도 멀티태스킹이 단시간에 많은 양의 일을 할 수 있는 좋은 방법이라 생각한다. 그러나 과학적 증거는 이러한 믿음이 옳지 않다고 말한다. "사람들이 동시에 두 가지 이상의 일을 하거나 여러 일을 잠깐씩 바꿔가며 할 때, 결과적으로 어느 일도 제대로 해내지 못했다." Michigan 대학의 '뇌 인지와 행동 연구소'의 소장인 David E. Meyer는 말한다. "멀티태스킹을 하는 사람들은 더 많은 실수를 했고 일을 하나씩 순차적으로 했을 때보다 시간도 더 오래 걸렸다." 그는 학생들이 숙제를 하면서 동시에 다른 일을 하려 할 때, 평소보다 400 퍼센트 이상 오래 걸릴 수 있다고 말한다. 왜 이런 일이 발생할까? 우리의 뇌는 단순히 여러 작업들을 묶어서 처리하지 않는다. 대신 뇌는 일의 우선순위를 매긴다. 따라서 우리가 음악을 들으면서 책을 읽을 때, 우리의 뇌는 먼저 음악에 집중할 것이고 음악이 끝난 후에야 책의 내용들을 받아들인다. 그러나 여러 일을 번갈아가며 집중하면서 뇌는 많은 에너지를 소비해야 한다. 결국, 어느 쪽도 효과적으로 해내지 못하는 것이다.」

21 ④

equivocal : 다의적인, 이중적인, 모호한   distinguish : 구별하다   recurrent : 반복되는

☞ ④ (A) 텔레비전의 이중적 면모에 대해 서술되어야 한다. 가족의 화합의 반대말인 '흩어지는'이라는 뜻의 'dispersing'이 적당하다. (B) 텔레비전의 문제점이 장점을 상쇄한다는 내용이므로, 'counterbalances' 가 적당하다.

① 모이는, 유지하다
② 모이는, (장점을) 상쇄하다
③ 흩어지는, 강화하다
⑤ 흔들리는, 강화하다

「가족생활에 대한 텔레비전의 기여는 이중적이다. 가족이 흩어지는 것을 막아주었지만, 또 한편으로는 가족의 화합을 방해했다. 가족이 함께 보내는 시간을 모두 텔레비전 시청으로 보내면서, 텔레비전은 가정 내의 관습, 게임, 회자되는 농담, 친숙한 노래, 공유하는 활동과 같은 한 가정 고유의 특성들을 모두 파괴시켰다. 그러나 부모들은 텔레비전이 지배하는 가정을 완전히 받아들여서 그 매체가 가족에게 가져다주는 문제점들을 보지 못하고 있다. 심지어 텔레비전 시청을 자제하려 노력하는 가정에서도, 텔레비전의 존재가 유발하는 역효과들은 그것의 장점을 상쇄한다.」

22 ⑤

simplify : 간단화하다   priority : 우선순위

☞ ⑤ (A) 요즘의 추세인 복잡화와는 달리 또 한편에서는 간단화 하자는 움직임이 있다고 소개한다. 따라서 'However'가 적당하다. (B) 단순화 운동을 주창하는 이들에 대해 정리하고 있으므로 'In short'가 적당하다.

① 더구나, 게다가
② 더구나, 즉, 짧게 말하면
③ 그러므로, 게다가
④ 그러나, 유사하게

「19세기의 미국 철학자 Henry David Thoreau는 "간단하게, 더 간단하게!"라는 말로 유명하다. 그러나 오늘날의 추세는 "복잡하게, 더 복잡하게!"인 듯하다. 많은 이들이 다른 어느 때보다 더 많이 일하고 더 많이 낭비하며 더 많이 빚지고 있다. 또한, 이들은 조금 휴식하고 친구, 가족과도 더 적게 함께한다. 하지만, 이와는 반대되는 자발적인 단순화 노력 역시 존재한다. 자발적 단순화를 주창하는 사람들은 스스로의 삶을 좀 더 단순하면서도 즐겁게 만들기 위해 다양한 노력을 기울인다. 어떤 이들은 주중에 일을 조금 덜 한다. 어떤 이들은 정원에 채소를 가꾸는데, 이것들은 유기농 음식을 제공할 뿐만 아니라 공기를 정화해 주고 가족과 함께 보내는 시간을 증대시킨다. 또 다른 이들은 불필요한 물건을 구매하지 않음으로써 소비를 줄인다. 짧게 말해 단순화 운동에 참여하는 이들은 '단순화'라는 Thoreau의 조언을 가장 중시하고 이에 따르는 것이다.」

23 ⑤

ignorance : 무지, 무식   pain-killing drug : 진통제   vaunt : 자랑하다

☞ ⑤ (A) 진통제는 고통을 잊게 해주는 것이므로, 'conceal'이 적절하며, (B) 진통제가 고통 메커니즘을 파괴하는 것이므로, 'deaden'이 적절하다. (C) 고통을 숨기고 억누르는 것을 의미하는 단어가 적절하다.

「고통의 본질에 대한 무지도 문제지만, 더욱 큰 문제는 진통제의 작용 원리에 대한 무지이다. 약효가 선전되는 대부분의 진통제들이 고통의 원인이 되는 상황을 해결하는 대신 고통을 감출 뿐이라는 것을 사람들은 잘 모르고 있다. 몸에 이상이 있다는 것을 뇌에 전달하는 역할을 하는 것이 고통의 역할인데, 진통제는 이러한 메커니즘을 파괴하는 것이다. 고통의 근본 원인을 인지하는 대신 고통을 억누르려고 하는 것은 결과적으로 건강의 파괴라는 큰 대가를 치르게 한다.」

24 ②

the theory of relativity : 상대성이론 father : ~의 아버지가 되다 illuminate : 설명하다, 조명하다

☞ ② (A) 모나리자를 그려낸 생각과 상대성이론을 발명한 생각을 연결시키는 것이므로 '(대량) 생산하다'는 뜻의 'spawned'가 맞다. (B) 천재들의 부모에 대한 연구에는 많은 오류가 있었으므로 아무것도 밝히지 못했다고 할 수 있다. 따라서 'nothing'이 적절하다. (C) 보통 사람들보다 조금 높은 122라는 아이큐 지수를 가지므로 '상당한'의 뜻을 가진 'respectable'을 merely의 수식을 받아쓰는 것이 옳다.

「천재들은 어떻게 아이디어를 생각해낼까? 모나리자를 만들어낸 생각과 상대성이론을 만들어낸 생각은 어떤 공통점이 있을까? 역사 속의 모차르트, 에디슨, 갈릴레오의 생각을 통해 우리는 무엇을 배울 수 있을까? 지난 수십 년간 학자들은 천재들의 전략을 분석하면서 천재들을 이해하려 노력했다. 1904년에 Havelock Ellis는 대부분의 천재들이 30살 이상의 아버지와 25살 이하의 어머니에게서 태어난 병약한 아이들이었다고 발표했다. 그러나 또 다른 학자들은 천재 중에서도 어머니가 없거나(Darwin), 아버지가 없거나(Dickens), 독신인 사람이(Descartes) 있었다고 지적한다. 결국 그 자료는 아무것도 설명하지 못했다. 학회에서는 지능과 천재성의 연관 여부에 대해서도 조사하려 했다. 그러나 평범한 물리학자들의 지능이 노벨상을 받은 엄청난 천재 Richard Feynman의 지능보다 높았는데, 그의 지능은 평균보다 조금 높은 122에 불과했다. 천재들은 일곱 살에 14개국의 언어를 구사하는 이들도 아니었고 특별히 더 똑똑한 이들도 아니었다. 창의성이라는 것은 지능과 일치하는 것이 아니다.」

25 ④

meditation : 명상 skeptic : 회의론자 adherent : 지지자 relapse : 재발 psychiatry : 정신 의학

☞ ④ (A) 명상의 효과에 대해 실체적인 증거들을 발견하고 있는 의미의 'tangible'이 적절하며, (B) 남편의 죽음이 우울증을 유발한 것이므로 'triggered'이 적절하다. (C) CBT를 발명하고 조직한 박사에 대한 설명이므로 '선구자'라는 의미의 'pioneers'이 적절하다.

「과학자들은 명상이 뇌에 실체적인 영향을 끼친다는 증거를 발견하고 있다. 회의론자들은 현대 삶의 스트레스들을 명상으로 푸는 것이 실용적인 방법이 아니라 비판한다. 그러나 명상의 지지자들이 그 믿음을 자연과학적 기술로 설명하지 못하던 시대는 지났다. Carol Cattley의 경우, 남편이 죽은 후 10대 이후 나타나지 않던 우울증이 재발했다. Carol은 의학의 도움을 구했고 약물과 '인지 행동 치료(CBT)'라 불리는 심리 치료를 통해 병을 치료할 수 있었는데, 이 심리치료는 주요 과정으로 명상을 포함하는 것이다. CBT의 선구자인 옥스퍼드 대학의 정신 의학자 Mark Williams는 CBT가 80%의 명상과 20%의 인지치료로 구성된다고 설명한다.」

26 ③

ingenuity : 창의력 substitute : 대체재 exponential : 기하급수적인

☞ 환경 비관론자들은 인간의 생활이 지구의 수용 범위를 초과해 발달하고 있고 이에 따라 지구가 파괴된다고 주장한다. 따라서 ③ upgrading을 '격하시키다, 타락시키다'라는 의미의 'degrading'으로 바꿔야 한다.

「인구와 환경문제의 심각성과 그에 대한 대책에 대해 전문가들의 생각은 엇갈린다. 어떤 이들은 인간의 창의력과 기술의 진보가 오염을 수용 가능한 수준으로 해결하고 부족한 자원에 대한 대체재를 개발하게 할 것이라 주장한다. 그들은 기술 낙관론자로, 기술 혁신을 통해 지구의 천연 자원을 보존할 수 있다고 믿는다. 그러나 대부분의 일류 환경학자들은 이에 대해 동의하지 않는다. 그들은 인간이 만든 주요 환경적·사회적 진보에 대해 찬사를 보내지만, 또 한편으로는 인간이 지구의 생명 유지 시스템들을 기하급수적인 속도로 파괴하고 있다는 증거를 제시한다. 그들은 지구 생명체 모두의 생명과 인간 경제를 보호하는 천연 자원들을 지키기 위해 더 많은 노력이 필요하다고 주장한다. 그들은 환경 비관론자로, 지구 환경이 악화되고 있고 세계경제가 지구의 수용 능력을 초과해 성장하고 있다고 주장한다.」

27 ②

juvenile delinquency : 청소년 비행 lucrative : 수지가 맞는 unremit : 용서받지 못하다 variant : 변수, 변화

☞ ② 50년대에 청소년 비행 영화에 대해 대중들이 우려와 압박을 보냈다는 이야기를 하고 있으므로,
   "challenges for the juvenile delinquency films in the 50's"이 적절하다.

   ① 50년대 영화 제작 환경
   ③ 50년대 비행청소년 영화의 도덕적 원칙
   ④ 50년대 비행청소년 영화의 성장과 소멸
   ⑤ 이익이 되는 장사였던 50년대의 비행청소년 영화

「1950년대 비행청소년에 대한 쏟아지는 지나친 우려는 영화를 통해 잘 알 수 있다. 비행청소년에 대한 묘사는 위험하지만 수지가 맞는 장사였다. 영화에 대한 대중적 관심이 시들해지는 시점에서 부모, 육아업체, 선생님, 청소년들, 사법관계자들이 거대한 관객층이 되어주는 비행 영화가 인기를 끈 것이다. 그러나 비행을 저지른 청소년에게 영화가 좋은 예가 되어야 한다는 대중의 압박이 거셌기 때문에 이 주제는 다루기 매우 위험했다. 더구나 대중문화가 비행을 야기한다는 비난은 당시의 관심을 반영한 것이었다. 만약 영화가 비행청소년이라는 주제를 다루고자 한다면, 매우 조심스럽게 진행되어야 한다는 것이다. 영화는 비행을 우호적으로 표현할 수 없었다. 따라서 모든 줄거리는 도덕적 세계관이라는 코드를 가져야 했다. 그러나 성공을 위해서 영화는 젊은 층으로부터 공감을 이끌어내야 했다. 그리고 이 젊은 층은 비행을 하나의 변화쯤으로 여기는 새로운 문화로부터 많은 영향을 받은 사람들이었다.」

28 ③

rigorous : 격렬한, 심한 assure : 설득하다 mercilessly : 자비 없이

☞ ③ 연습을 게을리 해도 괜찮다는 악마의 유혹에 넘어간 것이므로 '질질 끌다, 지연시키다'는 뜻의
   'procrastination'이 적절하다.

   ① 경쟁심 ② 집착 ④ 동요 ⑤ fastidiousness 까다로움

「10월 말쯤, 나는 공연을 위해 연습을 시작했다. 처음에는 연습 일정이 심하지 않아서 내 생활에 큰 무리를 주지 않았다. 그런데 그 시점에서 공연에 대해 걱정할 게 전혀 없다는 악마의 속삼임이 들렸다. 나는 그만 그 유혹에 넘어가고 말았는데, 1월 공연은 그 당시로서는 너무나 먼 얘기 같았기 때문이다. 그러나 연습 과정에 포함되는 세부적인 마감 시간들이 살금살금 다가와 머리를 들이밀고 나를 무자비하게 몰아치기 시작한 것은 그리 먼 훗날의 이야기가 아니었다. 벌써 크리스마스가 코앞이었고 공부해야 할 것들과 연습해야 할 것들이 모여 엄청난 책임감을 주고 있었다. 주어진 의무들은 나를 자비 없이 몰아치고 있었고 나는 1월 공연의 데드라인을 맞추기 힘들 것이라는 생각을 하며 악마가 나를 보고 낄낄 비웃고 있을지 모른다는 생각을 했다. 처음엔 큰 소리로 악마를 저주했다. 하지만 곧 이번 경험을 통해 내게 필요한 것은 마감 기한을 객관적으로 바라보고 악마에게 넘어가지 않도록 스스로를 관리하는 일이라는 사실을 깨닫게 되었다.」

29 ⑤

straightforward : 간단한 yardstick : 지표 suspense : 긴장감

☞ '외국어로 된 책을 선택하는 데에 있어서 가장 중요한 요소는 언어의 난이도가 아니라 _____이다.'에 들어갈 빈칸을 채워야 한다. 글에서는 재미와 긴장감 같은 동기들이 중요하다고 언급하고 있으므로 '동기를 제공함으로써 독자의 참여를 유도한다.'는 의미의 ⑤ stimulate the readers' involvement by providing incentives가 적절하다.

① 독자가 언어의 장벽을 극복하는 것을 돕는다.
② 사람들의 근본적 문제들에 대해 이야기한다.
③ 책을 읽는 데 소요되는 독자들의 시간과 노력을 정당화한다.
④ 외국어를 배우는 데에 신선한 통찰력을 제공한다.

「문학 작품의 언어가 간단하다면, 이것은 도움이 될 것이나 그 자체로서 외국 언어로 된 작품을 선택하는 일에 중요 지표가 되지는 못할 것이다. 흥미, 매력, 그리고 관련성이 더 중요하다. 외국의 언어로 된 작품을 이해하기 위해 드는 부가적인 시간과 노력을 정당화하기 위해서는 특별한 동기들이 존재해야 한다. 재미, 긴장감, 주제에 대한 신선한 통찰력이 독자들의 마음에 와 닿아야 한다. 이러한 동기들이 있어야 독자는 언어의 벽을 열성적으로 극복할 수 있는 것이다. 그렇지 않으면 다른 언어로 책을 읽는 것은 너무 어려운 일이다.」

30 ④

poultry : (닭 따위의) 가금류 minimize : 축소하다 consumption : 소비

☞ Red meat의 소비는 꾸준히 줄어들고 있는데 ④에서는 소비가 줄어드는 음식이 없다고 했으므로 도표의 내용과 일치하지 않는다.

「위의 그래프는 1970년부터 2000년까지의 음식 소비의 변화를 보여준다. 채소와 과일에 대한 소비는 30년 동안 20% 이상 증가했다. 소양고기와 가금 소비의 격차는 2000년에 들어 줄어들었다. 치즈의 소비는 꾸준히 증가한 반면 생선의 소비는 30년 동안 거의 일정하다. 이 기간 동안 어떠한 음식의 소비도 줄어들지는 않았다. 2000년 미국인들의 평균적인 과일과 채소 소비는 다른 어떤 음식보다 많다.」

31 ⑤

flock : 뭉치다 solitary : 외로운, 개별적인 incubate : (알을) 품다

☞ ⑤ 마지막 문장에서 확인할 수 있다.

① Whistling Swan의 부리는 검은색이다.
② Whistling Swan의 이름은 울음소리가 아닌 날갯짓 할 때 나는 소리에서 유래되었다.
③ Whistling Swan은 둥지를 연못이나 강가에 짓는다.
④ Whistling Swan의 암컷은 수컷의 도움을 받아 새끼들을 보살핀다.

「Whistling Swan은 온몸이 하얀 우아하고 아름다운 새로, 오직 부리와 발만 검다. 이름이 의미하는 바는 새가 내는 낮고 멜로디 있는 소리가 아니고, 날갯짓을 할 때 나는 소리를 딴 것이다. Whistling Swan은 믿을 수 없게도 3,725 마일을 날아서 이주한다. 이주 동안에는 모두 모여 이동하지만, 그들은 원래 느린 흐름의 강가나 연못 주위에 개별적으로 둥지를 만든다. 가장 좋은 둥지들은 세대를 거쳐 내려오면서 계속 이용된다. 암컷은 네다섯 개의 알을 낳고 수컷의 도움을 받아 한 달 정도 알을 품는다. 알이 부화하면 암컷과 수컷 모두가 새끼를 보살펴 식량이 있는 곳으로 유도한다. 새끼는 부화 후 두세 달이 지나면 날 수 있지만, 첫 겨울은 부모와 함께 보낸다.」

32 ③

wage : 수행하다 succumb : 굴복하다 stuff : 막다, 채워넣다 transform : 바꾸다

☞ ③ Ulysses와 그의 선원들은 사이렌보다 오르페우스의 노래가 달콤해서 사이렌의 유혹을 이겨낼 수 있었다.

　① 두 번째 문장에 평화를 위해 노력하는 것이 중요하다고 나와있다.

　② 사이렌의 유혹에서 벗어나기 위해 돛대에 몸을 묶은 것은 Ulysses이다.

　④ 오르페우스의 노래는 평화를 상징한다.

　⑤ 핵무기 경쟁에서 벗어나 인류 평화를 위해 인간의 천재성을 발휘하는 것이 옳다.

「"전쟁을 하면 안 돼요!"라고 말하는 것은 부족하다. 그러자면 평화에 대한 사랑과 그를 위한 희생이 요구된다. 우리는 전쟁의 박멸에만 초점을 둘 것이 아니라 평화의 확보를 위해서 힘써야 한다. Ulysses and the Sirens에 대한 흥미로운 이야기가 그리스 문학에 담겨 있다. Siren들은 달콤하게 노래를 불러 선원들을 자신의 섬으로 오게끔 하는 능력을 가지고 있었다. 많은 선박들이 바위에 충돌했고 선원들은 그들의 집과 의무와 명예를 잊고 노래에 빠져들었다. Siren들은 이들을 팔로 감싸안아 바다 깊은 곳으로 이끌어 죽게 만들었다. Ulysses는 Siren들에게 굴복하지 않으리라 다짐했다. 우선, 그는 자신의 몸을 돛대에 묶고 자신의 선원들에게 왁스로 귀를 막으라고 명령했다. 그러나 그와 선원들은 그들을 지키기 위한 보다 현명한 방법을 깨달았다. 그들은 Siren의 음악보다 더 아름다운 노래를 부르는 Orpheus를 배에 태웠다. Orpheus가 노래를 한다면 누가 굳이 Siren의 노래를 들으려 하겠는가? 우리는 평화를 의미하는 아름다운 음악과 조화로운 멜로디가 전쟁의 부조화보다 우월하다는 것을 알아야 한다. 어떻게든 우리는 누구도 승자가 될 수 없는 핵무기 전쟁에서 벗어나 인류 전체에 평화와 번영이라는 현실을 제공하기 위한 목적을 향한 발전적인 경쟁을 시작해야 한다.」

33 ②

cluster : 묶음, 다발 light year : 광년 naked eye : 맨눈 faint : 희미한

☞ ② Pleiades의 나이는 태양의 1/50 정도이다.

「Messier 45라고도 알려진 Pleiades는 가장 이른 시기에 생성된 성단들 중 하나이다. Kenneth Glyn Jones에 따르면, 역사상 처음으로 이 성단이 기록된 것은 Homer의 Iiad (about 750 B.C.)와 Odyssey (about 720 B.C.)를 통해서였다. Pleiades의 별들은 1억년 정도 전에 생성된 것이라 추측되는데, 이는 태양의 나이의 1/50 정도이다. 425광년이나 떨어져 잇지만, 적어도 6개의 별이 육안으로 관찰 가능하고 어두운 밤에는 12개 이상까지도 관찰할 수 있다. 현대의 관측 기술을 통해 Pleiades에는 500개 이상의 희미한 별들이 존재한다는 것이 밝혀졌고 그 범위가 (달 직경의 네 배에 이르는) 2도에 걸쳐있다는 사실이 확인되었다. 다른 개방된 성운에 비하면 별들이 빽빽이 배열된 편은 아니다. 이는 Pleiades 성운의 수명이 낮은 이유 중 하나이다.」

34 ④

인지하지 못하는 특권을 가지고 어디까지 일을 할 수 있는가에 대해서 깨닫고 난 후, 남성들의 억압이 대개 무의식 속에서 나온다는 것을 이해했다. 그리고 유색인 여성들이 그들이 만난 백인 여성이 억압적이라고 종종 비난했던 것이 기억났다. 나는 왜 우리가 우릴 그렇게 보지 않을 때도 당연하듯 억압적으로 보이는지 이해하기 시작했다. 나는 내가 노력하지 않고 얻은 피부색에서 오는 특권을 즐길 방법을 생각하기 시작했고 그것에 대해 망각하기까지 이르렀다. 학교 교육은 나에게 스스로를 억압하는 사람으로, 부당하게 해택받는 사람으로, 또는 망가진 문화의 참여자로 바라보는 것을 가르쳐주지 않았다. 나는 스스로를 도덕적 의식은 개인의 도덕적 의지에 달려있다고 생각하는 사람으로 생각하도록 배웠다. 교육은 나의 동료 Elisabeth Minnich가 지적했던 형식을 따랐다. 백인들은 자신들의 삶이 도덕적으로 중립이고 규범적이며 평균이고 또한 이상적이라고 생각하도록 배웠고, 그래서 백인들이 다른 사람들을 유익하게 할 때, 이는 "그들"이 좀 더 "우리"와 같도록 하는 것처럼 보인다.

35 ①

hardworking : 열심히 일하는 low-paid : 저임금의

☞ 이주 노동자들의 역할을 인정하고 있다. '가치를 인정하는, 감사하는'이라는 의미의 ① appreciating이 적절하다.

② 냉소적인   ③ 무관심한   ④ 거만한   ⑤ 꺼리는

「십년 전에 south Dallas에 사는 Jefferson Boulevard는 빈 점포가 많은 도시 내부 구역에서 식사를 했다. 오늘 날, 거기에는 800개의 점포들이 있고 근처 도로의 3/4은 이주 1세, 2세인 히스패닉 인이 차지하고 있다. "그들은 일을 하는 것에 매우 굶주려있다." Jefferson Area 연합의 대표 Jefferson Area Association는 말한다. 사회학자 Kasarda "이는 사회 전체에 엄청난 영향을 줄 것이다."라고 덧붙인다. 이주자들은 낮은 임금에도 근면 성실하게 일함으로써 현대 서비스 경제가 작동하는 데에 큰 역할을 했다. 많은 도시에서, 이주노동력이 없다면 호텔, 레스토랑, 보육시설과 같은 사업들은 큰 문제를 겪을 것이다.」

36 ③

literally : 문자 그대로 avalanche : 산사태 pulverize : 분쇄하다

☞ 앞뒤 문맥을 파악했을 때, 어느 것도 기후에 대해서는 언급하지 않고 있다. 따라서 'There is no doubt that the activity of Mount St. Helens has influenced our climate'는 내용과 무관한 문장이다.

「5월 18일 아침 8시 32분, St. Helens산은 말 그대로 산꼭대기가 날아가버렸다. 갑자기, 이 산은 전보다 1300 피트 낮아졌다. 동시에 Richter 강도 5의 지진이 발생했다. 이 지진은 눈과 얼음이 결합된 딱딱한 바위형태의 산사태를 야기했다. 200m/h의 속도로, 응고된 화산 가스와 바위 이물질이 화산의 측면으로부터 수평적으로 뿜어져 나왔다. (St. Helens산이 기후에 영향을 미친 것은 당연하다.) 미끄러지는 얼음과 눈이 녹으면서, 뿜어져 나오며 모든 것을 초토화시켰던 진흙과 파편들의 급류도 씻겨 내려갔다. 분쇄된 바위들이 먼지 구름을 형성해 대기 중으로 들어갔다. 결국 재와 가스의 구름과 함께 용암이 화산의 새로운 분화구를 덮었다.」

37 ④

theorize : 이론화하다 camouflage : 위장하다 vegetation : 식생

☞ Giganotosaurus의 피부색을 추측하는 과정을 담은 글이다. ④에서 치아 조직은 피부색과 무관하며 이는 뼈를 통해 알 수 있는 것으로 추측의 대상은 아니다.

「남겨진 Giganotosaurus의 뼈는 피부조직을 보여주지 못하기 때문에, 과학자들은 이들의 피부색에 대한 이론을 세워야 했다. 과학자들은 이 공룡의 색에 대해 근거 있는 추측을 하고자 노력했다. Giganotosaurus가 작은 동물을 먹잇감으로 삼았으므로, 이들의 색깔은 주변 환경과 어울려 위장하기 좋은 색이어야 했을 것이다. Giganotosaurus는 지금의 Argentina에 살았는데, 이곳은 아프리카의 사바나와 같이 풀이 많은 습지대였다. (이들은 초식 공룡보다 훨씬 큰 이빨을 가졌다.) 그러므로 이 공룡들은 주변의 식생들의 색과 가까운 색을 피부색으로 가졌을 확률이 높다.」

38 ③

take turns : 교대로 하다   redeem : 다시 생각하다   diversified : 다양화

☞ ③ 필자는 다수라는 권력에 대한 비판적 시각을 가지고 있다. 따라서 '다수는 효율성을 위해 고정되어야 한다.'는 의미의 'The majority should not be shifting, but fixed for effectiveness.'는 필자가 주장하는 민주적인 방법이라 할 수 없고 결국 부적절한 추론이다.

　① 필자는 다수라는 권력을 비판적으로 바라본다.

　② 다수가 지배하되 위압하지 않는 것이 바람직하다.

　④ '번갈아 하기' 시스템에서는 소수에게도 기회가 주어지기 때문에 소수자들도 활발히 참여할 수 있다.

　⑤ 독재정치는 왕이나 황제에게서만 나오는 것이 아니라, 다수가 지배하는 민주사회에서도 출현할 수 있다는 것이 필자의 생각이다.

「정치적사회적 차이를 인식할 때 '번갈아 하기'는 구성원의 동의를 얻고자 하는 것으로, 이 방법은 모두의 참여를 가능케 한다. '번갈아 하기' 접근법은 더 많은 지지자들이 있는 입장에 더 많은 기회를 주지만 또한 소수에게 인정받는 입장이라도 그들 개인의 관점이 표현될 수 있도록 한다. 나는 민주주의가 권력에 의한 지배를 옹호해야 한다고 생각하지 않는다. 다수라는 권력 역시 마찬가지이다. 대신, 민주주의는 스스로 평등하다고 생각하는 주체들이 공동의 포부를 이루기 위한 공정한 토론을 전제해야 한다. 이 전제를 다시 생각해보면, 우리는 의견 발표에 '번갈아 하기'라는 생각을 사용해야 한다. 특히 다양한 시민들이 존재하는 21세기에 들어서 이 접근법은 독재가 아닌 다수의 지배 시스템 하에서 투표와 발표가 성공적이냐 아니냐를 결정짓는 중요한 요소이다.」

39 ⑤

palm : 야자수   sap : 수액   savory : 맛있는

☞ ⑤ 다양한 맛의 음식을 먹으면서 인생의 행복과 지혜를 기원하는 인도의 풍습에 대한 글이므로 'Food for Luck and Wisdom in India'이 적절하다.

　① 인도 전통음식 요리법

　② 인도의 새해맞이 축제

　③ 음식과 건강의 관계

　④ 인도의 기쁨과 고통이라는 요소

「Classic Indian Cooking의 저자 Julie Sahni에 따르면, 10월 말에 인도해서 행해지는 신년 맞이 축제는 하나의 음식에 집중하는 것이 아니라 다양한 맛의 균형에 초점을 맞춘다. 쌀 반죽, 코코넛, 우유, 야자수액으로 요리되는 Appam은 barifi라 불리는 퍼지와 함께 대접된다. 그러나 Sahni는 닭고기 카레 수프(숙취에 좋은 음식)와 달면서 매운 초록 망고 처트니 같은 음식 역시도 요리된다고 말한다. 신년 맞이 축제 음식은 반드시 달면서 맛있고, 동시에 시고 매운 맛을 포함해야 하기 때문이다. "다양한 맛을 가진 음식을 먹는 것은 우리의 삶에 기쁨과 고통이라는 다양한 요소들이 주어지기를, 이러한 요소들을 우리가 기쁘게 받아들이기를 바라는 마음에서 비롯된 것이다."라고 Sahni는 이야기한다.」

40 ③

unforseen : 예측하기 어려운 varmint : 유해동물 endangered : 위험에 처한

☞ ③ 생물학적 다양성을 지켜내자는 것이 글의 요지이다. 따라서 'Maintenance of Biological Diversity'가
적절하다.

　① 위험에 처한 여러 생물종들

　② California Condor을 어떻게 지켜낼 방법

　④ 환경학자들의 접근법의 문제점

　⑤ 불쾌감을 주는 동물들을 지키는 법

「Mr. Halle은 유해동물까지 지켜내는 삶의 다양성을 사람들이 이해하고 도와주기란 어렵다는 사실을 안다. "우리가 지키기
위해 애쓴 모든 종류의 생물들이 있다. 환경학자들이 잘못하고 있는 것은 특정 종의 중요성만을 강조한다는 것이다. 수많은
이들이 캘리포니아로 향하죠. 제가 아는 한 더 절실한 도움이 필요한 곳이 있는데도 말에요." 그럼에도 불구하고 그는 생물학
적 다양성이 중요하고 인류는 생물들이 멸종했을 때 야기될 결과에 대해 염려해야 한다고 말한다. 설령 그것이 혐오감을 불러
일으킨다 해도, 모든 것은 필요가 있다. Jonathan Swift는 '벼룩은 그보다 더 작은 벼룩을 먹고 연명하죠. 그 작은 벼룩도
먹이를 찾아요. 이 사슬은 무한히 지속되죠.'라고 말한다. 결국 어떠한 생명체를 잃는다는 것은 이 거대한 먹이 사슬을 손상시
켜 예측하기 어려운 피해를 야기할 것이다.」

41 ③

defile : 더럽히다 extraordinary : 특별한 endow : 부여하다

☞ ③ 먼저 시각이 카메라를 통해 이용된 것이 나와야 하므로 (B)를 넣는다. 카메라의 거짓에 대한 내용이
이어지므로 그 뒤에는 (C)가 맞고, 마지막으로는 사진가에 대한 내용이므로 (A)가 되어야 한다.

「인간이 태어난 이래 시각은 중요한 감각으로 이용되어 왔고 오랜 시간 시각적 예술로도 빛을 발했다. 백 년 조금 넘게, 시각은
카메라를 통해서도 이용되었다.

(B) 잘 사용된다면, 카메라는 우리의 시각을 발전시키는 데에 특유의 큰 역량을 발휘한다. 그러나 잘못 사용된다면, 우리의
능력을 파괴하는 것도 사실이다. 이제 "카메라는 거짓말을 하지 않는다."라는 말이 얼마나 말도 안 되는 소리인지는 대부
분이 알 것이다.

(C) 그러나 카메라가 얼마나 뛰어난 거짓말쟁이인지를 많은 사람들이 알 것인가는 의문이 남는다. 카메라는 단지 기계일 뿐이고
사진가의 눈과 마음과 정신과 사진기술이 사진을 진실성을 좌우한다.

(A) 상대적으로 굉장히 적은 사진가만이 이러한 능력을 제대로 부여받았기 때문에, 그 결과는 대부분 안타까울 뿐이다. 지난
10~15년 간 카메라가 수천의 눈들을 타락시켰다는 것은 상당히 잘 남겨져 있는 사실이다.」

non-mainstream : 비주류의   conversely : 역으로

「최근 몇 년 동안, '타자'라는 용어는 차이, 다양성, 선입견, 인종차별에 대한 토론에서 가장 흔히 등장하는 단어가 되었다. 간혹 '타자'라는 단어는 이상하게 쓰이기도 한다. 너는 '다르게 될 수 있다. – 이 말은, 당신이 보통의 어떤 것보다 적고 작은 '다른' 범주의 포함될 수 있음을 의미한다. 주로, 주류가 아닌 소수집단에 속한 이들이 '타자화 되었다'고 표현된다. 그러나 편견과 선입견에 의해 차별 대우 받는 모든 이들에게도 이 단어를 사용할 수 있을 것이다. 우리 모두는 타자가 되었던 경험이 있다. 그러나 어떠한 집단들은 구조적으로 장시간 타자로 분류되었다. 타자들은 우리가 서로의 정체성을 어떻게 대우해야 하는지를 알려준다. 인종, 성, 민족, 종교, 문화의 부정당성에 대한 토론에서 이 용어는 단순히 선입견 이상의 것을 보여주는 것으로 매우 큰 의미가 있다. 선입견을 갖는다는 것은 어떤 것에 대해 싫어하고 부정적인 감정을 가진다는 것을 의미한다. 역으로 우리는 어떤 것에 대해 우호적인 선입견을 가질 수도 있다. 예를 들어 운동을 좋아하는 사람은 자신이 응원하는 운동 팀에 대해 좋은 선입견을 가질 것이다. 그러나 타인을 타자로 본다는 것은 우리 자신과는 완전히 다른 범주로 그를 보는 것이고, 더욱 중대하게는 우리보다 열등한 존재로 본다는 것이다.」

42   ④

☞ 타자화란 단순히 타인을 싫어하는 것이 아니라 우리보다 열등한 존재를 평가한다는 문제점을 가진다. 따라서 '~보다 열등한'이라는 뜻의 'inferior to'가 적절하다.

① 제한적으로   ② ~와 다른   ③ 동등한   ⑤ ~보다 더한

43   ⑤

☞ 긍정적 또는 부정적 의미로 사용될 수 있는 것은 선입견이다.

sophisticated : 정교한   battleplan : 전투전략   spirit : 몰래 데려오다   tight-knit : 촘촘한   slap : 때리다

「수 천 시간을 호주 해변의 청백돌고래의 행동 관찰에 보낸 연구자들은 수컷 돌고래들이 다른 어떤 비사육 동물보다도 정교한 사회적 연대를 갖는다는 사실을 발견했다. 제3의 무리에 맞서기 위해 하나의 수컷 돌고래 무리는 다른 돌고래 무리와 연합한다. 과학자들에 따르면, 이러한 전투전략은 실행되는 데에 상당한 수준의 정신 계산 능력을 요구한다고 한다. 그런데 이러한 복잡한 사회적 연대는 명랑한 성격만을 가지지는 않는다. 수컷들은 경쟁 무리들로부터 출산력 있는 암컷을 빼앗기 위해 결탁한다.

암컷을 몰래 데려오는 데에 성공한 후에도 수컷들은 위협적인 장관의 무리를 연출하면서 암컷이 무리에 머물러 있도록 촘촘히 모여 있다. 하나의 암컷을 두셋의 수컷이 둘러싸고 뛰고 활강하고 재주넘기를 하는데, 모든 동작들은 동시에 행해진다.

만약 암컷이 이러한 동작에 감명받지 않아 도망가려 한다면, 수컷은 암컷을 따라와 물고 지느러미로 암컷을 때리며 억지로 성교를 맺는다. 과학자들은 암컷을 지배하는 이러한 행위를 'herding'이라 이름 붙였지만, 그 이름이 행동의 공격성을 전달하지 못한다는 한계점을 알고 있다.」

44 ⑤

☞ 청백돌고래들의 사회적 연대에 대한 설명이 나와야하므로 (D)가 (A) 다음에 위치한다. 암컷을 뺏기 위한 노력이 서술되었으므로 뺏은 후 수컷의 움직임에 대해 설명하는 (C)가 나오고 그 뒤에 암컷의 반항 시 수컷의 대응을 보여주는 (B)가 나오는 것이 적절하다.

45 ②

☞ 돌고래들이 짝짓기를 할 때 쓰는 교묘한 방법에 대해 보여주므로, '구애 시 돌고래들의 교활한 과시 행동'을 뜻하는 'Dolphins Display Cunning in Courtship'이 적절하다.
   ① 돌고래 암컷과 수컷의 상호 의존 관계
   ③ 돌고래의 성 차이
   ④ 자신의 짝인 암컷을 위협하는 수컷 돌고래
   ⑤ 위험에 빠진 종들의 멋진 행동들

46 ⑤

☞ 돌고래 여러 마리가 함께 모여 구애를 성공시키므로 'social alliances'이 적절하다.
   ① 이타적 연합
   ② 매력적인 기술
   ③ 연령 집단
   ④ 방해되는 관계

47 48

workplace : 일터   accusation : 비난   discriminatrion : 차별   first-rate : 일류의

「이론이 어떻건, 실제 노동환경에서 생물학적 무능과 자연적 선호는 차별에 대한 비난을 반박할 때 주로 이용되는 반론 근거들이다. Harvard University의 학장인 Larry Summers은 경쟁이 차별을 불합리하게 만든다고 주장한다. 전 분야에서 차별이 만연하다면, 여성이 사회에 나와서는 안 된다는 데에 의견이 일치한다면 사실 차별은 문제가 되지 않을 것이다. 경쟁의 위험이 확실하지 않은 경우 역시 마찬가지다. 북서부 대학들이 아이비리그의 대학들이 멍청히 놓쳤던 일류 여학생들을 입학시키면서 대학을 발전시키는 것이 아이비리그의 대학들을 자극하는 것은 오래 걸릴 것이다. 일터에서의 여성과 소수자의 역사는 강력한 차별 금지법을 제정하는 것이 평등을 위한 진보를 가져온다는 것을 알 수 있다. 결국, 부와 명예를 고려할 때, 하버드는 여성을 위해 지구상의 다른 어떤 대학과도 충분히 경쟁할 능력이 있다. 그렇다면, 왜 하버드는 그렇게 하지 않는가?」

47 ④

☞ Northwestern대학은 이제 우수한 여학생들을 받아들이며 개선을 꾀하고 있다.

48 ②

☞ (A) 문장 뒷부분에 있는 '생물학적 능력의 결핍, 자연적 선호'을 받아 실제와 이론이 다르다는 것을 보여주므로, 'biological incapacity and natural preference'이 적절하다. (B) 아이비리그의 대학들이 받아들이지 않은 우수한 여학생들을 Northwestern 대학이 받아들였다. 따라서 'Ivies'가 적절하다.

49 50

interdependence : 상호의존 interpretation : 해석, 설명 conquest : 정복 inconsistency : 불일치 downplay : 경
시하다 bolster : 지지하다

「최근 보고서 "하나의 국가, 많은 인종들 : 문화 상호 의존성의 선언"에서 교사와 교수로 구성된 위원회는 공립학교가 다문화 교육을
실시하기를 추천한다. 무슨 말이냐 하면, 보고서는 미국이 다양한 민족 배경에 의해 성립되고 유지되고 있으며 미국의 역사는 계속되
는 발견과 과거의 해석으로 이루어진다는 것, 세상을 보는 방법은 하나가 아니라는 진리를 알아야 한다고 주장하는 것이다.
따라서 백인들의 서부 이동은 단순히 길들여지지 않은 야생에 대한 영웅적 정복일 수 있지만 한 편으로는 토착민에 대한 정복이라고
볼 수도 있는 것이다. 이주자는 백인만 있는 것이 아니고 아시아인도 될 수 있다. 흑인들은 단지 북부 백인에 의해 해방된 수동적인
노예가 아니고 그들 자신의 자유를 위해 싸운 적극적인 투쟁자들이다.
특히, 보고서에 따르면 교육 과정은 아이들이 '미국의 이상과 사회현실 간 불일치의 이유에 대해 비판적으로 평가하도록 가르쳐야
한다. 교육은 아이들이 현실이 이상에 다가가는 것에 기여할 수 있도록 정보와 지적 장치들을 제공해야 한다. 바꿔 말하면, 아이들에
게 실제로 어떤 일이 일어났는지를 보여주고 어떻게 하면 국가의 상황을 개선시킬 수 있는지 알리라는 것이다. 얼마나 애국적인가?
몇몇 구성원들은 다문화 교육이 채택되면 미국이 민족 갈등에 따라 분열될 것이라 반대한다. 그들은 위원회의 보고서가 민족성에
집중한 대가로 국가적 통합을 손상시켰다고 주장한다.
그러나 민족성을 경시하는 것이 국가 통합을 지지하지는 않을 것이다. 미국의 역사는 그 많은 사람들이 어째서, 어떻게 각지로부터
미국으로 이주해왔는지를 말해준다. 또한, 역사를 통해 우리는 그들이 더 나은 삶을 위해 얼마나 노력했는지, 어떻게 나라를 개선시켜
나갔는지를 엿볼 수 있다. 이러한 과정을 통해 그들은 서로 다른 그들 스스로를 모두 미국인이라 부르게 된 것이다.」

49 ①

☞ 역사를 보는 다양한 시각이라는 내용을 이어 (E)가 나오고 그 내용을 심화시켜 특히 교육과정에서 사회를
바라보는 시각에 대한 교육을 할 것을 주장하는 (C)가 이어진다. 그러나 이에 대한 반대의견도 존재하므
로 (B)를 넣어 반론을 확인하고, (D)를 통해 재반론하여 글의 논지를 강화한다.

50 ④

☞ 백인의 이주는 영웅적으로 볼 수도 있으나 한 편으로는 토착민에 대한 정복으로 볼 수도 있다는 내용이
본문에 언급되어 있다.
① 위원회의 모든 구성원들이 다문화교육과정의 도입에 동의한 것이 아니라 반대자들도 있었다.
② 이상과 실제의 괴리에 대한 교육을 하자고 주장하고 있다.
③ 마지막 문단을 통해 어긋남을 확인할 수 있다.
⑤ 흑인노예는 북 백인에 의해 해방되었을 뿐 아니라 스스로 해방을 위해 싸웠다.

01 ①

reserved : ~의 역할이었다, ~가 맡았다   retained : 유지하고 있는, 보유하고 있는

① 유지(보유)하는 ② 예약된 ③ 수정된 ④ 교체된 ⑤ 중단된

「Wagner(바그너)의 The Ring of the Nibelungs(니벨룽겐의 반지)는 오페라 전체가 가곡조라는 점이 특이하다. 또한 그의 오페라는 작곡가 자신이 직접 대본을 쓴다는 점이 색다르다. 대본 작곡은 보통 시인이나 문학계 명사가 맡는다.」

02 ⑤

odoriferous : 냄새나는   stinky : 구린 악취가 나는

① 해로운 ② 헛된 ③ 자연 분해되는 ④ 귀중한 ⑤ 악취가 나는

「본래 쓰레기 위기는 사람들이 농경지에 처음 정착하고 쓰레기가 지나치게 많아져도 주거지를 떠날 수 없을 때 일어났다. 그 후로, 모든 사회는 보통 악취가 나는 것들을 폐기하는 데 문제를 겪어 왔다.」

03 ①

belligerent : 적대적인, 공격적인   hostile : 적대적인

① 적대적인 ② 건방진 ③ 무관심한 ④ 사교적인 ⑤ 부도덕적인

「Michael은 매우 유능한 판매원이었다. 그는 에스키모들에게도 냉장고를 팔 수 있었다. 그러나 단체 프로젝트에서 Michael의 적대적인 태도는 그의 상사가 어찌할 바를 모르게 했다.」

04 ⑤

'rickety'는 '곧 무너질 듯한'이라는 뜻을 갖고 있다. 따라서 '불안정한, 위태로운'의 뜻을 가진 'precarious'가 올바른 정답이다.

① 사회적인 ② 우세한 ③ 은밀한 ④ 튼튼한 ⑤ 불안정한

「수상은 미국과의 위태한 동맹을 강화하고 재분배보다 경제 성장을 강조하고 싶어 한다.」

05 ②

sardonic : 냉소적인, 조소하는   cynical : 냉소적인, 부정적인

① 실수를 할 수 있는 ② 냉소적인 ③ 아부하는 ④ 카리스마 있는 ⑤ 너무 제멋대로인

「Shakespeare(셰익스피어)의 "Romeo and Juliet"(로미오와 줄리엣)의 현대판은 엇갈리는 평을 받았다. 한 냉소적인 평은 현대판 로미오와 줄리엣을 "무지한 *Sophist(소피스트)들의 진정한 걸작"이라고 불렀다.
*Sophist(소피스트): 기원전 5세기부터 4세기까지 그리스를 중심으로 활동했던 철학사상가」

06 ⑤

lucratives : 수익성이 좋은   well-paying : 이익을 창출하는, 보수가 좋은
① 한가한 ② (일 하기에) 좋은 ③ 너그러운 ④ 세련된 ⑤ 보수가 좋은
「당신의 경쟁자 중 한 명이 당신의 현재 직무와 어울리고 급여가 거의 두 배인 수익성이 좋은 위치를 제안했다.」

07 ②

☞ 글의 도입부에서 비버에 대한 수요가 늘었다고 한다. 이는 부지런한 설치류가 자연적인 댐을 건설할 수 있다고 추측되기 때문이다. 그렇기 때문에 사람들은 비버들을 다시 들여오려고 할 것이다. 의회는 주가 십억이 넘는 인공댐 건설 프로그램을 고려하고 있다는 것을 알고 나서 비버에 대한 연구를 진행하며 비버가 적은 비용으로 물 부족 문제를 해결할 수 있을 것이라고 생각한다.

「한때 가죽을 얻기 위해 사냥되었던 비버피 몸에 대한 수요가 아닌 본성에 대한, 구체적으로는 그들의 건축 능력에 대한 수요가 다시 많아졌다. 기후 변화 때문에 개울에 물이 적어짐에 따라 연구원들은 부지런한 설치류가 자연적인 해결책을 제공할 것이라고 (A)추측하고/반박하고 있다. 댐이 어떻게 물을 저장하는지에 대한 조사를 바탕으로, Washington주의 토지 의회는 10,000 miles의 적절한 서식지에 비버를 (B)금지하면/다시 들여오면 동물들의 자연적으로 새는 댐에서 천천히 흘려보낼 수 있는 650조 gallon이 넘는 물을 보유할 수 있다. 의회는 주가 십억이 넘는 인공댐 건설 프로그램을 고려하고 있다는 것을 알고 난 후 비버 (C)연구/종료를 시작했다. 의회는 비버가 적은 비용으로 해낼 것이라고 주장한다.」

08 ③

☞ 첫 번째 문장은 '그러나 (but)'로 연결되어 있다. 따라서 쉼표 앞뒤의 내용이 상반되는 내용이어야 한다. 쉼표 뒷부분에서 "동작이 의미를 대체하고 있는지는 확실하지 않다. (it can be asked whether motion is replacing substance.)"라고 말하며 모호성을 제시한다. 따라서 쉼표 앞부분은 명백한 내용이어야 한다. John F. Kennedy 이후로 여행을 하는 일이 관례가 됐고, 또한 Nixon은 해결책을 찾기 위해 그림을 찾아다녔다기 보다 경치를 보러 다녔다고 하는 게 맞다.

「대통령이 여행을 할 필요성은 (A)모호/명백하지만, 동작이 의미를 대체하고 있는지는 확실하지 않다. Nixon의 대륙 횡단은 Oval Office에서 한 연설에서부터 시작해서 Florida 남쪽, New Orleans, 그리고 태평양에서 멈춘 조작된 행사였다. 해안에서 해안까지 환희의 행진이었어야 했지만, 헛된 개념이었기 때문에 실패했다. John F. Kennedy 이후로, 다른 지역으로 날아가는 것이 (B)의무/혐오가 있어 왔다. 35,000 feet에 있다는 것은 대통령의 전능함을 증가시킨다. Kennedy는 마법 양탄자에 올랐을 때 사기가 충전됐다. 심지어 Nixon이 California에서 지상에 묶여 있을 때조차 소란스러운 California 고속도로를 돌았다. Nixon과 여행한 아마추어 심리학자들은 그가 문제로부터 도망가고, 해결책이 나타날 (C)십화/경치를 찾아다닌 것이라고 주장한다. 해결책은 전혀 나타나지 않을 수도 있다.」

09 ④

☞ 본문에서 "행복은 추구하는 그 자체 (happiness is in the pursuit itself)"에 있다고 말한다. 행복이라는 것은 유지할 수 있는 순수한 상태가 아니고 추구하는 그 과정 속에서 도래된다. 따라서 행복의 수용이라기보다는 행복을 추구하는 과정이 더 적합한 말이다.

「행복시장의 구매자와 판매자는 곤경의 즐거움에 대한 감각을 잃어버린 것 같다. 하늘은 그들이 어떤 게임을 하고 있는지 알지만, 그것은 따분한 게임 같아 보인다. 그리고 행복이 그의 외면에 있는 어떤 것도 필요로 하지 않는다는 생각을 가진 인디안 성자는 어떤 게임도 거부하는 것 같이 보이기 때문에 지루해 보인다고 추측한다. 서양의 약점은 행복을 살 수 없다는 착각에서 기인할 수도 있다. 어쩌면 동양의 약점은 완벽한 (따라서 고정적인) 행복 같은 것이 존재한다고 생각하는 데서 기인할 수도 있다. 행복은 부분적인 것 그 이상이 아니다. 인류의 순수한 상태는 존재하지 않는다. 행복이 무엇이든지 간에 그것은 가지거나 된 것이 아니라, 되어가는 것에 있다. 우리가 기억하기 위해 노력해야 할 것이자 창시자들이 우리에게 내재한 권리라고 선포한 것은 행복이 아니라 행복의 수용이다. 그들이 행복 시장을 예측할 수 있었다면 행복은 추구하는 그 자체, 인생에 참여하고 인생에 대해 드러내는 의미 있는 추구, 되어 간다는 기본적인 사실을 강조했을 것이다.」

10 ②

☞ 본문에서 "세상은 호기심을 게으른 호기심이라고 부르며 묵살한다."라고 말하며 부모들은 이러한 호기심이 인생을 힘들게 한다고 생각한다. 따라서 부모들은 자녀들의 호기심을 기르기 위해 최선을 다하는 것이 아니라 호기심을 막기 위해 최선을 다하는 것이 논리적 흐름에 더 부합한다.

「세상은 호기심을 그다지 좋아하지 않는다. 세상은 호기심이 신세를 망친다고 말한다. 호기심이 많은 사람들은 좀처럼 게으르지 않는데도 세상은 호기심을 게으른 호기심이라고 부르며 묵살한다. 부모들은 자녀들의 호기심을 기르기 위해 최선을 다한다. 왜냐하면 무엇이 불을 뜨겁게 하는지 왜 풀이 자라는지와 같은 대답 없는 일련의 질문들을 매주 마주치며 인생을 힘들게 하기 때문이다. 그들은 어린이들이 폭발해서 갑작스럽게 죽기 전에 어린이들의 조사를 중단시킨다. 호기심이 부모님의 훈육을 견뎌 내고, 폭발하기 전에 성장한 아이들은 대학교에 들어간다. 대학교에서 그들은 질문을 하고 답을 찾으려고 노력한다. 학자의 눈에는 그것이 대학의 주된 목표이다. 그곳은 호기심에 대한 세상의 거부감에 저항한다.」

11 ①

☞ to figure out about what kind of engineering she'd major in에서 figure out 자체가 이미 "~에 대해 찾아 내다"라는 의미를 내포하고 있으므로 'about'은 사용하지 않는 것이 맞다.

「Julie의 일 학년 주요 목표는 학업적으로 잘하고 어떤 종류의 공학을 할 것인지에 대해 찾아내는 것이었다. 그러나 그녀는 공학이 어렵고, 그것을 잘하기 위해서는 그녀가 지난 몇 년간 참가해 온 과외 활동을 줄여야 한다는 것을 알았다. 그녀는 고등학교에 다니는 동안 치어리더와 학생회의 일원이었다. 그녀는 피아노 레슨을 받았고, 작년에는 청소년 미스 Elkhart(학교를 대표하는 미인)이 됐고 그것은 그녀에게 대학 장학금을 받게 해주었다. 그렇다고 그녀가 앞으로 4년 간 책에 얼굴을 파묻을 것이라는 것은 아니다. 그녀는 수영을 하고 에어로빅을 하기 위한 시간을 만들고 싶었다. 그녀는 Purdue의 사교 생활, 특히 주말에 있는 남학생 사교 클럽에 들고 싶었다. 그리고 그곳에는 그녀의 남자 친구가 있었다. 그녀는 "나는 내가 나가고 싶을 때면 나갈 것을 안다."라고 하며 "그러나 숙제는 내 우선순위다."라고 말했다.」

12 ②

☞ but only because one will not give way to another one은 보통 the other과 짝지어서 나온다. 따라서 another가 아닌 the other를 사용하는 것이 맞다.

「전설에 따르면 기원전 5세기 초 그리스의 길가에서 서구 문명을 살려 낸 치킨을 찾았다고 한다. 아테네의 장군인 Themistocles는 페르시아 침입군에 맞서 싸우러 가는 길에 두 마리의 수탉이 싸우고 있는 것을 보기 위해 멈췄다. 그는 그의 부대에게 "지켜보라, 이 닭들은 자신들의 수호신을, 조상들의 기념을, 자유와 자녀들의 안전을 위해 싸우는 것이 아니고, 단지 한 마리가 다른 한 마리에게 굽히지 못해서 싸우는 것이다."라고 말했다. 이 이야기는 패배자에게 무슨 일이 일어났는지에 대해 설명하지도 않고, 또한 왜 군인들이 이러한 본능적인 싸움이 무의미하고 우울하기 보다는 영감을 준다고 생각했는지에 대해서도 설명하지 않는다. 그러나 역사는 용기를 얻은 그리스인들이 침략자를 격퇴하기에 이르렀고, 오늘날에 이르러서는 굽고, 튀기고, 기호에 맞춘 소스에 찍어 먹으면서 닭을 기리는 문명을 지켜냈다. 이 수탉들의 후손들은 만약 그들이 이러한 엄청난 생각을 할 수 있었다면 그들의 조상들이 대답해야 할 것이 많다고 생각했을 것이다.」

13 ②

☞ Those who had it gloried in it, and those who did not speak of it with longing. 문단의 시제는 모두 과거이다. 따라서 speak of가 아닌 spoke of를 사용하는 것이 올바르다.

「오늘날 어떤 사람들은 일을 단순한 네 글자 단어로서 생각한다. 하지만 경제 대공황 시기 내가 학부생이었을 때에 일은 굉장히 인기가 많은 단어였다. 그것을 가진 사람들은 기뻐했고, 가지지 못한 사람들은 간절하게 갈망하며 그것에 대해 얘기했다. 캐나다에서 대학을 마친 후에 옥스퍼드로 갔고, 그곳에서 나는 다른 정세를 보았다. 사람들은 일에 대해 얘기하지 않았다. 가끔 학생들은 "나는 지금 떠나야겠어."라고 말하며 파티를 떠났다. 모두가 그들이 일을 하기 위해 몰래 빠져나가는 것을 알았지만, 우리는 그것을 밝히기에는 지나치게 예의가 바랐다. 교수님들은 전혀 일하는 것처럼 보이지 않았다. 옥스퍼드의 매력 중 일부는 어떤 사람도 일하는 것처럼 보이지 않았다는 데 있었다. 그러나 나는 곧 옥스퍼드 비밀을 밝혀냈다. 모두가 뼈 빠지게 일하지만, 그것을 인정하는 것을 좋지 않은 꼴로 생각한다는 것이었다. 사람들은 그들이 주워 담아 배운 것을 받아 들여야 했다.」

14 ①

☞ "Behind that number is several corporate strategies including using armies of part-time workers."은 도치구문이다. 이 문장에서 주어는 "several corporate strategies"로서 복수 형태를 띠고 있다. 따라서 동사 역시 복수형으로 "are"을 사용하는 것이 맞다.

「40년 전에 Ray Kroc이 첫 번째 맥도날드 햄버거를 연 이후로 적어도 2억 명의 사람들이 맥도날드에서 일했다. 이러한 숫자 뒤에는 아르바이트 직원 군단을 포함한 여러 회사 전략이 숨어 있다. 게다가, 맥도날드에서 일하는 사람들의 시급은 최저 임금인 5.25 달러보다 조금 많고, 부가 급여는 거의 없다. 맥도날드와 체인점은 미국과 캐나다에서 50만 명 이상을 고용하는데 올해 피고용인들이 빈번히 맥도날드와 체인점을 떠나는 바람에 인원을 완전히 충족시키기 위해서는 훨씬 많은 수의 사람들을 고용해야 할 것이다. 그러나 이러한 격변에는 긍정적인 면도 있다. 패스트푸드 체인점들이 숙련되지 않은 신입 직원들에 맞춘 훈련에 집중하게 해주었다.」

15 ④

☞ ①, ②, ③, ⑤는 모두 사람들이 떼놓고 싶지 않은 애정이 담긴 물건을 지칭하지만 ④는 은색 반지를 지칭한다.

「많은 사람들이 차마 떼놓을 수 없는 애정을 담은 물건을 가지고 있다. ①그것은 가장 좋아하는 영화배우에게 싸인을 받은 오래 된 누더기 티셔츠일 수도 있다. ②그것은 또한 수많은 시험 동안 믿음직스러운 조수가 되어주었던 잉크가 다 나간 펜일 수도 있다. 다른 이들에게는 ③그것이 오래 전에 빛을 읽고 변색된 은색 반지 일 수도 있다. 반지는 더 이상 치장의 목적으로 쓰이지 않지만, ④그것은 돌아가신 할머니와 같이 사랑하는 사람에 대한 기억을 불러 낼 수 있다. 그 물건이 무엇이든지 간에 그것을 간직하는 이유는 표면적인 이유 때문이 아니라 ⑤그것이 우리의 과거 일부와 우리 가슴 속에 간직하고 있는 기억들을 대변하기 때문이다.」

16 ①

☞ 이것은 사람들이 더 높은 목표를 설정하고, 실패에 대해서 덜 두려워하며, 어려움에 당면했을 때 버틸 수 있게 해 준다고 했다. self-efficacy는 자기 효능감으로서 자신이 어떤 일이나 상황에 처했을 때 그 일을 내가 잘 해 낼 수 있을 것이라는 자신의 능력에 대한 신뢰와 믿음의 정도를 말하기 때문에 이것이 가리키는 말로 가장 적합하다.

① 자기 효능감 ② 균형 ③ 공감 ④ 자의식 ⑤ 관심

「이것은 성공과 실패에 대한 기대에 영향을 미칠 뿐만 아니라, 또한 목표를 설정하는 동기에 대해서도 영향을 준다. 만약 우리들이 외국어 학습과 같은 특정 분야에 이것에 대한 감각이 있다면, 우리는 더 높은 목표를 설정하고, 실패에 대해서 덜 두려워하며, 어려움에 당면했을 때 더 오래 버틸 수 있다. 하지만 이것에 대한 감각이 낮다면, 우리는 일을 아예 피하거나 문제가 생겼을 때 금방 포기해 버릴 것이다. 또한 이것은 귀속성에도 관련이 있어 보인다. 주어진 일에 대해 이것을 강력하게 가지고 있는 사람들은 실패를 노력의 부족 탓을 하고, 하지만 이것을 적게 가지고 있는 사람은 실패를 능력의 부족 탓을 한다. 당신은 실패가 능력의 부족 탓이라고 생각한다면 동기가 파괴된다는 것을 알 것이다.」

17 ⑤

☞ 본문에서 "Alice Cooper와 같은 다양한 유명 인사들이 필요한 금액을 조성하는 데 일조를 했다. (Various celebrities including Alice Cooper were instrumental in helping to raise needed funds.)"라고 말하기 때문에 유명 인사들이 교체 비용을 모금하는 데에 기여했다는 내용은 본문과 일치한다.

「Los Angeles의 북방 경계선을 따라 있는 언덕에 위치한 The Hollywood sign은 세계적으로 인정받은 유명한 지형물이다. 하얗게 페인트칠 된 50 feets 높이의 금속 글자는 Los Angeles 일대를 가로질러 머나먼 거리에서도 볼 수 있다. 사람들이 추측하는 것과는 달리 이 간판은 산업에서 Hollywood의 중요성을 기념하기 위해 사업체들이 지은 것이 아니다. 대신 그것은 1923년에 "Hollywoodland"라는 Los Angeles의 500 acresd의 주택 부지를 홍보하기 위해 지어졌다. 그 당시에 지어진 간판은 당연하게 "Hollywoodland"로 불렸다. 시간이 지나면서 사람들은 "Hollywood"로 줄여서 부르기 시작했고, 그 후에 그 간판은 1945년 Los Angeles에 기부되었고, 뒤에 네 글자는 없어졌다. 간판은 수년간 황폐하게 있다가 1973년에 글자 당 27,000 달러의 가격으로 완전 교체 되었다. Alice Cooper와 같은 다양한 유명 인사들이 필요한 금액을 조성하는 데 일조를 했다.」

18 ③

☞ 본문에서 "그들은 쌀, 밀, 목화, 소, 양 그리고 물소 등을 기른다. (They raise rice, wheat, cotton, cattle, sheep and water buffalo.)"라고 하지만, 물소를 숭배한다고 하지는 않았다.

「인도는 아시아 아대륙의 일부이고 10억이 넘는 사람들의 집이다. 중국만이 더 많은 인구를 가지고 있다. 인도 땅의 반 조금 넘는 공간이 농경에 적합하지만 인도인의 65퍼센트 정도가 농부나 농경 노동자이다. 그들은 쌀, 밀, 목화, 소, 양 그리고 물소 등을 기른다. 생산량을 늘리기 위해, 정부는 관개와 토지 개간 사업을 실행했다. 또한 새로운 종류의 작물과 비료도 사용됐다. 인도는 녹색 혁명의 혜택을 받고 있는 나라 중에 하나다. 불행하게도, 녹색 혁명에 대한 인도 초기의 바람은 씨앗과 비료의 높은 가격과 농약의 대량 사용으로 인해 환상에 불과하다고 증명됐다.」

19 ②

☞ 글쓴이는 본문에서 "Thoreau는 옹알이는 참을 수 없었지만 꽃, 잡초와 죽은 동물들을 가져 온 아이들에게는 관심을 보였다. (Thoreau had no tolerance for babble but was responsive to children who brought him flowers, weeds, and dead animals.)"라고 말했다. 따라서 죽은 동물들을 가져 온 아이들에게 화를 냈다는 보기는 글의 내용과 일치하지 않는다.

「Thoreau은 "많은 여행객들이 나를 보기 위해 온다."라고 말했다. 여행객에는 그의 친구, 학생, 목적 없는 방문객, 그리고 부자 방문객들보다 훨씬 흥미로운 빈민 구호소에서 온 사람들이 있다. Thoreau는 옹알이는 참을 수 없었지만 꽃, 잡초와 죽은 동물들을 가져 온 아이들에게는 관심을 보였다. 전체적으로, 그들은 "계산되지 않은 방문객" 어른들과는 달리 그들 자신을 즐겁게 했다. Thoreau가 의심하기를 더 파렴치한 사람들은 그가 숲 속으로 걸어 나갔을 때 와서 그의 서랍과 장롱을 뒤졌다. 대대수의 방문객들은 근처에 있는 Concord와 Lincoln이나 Boston에서 왔다. Thoreau는 "여자 아이와 남자 아이 그리고 젊은 여성들은 숲 속에 있는 것을 즐거워하는 것 같았다."라고 썼다. "그들은 연못과 꽃들을 보고 그들이 시간을 향상시켰다." 일을 하는 남자들은 심지어 농부들까지 고독과 직장 그리고 내가 살고 있는 곳과는 먼 거리에 대해서만 생각했다. 그리고 그들은 가끔 숲 속을 거니는 것을 좋아한다고 했지만, 실제로는 좋아하지 않는다는 것은 분명했다.」

20 ③

☞ 밑줄 안에는 상처를 입었을 때 경험했던 감정이 들어가야 한다. 보기 중에 상처를 입었을 때 느낄 만한 감정으로 '무기력함'이 가장 적절하다.

① 복수 ② 잊을 수 없음 ③ 무기력 ④ 은혜 ⑤ 무죄

「용서가 기분을 좋게 한다면, 왜 많은 사람들이 그렇게 큰 증오를 끌고 다닐까? 한 가지 이유는 그것이 그들이 상처를 입었을 때 경험했던 _____에 대해 보상을 해 줄 수 있기 때문이다. How to Forgive When You Don't Know How(당신이 어떻게 용서해야 할 지 모를 때 용서하는 방법)의 저자인 Mart Crunte는 "사람들은 화로 가득 차 있을 때 자신이 더 힘이 있다고 느낀다." "그러나 용서는 더 큰 힘을 불어 넣는다. 당신이 용서하면, 선택할 수 있는 힘을 되찾게 된다. 상대방이 용서 받을 자격이 있는지는 상관이 없다. 그러나 당신은 자유로울 자격이 있다."라고 말했다.」

21 ⑤

☞ 밑줄 안에는 미끄러지듯 지나가는 광경에 대해서 얘기하며 아름다운 나무, 도시 광장 그 어느 것도 광경에서 어긋나지 않는다고 말해야 한다.

① 아름다운 경치를 망치지 않는다.
② 운전자한테 피로를 더하지 않는다.
③ 과거를 떠올리게 하지 않는다.
④ 오락시설의 질을 개선하지 않는다.
⑤ 시야를 벗어나지 않는다.

「기차표는 인간사(人間事)라는 지상 최대의 쇼의 앞좌석 얻는 것이다. 시차 적응이나 운전자의 피로 없이 승객들은 혜택 받은 순례자로서 어떤 요구도 받지 않고 기차 안에 갇혀 있는 동안만큼은 시간이 잠시 멈춘다. 그는 창밖으로 펼쳐진 생생한 그림처럼 지나가는 삶의 증인이다. 그는 하루를 만드는 작은 순간들을 미끄러지듯 지나간다. 뒤뜰, 아름다운 나무, 도시 광장—아무것도, 만약 그가 원한다면, 그가 관찰하고 있던 것에 직접 들어가기 위해 어느 역에서든 내릴 수 있다. 세관 직원이 담배를 피우고 화물차에는 우유 캔들이 쌓여 있고 외국에 있는 불빛이 밝은 역에 한밤중에 도착하는 것만큼의 탐험은 없을 것이다.」

22 ④

☞ 밑줄 뒤에 글쓴이는 "열정이 그들을 장기전으로 인도한다. 밑줄의 앞부분에서 "문화부는 잘 보존된 조각 상들이 관광객들로부터 경제적 이윤을 만들어낼 것이라고 믿고, 재건에 들어가는 돈을 늘렸다. (The Culture Ministry has increased the money for restoration in the belief that better-kept statues will reap an economic return from visitors.)"라고 하며 복원 전문가들의 자세와 상반된 문화부의 입 장이 나온다. 문화부는 복원 사업이 관광객들을 끌어들이기 위한 장식품이라는 것을 강조하므로, 밑줄에 서는 복원 사업이 관광객들을 끌어들이기 위한 장식품이 아니라는 점을 제시해야 한다. 따라서 복원하는 일은 ④ "관광객들을 위한 장식품이라기보다는 도시의 영혼을 보호하기 위한 열정이다."가 적절한 답이 다. 또한 밑줄의 뒷부분에 글쓴이는 "가끔 열정이 그들을 장기전으로 인도한다.(Sometimes the passion led them to go to extraordinary lengths)"라고 말한다. 따라서 복원하는 일은 복원 전문가들의 열정 덕분이라는 점을 강조해야 한다. 따라서 열정 이외에 ① 돈을 벌기 위한 수리나, ③ 건축에 대한 더 많은 조사와 같이 다른 측면을 강조한 보기는 답이 될 수 없다.

① 돈을 벌기 위한 더 많은 수리이다.
② 유명해지기 위한 열망이라기보다는
③ 건축에 대한 더 많은 조사이다.
④ 관광객들을 위한 장식품이라기보다는
⑤ 사랑의 노동이라기보다는

「"산성비부터 기계적 손상에 이르는 공격 때문에 우리의 조각상 중 적어도 80퍼센트는 좋지 않은 상황이다." "우리 길은 마차를 위해 건설되었는데 현재는 차들이 조각상들을 향해 후진을 한다" 라고 문화부의 보호 감독이 말했다. 문화부는 잘 보존된 조각 상들이 관광객들로부터 경제적 이윤을 만들어낼 것이라고 믿고, 재건에 들어가는 돈을 늘렸다. 하지만, Branda씨와 그의 동료 복원전문가들에게 복원하는 일은 도시의 영혼을 보호하기 위한 열정 _____, 가끔 열정이 그들을 장기전으로 인도한다. 많은 밤들과 자정이 지나 Mr. Branda와 그의 동료들은 17세기 제자들의 석상을 포장하기 위해 강한 바람에 노출되어 있는 Charles 다리 기슭에 있는 St. Slavator 교회의 지붕에 올라갔다. 어둠 속에서 보호와 보수를 위해 크레인으로 조각상을 뽑아냈다.」

23 ①

☞ 글쓴이는 "Donne 세대는 그의 감정의 깊이를 존경했으나 그의 불규칙적인 운율과 모호한 언급 때문에 헷갈려 했다. (Donne's generation admired the depth of his feeling, but was puzzled by his often irregular rhythm and obscure references.)"라고 말하며 Donne 세대가 그의 작품을 이해하는 데 어려 움을 겪었다고 암시한다. 또한 밑줄 뒤에는 예시로 T.S. Eliot이나 W.B. Yeats 같은 작가들이 Donne의 심리적인 복잡성을 이해하고 존경했다고 말하기 때문에 밑줄 안에는 Donne이 20세기가 지나서야 그 진 가를 인정받게 되었다는 내용이 들어가는 것이 알맞다.

① Donne이 진가를 인정받게 되었다.
② Donne의 잊힌 작품들이 다시 쓰였다.
③ Jonson이 Donne을 잘못 판단했다고 인정했다.
④ Donne's 확실하지 않은 언급이 더욱 모호해졌다.
⑤ 시에서 운율이 더 자주 사용되었다.

「유명한 희곡 작가이자 17세기 John Donne와 동시대에 살았던 Ben Jonson은 Donne에 관하여 "어떤 상황에 따라서는 세상의 첫 시인이다"라고 했으나, 그럼에도 불구하고 그는 "억양을 지키지 않는 것에 대해서 교수형을 당해 마땅하다."라고 말했다. Donne 세대는 그의 감정의 깊이를 존경했으나 그의 불규칙적인 운율과 모호한 언급 때문에 헷갈려 했다. 20세기가 되어 감정과 암시를 찬양하는 현대 운동이 생기고 나서야 _____. T.S. Eliot이나 W.B. Yeats와 같은 작가들은 한 순간에는 여자와의 세속적으로 놀아나는 것을 과시하다가 다음 순간에는 비참하게 신에게 "힘을 굽혀서 저를 부수고, 날리고, 태워 새롭게 만들어주시옵소서"라고 간청할 수 있는 시인의 심리적인 복잡성을 존경했다.」

24 ③

☞ 글의 도입부에서 글쓴이는 "한 사람이 물을 수 있다. 왜 고전 작가들의 명성은 계속되는가? 정답은 고전 작가의 명성이 다수로부터 완전히 독립적이기 때문이다. (One may ask: Why does the great fame of classical authors continue? The answer is that the fame of classical authors is entirely independent of the majority.)"라고 말하며 고전 작가의 명성의 형성에 지대한 영향을 끼친 것이 다수가 아님을 강조한다. 또한 결론 부분에서도 글쓴이는 "그리고 죽음 후에 명성을 얻게 된 작가들의 경우, 적은 사람들의 완고한 보존에 의해 행복한 속편이 생겼다. the happy sequel has been due to the obstinate perseverance of the few."라고 말하며 소수에 의해 고전 작가의 명성이 지속되고 있다고 말한다. 따라서 정답은 ③ 열렬한 소수의 열정에 의해 강화되었다.(reinforced by the ardour of the passionate few)이 가장 적절하다.

① 엘리트 독자들에 의해 실력이 부족한 작가들과 동일한 취급을 받았다.
② 행인으로부터 명성을 얻어 왔다.
③ 열렬한 소수의 열정에 의해 강화되었다.
④ 자연스럽게 아류 작가들과 구분되었다.
⑤ 대중의 엄청난 존경에 영감을 받았다.

「한 사람이 물을 수 있다. 왜 고전 작가들의 명성은 계속되는가? 정답은 고전 작가의 명성이 다수로부터 완전히 독립적이기 때문이다. 만약 당신이 셰익스피어의 명성이 길거리에 있는 사람에 의존한다고 전제한다면 그의 명성이 2주일은 버텼을까? 고전 작가들의 명성은 열정적인 소수에 의해 만들어지고, 지켜져 왔다. 최고의 작가가 살아생전 엄청난 성공을 누렸지만, 대다수의 사람들은 아류 작가들을 인정하는 것만큼 최고 작가의 진가를 인정하지 않았다. 그는 항상 _____. 그리고 죽음 후에 명성을 얻게 된 작가들의 경우, 적은 사람들의 완고한 보존에 의해 행복한 속편이 생겼다.」

25 ⑤

☞ 글의 중반부에서 글쓴이는 "그들의 얼굴은 그들의 열정과 경험을 전하고 그들의 성격과 모순되지 않았다. (Their faces transmit their passions and experiences and never betray their character.)"라고 말한다. 마지막 문장에서도 어떠한 것에도 찌들지 않은 영혼의 모습이 얼굴에 그대로 나타난다는 뜻으로 해석되어야 알맞기 때문에 ⑤ 사치와 자기 진단에 때 묻지 않고(untainted by luxury and self-examination)가 가장 적절한 답이다.

① 서로의 고통과 슬픔을 비추며
② 그들의 따뜻한 영혼으로 채워주며
③ 영원히 내면의 평화를 찾으며
④ 현대인들의 몸과는 다르게
⑤ 사치와 자기 진단에 때 묻지 않고

「만약 당신이 영혼의 사진을 찍을 수 있다면, 그것은 미국의 남북 전쟁에 있는 노예와 군인들의 흑백 사진처럼 보일 것이다. 그들은 자신을 바라보고 외모를 걱정할 시간이 없었던 사람들이었고, 그리고 그것은 드러났다. 그들의 얼굴은 그들의 열정과 경험을 전하고 그들의 성격과 모순되지 않았다. 한 사진은 강한 눈빛과 뾰족한 수염을 갖고 있는 큰 남성을 보여준다. 다른 사진에서는, 눈 밑에 있는 다크서클이 엄마의 지혜를 보여준다. 작고 팽팽한 입술에서 아이의 의심이 보인다. 어떻게든, 상황은 _____ 그들의 영혼이 얼굴에 나타날 수 있게 해주었다.」

26 ⑤

☞ 글쓴이는 TV나 영화가 특정 상품을 광고하면서 사람들의 심리를 조작하고 있다고 말하고 있다. 이전에도 TV나 영화에서 배우들이 음료수를 마시고 차를 운전했지만, 현대에 와서 음료수의 상표와 차의 로고가 더 두드러져 보인다는 내용이 적합하고, (B)에서는 Y 대신 X 음료수를 선택한 사람의 심리 뒤에 광고의 영향이 있을 수도 있다고 제시하므로 ⑤ 유명한, 두드러지는(prominent) - 조작된(manipulated)이 적합하다.

「지난 번 봤던 영화에서 당신은 영웅이 어떤 음료를 마시고 있었는지 눈치 챘는가? 여자 스타가 운전하던 차는? TV와 영화에 나오는 배우들은 항상 음료를 마시고 차를 운전했지만, 지금은 음료의 이름과 자동차의 상징이 더욱 (A) _____. 광고주들은 TV와 영화에 내보내서 그들의 광고물을 노출시킬 수 있다는 것을 깨달았다. 영화 스튜디오는 소위 "매립물"이라고 불리는 것들 덕분에 돈을 벌 수 있다는 것을 깨달았다. 그래서? 다음에 당신이 음료 X를 Y 대신 주문한다면, 지난 번 봤던 영화에서 음료수 X가 나왔는지 Y가 나왔는지 생각해보라. 당신은 광고주와 영화 제작자들에 의해 (B) _____?」

27 ④

☞ (A)의 앞부분은 연쇄 반응이 일어난다고 말하고 있고 (A)의 뒷부분은 연쇄 반응이 '어떻게' 일어나는지에 대해서 확장 설명하고 있다. 따라서 '게다가'로 두 문장을 연결하는 것이 적절하다. 또한 (B)의 앞에는 지구를 위협하는 연쇄 반응의 발달에 대해 얘기하고 있고, (B)의 뒤에는 그 예로 소통과 기상 위성을 파괴할 수도 있다는 예시를 담고 있으므로 '예를 들어'로 앞뒤 두 문장을 연결하는 것이 적합하다.

「연쇄 반응은 지구에서 항상 일어나고 있다. 연쇄 반응은 화학 공장에서 하나의 들뜬 분자가 이웃들에게 플라스틱을 형성하기 위한 수많은 결합들을 촉발시킬 때 일어난다. (A) _____, 그들은 빠른 아원자 입자들이 무거운 원자에 부딪히고 그것을 분해시키며 솟구치는 에너지로 이러한 과정을 반복 확장하며 더 많은 입자를 만들어 내는 원자로에 있다. 전문가가 말하기를 현재 우주에서 지구를 초월하는 인류의 노력을 제한하며 위험하는 위험한 연쇄 반응이 진행되고 있다. (B) _____, 그것은 수십억 달러를 호가하는 최첨단 소통과 기상 위성을 파괴의 위험에 빠뜨릴 수 있다. 문제는 지구 근처의 궤도 일부가 수명이 다하거나 아직 활동하고 있는 위성들, 로켓과 수십억 개의 선회하는 파편들로 인해 쓰레기장이 됐다는 것이다.」

28 ③

☞ 글쓴이는 "1950년대 초에서 1990년대 초까지 지구에 도달하는 햇빛이 10퍼센트 줄었다. (The amount of sunshine that reaches the Earth dropped by 10 percent between the early 1950s and the early 1990s.)"는 현상을 제시하며 그 원인으로 "문제는 지구와 태양 사이에서 나타나는 것 같다. 그 중간에 오염이 생겼다.(The problem appears to be between the Earth and the Sun. Pollution has gotten in the way.)"라고 제시한다. 오염 때문에 지구의 일조량이 줄어들었다는 내용을 담고 있는 ③ 오염 : 부자연스러운 그늘 (Pollution : An Unnatural Sunshade)이 가장 적절하다.

① 태양에게 휴가를 주자
② 햇빛 : 많으면 많을수록 좋다
③ 오염 : 부자연스러운 그늘
④ 태양이 어두워지는 것을 어떻게 막을 수 있는가?
⑤ 고생 끝에 낙을 찾자

「1950년대 초에서 1990년대 초까지 지구에 도달하는 햇빛이 10퍼센트 줄었다. 과학자들은 그것이 태양의 문제가 아니라는 것을 알아냈다. 어떤 기구도 태양 광선의 어두워짐을 기록하지 않았다. 문제는 지구와 태양 사이에서 나타나는 것 같다. 그 중간에 오염이 생겼다. 오염물의 미립자들이 태양 광선을 다시 반사시킨다. 오염은 공기의 응축을 증가시킨다. 이러한 응축은 두껍고, 어두운 구름을 만든다. 이러한 이론을 입증하기 위해 과학자들은 오염이 적거나 아예 없는 곳을 가리킨다. 이러한 지역의 기구들은 햇빛이 예전처럼 밝다.」

29 ④

☞ 글의 앞부분에서는 초기에 이야기 말하기에 대해서 얘기하다 "이야기의 반대에 있고, 이야기를 완전히 교체하려고 하는 것은 소설이다. (What stands in opposition to storytelling, what is in the process of replacing it entirely, is of course the novel.)"라고 하면서 입에서 입으로 전해지는 구전 동화를 소설이 대체한다고 얘기한다. 따라서 ④ 이야기의 하락, 소설의 성공 (The Decline of Storytelling, the Rise of the Novel)이 가장 적절한 제목이다.

① 두 번, 한 번의 서술
② 이야기 : 살아있는 말하기 vs 죽은 글자
③ 현대 이야기의 고독한 영웅
④ 이야기의 하락, 소설의 성공
⑤ 공예가와 여행가 : 동전의 양면

「Walter Benjamin은 전통적인 이야기를 얘기할 거리를 갖고 여행에서 돌아온 여행자뿐만 아니라 그 지역에 뿌리박고 있는 지역 전통의 수호자와 동일시했다. 중세 시대에서는 거주하는 명공과 여행자가 업무 현장에서 만나서 하는 공예 기법 때문에 이 두 가지 이야기가 서로 관통할 수 있었다. 그러나 "역사의 세속적이고 생산적인 힘"의 역할을 통해 살아있는 말하기의 범주에서 묘사가 도래됐다. 이야기의 반대에 있고, 이야기를 완전히 교체하려고 하는 것은 불가분하게 인쇄의 발명과 책의 개념과 연결돼 있는 소설이다. 소설가들은 인간들과의 대화에 참여할 능력이 없고, 그에 따라 좋은 충고가 되는 지혜를 교류할 수 없는 고립돼 있는, 보이지 않으며 숨겨진 신이다.」

30 ③

☞ 글쓴이는 "1960년대에서 1970년대 사이에, 많은 심리학자들이 4개의 학술지를 분석했고 58에서 96 퍼센트에 이르는 본문이 대학생들에 근거했다는 것을 알았다. (During the 1960s and 1970s, several psychologists analyzed four journals in the field and found that 58 percent to 96 percent of the articles were based on studies with college students.)"라고 지적하면서 "그러나 대학생들이 대학생이 아닌 사람처럼 생각하고, 행동하고 느낄까? 또는 나이가 든 어른들이 하는 것처럼 행동할까? 이 두 문제에 대한 대답은 다 "아니다."(But do college students think, behave, and feel as their non-college peers do? Or, for that matter, as older adults do? The answer to both questions is "no.")"라고 얘기하며 대학생들에만 초점을 맞춘 심리학 연구에 대한 문제점을 제시한다.

① 대학생 : 현재와 과거

② 유전학 연구 : 작을수록 낫다?

③ 심리학 연구에서의 샘플링 오류

④ 심리학의 대학생들 : 지나치게 많은가?

⑤ 대학생과 나이가 든 어른들의 사고방식

「현대 심리학은 "대학 2학년의 행동 과학"이라고 불린다. 1960년대에서 1970년대 사이에, 많은 심리학자들이 4개의 학술지를 분석했고 58에서 96퍼센트에 이르는 본문이 대학생들에 근거했다는 것을 알았다. 최근에 나는 이 두 1991년 학술지에 있는 본문을 분석했고 77퍼센트의 리서치가 대학생들에 대해 행해졌다는 것을 알았다. Michigan 대학의 심리학자이자 학술지의 편집자 중 한 명인 Melvin Manis 편리가 다른 분야에서의 대상 선정도 좌우한다고 설명한다. 그가 말하길 "코끼리에 관한 유전한 역구는 매우 적다.", "많은 연구가 초파리를 이용했는데, 그것은 초파리들이 짧은 수명을 갖고 있기 때문만 아니라 훨씬 싸기 때문이기도 하다." 코끼리와 초파리가 비슷한 구조를 가지고 있어 상관이 없다. 그러나 대학생들이 대학생이 아닌 사람처럼 생각하고, 행동하고 느낄까? 또는 나이가 든 어른들이 하는 것처럼 행동할까? 이 두 문제에 대한 대답은 다 "아니다."」

31 ④

☞ 글쓴이는 어른들의 개입이 없는 어린이들의 사회에서 독재가 자행되고 있다고 하면서, "대다수의 아이들에게 다른 아이들에 대한 고려는 자발적으로 일어나지 않고, 가르침을 받아야만 하는데 권력의 행사 이외의 다른 방법으로는 쉽게 가르칠 수 없다. (Consideration for others does not, with most children, arise spontaneously, but has to be taught, and can hardly be taught except by the exercise of authority.)"라고 말하며 어른들의 개입의 필요성을 제시하고 있다.

① 보육에 있어서 자유의 중요성

② 여러 가지 학습 상황에 따른 아이들의 행동에 대한 이해

③ 어린이 사회에서 승자와 패자의 관계

④ 보육에 있어서 어른들의 참견의 필요성

⑤ 어린이의 리더십에 영향을 끼치는 여러 요소

「일부 자유 옹호자들이 지나치게 적은 중요성을 부여하는 것이 배려이다. 어른들의 개입이 없는 어린이들의 사회에서는 어른들의 독재보다 훨씬 잔혹한 강자의 독재가 있다. 만약 두, 세 살 정도의 두 아이가 같이 놀게 내버려두면 여러 차례의 싸움을 통해 누가 승자가 되고 누가 노예가 될 것인지를 알아낸다. 어린이의 수가 많아지면 한 명 또는 두 명이 완벽한 장악력을 갖게 되고, 다른 아이들은 어른들이 끼어들어 약자와 덜 공격적인 아이들을 보호할 때보다 훨씬 적은 자유를 갖는다. 대다수의 아이들에게 다른 아이들에 대한 고려는 자발적으로 일어나지 않고, 가르침을 받아야만 하는데 권력의 행사 이외의 다른 방법으로는 쉽게 가르칠 수 없다. 이것이 아마 어른들의 물러남을 반대하는 가장 중요한 주장일 것이다.」

32 ④

☞ 글의 초반부에 글쓴이가 "간접흡연이 질병을 유발한다는 것에 대한 연구가 계속돼 왔다. (The place of secondhand smoke in causing disease has been under study for years.)"라고 글의 화제에 대해서 언급한다. 그리고 중반부에서 서부에 있는 도시를 예시로 제시하며 글의 결론에서 "간접흡연은 심박동수를 늘리고 혈관의 확장 능력을 감소시킴으로써 심장 마비에 일조한다. (Secondhand smoke contributes to heart attacks by elevating heart rate and decreasing the ability of blood vessels to dilate.)"라고 주장한다. 따라서 ④ 간접흡연과 심장마비의 관계 (the relationship of secondhand smoke and heart attacks)가 글의 주제로 가장 적절하다.

① 직장 내 흡연의 영향
② 중간 규모 도시에서 심장 마비의 원인
③ 스트레스가 없는 직장 분위기의 중요성
④ 간접흡연과 심장마비의 관계
⑤ 공공장소와 직장 내 흡연 금지의 중요성

「간접흡연이 질병을 유발한다는 것에 대한 연구가 계속돼 왔다. 서부에 있는 중간 규모의 도시가 예상치 못하게 자료에 더해졌다. 공공장소와 직장에서의 흡연이 금지되었다가 6개월 후에 다시 금령이 풀렸다. 공공장소에서 흡연이 금지 되었을 동안, 심장 마비로 병원에 등록된 사람의 비율은 24였다. 일상적인 6개월의 기간 동안, 그 비율은 40이었다. 연구가들은 비율의 하락이 간접흡연의 악영향에 대한 증거라고 믿는다. 간접흡연은 심박동수를 늘리고 혈관의 확장 능력을 감소시킴으로써 심장 마비에 일조한다.」

33 ④

☞ 보통 글의 도입 부분과 결론 부분에서 주장이 언급된다. 이 글에서는 글의 결론 부분에서 주장이 제시 된다. 글의 결론 부분에서 "실제로는 많은 도시와 마을이 시작한 거대한 재활용 프로그램이 정부의 부족한 재정을 이용하는 가장 합리적인 방법이 아닐 수 있다. (In the real world, the sort of gigantic recycling programs that many cities and towns have embarked upon may not be the best use of scarce government funds.)"라고 말하며 쓰레기 재활용에 쓰이는 정부의 재정이 쓸 데 없는 것이라고 주장한다.

「만약 쓰레기 위기가 있다면, 그것은 우리가 쓰레기를 그 자체로 보는 것이 아니라 복잡하지만 감당할 수 있는 시민들의 문제로서 환경적인 위험이라고 생각한다는 것이다. 많은 오래 된 도시 매립지들이 수용 한계에 다다르고 있지만, 현실적으로 이 나라에 안전한 매립지를 위한 충분한 공간이 있고 앞으로도 있을 것이다. 우리는 쓰레기를 관리 문제로 생각하는 것이 아니라, 도덕적인 위기라고 생각한다. 결과적으로 재활용은 나무랄 데 없는 선행이고, 비용-이익 분석을 넘어선 것이다. 그러나 실제 상황에서 재활용에 쓰인 돈은 학교, 도서관, 의료와 치안에 쓰일 수 없게 된 돈이다. 실제로는 많은 도시와 마을이 시작한 거대한 재활용 프로그램이 정부의 부족한 재정을 이용하는 가장 합리적인 방법이 아닐 수 있다.」

34 ①

☞ 글 속에서 소녀는 산들 바람이 부는 들판 한 가운데서 자고 있다가 깨어서 하늘을 바라본다. 고요하면서도 차분한 느낌을 주기 때문에 ①이 가장 적절한 답이다.
① 차분하고 느긋한 ② 생생하고 즐거운 ③ 재밌고 즐거운 ④ 슬프고 무서운 ⑤ 급하고 절망적인

「태양은 그림자를 불러일으킬 만큼 서쪽 멀리 있었다. 작은 들판의 한 가운데에 그리고 건초 더미의 그늘 안에 한 여자아이가 자고 있었다. 여자 아이는 산들바람이 그녀를 깨웠을 때 길고 곤히 자고 있었다. 그녀는 눈을 뜨고 파랗고 하얀 하늘을 바라보았다. 그녀는 하품을 하고 긴 갈색 다리와 팔을 게으르게 뻗었다. 그리고 그녀의 머리와 빨간색 스웨터와 발목에 닿지 않을 정도의 길이인 파란색 면 치마에 붙어 있는 지푸라기들은 신경 쓰지 않고 일어났다. 그녀는 머리 위에서 게으르게 떠다니는 구름이 어떤 동물을 닮았는지 찾으려고 노력하면서 건성으로 하늘을 바라보았다.」

35 ②

☞ 문장의 뒤에 화자가 "나는 짜증이 났고, 내가 틀린 방식으로 삽질을 하는 것을 즐긴다고 말하고 싶었다. (I was annoyed and wanted to tell him that I enjoyed shoveling the wrong way.)"라고 말한다. 화자는 일이 힘들어도 즐기고 있지만 ②에서는 화자의 몸이 일을 거부한다고 얘기하기 때문에 글의 문맥에 맞지 않다.

「근처에서 일하고 있는 몇몇 남자들이 나를 보고는 웃었을 것이다. ① 노인 두 세 분 정도가 올바르게 삽질하는 방법을 가르쳐 주는 수고를 해주셨다. "너는 잘못하고 있어,"라고 한 남자가 나무랐다. ② 아침 7시 정도에 시작해서 나는 내 몸이 처음 하는 삽질을 거부하는 것을 느꼈다. "등에 너무 많은 힘을 주지 마,"라고 남자가 가르쳤다. ③ 나는 참을성 없이 듣고, 멍하니 보다가, 삽을 쥐고 있는 일 때문에 굵어진 손가락을 보았다. 나는 짜증이 났고, 내가 틀린 방식으로 삽질을 하는 것을 즐긴다고 말하고 싶었다. 거의 그럴 뻔 했지만, 끝내는 아무 말도 하지 못했다. ④ 대신 나는 내가 몇 주 간의 노동이 노동자 세계에서 인정받을 수 있게 해 줄 것이라고 기대했다면 내가 내 자신을 속이고 있었던 것이라는 것을 깨달았다. 내 부모님이 "진짜 일"이라고 하신 것을 3개월 만에 배울 수는 없었다. 나는 노력과 피곤의 감각을 즐길 수 있었다. ⑤ 우리 부모님이 내 나이에 이런 일을 했다면 이러한 감각들이 무서웠을 것이다. 피로는 그들의 몸과 마음에 다른 종류의 피해를 주었을 것이다.」

36 ②

☞ 문장에서는 서양인들이 혈액형과 성격 사이의 관계에 대한 개념에 대해 이해하지 못한다고 주장하고 있다. 따라서 두 개의 상반되는 개념 사이의 관계에 관심을 가지고 이해하고 있다는 ②는 글의 흐름에 맞지 않는다.

「"당신의 혈액형은 무엇입니까?"는 서양의 시각에서 봤을 때 흔치 않은 질문이다. 한국인과 일본인의 시각에서, 이러한 질문은 일반적이다. ① 이러한 문화의 사람들은 구체적인 성격과 특징이 혈액형에 관련이 있을 것이라고 생각한다. ② 그러나 요즘에는 더 많은 서양인들이 뚜렷이 다른 두 가지 특성 사이의 관계에 더 많은 관심을 두고 있다. ③ 이러한 믿음은 서양의 점술학과 별자리와 매우 흡사하다. ④ 대부분의 서양인들은 혈액형과 성격의 관계에 대한 개념을 모르고 있기 때문에 이러한 질문을 들으면 놀란다. ⑤ 사실, 많은 서양인들이 자신의 혈액형조차 모른다.」

37 ④

☞ 위에 제시된 문장은 긍정적인 방향으로 여가가 증가한다는 내용이다. 문장이 "만약, 대신해서(If, instead,)"로 시작하기 때문에 문장 앞에는 부정적인 방향으로 여가가 증가하는 현상에 대한 언급이 나와야 하고, 문장의 뒷부분에는 긍정적인 방식의 여가에 대한 보충 설명이 나와야 한다. 따라서 앞에는 "서로에게 그리고 경제를 관장하는 부자 엘리트 집단에게 채찍질을 하는 광범위한 사회 격변, 전례 없는 폭력, 열린 전쟁이 될 것이다. (The more likely course would be widespread social upheaval, violence on an unprecedented scale, and open warfare, with the poor lashing out at each other as well as at the rich elites who control the global economy.)"이 나오고 뒤에는 "자유 시간은 지역 사회의 유대를 재건하고, 민주주의의 유산에 다시 활기를 찾는 데 쓰일 수 있다. (That free time could be used to renew the bonds of community and rejuvenate the democratic legacy.)"는 내용이 따라 오는 ④가 위에 제시된 문장이 들어갈 만한 가장 적절한 장소이다.

「만약, 대신해서, 개화된 방식을 추구해서 노동자들이 짧은 노동 시간과 충분한 급여와 함께 생산성 증가로부터 이익을 얻을 수 있게 한다면, 현대사의 어느 부분보다도 더 많은 여가가 존재할 것이다.
미래에는 더 많은 수의 사람들이 일을 적게 하고 더 많은 시간을 갖게 될 것이다. (①) 그들의 "자유" 시간이 강요되고, 본의 아닌 것, 강요된 시간제 직업, 해고, 그리고 실업의 결과이든지, 생산성 향상, 짧은 노동 시간, 더 나은 급여 때문에 생긴 여가인지는 정치 분야에서 해결되도록 남아 있다. (②) 역사에서 유래가 없는 거대한 실업이 사람 대신 기계가 대체하면서 생긴 결과라면 연민 어리고 보살피는 사회는 나타나기 어렵다. (③) 서로에게 그리고 경제를 관장하는 부자 엘리트 집단에게 채찍질을 하는 광범위한 사회 격변, 전례 없는 폭력, 열린 전쟁이 될 것이다. (④) 자유 시간은 지역 사회의 유대를 재건하고, 민주주의의 유산에 다시 활기를 찾는 데 쓰일 수 있다. (⑤) 새로운 세대는 민족주의의 한계를 뛰어 넘고 서로와, 공동체와 더 큰 생물권에 대한 헌신을 공유하는 전 인류의 구성원으로서 생각하고 행동하기 시작 할 수 있다.」

38 ⑤

☞ 본문에서 글쓴이는 "기계는 우리 삶의 나쁜 면에 어느 정도 기여한다. 그렇지만 아무도 기계 없이 살고 싶어 하지 않는다. 기계와 그것들이 주는 편리와 즐거움에 익숙해져서 사람들은 기계가 중요한 역할을 하지 않는 사회에 대해서는 상상할 수 없다. (Machines certainly contribute to much that is bad in our lives. Yet no one is eager to do without machines. Having become used to them, to the convenience and entertainment and stimulation they provide, people cannot imagine a life in which machines do not play a major role.)"라고 말하며 사람들의 기계에 대한 의존성에 대해 얘기한다. 그리고 밑줄 친 문장은 이러한 본문을 요약하는 내용이다. 따라서 기계가 해로운데도 불구하고 기계에 의존하는 사람들이라는 점을 시사해야 한다. 따라서 (A)는 기계의 해로움을 언급하고, (B)에는 기계에 대한 사람들의 의존성을 언급해야 하므로 ⑤ 해로운 (harmful) − 필수적인 (indispensable)이 적절하다.

기계는 가끔 골치 아프고, 불만스럽고 그리고 심지어는 (A) ; 그러나 그것들이 주는 이익에 익숙해지고 나면, 그것들이 당신의 일생 생활에 (B)하다고 느낄 것이다.

	(A)	(B)
①	중독성 있는	불필요한
②	실망스러운	불필요한
③	해로운	불필요한
④	중독성 있는	필수적인
⑤	해로운	필수적인

「당신은 당신의 곁에 있어 줄 텔레비전에 의존하는 사람 중에 하나이거나, 컴퓨터에 말을 하다가 걸렸을 수도 있다. 그러나 당신과 기계와의 관계가 모두 애정의 관계는 아니다. 당신은 자신의 의식이 있는 컴퓨터나 시동이 걸리지 않는 차, 매번 빵을 태우는 토스터기, 당신의 돈을 먹는 자판기 등과 같이 특정한 기계들을 싫어할 지도 모른다. 기계들이 보통 당신의 삶을 쉽게 만들도록 설계 됐지만, 가끔 그것들이 당신의 삶을 비참하게 만들지 않으면 불만스럽게 만든다. 기계는 우리 삶의 나쁜 면에 어느 정도 기여한다. 총은 높은 범죄율에 기여한다. 자동차는 공기 오염과 사고를 증가시킨다. 그리고 기계는 가끔 사람들이 직장을 잃게 한다. 그렇지만 아무도 기계 없이 살고 싶어 하지 않는다. 기계와 그것들이 주는 편리와 즐거움에 익숙해져서 사람들은 기계가 중요한 역할을 하지 않는 사회에 대해서는 상상할 수 없다. 기계는 가끔 골치 아프고, 불만스럽고, 그리고 심지어는 (A) _____ ; 그러나 그것들이 주는 이익에 익숙해지고 나면, 그것들이 당신의 일상생활에 (B) _____ 하다고 느낄 것이다」

39 ②

☞ 첫 번째 문단에서는 진실이 논리학의 법칙을 거부할 수도 있고, 거짓이 오히려 논리학의 법칙에 순응할 수 있다는 내용을 제시한다. 따라서 그 뒤에는 논리학자들이 진실의 여부보다는 논리의 법칙에의 순응 여부를 더 중시한다는 내용이 나오며 새로운 단어 "유효함(valid)"와 "유효하지 않음(invalid)"를 소개하는 (A)문단이 오는 것이 적절하다. (C)는 "Valid"라는 단어의 기원을 설명하기 때문에 단어를 처음 언급한 (A)문단 뒤에 따라 오는 것이 자연스럽다. 마지막으로 (B)는 유효성에 대한 예시를 제시하기 때문에 단어에 대한 정의를 제시한 (A)의 뒤를 따르는 것이 적합하다.

「논리는 진실을 촉진한다. 그러나 우리는 이 단어들의 일반적인 의미 속에서 특정한 설명이 진실인지 혹은 거짓인지에 대해 알거나 신경 쓰지 않고 논리적으로 나아갈 수 있다. 일반적인 연설에서 진실은 사실에 의거한 진실이고, 거짓은 그 반대를 의미한다. 이제 특정한 사실에 의거해 진실인 특정한 진술이 그 내용에서 논리의 법칙을 위반할 수도 있다. 그리고 사실에 의거해 거짓인 진술이 그 내용에서 논리의 법칙을 따를 수 있다.」

(A) 이와 같이 논리학자들은 사실에 직접적으로 관심을 가지지 않고, 논리의 법칙의 준수 여부에 더 관심이 있다. 따라서 그는 논리학 법칙에 순응하는 것과 순응하지 않는 것들을 차례로 설명하기 위해 유효함과 유효하지 않음이라는 한 쌍의 전문적인 단어를 쓴다.

(B) 유효한 여권은 실수를 할 수도 있지만, 적절하게 서명을 하고 날짜가 지나지 않았다면, 그 역할을 다해서 장벽을 넘을 수 있게 할 수도 있다. 반면에 그것이 눈 색깔과 다른 사실들을 올바르게 제공할 수 있을지라도, 그것이 날짜가 지났다면 효과가 없을 것이고 따라서 유효하지 않다.

(C) 이러한 단어들의 도움으로 그는 특정 서술이 사실에 의거해 진실인지 아닌지에 대해 전념할 필요 없이 추론의 법칙을 세울 수 있다. 유효함을 뜻하는 Valid 는 강함을 의미하는 라틴 단어 validus에서 온다.」

40 41

「이만큼 알려져 있다. This much is known. 뉴런 (신경 세포) 28번은 전기 신호를 발사하고, 28번의 연결고리 중 하나가 뉴런 29번에 닿는 시냅스 (신경 접합부)에서 화학적 변화가 29번의 전기 신호를 촉진시킨다. 그 신호는 뉴런 30번으로 전달되고, 계속적으로 반복된다. 만약 28번과 29번의 연결이 충분히 이루어지면, 두 뉴런 간의 유대가 더욱 강해진다. 이러한 중요한 결합으로 기억이 만들어지는 것으로 보인다. 온몸에 있는 세포들과 달리, 뉴런은 분열하지 않는다. 사람이 65세 또는 70세에 이르게 되면, 뉴런 28번과 그 이웃 뉴런 세포들은 죽거나 아주 약해져서 효과적으로 전기 신호를 전달 할 수 없게 된다.
그러나 아직도 수십억의 뉴런들이 남아 있다. 그리고 뇌가 새로운 뉴런들을 생성할 수 없지만, 뉴런들은 새로운 시냅스를 생기게 할 수 있고, 따라서 새로운 연결 고리를 만들 수 있다. 한 연구가가 실험용 쥐에게 매일 새로운 장난감을 공급하고 우리 안에 활로와 터널을 바꾸어 보았다. 그가 쥐들의 뇌를 꺼내 보았을 때, 장난감과 새로운 장식을 받지 못한 쥐들보다 훨씬 많은 시냅스를 발견했다. 사람들의 뇌 역시 계속적으로 자극을 받고 도전을 받는다면 더 많은 시냅스를 생성할 것이라고 생각하는 것은 좋은 추측이다. 따라서 뇌가 줄어들고 있을지라도 기억을 남기기 위해 더 많은 길들을 만들지도 모른다. 만약 뉴런 28번 길이 더 이상 쉽게 지나갈 수 없게 되면, _____. 속임수로 뇌가 만들 수 있게 강요한다.」

*synapse : 신경세포의 자극 전달부

40 ②

☞ 첫 번째 문단에서는 신경 세포 뉴런과 신경 접합부인 시냅스가 어떻게 기억을 만들어내는지 그리고 뉴런이 분열을 하지 않는다는 한계점에서 얘기한다. 그리고 두 번째 문단에서는 이어서 이러한 뉴런의 한계를 극복하고 어떻게 사람의 뇌가 기억을 이어가는지 설명한다. 특히 두 번째 문단에서 글쓴이는 "그러나 아직도 수십억의 뉴런들이 남아 있다. 그리고 뇌가 새로운 뉴런들을 생성할 수 없지만, 뉴런들은 새로운 시냅스를 생기게 할 수 있고, 따라서 새로운 연결 고리를 만들 수 있다. (Still, there are billions more neurons remaining. And even though the brain cannot grow new ones, the neurons can probably sprout new synapses and thereby form new connections with one another.)"라고 시작하면서 제약을 극복할 수 있는 신경세포의 구조에 대해서 주로 얘기하고 있다. 따라서 ② 쇠약해지는 기억을 극복하기 위한 뉴런의 구조 (the mechanism of neurons for overcoming weakening memory)이 가장 적절한 대답이다.

① 새로운 기억을 만드는 데 있어 뉴런의 중요한 역할
② 쇠약해지는 기억을 극복하기 위한 뉴런의 구조
③ 인간과 쥐 뇌의 기억 능력의 유사성
④ 전기 신호를 촉진하고 전달하는 뇌세포의 역할
⑤ 재생산을 위한 자극과 도전에 대한 뇌세포의 수요

41 ①

☞ 밑줄이 있는 문장의 바로 앞 문장에서 화자는 "뇌가 감퇴하고 있을지라도 기억을 낳기 위해 더 많은 길들을 만들지도 모른다. (So the brain—even while shrinking—may be able to blaze ever more trails for laying down memory.)"라고 말한다. 따라서 밑줄 친 내용도 앞 문장과 맥락을 같이하는 내용이 나와야 한다. 밑줄 바로 앞의 내용이 뉴런 28번 경로가 막혔을 경우를 제시하고 있으므로 그럴 경우에는 뇌에서 다른 수많은 경로를 제시할 것이라는 내용이 나와야 적절하다. 따라서 교체 경로의 수에 거의 제약이 없어서 기억을 만들어 낼 수 있다는 내용으로 ①"교체 경로의 수는 거의 제약이 없다(the number of alternate routes may be virtually limitless)"가 가장 적절하다.

① 교체 경로의 수는 거의 제약이 없다.
② 뇌의 기억 능력이 잠시 멈춘다.
③ 뉴런이 통로를 더욱 강하게 만들 수 있을 것이다.
④ 뇌는 그것을 연장시킴으로써 다시 살리기 위해 노력할 것이다.
⑤ 뇌는 전기 신호를 전달하기 위해 새로운 뉴런을 생성할 것이다.

42 44

「(A) 일반적으로 젊은 성인들이 학교에서 얼마나 적게 배웠는지 알게 되면, 그들은 보통 그들이 다닌 학교나 그 곳에 자신들이 시간을 보낸 방식에 문제가 있다고 생각한다. 그러나 사실은 최고로 좋은 학교를 졸업한 최고의 졸업생들도 계속해서 배워나가야 한다.
(B) 그러나 그냥 읽기만 하지 마라. 똑같은 책을 읽은 다른 사람들과의 토론 없이 읽기만 한다면 그다지 유익하지 않다. 그리고 토론 없이 읽기는 완벽한 이해를 돕는 데 실패할 수 있다. 그래서 훌륭한 책들이 제공하는 내용이 없는 토론은 _____ 의 교환보다 조금 나은 상태로 퇴보될 수 있다.
(C) 그들이 어떻게 해야 할까? 작년에 출판된 책에서, 나는 "학교교육이 끝나고 난 후에도 스스로를 위해 배움을 계속하고 싶은 사람들이 어떻게 하면 될까?"에 대해 대답하려고 노력했다. 이 중요한 질문에 대한 간략한 정답은 읽고 토론하는 것이다.
(D) 학교 교육이 지적인 규율과 그것을 수행하기 위한 능력을 제공했다면 이 처방을 진지하게 받아들이는 사람들에게 더 낫다. 그러나 아주 많은 독서와 그에 따른 통찰력 있는 토론을 하고 학교와 대학을 졸업한 운 좋은 사람들 역시 지식인이 되기 위해서 아직 갈 길이 멀다.」

42 ②

☞ (A)에서 화자는 학교를 졸업한 후에도 공부를 지속해야 한다고 주장한다. 따라서 다음에는 어떻게 공부를 지속해야 하는지에 대한 설명이 와야 적절하므로 (C)가 타당하다. 그리고 나서 왜 토론이 독서를 동반해야 하는지에 대해 설명한 (B)가 흐름에 맞고, 마지막으로 진정한 지성인이 되려면 아직 갈 길이 멀다고 일박적인 미래에 대한 예측을 제시한 (D)가 결론 문단으로 가장 적합하다.

43 ①

☞ (D)에서 화자는 "학교교육이 끝나고 난 후에도 스스로를 위해 배움을 계속하고 싶은 사람들이 어떻게 하면 될까?(How should persons proceed who wish to conduct for themselves the continuation of learning after all schooling has been finished?)"라고 스스로 질문을 던지며 그 질문에 대한 답으로

"읽기와 토론 (Read and discussion)"을 제시했다. 화자는 계속해서 학교 교육이 끝나고 나서도 읽기와 토론을 통해 지성을 함양해야 한다고 얘기하므로 주제는 '배움을 지속하는 데 있어서 독서와 토론의 중요성'이 가장 적절하다.

① 배움을 지속하는 데 있어서 독서와 토론의 중요성
② 평생 교육에 대한 학교 교육의 기여
③ 젊은 성인들에 대한 학교 교육의 문제성
④ 젊은 성인들에게 방대한 독서의 필요성
⑤ 학교 교육 동안 독서와 토론에 영향을 미치는 요소

44   ③

☞ 빈칸 앞에 'degenerate'이라는 말이 나온다. 'degenerate'은 퇴보한다는 뜻으로 부정적인 의미를 지니고 있다. 문장은 "~의 교환보단 조금 나은 상황으로 퇴보한다."라는 뜻을 가지고 있으므로 밑줄 안에는 부정적인 단어가 나와야 한다. ①, ②, ④, ⑤는 다 긍정적인 의미를 가지고 있으므로 ③이 가장 적절하다. 또한 화자는 문단에서 내용이 없는 토론의 단점을 지적하는 것이므로 내용이 없는 토론은 '표면적인' 의견 교환에 불과한 것이다.

① 비판적인 질문   ② 깊이 있는 학교 교육   ③ 표면적인 의견   ④ 통찰력 있는 이해   ⑤ 지적인 규율

45   47

「(A) 하루는 어부가 배를 타고 바닷가에 나가서 그물을 던지려는 참에 그의 바로 앞에서 익사 직전의 남자를 보았다. 용감한 동시에 날렵한 사람으로서, 그는 뛰어내려서 보트를 잡아당기는 갈고리 장대를 붙잡고 남자의 얼굴을 향해 던졌다. 그것은 그의 눈에 안착해서 눈을 찔렀다. 어부는 그를 배로 끌어왔고 그물을 던지지 않은 채 물가로 돌아 왔다. 어부는 남자를 집으로 데려가서 그 남자가 시련을 극복할 때까지 최선의 관심과 치료를 제공했다.

(B) 다른 사람이 즉각적으로 말했다. "신사 여러분 내가 그의 눈을 망친 것은 사실이지만, 내가 한 일이 잘못된 것이라면, 그것이 어떻게 생긴 일인지 설명하겠습니다. 이 남자는 바다에서 익사할 뻔한 죽을 위기에 처해 있었습니다. 나는 그를 돕기 위해 갔습니다. 내가 갈고리 장대로 그에게 상처를 입힌 것은 사실이지만, 그를 위해서 한 일입니다. 나는 그를 구했습니다. 내가 어떤 말을 더 할 수 있을지 모르겠습니다. 부디 저에게 정의를 보여주세요!"

(C) 재판소는 무엇이 옳은 것인지에 대한 판결을 내리지 못하고 어쩔 줄 몰랐으나 그 곳에 있던 한 바보가 그들에게 말했다. "무엇을 망설입니까? 첫 번째 화자를 얼굴에 상처를 입은 바다로 다시 던지고, 그가 다시 살아남을 수 있다면, 피고인은 그에게 잃어버린 눈에 대한 보상을 하면 됩니다." 사람들 모두 한 입을 모아 부르짖었다. "당신이 틀림없이 맞습니다! 나라면 그렇게 했을 것입니다!" 그래서 판결이 났다. 남자가 자신이 그 추위를 버텨냈던 바닷가로 다시 던져질 것이라는 것을 들었을 때, 그는 죽어도 다시 돌아가지 않고 싶었다. 그는 착한 남자를 모든 법적 책임으로부터 해방시켰고, 그의 초반 태도는 비판을 받았다.

(D) 오랜 기간 동안, 남자는 그가 눈을 잃은 것이 엄청난 불행이라고 여기며 계속해서 손실에 대해 생각했다. "그 사악한 남자가 내 눈을 빼앗았고, 나는 그에게 아무 잘못도 하지 않았어. 나는 가서 그에 대한 항의를 제기할 거야. 왜냐고, 나는 그가 배겨나지 못하게 할 거야." 따라서 그는 치안 판사에게 가서 항의를 제기했고, 치안 판사는 사건을 듣기 위해 날을 잡았다. 두 사람 모두 그 날이 오기를 기다렸고, 법정으로 갔다. 눈을 잃은 사람이 당연한 듯이 먼저 말을 했다. "신사 여러분, 저는 제 눈을 잔인하게 갈고리 장대로 뽑아 버린 이 남자에 대한 항의를 제기합니다. 나는 이제 장애인이 됐습니다. 저에게 정의를 보여주세요. 그것만이 내가 원하는 것입니다. 다른 할 말은 없습니다."」

45 ④

☞ (A)는 어부가 물에 빠진 남자를 보고, 구하는 내용을 설명하고 있다. (D)에서는 눈을 잃은 남자가 억울해 하며 자신을 구해준 어부를 고소하는 내용이 나오는 것이 적절하다. 또한 (D)의 중반부에 "The one who had lost an eye spoke first, as was appropriate." 문장에서 볼 수 있듯이 눈을 잃은 남자가 먼저 얘기를 시작한다. 이 문장에서 'the one'은 (B) 문단의 머리말인 'The other'과 보통 짝을 지어 나오는 말임을 주의해서 본다. ("One … The other") 따라서 형식적인 면에서 (B)가 (D)의 뒤에 나오는 것이 적절하다. 또한 내용적인 면에서도 남자가 말을 하고 뒤에 그 남자를 구해 준 어부가 해명을 하는 것이 적절하기 때문에 (B)가 (D)뒤에 나와야 한다. 마지막으로 재판의 결과를 제시하는 (C)가 나와야 글의 흐름이 어색하지 않다.

46 ②

☞ 처음에 남자는 자신을 구해 준 어부를 고소했다. 그러나 사람들이 남자를 다시 바닷가에 빠뜨리기로 하자 남자는 자신이 추위 속에서 고통 받았던 순간을 떠올리며 어부를 풀어 주었다. 이 글은 은혜를 잊지 말라는 교훈을 주고 있다.
① 그것은 모두 지난 일이다.
② 먹이 주는 사람의 손을 물지 마라.
③ 아름다움은 보는 사람의 생각에 달린 것이다.
④ 겉보기로 판단해서는 안 된다.
⑤ 남의 떡이 커 보인다.

47 ③

☞ Then they all cried out as one man, "You're absolutely right! That's exactly what we'll do!" 문장에서 볼 수 있듯 'all'과 'we'와 같이 함께임을 강조하는 말이 쓰였다. 남자가 한 말에 '우리'라면 그렇게 할 것이라고 모두가 한 사람이 된 것처럼 '다같이' 부르짖었다. 따라서 '만장일치로'라는 말이 단어가 가장 적합하다.
① 독특하게 ② 자비롭게 ③ 만장일치로 ④ 그가 믿는 것처럼 ⑤ 차례로

48 50

「나는 선천적으로 시골 사람은 아니다. 하지만 아주 오래 전에 시골을 강요당했다. 우리는 1942년, 나의 고향인 Cardiff에서 15마일 떨어진 농장으로 대피하였다. 우리는 Cardiff항으로 향하면서 폭격기들이 시골하늘을 누비는 것을 보았다. 우리는 그 농장에서 6개월 동안 있으면서 엄청난 변화를 겪었다. 이 모든 변화는 내가 아침에 학교를 가려 나가는 순간 시작되었다. 우리 어머니는 창문 앞에서 소 한 마리가 평야를 가로지르는 것을 보고 계셨다. 어머님은 말씀하셨다. "저 소는 어디로 가고 있는 걸까, 그리고 언제쯤 도착할까?" 우리 어머님은 평소 실용적인 분이셨기 때문에 나는 순간 이 시골이 어머님을 변화시켰다고 생각했다.

그 날 아침 역으로 가는 길에 꾸물거리는 바람에 나는 학교 가는 기차를 놓쳤다. 엄마의 궁금증은 나를 불안하게 만들었다. 나는 다음에 오는 기차를 탔다. 그러나 나는 하루 종일 집중할 수 없었고 학교가 끝난 후 역으로 가는 길에 나는 내가 산울타리 꽃을 공부하며 즐거움을 찾는 나를 발견했다. 농장에 있는 집에 도착했을 때 나는 말했다. "오늘 울타리에 있는 예쁜 꽃들을 봤어. 그 꽃들의 이름을 알았으면 좋겠어."

그 후에 엄마와 나는 매일 산책을 갔다. 처음에 우리는 도시에 있을 때 습관처럼 서로에게 말을 거의 하지 않았다. 왜냐하면 도시의 화제는 하지 않은 숙제, 청소하지 않은 서랍과, 연습하지 않은 피아노와 같이 (A)_____로 덮인 얘기할 필요가 없는 것들이었다. 시간이 지나면서, 우리는 산울타리 꽃을 구분하기 시작했다. 우리는 또한 새를 구경하고 새롭게 찾아낸 새들의 이름을 음미했다. 또한,

폭격기가 멈춘 밤에는 오리온, 북두칠성, 대웅성 같은 별들을 바라보며 속삭였다.
Cardiff에 돌아왔을 때, 우리는 도시의 (B)_____로, 시험과 깨끗한 서랍과 같은 엉터리 우선순위로 돌아왔다. 그러나 우리는 자주 서로를 바라보고 웃으며 시골의 마법, 모든 것을 올바른 자리로 옮겨 놓은 마법 지팡이를 떠올린다. 그리고 많은 해가 지나고 난 지금까지도 나는 아직도 사람들이 가득한 거리에 개가 돌아다니는 것을 보며 그것이 어디로 가는지 궁금해 한다.」

*round the bend : 정신이 나간

---

48 ③

☞ "I found myself studying the hedgerow flowers and finding pleasure in their discovery. ~ Thereafter we took walks every day, my mother and I." 화자는 학교가 끝나고 역으로 가는 길에 산울타리 꽃을 보며 즐거워하는 자신의 모습을 발견하였다. 그리고 그 후로 화자와 엄마는 매일 산책을 갔다.

49 ③

☞ 마지막 문단에서 화자는 "But often we would smile at each other as we recalled that rural magic ~" Cardiff에 돌아와서도 시골의 마법을 떠올린다고 했다. 처음에는 시골 생활을 낯설어 하던 화자가 시골에 오게 된 후로 자연에 관심을 갖게 되고, 엄마와 더 교감하게 되기 때문에 시골은 화자에게 있어서 새로운 세상 같다.

① 시골의 아름다움으로부터 환멸을 느꼈다
② 전쟁 기간 동안 위험했던 지난 날
③ 시골 마법 : 새로운 세계로 눈을 뜸
④ 시골 감옥으로부터 예상치 못한 탈출
⑤ 전쟁에서 살아남기 : 시들지 않는 산울타리 꽃

50 ⑤

☞ "At first we said little to each other, as was our wont in the city."라는 말에서 비추어 보았을 때 도시 사람들은 서로 얘기를 잘 하지 않는 습관을 가지고 있다. (A)와 (B)모두 도시의 특성에 대해 설명하는 부분으로 위의 문장에서 유추해 보면 '고요함'이 가장 적절한 단어이다.

① 설득력 ② 돌진 ③ 선율 ④ 수수께끼 ⑤ 고요

01 ③

coined : 만들어진   classified : 분류되는

☞ deemed는 '여겨지는'의 뜻으로 considered와 같은 의미로 쓰인다.

「한 종류의 연구에 부적절한 것으로 <u>여겨지는</u> 실험적 방법은 다른 종류의 연구에 대한 선택의 방법이 될 수 있다.」

02 ②

monument : 기념물   legalize : 합법화하다   clarify : 명확하게 하다

☞ wield는 '휘두르다, 행사하다'의 의미로 '고용하다, 사용하다'의 employ와 바꿔 쓸 수 있다.

「세계 유적지는 국가들의 내전으로 위협당해 왔다. 전문가들은 위험에 처한 박물관, 기념물, 그리고 역사적으로 중요성을 가진 다른 지역들을 감시하고 보호하기 위해 위성 기술을 <u>사용하고 있다.</u>」

03 ④

colon cancer : 대장암   demagogue : 선동 정치가   benefactor : 후원자

☞ quack 돌팔이 의사 = charlatan 사기꾼, 돌팔이

「그가 대장암 진단을 받았다는 사실을 받아들일 수 없어서, Michael은 그의 의사가 <u>돌팔이 의사</u>인 것을 의심하고 다른 의견을 알아보기로 결심했다.」

04 ③

incite : 선동하다   appease : 누그러뜨리다, 달래다

☞ hector 위협하다, 비난하다 = criticize 비평하다, 비난하다

「아리스토텔레스는 물질적인 것에 대한 욕구에 대항하는 독실함을 가진 학생들을 <u>비난하지</u> 않았다. 그에게, 돈에 관한 관심은 좋은 것이고, 좋은 것들 중 하나인 돈을 가진 사람들은 관대함을 행할 수 있다는 것이다.」

05 ①

sneaky : 교활한   elusive : 찾기 힘든, 교묘한   fragile : 허술한

☞ sockdolager 결정적 한 방, 결정타 = decisive blow 결정적 날림

「권투 해설자는 그 헤비급 챔피언에 대해 말했다. "그의 왼쪽 훅은 정말 <u>결정타</u>군요. 그런 충격을 견딜 수 있는 건 탱크나 가능하겠지요."」

06 ③

inadequacy : 부적절함 biodiversity : 생물의 다양성 substitute A for B : B를 A로 대체하다 throughput : 처리량, 생산량

☞ (A) strength 강화 / weakness 약화

　 (B) less 덜 / more 더

　 (C) maximize 최대화하다 / reduce 줄이다

「최근에 진정한 부의 척도로써 GDP의 부적절성에 대한 인식이 증가해 왔다. 경제 자본 형성에 대한 배타적인 초점은 있으나, 다른 형태의 자본에 관한 참고 없이 – 자연 환경의 건강과 생물의 다양성, 지역 사회의 강화, 그리고 사람들의 복지와 행복. 한 사회는 더 균형 잡히고 통합된 방법으로 자본의 다양한 형태를 의식적으로 발달시켜야 한다. 사회는 어떻게 삶의 질이 유지되고 심지어 향상될 수 있는지를 증명하고, 동시에 소비와 물질 생산량을 상당히 줄이면서 경제적 부를 다른 형태의 자본으로 대치해야 한다.」

07 ⑤

culprit : 장본인, 범인 enormous : 거대한 statistic : 통계 startling : 놀라운

☞ 많은 시나리오가 있지만 이야기의 부족으로 영화의 성공이 매우 힘들다는 내용으로 보아 좋은 이야기를 만드는 것이 어렵다는 것을 알 수 있다.

「특히 영화를 위해 좋은 이야기를 창작하는 작가들에 대한 지속적인 요구가 있다. 그러나 사용하지 않는 이야기와 시나리오에 대한 훨씬 더 큰 공급이 있고, 그것을 절대 영화로 만들지는 않을 것이다. 사실, 매년 100,00개 이상의 대본이 쓰여 지고, 오직 몇 백 개만이 실제로 영화를 만든다. 그때가 되서도, 이 영화들의 대부분은 성공하지 못한다. 보통 대본이 문제이고, 가장 흔한 대본 문제는 이야기의 부족이다. 믿거나 말거나, 영화를 위한 좋은 이야기와 시나리오를 만드는 과정에 거대한 관심을 준다. 그러나 이러한 통계는 단지 좋은 이야기를 만드는 것이 얼마나 쉬운지(→어려운지)에 대한 놀라운 증거일 뿐이다.」

08 ⑤

correspond : 부합하다, 일치하다 military organization : 군대 제도 obliged : 의무를 지닌 self-renewing : 자기 혁신의 militia : 민병대, 의용군 naval service : 해군 복무 disband : 해체하다 vassal : 신하 tenant : 소작인 serf : 농노 overlord : 지배자, 권력자

☞ 마지막 부분에 개인적인 전쟁을 하거나 지배자의 군대에 합류하기도 한다는 내용으로 보아 자신만의 군대를 조직한다(organize)는 것이 더 적절하다.

「다른 형태의 통치에 대해서는 다른 종류의 군대 제도가 부합된다. 중세 시대에, 독립적인 도시들은 보통 자신들만의 군대와 그것을 행할 의무를 가진 시민들을 만들었다. 시민들은 절대로 모든 도시의 인구를 포함하지 않았고, 종종 자문 위원회의 선출된 구성원으로 좁혀졌다. 베니스와 많은 해양 도시들의 경우, 병역의무는 민병대뿐만 아니라 해군 복무로 구성되어 있었다. 장원제도에서, 지주는 종종 그들 자신의 신하, 소작인, 농노로 이루어진 군대를 해체하고(→조직하고), 때때로 그들 자신들의 개인적인 전쟁을 하거나, 또 다른 때에는 본국으로 돌아오기 전에 전쟁 기간 동안 지배자의 군대에 합류하기도 한다.」

09 ③

outrank : ~보다 더 높다 coincide : 일치하다, 동시에 일어나다 flood : 폭부, 쇄도 combustion : 연소 compensate for : ~을 보상하다, 보충하다 glaring : 두드러진, 명백한 slash : 긋다, 베다, 줄이다

☞ 인간의 나쁜 운전 습관을 언급한 것으로 보아 '효율성'보다는 '문제(problem, issue)'라고 바꾸는 것이 적절하다. 또는 본문에서 언급한 '고려사항(consideration)'도 가능할 것이다.

「작년에, 미국 차 구매자들은 차를 살 때, 심지어 질과 안전보다 더 높게 연료 경제를 가장 중요한 고려사항이라고 말했다. 그 변화는 시장에서의 하이브리드와 고효율 내부연소 엔진에 대한 폭주와 아주 잘 일치한다. 그러나 그것들은 엔진이 효율적인 만큼이나 한가지의 명백한 **효율성(一문제)**은 보충해주지 못한다.: 우리. 나쁜 운전 습관은 연료 경제를 1/3만큼이나 줄일 수 있다. 그것을 최대화하기 위해, 기술자들은 차를 다시 만들뿐만 아니라; 그들은 운전자들도 다시 만들 필요가 있다.」

10 ④

insensitivity : 무감각   inactivate : 비활성화하다   axon : 축색 돌기   thrust : 찌르다
☞ 특정 과거 사실에 대한 묘사이므로 단순 과거시제를 써야 한다. 따라서 ④는 died로 바꾸는 것이 옳다.

「통증에 대한 무감각은 위험하다. 통증 축색돌기를 비활성화하는 유전자를 가진 사람들은 반복적인 부상으로 고통을 겪고 일반적으로 위험을 피하는 것을 배우지 못한다. 이 질환을 가진 한 소년이 파키스탄에서 그의 팔을 칼로 찌르거나 타고 있는 석탄 위를 걸으면서 거리 연극을 했다. 그는 14살에 지붕에서 떨어져 죽었다. 그럼에도 불구하고, 비록 우리가 고통을 없애길 원하겠지만, 그것을 통제할 수 있는 것이 좋을 것이다.」

11 ④

residential : 주택지의, 거주의   rearrange : 재배열하다   grid : 격자   transpose : 바꾸다   inspiration : 영감
☞ 앞에서 언급한 photographic food diary를 선행사로 받으며, 뒤에 이어지는 절이 완전한 문장의 형식을 띠고 있으므로 관계부사 where가 와야 한다.

「Menno Aden은 건축물과 공간의 디자인과 거기에 사는 사람들에 대한 영향력에 매료되어 있다. 그 41세 예술가는 그의 고향 베를린에서 각각의 이미지들을 격자무늬나 모자이크 방식으로 재배열하고, 때때로 그것들을 영상 작품으로 바꾸면서, 주택지 발달의 외부와 기업 건물들의 내부를 탐구했다. 그러나 그의 최근 프로젝트에 대한 영감은 음식 일기 사진에서 나왔다. 그 사진에서 그는 의자 위에 서거나 그의 카메라를 아래로 향하게 하여 그의 식사를 찍었다. 이러한 관점은 음식보다는 공간에 대해 더 많은 강조를 두었고, 그는 전체 방의 머리 위 조명을 찍을 수 있는지에 대해 궁금해 했다.」

12 ①

amendment : 개정   Constitute : 헌법   deprive : 빼앗다   due process of law : 정당한 법적 절차
compensation : 보상   authorize : 권한을 부여하다   revolve around : ~을 중심으로 돌다
☞ ①은 "경쟁적으로 다루어지는, 문제화 되는"의 의미이므로 contesting은 contested로 바꿔야 적절하다.

「환경보호 목적을 위해 지역 토지 이용통제를 사용할 때 가장 경쟁적인 문제 중 하나는 "취득"문제이다. 미국 헌법에 대한 다섯 번째 개정은 다음과 같은 내용을 포함한다.: "어느 누구도 정당한 법적 절차 없이 생명, 자유, 재산을 빼앗겨서는 안 된다.; 또는 적절한 보상 없이 공공의 사용을 위해 개인 재산을 빼앗을 수도 없다." 이것은 정부에게 개인 재산을 취할 수 있는 권한을 부여했지만, 오직 그것이 공공의 목적을 위해서이거나, 소유주가 적절한 보상을 받았을 경우에만 이다. 땅은 물리적으로 취해질 수 있다. (예를 들어, 공원이나 고속도로를 위해) 그리고 주요 문제는 얼마나 많은 보상이 이루어져야 하는 지를 중심으로 삼는다.」

13 ④

accumulate : 쌓다, 축적하다 cave in : 무너지다 beam : 기둥 pin down : ~을 꼼짝 못하게 잡다 squeal : 꽥
소리를 지르다 offspring : 자손, 새끼 restrain : 저지하다, 억누르다

☞ ④는 엄마 돼지를, ①②③⑤는 새끼 돼지를 가리킨다.

「농장에 여느 때처럼 겨울이 시작되었다. 그러나 오후에, 모든 지옥이 나른함을 깼다. 돼지우리 지붕에 쌓여 있었던 눈이 너무
많았던 것이다. 지붕은 무너졌고 무거운 나무 기둥이 새끼 돼지들 중 한 마리를 가두었다. 그 기둥은 새끼 돼지를 꼼짝 못하게
잡았고 그것은 움직일 수가 없었다. 내가 그 현장에 도착했을 때, 새끼 돼지는 고통으로 꽥 소리를 질렀다. 내가 그 기둥을
들어내려고 했으나 예기치 못한 걸림돌에 부딪히게 되었다. 엄마 돼지가 새끼 돼지를 보호하고 있었다. 엄마 돼지는 어느
누구도 자기 새끼 근처에 접근하는 것을 허락하지 않았다. 엄마 돼지는 내가 도우려고 하고 있다는 것을 거의 이해하지 못했
다. 다른 농장의 일꾼이 줄로 엄마 돼지를 저지했을 때가 되서야, 나는 새끼 돼지에게 다가가 그를 풀어줄 수 있었다.」

14 ④

frugal : 검소한 scrimp : 절약하다

☞ 한 달에 13,000위안을 벌고 반을 저축한다고 하였으므로 ④가 옳다.

「27세의 변호사 Kevin Han은 검소하다. 아침 식사는 5위안의 두유 한 컵과 잘 익은 계란 하나다. 그는 베이징에 있는 그의
직장의 카페에서 약간의 고기 덩어리와 야채와 함께 흰 쌀밥으로 20위안의 점심식사를 한다. 그는 저녁 식사로 같은 돈을
쓴다. 그는 온라인으로 옷을 사고, 싼 임대 아파트에서 살고, 직장에 지하철을 타고 다닌다. (왕복 4위안) 만약 그가 자신의
집을 사야 한다면 절약은 필수다. 그는 한 달에 13,000위안을 벌고 반을 저축한다. "나의 부모님은 부자가 아니다. 그래서
나는 혼자 모든 것을 절약해야 한다."」

15 ⑤

「Ed Sheeran은 Radio City Music Hall show에서 매진된 관객들에게 세레나데를 연주한 후 이렇게 말한다. "나는 집에 가서
TV를 볼 거야." 22세의 그래미 후보자 싱어 송 라이터는 정말 그가 누구인지 말고는 다른 어떤 것에 대한 관심이 없다: 너의
부모님이 들어봤을지 모르는 대중가요 래퍼. 이제까지, 이러한 신선한 접근이 그를 있게 해준 것 같다. 우리를 믿지 못한다
고? 그의 6백 5십만 명 이상의 트위터 추종자들과 단지 그를 보기 위해 수많은 콘서트에 오는 수천 명의 소리 지르는 소녀들
에게 물어보라. 몇몇은 Ed가 하룻밤에 이루어진 음악의 돌풍이라고 생각한다. 그러나 그는 England Halifax 출신으로 음악에
대한 사랑이 어릴 때부터 키워졌던 예술적 가정에서 성장했다.」

16 ④

emerge from : ~에서 벗어나오다 bankruptcy court : 파산 법원 diversify : 다각화하다 turn around :
호전시키다 delve into : ~을 캐다

☞ 방콕에서 떨어진 지역에서 투자를 했다는 내용으로 보아 ④는 일치하지 않는다.

「5년 전에 Pete Bodharamik는 35세로 큰 도전을 갖고 있었다. 그는 그의 아버지가 1982년에 시작했던 Jasmine 국제 통신
지주회사를 이어 받았다. 그것은 그의 아버지가 1990년대에 빌린 돈으로 회사를 다각화한 후에 파산 법원에서 있었던 수년에
서 벗어나면서, 힘든 시간을 겪고 있었다. 그리고 Pete가 상황을 호전시킬 유일한 사람이라는 기대는 크지 않았다. 그러나
Pete는 새로운 형태의 매체에 관한 내용을 조사하고 대중문화와 연예에 대한 그의 사랑을 추구하면서 그의 시간을 보냈다.
그는 방콕에서 떨어진 지역에서 Jasmine의 한정된 방송 네트워크를 확장하는데 집중적으로 투자했는데, 그곳은 경쟁이 거의
없었다. 그는 영화, TV 쇼, 음악 비디오, 게임과 때때로 그가 시작했던 미디어 회사에서 만들어진 다른 풍부한 내용으로 그러
한 네트워크를 꾸렸다.」

17 ③

enlist : 등록시키다, 입대시키다 apprentice : 실습생, 견습생 posthumously : 죽은 후에 enshrine : 소중히 모시다

☞ Sousa의 제안으로 sousaphone을 만들었다.

「John Philip Sousa는 6세의 나이에 바이올린을 연주함으로써 그의 음악 교육을 시작했다. 13세에, 해군 군악대의 트럼본 연주자인 그의 아버지는 Sousa를 미 해병대에 견습생으로 입대시켰다. 그의 견습생 생활을 마치고 몇 년 후에, Sousa는 극장 오케스트라 단원이 되었고, 거기서 지휘를 배웠다. 행진 금관악기 베이스, 수자폰은 디자인에 있어서 Sousa의 여러 제안으로 필라델피아 악기 제작자 J. W. Pepper에 의해 1893년에 만들어졌다. 그는 해군 악대를 떠나고 몇 년 후 Sousa 밴드를 조직했다. 그의 밴드는 파리 세계 박람회를 포함하여 미국과 전 세계에서 연주하였다. Sousa는 펜실베이니아에서 77세의 나이에 심장마비로 죽었다. 그는 그 전 날 Ringgold 밴드와 함께 "The Stars and Stripes Forever"의 리허설을 지휘했다. 그는 죽은 후에 1976년 위대한 미국인으로 명예의 전당의 일원이 되었다.」

18 ①

aspirational : 야심찬, 희망적인 emphatically : 단호하게 antiquated : 구식의 rhetoric : 수사법, 표현 disregard : 무시하다 constrained : 억압된, 제한된 optimization : 최적화 parameter : 변수, 한도 allocate : 할당하다 scarcity : 부족

☞ 제한된 자원에 대해 모든 인간이 다 가질 수 없음은 균형에 대한 기본 개념이 잘 설명해 준다.

「아마 인류를 위해 만들어진 가장 큰 함정은 다음과 같은 문구일 것이다. "모든 것을 가지기." 연설, 머리기사, 기사들에서 오르내리면서, 이 세 단어는 야심찬 것처럼 의도되었으나 대신에 우리 모두가 부족한 것처럼 느끼도록 만든다. 나는 단호하게 "네, 나는 다 가지고 있어요."라고 말하는 사람을 만나본 적이 없다. 왜냐하면 우리가 가진 것이 무엇이든지간에, 어느 누구도 다 가질 수는 없기 때문이다. "모든 것을 가지기"라는 구식의 표현은 모든 경제적 관계의 기본을 무시한다.: 균형에 대한 생각. 우리 모두는 직업, 아이들, 관계와 같은 변수에 근거된 유용성을 최대화하려고 하고, 시간 자원을 할당하는데 최선을 다하면서 존재하는 제한된 최적화를 다루고 있다. 그러므로 이러한 자원의 부족 때문에, 우리 중 누구도 "모두 가질"수 없고 그렇다고 주장하는 사람들은 대부분 거짓말을 하는 것이다.」

19 ②

sustainability : 지속 가능성 feature : 특집으로 다루다, 집중 조명하다 outcome : 결과 substitute : 대체물, 대리인

☞ 앞에서 인간의 시간 사용에 관한 유형은 생태학적 결과의 핵심 추진 요인이고, 일을 더 빨리 하는 것은 큰 피해를 준다고 말했기 때문에, 더 무거운 생태학적 발자취를 갖게 되고 1인당 더 큰 에너지 사용을 하게 되는 요인은 시간에 억압받는 가정과 사회라는 것을 추론할 수 있다.

「생태학적 지속 가능성에 대한 논의는 주로 온실 가스 방출, 생물의 다양성, 그리고 다른 자연적 세계에 대한 측정에 초점을 맞춘다. 그것들은 생산과 인구에 있어서 경제적, 사회적 경향을 포함한다. 그러나 그것들은 시간 사용에 관해서는 거의 집중 조명하지 않는다. 그러나 인간의 시간 사용에 관한 유형들은 생태학적 결과의 핵심 추진 요인이다. 사람들은 그들의 일상생활과 활동을 수행하기 위해 시간, 돈, 그리고 천연 자원을 혼합한다. 기업들은 생산을 하기 위해 시간, 물적 자본 그리고 천연 자본을 혼합한다. 어느 정도로, 시간과 천연 자원은 서로에 대한 대체물이다 : 일을 더 빨리 하는 것은 보통 지구에 거대한 피해를 준다. 그래서 시간적 스트레스를 받는 가정과 사회는 더 무거운 생태학적 발자취를 갖게 되고 1인당 더 큰 에너지 사용을 하게 된다.」

20 ①

inmost : 가장 깊은 속의   disposition : 기질, 성향   gymnasium : 체육관, 단련장   moderation : 절제, 중용
ferocity : 잔인함   defer to : ~의 의견에 따르다

☞ 플라톤이 말하기를 시나 음악이 젊은이들을 파괴하고 있다고 했고 따라서 국가가 젊은이들을 통제하고
  훈련시키려면 정치학에 따라 미학이 통제되어야 한다는 내용이다.

「그의 공화국에서 플라톤은 젊은이들을 타락시키는 것에 대해 시인을 비판했다. 또한, 그는 이상적인 공화국은 시와 연극을
통제하는 것보다 훨씬 더 강하게 음악을 통제한다고 말한다. 플라톤이 말하기를, 음악적 리듬은 "그것들을 영혼의 가장 깊은
곳으로 밀어 넣는" 대단한 능력을 갖고 있다. 때때로 음악은 단련장에서의 시간으로 너무 힘든 시민들의 기질을 부드럽게
해주기 때문에 좋다. 그러나 대개 음악에 대한 기호는 우리가 영혼에서 추구하는 절제를 위협하고 잔인함에 불을 지핀다.
만약 국가가 젊은이들을 잘 훈련시키고 싶다면 <u>미학은 정치학의 의견에 따라야 한다.</u>」

21 ③

adore : 정말 좋아하다   descend : 내려가다   mitochondria : 미토콘드리아   meander : 거닐다

☞ 빨리 타건, 느리게 타건 자전거 타는 것을 즐긴다는 내용으로 안장(자전거의)을 정말 좋아함을 알 수 있다.

「나는 빠른 것을 아주 좋아한다. 나는 마치 내가 중력의 경계를 탈출하는 것처럼 하강과 회전으로 내려가는 것을 좋아한다.
비록 사진 속에서 내가 자전거 선수와 닮았지만, 그리고 가끔 내가 평범한 사람이라는 사실이 가능한 한 빨리 가려고 노력하
는 것을 막지는 못하지만, 나는 자랑스러운 평범한 사람이다. 나는 내 자신을 어려움 속에 밀어 넣을 때 내 자신에 관한 중요
한 뭔가를 발견한다. 나는 똑같이 느린 것을 아주 좋아한다. 내가 똑바로 앉아 회전을 할 때, 나는 세상을 보고 활기를 느끼고
내 공동체와 연결되어 있음을 느낀다. 나는 내가 청바지를 입고 농장으로 페달을 밟고 달리거나, 시골길을 거닐 때 자전거
선수로써 더 완벽함을 느낀다. 나는 정말로 <u>내 안장을 사랑한다.</u>」

22 ②

alter : 바꾸다   coordination : 합동, 조정력   pursuit : 취미   heritability : 상속 가능성, 유전력
roundabout : 대략적인, 간접적인

「정확히 어떻게 유전자가 주어진 행동의 가능성을 증가시키는지는 복잡한 문제이다. 몇몇 유전자는 뇌의 화학물질을 통제하지
만, 다른 유전자들은 행동에 간접적으로 영향을 끼친다. 너의 유전자가 너를 매우 매력적으로 만든다고 가정해 보자. 그 결과,
낯선 사람들은 너를 향해 미소 짓고 많은 사람들이 너를 알고 싶어 한다. 너의 외모에 대한 그들의 반응은 너의 성격을 변화시
킬 것이고, 그리고 만약 그렇다면, 유전자는 너의 환경을 바꿈으로써 너의 행동을 바꿨다. 또 다른 예로, 키, 달리기 속도,
조정력에 있어서 평균보다 보다 더 많은 능력을 조장하는 유전자를 갖고 태어난 한 아이를 상상해라. 그 아이는 농구에서
일찍 성공을 보여주고, 곧 점점 더 많은 시간을 농구하면서 보내게 된다. 곧 그 아이는 다른 취미 - TV 보기, 장기 두기,
우표 모으기 - 에는 더 적은 시간을 보내게 된다. 따라서 많은 행동에 관해 측정된 유전력은 일부 다리 근육에 영향을 끼치는
유전자에 달려있을지도 모른다. 이것은 가설적 예이지만, 다음과 같은 요점을 설명해준다.: <u>유전자는 간접적인 방법으로 행동
에 영향을 끼친다.</u>」

23 ①

smattering : 조금   tally : 총계를 내다   staggering : 충격적인

「지구의 상층부 대기 - 자외선 방사로 넘쳐나며, 거의 산소가 없는 영하의 - 는 살 수 없는 공간이다. 그러나 지난겨울,
Georgia 기술 연구소 과학자들은 수십억 개의 박테리아가 실제로 거기에서 번성하고 <u>있는</u> 것을 발견했다. 매우 적은 미생물
을 기대하면서 연구자들은 NASA 제트 비행기로 지구 표면 상공 6마일로 날아갔다. 거기서, 그들은 입자를 모으는 필터를
통해 바깥 공기를 펌프질했다. 지상으로 돌아와서 그들은 유기체를 계산했고, 그 수는 충격적이었다.: 그들이 <u>먼지</u>나 다른
입자라고 가정했었던 것의 20%가 살아 있었다. 지구는 박테리아 거품으로 둘러 쌓여있는 것 같다.」

24 ④

billionaire : 억만장자   philanthropy : 자선 활동   nothing less than : 다름 아닌   uplift : 고양시키다
morality : 도덕성   underpin : 뒷받침하다   congenial : 마음이 맞는

☞ 억만장자 Chang은 자신의 그룹이 도덕성을 기본으로 성장했다고 믿고 자신이 번 돈으로 사회의 도덕성을 고양시키려고 한다. 따라서 "기업가가 도덕성의 전도에 눈을 돌리다."라는 제목이 적절하다.

「억만 장자가 그들의 부를 창출한 후에 자선활동으로 눈을 돌릴 때, 그들은 종종 가난한 학생들을 위해 장학금을 대고, 건강관리를 향상시키는 데 애를 쓰고, 또는 예술에 기여한다. Chang Yung-Fa의 임무는 다름 아닌 사회적 가치를 재조직하는 것이다. 5년 전 그는 만화 잡지 Morals를 시작했고, 그것은 타이완과 전 세계에서 사람들의 도덕성을 고양시키고 있다. 그가 돈을 벌든지, 잃던지 간에 도덕성은 85세의 Chang이 하는 많은 것을 뒷받침해준다. 그는 그의 Evergreen 그룹 – 세계에서 가장 많은 부의 갖고 있는 운송회사, 호텔, EVA 항공, 섬의 주요 공항으로 가는 장거리 버스를 포함하는 – 은 회사의 도덕성을 배경으로 하는 마음 맞는 직원 관계 때문에 매우 번창한다고 믿는다.」

25 ②

reignite : 다시 일으키다, 다시 불을 붙이다   astronomer : 천문학자   telescope : 망원경   optimum : 최적의
frigid : 몹시 추운   crater : 분화구   proponent : 지지자

☞ 거대한 망원경을 달에 설치하여 달을 관찰하는 임무를 설명하고 있다.

「아마 달 프로그램을 다시 일으키는 것에 가장 흥분한 과학자들은 달 전문가가 아니라, 넓은 범위의 대상을 연구하는 천문학자들 일 것이다. 그러한 과학자들은 달의 건너편에 직경 30미터의 거대한 망원경을 설치하는 새로운 임무를 좋아할 것이다. 하나의 망원경이 최적의 작동을 위해 필요로 하는 두 가지는 극심한 추위와 매우 작은 진동이다. 달의 온도는 어두운 쪽에 있는 분화구에서는 섭씨 영하 200도 정도로 몹시 추울 수 있다. 진동의 활동이 없기 때문에 달은 안정된 기반이다. 영구적인 어둠은 망원경의 지속적인 사용이 가능하다는 것을 의미한다. 지지자들은 이러한 상태에서 달에 설치된 망원경은 Hubble 망원경이 10년 걸린 것에 대한 대체로 17일 안에 많은 것을 성취할 수 있다고 주장한다.」

26 ③

optimism : 낙천주의, 긍정   stave off : 늦추다, 피하다   traction : 견인, 끌기   fare well : 잘 지내다   meta : 더 높은, 초월한   inclined to : ~하고 싶어지는   upbeat : 긍정적인   distraught : 괴로운, 제 정신이 아닌
solace : 위로   downfall : 몰락, 쇠퇴

☞ 긍정이 암 환자들에게 도움이 된다는 증거 없는 믿음으로 오히려 해가 될지도 모른다는 내용이다.

「긍정은 당신을 살아있도록 해 준다 – 또는 적어도 암을 피하게 해 준다 – 라는 믿음은 1979년 Lancet 의학 잡지에서 유방암 환자들이 회복한 것에 대한 연구를 발표하고 난 후 관심을 끌었다. 그 때 부터, "건강한 정신"을 가진 환자들이 절망감을 갖고 있는 사람들보다 더 잘 생활한다는 것이 가정의 신념이 되었다. 그러나 최근의 몇몇 더 깊은 분석들은 긍정이 정말로 암 환자들의 생명을 연장시켜주는지에 대한 확실한 증거가 부족하다는 것을 발견했다. 결정적인 자료의 부족에도 불구하고, 긍정적 사고의 힘에 대한 믿음은 너무 퍼져서 실제로 해를 끼칠지도 모른다. 암 환자들은 그들이 괴로울 때조차도 긍정적으로 행동하고 싶어지고, 위로나 치료를 찾는 것 대신에 그들의 절망을 숨기거나, 만약 그들의 질병이 진행되면 자신을 비난할지도 모른다.」

27 ①

gravitation : 만유인력   derive : 끌어내다   occupy : 사로잡다, 점령하다   endeavor : 노력

☞ 태양계를 이해하려는 많은 과학자들의 노력에 대한 글이다.

「사모스의 에게 해 제도의 아리스타르코스는 지구와 다른 행성들이 태양 주변을 움직인다고 먼저 주장했다. - 그것은 2,000년 후에 코페르니쿠스가 그것을 다시 주장할 때까지 천문학자들에 의해 거절당했던 생각이었다. 코페르니쿠스 이후, 덴마크의 천문학자 Tycho Brahe가 Hveen의 Baltic섬에 있는 그의 관측소에서 화성의 움직임을 관찰했다.; 그 결과 Johannes Kepler 는 화성과 지구와 다른 행성들이 태양 주변을 타원으로 움직이고 있다는 것을 보여줄 수 있었다. 그러고 나서 Isaac Newton 은 그의 만유인력의 법칙과 운동의 법칙을 주장했고 이것들로부터 전체의 태양계에 대한 정확한 묘사를 끌어내는 것이 가능 했다. 이것은 다음 세기의 몇몇 가장 훌륭한 과학자들과 수학자들의 마음을 사로잡았다.」

28 ①

self-interest : 사리사욕   adapt : 맞추다   discipline : 훈육, 규율   effectual : 효과적인   restrain : 억제하 다   fraud : 사기, 속임수   negligence : 부주의, 과실   self-command : 자제, 극기   propriety : 예절, 적절 성   prudence : 신중, 사리분별   defer : 보류하다, 유보하다   gratification : 만족감

☞ 시장 경제에서 성공하기 위해서는 자기 절제와 훈육이 필요하다고 말하고 있다.

「교환을 기초로 하는 상업 사회에서, 모든 사람은 "어느 정도 상인이 된다." 노동 분업과 다른 사람들에 대한 결과를 초래하는 의존성과 함께 시장에서의 사리사욕에 대한 추구는 다른 사람들의 기대에 대해 그의 행동을 맞추게 되는 결과를 낳는다. 그러 므로 시장 그 자체는 훈육의 기관이다. Adam Smith가 다음과 같이 썼다. "노동자에게 행해지는 실질적이고 효과적인 훈육은 그의 기업에 대한 훈육이 아니라 그의 고객에 대한 훈육이다. 그것은 속임수를 억제하고 그의 과실을 바로잡는 실직에 대한 두려움이다." 다른 사람들과의 경제적인 교환에 성공하기 위해서는, 개인은 Smith가 "예절"이라고 부르는 적당한 수준의 자제 를 개발시키도록 이끌어진다. 시장이 장려하는 특징은 신중함과 장기간의 이익을 위해 단기간의 만족감을 보류하는 능력을 포함한다.」

29 ②

purport : 주장하다   ailment : 가벼운 질병   measle : 홍역   epilepsy : 간질   rhinoceros : 코뿔소   poaching : 불 법 침입   legalize : 합법화하다   stockpile : 비축량   confiscated : 몰수된   black-market : (불법)암시장

☞ 금지법에도 불구하고 코뿔소가 멸종 위기에 처하게 되었으나 합법적으로 강하게 규제를 한다면 오히려 코뿔소를 살릴 수 있을 것이라고 주장한다.

「열부터 홍역, 간질에 이르기까지 다양한 질병을 치료하는 것으로 주장되는 코뿔소 뿔은 수천 년 동안 중국 의학에서 재료로 소중히 여겨져 왔다. 그들의 뿔을 위해 사람들이 찾는 하얀 코뿔소는 1910년까지 남아프리카에서 개체 수가 100마리까지 떨어지는 것을 보았다. 오늘날, 코뿔소 부위의 판매에 대한 1977 금지법에도 불구하고 아프리카의 코뿔소는 다시 한 번 멸종 의 위기에 처해 있다. 금지법이 코뿔소의 불법적인 침해를 막지 못해왔기 때문에, 역설적으로 코뿔소 뿔에 대한 매우 규제된 거래를 합법화하는 것이 결국 그 동물들을 구할 수 있었다. 코뿔소 뿔은 그 동물들을 다치게 하지 않고 자르거나 깎을 수 있고, 그 뿔들은 다시 자란다. 만약 하나의 중앙 조직이 강하게 통제를 한다면, 현재의 수요는 몰수된 암시장의 뿔의 비축량과 자연사한 코뿔소로부터 모은 뿔과 함께 합법적인 뿔의 절단으로 만족될 수 있을 것이다.」

30 ②

vegetate : 하는 일 없이 지내다 dusk : 해질녘 fetch : 데려옴, 지참 oblige : 의무적으로 ~하다, 돕다, 베풀다 snug : 아늑한

☞ 더운 여름, 아무것도 하지 않고 편안한 오후를 보내는 모습이다.

「매우 더운 여름이었다. 태양은 밝게 비추고 있지만, Jake는 뒷마당 그늘에서 편안했다. 그는 오른손에 차가운 한 잔의 차와 왼손에 읽기 좋은 책 하나를 가지고 있었다. Jake는 세상에 신경 쓸 것이 하나도 없었다. 오늘, 그는 해질녘까지 앉아서 하는 일 없이 시간을 보낼 것이다. 그의 명랑한 강아지는 공을 가지고 놀고 있었다. 그녀는 마치 그를 게임에 초대하는 것처럼 Jake를 바라보았다. 그러나 그는 오늘 그녀를 보살피지 않을 것이다. 오직 리히터계로 지진의 강도 10만이 그를 그의 아늑한 둥지에서 끌어낼 수 있었다.」

31 ①

cultivation : 배양 trillion 조 unsustainable : 지속 불가능한 in vitro meat : 배양육 culture : 배양하다 hang-up : 콤플렉스, 장애 mouth-wateringly : 군침이 돌게

☞ 배양육의 생산에 대한 어느 정도의 문제가 있긴 하지만 사실 이전보다 더 효율성이 있는 방법이라는 내용으로 쓰레기 재활용에 관한 이야기는 흐름에 맞지 않다.

「세포 배양의 진보 덕택에, 연구자들은 실험실에서 실질적이고 먹을 수 있는 고기를 기르는 것에 이전보다 더 가까워졌다. 미국에서 매년 음식을 위해 죽임을 당하는 90억 동물들을 기르는 것에 대한 윤리를 뛰어 넘어, 공장식 농장은 거대한 양의 쓰레기를 만들어 낸다. ①과학자들은 이러한 쓰레기를 재활용하기 위한 효율적인 방법을 생각해내려고 애쓴다. ②2조 파운드의 동물 쓰레기는 공기와 물을 오염시킨다. ③오염 문제 이외에도, 고기에 대한 세계의 수요는 2050년까지 60% 증가할 것으로 예상되고, 닭, 돼지, 소들을 먹이기 위해 필요한 농지와 곡물의 양은 지속 불가능할지도 모른다. ④그러나 배양육을 생산하는 것 – 동물 세포에서 배양되고 실험실에서 자라는 근육조직 – 은 어떠한 장애도 없다. ⑤사실, 그것은 45% 더 적은 에너지와 99% 더 적은 땅을 사용하면서, 존재하는 고기 생산 방법과 비교하여 매우 효율성이 있다.」

32 ④

sparkling : 뛰어난, 반짝이는 obscure : 모호하게 하다 vital : 필수적인 eager to : 몹시 ~하고 싶어 하는 articulate : 분명히 표현하다 initiate : 시작하다 instinctively : 본능적으로

☞ 아이가 자극을 받고 스스로 대답을 찾은 후에 대화를 시작한다는 내용으로 보아 ④번은 전체 흐름과 어울리지 않는다.

「유아의 뛰어난 대화의 부족은 우리 모두가 의사소통을 할 수 있는 능력을 갖고 태어난다는 사실을 모호하게 만들지도 모른다. ①언어에 대한 능력은 눈, 귀, 팔, 다리, 그리고 중요한 기관들과 함께, 분만실 안의 작고, 울부짖는 몸속에 존재한다. ② 그 능력은 자극을 받는다. – 우리는 단어를 만들기 위해 사람들이 말하는 것을 들을 필요가 있다. – 그러나 우리는 몹시 말하고 싶어 한다. ③신생아는 질문에 대한 대답을 천천히 기다리고 있다.: "내가 내 주변에 있는 물체들을 뭐라고 부를까요? 어떻게 내가 긍정적이고 부정적인 문장들을 만들까요? 어떻게 내가 사물과 사람들에 대한 감정을 표현할 수 있을까요?" ④ 아기가 그러한 질문에 명확하게 표현을 할 수 있을 때가 되서야, 부모는 대화를 시작한다. ⑤아이의 뇌는 본능적으로 이러한 질문에 대한 대답을 찾고, 그때 스펀지처럼 모든 것을 흡수한다.」

33 ⑤

outspend : ~보다 많이 쓰다   oddly : 이상하게도   uninsured : 보험에 들지 않은   viable : 실행 가능한
clinician : 임상의사

☞ 주어진 문장의 all of those people은 앞에서 언급한 보험에 들지 않은 사람들을 일컫는 것으로 ⑤에 들어
가는 것이 적절하다.

「건강관리에 관해 세계의 모든 다른 선진국들보다 많은 비용을 쓰려고 하는 나라로, 미국은 이상하게도 의사가 부족하다. 우리
는 100,000명 당 30명의 약 전문 의사를 가지고 있다. 그것은 다른 산업 국가보다 훨씬 적다. 당신은 미국의 의사 부족과
베이비붐 세대가 은퇴를 하면서 얼마나 상황이 더 나빠지고 있는지에 대한 머리기사를 본 적이 있을 것이다. 이것은 막 의료
보험 제도에 가입하려는, 이전에 보험에 들지 않은 수백 만 명의 사람들에 의해 더 나빠지기만 한다. 그러한 모든 사람들을
누가 관리해줄 것인가? 가장 실행 가능한 해결책은 진보되고 전문적인 훈련을 받고 의사들처럼 많은 것을 하도록 자격을
받은 간호사와 임상의사의 수를 늘리는 것이다.」

34 ⑤

depict : 묘사하다   biblical : 성서의   mosque : 회교 사원   exclusive : 배타적인   sacred : 신성한   secular : 세속
적인   plain : 소박한   exquisite : 정교한, 강렬한   geometric : 기하학적인

☞ 유럽과 중동의 예술은, 전자는 성서의 이미지를 포함했고, 후자는 기하학적인 문양을 사용했다는 점에서
달랐다.

「수백 년 동안 유럽에서, 종교적 예술은 거의 존재하는 유일한 예술 유형이었다. 교회와 다른 종교적 건물들은 성경에 나오는
사람들과 이야기를 묘사한 그림으로 가득 채워져 있다. 비록 대부분의 사람들이 읽을 수는 없었지만, 그들은 교회 벽 그림
속에 있는 성서의 이야기들을 여전히 이해할 수 있었다. 반대로, 중동 예술의 주요 특징 중 하나는 인간과 동물의 이미지가
없다는 것이었다. 이슬람법에 의해, 예술가들은 양탄자나 그릇과 같은 일상의 작은 물건들을 제외하고는 인간과 동물의 형상
을 베끼는 것이 허락되지 않았다. 따라서 궁전, 회교 사원, 다른 건물들 위에, 이슬람 예술가들은 배타적인 아라베스크 무늬를
만들었다. - 원, 사각형, 삼각형과 같은 모양이 있는 매우 아름다운 장식.」

35 ②

prospect : 희망, 가망   take a turn for the worse : 차차 나빠지다   bluster : 거세게 불다   engulf : 에워싸다
undo : 망치다, 실패하게 만들다   spell : 잠깐의 시간   sensation : 느낌   trickle : 흘러내리다   anticipate :
기대하다, 예상하다   compact : 압축하다   drip off : 방울방울 흐르다   ritual : 의식

☞ 악화된 상황에서 조금 걸어 나아가(A) 눈 덩어리로 물을 만들고(C) 그것을 즐기고 있는(B) 내용이다.

「달을 보고 판단했을 때, 나는 폭우에 갇힌 지 거의 4주가 되었다는 것을 알았다. 나는 1월 6일에 날짜 세는 것을 멈췄다.
왜냐하면, 그 날 나의 희망이 갑자기 더 나빠졌기 때문이다.

(A) 거센 구름은 태양이 할 수 있는 희망적인 것들을 재빨리 망치면서 눈으로 내 산비탈을 에워쌌다. 그러나 나는 해가 잠깐
나는 동안 약간의 걸어 나갔다.

(C) 나는 눈을 얼음 덩어리로 뭉쳐서 햇빛에 놓으면, 마실 수 있는 물이 바닥에 생길 거라는 것을 알게 되었다. 이것은 내
입 속에서 눈이나 얼음을 녹이는 것보다 훨씬 쉬웠다. 눈 덩이를 녹이는 것이 내 일상의 의식 같은 일이 되었다.

(B) 내 목구멍에 흘러내리는 시원한 물의 느낌이 너무 좋아서 나는 그것에 거의 중독되었다. 나는 미리 몇 시간 동안 작은
즐거움을 기대했다.」

「지구 가까이의 물체(NEOs)는 주기적으로 지구의 궤도를 건너 우리의 행성으로 가까이 오는 거대한 물체에 대한 현대 용어이다. 그것들은 소행성, 유성체, 혜성을 포함한다. 거의 모든 소행성은 화성과 목성 사이에 위치하여 소행성대에 갇혀 있다. 천 개 이상의 소행성이 적어도 1마일의 넓이라고 추정되고 있다. 아마 몇 묶음은 3마일 또는 그 이상의 넓이일 것이다. 소행성은 먼지 입자나 작은 돌덩이도 해당되기 때문에 크기에 있어서 더 낮은 제한은 없다. 그러나 어떠한 소행성도 대기를 지닐 만큼 크지는 않다. 무엇이 소행성을 만들었을까? Isaac Asimov는 소행성은 한 작은 행성의 거주자들이 핵에너지를 발견했고 그들의 세계를 작은 파편 조각으로 날려 버리고 남은 부분이라는 한때 유행했던 과학 허구적 생각을 제기했다. 그러나 심지어 핵폭발조차도 소행성대를 형성할 만큼 거대하지는 않을 것이다. 일반적인 과학적 의견은 소행성이 하나의 행성으로 통합되지 못한 물질이라는 것이다. 거대한 NEO의 최근 출현 중 하나는 시베리아에서의 1908년 충돌이었다. 그것은 주변 수마일의 나무들을 부쉈고, 순록 떼를 죽였다. 지구는 비슷한 충격을 증명하는 눈에 보이는 수십 개의 분화구들의 자국이 있다. 거대한 NEO의 충격은 6천 5백 년 전, 공룡을 포함한 생명의 거대한 멸종을 일으켰다고 믿어진다.」

36 ⑤

☞ 주어진 문장의 It은 앞에서 언급한 시베리아의 충돌을 의미한다.

37 ②

asteroid : 소행성 meteoroid : 유성체 remnant : 나머지, 남은 부분 inhabitant : 거주자 fragment : 조각, 파편 prevailing : 우세하는, 일반적인 testify : 증언하다, 증명하다

☞ Isaac Asimov가 제기한 의견으로 위에서 언급하고 있다.

「두 가지 사적 사실은 컴퓨터 보안 분야에서 다루어질 필요가 있는 기본적인 문제를 강조한다. 먼저, 모든 복잡한 소프트웨어 시스템은 결국 나중에 수리를 필요로 하는 결함이나 고장을 드러냈다. 둘째, 다양한 보안 공격에 취약하지 않은 컴퓨터 하드웨어, 소프트웨어 시스템을 만드는 것은 매우 어렵다. 이 어려움에 대한 설명은 1990년대 초기에 Microsoft에 의해 도입된 윈도우 NT 작동 시스템이다. 윈도우 NT는 높은 수준의 보안을 가질 것으로 약속되었다. 슬프게도, 윈도우 NT는 이 약속을 이행하지 못했다. 이 작동 시스템과 뒤를 이은 윈도우 버전은 다양한 범위의 보안 약점으로 매우 어려움을 겪어 왔다. 강한 컴퓨터 보안을 제공하는 것과 관련된 문제는 디자인과 실행 둘 다를 포함했다. 어떤 하드웨어나 소프트웨어 모듈을 디자인 할 때, 사실 그 디자인이 의도된 수준의 보안을 제공해 준다고 장담되기는 어렵다. 이 문제는 많은 예기치 못한 보안 약점을 낳았다. 비록 디자인이 어느 정도 정확할지라도 또 다른 약점의 요인들을 제공하면서 문제와 고장 없이 디자인을 만들기는 어렵다.」

38 ③

☞ 컴퓨터 보안 문제를 해결할 수 있는 시스템을 만들기는 어렵다고 말하고 있다.

39 ⑤

subsequently : 나중에 extraordinarily : 엄청나게, 매우 vulnerable : 취약한 successor : 후임 implementation : 이행, 실행, 충족 assure : 장담하다 unanticipated : 예기치 못한 vulnerability : 취약성, 약점 plague : 성가시게 하다

☞ 다양한 보안 공격에 취약하지 않은 시스템을 만들기는 어렵다는 내용에 대해 윈도우 NT와 그 뒤를 이은 버전을 예로 들었기 때문에 보안 문제로 어려움을 겪는다는 내용이 적절하다.

40 42

「많은 이야기들처럼, the Bell Witch가 누구인지, 어떤 사람인지에 관한 세부사항들은 버전마다 다르다. 일반적인 이야기는 그것이 John Bell의 인색한 늙은 이웃인 Kate Batts라는 이름을 가진 여자의 유령이었다는 것이다. Batts는 Bell이 그녀에게 땅 구매에 관해 사기를 쳤다고 믿었고, 그녀의 임종에서 John Bell과 그의 가족들에게 그녀가 귀신으로 나타날 것이라고 다짐했다. 이 버전은 1933년에 출판된 Tennessee의 안내책자에 나온다.: "분명, Bell 가족들은 늙은 Kate Batts의 악의적인 영혼에게 수년 동안 고통을 당했다. John Bell과 그의 딸 Betsy가 주 목표였다. 다른 가족 구성원들에 대해서는, 그 마녀는 무관심하거나, 또는 Bell 부인에게는 우호적이었다. 어느 누구도 그녀를 본 적은 없었지만, Bell 집에 오는 모든 방문객들도 그녀의 소리를 들었다. 늙은 Kate의 영혼은 John과 Betsy를 이리저리 끌고 다니며 괴롭혔다. 그녀는 그들에게 가구와 접시를 던졌다. 그녀는 그들의 코를 당기고, 머리카락을 홱 잡아당기고, 바늘로 그들을 찔렀다. 그녀는 그들이 밤새 잠을 못자도록 소리를 질렀고, 식사 시간에 그들의 입에서 음식을 낚아챘다." Bell Witch의 소식은 빨리 퍼졌다. 귀신이 나타난다는 소문이 Nashville로 퍼졌을 때, 가장 유명한 시민 중 한 사람인 Andrew Jackson 장군이 친구들의 한 무리를 모아 그것을 조사해보기로 결심했다. 그 미래의 미국 대통령은 그것을 거짓말이라고 폭로하거나 그 영혼을 보내버리기를 원했다. Jackson과 그의 일행들이 여행을 하고 있었을 때, 갑자기 마차가 멈췄다. 남자들은 마차를 밀어 보았지만, 움직이지 않았다. 그 때 수풀 속에서 다음과 같이 말하는 목소리가 들려왔다. "좋아, 장군. 내가 마차를 움직이게 해주지. 나는 오늘 밤 당신을 볼 거야." 놀란 남자들은 목소리의 근원지를 찾을 수 없었다. 말이 그 때 예기치 못하게 가던 길을 걷기 시작했고, 마차는 다시 움직였다. Jackson은 정말로 그 날 밤 그 마녀와 만나게 되었고, 그가 Bell가의 마녀보다는 영국과 싸우는 것이 낫겠다고 소리치며 다음 날 아침 떠났다.
Bell가의 마녀 현상에 대한 몇 가지 설명이 시간이 지나면서 밝혀졌다. 한 가지는 그 귀신은 Betsy와 Betsy가 사랑했던 Joshua Gardner라는 소년의 학교 선생님 Richard Powell 에 의해 만들어진 거짓말이라는 것이었다. Powell은 Betsy를 정말 사랑했고 Gardner와 그녀의 관계를 깨기 위해 뭔가를 하기로 했다. 다양한 속임수를 통해, Powell이 Gardner를 겁주기 위해 유령 같은 모든 효과를 만들었다. 사실, Gardner는 결국 Betsy와 헤어졌고 그 지역을 떠났다. 그러나 어떻게 Powell이 그 모든 효과를 완성했는지에 대해서는 만족스러운 설명이 없었다. 그러나 Powell은 승자가 된 것이었다. 결국, 그는 Betsy Bell과 결혼했다.」

40 ①

☞ Bell 가족에게 있었던 유령 사건에 관한 이야기이다.

41 ⑤

☞ (E)는 딸 Betsy를 가리키고 나머지는 유령 Kate Batts를 가리킨다.

42 ④

mean : 인색한 deathbed : 임종 haunt : 따라다니다, 귀신으로 나타나다 torment : 들볶다, 고통을 주다 malicious : 악의적인 lead someone on ~ merry chase : ~를 목적 없이 이리저리 끌고 다니다 yank : 홱 잡아당기다 snatch : 잡아 뺏다 hoax : 거짓말

☞ Jackson 장군이 Bell의 집에서 나오면서 차라리 영국과 싸우겠다고 말한 것이지 영국과 싸우기 위해 남부에서의 전투를 중지한 것은 아니다.

43 45

(가) 나는 내가 13살이었을 때 여름, 조부모님의 현관에서 Veranda Beach에 대해 처음 들었다. 여유로운 밤은 흐린 청색의 언덕과 비 냄새로 찬 공기를 남겼다. 대화가 다가오는 여름으로 바뀌었을 때, 마지막 그림자가 황혼으로 녹아들었다.

(라) "계획은?" 할아버지가 물으셨다. 의자를 뒤로 기울이면서, 아버지가 대답하셨다. "그냥 Veranda Beach" 그들은 모두 빙그레 웃었다. 내 가슴이 마구 뛰었다. Veranda Beach? 어디 있었지? 언제 가지? "왜, 너 벌써 거기 있잖아."아버지가 놀리셨다. 그들이 나에게 끔찍한 진실을 말했을 때 부드러운 웃음소리가 퍼졌다. 우리는 어디에도 가지 않을 것이다. Veranda Beach는 앞 현관이었다. 내 사춘기 영혼이 <u>곤두박질쳤다</u>. 그들은 그 지루한 현관에서 무엇을 보았을까? 그들은 다른 먼 곳에 있는 풀이 분명 더 푸를 거라는 것을 몰랐나?

(나) 음, 여름은 지나갔고, 나이와 함께 지혜도 갖게 되었다. 나는 그 앞 현관이 모험할 적이 없다는 것을 깨달았다. 그것은 세상 위에 있는 창문이고 어떻게 그 세상이 돌아가는지에 대한 교훈이었다. 게다가, 열의는 오늘까지 계속된다. – 새로운 교훈을 옛 것에 더하면서. 우리 가족의 현관에서, 나는 삶과 사랑, 희망, 그리고 꿈, 그리고 약속과 신뢰를 배웠다. 어느 날 그것은 내 여동생과 내가 끔찍한 남부 억양을 뽐내고 Rhett Butler를 위해 지평선을 바라보았을 때, Tara로 가는 정문이었다. (영화 '바람과 함께 사라지다'를 인용) 다음 날, 그것은 성 요새이고 바다의 배였다. 어른들에게는, 가벼운 농담과 체커 게임을 북돋았다; 세금에 관한 이야기와 수표책에 관한 것이 아니라. Veranda는 작은 것들을 즐기는 장소였다. 삶은 거기서 더 느렸다.

(다) 지금, 여러 번의 veranda를 경험한 후에, 나는 현관 감정가가 되었다. 이번 여름 나는 어린 시절의 이야기를 되새기면서, 현관 난간에 앉아서 시간을 보내고 있다. 나는 새로운 세대가 레몬에이드 물병에 땀 흘려 그들의 이름을 쓰는 것을 볼 때, 그들도 또한 Veranda Beach에 대한 교훈을 배우고 있기를 희망한다. 바람에 대해 강해져라. 화려하고 창의적이 되어라 – 예기치 못한 방법으로 자라라. 유성을 관찰하라. 또한, 때때로 갈 곳이 있는 것보다 너 자신이 있을 곳을 갖는 것이 더 좋다는 것을 알아라.」

43 ⑤

☞ (라) Veranda Beach에 대한 설명이 나오고, (나) Veranda Beach가 필자에게 의미하는 바를 언급하고, (다) 나이를 먹고 Veranda Beach를 통해 배운 것을 떠올린다.

44 ③

☞ Veranda Beach가 필자에게 의미하는 바를 보여주는 내용이다.

45 ①

porch : 현관 awful : 끔찍한, 지독한 accent : 억양 scout : 정찰하다, 조사하다 fortress : 요새 lighthearted : 걱정이 없는, 마음이 가벼운 banter : 농담을 주고받다 connoisseur : 감정사 perch : 앉아 있다, 위치하다 tip : 기울이다 chuckle : 빙그레 웃다 pound : 마구 치다 tease : 놀리다

☞ (A) Veranda Beach를 가볍고 즐거운 장소로 묘사했기 때문에 내용상 encourage가 적절하다. (B) 어디에도 가지 않고 집 앞 현관에 있을 거라는 말에 필자가 실망함을 보여주는 표현으로 plunge가 적절하다.

01 ①

incur : 초래하다   withdraw : 인출하다

☞ doled out은 '유통되는'의 뜻으로 해석되어 distributed가 적절하다.

「내 조부에 의해 유통된 은화는 그들과 우리를 믿지 못하는 내 부모에 의해 유지되었다.」

02 ②

customize : ～을 주문받아 만들다   invoke : 일으키다   traverse : 횡단하다   strip : 빼앗다   circumvent : 우회하다

☞ conjuring up은 '～을 일으키는' 뜻으로 해석되어 invoking이 적절하다.

「잡지 제목은 독자들의 기대를 형성하는데 큰 역할을 한다. 그것들은 독자들의 마음에 특별한 연관을 불러일으키는 큰 글씨로 쓰여 진다.」

03 ④

duality : 이중성   obscurity : 불명료   viciousness : 잔인함

☞ malleability 순응성, 유연성＝plasticity 유연성

「20세기는 유전학과 인종에 대한 나치 사이비과학에 의해 야기된 끔찍한 대량학살을 보았지만, 그것은 또한 인간 본성의 유연성에 대한 마르크스주의 사이비과학에 의해 야기된 끔찍한 대량학살도 보았다.」

04 ⑤

deprive : 빼앗다.

☞ coveted는 '열망하는, 탐내는'의 뜻으로 '부러워하다'의 의미를 가진 envy와 상통한다.

「귀족의 과두 권력은 농부, 노동자, 상인을 포함한 평민, 로마 시민의 다른 계층에 의해 열망되었다.」

05 ④

elongate : 연장하다.

☞ non sequitur 불합리한 추론 ＝ irrelevant 부적절한

「"내 작은 동생을 뉴욕에 데려가줄래?" 10년 동안 외국인으로서 살았더니 나는 불합리한 대화에 익숙해졌지만 그 개시자는 나를 과묵한 채로 그대로 두었다.」

06 ②

colony : 식민지 declare : 선언하다.

☞ 'attempted to'는 동사로 쓰인 것이 아니다.

「볼링은 식민지에서 매우 인기였다. 처음에 그것은 나인핀스라고 불리었다. 나인핀스는 사실은 식민지 사람들에 의해 경기된 여러 볼링 게임들 중의 하나였다. 다른 종류의 볼링은 큰 공을 굴리고 잔디 위에 있는 작은 공에 최대한 가까이 정지시키도록 시도하는 경기자들을 포함했다. 그 타켓 공에 가장 가까운 경기자가 승리자로 선언되었다. 이 볼링의 형식은 흙에 그려진 선에 동전을 던지는 현대 게임과 유사했다. 동전 던지기에서는 선에서 가장 가까운 돈의 경기자가 승리한다.」

07 ②

layout : 배치, 설계 orchestrate : ~을 편성하다 retailers : 소매상인 subtle : 미묘한

☞ orchestrate는 타동사로서 목적어를 수반해야 한다. 능동태 형태인 'has orchestrated' 뒤에 목적어가 없으므로 수동태 형태로 바뀌어야 한다.

「다음에 당신이 소매점을 시작할 때 - 전자기기, 하드웨어 또는 하이패션을 팔든 아니든 - 멈추고 주의 깊게 당신의 환경을 생각해라. 상점의 설계와 전시를 생각해라. 배경음악을 들어라. 냄새를 맡아라. 기회는 설계와 조명에서부터 음악까지 상점에서 모든 것이고 심지어 냄새는 당신의 쇼핑경험을 형성하는데 도움을 주기 위해 편성된다. - 그리고 당신의 지갑을 열기 위해. 대부분의 경우에, 너무 미묘해서 당신은 당신에게 무슨 일이 일어나는지 깨달을 수 없는 방식으로 영향을 받는다. 이와 같이, 상점에 들어가면 쇼핑자로서 당신이 어떻게 움직이고 돌아다니는지는 정말로 당신에 달려있지 않다. 다음에 당신이 상점에 방문할 때, 당신의 쇼핑 행동에 영향을 주기 위해서 소매상인들이 하는 미묘한 것들을 발견 할 수 있는지 확인해봐라.」

08 ③

fiberglass : 섬유유리 terra-cotta : 테라코타(질그릇 토기) drainage hole : 배수구 drain away : 배수되어 없어지다 topple : 앞으로 꼬꾸라지다, 쓰러지다

☞ '반드시 ~해라'는 be sure to V형태로 와야 한다.

「좋은 화분을 위한 넘버원 추천 : 크게 생각해라. 작은 용기는 건강한 뿌리 성장을 위한 흙이 너무 적고 물을 댄 상태로 유지하게 위해서는 일이 너무 많다. 그래서 용기가 클수록 더 좋다. 윤이 나는 섬유유리와 형성된 플라스틱 용기는 유약을 바르지 않은 질그릇 토기보다 수분을 더 많이 가지고 있다. 종류에 상관없이, 반드시 배수구를 가지고, 물이 배수되어 없어지게 허락하여 땅으로부터 약 반 인치를 키우기 위해서는 화분 발 또는 심을 사용해라. 섬유유리와 플라스틱 화분은 극심한 날씨에도 질이 저하될 가능성이 적고 이동하기에도 쉽다. 그러나 무거운 용기는 바람에 꼬꾸라지는 것을 예방하기 위해 필요한 토대를 큰 식물에게 줄 수 있다. 더 가벼운 화분은 꼬꾸라지는 것을 방지하기 위해 보호 받아야 된다.」

09 ③

disadvantaged : 혜택 받지 못한, 가난한 acquisition : 취득, 획득 deceptive : 속이는 materialism : 물질주의 barrier : 장벽, 장애물

「개인 소비자 행복에 대한 마케팅의 영향은 가난한 소비자에 대한 높은 물가, 속이는 관습, 그리고 부족한 서비스로 비판받아 왔다. 사회에 대한 마케팅의 영향은 거짓 욕구 창조와 심한 물질주의, 너무 적은 사회적 재화, 그리고 문화 오염으로 비판받아왔다. 비평가들은 참가에 장벽을 만드는 관행과 획득을 통해 경쟁을 감소시키고 경쟁자들에게 해를 입히는 다른 사업에 대한 마케팅의 영향도 또한 비판했다. 이러한 우려는 정당화된다. 일부는 그렇지 않다.」

10 ③

free – standing : 독립해 있는   jumble : 뒤범벅이 된   costume : 의상   props : 소도구   gear : 장비

☞ '그날의 연극을 위해 필수적인'이므로 inessential은 적절하지 않다.

「무대 벽과 건물의 뒤 사이에 있는 무대 뒤는 분장실로 알려져 있다. 여기에는 의상과 소도구들이 <u>저장되어</u> 있고 배우들은 준비를 한다. 초기에 분장실은 <u>독립해있는</u> 구조였으나 지금은 건물에 붙박이로 되었다. 바로 무대 뒤는 꽉 차고 뒤범벅이 된 방이다. 그 곳은 그날의 연극을 위해 필수적인 모든 사람과 모든 것들이 준비된 상태로 모여 있다. 의상은 어디나 걸려있 다. 연극에서 여러 번의 변화를 가진 배우들은 <u>순서대로</u> 옷을 유지하려고 노력하는 동안에 옷을 입거나 옷을 벗거 나 해야 한다. 테이블과 벤치는 배우들의 장비, 가짜 턱수염과 가발, 그리고 메이크업으로 <u>덮여있다</u>.」

11 ⑤

enforcement : 집행   criterion : 기준   intimidation : 위협   extract : 이끌어내다

☞ 경찰들이 조사하길 원하는 다른 지역 또는 무엇이든 통제한다는 뜻으로 해석되므로 '부분적으로'의 뜻인 partially는 적절하지 않다.

「원칙적으로 법집행 관리들은 동의에 바탕 하여 조사를 수행한다. 유효한 것으로 여겨지기 위해서는 동의 조사는 두 가지 기준 을 충족시켜야 한다. 첫째, 허가는 자유롭고 자발적으로 주어져야 한다. 둘째, 동의를 승인한 개인은 그렇게 할 권한을 가져야 한다. 허가가 얻어지면 경찰은 <u>합법적으로</u> 조사를 할지도 모르나, 그 조사는 동의를 주는 사람에 의해 부과된 제한을 넘어 확장할 수는 없다. 동의의 요구된 자발적인 본성은 허가가 <u>위협</u>의 결과로 주어질 수 없다는 것을 의미한다. 만약에 경찰이 실제로 또는 위협된 육체적인 힘에 의해 또는 속임수에 의한 동의를 이끌어냈다면, 그 허가는 <u>무효하고</u> 그에 기인한 조사 또한 그렇다. 두 번째 요구는 오직 <u>정당화된</u> 개인이 조사에 허가를 줄 수 있다는 것이다. 일반적으로 그러한 허가는 소유하고, 점유하는 성인에 의해서만 주어져야 한다. 그렇지 않다면 <u>부분적으로</u> 집, 자동차, 사무실 또는 경찰들이 조사하길 바라는 다른 지역 무엇이든 통제할 것이다.」

12 ⑤

deploy : 배치하다   cannot help but do : ～하지 않을 수 없다   vulnerable : 취약한   heal : 치유

☞ aggravating은 '악화하는'의 의미이므로 '적극적인'을 의미하는 aggressive가 적절하다.

「환자들 삶의 질 촉진에 도움을 주기 위한 사회적인 지원과 간호를 배치하는 의학 시스템은 그들의 치유 가능성을 높인다. 예를 들면, 다음 날 중요한 수술을 기다리면서 침대에 누워있는 환자들은 <u>걱정하지</u> 않을 수 없다. 어느 상황에서 사람이 느끼 는 것이 강하게 <u>다른 사람에게</u> 전달되는 경향이 있다 : 스트레스가 쌓이고 취약한 사람들이 느낄수록 그들은 더 예민해지고 그들의 감정을 따라가기 쉽다. 만약 걱정하고 있는 환자가 수술을 직면한 다른 환자와 함께 방을 쓴다면, 그 둘은 서로 더 <u>불안하게</u> 만들 것이다. 그러나 만약 그녀가 성공적으로 수술에서 막 나온 환자와 방을 함께 쓴다면 - 그리고 상대적으로 안도 하고 침착한 - 그녀에게 미치는 감정적인 효과는 더 적극적이 될 것이다.」

13 ②

point a finger : 손가락질 하다   reciprocate : 응답하다   salute : 경례를 하다   doff : (경의를 표하며) 모자 를 벗다   crowd : 군중

☞ ①③④⑤는 모두 이튼에 있었던 전통을 말하는 것이나, ②의 it은 가주어로 쓰인 것이다.

「이튼에 'capping'이라고 알려진 <u>전통</u>이 있었다. - 소년들이 모자를 벗는 행위를 단축하는 것과 같이 그들의 교사에게 손가락질 함으로써 거리에서 교사에 경례를 할 때 ; 이는 교사에 의해서 응답된다. 최근에 정부가 기꺼이 'respect'라고 불리는 것의 승격을 추진했음에도 불구하고 <u>이 전통</u>은 멸종되었다. 나는 그것이 너무 많은 시간과 노력이 걸리고 너무 많은 차이를 보인다고 생각한다. - 그래서 많은 비슷한 문화와 같이, <u>그것은</u> 현대 영국에서 운명 지어졌다. 공평하게 보아, 위에 글로 표현된 바로 직후 나는 TV에서 많은 골퍼들이 군중에 경례하기 위해 <u>그 예전의 관습을</u> 아직도 따른다는 것을 언급하기를 응원 받았다.」

14 ④

sporadically : 이따금   anticipation : 기대

☞ 그는 기대형성 하는 것에 대해서 마스터라고 했으므로 자신의 행보에 대한 궁금증을 잘 유발 시킨다.

「Garth Brooks는 좋은, 긴 은퇴를 가졌다. 지금 그것은 끝났다. Nashville에서 목요일 뉴스 회의 동안 52세인 Brooks는 가장 가능성 있는 월드 투어를 위한 계획을 포함해 그의 컴백 세부세항을 발표할 예정이다. 미국 앨범 판매에서 비틀즈와 엘비스 프레슬리 바로 뒤 순위인 국가 슈퍼스타는 그의 세 딸을 키우기 위해 2001년에 음악 시장에서 떠났다. 그 이후로 그는 오직 이따금 공연하고 음악을 발매했다. Brooks의 가장 어린 딸, Allie가 가을에 대학에 들어가면서 그의 복귀를 위한 무대는 세워졌다. 그는 기대형성에 있어 마스터다 : 지난주 그의 홈페이지는 그의 진짜 발표하기로 한 날에 대해 소식을 애타게 했다.」

15 ⑤

authority : 당국, 권위   misgiving : 불안, 의혹

☞ 보이 스카우트, 걸 가이드와 9개의 그룹이 참여한다고 했으므로 ⑤이 내용과 일치한다.

「이 여름을 시작하면서 홍콩 정부는 저작권이 있는 노래와 영화의 불법적인 복제를 위해 200,000 청소년들이 인터넷 토론장을 검색하고 당국에 그것을 보고하도록 계획하고 있다. 그 캠페인은 연예 산업을 즐겁게 하겠지만, 시민 자유 옹호자들 사이에게는 불안을 유발한다. 소위 Youth Ambassadors 캠페인은 주된 홍콩 영화와 가수 스타와 여러 홍콩 정부 장관들 앞의 스타디움에서 1,600명의 청소년이 그들의 참가를 서약하면서 수요일에 시작할 것이다. Youth Ambassadors는 인터넷 상에서 질서를 유지시키기 위해 청소년에 대한 새로운 의존을 상징한다. 9살에서 25살까지 이르는 보이 스카우트, 걸 가이드 그리고 9개의 다른 미숙한 청소년 그룹들의 모든 멤버들이 참가할 것으로 예상된다.」

16 ②

backcountry : 시골의   world-class : 세계일류의

☞ 눈사태 발생에 훈련된 시골 가이드에 의해 운영된다는 의미이며, 참가자가 안전 교육을 받아야 되는다는 내용은 없다.

「Utah는 Interconnect Adventure Tour로 뛰어난 스키어에게 하루에 최대 다섯 가지 세계 일류 리조트에서 스키를 탈 수 있는 기회를 제공한다. 그 투어는 미국에 의해 주어진 특별한 사용 허가 하에서 Ski Utah에 의해 운영된다. 국립 산림 서비스는 눈사태에서 안전과 통제에 훈련된 시골 가이드에 의해 운영된다. 투어에 등록하려는 스키어들은 다양한 눈 상태에서 스키 경험을 가지고 건강한 몸 상태에 있어야 한다. 각 참여자들의 능력은 투어 출발하기 전에 테스트 된다. 일요일, 월요일, 수요일 그리고 금요일에 운영하는 투어는 Park City에서 시작하고 Park City, Brighton, Solitude, Alta 그리고 Snowbird에 데려간다; 그것은 끝나기 위해서는 8시간 걸리고, 점심을 위한 휴식이 포함된다. 화요일, 목요일 그리고 토요일에 운영하는 투어는 Snowbird에서 시작하고 Snowbird, Alta, Brighton 그리고 Solitude를 포함한다.」

17 ②

warehouse : 창고   disassemble : 분해하다, 해체하다   gut : 용기   prophetic : 예언의   multistate : 여러 주에 걸친

☞ 사업에 대한 구상은 인도 여행을 다녀 온 이후에 착안하였다.

「그가 막 시작한 유기농 홈 배달 사업을 위해 창고로 제공된 차고에서 보드상자를 해체할 때조차 David Gersenson의 용기는 그에게 택배유기농은 더 큰 것을 위한 운명이라고 말했다. "내가 그 박스를 다 부쉈을 때 나는 이것들이 갑자기 팔려나갈 것을 알았다." 그는 그 회사의 미래를 예견했던 1997년 그 순간을 회상했다. Upper Bucks County에서 약 700달러로 시작한 그 사업은 인도로 여행 중 유기농 제품을 먹은 후 그의 20대 초반에 계획을 세웠다. Gersenson의 비전이 예언적인 걸 증명했을 때, 그는 유기농 택배가 오늘날 다국적기업이 되게 하는 방법을 따라서 그가 했던 전략적인 결정의 결과를 예상할 수 없었다. 유기농 생산물의 그 온라인 식품가게는 전국 5개 수도권 시장에서 200명이 넘는 사람을 고용했고, 2013년에 2,600만 달러의 수입을 기록했고 올해에는 4천만 달러 이상 성장할 것이 예상된다.」

18 ④

entail : 수반하다, 필요로 하다　reap : ~을 받다　pluralist : 다원론자　calculate : 측정하다 생각하다
imply : 암시하다, 함축하다

☞ 빈칸을 포함한 문장은 앞의 내용과 반대되는 내용이므로 다원론자들의 주장은 의심스럽다는 ④의 내용이 적절하다.

「임금 인상은 노동조합 멤버들과 파업한 사람들과 함께 똑같이 위협받는 노동단체 일원이 아닌 노동자 또는 임금 요구 조장에 파업을 선택하지 않은 노동자들에게 공공이익이다. 이것은 그룹 멤버들이 필요로 할지도 모르는 다양한 비용 없이 이익을 받으면서 개인들에게 무임승차자(비조합원)가 되는 기회를 만들어낸다. 이 분석은 공공이익의 존재가 그 이익을 발전하거나 또는 방어하기 위한 조직의 형성을 초래한다는 보장이 없음을 내포하기 때문에 중요하다. 모든 그룹은 어떤 종류의 정치적인 목소리를 가진다는 다원론자의 가정은 _____, 그것은 또한 큰 그룹의 비용으로 작은 그룹에게 종종 권한을 부여할 수도 있다는 주장을 한다. 큰 멤버십은 무임승차를 조장한다. 왜냐하면 참여하는데 그들의 실패로 인해 그룹의 효과성이 조금 감소된다고 개인들이 생각하기 때문이다.」

19 ①

contend : 주장하다　no amount of : 아무리~일지라도　voidness : 공허함　inferiority complex : 열등감

☞ 미국은 유럽으로부터 왔고, 지속적으로 유럽인과 미국인들 모두 지속적으로 들여다보는 거울이라고 했으므로 열등감을 나타내는 'an inferiority complex'가 적절하다.

「놀랄 것 없이, 많은 이들은 미국이 _____으로 태어났다고 주장한다. 미국인 이야기는 유럽에서 왔다. 미국인 신화는 독특하지 않다. 유럽인들은 그들이 누구인지 미국인들에게 말했다. 미국 정부의 형식은 유럽에서 빌려왔다. 위대한 자본주의자들이 그들의 입장을 가질 때까지 미국인들은 왕과 여왕 그리고 성도 없었다. 아무리 부와 권력이 공허함을 지우려고 했을지라도 수백만의 미국인들은 등급의 터치를 잡고 맛보기 위해 매년 여름에 유럽으로 여행했다. (뒤집어서 반대도 사실이다, 수백만의 유럽인들은 마지막 국경을 보기 위해서, 그리고 유럽인들이 그들에게 준 유산을 가지고 미국인들이 무엇을 했는지 보기 위해서 매년 여름에 미국을 여행했다. 미국은 미국인들과 유럽인들이 어떤 이유로든 그들이 보기에 길들여진 것을 발견하기를 바라면서 지속적으로 살펴보는 거울이다.」

20 ④

meditation : 명상　cognitive : 인식의　illusory : 가공의　distort : 왜곡하다.

☞ ① 그렇게 하는데 성공하다
　② 시도하다
　③ 가는 것이 허용되다
　⑤ 서로 의존하다

「명상의 습관으로 전반적인 인지시스템은 몸의 행동을 통제하는 이미지 된 나에 대해 덜 집중하는 방식을 만드는데 훈련되고 무엇을 할지 결정한다. 가공의 나 자신은 천천히 방종하고 세상은 그것의 필요에 의해 더 명확하고 덜 왜곡돼 보인다. 감정은 생겨나고 빠진다. 생각 형태는 잊어버린다. 그러한 방식은 자유롭게 흐르는 듯 느껴지고 자신이 만든 환상의 어리석음과 함께 웃을 수 있다. 우리의 대부분으로서 스스로의 방어하는 방법과 심하게 묶이게 되는 것이 대부분의 시간들인 것과는 꽤 다르다.」

21 ②

preeminent : 탁월한　reproduction : 복제, 재생산　diminish : 감소하다　reverence : 존중

☞ 멀티미디어 복제의 장점에 대해 설명하고 있다. 멀티미디어 복제를 본 사람들은 원본을 보고 싶어 한다는 뜻으로 'want to see the originals'이 적절하다.

「대부분 것들과 마찬가지로 미술은 당신이 그것에 대해 무언가를 알 때 더 즐겁다. 당신은 그림을 감탄하면서 Louvre을 따라 한 시간 동안 걸을 수 있으나, 그 경험은 박식한 누군가가 당신과 함께 걸을 때 더 흥미롭다. 멀티미디어 자료는 당신이 집에 있던지 또는 미술관에 있던지 안내하는 역할을 한다. 그것은 당신이 작품에 대해 탁월한 학자의 강의의 일부를 들을 수 있게 한다. 그것은 당신에게 같은 작가에 의한 또는 다른 시대로부터 다른 작품들을 언급한다. 당신은 심지어 더 가까이 보기 위해 줌인 할 수 있다. 멀티미디어 복제와 프레젠테이션은 미술을 더 접근하기 쉽고 가까이하기 쉽게 만든다면 복제를 본 사람들은 _____, 복제에 대한 노출은 실제 미술에 대한 존중을 감소시키기보다 증가시킬 가능성이 있고 더 많은 사람들이 미술관과 갤러리에 가도록 장려한다.」

22 ①

portent : 전조, 조짐   perch : 자리잡다, 앉다   dictator : 독재자   weep : 울다   heed : 주의하다
conspirator : 음모자

☞ Caesar가 죽기 전에 나타났던 전조들에 대한 설명이다. Caesar가 이러한 전조들을 믿었더라면 더 오래 살았을 것이라는 가정법 과거완료 형태이다.

If 주어 had pp, 주 might have pp

여기서는 if가 생략되고 had가 앞으로 나온 형태이다.

「_____, 그는 더 오래 살았었을 것이다. 전설에 따르면, 많은 나쁜 조짐들이 그의 죽음에 앞섰고, 그들 사이에서, Plutarch에 따르면 "천국에서 빛, 밤에 들었던 소음, 토론회에 자리 잡은 야생의 새" 그리고 유명하게, 그 독재자는 점쟁이에 의해서 "3월 15일을 경계하라"는 경고를 받았다. 그의 마지막 날 아침, 그의 아내인 Calpurnia는 그에게 그녀가 자는 동안 끔찍한 꿈을 꿨다고 말했다; 울면서 그녀는 그에게 Senate에 가지 말라고 부탁했다. Caesar는 깜짝 놀랐다. Plutarch가 말하길 "그가 이전에는 Calpurnia에게서 여자다운 미신을 발견하지 못했으니까" 그는 그녀의 경고를 주의하기로 결정했지만 Senate가 이탈리아를 제외한 모든 로마 주의 왕으로 그를 선언하는 날을 계획했다고 그에 대한 음모자 중의 한사람인 Decimus Brutus가 넌지시 말했을 때 그의 마음을 바꿨다.」

23 ③

distinguish : 구별하다, 구분하다   boredom : 지루함   intermittently : 때때로   heed : 주의를 기울이다
little more than : ~에 지나지 않는   look away : 눈길을 돌리다   look back at : ~을 되돌아보다

☞ disguise는 '위장하다, 가장하다'라는 뜻으로 뉴스는 우리의 존재를 위장하려고 노력하지 않는다.

「TV 뉴스를 구별하는 특징 중의 하나는 (그리고 다른 소위 '정보의 쇼') 드라마와 같지 않고 뉴스는 _____ 하려는 시도 를 하지 않는다. 우리는 항상 직접적으로 알게 되고, 공개적으로 이야기한다. ; 우리는 TV 앵커들을 볼 때 자신의 고양이와 함께 하는 것일지도 모르는 요란한 콘테스트의 종류에서 그들은 바로 우리를 되돌아본다. 이 콘테스트에서 우리는 항상 깜빡이거나 눈길을 돌리고, 더 쉽게 지루함에서 벗어난다, 왜냐하면 단지 때때로 주의를 기울이게 되는 정보의 '흐름'과 진행 중인 전자기기의 일부분에 지나지 않기 때문이다. 우리는 눈길을 돌리지만, 그들의 존재로, 그들의 날의 포커스이기 때문에 앵커들은 결코 그러지 않는다. 우리는 우리가 그들을 지켜본다고 생각하지만, 그들이 우리를 또는 사실상의 우리를, 심지어 힘들더라도, 지켜본다.」

24 ①

retrospect : 추억, 회고   prestigious : 일류의   enormous : 거대한   leverage : 영향력   drive up : 끌어 올리다   gobble up : 게걸스럽게 먹어치우다   albeit : 비록~일지라도   cautionary : 경고적인

☞ rein 억제하다

「회고에서, 매사추세츠는 1994년에 (A)심각한 실수를 한 것처럼 보인다. 그때 두 개의 가장 일류의 비싼 병원을 —하버드와 제휴한 두 개의 Massachusetts General Hospital 과 Brigham&Women's Hospital — 파트너 헬스케어로 알려진 하나의 시스템에 합병 했다. 수사는 합병이 보험회사로부터 지나친 변상을 요구함으로써 보스턴 지역에서 헬스케어 비용을 끌어올리는 거대한 시장 영향력을 병원에게 주었다는 걸 기록했다. 그것은 전달된 케어의 질 또는 복잡함과는 관련이 없는 것이었다. 지금, 뒤늦게, Attorney General Martha Coakley는 비록 일시적일지라도 게걸스럽게 먹어치울 수 있는 의사 관행의 수를 제한하고 파트너의 가격 인상을 최소한으로 늦추는 협상된 동의를 가지고 병원들을 (B)억제하려고 노력하고 있다. 매사추세츠에서의 그 경험은 큰 병원의 합병 위험성에 대해 다른 주에게 경고적인 이야기를 제공한다.」

25 ①

adhere to : ~을 고수하다 hospitality : 환대 maintain : 관리하다 corruption : 부패 bidding : 입찰
☞ 법에 의해 결정된 공급자 선정 과정에 대해 설명하고 있다.

「당신은 Cross—Continent Enterprise(CCE) 과정을 따르고 공급자 선정을 둘러싼 내부통제 시스템을 고수해야 한다. 공급자 선정은 선물, 환대, 보상의 수령에 의존해서는 안 된다. 공급자 선정이 상품 또는 서비스의 공급을 위한 공식적이고 구조화된 초청(종종 'tender'라 부른다.)일 때 우리가 우리의 내부통제를 지원하는 문서를 관리하는 게 제일 중요하다. 공공분야에서 그러한 tender과정은 공공재산의 사용을 위한 그러한 경쟁이 부패로부터 공개적이고 공평하고 자유롭다는 것을 보장하기 위해 법에 의해 구체적으로 요구되고 결정된다. tender과정은 적절한 계약을 위한 어떠한 경쟁이 tender에 반응하여 수행되고, 어떠한 관계자도 계약을 위해 이전 비밀협상으로 독립적인 부당한 이익을 얻어서는 안 된다는 이해 위에서 제안하기 위해 다른 관계자를 위한 초청을 포함한다. 그 곳은 입찰 과정이 자격이 있는 입찰자에 공개되고 밀봉된 입찰은 감시를 위해 공개되고 규정과 가격에 따라서 선정된다.」

26 ①

molecule : 분자 wavelength : 파장 diameter : 직경, 지름 atom : 원자 absorb : 흡수하다 radiate : 빛을 내다
☞ 파장의 길이에 따라 색이 다르다는 설명을 하고 있다.

「빛이 지구의 대기에 부딪힐 때 다른 색들은 다른 방식으로 반응한다. 그들의 일부는 가스 분자에 의해 흡수된다. 반면에 다른 것들은 그렇지 않다. 더 긴 파장의 색의 대부분은(빨강과 오렌지색 같은)대기에 직선으로 통과하여 영향 받지 않지만, 짧은 파장의 색들은(보라색과 파란색 같은) 가스 분자에 의해 흡수된다. 왜냐하면 이러한 색의 파장(각 파동의 정점 사이의 거리)은 산소 원자의 직경과 크기가 같기 때문이다. 가스 분자는 그리고 나서 이러한 색을 내고 하늘이 파란색으로 보이도록 야기하면서 하늘을 가로 질러 흩뿌린다.」

27 ⑤

not necessarily : 반드시~는 아닌 mismatch : 부조화 sensitivity : 세심함 parenting : 육아
☞ 심리학에서의 육아와 엄마들이 생각하는 육아 차이에 대해 설명하고 있다.

「관찰연구는 아이들 주위에 엄마들이 하는 어떤 것들에 대한 정보를 제공하지만 그러나 아이들에 관한 감정, 생각, 믿음, 보육과 그들 자신에 관해서는 그렇지 않다. 엄마들은 심리학의 그것과 반드시 일치하는 것은 아닌 아이들과 육아에 대해 다양한 견해를 가진다. 그리고 이것들은 그들이 그들의 아이들과 어떻게 상호작용하는지 영향을 준다. 일부의 엄마들은 아이들에 대해 세심해 지는 것이 쉽지 않다. 이는 아마도 그들이 쉽게 그들의 아이들과 결부할 수 없기 때문일 것이다. 왜냐하면 그들이 우울하거나 고립되거나 또는 세심함은 아이들과의 관계에서 중요하다고 믿지 않기 때문이다. 일부 엄마들에게는 그들의 행동, 감정과 심리학에 의해 처방된 그것들 사이에 부조화가 있을지 모른다. ; 그리고 그들 자신의 필요와 그들의 아이들의 그것 사이에서 충돌이 있을지도 모른다.」

28 ③

weary : 피곤하게 하는, 지친   conquer : 정복하다   unrest : 불만   occupation : 점령   religious : 종교의
vibrancy : 진동   sculpture : 조각품   mingle : 어울리다, 섞이다   temple : 신전
☞ 결합을 통해 문화가 섞이게 되는 것을 설명하고 있다. interchange은 '교환'의 뜻이다.

「알렉산더 대왕은 기원전 332년에 이집트의 그리스 로마 시대를 개시했다. 서부 아시아 일부를 정복한 후에, 마케도니아의 장군은 국외자에 의해 불만과 점령의 수 백 년 이후에 정치적으로 지친 사람들에 의해 이집트에서 환영받았다. 아직도 풍요로운 이집트 문화에 있어서의 그리스의 영향력의 결합은 지중해에 걸쳐 돌고 있는 사회적이고 종교적인 변화를 일어나게 하는데 도움을 줬다. 이 새로운 시기의 진동에 이집트의 옷 스타일과 조각품은 그리스와 로마를 위해 그들의 방식으로 작업했고, 반면에 이집트의 신과 반신은 그리스와 로마의 신화에서 그들의 상대와 섞이었다. 그 어머니 하느님 이시스는 결국 시저스의 땅에서 그녀를 위한 신전을 지었고, 반면에 많은 고대인들의 신과 영웅들은 이집트 도처에서 신전에 영예를 가졌다.」

29 ④

lapse : 실수, 과실   embark on : ~에 착수하다   give in to : ~에 굴복하다   traffic tie-up : 교통정체
slow down : 느긋해지다   urge : 욕구
☞ 변화하려고 노력하는 중에 직면한 가끔의 일탈은 비정상적인 것이 아니다. 첫 문장에서도 나왔듯이 그러한 실수는 단지 하나의 사건일 뿐이다.

「당신이 변화시키려고 노력했던 옛날의 행동을 시작하는 그 시기에 실수는 하나의 사건이다. 실수를 극복하는 열쇠는 고속도로 위에서 당신을 지연시키는 도로 건설과 교통정체와 같이 때때로 그것들에게 기대하는 것이다. 당신이 장거리 자동차 여행에 착수한 마지막 시간에 대해 생각해봐라. 변화는 당신이 느긋해지는 태도에 따라오는 당신이 직면한 어떤 것이다. –그러나 당신은 포기하거나 차를 돌리거나 집으로 향하지 않는다. 비록 예상했던 것보다 더 오래 걸린다고 할지라도 당신은 아직도 의도된 목적지에 이르고 있다. 개인의 변화도 이와 같다. 더 많은 과일과 야채를 더하면서 당신의 접시에 균형을 맞춘다고 말해보자, 그러나 갑자기 패스트푸드 햄버거를 먹고 싶은 욕구에 굴복한다. 당신은 실수를 한 것이다.」

30 ⑤

gnat : 각다귀   mosquito : 모기   crawl : 기어가다   stuffy : 답답한   dull : 따분한, 흐릿한   get rid of : ~을 처리하다, 없애다
☞ ⑤ reminiscent 연상시키는, 추억에 잠긴 듯한   displeased 불쾌한

「낮 동안 공기는 뜨겁고 건조하고 먼지의 입자들로 가득 차 있다. 밤에 좀 시원해 질 때 숲에서 각다귀와 모기는 나를 더 많은 그들의 부재에 대해 감사히 여기도록 했다. 내 오두막은, 내 방의 10배가 되는 헌팅 캠프에서, 가깝고 답답하게 보였고 내가 침대에 누웠을 때 나는 거대한 거미를 들었고, 일부는 여러 인치를 가로질러서, 지붕의 나뭇잎에 기어갔다. 때때로 하나는 흐릿한 쿵 소리와 함께 침대에 떨어졌고 성큼성큼 걷기 전까지는 잠시 그곳에 놓였다. 처음에 나는 그것들을 없애기 위해 적극적인 캠페인을 수행했으나 그것은 소용없었고 –그리고 모기망은 참을 수 없이 뜨거웠을 텐데. 숲의 익숙한 밤소리는 근처 호텔 무도회 집으로 돌아오는 술 취한 소리에 의해 대체되었다.」

31 ④

conclusively : 최종적으로, 결정적으로   radiation : 방사능   conventional : 전통적인   autopsy : 사후분석
☞ CT검사에서 더 적은 방사능으로 검사를 할 수 있는 방법에 대해 설명하고 있다. 그러나 ④의 내용은 CT검사에서 방사능이 얼마나 나오는지에 관한 내용이다.

「CT방사능을 위한 새로운 안전기준을 최종적으로 설정하기 위해서 연구원들은 CT검사를 받은 사람들 사이에 암의 수를 직접 조사하기 시작한다. 다른 나라로부터 약 12개의 그러한 연구는 다음 몇 년 이내에 발행될 것이다. 그러는 동안 일부 연구원들은 좋은 이미지가 전형적인 CT검사에서 발생되는 그것보다 더 적은 방사능 투여량으로 만들어 질 수 있는지 테스트하기 시작했다. Mass General Hospital에 있는 방사능 연구자들은 그러한 조사를 수행하는 특이한 방법을 가지고 있다. ④ 하나의 CT 검사는 사람의 몸이 전통적인 엑스레이의 방사능에 150에서 1,100번 사이를 겪게 한다. 그러한 방법으로 그들은 사람들을 아프게 만드는 걱정 없이 몸을 많이 스캔한다. 그리고 의학문제를 정확하게 식별하는 스캔인지 아닌지 점검하기 위해 사후분석을 실시한다. 생활 모집, 인간지원자 호흡 대신에 그들의 연구를 위해 그들은 시체와 일한다.」

32 ②

salient : 중요한, 핵심적인   perceive : 인지하다   noticeably : 두드러지게, 현저히
☞ 원주민들과 언어 학습자들의 언어 행위 차이에 대한 설명이다. ②는 언어행위의 부재가 중요하다는 내용으로 전체 흐름과 관계없는 문장이다.

「외국어 학습자들은 같은 문맥에서 원주민들보다 다른 언어행위를 행한다. 또는 대안적으로 그들은 전혀 어떤 언어행위도 행하지 않을지도 모른다. 이것의 좋은 예는 그들이 말하고 또는 행하는 방법을 결정하는데 유연성을 가진 진정한 대화와 역할놀이에서 나온다. 학업의 충고 시간에 원주민들과 학습자들은 다른 언어행위를 가진다. 원주민들은 권고 시간에 대하여 학습자들보다 더 많은 제안을 만들어내고, 반면에 학습자들은 원주민보다 권고 시간에 대하여 더 많은 거절을 만들어낸다. ② 게다가 충고 언어행위의 부재는 학업의 충고자들에게 중요했다. 제안과 거절의 두 언어행위는 똑같은 기능을 제공한다. 원주민들은 제안을 만들어냄으로써 학업 강의 시간에 통제를 행사한다. 학습자들은 충고자들의 제안을 막아냄으로써 거절을 통해 그렇게 한다. 두 학생 그룹이 그들이 궁극적으로 취하는 과목을 결정하는데 참여할지라도, 인터뷰에서 그 결과로 초래되는 하모니의 느낌은 현저히 다르게 충고자들에 의해서 인지된다.」

33 ⑤

toad : 두꺼비   secrete : ~을 분비하다   fluid : 체액   secretion : 분비액   bark : 나무껍질   seabed : 해저
painkiller : 진통제   venom : 독   tropical : 열대의   snail : 달팽이
☞ 주어진 문장을 해석하면 '다른 장래성이 있는 선두는 전통적이고 현대적인 의학 시스템에 의해 사실상 아직 손대지 않은 중요한 원천으로부터 온다. -바다'
⑤ 앞에서는 현재 쓰이고 있는 약들을 설명했고, ⑤ 다음문장에서 장래성 있는 약을 설명하고 있으므로 주어진 문장은 ⑤에 들어가야 한다.

「모든 개구리와 두꺼비는 방어적인 체액을 분비한다. 체액의 대부분은 항생물질을 가진다. 그것은 중국 민속 치료자들이 개에게 물린 상처와 같은 고통을 두꺼비 분비액으로 치료하는 이유이다. 그 분비액은 때때로 그들을 놀라게 하기 위해 거울을 이용하여 두꺼비를 둘러쌈으로써 얻어진다. 그러한 방법은 이상하게 들리긴 하지만 서부나라에서 사용된 약의 높은 비율은 자연 또는 자연에서 발견된 화학 제조법으로부터 나온다. 스테로이드, 페니실린, 디기탈리스, 모르핀, 그리고 아스피린은 약간의 예시이다. 의학에서 가장 즐거운 발견중의 하나는 택솔이다. 그것은 흉부암과 난소암과 싸우며 재목의 나무껍질로부터 얻을 수 있다. (⑤) 후보들은 Antarctic 해저로부터의 항암제와 열대 중심부 달팽이의 독으로부터의 진통제를 포함한다.」

34 ②

culmination : 최고조, 정점   capacity : 수용력   conventional : 전통적인, 관습적인   continuum : 연속체   a series of : 일련의   substantial : 상당한   respectively : 각각   conceptualize : 개념화하다   locomotive : 기관차
☞ 해석 : 역사에서 그 영화의 출현은 시간과 공간의 경계를 뛰어넘도록 도와주는 과학기술의 성취의 최고조를 나타낸다.
② advent 출현   surpass 뛰어넘다

「시공적인 중간매체로서 영화의 지위는 그것의 기술적으로 주어진 능력만큼이나 그것의 역사적인 맥락에도 빚지고 있다. 19세기 말에 첫 출현 하면서 영화는 시간과 공간의 전통적인 경계를 붕괴시키기 위한 기술의 수용력을 강조하는 일렬인의 발명 중 정점의 후보로 나섰다. 영화는 전신과 전화로부터 기관차와 자동차를 통해 그리고 축음기와 사진으로 늘어지는 연속체의 일부로 작동되었다. (전신과 전화는 상당한 거리에 의해 분리된 두 위치 사이에 일어나는 커뮤니케이션을 가능하게 했다.)(기관차와 자동차는 그들의 승객들이 이전과는 달리 월등한 스피드로 상당한 지역에 여행하는 것을 가능하게 했다. 그것 때문에 여행 시간을 붕괴하면서)(축음기와 사진은 소리와 이미지를 각각 광전과정을 거쳐 현실로부터 소리와 사진 캡처를 통해 시간을 멈추었다.) 영화는 공간과 시간을 나타내고 개념화하는 방법의 전통적인 감각을 확장하는 최신의 발명품이다.」

35 ④

a close circle of friends : 친한 친구 사이   gaze into : 응시하다   reassure : 안심시키다

「당신은 새로운 근처에 이사를 했고 사람들을 만나기 어렵기 때문에 마음이 울적한 것을 상상해봐라.

(B) 재미로, 당신은 어떤 미래가 당신에게 있는지 알아보기 위해 지역 점쟁이에 가기로 결정한다. 점쟁이는 그녀의 수정 구슬을 응시하고 웃으면서 미래가 밝다고 말한다. 그녀는 몇 달 안에 당신이 가깝고 충실한 친구들에게 둘러싸일 것이라고 말한다.

(C) 당신은 그녀의 말에 의해 안심하고 당신이 도착했을 때보다 더 행복하게 돌아간다. 당신은 이제 미래에 대해 행복하고 자신 있게 느끼고, 당신은 더 웃고 더 밖으로 나가서 더 많은 사람들과 이야기 한다.

(A) 몇 주 후에 당신은 당신이 정말로 친한 친구들에 의해 둘러 싸여 있는 걸 발견한다. 사실은, 점쟁이는 미래를 실제로 보지 못하지만 대신에 실제로 그것이 일어나게 도와주는 것은 가능하다.」

36 37

「인도델리공과대학에 있는 Balak교수는 Smartcane™ 뒤에서 팀을 이끌었고, 그것은 널리 사용되는 흰 지팡이에 만들어짐으로써 인도의 복잡한 거리 사이에 시각 장애인을 안내하기 위해 초음파를 사용하는 새로운 장치이다. "흰 지팡이는 사용자들에게 많은 정보를 제공하는 훌륭한 장치이다." 그가 말했다. "그러나 허리 높이 위에 있는 장애물을 감지하는 것은 취약하고 당신의 길에 돌출된 나뭇가지 같은 땅 위에서 접점을 가지고 있지는 않다. 그 영리한 기술 버전은 표준 흰 지팡이에 부착된 장치를 거쳐 초음파를 보내는 대신에 그것은 그들의 복귀로 그것들을 탐지하고 사용자들에게 그들 길에 있는 장애물을 알리기 위해 진동을 사용한다. 현실적인 이익은 보통의 지팡이가 단순히 제공할 수 없는 정보들을 제공하면서, 무릎 위 45도 범위를 스캔하는 초음파로부터 온다. 사람들은 그들이 걸을 때 지팡이를 왼쪽에서 오른쪽으로 움직인다. 한 면에서 감지된 진동은 그들이 다른 방향으로 가야한다는 걸 의미한다. 진동의 패턴과 강도의 차이는 사용자에게 그들의 길에 방해되는 물체의 거리를 말해준다. 그 거리는 3미터까지이다.」

36 ②

ultrasound : 초음파 stick out into : ~로 돌출되다 intensity : 강도 sonar : 음파 divert : 방향을 바꾸다

☞ 해석 : Smartcane™ 에서 그 팀은 이 도전에 대해 그들의 환경으로 불러들이기 위해 음파를 방출하고 인근의 물체들로부터 그들 사방에 방향을 바꾸게 하기 위해 다시 회복되는데 메아리를 이용하는 박쥐와 같이 동물의 기술을 복제함으로써 성공했다.

(B) 이전에는 허리 높이 위에 있는 장애물을 감지하지 못하는 등의 취약점을 설명했고, 이와 관련해서 (B)에서 'this challenge'로 표현 되었다. (B)는 이 문제를 어떻게 해결했는지에 대한 문장이다. 그리고 (B)이후에는 영리한 기술 버전의 이점을 설명하고 있다.

37 ⑤

☞ 초음파를 이용하여 장애물을 식별하고 사용자에게 장애물을 알리기 위해 진동 패턴을 사용한다.

38 39

「오래전에, 내가 82번째 공수부대에서 어린 중위였을 때 노스캐롤라이나 포트 브랙에서 필드 문제에 대해 사태를 파악하려고 노력했다. 내가 지도를 공부하면서 서 있을 때 많은 후배 장교의 고참병인 소대장이 다가왔다. "당신은 우리가 있는 곳을 알아낸다. 중위?" 그가 물었다. "글쎄, 지도에서 말하기를 저기 위로 언덕이 있어야 하는데, 나는 보이지 않는다." 나는 대답했다. 그가 말했다. "지도가 땅과 일치하지 않는다면 지도가 틀린 것이다." 심지어 그때 나는 심오한 진실을 들었다는 것을 알게 되었다.

많은 해에 걸쳐 나는 사람들의 이야기, 특히 예측에서 벗어나는 모든 방법을 듣는데 시간을 썼다. 나는 삶을 관통한 우리의 통로는 우리가 걸어가는 땅에 순응하기 위해 우리의 머리에 지도를 가지려는 노력으로 이루어져있다는 것을 배웠다. 이상적으로 이 과정은 우리가 성장할 때도 일어난다. 우리의 부모는 우리에게 그들이 배웠던 것을 주로 예를 들어서 가르친다. 불행하게도 우리는 전반적으로 이 강의를 거의 수용하지 못한다. 그리고 종종, 시행착오의 빈번하게 고통스러운 과정을 통해 우리가 알게 되는 많은 것을 위해 우리 부모의 삶은 그들이 전달하기에는 유익한 것이 없다고 우리에게 말한다.」

38 ④

orient oneself : ~에 순응하다, 사태를 파악하다 veteran : 고참병 go awry : 실패하다, 예측에서 벗어나다 convey : 전달하다 platoon : 소대 sergeant : 병장

☞ 과거의 경험을 우리 성장기에 연관시켜 삶에서 개인적인 경험의 중요성에 대해서 말하고 있다.

① 지도를 읽는 방법을 학생에게 가르치는 이유
② 부하에게 리더십을 옮기는 어려움
③ 우리 마음에 그려진 지도의 가치
⑤ 아이들에게 직접 경험을 노출시키는 방법

39 ①

receptive : 수용적인 inappropriate : 부적절한 restricted : 제한된 addicted : 중독된
conductive : 전도하는

☞ 앞 문장에서 우리의 부모들이 우리에게 그들이 배운 것을 가르친다고 했고, 해당 문장 앞에서는 '불행히도'를 의미하는 unfortunately가 나왔다. '부모가 우리에게 가르치지만 불행히도 수용하지 못한다.'의 의미로 receptive가 들어가야 한다.

40 42

「수렵 · 채집인은 약 50,000년에 오스트레일리아에 도달했다. 불과 원시도구들로 무장한 그들은 그들이 식민지화되는 환경에 상당한 영향을 미쳤다. 화석 기록은 오스트레일리아에서 많은 큰 포유동물의 갑작스런 멸종을 보여준다, 그것은 인간 식민지화와 동시에 나타난 것이다, 그러나 원인과 결과에 대한 증거는 분명하지 않다. 그 멸종이 인간 활동에 의했는지, 아니면 많은 종이 (B)적응할 수 없는 빠른 기후변화에 의했는지에 관한 일부 논쟁이 있다. 최근 플라이스토세 동안, 인류는 오스트레일리아에 도착했고 큰(몸무게가 44kg을 초과) 유대동물과 새의 85%는 멸종했다. 이것은 단지 우연의 일치인가? 닥터 David Miller는 에뮤에 관련된 거대한 새(큰 날지 못하는 새)의 멸종 원인에 관한 증거를 조사했다. 멸종의 시기는 단지 알맞은 기후변화의 시기와 일치하고, 그는 이 새의 서식지에 대한 인류의 영향이 가장 가능성 있는 원인이라고 결론을 내렸다. 그러나 닥터 Susan Bowman은 원시 인구가 지금보다 더 상당히 밀집되지 않는 한, 인류 약탈이 오스트레일리아의 그러한 다량의 거대동물 멸종의 직접적인 원인이라는 설득력 있는 증거가 아니라고 주장했다. 더 가능성 있는 시나리오는 이른 원시 인구에 의한 불의 사용의 영향이 지형을 너무 빨리 변화 시켜서 많은 종이 살아남을 수 없었다는 것이다. 불타는 원시 지형은 유럽인들의 도착 전에 전형적인 오스트레일리아 초원 지역 사회의 구조에서 중대한 영향을 맡았다. 이것은 풀을 뜯는데 적응한 일부 종에게는 적절한 서식지를 만들어 줬지만 관목이 무성한 초목에 의지하여 풀을 먹는 종에게는 적대적이었다. : 브라우징은 많은 멸종된 종의 특징이다.」

40 ③

primitive : 원시사회의 extinction : 멸종 colonize : ~을 식민지로 하다 mammal : 포유류 colonization : 식민지화 marsupial : 유대동물 coincidence : 우연의 일치 correspond : 일치하다 predation : 약탈 aboriginal : 원시의 megafauna : 거대동물 adapt : ~을 적응시키다 scrubby : 관목이 무성한 vegetation : 초목 suitable : 적절한

☞ 수렵 · 채집인이 약 50,000년 전에 오스트레일리아에 도달한 것으로 시작하는 이 글은 포유동물의 멸종에 대한 가능성 있는 원인들을 설명하면서 오스트레일리아에 도착한 인류에 대해 설명하고 있다.

41 ②

equivocal : 분명하지 않은 dense : 밀집한

☞ 멸종의 원인에 대한 설명으로 '많은 인종이 적응할 수 없는 빠른 기후변화'의 뜻이 되어야 한다. 그러므로 able이 아니라 unable이 들어가야 한다.

42 ⑤

☞ 마지막 문장에서 초원 지역사회가 grazing에 대해서는 적절한 서식지를 만들었지만, browsing에 대해서는 적대적이라고 나와 있다. browsing은 많은 멸종된 종의 특징이다.

「(가) 적어도 미국에 따르면 당신이 두 조각의 빵 사이에 조금의 고기를 놓으면 당신은 샌드위치를 갖는다. 농무부는 고기와 가금류의 고기의 안전과 표시를 시행한다. "우리는 전통적인 닫힌 얼굴의 샌드위치에 대해 이야기 한다." USDA 식품 안전에서 일하는 Mark Wheeler이 말했다. "샌드위치는 둥근 빵 또는 비스킷인 두 개의 조각 빵 사이에 고기 또는 가금류의 고기를 채워 넣은 것이다." 그것은 부리토, 랩 샌드위치 또는 핫도그를 제외한다.

(라) 그러나 USDA가 샌드위치를 정의해야하는 유일한 장소는 아니다. 전국에 걸쳐 주로 검사와 세금 용도를 위한 사법권이 중요하다. 컴퓨터 개발자인 Noah Veltman은 애매한 정부 메모를 읽는 괴상한 취미를 가졌다. 그가 말하길, "나의 새로운 뉴욕의 국가는 샌드위치를 위한 특별한 세금 범주를 가진다. 그래서 그들은 샌드위치가 클럽 샌드위치, BLT, 핫도그와 부리토를 포함한다고 설명하는 이 메모를 발행한다. 그러면 당신은 부리토가 정말로 샌드위치인가? 궁금해 한다. 뉴욕은 '예'이고, USDA는 '아니오'이고 그것을 검열할 때는 차이가 발생한다.

(나) 논쟁은 2006년에 너무 뜨거워져서 Qdoba Mexican Grill의 부리토가 샌드위치의 자격을 갖추는지에 대한 계약 논쟁이 재판에 회부되었다. 요리사와 음식 비평가를 포함하는 전무가 증인들은 증언했고, 더 많은 심사숙고를 하고, 결국에는 상급법원 Judge Jeffrey Locke는 부리토가 샌드위치가 아니라고 정했다. 그것이 매사추세츠에 정착고되었다. 그러나 모든 곳에서 확실한 정의를 위해서는 당신은 가장자리의 케이스를 찾아야한다. 연방정부의 관리에 따르면 아이스크림 샌드위치는 정말로 샌드위치가 아니다. 그러나 부리토는 왠지 그렇다. 그러나 뉴욕에서는 이유를 설명하지 않았다. −적어도 아직까지.

(다) 모두 무슨 말을 하나? 얇게 썰린 빵은 우리에게 샌드위치를 가져왔다. 그러나 그것은 변화하고 있다. 음식 트렌드는 휙 들락거린다. 그리고 모든 혁신을 따라잡는 것은 규제기관에게는 지는 게임이다. 샌드위치든 스마트폰이든 정부는 대중을 보호하기 위해 이러한 것들을 분류하려고 시도한다. 그러나 혁신은 기준이 변하는 것보다 더 빨리 움직인다. 펠트만은 몇 번이고 본다. "이 메모들을 쓰는 사람들은 분류할 수 없는 것을 분류하려는 시도의 업무에 있다. 인간의 무한히 변화가 있는 유형이다. 당신은 실제로 모든 것에 들어맞는 것을 위한 계획을 따라잡지 못할 것이다". Veltman이 말했다.」

43 ④

enforce : 시행하다 poultry : 가금류의 고기 exclude : 제외하다 go the trial : 재판에 회부되다 fed : 연방 정부의 관리 witness : 증인 solid : 확실한 unclassifiable : 분류할 수 없는 scheme : 계획, 설계 infinitely : 무한히 weird : 기묘한, 괴상한 obscure : 애매한 jurisdiction : 사법권, 재판권

☞ (가)에서 샌드위치에 대한 USDA의 견해가 나온다. (라)에서 'But'으로 시작하여 USDA의 견해에 반대 입장으로 뉴욕이 나온다. (나)에서는 이 뜨거운 논쟁으로 인해 재판에 회부된 내용이 나오고 (다)에서는 규정이 변화를 따라가지 못하는 현상에 대한 설명이 나온다.

44 ④

☞ (다)에서 변화가 너무 빨라서 규정들이 변화를 따라가지 못한다는 내용이 주를 이루고 있다.

45 ①

edge 가장자리, 모서리 regulator 규제 기관 lucid 명료한

☞ (A) 샌드위치의 정의가 각각 다르기 때문에 모든 곳에서 쓰이는 확실한 정의를 위해서는 가장자리에 있는 경우까지 모두 찾아봐야 한다.
(B) 규정이 변화를 따라가지 못한다는 내용으로 '혁신은 규제기관에게는 지는 게임'이다.

2016학년도 정답 및 해설

01 ①

ephemeral : 수명이 짧은, 단명하는
① 순식간의, 잠깐 동안의 ② 남은, 잔여[잔류]의 ③ 끊임없이 계속되는 ④ 전설적인, 아주 유명한 ⑤ 남의 말을 잘 믿는, 잘 속는

「누가 그 영화 스타의 명성이 <u>단명할</u> 것이라고 추측이나 했었는가?」

02 ①

cajole : 꼬드기다, 회유하다   to no avail : 아무 효과가 없어, 헛되이
☞ cajole은 '꼬드기다, 회유하다'
① 구슬리다, 달래다 ② (약자를) 괴롭히다, 왕따시키다 ③ 중상모략[비방]하다 ④ (특정한 반응을) 유발하다
⑤ 최면을 걸다, 혼을 빼놓다

「Karen은 그의 친구가 그녀를 쇼핑몰에 태워다 주도록 꼬드기려고 애썼지만, 효과가 전혀 없었다.」

03 ⑤

fastidious : 까다로운, 세심한 주의가 필요한 premises : 부지[지역], 구내, 점포 spotless : 티끌 한 점 없는, 청결 하게 to a fault : 결점이라 할 만큼, 지나치게
☞ fastidious는 '세심한, 꼼꼼한'
① 아주 위험한 ② 서서히 퍼지는 ③ 파산한 ④ 앙심을 품은, 보복을 하려는 ⑤ 꼼꼼한, 세심한

「그녀는 점포 안을 티끌 한 점 없이 유지하는 것에 대해 거의 지나칠 정도로 굉장히 꼼꼼하다.」

04 ②

☞ quandary는 '진퇴양난'
① 유대, 끈 ④ 황홀감, 황홀경 ⑤ 짜증나게 함, 짜증

「꿈은 사람들이 그날의 정서적 진퇴양난을 겪어 나가는 것을 돕는다. 이것은 내장된 치료사를 갖고 있는 것과 같다.」

05 ④

☞ discreetly는 '신중하게'
① rashly 성급하게, 무분별하게, 경솔하게 ⑤ impartially 치우치지 않고, 편견 없이

「그는 나를 Clare와 같은 수준으로 승진시킬 것이다. 그는 나에게 신중하게 얘기해 줘서 그녀는 질투하지 않을 것이다.」

06 ④

tend : 돌보다, 보살피다   diarrhea : 설사   pick one's way : 조심하며 걷다

☞ ④ what과 관련된 어법 문제는 what 이 유도하는 문장에 유의함. what 뒤에는 문장구성 요소가 완벽한 것이 오지 않음. ④ 문장은 it ~ that … 가주어ㆍ진주어 구문의 문장임.

「나는 한때 파푸아뉴기니의 해변 마을에 살았다. 그곳의 아이들은 자신의 부모와 함께 살지 않고 그들이 원하는 대로 집집마다 옮겨 다녔다. 10살 된 아이들이 아기들을 업고 다니거나, 요리하기 위하여 불을 다루는 것을 목격할 수 있었다. 14살쯤이 되면 그들은 자신감과 자부심을 갖고 어른들의 일을 했다. 그 마을에서 가장 새롭고 가장 흥미로운 일은 내가 12명쯤 되는 아이들을 내 베란다에서 재웠던 것이었다. 열대 지방의 설사가 한 밤 중에 찾아왔을 때, 나는 카펫 위에 있는 작은 갈색 몸들 (아이들) 사이로 나가려고 조심스럽게 걸어야만 했다. 마을 전체가 부모의 일과 즐거움을 공유하였기 때문에, 이곳은 부모가 되기에 쉬운 곳이라는 생각이 내게는 들었다. 사실 그곳에 있었던 어느 어른이나 부모였다.」

07 ④

plunge : 거꾸러지다, 급락하다, 가파르게 내려가다   peril : (심각한) 위험, 위험성, 유해함   strip of : ~을 빼앗다   prosperous : 번영한, 번창한   executive : 경영진, 경영 간부 C.E.O = chief executive officer(최고 경영자)

☞ ④ be 동사 관련 문제일 경우에는 단, 복수 문제 일 가능성에 유의함. Those fears가 주어이고, 접속사 and에 의해 동사가 병렬로 연결됨. 동사 형태가 were로 나와야 함.

「대단히 부유하게 태어났지만 10대였을 때 급격히 가난에 빠졌기 때문에 나는 성공을 달성하는 비결보다는 성공을 상실하는 위험에 대해 더 많이 알면서 자랐다. 비록 우리 부모님이 중년에 모든 것을 빼앗긴 후에 회복했지만, 그들은 풍요로운 마음 가짐을 결코 되찾지는 못하셨다. 그리고 나는 그들의 성공보다는 공포를 더 완전히 흡수했다. 이러한 공포는 재정적으로 성공적이고자 하는 내 욕구에 불을 붙였고, 부분적으로는 사람들에게 성취하는 법을 가르치면서 내가 생계를 유지하도록 몰아갔 던 것이었다. 나는 어른이 되어 수천 명의 회사 경영진들과 프로 운동선수들이 가치 있는 성공 원리를 사용하면서 그들의 목표를 달성할 수 있도록 영감을 불어넣어 주는 동기 부여 연설가가 되었다.」

08 ⑤

myth : 신화, 미신, 통념 gem : 보석   curse : 저주하다   cursed : 저주 받은   intrigue : 음모 prospector : (금, 광물 등 을 찾는) 탐사[탐광]자   monarch : 군주   curb : 제한(억제)하다   cultivate : 조성하다, 장려하다

☞ ⑤ the belief that anyone who took a stone from a mine would be cursed may have deliberately cultivated to curb losses of a valuable national assets. 이 문장의 주어는 the belief 임. 이런 유형의 문제는 항상 주어와 동사의 관계를 생각하는 습관이 필요함. 주어 the belief는 동사와 함께 쓰일 때 cultivate the belief의 형태를 취함. 그러므로, may have been deliberately cultivated가 되어야 함.

「보석과 연관된 수많은 신화와 전설들이 있다. 어떤 것은 저주받은 보석에 대하여 이야기한다. 또 다른 것은 특별한 치유의 힘이 있거나 혹은 (보석을) 갖고 있는 사람을 보호하거나, 행운을 가져다주는 보석에 대하여 이야기한다. 또 어떤 것들 은 가장 크다고 알려진 다이아몬드들은 수세기 동안 되풀이 되어 말해져 왔던 그것들과 관련된 전설을 갖고 있다고 이야기 한다. 그리고, 현재 없어진 많은 이야기들은 음모와 살인에 대한 이야기들로 둘러싸여 있다. 약간의 광산들은 저주받았다고 여겨지 는데, 아마도 이것은 원치 않았던 탐사자들을 멀리하고자 광산 소유주들이 퍼트렸던 소문일 것이다. 예를 들어, 모든 보석들 이 왕실의 소유였던 미얀마에서는 귀중한 국가 자산의 손실을 막기 위해 광산에서 보석을 가져가는 사람은 누구나 저주를 받을 것이라는 믿음을 의도적으로 조장했었을 수 있다.」

09 ①

landline : 일반 전화 pinpoint : ~의 위치를 정확히 나타내다 overlook : 간과하다, 눈감아 주다 in a matter of seconds : 순식간에 triangulation : 삼각 측량 circulation : 순환, 유통 cell tower : 기지국 approximate : ~을 어림잡다, ~에 가까워지다 radius : 반지름, 반경 diameter : 지름

☞ 일반전화와 휴대전화로 911 긴급전화를 했을 경우에, 전화를 건 사람의 위치를 파악하는 시간은 일반전화가 훨씬 빠르며, 휴대전화로 전화를 하면, 삼각측량법에 의해 한 블록의 반경에서 위치를 찾아낸다는 내용에 어울리게 어휘를 사용하면 됨.

「지난 여름, 캘리포니아에 사는 26세 여성이 응급상황을 신고하기 위해 911에 전화했다. 만약 그녀가 일반 전화로 긴급 전화를 했었더라면, 최초의 응답자는 금방 그녀의 위치를 정확히 찾아낼 수 있었을 것이다. 하지만 현재 911 시스템은 1960년대에 고안된 이후로 대체로 변화가 없었기 때문에, 경찰은 그녀가 위치 할 수 있는 곳을 결정하기 위해 그녀의 휴대폰에 의해 제공되는 부정확한 정보를 사용할 수밖에 없었다. 긴급신고 전화가 휴대폰으로 걸려오면, 통신 회사는 전화기의 위치를 어림잡아 측정하기 위해 신호의 세기와 신호가 수많은 기지국에 도달하는 데 걸리는 시간을 비교하는 삼각 측량법을 사용한다. 이 기술은 그녀가 한 블록 반경 안에 있다는 것을 알아냈으며, 그녀를 찾는 데 20분 이상 걸렸다.」

10 ③

account for : ~을 설명하다 thence : 거기서부터, 그때부터 realm : 영역[범위], 왕국 as opposed to : ~와는 대조적으로, ~이 아니라 annal : 1년간의 기록 speculate : 사색하다, 추측하다 be bound : 구속되다 fetter : 속박, 족쇄 inherited : 상속한, 승계한 orthodoxy : 정설, 정통적 관행

☞ 역접의 접속사 but의 쓰임에 유의하면, familiar와 ordinary의 의미와 접속사 but의 쓰임을 생각할 때, 서로 반대의 의미는 아니므로, ordinary를 'exceptional(특출한, 예외적인)'으로 바꾸는 것이 필요함.

「모든 역사에서 그리스의 갑작스런 문명 발생만큼 놀랍거나, 설명하기 어려운 것은 없다. 문명을 이루고 있는 많은 것들은 이미 이집트와 메소포타미아에 수천 년간 존재해 왔고, 거기서 부터 인접 국가들로 확산되었다. 그러나, 특정 요소들은 그리스인들이 그것들을 제공할 때까지는 부족한 상태였다. 그들이 예술과 문학에서 성취한 것은 누구에게나 친숙하다, 그러나 그들이 순전히 지적인 영역에서 성취했던 것은 훨씬 더 평범하다(→ 특별하다). 그들은 수학, 과학, 철학을 고안해 냈다; 그들은 처음으로 단순한 기록과 대조되는 것으로서 역사를 기록하였다; 그들은 세상의 본질과 삶의 목적에 대해 대대로 이어져 내려온 어떤 통설의 속박에 구속받지 않고 자유롭게 사색하였다.」

11 ④

dispel : 떨쳐 버리다, 없애다 gloom : 어둠, 우울 illuminate : 비추다, 밝히다 candlepower : 촉광, 광도 arc 호(弧), 둥근[활] 모양 dimly : 희미하게 serviceable : 실용적인, 쓸 만한 incandescent bulb : 백열전구

☞ 전기 램프의 등장이 12촉광으로 도시를 희미하게 밝혀주던 가스등을 대체하였을 것이므로 ④ established ⇒ removed로 바꾸어야만 함.

「일반 시민들에게 밤에 도시의 어둠을 없앴던 전깃불은 시대가 변했다는 가장 극적인 증거를 제공해 주었다. 석탄에서 나오는 가스를 밝게 하는 가스등은 19세기 초 이후로 사용되고 있었다. 하지만 12촉광의 램프는 도시의 공공장소를 단지 희미하게 밝혀주었다. 전기의 첫 번째 상업적인 사용은 더 나은 도시 조명 시설을 위한 것이었다. 1878년 필라델피아의 Wanamaker 백화점에 설치된 Charles F. Brush의 둥근 전기 램프는 눈부신 빛을 밝혔고, 곧 전국의 도시 거리와 공공건물에 가스등을 세웠다(→ 없앴다.) 그리고 나서 1879년 Thomas Edison의 실용적인 백열전구 발명 덕분에 전깃불은 미국인의 가정으로 들어왔다. Edison의 좌우명 – "빛이 있으라!" – 은 현대 도시의 경험을 진정으로 묘사하였다.」

12 ④

track : 추적하다 probiotic yogurt : 프로바이오틱 요구르트 strain : 종류, 유형 extinguish : 소멸시키다, 끄다 hygienic : 위생적인, 건강에 좋은 hygiene : 위생, 위생학 immunity : 면역력

☞ 문단의 주된 내용이 키스를 통해 세균이 얼마나 확산되는가에 대한 것이므로, 연구의 대상자들이 키스를 통해 8천만 마리의 박테리아를 상대방에게 옮겼다는 것이 적절한 어휘 사용임.
　따라서 'extinguished(소멸시켰다)' ⇒ 'transfer(옮기다)'로 바꾸는 것이 적절함.

「키스하는 동안 사랑 외에 다른 무엇이 전달될까? 네덜란드의 연구자들은 키스가 어떻게 21쌍 커플의 구강 박테리아에 영향을 미치는가를 추적했다. 그들은 세균의 확산을 추적하기 위해 각 커플 중 한 사람에게 특정 박테리아 종류의 프로바이오틱 요구르트 음료를 마시도록 요청했다. 그러고 나서 그 사람은 그나 그녀의 파트너와 10초 동안 키스를 나누도록 요청받았다. 평균적인 키스는 8천만 마리만큼의 많은 박테리아를 소멸시켰다(→ 옮겼다). 비록 이것이 매우 위생적인 것처럼 들리지는 않지만, 전문가들은 누군가의 박테리아에 대한 노출이 실제로는 당신의 면역력을 강화시키는 것에 도움이 될 수 있다고 말한다.」

13 ④

give birth to : 출산하다. ~의 원인이 되다 airborne : 비행 중인, 하늘에 떠 있는 pros : 찬성 cons : 반대 vector : 방향, 궤도, 진로

☞ ④는 지상에서 다니는 자동차를 지칭하며, 나머지는 하늘을 나는 자동차를 지칭함.

「공중을 나는 자동차를 만드는 것이 사실은 그렇게 어려운 일은 아니다. 최초의 작동 모델은 1947년에 나왔다. 진짜 과제는 말이 되는 비행 자동차를 만드는 것으로 판가름 나는 것이다. Tesla와 SpaceX의 CEO인 Elon Musk는 왜 그는 그의 두 회사를 결합시켜서 로켓 자동차를 탄생시킬 수 없는지 질문을 계속 받았다. 그는 최근 트위터에 "비행 자동차에 대한 찬성 : 3차원에서 빠르게 움직임. 반대 : 두 방향으로 움직이는 것보다 차가 머리 위에 떨어질 위험이 훨씬 더 큼"을 포함해서 일련의 응답을 했다. 그리고 유명한 투자가인 Peter Thiel은 "우리는 진짜 하늘은 나는 자동차를 원했다. 그 대신 우리는 쓰레기 같은 것을 얻었다."라고 말하면서 돌아다니고 있다.」

14 ①

neurologist : 신경학자 renowned : 유명한, 명성 있는 autism : 자폐증(자폐범주성 장애 autism spectrum disorder) utter : 말로 표현하다, 말하다 splash : (물탕을) 튀기다. 첨벙거리다 spectrum : 스펙트럼(같은 성질을 갖도록 적당한 폭으로 구분한 연속적인 주파수의 범위) patty : 패티(간 고기 등을 얇게 원형으로 만든 요리) compassion : 연민, 동정심 Temple Grandin : 1947년 출생, 현재 콜로라도 주립대 교수, 동물학자

☞ 문단의 초반에 Temple Grandin을 a renowned animal scientist born with autism이라고 말하고 있으므로, ①이 글의 내용과 일치함.

「신경학자, 소, 패스트푸드 식당은 무엇을 공통으로 갖고 있을까? 그들은 모두 자폐증을 가지고 태어난 유명한 동물 과학자 Temple Grandin이라는 한 여성에게 많은 빚을 지고 있다. 그녀는 4번째 생일 때까지 단 한마디도 말하지 못했지만, 그 유명한 신경학자 Oliver Sacks 덕분에 그녀는 1995년에 대중의 인식 단계로 첨벙 뛰어 들었다. (대중들이 그녀를 알게 되었다). 하지만 많은 정신 장애와 마찬가지로, 자폐는 스펙트럼성 장애의 하나인데, Temple은 스펙트럼의 한 쪽 끝에 있었다. 이 끝에서 살아가는 것이 그녀가 자폐 아동들에게 뛰어난 영감의 원천이 되도록 했다. 그녀는 또한 다른 포유동물, 소에게는 희망의 원천이었다. 동물의 마음을 들여다보는 그녀의 독특한 창을 사용하여, 그녀는 스트레스를 감소시켜서 소들의 삶의 질을 증진시켜주는 소 축사를 개발하였다. 그리고, 패스트푸드 산업은 소를 패티에 계속 사용하고 있음에도 불구하고, Grandin 버거의 윤리와 연민을 고맙게 여겨 왔다.」

15 ③

slender : 날씬한, 호리호리한, 가느다란 filefish : (어류) 쥐치 camouflage : 위장하다, 감추다 sea fan : 산호충의 일종, 부채꼴 산호 gorgonian : 부채뿔산호 coloration : (생물의) 천연색 longitudinal : 세로(방향)의, 길이의 longitude : 경도 stripe : 줄무늬, 줄

☞ 문단의 내용과 일치하는 것을 고르는 사실적 이해의 문제. 글의 중간 부분 'It took them just two seconds to match the color ~'를 참고하면 ③이 글의 내용과 일치함.

「지금 보이다가도 보이지 않는다. 날씬한 쥐치는 그것의 천적을 피하는 교묘한 방법을 갖고 있다. 이것은 거의 눈에 보이지 않게 되는 능력을 진화시켜 왔다. Brown 대학의 Justin Allen은 그녀가 카리브해에서 이 물고기를 봤을 때, 얼마나 빨리 그것들이 스스로를 위장시키는지에 놀랐다. 이 물고기가 헤엄치며 지나간 부채뿔산호의 색깔에 맞추는 데는 단 2초가 걸렸다. 어떻게 된 일일까? 어떤 물체가 무엇인지 파악하기 위해, 당신은 배경과 구별될 수 있도록 그 물체를 표시하는 테두리를 인지할 필요가 있다. Allen은 쥐치가 "가짜 테두리"를 만들기 위해 배색을 바꾼다는 것을 알아냈다. 예를 들어, 쥐치는 진짜 테두리처럼 보이는 어두운 세로 방향의 줄무늬가 몸에 나타나게 할 수 있다. 눈은 이 가짜 테두리를 보게 되는데, 그래서 이 물고기의 진짜 윤곽을 파악하지 못 할 수 있다.」

16 ⑤

ambiguous : 애매모호한 wrought : 만들어진 surge : 급증, 급등, (갑자기) 밀려듦[솟아오름] infuriate : 극도로 화나게 만들다 policy : 보험 증권(증서), 정책 sue : 고소하다 suit : 소송, 고소 credibility : 신뢰 coverage : (보험의) 보상 범위

☞ 마지막 문장에서 주택소유자들은 lost the suit라고 했으므로 ⑤의 내용은 일치하지 않음.

「실망을 초래하는 혼돈과 오해의 근원은 종종 보험계약서의 복잡하고 애매모호한 용어이다. 미시시피 주 Gulf 해안에서 발생한 허리케인 Katrina에 의해 만들어진 수십억 달러의 피해는 Katrina의 엄청난 폭풍이 수천 채의 집과 회사를 손상시키고 파괴시켰을 때 발생했다. 주택소유자들은 그들의 보험 증서는 물이 아니라 바람에 의한 손해만 보장해 준다는 사실을 깨달았을 때, 극도로 화가 나서 보험 회사를 고소하기 위해 주 정부와 함께 협력했다. 그들은 보험이 수해를 보장하지 않는다 할지라도 Katrina의 엄청난 바람이 그들의 재산에 피해를 입힌 물 장벽을 몰고 왔기 때문에 보상해 주어야 한다고 주장했다. 주택소유자들은 소송에서 패했지만, 보험회사는 많은 신용을 잃었고 사람들은 그들의 보상 범위가 계약서에 나타나 있는 것 보다 훨씬 더 적은 것을 걱정하게 되었다.」

17 ⑤

benchmark : 기준(점), 척도 invitational : 초청선수 경기 scorching : 맹렬한, 타는 듯한 smash : 깨다, 부서지다 dash : 단거리 경주

☞ would have p.p. (가정법 과거완료 주절의 구문) '~였었을 것이다'라는 과거사실의 반대를 가정하는 구문으로 대회에 참가했었다면 그랬을 것이었다는 의미이므로 ⑤의 3등을 차지했다는 내용은 본문의 내용과 일치하지 않음.

「11초는 100미터 달리기에서 성인 여성과 소녀를 구분하는 기준점이다. 지난 토요일, 시애틀 주 Brooks PR 초청 경기에서 16세의 Candace Hill은 10.98초의 뜨거운 승리로 엘리트 그룹에 합류하면서, 미국 유소년과 세계 청소년 기록을 깨고, 11초 장벽을 깬 최초의 미국 여고생이 되었다. 지난달 조지아 주 Rockdale County 고등학교에서 2학년을 마친 Candace는 다섯 차례의 국내 챔피언이고, 이미 100미터, 200미터 단거리 경주에서 조지아 주 기록을 이미 보유하였다. 그녀가 기록을 세운 경주는 올해 NCAA(미국대학경기협회) 선수권대회에서 3등에 입상할 수 있었던 기록이었고, 이번 시즌 세계 10위 기록과 같은 것이었다.」

18 ⑤

fraught : ~로 가득 찬, ~ 투성이인(with) enact : 제정하다 unspoiled : 훼손되지 않은, 약탈당하지 않은 exploit : 이용하다, 착취하다 gratitude : 감사, 고마움 abuse : 학대하다, 남용하다 hostility : 적대감 contradiction : 모순

☞ 연간 600억 달러 규모의 애완동물 산업이 있는 미국에서도, 매년 수십억 마리의 동물들이 이런 저런 이유로 죽임을 당하고, 동물을 착취한다는 내용으로 보아, 인간이 동물을 다루는 방식은 모순이라는 것이 내용과 일치하므로, ⑤이 정답임.

「사람들의 동물과의 관계는 <u>모순</u>투성이다. 사람들은 동물에 대한 사랑과 감사하는 마음을 표현하고, 동물에 대한 학대를 금지하는 법을 제정했다. 미국은 개, 고양이, 앵무새, 햄스터, 그 밖의 다른 애완동물들을 합친 것이 사람 수보다 더 많고, 그것들을 관리하는데 연간 600억 달러의 산업이 있는 애완동물 친화적인 사회이다. 수백만 명의 미국인들은 어느 정도 야생동물에 관여하고 있고, 약간의 가장 행복한 순간을 훼손되지 않은 환경에서 보낸다. 그러나 동시에, 음식, 옷, 연구, 다른 목적을 위해 매년 수십억 마리의 생명체들이 죽임을 당하고 학대를 당하는 가운데, 그들은 대규모로 동물들을 착취하고 있다.」

19 ①

preoccupy : ~을 열중하게 하다 preoccupied : 열중한, 정신이 팔린 preoccupation : 몰두, 선입관, 편견, conform : 순응하다, 따르다 validation : 확인 anonymous : 익명의 obsession : 강박 상태, 집착 acquaintance : 아는 사이, 아는 사람 domain : 영역 prompt : 촉발하다, 자극하다 misgiving : 의혹, 염려, 불안 impose : 부과하다, 강요하다

☞ 소셜 네트워킹 서비스의 사용이 상승하는 이유는 보통사람들도 마치 유명 인사들의 경우처럼, 다른 사람들로부터 확인, 인정받고자 하는 욕구가 있다는 내용으로 미루어, 빈칸에는 ① '다른 사람들로부터의 인정을 추구한다'는 것이 적절함.

「우리는 아주 사회적인 동물이어서 다른 사람이 우리들에 관하여 생각하는 것에 완전히 사로 잡혀있다. 순응하라고 하는 사회적 압력은 집단에 의하여 평가를 받는 것과 연루되어 있다. 왜냐하면, 결국 대부분의 성공은 다른 사람이 생각하는 것에 의해 실제로 정의되기 때문이다. 이렇게 사로잡힌 생각은 현대 우리의 유명인들의 문화에서 명백하다. 그리고, 특히, 소셜 네트워킹의 증가로 해서, 보통 개인들은 상당한 양의 시간과 노력을 <u>다른 사람들로부터의 인정을 추구하는</u> 데 소비한다. 이 지구상에 17억 명이 넘는 사람은 다른 사람들과 공유하고, 그들로부터 확인을 구하기 위해 인터넷 소셜 네트워킹 서비스를 이용한다. 공연예술 학교에 대한 유명 뮤지컬 시리즈의 등장인물인 Rachel Berry는 "오늘날 익명이 된다는 것은 가난해 지는 것 보다 더 나쁜 일이다."라고 말했을 때, 그녀는 비록 현대인들이 주로 익명이거나 약간 아는 사이라 할지라도 많은 사람들에 의해 선호되고 싶은 욕망과 명성에 대한 우리 현대인의 강박증을 그대로 반영해 주었다.」

20 ⑤

originality : 독창성 nowhere : 아무데도 ~ 없다 accompaniment : 반주 novel : 새로운, 신기한 as it were : 말하자면, 이를테면 incessantly : 끊임없이 strain : 긴장시키다, 최대한으로 활동 시키다 obscure : ~을 약화시키다, ~을 불명료하게 하다 plethora : 과다, 과잉 desolation : 황량함, 적막함 command of words : 말의 구사력 redundancy : 불필요한 중복[반복], 장황함

☞ Mozart의 음악적 천재성에 대한 문단의 내용으로 보아, 빈칸에 들어갈 적절한 것은 ⑤ '풍부한 아름다움'이다. Mozart의 완벽한 아름다움은 우리들이 모두 받아들일 수 없을 정도여서, 그것이 유일한 결점일 수도 있다는 내용에서 추론이 가능함.

「Mozart의 음악적 천재성의 가장 충실한 묘사를 얻기 위해, 예술에 대한 심오한 지식을 아름다운 멜로디를 만드는 가장 행복한 재능과 결합시키고, 그런 다음 이 둘을 가능한 가장 최고의 독창성과 결합시켜 보자. 그의 작품 어디에서도 우리가 이전에 들어왔던 생각을 지금까지 찾을 수가 없다. 심지어 그의 반주조차도 항상 새롭다. 말하자면, 한 작품은 하나의 개념에서 다른 개념으로 쉬지 않고 끊임없이 움직여 간다. 그래서 가장 최근 것에 대한 감탄은 전에 지나간 것에 대한 감탄을 항상 흡수한다. 그리고 심지어는 우리의 모든 힘을 바짝 긴장시킴으로서 우리는 우리 영혼에게 주어지는 그 모든 아름다움을 좀처럼 받아들일 수 없다. 만약 어떤 잘못을 Mozart에게서 찾아내야만 했었다면, 그것은 확실히 단지 이것일 수 있다. 그렇게 풍부한 아름다움은 영혼을 거의 지치게 하고, 전체의 효과는 때때로 그것 때문에 애매모호해진다. 하지만 유일한 결점이 너무나도 위대한 완벽함에 있는 예술가는 행복하다.」

21 ①

legal domain : 법적인 영역 rhetoric : 수사학, 미사여구 Common Law : 관습법, 불문법 be doomed to : ~ 할 수밖에 없는 운명이다 dominance : 지배, 우세 testimony : 증거 threaten : (나쁜 일이) ~의 징조 (조짐)를 보이다, 위협하다 purport : ~을 의도하다, 주장하다 emblem : 상징 watchword : 표어, 좌우명 terminology : 전문 용어 eloquence : 웅변, 능변 subjective : 주관적인

☞ 현미경, 망원경 등은 모두 시각적인 정보와 관련 있다는 사실을 고려하면 빈 칸에는 ① '시각적 증거'가 적절함.

「하나의 그림은 천 마디 말의 가치가 있을 수 있지만, 수세기 동안 말은 법적 영역을 지배했다. 언어를 사용하는 예술인 수사학은 항상 변호사의 트레이드마크가 되었고, 특히 관습법에서의 재판은 말에 의한 싸움으로 널리 이해되어 왔다. 아, 모든 영광은 지나갈 운명이어서, 19세기 후반부에는 말을 사실을 전달하는 열등한 방식으로 바꾸도록 위협했던 기계가 만든 증거의 새로운 수준에 의해 추진되는, 새로운 설득의 방식이 우세해지는 것을 보게 되었다. 현미경, 망원경, 고속 카메라, X-ray관과 같은, 항상 기민하고 결코 어떤 일에 연루되지 않는 기계들이 만약 그렇지 않다면 인간에게 종종 접근 불가능한 더 풍부하고, 더 낫고, 더 진실한 증거를 전달하는 것으로 주장이 되었다. 이러한 새로운 형태의 기계적 객관성을 위한 상징은 시각적 증거였다. "자연이 스스로 말하게 하라."는 표어가 되었고, 자연의 언어는 사진과 기계적으로 그려진 곡선의 언어인 것처럼 보였다.」

22 ②

track : (음반 · 테이프에 녹음된 음악) 한 곡 lyric : (노래의) 가사 the theory of processing fluency : 정보처리 유창성 이론 digest : 완전히 이해하다, 소화하다 be in on the secret of : ~의 비밀을 알고 있다 saturate : 포화시키다, 흠뻑 적시다 stand-up : 혼자 서서 하는 코미디 loop : 고리 모양을[으로] 만들다 punch line : 핵심이 되는[결정적인] 구절, 급소를 찌르는 말 exert : (권력 · 영향력을) 가하다(행사하다) likelihood : (어떤 일이 있을) 가능성 decode : 해독하다

☞ 노래는 '가사가 단순하고 반복적일수록 사람들이 좋아한다.'라는 문장을 고려할 때, 빈칸에는 ② '사람들은 그것에 그만큼 더 긍정적으로 반응한다'가 적절함.

「소비자 심리학 저널에 실린 연구는 1958년부터 2012년까지 빌보드의 Hot 100 목록에 오른 모든 1위곡과 90위를 절대 깨지 못했던 노래들을 비교함으로써 반복의 힘을 탐구했다. 조사자들은 노래 가사가 더 단순하고 더 반복적일수록, 그 만큼 차트의 높은 순위에 오를 가능성이 더 좋아진다는 것을 관찰했다. 그러한 노래들은 또한 덜 반복적인 노래보다 차트 순위가 더 빨리 올라갔다. 이러한 발견은 메시지가 이해하기 더 쉬우면 쉬울수록 사람들은 그 만큼 더 긍정적으로 그것에 반응한다는 정보처리 유창성 이론을 뒷받침 한다. 음악가들이 이러한 비밀을 알고 있는 유일한 사람들이 아니다. 비슷한 전략은, 광고내용을 충분히 담고 있는 슬로건을 통한 광고에서, 그리고 심지어는 코미디에서도 사용된다. 혼자 서서 하는 코미디는 종종 한 공연 세트에서 똑같은 핵심 구절을 반복한다.」

23 ②

attribute A to B : A를 B의 탓으로 돌리다 Big Bang : 대폭발설(100~150억 년 전에 우주가 생겼을 때 있었다고 함) subsequent : 그 다음의, 차후의 snapping : 찰깍(딱)소리 내는 것 liana : (식물) 리아나 (열대산 칡의 일종) ironwood : 경질(硬質) 목재 meteorologist : 기상학자 ethology : 동물 행동학 evolutionary biologist : 진화 생물학자 usurp : (권력, 지위를) 빼앗다 give rise to : ~을 생기게 하다, ~을 낳다 evoke : ~를 되살려내다, 환기(喚起)하다 controversy : 논란, 논쟁 adequacy : 적당함, 타당성 creationist : 천지 창조론자

☞ 우주의 기원, 언어의 다양성을 비롯한 자연 현상에 이르기 까지 과학에 의해 설명되는 현실을 이야기하고 있는 내용으로 보아, 빈칸에는 ② '과학에 의해 점점 더 빼앗겼다'가 적절함.

「현대 서부 사회에서, 종교의 본래 설명적 역할은 <u>과학에 의해 점점 빼앗겨</u> 왔다. 우리가 알고 있는 것처럼 우주의 기원은 이제는 빅뱅과 그 이후에 일어나는 물리학 법칙의 작용 탓으로 여겨지고 있다. 현대 언어 다양성은 바벨탑이나 뉴기니의 경질 목재를 들고 있는 리아나의 찰깍 소리와 같은 기원 신화에 의해 더 이상 설명되지 않는다. 하지만 그 대신에 언어 변화의 역사적 과정을 관찰함에 의해서 적절하게 설명되는 것으로 여겨진다. 일출, 일몰, 그리고 조수의 설명은 이제 천문학자에게 맡겨져 있고, 바람과 비의 설명은 기상학자에게 맡겨졌다. 새의 노래는 동물 행동학에 의해 설명되며, 인간을 포함한 각각의 식물과 동물 종의 기원을 해석하는 것은 진화 생물학자에게 남겨져 있다.」

24 ⑤

illustrate : 예증하다, 설명하다 deify : 신격화하다 take over : 인수하다 Spaniard : 스페인 사람 ritualistic : 의식의 shed : (악습 등을) 버리다 be in line with : ~와 일치하다 maize : 옥수수 tribute : 공물, 조공 degradation : 불명예, 체면손상, 격하(格下) relevant : 관련된, 적절한 subordinate : 부수적인, 예속되는 inquisition : 조사, 심문, 종교재판 staff of life : 생명의 양식, 주식 secularization : 세속화

☞ 마야인에게 담배는 종교적인 의미가 중요하고, 즐거움을 주는 특성은 상대적으로 (A) '부수적(subordinate)' 이라는 내용이 적절함. 그리고, 스페인 사람들에게는 담배는 단지, 개인에게 즐거움을 주는 수단이 되었던 것처럼, 옥수수, 카카오의 경우도 종교적 의미를 상실하고 단지 상품의 역할로 degradation(가치의 격하)가 이루어졌으므로, (B)에는 '세속화(secularization)' 했다는 표현이 들어가는 것이 적절함.

「담배의 용도는, 담배가 스페인의 혹은 그 점에 있어서 모든 서양 문화의 한 부분이 되었을 때, 마야인의 눈에는 거의 종교의 한 요소였던 것(담배)에 어떤 일이 일어났었는지를 설명한다. 마야인에게 담배는 종교적인 생활에서 매우 중요한 역할이 있었다. 이것은 질병의 예방과 치료에서 중요한 요소였고, 어떤 지역에서는 신격화되었다. 담배의 즐거움을 주는 특성은 마야인의 눈에는 다른 기능들에 비해 꽤 부수적인 것이었던 것 같다. 그러나 담배가 스페인 사람들에게 넘어갔을 때, 그것은 단지 개인에게 즐거움을 주는 상품으로서 존재했다. 마야의 의식적이고 공동체적 모든 연관성은 사라졌다. 이러한 과정은 스페인 사람들이 흡수했던 정복된 원주민들의 문화적 요소를 세속화하는 것과 일치했다. 옥수수는 더 이상 사랑받는 신성한 생명의 양식이 아니었다. 이것은 정복자를 위한 공물과 상업적 거래의 물건이 되었다. 카카오도 똑같은 불명예를 겪었다.」

25 ⑤

ballad : (이야기를 담은) 발라드(시나 노래) dashing : 늠름한, 멋진, 근사한 yeoman : 소지주 rectify : (잘못된 것을) 바로잡다 outlaw : 도망자, 범법자 medieval : 중세의

☞ 로빈 후드 전설에서 로빈 후드의 캐릭터가 어떻게 변했는지에 대한 글의 내용으로, 자작농이었던 로빈 후드가 인기를 얻어감에 따라 영웅적인 범법자로 바뀌었으므로, 제목으로 가장 적절한 것은 ⑤ '로빈 후드 캐릭터의 변화'가 적절함.

「최초의 로빈 후드 이야기는 1450년에 출간되었다. 그런데 그것은 우리가 대중문화에서 알게 되었던 멋진 영웅을 묘사하지 않고 있다. 그는 가끔씩은 거칠고 잔인한 자작농이었다. 전설은 그가 부자들로부터 훔친 돈을 가지고 때때로 가난한 사람들을 도와주었던 도둑에 더 근거를 두었던 것 같다. 그는 숲속에 이상적인 사회를 세우고 싶어 하지 않았다. 그와 그의 부하들은 주로 사회적 부정을 바로잡고 잘 살기를 추구했다. 로빈 후드는 17세기쯤에는 아주 인기가 있어서 사람들은 그의 이름을 따서 장소나 배의 이름을 지었다. 19세기쯤에는 많은 이야기와 노래들은 로빈 후드 전설에 중요한 변화를 가져왔다. 자작농이던 그의 기원은 사라졌고, 그는 점차적으로 가난한 사람들의 권리를 방어하는 Sherwood 숲의 영웅적인 범법자가 되었다.」

26 ②

soothing : 누그러뜨리는, 진정하는 ambivalent : 반대 감정이 병존하는, 애증이 엇갈리는 overbearing : 고압적인, 남을 지배하려 드는 volatile : 변덕스러운 mercurial : 변덕스러운 loom : 어렴풋이(흐릿하게) 보이다[나타나다] archetype : 전형 assassin : 암살범 boss : ~를 쥐고 흔들다

☞ 대인관계 속에서 혈압이 어떻게 변화하는가에 대한 글의 내용을 고려해 볼 때 적절한 제목은 ② '불편한 관계 : 너의 몸은 거짓말하지 않는다'가 적절함.

「한 연구에서 백 명의 남녀들은 누군가와 교류할 때 마다 혈압의 측정치를 기록하는 장치를 달고 있었다. 그들이 가족이나 즐거운 친구와 있었을 때, 그들의 혈압은 떨어졌다. 즉, 이러한 교류는 즐거웠고 마음을 진정시켜주었다. 그들이 골칫거리인 누군가와 만났을 때, 혈압상승이 있었다. 하지만 가장 큰 상승은 그들이 애증을 느꼈던 사람들, 즉 고압적인 부모님, 변덕스러운 파트너, 또는 경쟁적인 친구와 함께 있는 동안 나타났다. 변덕스러운 상사는 (혈압상승을 유발하는) 전형적인 사람으로 어렴풋이 나타나지만, 이러한 역학은 우리의 모든 대인 관계 속에서 작용한다.」

27 ⑤

comtemporary : 동시대인 Koto : 일본의 전통 현악기로 우리나라의 가야금과 유사함 Venda : 남아프리카 의 부족 sitar : 시타르(기타 비슷한 남아시아 악기) Chopi xylophone : 모잠비크의 Chopi족이 연주하는 목 재 건반 psyche : 마음, 정신, 심령 divergence : 확산, 차이, 발산 nourish : 풍요롭게 하다 universality : 일반성, 보편성 transcend : 초월하다

☞ 음악의 심층구조에는 시간과 문화를 초월하는 공통적인 요소가 있다는 글의 내용을 설명하기 위해, 바흐 와 베토벤의 음악, 비틀즈의 음악, 일본의 Koto 음악, 인도의 시타르 음악, Chopi 실로폰 음악 등을 예로 들면서, 이러한 음악들이 아직도 우리들을 즐겁게 한다고 하였으므로, 주제로 가장 적적한 것은 ⑤ '시간 과 문화를 초월하는 음악의 보편성'이 가장 적절함.

「바흐와 베토벤의 동시대 사람들에게 즐거웠던 음악은 우리가 그들의 문화를 공유하지 않고 있는데도 불구하고 여전히 즐겁다. 비록 비틀즈가 유감스럽게도 해체되었을지라도 초기 비틀즈의 노래들은 여전히 아주 신이 난다. 비슷하게도, 수백 년 전에 작곡되었음에 틀림없는 Venda 부족의 노래들은 여전히 나를 신나게 한다. 우리들 중 많은 사람들은 일본의 Koto 음악, 인도의 시타르 음악, Chopi 실로폰 음악 등에 의해 전율을 느낀다. 나는 우리가 연주자와 정확히 똑같은 방식으로 음악을 받아들인다고 말하는 것은 아니지만, 우리 자신의 경험은 서로 다른 문화 상호간의 의사소통의 가능성이 있음을 암시한다. 비록 표면 구조에는 나타나지 않을 수 있지만, 음악의 심층 구조 수준에는 인간의 마음에는 공통된 요소들이 있다는 사실에서 나는 이것에 대한 설명을 찾을 수 있다고 확신한다.」

28 ③

notable : 주목할 만한, 유명한, 중요한 quote : 인용구 measure up : (기대, 필요에) 부합하다, 미치다
tremendous : 엄청난, 놀랄만한, 굉장한 figure : 인물 emulate : 모방하다

☞ 롤 모델을 선택할 때, 자신의 능력으로 도달할 수 없는 일을 성취했던 사람을 롤 모델로 선택하면 좌절과
패배의식만을 가져올 수 있으므로, 자신의 직장동료 혹은 가족을 롤 모델로 선택하는 것이 오히려, 대단
히 가치 있는 일이라는 내용을 고려해 볼 때, 주제로 가장 적절한 것은 ③ '도달 가능한 롤 모델을 선택하
는 것의 중요성'이다.

「우리는 종종 영감을 불러일으키는 사람들과 훌륭한 성공에 관한 이야기를 보게 된다. 우리들 중의 약간의 사람들은 그들의
사진을 벽에 붙이거나, 그들의 유명한 인용구를 가위로 오려낸다. 하지만 만약 이러한 영감을 불러일으키는 사람이 우리가
결코 하지 않을 일을 혹은 우리가 결코 할 수 없을 일을 했다면 이것이 우리에게 무슨 도움이 되는 것인가? 우리들 중 많은
사람들에게 롤 모델의 선택은 비교를 초래한다. 그런데, 만약 우리의 능력과 결과가 그들에게 미치지 못하면 롤 모델은 영감
의 존재가 아니라 좌절과 패배의 근원으로서의 역할을 한다. 당신이 성취할 수 있고 성취하고 싶은 일을 성취했던 누군가를
롤 모델로 선택하라. 굉장한 성공을 경험했지만 그들의 경험이 당신의 경험과 공통점이 적은 유명한 운동선수, 지도자, 혹은
역사적 인물보다는 차라리 당신이 존경하는 직장동료나 가족을 롤 모델로 이용할 때 놀랄만한 가치가 있다.」

29 ③

endangered : (동식물이) 멸종 위기에 처한 grizzly bear : (북미 서부지역의 큰) 회색 곰 cub : (곰 · 사자 ·
여우 등의) 새끼 keen : 날카로운, 예민한, 열심인 rat race : 극심한 경쟁, 쫓고 쫓기는 경쟁 mindlessly
: 아무 생각 없이, 분별없이 moderation : 적당함, 온건, 절제 pocket : ~을 포켓에 넣다, ~을 착복하다
outweigh : ~보다 뛰어나다, ~보다 무겁다 cheat : 부정을 저지르다 mirror : ~을 반영하다

☞ 부모의 행동이 자식들에게 영향을 준다는 글의 내용을 새끼 곰이 어미 곰을 관찰하면서 살아가는 법을
배운다는 것을 예를 들어서 설명하는 글의 내용으로 보아, ③ '좋은 부모는 좋은 본보기를 보이는 것으로
시작해서 끝난다.'가 이 글의 요지로 가장 적절함.

「나는 최근에 British Columbia(캐나다 서해안에 위치한 주) 해변의 멸종 위기에 처한 회색 곰에 대해 읽고 있었다. 저자는
새끼 곰들이 먹이를 찾아다니거나 먹을 때 그들의 어미 곰들의 기술을 얼마나 예리하게 관찰했는지를 강조했다. 새끼 곰들이
어미 곰들의 시범에서 배운 것은 생사가 걸린 문제였다. 그러한 지식 없다면 새끼 곰들은 아마 살아남지 못할 것이다. 똑같은
원리가 우리에게도 적용된다. 우리가 극심한 생존 경쟁 같은 삶을 살 때, 우리 아이들은 어떻게든 그렇지 않을 것이라고 어떻게
믿을 수 있는가? 우리가 아무 생각 없이 얻고 쓸 때, 우리의 아이들이 어떻게든 물건과의 관계 속에서 의미와 절제를 알
수 있을 것이라고 (어떻게 믿을 수 있을 까?) 만약 내가 계산대에서 받은 추가 거스름돈을 돌려주지 않거나, 주인을 찾으려는
노력 없이 주운 돈을 주머니에 넣는 것과 같은 작은 일들에 대해 주기적으로 부정한 짓을 저지른다면, 나는 아이들에게 그
행동을 가르치고 있는 것이다.」

30 ②

hurl : 내던지다 mingle : 섞이다, 어우러지다 awakening : 각성 terrific : 엄청난, 멋진, 훌륭한 explosion : 폭발
absent-mindedly : 멍하니, 넋을 잃고 deck : (배의) 갑판 throb 진동, 욱신거림 be accustomed to : ~에 익숙해
지다 board : (배에) 타다 abruptly : 갑자기, 불쑥 cease : 멈추다 tremble : 떨다 distract : 주의를 산만하게
하다, 초점을 흐리다 stimulate : 자극하다, 촉진시키다

☞ Dave가 배를 타고 여행하는 중에 겪었던 사고를 묘사하는 글의 내용으로, 그는 자다가 침대에서 떨어져
깨어났고, 폭발이 있었고, 항상 들리던 엔진 소리가 멈추었다는 것을 깨닫고 전등을 켜려 하지만 켜지지
않는다. 이와 같은 내용을 으로 보아, ② '혼란스럽고 불안한' 상황이 필자의 심경으로 가장 적절함.

「Dave는 어떻게 그것이 일어났는지 전혀 확실치가 않았다. 그는 그가 침대에서 내던져 졌을 때 깨어났고, 화들짝 잠이 깬 상태와 뒤섞여 엄청난 폭발이 있었다는 것만 알았다. 잠시 동안, 그는 감각을 회복하기 위해 애쓰면서 그의 방 갑판 바닥에 멍하니 누워 있었다. 그러고 나서 그는 그가 배에 탄 이후로 지난 일주일간 익숙해졌던 엔진의 꾸준한 진동소리가 갑자기 멈췄다는 것을 천천히 깨달았다. 무슨 일이 일어난 것인가? 그는 일어났고, 전등 스위치를 찾아 나아가며 떨리는 손으로 전등을 켰다. 아무 일도 일어나지 않았고, 그는 다시 시도해 보았다. 불은 켜지지 않았다.」

31 ③

on the face of it : 표면상, 언뜻 보기에는 ramify : 가지를 내다, 분파시키다, 작게 구분되다 a host of : 다수의 foster : 조성하다, 발전시키다 fertilizer 비료 pesticide : 살충제 contamination : 오염 groundwater 지하수 monoculture : 단일 재배, 단종 재배 biodiversity : 생물 다양성 undermine : 손상시키다, 약화시키다 stability : 안정, 안전

☞ 산업화된 농업은 표면상으로는 세계 기아문제를 해결할 것 같았지만, 실상은 많은 분파된 문제들을 야기하고 있다는 글의 내용으로 보아, ③ 산업화된 농업을 빠르게 확산시키고자 한다는 내용은 글의 흐름과 관계없는 문장임.

「표면상으로는 산업화된 농업은 영구적인 세계 기아 문제에 대한 매우 환영받는 해결책이 된다고 약속했다. ① 하지만 작가이자 농부인 Wendell Berry가 관찰했던 것처럼, 소위 약간의 해결책들은 새로운 문제들의 분파형태를 야기시켰다. ② 과거 수십 년 동안, 산업적 농업은 확실히 사람과 지구 건강에 영향을 미치는 많은 새로운 문제들을 만들어 왔다는 것이 점점 명백해졌다. ③ (그래서 새로운 기술에 의해 제시된 기회를 인지하고 있는 기업과 정부는 산업화된 농업의 급속한 확산을 조성했다.) ④ 예를 들어, 비료와 살충제의 사용은 암의 더 높은 발생 비율과 토양, 개울, 지하수의 오염으로 이어져 왔다. ⑤ 단일 재배 농업은 생태계의 생산성과 안전성을 약화시키면서, 생물 다양성의 손실로 이어져 왔다.」

32 ③

artfully : 교묘하게, 솜씨 있게 grain bowl : 곡물 사발 simmer : 부글부글 끓다, 서서히 끓이다 broth : 국 become obsessed with : ~에 사로잡히다, ~에 집착하게 되다 virtuously : 고결하게, 정숙하게 fortify : 강화시키다, 영양가를 높이다 square meal : 실속 있는 식사, 충실한 식사 sedentary : 앉아서 하는 enterprising : 진취적인 enterprise : 기업, 진취적 기상 wholesome : 건강에 좋은 door-to-door : 택배의 answer the call : 요구에 응하다, 부름에 응하다 the juice cleanse : 해독 주스

☞ 바쁜 현대 사회에서 다양한 종류의 건강한 배달 음식이 성행하고 있다는 내용의 글이다. 따라서 좌식 생활습관과 관련된 내용의 ③은 전체 흐름과 관계없는 문장이다.

「솜씨 있게 만들어진 곡물 그릇부터 천천히 끓여진 인기 있는 시골 국물까지, 메시지는 명확하다. 아름다움과 건강의 조합은 영양에 집착해 왔다. ① 오늘날, 고결하게 먹는 것은 단지 날씬함을 유지하기 위한 수단이 아니다. 이것은 점점 더 건강하고 바쁜 삶을 위해 신체를 강화시키는 중요한 단계이다. ② 하지만 점심이 이메일과 함께 제공되는 이러한 다중 작업의 시대에서, 모든 사람들은 너무도 종종 충실한 식사를 제외하고는 접시에 너무 많은 것을 담는다. ③ (이러한 로컬 푸드의 적절한 영양분 부족은 앉아서 하는 생활 스타일에 의해 단지 악화된다.) ④ 전국적인 요구에 응하는 것이 진취적인 젊은 요리사들과 건강한 음식을 택배의 편리함과 결합시킨 기술 선구자들에게 널리 퍼진 물결이다. ⑤ 만약 지난해가 해독 주스에 의해 지배당했다면, 올해는 디자이너의 음식 배달의 해가 될 듯하다.」

33 ②

range from ~ to : 범위가 ~에 미치다 accounting : 회계 practice : (변호사, 의사 등 전문직의) 개업(장소) mounting : 증가하는 empathetic : 공감적인

☞ The advice (그 조언)을 듣고 필자가 자신이 느낀 바를 서술을 시작하는 ②에 주어진 필자의 삼촌이 충고하는 내용이 오는 것이 글의 전체적인 흐름으로 보아 적절함.

「내 딸 중 하나가 최근에 결혼했다. 그리고 나는 그날 밤을 200명의 모든 연령대 사람들과 함께 축하하며 보냈다. ① 그들의 범위는 3살짜리 손녀들부터 2차 세계대전에 참전하여 싸웠고 50년간 성공적인 법률 회계 사무소를 운영했던 85세의 삼촌에 이르기까지 걸쳐 있었다. ② 어느 순간, 그는 내 등을 두드리며 얘기했다. "얘야, 너는 오늘 밤 여기 있는 모든 사람들과 얘기를 하도록 확실히 하고, 그들이 이 문으로 들어왔을 때 느꼈던 것 보다 나갈 때 자신에 관하여 더 좋게 느끼는지를 확인해 보아라." 그 조언은 내가 정신적으로 예리하다는 것이 무엇을 의미하는지 생각하게 만들었다. ③ 비록 배우고 기억하는 우리의 능력이 성인기를 통하여 점차적으로 쇠퇴할지라도, 중요한 정보와 경험을 이해하는 능력은 증진한다는 증거가 점차 늘어나고 있다. ④ 이것이 지혜라고 알려져 있으며, 이것은 과학자들이 막 연구하기 시작한 것이다. ⑤ 이것의 전형적인 요소들은 적절한 판단, 정신적 통찰력, 길고 다양한 인생 경험, 감정 통제, 공감 이해, 그리고 물론, 지식을 포함한다.」

34 ①

life expectancy : 기대수명 fretful : 화 잘 내는, 초조해 하는 apocalypse : 파멸, 대재난, 인류 종말의 날 provocative : 도발적인, 화나게 하는 tapestry : 태피스트리(색실로 짠 주단)

☞ 미국인들은 평균 기대 수명이 증가하고, 예전보다 더 건강한 삶을 살고 있지만, 건강에 대한 자극적인 경고로 인해, 그 어느 때 보다도 건강에 대하여 불안해하고 있다는 내용으로 보아 빈칸 (A)에는 healthier, (B)에는 anxiety가 적절함.

「평균적인 기대수명은 수십 년간 꾸준히 늘어 왔으며, 흡연과 햇빛의 노출에 의해 야기되는 암을 제외하고 암에 의한 사망률은 떨어졌거나 비교적 안정된 상태를 유지하고 있다. 하지만 연구는 사람들이 그들의 건강에 대해 지금 보다 더 초조해 했던 적이 결코 없었다는 것을 반복적으로 보여주고 있다. "사람들은 단지 그들이 향하는 곳 어디에서나 종말을 보는 것 같다."라고 Bruce Ames가 말했는데, 그는 자연 살충제가 인간이 만든 것보다 적어도 10,000배 더 흔하다고 제일 먼저 지적했던 사람들 중의 한 사람이었다. "물론 약간의 주목해야 할 위험성은 있다. 하지만 모든 사람들은 단지 약간 긴장을 풀고 즐겨야 한다." 때때로, 그렇게 행하는 것은 어려워 보인다. 너무 많은 콜레스테롤, 충분하지 않은 비타민 A, 그리고 충분하게 운동 하지 않는 사람들에게 어떤 일이 일어날 수 있는지에 대한 도발적인 경고는 미국인들의 다양한 삶의 일부분이 되었다. 어떤 사람들에게, 암은 모든 음식에 숨겨져 있는 것 같다.」

→ 비록 미국인들이 예전보다 더 건강해졌지만, 그들은 그들의 건강에 대해 높은 수준의 불안감을 경험하고 있는 것 같다.

35 ④

flit : 경쾌하게 움직이다 give over to : ~에 빠지다, 몰두하다 fabric : 직물, 구조, 조직

☞ 사람들이 여행을 할 때 여행자가 되기보다는 관광객이 되려고 한다는 것이 주어진 글의 내용이므로, 주어진 글 다음에는 이러한 관광객이 되려는 사람들의 특징을 설명하는 (C)가 오는 것이 적절하며, however가 글의 내용을 연결해주면서 진정한 여행자가 되기 위한 태도를 말해주는 (A)가 적절한 글의 내용으로 와야 하며, 마지막으로 여행자의 태도를 취했을 때 사람들이 깨닫게 되는 내용인 (B)가 마지막에 오는 것이 적절함.

「많은 사람들은 여행자가 되기를 원하지 않는다. 그들은 차라리 진실로 그들 자신의 삶을 결코 떠나지 않으면서 다른 사람의 삶의 표면 위를 날아다니는 관광객이 되고 싶어 한다. (C) 그들은 그들이 가는 곳이 어디든지 그들의 세계를 가지고 가려고 노력하거나 그들이 떠나온 세계를 다시 만들어내려고 노력한다. 그들은 그들 자신의 이해의 안전성을 위험에 처하게 하고 그들의 경험이 진실로 얼마나 작고 제한적인지를 알고 싶어 하지 않는다. (A) 하지만, 진정한 여행자가 되기 위해, 당신은 기꺼이 당신 자신을 그 순간에 맡기고 당신 세계의 중심으로부터 당신 자신을 꺼내야만 한다. 당신은 사람들의 삶과 당신 스스로를 발견하게 되는 장소를 완전히 믿어야만 한다. (B) 그들의 일상생활의 구조의 일부가 되어, 당신은 이 세상에서 삶의 가능성은 끝이 없으며, 언어와 문화의 차이 아래에서 우리들 모두는 사랑하고, 사랑받고, 슬픔보다는 더 많은 즐거움이 있는 삶을 살아간다는 같은 꿈을 공유한다는 것을 깨달을 것이다.」

36 37

grab : 먹다, 꽉 잡다 domesticated : 가축화된 carnivore : 육식동물 egalitarian : 평등주의의 pack : 무리(떼) dictatorial : 독재적인, 군림하는 subordinate : 종속적인, 하위의 growl : 으르렁 거리다 obedient : 순종적인, 복종하는 feat : 위업, 공적 baffle : 도저히 이해 할 수 없다, 완전히 당황하게 만들다 determine : 밝혀내다 ancestry : 가계, 혈통 canis familiaris : 개

「2008년부터 Zsófia Virányi와 오스트리아의 늑대 과학 센터에 있는 그녀의 동료들은 무엇이 개를 개로 만들고, 무엇이 늑대를 늑대로 만드는지를 알아내기 위해 개와 늑대를 키워 왔다. "당신은 고기 한 조각을 테이블 위에 남겨 놓고, 개 한 마리에게 '안 돼!'라고 얘기 할 수 있다. 그러면, 그 개는 먹지 않을 것이다."라고 Virányi는 말하고 있다. "하지만 늑대는 당신을 무시한다. 늑대들은 당신의 눈을 똑바로 쳐다보면서 고기를 먹을 것이다." 그리고 이 일이 일어날 때, 그녀는 어떻게 늑대가 (A)가축화된 개가 되었는지 다시 궁금해 한다. "당신은 당신과 함께 살면서 그렇게 행동하는 큰 육식동물을 기를 수는 없다."라고 그녀는 말한다. "당신은 '안 돼'를 받아들이는 개와 같은 동물을 원한다."
개가 절대적인 거절을 이해하는 것은 아마도 늑대의 무리들처럼 평등주의적이지 않고 독재적인 (B)그들의 무리 구조와 관련 있을 것이라고 센터의 연구자들이 발견했다. 늑대들은 함께 먹을 수 있다는 것에 Virányi는 주목한다. 비록 주도적인(힘이 강한) 늑대가 이빨을 번득이며 종속된(힘이 약한) 늑대에게 으르렁거릴지라도, (C)낮은 서열의 늑대는 물러나지 않는다. 하지만 똑같은 상황이 개의 무리에서는 적용되지 않는다. "종속된 개들은 주도적인 개들과 좀처럼 동시에 먹으려고 하지 않을 것이다."라고 그녀는 말하고 있다. "그들은 심지어 시도하지도 않는다." 그들의 연구는 또한, 개들은 인간과 함께 과제에 대해 협력하는 것을 기대하기 보다는 차라리 단지 해야 할 일을 듣기를 원한다는 것을 시사해 준다.
어떻게 독립적이고 평등주의적인 늑대가 (D)순종적이고 명령을 기다리는 애완동물로 바뀌었는지 와 이러한 업적을 달성함에 있어서 고대 인간이 어떤 역할을 했었는가가 Virányi는 도저히 이해할 수가 없다. 그녀 혼자만 그런 것이 아니다. 비록 연구자들이 양부터 소, 닭, 기니피그까지 거의 모든 가축화된 종들의 시간, 장소, 혈통을 성공적으로 밝혀냈음에도 불구하고, 그들은 (E)우리의 가장 친한 친구인 개에 대한 이러한 문제를 계속해서 토론하고 있다.」

36 ③

☞ (C)는 늑대 중에 낮은 서열에 속하는 '늑대', 나머지는 모두 '개'를 지칭함.

37 ③

☞ 글의 두 번째 문단에서, 늑대는 평등주의적인 속성이 있어서, 먹이를 먹을 때 강한 늑대가 으르렁거려도, 약한 늑대가 물러서지 않는다고 했으므로 ③은 글의 내용과 일치하지 않음.

38 39 장문의 이해

costly : 많은 돈(비용)이 드는 incentive : 동기, 이유 optimal : 최적의, 최상의 appliance : 가정용품 manufacturer : 업체, 제조업자 interest-rate : 이율 equate : 동일시하다, 일치하다

「왜 사람들은 모든 이용 가능한 정보를 이용하여 그들의 예상을 최고로 가능한 미래의 추측과 (일치시키려고) 노력할까? 가장 간단한 설명은 사람들이 그렇게 하지 않으면 많은 돈이 든다는 것이다. 통근하는 Joe는 가능한 한 정확하게 그가 운전해서 직장으로 가는 데 걸리는 시간을 예상하기 위한 강한 동기를 갖고 있다. 만약 그가 운전 시간을 짧게 예측한다면, 그는 자주 회사에 늦을 것이고, 해고당할 위험도 있을 것이다. 만약 그가 길게 예측한다면, 그는 평균적으로 너무 일찍 회사에 도착할 것이고 수면 혹은 여가 시간을 불필요하게 포기하게 될 것이다. 정확한 예상이 바람직하며, 그리고 사람들이 예상을 모든 이용 가능한 정보를 사용하여 최적의 예측과 일치시키려고 노력하고자 하는 동기는 강력하다.

그와 똑같은 원리는 사업에도 적용된다. 가정용품 제조업체가 이율의 변동이 가정용품 판매에 중요하다는 사실을 알고 있다고 가정해 보자. 만약 회사가 이율을 잘못 예측 한다면, 너무 많거나 너무 적은 제품을 만들 수 있기 때문에, 더 적은 이익을 올릴 것이다. 회사가 이율을 예측하는 것에 도움을 주기위하여 모든 가능한 정보를 얻고, 미래의 이율 변동에 대한 가장 최고의 가능한 추측을 하기 위해 그 정보를 이용하고자 하는 동기는 강력하다. 예상을 최적의 예측과 일치하는 것에 대한 동기는 특히 금융시장에서 강력하다. 이러한 시장에서, 미래에 대한 더 나은 예측을 하는 사람들은 부자가 된다.」

38 ②

☞ 금융시장에서 최적의 예측을 하고자 노력하는 동기는 분명하다. 돈과 관련되어 있기 때문이므로, 이 글의 제목으로는 ② '최적의 예측으로 보상을 얻어라.'가 적절함.
① 가능한 한 목표를 높게 잡아라
③ 이율을 조절함으로써 이익을 극대화시켜라
④ 사업에서의 이론과 실제사이의 차이
⑤ 통근거리는 생산성에 어떻게 영향을 주는가?

39 ①

☞ 문단의 마지막 부분에 The incentives for equating expectations with optimal forecast ~에서 equating을 대체할 수 있는 낱말은 ① match(맞추다, 일치시키다)가 빈칸에 들어가기에 적절함.

40 42

Kohler : (1887-1967) 독일의 심리학자, 게슈탈트 심리학 발전에 공헌, 통찰 학습 이론을 주창 expend : (많은 돈, 시간, 에너지를) 쏟다, 들이다 pulley : 도르래 exhaustion : 기진맥진 moderately : 적당하게 conversely : 반대로 underlie : 기저를 이루다, 기초가 되다 indispensible : 불가결의, 필수적인, ~에 절대 필요한 instrumental : 중요한 social loafing : 사회적 태만 a tug-of-war : 줄다리기 exert : (힘, 노력 등을)쓰다, 행사하다 plummet : 수직으로 떨어지다, 갑자기 내려가다 boost : ~을 끌어 올리다, 늘리다

「동기 이득은 집단 과제에서 집단 구성원들이 기울이는 노력을 증가시키는 환경을 말한다. 능력이 덜한 구성원이 더 열심히 일한다는 동기 이득은 Köhler 효과로 알려져 있다. 몇몇 연구에서 운동선수들은 탈진할 때까지 도르래에 부착된 막대를 감았다. 그들은 이것을 처음에는 개인별로 했고, 그런 다음에 2명의 그룹으로 했다. 운동선수의 짝이 적당히 서로 다른 능력을 가지고 있을 때, 동기 이득은 발생했다. (A) 반대로, 운동선수들이 동등한 혹은 매우 동등하지 않은 능력을 가지고 있을 때, 동기 이득은 나타나지 않았다. 동기 이득의 책임이 있었던 사람은 다름 아닌 그 집단에서 더 약한 구성원이었다. Köhler 효과의 기저를 이루고 있는 심리적 메커니즘은 사회적 비교(특히 누군가가 그들의 팀원이 더 유능하다고 생각할 때)와 자신의 노력이 집단에 절대 필요하다는 느낌이다. 집단 구성원들은 그들이 개인적으로 높게 평가하는 결과를 얻는데 그들의 노력이 중요하다고 예상할 때 집단 과제에서 기꺼이 노력 한다. 게다가 특히, 어떤 팀에서 가장 약한 구성원은 모든 사람들이 시기적절하게 사람들의 수행에 대해 피드백을 받았을 때 더 열심히 일할 가능성이 더 많다.

집단속에서 더 흔히 관찰되는 것은 사회적 태만이라고 또한 알려져 있는 동기 상실이다. 프랑스 농업 기술자 Max Ringelmann은 말, 소, 기계, 그리고 사람에 의해 공급된 농장 노동의 상대적 효율성에 관심을 갖고 있었다. 특히, 그는 줄다리기에서처럼 수평적으로 짐을 끄는 상대적인 능력에 대해 궁금해 했다. 그의 한 실험에서, 14명의 남자들 집단이 짐을 끌었고, 그들이 발생시킨 힘의 양이 측정되었다. 각각의 사람이 독립적으로 끌 수 있는 힘도 역시 측정되었다. 줄다리기 팀의 크기가 증가함에 따라 한 명당 평균적인 끄는 힘에는 꾸준한 감소가 있었다. 혼자서 줄을 끄는 한 사람은 평균 63킬로그램의 힘을 발휘했다. (B) 하지만, 3명의 집단에서는 한 사람당 힘은 53킬로그램으로 떨어졌고, 8명의 집단에서는 혼자 하는 사람에 의해 발휘됐던 노력의 절반보다 작은 겨우 31킬로그램으로 곤두박질쳤다. 이것은 팀워크의 근본적인 원리를 보여주었다. 즉, 집단속에 사람들은 종종 혼자일 때 그들이 일하는 것만큼 열심히 일하지 않는다.

40 ②

☞ 동기 이득과 동기 상실에 대한 글의 내용으로 이에 대한 실험의 예들을 제시해주는 글의 흐름으로 보아, ② '팀워크에서의 동기의 영향'이 글의 제목으로 가장 적절함.

41 ②

☞ 동기 이득은 두 사람이 적당히 다른 능력을 가지고 있을 때라 발생한다는 글의 내용과 ②는 일치하지 않음.
① Koher 효과는 능력이 덜한 사람이 집단속에서 더 열심히 일할 때 발생한다.
② 동기 이득은 같은 능력의 사람들이 함께 일할 때 발생할 가능성이 있다.
③ 가장 힘이 약한 구성원은 적적한 피드백이 제공될 때 더 열심히 일하는 경향이 있다.
④ Max Ringelmann은 서로 다른 집단 간의 노동의 효율성을 연구했다.
⑤ Max Ringelmann은 사람들은 집합적으로 일할 때 노력을 덜 기울인다는 것은 알아냈다.

42 ③

☞ 빈칸(A)를 중심으로 앞부분에는 동기 이득 발생 상황, 뒷부분에는 동기 이득이 발생하지 않는 상황에 대한 내용으로, 서로 반대되는 상황을 연결해주는 'Conversely(반대로)'가 적절함.
빈칸(B)를 중심으로 사람들이 혼자서 일할 때 쓰는 힘의 크기와 집단 속에서 일할 때 한 사람당 쏟아내는 힘의 크기에 대해 서술하고 있으므로, 빈칸을 중심으로 서로 상반되는 내용을 연결해 주는 'However(하지만)'가 적절함.

rhinovirus : 리노바이러스, 감기바이러스 panoply : (많은 수의 인상적인)모음, 집합 nary : ~가 아닌, 하나도 ~ 없는 sniffle : 훌쩍거림 quarantine : 격리하다 pick up : (감기에)걸리다 lest : ~하지 않도록 nasal : 코의 secretion : 분비물 mucus : 점액 antibody : 항체 numerical : 숫자의 come down with : ~(병)에 걸리다 rocky : 험난한, 고난이 많은 deficiency : 결핍 susceptibility : 민감성, 감수성 health hazard : 건강상 유해한 것 perpetual : 끊임없이 계속되는 counterintuitive : 반직관적인, 직관에 어긋나는 vibrant : 활기찬, 생기 넘치는 suppress : 억누르다 cortisol : 코티솔 (부신 피질에서 생기는 스테로이드 호르몬의 일종으로 스트레스 호르몬으로 알려져 있음) enhance : 향상시키다. ~을 높이다

「Carnegie Mellon 대학교의 심리학자 Sheldon Cohen은 의도적으로 수백 명의 사람이 감기에 걸리게 했다. 신중하게 통제된 조건하에서, 그는 자원자들을 흔한 감기를 야기하는 리노바이러스에 체계적으로 노출시켰다. 이 바이러스에 노출된 사람의 약 3분의 1 정도는 완전한 (감기)증상들을 나타났던 반면, 나머지는 훌쩍거림도 없이 걸어 나갔다.

첫날, Cohen의 실험 자원자들은 그들이 노출되기 전에 다른 곳에서 감기에 걸리지 않았다는 것을 확실히 하기 위해 24시간 동안 격리되었다. 그다음 5일 동안, 자원자들은 다른 자원자들과 함께 특별한 구성단위로 수용되었다. 그들은 누군가를 재 감염시키지 않기 위해서 최소한 서로 서로 3피트는 떨어져 있었다. 이러한 5일 동안 그들의 코 분비물은 특정한 리노바이러스의 존재뿐만 아니라 (점액의 총 무게와 같은) 감기의 전문적인(의학적인) 지표에 대하여 검사되었다. 그리고 혈액 샘플은 항체에 대하여 검사되었다.

우리는 낮은 비타민 C 수치, 흡연, 수면 부족 모두가 감염의 가능성을 증가시킨다는 것을 알고 있다. 문제는 스트레스가 많은 인간관계가 이 목록에 추가될 수 있냐는 하는 것이다. Cohen의 대답은 물론 그렇다 이다. Cohen은 누군가를 감기에 걸리게 하지만 다른 사람들은 건강함을 유지하게 하는 요인들에 정확한 수치 값을 부여했다. 순탄치 않은 인간관계를 비타민 C 결핍과 수면 부족과 똑같은 인과 관계의 범위에 놓았을 때, 현재 진행 중인 개인적 갈등이 있는 사람들은 감기에 걸릴 가능성이 다른 사람들 보다 2.5배였다. 한 달 혹은 그 이상 지속되는 갈등은 그 민감성을 증가시켰지만, 가끔씩 일어나는 논쟁은 건강상 위험을 제공하지는 않았다. 끊임없이 계속되는 논쟁이 우리의 건강에 해롭기도 하지만, 우리 스스로를 고립시키는 것은 더 나쁘다. 풍부한 사교적 관계망을 갖고 있는 사람들과 비교했을 때, 가장 적은 친밀한 관계를 갖고 있는 사람들은 감기에 걸릴 가능성이 4.2배 더 많았다.

우리가 더 사교적이면 사교적일수록, 우리는 감기에 그 만큼 덜 민감해진다. 이 생각은 우리의 직관에 어긋나는 것 같다. 우리가 더 많은 사람들과 교류할수록 우리는 감기바이러스에 노출될 가능성을 증가시키고 있는 것은 아닌가? 확실히 그렇다. 하지만 활기찬 사교 관계는 코티솔을 억제하고 스트레스를 받는 면역 기능을 향상시키면서 우리의 좋은 기분을 북돋아 주고, 우리의 부정적인 기분을 제한한다. 인간관계 그 자체가 그것들이 제기하는 바로 그 감기 바이러스에 대한 노출의 위험으로부터 우리를 보호해 주는 것 같다.

43 ④

☞ 흔한 감기에 관한 실험으로부터 사람들과의 관계도 감기에 걸릴 확률에 영향을 미친다는 글의 내용을 고려해 볼 때, 이 글의 제목으로 가장 적절한 것은 ④ '흔한 감기 실험에서 나온 흔치 않은 결과가 적절함.

① 인간신체에서의 항생물질 신진대사의 본질
② 리노바이러스 노출 : 최고로 정밀한 방법론
③ 더 많은 사교적 교류, 그 만큼 더 심한 감기
⑤ 사이버 공간에서 발견된 새로운 건강상 위험

44 ④

☞ 사람들과의 활기찬 관계가 많으면 많을수록 우리는 감기에 덜 민감해지는 것 같다는 것이 이 글의 전체적인 내용이므로, 빈칸에는 ④ '~로부터 우리를 보호하다'가 들어가야, 사람들과의 관계가 감기 바이러스 노출의 위험으로부터 우리를 보호한다는 내용으로 적절한 문맥이 됨.

45 ④

☞ 문단의 사실적 내용에 대한 문제로서, 두 번째 문단 마지막 부분에서 점액의 무게 등 코 분비물(nasal secretions)을 검사한다는 내용과 ④는 내용과 일치함.

01 ①

attorney : 변호사 categorically : 명확히, 절대적으로

☞ categorically (명백하게)의 뜻을 지닌 단어는 보기 중 ①번 unequivocally이다.

① 명백하게 ② 전형적으로 ③ 무례하게 ④ 마지못해서 ⑤ 악의를 갖고, 심술궂게

「변호사들이 우리의 제안을 <u>명백하게</u> 거절했기 때문에 새로운 행동 계획을 고안해야 할 시간이었다.」

02 ③

bout : 병치레 media tycoon : 언론계 거물 turn over a new leaf : 새 사람이 되다 denounce : 맹렬히 비난하다, 고발하다 opulent : 호화로운

☞ opulent(호화로운, 사치스러운)의 뜻을 지닌 단어는 보기 중 ③번 luxurious이다.

① 부도덕한 ② 자랑스러운 ③ 호화로운 ④ 건강하지 못한 ⑤ 무능한

「언론계 거물인 그가 암과의 긴 투병에서 승리를 거둔 후, 그의 <u>사치스러웠던</u> 삶의 방식을 비난하며 새로운 사람이 되기 위해 노력했다.」

03 ①

sanction(s) : 제재(국제법위반을 범한 국가에 대한 대응) contentious : 논쟁을 초래할

☞ contentious(논쟁을 초래할)의 뜻을 지닌 단어는 보기 중 ①번 controversial이다.

① 논쟁의 여지가 있는 ② 복잡한, 복합적인 ③ 찾기 힘든 ④ 비밀스러운 ⑤ 성과 없는

「그 나라에 대한 제재는 가장 <u>논쟁이 되는</u> 쟁점이 될 것으로 여겨진다.」

04 ①

give way to : ~에 양보하다 assumption : 추정, 상정 intellectual : 지식인

☞ its days <u>are numbered</u>의 영영사전 의미를 보면 something cannot continue much longer이므로 이는 ~이 지속되지 못함을 의미하여 보기 ①의 limited가 답이 된다.

① 제한된 ② 만연된 ③ 보존된 ④ 가속화된 ⑤ 겹쳐진

「"자본주의 시대가 <u>지나갔고</u>, 자본주의자들이 사회주의자들에게 시대를 내어 주어야한다"라는 가정은 대서양 양쪽 지식인들에게 널리 퍼져 있었다.」

05 ⑤

presumptuous : 주제넘은, 건방진

☞ presumptuous(주제넘은, 건방진)의 뜻을 지닌 단어는 ⑤의 arrogant and disrespectable이다.

① 주의를 기울이는/ 경계하는

② 정확한/ 정밀한

③ 근면 성실한/ 부지런한

④ 성취할 수 있는/ 실용적인

⑤ 거만한/ 존경할 가치가 없는

「많은 정치인들은 그 나라의 경제헤게모니가 주제넘은 것이라 여겼다.」

06 ④

apparently : 분명히, 명확히   exceed : ~을 초과하다   decomposer : 분해   accumulate : ~을 축적하다
immense : 거대한   relatively : 상당히   carbon dioxide : 이산화탄소

☞ ④번의 fossil fuels recovering from the earth에서 지구에 화석연료가 뒤덮여져 있는 수동의 의미이므로 fossil fuels (which are) recovered from the earth가 되어야 한다.

「이 땅의 식물들과 해양생물들의 성장속도가 순환을 하기 위한 분해 능력을 초과했을 때인 수백만 년 전 정상적인 에너지 흐름의 중요한 중단이 생겨났다. 에너지가 풍부한 유기체의 축적된 층들이 겹겹이 쌓인 흙의 압력을 받아 점차적으로 석탄이나 석유로 변했다. 우리가 지금은 태워버림으로써 풀어 놓을 수 있는 그 에너지가 그 분자 구조 안에 저장되어 있다. 그리고 우리의 현대 문명화는 지구에 덮여져 있는 그러한 화석 연료로부터 거대한 양의 에너지를 얻고 있다. 화석 연료를 태움으로써 우리는 대부분의 저장된 에너지를 환경에 열로 내보낸다. 우리는 또한 수백만 년 동안 천천히 제거되어 왔던 거대한 양의 이산화탄소를 상당히 짧은 시간 내에 대기 중으로 돌려보내고 있다.」

07 ④

readily : 비교적   renewable : 재생 가능한   comprise : ~으로 구성되다   properties : 특징, 성질   extract : ~을 추출하다   deplete : 고갈시키다

☞ ④번 be동사 are의 주어는 A wide variety of minerals로 이 명사구의 핵심 명사는 바로 variety로 variety는 단수 취급을 해야 하므로 are는 is가 되어야 한다.

「지구는 인간에게 매우 중요한 많은 자원들을 갖고 있다. 어떤 자원은 비교적 재생가능하고 다른 자원은 재생하기 위해 비용이 들고, 아예 재생되지 않는 자원도 있다. 지구는 다양한 광물로 구성되어 있는데, 그 광물의 특징은 광물을 구성하고 있는 구성요소 뿐만이 아니라 광물이 어떻게 형성되었는지에 관한 역사에 따라서도 달라진다. 광물의 풍부함의 영역은 거의 없음부터 무한대까지이다. 하지만 환경으로부터 그 광물을 추출해 내는 난이도는 그 광물의 풍부함만큼 중요한 사안이다. 다양한 광물은 아연, 알루미늄, 마그네슘, 구리와 같이 공업 물질에 필수가 되는 자원들이다. 좋은 자원들 중 많은 부분이 고갈되어지고 있고 이는 그러한 광물들을 얻기가 점점 더 어려워지고 비용이 많이 들게 만들고 있다.」

08 ②

utilitarian : 공리주의의 defense : 방어, 수호 liberalism : 자유주의 compatible : 양립될 수 있는 autonomy : 자율성 frontispiece : 삽화 contemporary : 동시대의, 동년배

☞ ②번의 being noted가 수동분사구문으로 사용되었는데 주어인 존 스튜어트 밀이 이하의 내용을 언급했다는 능동의 의미이기 때문에 noting이 되어야 한다.

「유럽 대륙에서 칸트는 자유주의의 공리주의 옹호를 거부했고, 대신 인간이 좋은 삶에 대한 자신만의 개념을 자유로이 선택하는 사람에게만 올 수 있는 자율성을 위한 양립 가능한 경우를 내세웠다. 존 스튜어트 밀은 다른 독일 자유주의자들에게 영감을 얻었고, 그의 저서인 자유론의 삽화에서 동년배인 훔볼트를 언급했다. 하지만 독일과 영국계 미국의 자유주의로의 집중의 시대는 금방 지나갔다. 헤겔, 마르크스 그리고 독일 지식인들은 자유주의 사회를 강조하기 위한 개인주의의 민족성의 결함을 집중적으로 밝혀냈다. 칸트에서 헤겔로 또 마르크스로의 생각의 전환은 매우 극적이어서 플라톤에서 아리스토텔레스 또 아우구스티누스에게로의 생각의 전환과 견주어 볼 만하다.」

09 ①

balk at : ~을 망설이다 far-flung : 먼 prohibitive : 비싼 affordable : (가격이)알맞은 constrain : ~하지 못하게 하다 enable : ~을 가능하게 하다 subsidy : 보조금 notoriously : 악명 높게 consolidated : 합병된, 통합된

☞ (A) low-income families can find the fees [prohibitive/affordable] 낮은 소득의 가정은 비용이 비싸다고 여기는 것이므로 prohibitive가 적절하다.

(B) [constraining/enabling] kids to learn digitally and adults to work via the cloud~ enable + 목적어 + to부정사는 "목적어로 하여금 ~을 가능하게 하다"라는 의미이다. 아이들과 성인으로 하여금 배우고 일하는 것을 가능하게 해준다는 의미이므로 enabling이 되어야 한다.

(C) [increased/ decreased] competition for a notoriously consolidated industry에서 과열된 경쟁이란 의미이므로 increased가 되어야 한다.

	(A)	(B)	(C)
①	가격이 비싼	~을 가능하게 하는	증가된
②	가격이 비싼	~을 가능하게 하는	감소된
③	가격이 비싼	~을 억제케 하는	감소된
④	가격이 적합한	~을 억제케 하는	증가된
⑤	가격이 적합한	~을 가능하게 하는	감소된

「우리 대부분은 브로드밴드 인터넷을 당연시 여기지만, 미국인 5명 중 1명은 브로드밴드 인터넷 접속이 어렵다고 미국연방 통신위원회는 말한다. 교외 지역에서는 텔레콤 회사들은 멀리 떨어진 집에 인터넷 선을 설치하는 것의 비용 때문에 망설이는 반면 소득이 낮은 가족은 설치비용이 너무 (A)비싸다고 한다. 브로드밴드의 갭을 좁히는 것은 가장 최신 드라마를 방영하는 것보다 훨씬 의미 있다. 고속 인터넷은 현대의 삶에 필수적인 도구이며, 아이들이 디지털로 배우고 어른들이 클라우드를 통해 일하는 것을 (B)가능하게 해준다. 미국연방 통신위원회는 최근 적은 브로드밴드 보조금을 승인했지만, 진짜 해결책은 악명 높은 합병 회사들 간의 (C)고조된 경쟁에 있다.」

10 ③

predisposition : 성향, 경향   in vain : 헛되이

☞ (A) [innate/ acquired] ideas and predispositions~ 인간이 세상으로 나올 때 무엇인가를 배우기 위한 타고난 아이디어와 성향들을 지니고 온다는 의미이므로 innate가 적절하다.

(B) [adopt/ ignore] almost everything and home in only what is most important and interesting. 대부분의 것들은 무시해 버리고 가장 중요한 것들만 택한다는 의미이므로 ignore가 적절하다.

(C) [discriminating/ integrating] nature of our genes에서 우리 유전자의 차별적인 본성(중요한 것에 집중하는 능력)이라는 의미이므로 discriminating이 적절하다.

	(A)	(B)	(C)
①	습득된	무시하다	통합적인
②	습득된	무시하다	차별적인
③	타고난	무시하다	차별적인
④	타고난	채택하다	통합적인
⑤	타고난	채택하다	차별적인

「진화학자인 헨리 플롯킨이 이야기하기를, 세상의 수많은 유기체의 세대를 거쳐 지식을 얻으면서, 진화는 필요의 기준에 선택적으로 연관된 지식을 보존하고, 그 집약된 지식은 종의 유전자 풀 내에서 존재한다. 그러한 집약된 지식은 개인에게 전해지고, 그 개인들은 특정한 방법으로 어떤 것들을 배우기 위해 (A)타고난 아이디어와 성향들을 가지고 세상으로 온다. 다른 말로 하자면, 당신이 사바나에서 사냥을 하거나 혹은 유튜브에서 수백만의 비디오들 중에서 고를 때에도, 당신의 뇌는 거의 대부분의 것들은 (B)무시하고 오로지 중요하고 흥미로운 것들만 고르도록 프로그램화 되어 있다. 반면에 당신은 아무 나무나 바위에 창을 찌르는 것처럼 무한히 많은 비디오 링크들 사이에서 헤매며 그 중 가치 있는 것을 찾아내기를 헛되이 희망한다. 우리 유전자들의 (C)차별화된 본성을 이해함으로, 우리는 기억 속에 남겨두고 집중할 만한 이야기의 기초를 구성하기 시작한다.」

11 ④

exert : ~을 가하다   gravitational pull : 중력   attraction : 끌어당김, 매력   counterintuitive : 직관에 반대하는

☞ 이 글에 따르면 그린란드와 남극에서 가까운 곳은 빙하가 녹을 때 오히려 해수면이 하강하고 그린란드와 남극에서 먼 곳은 해수면이 높아진다는 것을 알 수 있다. 그러므로 ④번 the places farther away from the melting ice that will see the biggest ④drop in sea level.에서 먼 곳은 해수면이 높아지는 것이므로 ④번 drop은 rise로 변경되어야 한다.

「해안가를 따라 이어지는 해수면의 상승은 지구의 커다란 두 얼음덩이인 그린란드와 남극대륙에서 그 해안이 얼마나 떨어져 있는가에 달려있다. 두 반구(그린란드와 남극대륙)에서 가장 가까운 나라들이 빙하가 녹을 때 가장 큰 수면상승이 일어날 것이라고 생각하기 쉽지만 실상은 그리 ① 간단하지 않다. 그린란드와 남극대륙의 거대한 얼음덩이들은 그 주변의 바다에 강한 중력을 ② 가하는데, 그 얼음이 녹을 때 중력(끌어당김)이 약화되면서 해수면이 낮아진다. 게다가 얼음의 무게에 대한 가중이 없어지면서 육지가 상승하여 해수면 위로 약간 ③ 올라오게 된다. 이 효과가 거리가 멀어지면 감소하는데, 빙하가 녹는 곳으로부터 멀리 떨어진 곳의 해수면이 가장 크게 ④내려가는 것을 보면 알 수 있다. 해류는 빙하가 녹은 물이 지구의 양구 주변으로 흘러가도록 돕는다. "그것은 정말로 놀랍고 다소 ⑤ 직관에 반대되는 결과이지만, 그것은 사실이다."라고 하버드 대학교의 지구물리학자인 Jerry Mitrovica씨는 말한다.」

12 ②

simultaneously : 동시다발적으로 effortlessly : 쉽게 microscopic : 미세한 algae : 조류 profusion : 풍부 graze : 풀을 뜯어먹다, 먹다 swarm : 군중 crustacean : 갑각류

☞ 아델리 펭귄이 살고 있는 곳은 남극대륙으로 얼음이 꽁꽁 언 차가운 물에서 쉽게 수영을 하며 물 안, 밖으로 자유롭게 다니고 얼음 속에 있던 조류가 크릴새우의 먹이가 되고 또 크릴새우가 펭귄의 주요 먹이가 되는 것으로 보아 얼음이 펭귄의 존재를 위태롭게(endanger) 만든다는 내용은 적절하지 못하다.

「네 개의 작은 머리들이 끝없이 얼음으로 둘러싸인 짙은 남색 바다 위를 동시다발적으로 튀어 올라온다. 그들은 물고기만큼 ① 쉽게 수영을 할 수 있기 때문에 이 물을 떠나는 것을 꺼려하고 주저한다. 그들은 아델리 펭귄이며, 얼음은 그들의 존재를 ② 위태롭게 만든다. 펭귄들은 원을 그리며 뛰어 오르고 남극 해안가를 둘러싸고 있는 이 ③ 차가운 물을 아주 쉽고 완벽하게 들어왔다 나왔다 한다. 그들의 먹이는 이 꽁꽁 언 바다에 묶여있다. 얼은 바다의 층 안으로 햇살이 그 위를 비출 때면 미세한 조류들이 풍부하게 있음이 보인다. 여름이 시작되면서 얼음이 녹으면 얼었던 조류들이 물로 빠져나와 새우모양의 갑각류인 크릴새우 떼에게 ④ 잡아먹힌다. 그러면, ⑤ 차례로 이 크릴새우는 아델리 펭귄의 주요 먹이가 된다.」

13 ④

cognition : 인지 variation : 다양성 identical twin : 일란성 쌍둥이 fraternal twin : 이란성 쌍둥이 adoptive : 입양으로 맺어진 temperament : 기질, 성질 rear 기르다, 양육하다 neuroscience : 신경과학

☞ 이 글의 요지는 인간의 주요 성격이나 특징이 유전자에 따라 정해진다는 것이다. 그래서 "기질과 성격은 생애 초기에 나타나며 평생 예측 가능하다"라는 내용이 되어야 하므로 ④번의 unpredictable이 적절하지 않다.

「인간게놈은 복잡한 유기체의 구성요인을 안내하기 위한 ① 거대한 양의 지식을 포함하고 있다. 다양한 경우에서 어떤 특정한 유전자들은 인지적 측면, 언어적 측면, 성격에 연관이 될 수 있다. 심리적인 특성이 다양할 때 그 다양함은 대부분 유전자의 ② 다름에서 온다 : 일란성 쌍둥이는 이란성 쌍둥이 보다 훨씬 유사하고 생물학적 형제, 자매가 입양된 형제, 자매보다 훨씬 유사하다, 그들이 함께 ③ 길러졌든 따로 길러졌든지 간에. 사람의 기질과 성격은 생에 초기에 나타나며 이는 평생 동안 ④ 예측가능하지 않은 상태로 남는다. 성격과 지능 둘 다 문화 내의 가정환경과는 큰 영향이 있지 않다. 같은 가족 내에서 양육된 아이들이 유사한 것은 그들의 ⑤ 공유된 유전자 때문인 것이다. 더욱이 신경 과학은 뇌의 기본 구조는 유전적인 통제 하에 발달한다는 것을 보여준다.」

14 ②

yellow fever : 황열병 commemorate : ~을 기념하다

☞ Reed씨는 버지니아 대학과 뉴욕 대학교의 벨뷰 단과대학 두 곳에서 의사 학위를 두 번 취득했다.

「의사 Walter Reed는 미국의 군의관으로 1901년에 황열병이 특정한 종의 모기에게서 전염된다는 사실을 밝혀냈다. Reed는 버지니아 주에서 태어났고 1869년 버지니아 대학에서 의학박사 학위를 취득했다. Reed는 그의 두 번째 박사학위를 1870년 뉴욕 대학교의 벨뷰 단과대학에서 취득했다. Reed는 미군에 의사로서 입대했다. 그리고 1876년 결혼을 했다. Reed 부부는 아들과 딸 각 한 명이 있었고 후에 원주 미국소녀를 입양했다. Reed는 Army Medical Museum(군 의학 박물관)에서 큐레이터로 역임했고 이 박물관은 후에 National Museum of Health and Medicine(국가 건강 의학 박물관)이 되었다. 그는 수천 명의 군인들을 죽게 만든 황열병을 공부하기 위해 쿠바로 갔다. 다른 의사들의 도움으로 Reed는 황열병이 모기에게서 전염된다는 것을 확신했다. 이 발견이 수많은 삶을 구했다. 그의 업적을 기념하기 위해서 미국의 많은 병원들이 Reed의 이름을 따서 이름을 지었다.」

15 ⑤

commission : ~을 의뢰하다   comprise : ~으로 구성되다   perilous : 위험한

☞ 루이스와 클락은 미국 원주민 소녀인 Sacajawea의 도움을 받았다.

「1803년 미국 정부는 프랑스로부터 루이지애나 땅 전체를 사들였다. 그 영역은 미시시피 강으로부터 로키산 중턱까지 뻗어있지만, 그 누구도 어디가 미시시피 강이 시작하는 곳인지, 정확히 로키산이 어디인지 확신하지 못했다. 토마스 제퍼슨 대통령은 이 지역에 탐사를 의뢰했다. 이 탐험단은 대장 메리웨더 루이스와 중위 윌리엄 클락의 통솔 하에 미군 지원자들로 구성되었다. 그들의 위험한 탐험은 1804년 5월부터 1806년 9월까지 이어졌다. 그들의 일차 목적은 새롭게 취득한 이 영토를 탐험하고 지도를 만들며 미 대륙의 서쪽 절반을 가로지르는 실용적인 길을 찾아내는 것이었다. 루이스와 클락은 43명의 군사와 떠났고 2년을 유지했다. 그들은 이름이 Sacajawea(Bird Woman이라는 의미)인 16세의 원주 미국소녀를 알게 되었다. 이 원주 소녀의 도움으로 루이스와 클락은 인디언들로부터 말을 얻었고 이 덕분에 큰 어려움 없이 인디언 영토를 지나갈 수 있었다.」

16 ⑤

migrate : 이동하다, 이주하다   depleted : 고갈된   endangered : 멸종된

☞ ⑤번의 태평양에서 멸종위기 종으로 공표된 것이 아니라 대서양(Atlantic)에서 멸종위기 종으로 공표되었다.

「Halibut은 북대서양과 북태평양의 가자미류(넙치과) 생선에 주로 붙여지는 이름이다. Halibut은 위쪽은 어두운 갈색이고 하얀색 배를 가지고 있으며 육안으로 잘 보이지 않는 비늘을 가지고 있다. Halibut은 태어날 때 머리 양쪽에 눈을 가지고 있다. 6개월이 지난 뒤 한 쪽 눈이 다른 쪽으로 이동을 한다. Halibut은 신선할 때 데쳐먹거나 튀겨먹거나 구워먹는다. Halibut은 지방 함유량이 매우 적기 때문에 연어처럼 훈제를 하는 것은 매우 어렵다. 최근에 대서양에서 어류 남획으로 인해 Halibut이 고갈되면서 멍종위기 종으로 공표되었다.」

17 ⑤

inadvertently : 우연히   deliberately : 고의적으로   deceive : ~을 속이다, 기만하다   innocuous : 무해한
invasive : 악성의   prevailing : 우세한

☞ 본문에서 the extinction phase will eventually end라는 부분에서 귀화식물들이 멸종을 초래하더라도 그 과정은 결국에는 멈추게 되어 있다고 언급되었기 때문에 ⑤번 문장은 글과 일치하지 않는다.

「생태학자들은 일반적으로 귀화식물(종)을 사람들이 우연히 혹은 고의적으로 새로운 장소에 그것을 옮겨 놓은 것이라고 정의한다. "아주 적은 분포의 귀화식물(종)도 새로운 서식지에서 문제를 일으킬 있다"라고 생태와 진화생물학 교수는 말한다. 그러나 생태학자들은 이 식물들의 외향적인 모습에 속기 쉽고 오로지 그들의 나쁜 영향이 보고되지 않았다는 이유만으로 많은 이국적인 식물들이 받아들여지기도 한다고 경고한다. 더욱이 이 외래종은 수십 년간 무해한 상태로 있다가 갑자기 악성으로 바뀐다. 그러한 불확실성 때문에 생태학자들은 강한 조취가 취해져야 한다고 주장한다. 그들의 주장은 자연 생태 시스템에서 외래적인 종들을 제거하자는 것이다. 하지만 많은 전문가들은 생태계가 더 자연적이었던 그 때로 돌아가자는 과학적 의견에 의문을 가한다. 심지어 생태계에서 이국적인 요소들을 모조리 제거해야 한다고 주장하는 생태학자들조차 그들의 목표가 실용적이지 못하다는 것을 인정한다. 아리조나주의 대학교 교수인 Rosenzweig는 악성 귀화식물들이 생태계의 다양성을 감소시킨다는 우세한 견해에 도전하고 있다. 외래종들은 환경에서 종의 숫자를 증가시킨다. 심지어 귀화식물들이 멸종을 초래한다 하더라도 그 멸종 단계는 결국 끝나게 되고, 새로운 종이 진화를 시작할 것이라고 Rosenzweig 교수는 설명한다.」

18 ④

statute : 법규 Constitution : 헌법 devise : 고안하다 refine : 개선하다 amend : 개정하다 cumbersome : 복잡한, 까다로운

☞ 헌법을 개정하는 과정은 매우 복잡하기 때문에 그것을 개정하는 것이 아니라 현대에 맞게 유동적으로 해석하는 과정이 필요하므로 빈칸에는 ④번 flexible이 와야 한다.

① 더 이상 쓸모가 없는 ② 번역된 ③ 간결한

④ 유동적인, 융통성 있는 ⑤ 비판을 잘하는

「판사들은 집단의 복지에 중요한 영향을 줄만한 행동 강령을 고안하고 수정하는데 도움이 되기 위해 법규와 헌법을 읽는다. 사회(집단)는 200여 년 전에 살았던 사람들이 썼던 헌법에 의해 그들의 행동이 통제받는 것을 늘 달가워하지는 않는다. 하지만 헌법을 개정하는 과정은 매우 복잡해서, 판사들은 원래 법규(헌법)를 유동적으로 해석해서 사용하는 과정을 거치도록 압박을 받는다.」

19 ②

☞ 필자는 좋은 것을 친구와 각각 경험하는 것보다 그 자리에서 함께 경험하는 것이 각각 경험하는 것을 합친 것 이상이라고 어필하고 있다.

① 나눠질 수 있다.

② 합계보다 더 크다.

③ 합쳐진 양과 같다.

④ 기억 속에 훨씬 오래 유지된다.

⑤ 고려하지 않는다.

「예를 들어 내가 그랜드캐니언에 가서 그 광경을 보는 것이 너무 즐거워서 내 친구에게 "네가 여기에 있었으면 정말 좋았을 텐데"라고 엽서를 쓴다고 하자. 이 친숙한 말로 내가 말하고자 하는 바가 무엇일까? 내가 친구와 함께 이 광경을 공유했다면 그랜드 캐니언을 보는 기쁨이 훨씬 더 컸을 것이라는 의미이다. 나 혼자서 그랜트캐니언에서 좋은 것보다는 친구와 함께 이 경험을 공유하는 것이 훨씬 더 좋다는 것이다. 다른 말로 하자면, 내 엽서의 의미는 그랜드캐니언을 함께 보는 기쁨의 특별한 감정을 친구와 공유하는 것이 각각 다른 날에 나와 내 친구가 각자 그랜드캐니언을 보는 기쁨을 합친 것 이상이라는 것이다.」

20 ③

sag down : 축 쳐진 furtive : 음흉한 meanest : 사소한, 작은 despise : 경멸하다 flea : 벼룩

☞ 이 글의 제시된 코요테를 서술하는 단어들을 보면 poor, out of luck, friendless이므로 이러한 이미지들은 함축하고 있는 것은 allegory of want(궁핍함, 빈곤함)이다.

① 노여움의 전형 ② 사디즘(가학증)의 비유

③ 빈곤의 풍자 ④ 효율성의 상징

⑤ 우세의 비유

「코요테는 길고 마르고 약하고 불쌍해 보이는 뼈대에 회색의 늑대 털가죽으로 덮여있고, 털이 부성한 꼬리는 늘 축 쳐져있다. 음흉하고 사악한 눈빛과 길고 날카로운 얼굴에 입술이 살짝 들려 있고 이빨이 나와 있다. 코요테는 온몸으로 슬슬 도망치는 표현을 한다. 코요테는 살아 숨 쉬는 빈곤의 풍자이다. 그는 항상 굶주려 있다. 코요테는 항상 가난하고 불운하고 친구가 없다. 아주 작은 생물체들도 코요테를 경멸하는데 심지어 벼룩도 코요테를 눈 깜짝할 사이 떠나버린다.」

21 ①

intact : 온전한, 전혀 다치지 않은

① 그들의 결과물을 선택했다.
② 특별한 종류의 호두를 재배했다.
③ 새로운 장비를 사용했다.
④ 판매용 호두를 섞었다.
⑤ 교훈을 어려운 방식으로 배웠다.

「내가 어릴 때 나는 음식 생산자들이 완전한 호두 알맹이로 병을 어떻게 채우는지 매우 놀라웠다. 그들은 알맹이를 온전하게 한 상태로 호두껍데기를 깼다. 내가 그것을 시도해 보았던(호두껍데기 깨기) 대부분 경우에 결국 호두껍데기와 알맹이가 섞이고 말았고 가까스로 온전한 알맹이를 꺼내는 것은 10번에 1번쯤 가능했다. 그러나 후에 나는 제조업자들이 나보다는 더 성공 확률이 높을 수는 있지만, 그들 역시 종종 껍데기와 알맹이가 섞인다는 것을 알게 되었다. 그러나 나는 또한 그들이 뭔가 다른 것을 한다는 것을 알았다; 그들은 <u>그들의 결과물을 선택했다</u>. 그들이 성공을 했을 때(호두 알맹이를 제대로 분리했을 때) 그들은 "Whole Walnuts(온전한 호두 알맹이)"라고 라벨을 붙인 병에 호두를 집어넣었다. 반면 호두 알맹이를 제대로 분리하지 못했을 때 그들은 호두를 껍데기에서 분리해 내어 "Walnut Pieces(호두 조각들)"이라 라벨을 붙인 병에 집어넣었다.」

22 ①

surrender : (권리 등을)포기하다, 내어주다 to the extend that : ~할 정도까지 reciprocally : 서로, 상반되게 disarming : 무장해제 animosity : 적대감 compromise : 타협 conducive : ~에 좋은
☞ 밑줄 친 부분의 앞 문장에서 reciprocally라는 단어를 사용해서 서로 쌍방이 상대와의 전쟁을 포기하는 것을 알 수 있다. 이는 ①번에 나오는 mutual disarming이라는 단어로 이어질 수 있다.
① 이 상호 무장해제는 각 개인의 이익을 위해서이다.
② 이 공유된 무관심은 사회 평화를 촉진한다.
③ 이 상호 권리 포기는 적대감을 의미한다.
④ 이 사회적 타협은 자연권을 강화하는데 좋다.
⑤ 이 전쟁 규제는 약한 무리들에게 이롭다.

「홉스의 특정 어휘인 "natural rights(자연권)"은 우리가 이미 자연 상태에서 가지고 있는 것이다: 우리의 생명보존을 위해 무언가를 할 수 있는 권리이다. 홉스는 자연권의 첫 번째 법칙을 자연 상태에서 죽음에 대한 두려움으로부터 가져 온다. 그리고 두 번째 법칙을 첫 번째 법칙에서 가져 온다: 당신이 당신의 자연권을 나와의 전쟁을 위해 포기하는 만큼 나도 기꺼이 나의 자연권을 당신과의 전쟁을 위해 포기할 것이다. <u>이 상호 무장해제는 각 개인의 이익을 위해서이다</u>. 각각의 개인은 전쟁권리를 포기하기를 동의하면서 자신에게 "좋은" 어떤 것을 구하고, 이 "좋은"것은 바로 인간의 안전보장이다.」

23 ③

indispensable : 필수적인 empower : 권한을 부여하다 autonomous : 자율적인
☞ 마지막 부분에 학습자가 다른 학습자를 통해서(through) 배운다는 것을 보아 학습자들이 직접 그 행동을 배우기보다는 그 행동이 일어나는 상황 전체를 통해 배운다는 내용이므로 빈칸에는 ③번 내용이 와야 한다.
① 그들은 다른 사람들을 이해하기 위하여 그들 자신의 통찰력에 의존한다.
② 그들은 전반적인 문화 융통성을 광범위하게 향상시킨다.
③ 다른 사람들이 그것을 바라보는 방식의 상황을 보려고 한다.
④ 그들은 다른 사람들의 숨은 의도를 예측하는 것을 배운다.
⑤ 그들은 그들 스스로 자율적 학습에 참여하도록 권한을 부여한다.

「자극 혹은 사회적 증진형태로서의 사회적 학습은 많은 사회적 종들의 인지적 발달에서처럼 인간 발달에 있어서 중요한 역할을 한다. 그러나 어떤 측면에서 인간은 다른 사람으로부터 질적으로 다른 방식으로 배운다. 사람은 가끔 소위 문화학습이라고 불리는 것에 참여한다. 문화학습에서 학습자들은 그들의 관심을 다른 개인의 활동에만 두는 것이 아니라, 그보다 <u>다른 사람들이 그것을 바라보는 방식</u>의 상황을 보려고 한다. 이는 학습자가 다른 사람으로부터 배우는 것이 아니라 다른 사람을 통해 배우는 것이다.」

24 ④

☞ (A)의 앞뒤에는 상반되는 내용(GDP가 국가 경제발달수치라는 내용과 – GDP가 오해를 불러일으킬 소지가 있다는 내용)이 나오므로 (A)에는 대조를 나타내는 접속사가 와야 하고 (B)는 앞부분(GDP가 오해를 불러일으킬 수 있다는 것의 증거)에 관한 부연 설명이므로 부연접속사가 오는 것이 적절하다.

	(A)	(B)
①	대조적으로	그러나
②	대조적으로	예를 들면
③	더욱이	그러므로
④	그러나	더욱이
⑤	그러나	대조적으로

「국가를 비교하는 기본적인 기준은 그들의 경제발달 수준이다. 경제학자들이 경제적 발달 수치를 측정하기 위하여 가장 흔하게 사용하는 도구는 바로 GDP(국내총생산)이다. GDP(국내총생산)는 한 국가의 1인당 총생산 평균의 기준점을 제공한다. <u>하지만</u>, GDP통계는 꽤 오해의 소지가 될 수 있다. 그 중 하나는 어떤 국가의 사람들이 다른 사람들보다 훨씬 돈을 많이 벌 수도 있지만 그 실제 수치가 그 국가의 생활에 필요한 상대적 비용에 고려되지 않을 수도 있다. <u>더욱이</u> 국가 통화의 환율이 오르고 내릴 때 그 국가가 훨씬 부자처럼 혹은 더 가난하게 보일 수 있다.」

25 ③

BMI : 체질량지수 aggregate : 합계, 총액

☞ 이 글의 요지는 과체중일수록 건강유지 비용뿐 아니라 의복, 생명보험 등에 드는 비용도 늘어난다는 내용이므로 제목은 The Price You Pay for Extra Pounds이다.

① 건강관리의 늘어나는 비용
② 살을 빼라, 그러면 병의 위험도 낮아진다.
③ 몸무게 증가에 지불하는 비용
④ 비만인 사람들이 옷을 사는데 더 많은 돈을 지불하는가?
⑤ BMI(체질량지수) : 몸무게의 정확한 지표는 아니다.

「당신이 좀 뚱뚱하다면 건강관리부터 시작해서 추가로 비용이 가해진다. 2013년 Duke 연구에 따르면, 연구자들은 BMI(체질량지수)에 따라 건강관리에 드는 비용을 조사해 보았다. BMI(체질량지수)가 19인 사람의 평균 연간 건강관리 비용은 약 $2,541이다. 과체중이라 여겨지는 BMI(체질량지수)가 25인 사람들의 평균 연간 건강관리 비용은 약 $2,8930이다. 비만이라 여겨지는 BMI(체질량지수)가 33인 사람들의 평균 연간 건강관리 비용이 $3,439에 달한다. "정상 체중을 벗어나는 시점으로부터 병의 위험도는 증가하기 시작한다."라고 대표 연구가인 Truls Ostbye는 말한다. 체중 증가는 단순히 병원비용 증가에서만 끝나지 않는다. 2010 Mckinsey 연구는 비만인 미국인들이 옷을 사는데 추가로 들이는 비용의 총계가 300억 원에 달한다고 한다. 또한 비만인 40세 남성이 생명 보험에 들이는 비용은 두 배가 넘는 것으로 추정된다.」

26 ③

employ : 기술, 방법을 쓰다 obsolescence : 노후화 provoke : 유발하다, 도발하다 out of nowhere : 아무도 모르게 unadorned : 아무런 장식이 없는 piece of junk : 고물덩어리 hilarious : 우스꽝스러운

☞ 이 글의 요지는 새로운 광고와 새로운 마케팅 전략을 소개하고 있다. 예전에는 경쟁시장의 사다리의 꼭대기에 오르는 것이 목표였다면 이제는 그러한 경쟁을 벗어나는 새로운 기법이 등장하는 것이므로 제목은 New Ad : Step Down From Your Ladder가 정답이다.

① 경제적 어려운 시기 : 작게 생각하라
② 자동차 경쟁 사다리의 꼭대기
③ 새로운 광고 : 사다리의 꼭대기에서 내려오기
④ 자동차가 당신의 사회적 지위를 나타내는가?
⑤ 국제적 자동차 경쟁 : 크기의 중요성

「자동차 경쟁시장의 사다리에 오르는 것은 어려운 일이며, 그 꼭대기 위치를 유지하는 것은 더 어려운 일이다. 쉐보레(자동차회사)는 매년 노후화된 관행을 이용하여 완전히 새롭게 디자인되고 일반적으로 더 큰 자동차 모델을 내놓는다. 어제의 탑모델이었던 자동차는 내일이면 작고, 우스꽝스럽고 시대에 뒤처져 보인다. 당신이 상상할 수 있듯이, 이러한 모든 것들이 미국사회 전반에 불안을 야기한다. 그러던 중 1959년, 아무도 모르게 신문 광고의 한 페이지가 "작게 생각하라"라는 헤드라인과 함께 아무 장식이 없는 폭스바겐 비틀 자동차 이미지가 실렸다. 그 광고는 비틀 자동차가 현대적이고 효율적인 것 외에는 다른 어떤 것도 이야기 하지 않았고 광고는 심지어 그 자동차를 현대의 고물덩어리에 해당하는 슬랭인 "fivver(싸구려 소형차)"라 불렀다. 사람들은 그 광고가 놀라우리만큼 솔직하고 우스꽝스러우며, 마케팅 담당자들이 수년간 마음에 품고 있던 불안을 공식적으로 표출하도록 해 주었다고 했다. 내가 꼭 사다리의 꼭대기에 올라가야만 하는가? 무슨 상관인가?」

27 ①

obdurate : 고집 센 refusal : 거부 absurd : 우스꽝스러운 hygienic : 위생적인 contend : ~를 설득하다/deter : ~을 막다 ingestion : 섭취 dissuade : 설득하다 contagious : 전염되는 railcar : 철도차 lice 이 wasp : 말벌

☞ 역겨움이 우리 몸을 지키는 중요한 역할을 하고 있는 것에 관한 내용이므로 주제는 ① the role of disgust in keeping people safe가 된다.

① 사람들을 안전히 지키는 역겨움의 역할
② 적절한 영양을 얻는 것의 이득
③ 위험함과 전염 사이의 차이점
④ 해로운 물질을 피하는 것의 중요성
⑤ 좋은 위생 행동을 연습하는 것의 필요성

「역겨움에 대한 감정적인 반응은 종종 어린 아이들이 특정 야채를 먹을 때 끈질기게 거부하는 것으로 연관된다. 아이들이 역겨워하는 것이 영양이 있는 음식을 아이들에게 먹이려고 하는 부모들에겐 우스운 행동처럼 보일 수 있지만, 과학자들은 역겨워하는 그 행동을 이성적으로 설명할 수 있다고 한다. 이 이론은 사람들이 역겨워하는 그 행동을 낯설거나 해로운 물체에 대한 보호행동으로 간주한다. 최근의 연구는 역겨움이 위험한 물질의 섭취를 막을 뿐만 아니라 사람들로 하여금 잠재적으로 전염성 있는 상황에 들어가는 것을 막게 해준다고 말한다. 예를 들면, 연구는 붐비는 철도차가 텅 빈 철도차보다 더 역겨움이 나고 이가 말벌보다 더 역겨움이 난다고 단언한다.」

28 ②

perish : 소멸되다

☞ 과학자로서 논문을 쓰거나 글을 쓸 때 중요한 것은 그것이 다른 사람들에게 얼마나 영향을 주고 받아들여 지는지에 관한 내용이므로 주제는 ② the importance of influencing others in scientific writing이다.

① '더 많이 글을 쓸수록, 더 좋다'라는 오래된 신념

② 과학적 쓰기에 있어서 다른 사람들에게 영향을 주는 중요성

③ 탐구되지 않은 분야에서 조사를 해야 하는 필요성

④ 저널 수용에 필요한 우호적인 동료들의 견해

⑤ 출판에 있어서 직업 윤리 의식과 엄격한 자질 통제

「과학자로서의 성공은 단지 우리가 머릿속에 가지고 있는 아이디어의 기능과 우리가 손에 쥐고 있는 정보의 기능 뿐 만이 아니라 우리가 그 아이디어나 정보를 기술하는 언어의 기능에도 관련돼 있다. 우리는 "논문을 출판하는 것 혹은 도태되는 것"이 우리의 전문가적 삶을 지배한다는 것을 알고 있다. 그러나 "논문을 출판하는 것 혹은 도태되는 것"은 생존에 관련된 것이지 성공에 관련된 것은 아니다. 과학자로서 논문을 출판했다고 해서 성공하는 것은 아니다. 과학자로서 그 논문이 인용되는 것이 성공하는 것이다. 당신의 작업을 중요하게 만드는 것이 중요하다. 성공은 당신이 출판해 낸 페이지 수에 의해 정의되는 것이 아니라 그 논문의 영향력에 있는 것이다. 당신의 동료들이 당신의 작품을 이해하고 그들 자신의 것으로 하기 위한 동기를 받기 위해 사용한다면 당신은 성공한 것이다.」

29 ⑤

vegan : 엄격한 채식주의   pledge : 맹세, 약속   allegiance : 충성   cult : 추종   attainable : 이룰 수 있는 counteract : 대응하다   fidgeting : 꼼지락 거리기   excruciating : 괴로운

☞ 장수를 하기 위해서 우리가 생각하는 만큼 철저한 식단관리나 운동, 명상 등을 하지 않고 작은 변화만으로도 가능하다는 내용이기 때문에 요지는 ⑤ Achieving longevity is not as difficult as one might imagine이 된다.

① 건강한 삶의 방식으로 사는 것은 행하는 것보다 말이 쉽다.

② 식단의 변화는 당신을 더 오래 살게 해준다.

③ 주로 앉아서 지내는 사람들에게 운동을 하는 것은 중요하다.

④ 신체적 건강과 정신적 건강은 열심히 일함으로 성취된다.

⑤ 장수를 하는 것은 우리가 상상하는 것만큼 어려운 것은 아니다.

「건강한 생활 습관의 지속되는 효과를 얻기 위해서 반드시 채식주의자가 되거나 운동을 하겠다고 굳게 맹세를 하거나 하루 종일 명상할 필요는 없다. 사실상, 최근의 연구(과학)에서는 정 반대의 결과를 보여주었다. 건강한 삶을 유지하는 것은 아주 작은 변화만으로 이룰 수 있고 이 변화는 전혀 어려운 것이 아니고 이것이 당신을 우울하게 만드는 것도 아니다. 연구가들은 예를 들면 몇 시간씩 헬스장에 가 있는 것이 오랜 시간 앉아 있는 것의 부정적인 효과를 대응할 수 없다는 것을 알아냈다. 그러나 그것은 조금씩 움직이는 단순한 것만으로도 가능하다. 그들은 또한 당신이 먹는 것을 줄이는 것을 고통스러울 정도로 할 필요가 없다는 것과 그것이 당신이 장수할 수 있는 가능성을 높여줄 수 있다는 것을 밝혀냈다.」

30 ②

nausea : 구역질

☞ David가 힘들었던 직장을 그만두고 새로운 시작을 향해 첫 발을 내딛는 것이므로 David의 심경은 ② relieved and hopeful이 된다.

① 슬프고 불안해하는

② 안심되고 희망적인

③ 지루하고 무관심한

④ 긴장되고 혼란스러운

⑤ 텅 비고 포기한

「엘리베이터가 내려가기 시작했을 때 David의 얼굴에는 미소가 퍼졌다. 어지러움과 구역질이 사라졌다. 가슴을 짓누르던 압박감도 사라졌다. 그가 드디어 해냈다. 그는 직장을 그만두고 악몽 같은 시간들에 작별을 고했다. 그는 그 우울한 아침을 떠나기 위해 묘책을 발견했다. 그는 이제 텅 빈 엘리베이터에 서서 빨간색 디지털 숫자가 점점 내려갈 때 마다 웃음을 띠었다. 엘리베이터가 중간층을 지나갈 때 살짝 흔들렸다. 엘리베이터가 멈추고 David는 엘리베이터에서 내려서 에스컬레이터로 갈아탔다. 누군가가 "David 어디 가는 거야?"라고 묻자 David는 마치 모든 것이 감시를 당하는 것처럼 그냥 웃으며 손짓만을 했다. 그는 밖으로 나왔고 축축하고 음울해 보였던 공기가 이제는 새로운 시작의 약속을 보여주는 것 같았다.」

31 ⑤

notably : 현저히 far-fetched : 설득력 없는 passage : 구절 starchy : 녹말이 많은 undeniable : 부인할 수 없는

☞ 이 글의 요지는 파스타의 기원이 중국이라는 것이 오해에서 나온 잘못된 내용이라는 것이므로 ⑤번 문장은 전체 흐름과 관계없다.

「파스타의 인종적 뿌리는 오랜 시간 동안 논란이 되어왔다. ① 많은 이론들은 꽤 받아들여졌고 또 어떤 이론들은 아예 설득력이 없다. ② 13세기 탐험가인 마르코 폴로의 글에 기반을 둔 현존하는 신화는 파스타가 중국에서 이탈리아로 왔다는 내용으로 Polo's Travels란 책의 유명한 구절을 잘못 해석한 것에서 기인했다. ③ 그 책에서 폴로는 파스타처럼 생긴 어떤 것이 열리는 나무를 언급했다. ④ 그것은 야자나무로 파스타와 닮은 녹말이 많은 음식을 생산하는데 그것이 파스타는 아니다. ⑤ 아시아가 원산지인 이 나무는 파스타가 중국에서 기원되었다는 부인할 수 없는 증거를 제공했다.」

32 ④

communal : 공동의 deterrent : 제지하는 것

☞ 이 글은 '비서구 문화에서 법, 관습, 종교적 믿음의 차이가 서양과는 다르다'는 요지를 가지고 작은 마을에서 "도둑"의 개념을 예를 들어 설명하고 있다. ④번은 이 요지를 벗어나는 내용이며 또한 ③번과 ⑤번 문장이 작은 마을에서의 "도둑"의 개념을 이어 설명하고 있으므로 ④번 문장이 어울리지 않는다.

「정의의 개념에 있어서 또 다른 점은 법이 무엇인지에 대한 사회의 다양한 의견이다. 서양에서는 "법"을 "관습"과는 매우 다르게 여긴다. 또한 "죄"(종교적 법칙을 어기는)와 "범죄"(정부의 법을 어기는) 사이에도 큰 차이가 있다. ① 그러나 많은 비서구 문화에서는 관습, 법, 종교적 믿음 사이에 큰 차이가 없다. 다른 문화에서는 관습, 법, 종교적 믿음이 서로 다르지만 서구에서와는 차이를 보인다. ② 이러한 이유들 때문에 한 국가에서 범죄로 여겨질 수 있는 행동이 다른 국가에서는 받아들여질 수도 있다. ③ 예를 들어, 세계의 대부분에서 도둑을 범죄자로 보지만, 공동생활을 하고 물건을 공유하는 작은 마을에서는 도둑이라는 단어의 의미가 거의 없다. ④ 작은 마을에서는 모든 사람들이 재판관이 될 수 있다. 그러한 사회에서는 사람들의 행동을 사회적으로 허가하지 않는 것은 강력한 처벌의 역할을 하면서 또 범죄를 제지하는 역할도 한다. ⑤ 묻지 않고 어떤 물건을 가지고 간 사람은 그저 예의바르지 못한 사람으로 받아들여진다.」

33 ④

speculate 추측하다

☞ ③번 문장에 카멜레온이 주변의 환경에 따라 색깔을 변화하는 내용이 나오고 ④번 문장에 also라는 단어를 사용하며 사람 또한 카멜레온처럼 주변 사람들과 어울리기 위해 행동을 조절한다는 내용이 나오므로 주어진 문장은 ④번에 들어가야 한다.

「당신이 다른 사람과 상호작용을 할 때 당신은 어떤 면에서든 그들을 모방하고 있다는 사실을 발견하게 될 것이다. ① 예를 들어 당신은 무의식적으로 친구의 말 패턴이나 억양을 따라하게 된다. ② 사회 심리학자들은 이러한 종류의 모방을 카멜레온 효과라고 명명한다. ③ 카멜레온은 주변 환경과 섞이기 위해 자신들의 색깔을 자동으로 변화시킨다. ④ (사람은 또한 자동으로 그들의 행동을 주변의 다른 사람들과 어울리기 위해 조절한다.) 이러한 형태의 모방은 "사회적 유대감"으로 추측되어진다. ⑤ 동일한 행동을 취함으로서, 사람들은 그들 자신의 주변에 있는 다른 사람들과 더 유사하게 만든다.」

34 ③

☞ 이 글의 요지는 유명한 브랜드(나이키와 3M)를 사용할 때 수행능력이 높아진다는 내용이므로 (A) enhanced, (B) popular를 유추할 수 있다.

	(A)	(B)
①	향상되었다	포괄적인
②	향상되었다	육상의
③	향상되었다	저명한
④	감소되었다	유명한
⑤	감소되었다	평범한

「특정 상표의 생산품이 특별히 효과적일 것이라는 생각은 일종의 플라시보 효과를 가질 것이라고 조사자들이 발견했다. 일련의 연구에서 참가자들은 골프실력과 수학실력을 실험하기 위해 거의 똑같은 도구를 받았다. 유일한 차이점은, 절반의 퍼터는 나이키 라벨이 붙어있었고, 시험을 보는 사람들에게 주어진 귀마개의 절반은 3M에서 만든 것이라고 이야기해 주었다. 나이키 퍼터를 사용하고 있다고 생각했던 사람들은 실제로 공을 넣기 위해 평균적으로 더 적은 퍼팅을 했고, 수학 시험을 보는 동안 3M 귀마개를 착용하고 있다고 생각한 참여자들이 더 많은 정답을 했다. 처음에 아주 낮은 자신감을 보였던 사람들도 약간의 업그레이드를 통해 자신감을 얻는 것으로 밝혀졌다.」

참여자들이 더 (B) 유명한 상표를 사용하고 있다고 믿었을 때 평균적으로 시험에서 참여자들의 수행능력은 (A) 향상되었다고 연구는 밝혔다.

35 ⑤

taste bud : 미뢰(맛봉오리)   amniotic fluid : 양수   shudder : 몸서리치다

☞ 먼저 주어진 글의 different taste preferences(다양한 입맛)는 [C]에서 spicy food(매운 음식)의 예로 이어진다. [C]의 말미의 early in life(생애초기)는 [B]의 amniotic fluid(양수)나 in utero(자궁 내)로 이어진다. [B]의 말미의 taste buds(미뢰)는 [A]에서 구체적으로 설명되고 있으므로 글의 순서는 [C]-[B]-[A]이다.

「당신이 가족들과 친구들과 함께 식사를 할 때 당신은 사람들이 매우 다른 입맛을 가지고 있다는 것을 알게 될 것이다. [C] 예를 들어 어떤 사람들은 매운 음식을 좋아하지만 반면 다른 사람들은 고춧가루를 떠올리기만 해도 몸서리친다. 음식에 대한 선호는 생애초기 사람들이 경험한 맛의 차이에 의해 설명되어진다. [B] 사실상, 엄마가 먹는 음식은 양수의 맛을 변화시켜서 몇몇 음식에 대한 선호도는 자궁 내에서 이미 만들어진다. 그러나 사람들은 또한 그들이 가지고 있는 미뢰의 개수에서 상당한 차이점을 보인다. [A] 평균적인 미뢰의 수보다 훨씬 더 많은 미뢰를 가지고 있는 사람들의 그룹을 미각이 뛰어난 사람이라고 부른다. 다른 사람들의 혀에 있는 미뢰의 밀도에 있어서의 다양성은 유전적으로 나타난다. 여자들은 남자들보다 훨씬 미각이 뛰어난 사람들일 가능성이 있다.」

36 37

conversion 전환/ defend 방어하다/ vent 감정, 분통을 터뜨리다/ undermine 약화시키다/ thwart 좌절시키다/ lofty 고귀한/ contend 주장하다/ entrust 맡기다/ pecuniary 금전의/ parochial 지역의/ bickering 논쟁/ faction 파벌/ fanatical 광적인/ obsession 집착/ setback 차질

「1929년 대공황이 닥쳤을 때조차도 새로운 공학기술로의 대전환의 가치가 매우 효과적이어서 미국인들은 계속해서 기술적 전망을 옹호했다. ① 그들은 대신 국가의 새로운 영웅들—엔지니어들—의 고귀한 목표를 무너뜨리고 좌절시키는 탐욕스러운 사업가들에 대한 두려움과 분노의 분통을 터뜨렸다. ② 몇몇 미국인들은 경제학자이자 사회학자인 소스타인 베블런의 초기 비판에 동의했다. 그는 1921년 오로지 국가의 경제를 전문적인 엔지니어들(엔지니어들의 고귀한 기준은 금전적이고 지역적인 염려 우위에 있었다)에게 맡김으로서 경제가 살아나고 국가는 새로운 가능성이 열릴 것이라고 주장했다. ③ 그 지도자들 사이의 내부적 논쟁은 분열과 파벌로 이어졌다. ④ 그때 또 히틀러가 일약 떠오르게 되고 제3제국의 기술적 효율성에 맹신적으로 집착하는 것이 사상가들로 하여금 미국 내에서 기술적 독재에 대한 기술전문가들(테크노크래트)의 요구를 재고하도록 했다. ⑤ 세상을 기술적으로 보는 견해는 1945년 미국이 일본 도시들에 원자 폭탄을 투하하면서 더 차질을 빚게 되었다. 전 세계는 갑자기 기술-유토피아적 견해의 어두운 측면을 보게 된 것이다. 전쟁 이후 세대는 현대 기술의 놀라운 힘이 미래를 창출해 낼 뿐 아니라 파괴할 수도 있음을 늘 염두에 두고 살게 되는 첫 세대가 되었다.」

36 ③

☞ ③번 앞부분의 내용은 미국에서 기술의 진보가 경제를 살리고 새로운 세상을 열 것이라는 내용이지만 ③번 문장 이후 지도자들의 분열이 생기는 것이 보아 주어진 내용—테크노크라시 시대는 짧았다는 내용이 ③번에 들어가야 한다.

* 테크노크라시는 과학 기술 분야 전문가들이 많은 권력을 행사하는 정치 및 사회체제

37 ①

☞ 윗글의 주제는 마지막 문장에도 나와 있듯이 기술이 미래를 창출하는 밝은 면도 있지만 미국이 일본에 원자 폭탄을 투하하는 것 같은 어두운 면, 즉 기술 발달의 양면성을 설명하고 있으므로 주제는 ①번이 되어야 한다.

① 테크노크라시의 전망과 몰락
② 민주주의와 기술의 달콤함
③ 기술 중심으로 세상을 보는 견해의 피할 수 없는 도래
④ 더 나은 사회를 위한 기술 중심 사상의 공격적인 접근
⑤ 테크노크라시의 장점과 단점의 불균형

38   39

aggression : 공격, 침략   aggressor : 공격자   alleviate : 완화하다   retribution : 응징   retaliation : 보복
engender : ~을 낳다 feud : 불화 liability : 책임감, 부채 inflict : ~을 가하다 bilateral : 쌍방의 kinship : 친족
deterrent : 제지 savagery : 야만성

「국가나 조직화된 단체가 공격을 받은 피해자나 그들의 가족으로부터 가해자를 잡고 벌하는 책임을 인수하기도 전에, 복수관행의 문제
를 완화시키는 관습은 진화했다. 이 중 하나가 응징의 원칙인데, 즉 눈에는 눈과 같은 잘못한 것에 대한 정확한 보복이다. 잔인하다기
보다는, 그 단어의 현대적 함축이며, 이 응징은 불화를 야기하는 과잉행동을 줄인다. 또 다른 (A) 원칙은 보상금인데 가해자에게 책임
을 부여하며, 희생자나 희생자 가족이 부상에 대한 보상으로 돈을 받는 것을 권고 받는 것이다. 돈이나 물건을 주는 것은 폭력 행위보
다는 사회에 훨씬 덜 대가가 따르고, 폭력행위로 되갚는 것은 단지 한 사람이 다른 사람에게 부를 주는 것 보다 사회적 손실을 가하고
또 다른 폭력을 나을 것이다. 다른 (B) 관습은 쌍방 친족관계이다. 아이슬란드인들은 아빠와 엄마 둘 다를 통해 친족을 맺는다. (보통
많은 사회는 오로지 아빠를 통해서만 또는 오로지 엄마를 통해서만 친족을 맺는다.) 이는 가족을 강화시킴으로써 공격을 제지함으로
복수에 대한 신뢰성을 높일 뿐만이 아니라 논쟁자가 논쟁의 양 쪽 측면의 모두와 친족이 될 수 있다. 일리아드에서는 동정과 감정이입
이 복수의 야만성을 제한할 것이라고 언급했다.」

38   ④

☞ (A)와 (B)의 공통으로 들어갈 단어는 복수나 응징에 대한 정도가 점점 약화(온화해짐)되고 있다는 의미이
   므로 moderating이 알맞다.
① 수정하는
② 처벌하는
③ 모순되는
④ 중도의, 온건한
⑤ 매혹적인

39   ②

① 국가가 가해자를 처벌할 책임을 맡기도 전에 복수관행 문제를 완화시키는 관습이 진화했다.
② 눈에는 눈 원칙은 피해자의 과잉대응 가능성을 줄였다.
③ 피해자에 대한 물질적 보상은 가해자에게 부여된다.
④ 가족을 강화시킴으로써 공격을 제지한다고 언급하고 있다.
⑤ 마지막 문장을 보아 일치하지 않는다.

eloquent : 설득력 있는 swerve : 방향을 바꾸다

[A] 미국의 많은 주들은 개인이 오토바이를 탈 때 헬멧을 써야한다는 법을 가지고 있다. 이러한 법들은 종종 그 법의 유일한 목적이 오토바이를 타는 사람들이 부상당하는 것을 보호하기 위한 것이라는 이유로 도전받는다.

[B] 대학에 다닐 때 나는 헬멧 쓰기를 거부하며 오토바이를 타는 친구가 있었다. 그는 다른 친구들에게 종종 조롱을 당했는데, 이는 그가 다음과 같은 다소 설득력 있게 방어를 하는 그의 어리석음 때문이었다. "보라고, 나는 부르주아적 삶이 아주 싫증이 났어. 나는 모험을 하기 위해 나왔다고. 그것이 바로 내가 오토바이를 타는 이유야. 나는 위험해지는 것을 원해. 스릴은 위험한 것이야. 그리고 내가 더 위험할수록 스릴은 더 커지는 법이야.

[C] 이 에피소드로부터 헬멧을 쓰지 않은 오토바이 운전자는 결국 다른 행동에도 연관이 있을 것으로 보인다. 대중이 걱정하는 것은 오토바이 운전자에게 무슨 일이 일어나는가가 아니다. 대중은 그 무모한 행동을 하는 사람으로부터 생기는 일의 대가를 걱정하는 것이다. 모든 사람의 삶의 방식이 그가 공공 자원에 부여하는 세금이나 부담의 관점에서 똑같지 않다. 내 무모한 친구는 공공에게 그를 그냥 내버려 둘 뿐 아니라 그의 선택을 지지하라고 요구하는 이기주의자의 극적인 예로 보인다.

[D] 헬멧 없이 오토바이를 타겠다는 내 친구의 결정은 오로지 그 자신에게만 영향을 줄까? 길에서 돌맹이나 다른 물체가 갑자기 튀어 올라 그가 다른 곳으로 방향을 바꿀 수도 있다. 이는 그 자신에게 상처만 입히는 것이 아니라, 헬멧을 썼더라면 피할 수 있었던 두뇌 외상이 생길 수도 있다. 내 친구는 혼자 남겨질리 없고 앰뷸란스 운전자에게 이송되어 의사와 응급의료진의 손을 거치게 된다. 귀중한 시간과 돈이 그의 스릴을 찾는 행위에 들어가게 된다. 의료진들은 내 친구의 쪼개진 두개골에서 뇌 조직을 되돌려 놓기 위해 바쁘기 때문에 다른 환자를 볼 수 없게 된다. 병원 공간과 자원은 모두 세금으로 운영되고, 응급의료진이나 의료보험과 자동차 보험 모두 우리 모두에게 주어진다.

40 ②

[B]에서 필자의 친구의 구체적인 이야기(헬멧을 쓰지 않고 오토바이를 타는 이유-스릴을 위한)가 나오고 [D]에서 이 친구가 사고를 당할 경우의 이야기가 나온다. 사고를 당할 경우 본인이 다치는 것뿐만이 아니라 다른 시간과 비용이 들고 있음을 설명한다. [C]에서는 이 에피소드에서 얻을 수 있는 결론을 도출하고 있으므로 글의 순서는 [B]-[D]-[C]이다.

41 ④

① 헬멧을 쓰지 않는 오토바이 운전자의 마음
② 사고 없는 사회를 위한 팁
③ 위험 감수를 하는 사람들과 그렇지 않은 사람들의 생활방식
④ 다른 사람들의 희생을 요구하는 개인의 자유
⑤ 교통법칙 위반자들의 논란 많은 규제

42 ②

(b)를 제외한 he는 필자의 친구를 지칭하고 있지만 (b)는 앞에 나오는 everyone을 받고 있다.

43   45

serendipitous : 우연히 발견하는   ubiquitous : 아주 흔한

나는 항상 마술에 흥미가 있었다. 내가 10살이 되었을 때 나는 손수건을 사라지게 할 수 있었고, 카드의 순서를 바꾸지 않고 완전하게 섞을 수 있었다. 10대 초반 런던에 있는 잘 알려진 마술 협회에 들어갔다. 20대 초반이 될 때 까지 미국의 일류 쇼에서 공연을 하기 위해 여러 번 초청받았다.

이 매혹적인 속임수와 착각의 세계에 대한 나의 열정은 우연한 기회에 시작되었다. 내가 8살이었을 때 체스의 역사에 대한 학교 프로젝트를 완성해야 했다. 성실한 학생이었기 때문에 나는 그 주제에 관한 책을 찾기 위해 동네 도서관을 방문하기로 결정했다. 나는 도서관의 선반을 잘못 찾았고 마술에 관한 몇몇 책을 우연히 보게 되었다. 나는 호기심이 생겼고 마술사들이 불가능한 것을 이루는 것의 비밀들에 관한 모든 것을 읽기 시작했다. 만약 내가 올바른 선반을 찾아서 체스에 관한 책을 읽었더라면 어떤 일이 일어났을지 모르겠다.

많은 사람들은 어떻게 계획하지 않았던 우연이 종종 직업 선택에 있어서 중요한 변화를 낳는지에 대해 보고해 왔다. 우리들은 중요한 계획되지 않았던 사건들이 직업에서 어떻게 영향을 주는지, 그리고 수많은 사소한 계획되지 않았던 사건들이 최소한 어떻게 작은 영향을 주는지에 관해 이야기할 수 있다. 영향력 있는 계획되지 않은 사건들은 사실 특별한 것들이 아니다(흔히 일어난다). 그것들은 사실 매일 매일 일어나는 것이다. 세렌디피티(우연히 일어나는 것)는 사실 우연히 발견되는 것이 아니라, 아주 흔한 일이다.

조셉 퓰리처를 예로 들어보자. 그는 헝가리에서 태어났다. 어릴 때 퓰리처는 좋지 않은 건강과 나쁜 시력으로 고생을 했다. 그가 17살이 되었을 때 그는 더 나은 삶을 위해 미국으로 갔다. 그러나 그는 거기서 직업을 찾지 못했다. 퓰리처는 동내 도서관에서 체스를 두며 많은 시간을 보냈다. 그러던 중 그는 우연히 지역 신문사의 편집장을 만나게 되었다. 이 기대되지 않았던 만남이 퓰리처가 주니어 기자로 직업을 얻게 만들었다. 그는 신문사 일에서 꽤 성공적이었고 편집자가 돼 결국 잘 알려진 신문사 두 개를 직접 소유하게 되었다.

43   ②

① 성실함은 항상 결실을 맺는다.
② 기회들이 모여서 진짜 기회가 된다.
③ 조셉 퓰리처 : 알려지지 않은 일화
④ 명성과 직업 선택
⑤ 오래 기억되는 마법의 순간

44   ③

이 글의 요지는 우리의 인생에 영향을 주는 우연한 사건들은 특별히 일어나는 것이 아니라 우리의 삶속에서 흔히 일어난다는 내용이므로 ③ are not uncommon이 답이 된다.
① 미리 만들어진 것이다.
② 환영되지 못한다.
③ 흔한 일이다.
④ 미래를 예측할 수 있다.
⑤ 영향력을 잃을 수 있다.

45   ④

퓰리처는 도서관에서 체스를 두고 있었지만 체스 기사가 된 것은 아니다.

01 ②

deceive : 속이다   vanguard : 선두, 선봉   revolution : 혁명
① 혼란, 소동   ② 맨 앞, 선두   ③ 보호   ④ 반대   ⑤ 준비
「그 운동에 참여한 학생들은 속아서 그들이 혁명의 <u>선두</u>에 있다고 생각했다.」

02 ①

collude : 공모하다   conclude : 결론 내리다. 판단 내리다.   manufacturer : 제조업자   minor : 미성년자
① 협력하다   ② 제안하다   ③ ~인 척하다   ④ 의도하다   ⑤ 개입하다.
「정부는 그 제조업자들이 미성년자들에게 그들의 제품을 파는 데 <u>공모했다</u>고 결론 내렸다.」

03 ④

penchant for : ~에 대한 애호   demise : 몰락, 종말, 죽음   fortune : 재산
① 강박   ② 적성   ③ 비난   ④ 의향, 성향   ⑤ 낭비
「삶에서 더 좋은 것들에 대한 그의 <u>애호</u>는 그의 가족 재산의 몰락으로 이끌었다.」

04 ①

sternest : 가장 엄격한, 가혹한   cabin : 오두막(n), 가두다(v)   at most : 기껏해야   Anglo-American : 영국계 미국인
① 한정하다   ② 꾸짖다   ③ 소개하다   ④ 보호하다   ⑤ 예를 들다.
「롤즈에게 가장 가혹한 비판가들은 그를 오직 미국인이나, 기껏해야 영국계 미국인 청중들에게만 관련된 인물로 <u>한정하려(가두려)</u> 노력했다.」

05 ④

pending lawsuit : 미결 소송/ meet : 충족시키다/ pharmaceutical : 제약의/ representative : 대표
① 명백한   ② 간결한   ③ 근거 없는   ④ 우회적인   ⑤ 달래는
「미결 소송에 대한 질문들은 제약회사 대표에 의한 <u>에둘러</u> 말하는 대답들로 충족되었다.」

06 ②

legislative 입법의 on the dot 정확하게 podium 단상 jaunty : 활발한 detour : 우회로 refreshments
: 다과, 음식

☞ 4시 정각에, 부시대통령은 청중들 앞에 호명되었고, 그가 의기양양하게 걸어왔다. 부시대통령이 자신을
호명한 것이 아니라 호명된 것이기 때문에 ② 동사의 형태를 was announced(수동태)로 고쳐야 한다.

「나는 백악관의 입법부 직원에 의해 즉시 환영을 받았고 Gold Room으로 안내 받았으며, 그곳에는 하원과 상원 의원들 대부분
이 이미 모여 있었다. 4시 정각에, 부시대통령이 호명됐고, 그는 최소한의 우회로를 유지하기를 원하며 예정대로 진행 중임을
나타내는 의기양양하고 확신에 찬 걸음걸이와 함께 활발하고 건강한 모습으로 단상으로 걸어왔다. 백악관 반대편에 있는 다
과와 그와 영부인과의 사진촬영을 하도록 우리를 초대하기 전에, 10분 정도 그 방에서 농담을 하며, 국가가 힘을 합쳐야 한다
고 요청하며, 대화했다.」

07 ⑤

breathtaking view : 숨이 막히는 경치 improbable : 가능할 것 같지 않은 itinerant : 돌아다니는 toils
of an odyssey : 경험(수고)이 많은 여정

☞ without 가정법 과거 완료(과거사실에 대한 가정), '~가 없었더라면, ~ 이었을지도 모른다.'이므로 문장
의 동사를 would have been으로 고쳐야 한다.

「샌프란시스코 자이언츠 투수 라이언 보겔슨(Ryan Vogelsong)과 그의 아내 니콜(Nicole)은 아파트 옥상 데크에서 7월 4일
불꽃놀이를 지켜보았다. 그리고 그 데크는 베이 브리지, 알카트라즈 섬 및 코잇 타워와 같은 랜드 마크의 숨 막히는 전경을
제공한다. 또한 그들은 샴페인으로 내셔널 리그의 올스타 팀으로 간 그의 선택, 순회 경력에서 믿을 수 없이 높은 점수를
– 적어도 지금까지는 – 축하했다. 샌프란시스코 크로니클 (San Francisco Chronicle)은 최근 그를 Cy Young 상 후보로
지명했다. Vogelsong(34세)은 8-1의 기록과 방어율 2.23의 월드 시리즈 챔피언을 기록한 동화 같은 시즌이었다. 올해의 업
적은 보겔슨이 전에 야구에서 했던 모든 것을 덮어 버리지만, 샌프란시스코, 피츠버그, 일본 및 베네수엘라뿐만 아니라 10개
의 마이너 리그 도시에서 머물렀던 경험이 많은 여정이 없었더라면 가능하지 않았을지도 몰랐다.」

08 ⑤

absence : 부재 rank : 지위에 오르다 inequality : 불평등 motivated : 동기부여 된 it gets to the point
where : ~에 지점에 이르다 have impressions on/of N : ~에 대한 인상을 받다, 가지다

☞ ⑤ 목적격 관계대명사절로 the impressions (that) other people have (목적어생략 = impressions)
on/of me가 적절하다.

「루소에게 자연 상태와 비교가 부재한 것은 중요하다. 지속적인 관계와는 별개의 삶을 살아온 생물체는 아직 인간의 지위에
오르는 정신으로 진화하지 못했을 수도 있다고 주장하면서, 루소는 두 가지 큰 결론을 이끌어 냈다. 첫째, 자연의 불평등
– 더 큰 체력, 더 나은 음성, 또는 더 높은 지능 – 들은 오직 우리가 소유하게 되는 한 가지 자질이 다른 사람들에게서 우리가
존경, 칭찬, 가치를 얻어낼 때에만 중요해 진다. 두 번째 결론은 자연인은 정직하다는 것이다. 사회에서 우리는 항상 다른
사람들이 우리에 대해 무엇을 생각하는지를 염려한다. 우리는 우리의 명예와 다른 사람의 존경을 획득하도록 하는 데에 동기
부여된다. 자신의 자아가 다른 사람들이 나에 대해 가지는 인상들로부터 유래하는 지경에 이르렀다.」

09 ②

void : 빈 공간, 공동 distinct : 뚜렷한, 구별되는 mortal : 죽을 운명의 despair : 절망 grasp : 파악하다, 이해하다 unappeasable : 가라앉을 수 없는

「우주가 원자와 빈 공간으로 이루어져 있다는 것, 세상은 창조주에 의해 우리를 위해 만들어지지 않았다는 것, 우리는 우주의 중심이 아니며, 우리의 감성적인 삶들은 모든 다른 생명체들의 물리적인 삶과 (A) 구별되지 않는다는 것, 우리의 영혼은 다른 신체들과 마찬가지로 죽을 운명이며, 물질에 불가하다는 것, 이러한 모든 것들은 (B) 절망의 원인이 아니다. 반면에, 일이 실제로 이루어지는 방식을 파악하는 것은 행복의 가능성을 향한 중요한 단계이다. 인간은 행복하게 살 수 있지만, 우주의 중심이라고 생각하지는 않는다. 가라앉을 수 없는 욕망과 죽음에 대한 두려움은 인간의 행복에 대한 주요 (C) 장애물이지만, 이성의 행사를 통해 극복될 수 있다.」

10 ④

explicit : 명시적인 witness : 목격하다 physiological : 생리적인 disabilities : 장애 significant : 중요한 dental : 치과의 coronary : 관상동맥의 conductive : 전도되는 attest : 입증하다

「명백한 일련의 관습으로서의 음악 치료법은 21세기 서양에서 처음으로 발전했다. - 특히나, 의사와 간호사가 음악이 부상당한 사람들로의 심리적인, 생리적인, 인지적이고 정서적인 상태에 영향을 끼쳤던 효과를 목격했을 때인 세계 1차 대전 동안. 음악의 (A) 의학적 속성에 대한 최초의 주요 학술 연구는 세계 2차 대전 동안 공장과 군 병원에서 음악 치료의 지속적인 사용에 대한 부분적인 반응으로써 1948년 출판되었다. 음악 요법은 현재 정신적 또는 신체적 장애나 질병을 가진 사람들에게 (B) 널리 사용되었다. 가장 중요한 기능 중 하나는 수술을 겪고 회복중이거나, 주로 치과, 화상, 관상동맥 치료를 준비 중인 사람들을 편안하게 해 주는 것이다. 느리고 꾸준한 템포, 레가토 구절, 완만한 리듬, 예측 가능한 변화, 단순한 지속 멜로디를 가진 음악이 이완에 (C) 도움이 된다(전도된다)는 것은 이미 잘 입증되고 있다.」

11 ④

spiritual : 영적인 controversial : 논란의 여지가 있는 resilience : 회복력 religious : 종교적인 interpretation : 해석 anti-discriminatory : 반차별적인

☞ exclude를 include로 바꿔야 한다.

「영(정신)적 차원은 복잡하고 논쟁의 여지가 있는 영역으로 전체적인 접근법에서 간과되기도 하지만 신체적, 정신적, 감정적 측면에 큰 영향을 줄 수 있는 ① 필수적인 요소로 점차 더 많이 인식되고 있다. 불행히도 영성과 회복력을 연구하는 대부분의 연구는 영성을 ② 쉽게 측정하고 통제되는 단일 실체로 취급한다. 영성은 실제로 복잡한 ③ 다차원적인 현상이다. 그러므로 영성에 대한 광범위한 해석을 ④ 배제한(→ 포함하는) 연구는 우리의 이해를 넓히기 위해 중요하다. 단지 종교적인 정의를 사용하여 영성을 해석하는 사람들이 있다. 기독교 해석으로 미국과 영국에서 흔히 볼 수 있는 영성에 대한이 ⑤ 좁은 종교적 해석은 반차별적 관행에 자부심을 느끼는 정부 기관에 적절하지 않다.」

12 ②

pervasive : 팽배한, 만연한 attitude : 태도 lack : 부족하다 resemble : ~와 닮다

☞ lively를 unlively로 바꿔야 한다.

「한 가지 이론에 따르면, 특정 한계 내에서 의사소통자들이 더 비슷할수록, 그들의 의사소통은 더욱 효과적이다. 한 가지 제한 조건은 사람들 사이의 유사성이 너무 ① 만연하여 모든 주제에 대해 동일한 태도와 신념을 가지고 있다면 의사소통의 필요성이 없다는 것이다. 예를 들어, 모든 사람이 영화에서 정치에 이르기까지 모든 주제에 대해 합의한 파티에서 대화가 ② 활발(→ 활발하지 않게)하게 진행될 수 있다. 반면에 거의 모든 면에서 ③ 다른 사람들은 경험을 공유하고 아이디어를 교환 할 수 있는 기반이 부족하다. 이 이론에 따르면, 이상적인 상황은 사람들이 많은 유사점을 지니고 있지만 상대방의 태도에 영향을 주고 흥미를 불러일으킬 당면한 주제에 대한 그들의 태도에 있어 충분히 다른 상황이다. 그러나 유사성은 명확히 ④ 만연하다. 결국, 태도 영향의 목표는 상대방의 태도를 변화시켜서 자신의 태도와 더욱 ⑤ 비슷하게 만드는 것이다.」

13 ①

combatant : 전투원 battlefield : 전장 hybrid : 융합 fuse : 융합시키다 potential : 잠재적인 magnitude : 규모

☞ clarified를 unclarified로 고쳐야 한다.

「4차 산업 혁명은 갈등의 규모와 그 성격에 영향을 미칠 것이다. 전쟁과 평화 사이의 구분, 그리고 누가 전투원이고 누가 비전투원인지가 불편하게 ① 명확해지고(→ 불명확해지고) 있다. 유사하게, 전장은 점차적으로 국지적이며 전 세계적이다. ISIS와 같은 조직은 ② 주로 중동의 특정 지역에서 운영하지만 반면에 소셜 미디어를 통해 100개 이상의 국가에서 전투원을 모집하고 관련 테러리스트 공격은 지구 어디에서나 발생할 수 있다. 현대의 갈등은 전통적으로 전장 기술과 이전에 주로 무장한 비국가 행위자들과 관련되었던 요소들을 결합하면서 본질적으로 점차 ③ 혼합되고 있다. 그러나 점점 더 예측할 수 없는 방식으로 서로 ④ 융합하는 기술과 국가와 무장한 비국가 행위자가 서로 배우는 기술로 인해 잠재적인 변화의 규모는 아직 완전하게 ⑤ 인식되지 못하고 있다.」

14 ④

identifiable : 신원을 확인 할 수 있는, 인식 가능한 offend : 기분을 상하게 하다 nationalistic : 민족주의적 steppe : 초원 nomadic : 유목의 assemble : 조립하다

① 대부분의 몽골인은 그것을 yort라고 부르길 선호한다.
② 당신은 오직 Ulaan Baatar에서만 그것을 발견할 수 있다
③ 그것은 나무와 벽돌로 만들어져 있다.
④ 그것은 3시간이나 더 적은 시간으로 지어질 수 있다.
⑤ 그것은 현대적인 여행객에게는 추천되지 않는다.

「게르(ger)라고 알려진 몽골 전역에서 보이는 크고 희게 보이는 텐트는 아마 이 나라의 가장 인식 가능한 상징일 것이다. ("yort"라는 단어는 러시아 사람들이 서쪽으로 소개 한 투르크어 단어이다. 몽골인들의 민족주의적인 감수성을 해치고 싶지 않다면 "게르(ger)"라는 단어를 사용해라.) 대부분의 몽골인은 여전히 Ulaaan Baatar라는 교외 지역에서 게르(ger)에 산다. 왜 그런지를 이해하는 것은 어렵지 않다: 나무와 벽돌은 부족하고 비싼데, 특히 대초원에서는 동물 가죽이 싸고 쉽게 얻을 수 있다. 유목민들은 분명히 유연성과 이동성을 가져야 하고 게르(ger)들은 쉽게 이동될 수 있다. 크기에 따라, 게르(ger)는 1∼3시간 내에 조립될 수 있다. 기회가 생기면, 게르(ger)에 머물고 방문할 수 있는 기회는 놓쳐서는 안 된다.」

15 ⑤

geyser basin : 간헐천 지대 ranger : 공원 관리인 bison : 들소 eliminate : 제거하다 distaste : 혐오, 증오

① 야생동물은 1900년대에 과학적으로 관리되기 시작했다.
② 1872년에 정확한 동물의 개체수는 알려지지 않았다.
③ 엘크들은 그들의 자연적 포식자가 제거된 후에 번성했다.
④ 4619마리의 엘크들이 1962년에 살해당했다.
⑤ 대중들의 의견이 늑대들의 총격을 중단시켰다.

「Yellowstone National Park는 간헐천 지대를 보호하기 위해 1872년에 만들어졌다. 그러나 2백만 에이커에 이르는 공원은 정부를 야생동물 산업에 착수시켰고, 반 세기가 더 지나서야 과학적 야생동물 관리가 시작되었다. 공원이 설립되었을 때 동물의 개체수와 먹이 행동에 대한 상세한 기록은 없다. 초기 공원 관리원들은 소를 먹이는 것처럼 엘크와 들소를 먹이고 늑대를 죽이기 시작했다. 1926년 연방의 지시에 따라 마지막 늑대가 제거되었다. 그 다음 엘크는 잔디, 솔, 그리고 그들이 도달할 수 있는 나무의 어떤 부분이든지를 먹어치우고, 공원에 개체수를 퍼뜨렸다. 그래서 1934년에 순찰 경비대원들이 그들을 쏘기 시작했다. 기록에 따르면 1962년에만 4,619마리가 사망한 것으로 나타났다. 1967년 공중의 혐오로 인해 파크 서비스는 총격을 중단시켰다. 그러나 공원은 회복하지 못했다.」

16 ⑤

unpopulated : 사람이 살지 않는   shower : 퍼붓다   wayward : 다루기 힘든   axis : 축   oomph : 힘
① 장엄한   ② 순식간의   ③ 참사의   ④ 보편적인   ⑤ 비직관적인

「좋은 로켓 발사 부지는 몇 가지 중요한 특징이 있다. 바다 근처에 사람이 살지 않는 지역이 선호되며, 그래서 어느 누구도 다루기 힘든 불타고 있는 금속으로 폭격당하지 않는다. 그것이 적도에 있으면 또한 좋다 – 모든 구가 축을 중심으로 회전하는 것처럼 지구는 중간에서 가장 빨리 회전하며 그것은 로켓 부스터에게 추가적인 힘을 제공한다. 다시 말해, 최고의 부지는 열대 지방의 외딴 곳에 있는 경향이 있다. 그런 장소들이 가장 가난한 지역들에 있다는 것은 많은 발사들에게 비직관적인 느낌을 준다: 미래적인 기계들(로켓들)이 열대우림들과 판자촌들을 위로 올라가도록 하는 데에 수십억 달러가 들러가는 것」

17 ③

distinguish : 구별하다   assumption : 가정   inference : 추론   conclusion : 결론   inductively : 귀납적으로   alien : 이상한, 낯선   terminology : 용어
① 용어의 혼란은 잘못된 논리를 더욱 악화시킨다.
② 논리적 생각은 과학적 연구의 전조이다.
③ 추론할 수 없는 무능력의 예가 풍부하다.
④ 일반화들은 철저한 검증의 대상이다.
⑤ 귀납적 논리는 학계에서 만연하다.

「추론할 수 없는 무능력의 예가 풍부하다. 분석가가 사실과 추론을 구별하지 못하거나 추론이 사실이라는 가정 하에 작업하고 있는 분석가들을 발견하는 것은 흔하다. 비록 귀납적으로 도출된 일반화가 논리적 증거의 대상이 아니더라도 그의 결론이 증거로부터 "논리적으로" 따라 왔다는 분석가의 말을 듣는 것은 드문 일이 아니다. 다른 유형의 탐구는 다른 유형의 "증거"의 대상이라는 것은 많은 연구자들에게 낯선 개념이다. 그리고 추론과 암시라는 단어의 흔한 잘못된 사용은 용어에 대한 지식의 부족뿐만 아니라 논리의 기저에 깔린 개념들에 대해서 친숙하지 않다는 것도 반영한다.」

18 ③

doublespeak : (일부로) 모호한 말   press release : 언론공개   compliance : 준수, 순응   publish : 제정하다   crack down : 엄중히 단속하다   fluctuational : 변동하는   predisposition : 경향/ juxtaposed : 병행하는   increment : 임금인상
① 해고 통지서   ② 유예된 모든 탄원서   ③ 급여 동결   ④ 공석 없음   ⑤ 조기 은퇴

「모호한 말은 정부 사람들이 대중과 이야기를 나누든, 서로 이야기를 나누든 간에 정부에서 흘러나온다. 국토 관리국 (Bureau of Land Management)은 1986년에 "법정 요구 사항을 준수하는 행정 절차를 추가하려는 움직임에 따라 내무부 국토 관리청 (Department of Land Management, BLM)은 연방 석탄계약 자격에 관한 규칙 제정한다."고 언론에 발표했다. 이 모호한 말은 단순히 BLM이 석탄계약을 단속할 계획임을 의미한다. 급여 인상을 요청한 상무부 관계자는 "정부 표준과 병행하여 당신의 지위의 생산 능력이 변동하는 경향상 임금 인상을 옹호하는 것은 금전적으로 부적절하다"고 전했다. 다시 말해, 급여 인상은 없다.」

19. ①

rejuvenate : 다시 젊게 하다   generate : 발생시키다   inject : 주사하다   counterpart : 상대방, 경쟁자   decline : 감소하다. 쇠퇴하다
① 시계를 되감아라.
② 제때의 바늘 한 번이 아홉 바느질을 던다.

③ 시간은 아무도 기다려주지 않는다.

④ 노인을 공평하게 다룬다.

⑤ 시간의 속도를 높여라.

「시계를 되감아라. 우리는 노인 생쥐의 근육을 젊어지게 할 수 있는 호르몬을 발견했다. 오스테오칼신(Osteocalcin) – 뼈에서 분비되는 호르몬 – 은 연료를 태우는 근육의 능력을 강화시키고 에너지를 발생시킨다고 컬럼비아 대학(Columbia University) 연구원은 발견했다. 연구팀이 늙은 쥐에게 그 호르몬을 주사했을 때, 쥐들에게는 상당한 시간인 일 년이나 더 늙었음에도 불구하고 그 늙은 쥐는 젊은 쥐만큼이나 멀리 달릴 수 있었다. 호르몬을 받지 못한 늙은 쥐는 절반만 달릴 수 있었다. 오스테오칼신 수치는 생쥐와 인간 모두에서 나이가 들어감에 따라 감소하며, 이제는 호르몬이 사람의 근육 기능을 향상시킬 수 있는지 여부를 테스트 할 계획이다.」

20 ⑤

capitalism : 자본주의   exigency : 성급함   institutionalized : 제도화된

① 지적 영영에서 빛나는 불빛

② 관료적 요구로부터 해방된

③ 난공불락의 요새

④ 당면한 도덕적 문제들에 취약한

⑤ 생각의 감옥

「인간의 필요성들이 생산의 성급함에 희생되는 자본주의의 쇠우리처럼, 현대 사회의 과학 또한 생각의 감옥이 되었다. 제도화된 과학 및 학문 영역 내에서, 창의력과 혁신은 다양한 전문적인 훈련들을 아우르는 전문화된 성취기준으로 수반되어야 한다.」

21 ①

anus : 항문   fart : 방귀를 뀌다   rumble : 천둥과 같은 소리   rectally : 직장으로   punctuate : 마침표를 찍다

① 의지대로   ② 조용하게   ③ 간헐적으로   ④ 보람 없이   ⑤ 무심코

「19세기 후반과 20세기 초반, 프랑스 요셉 푸홀(Joseph Pujol)은 그의 항문에 공기를 끌어 들여 의지대로 방귀를 뀔 수 있는 그의 능력으로 유명했다. 그는 자신을 "The Fartiste"라는 프랑스어인 Le Petomane고 부르면서, 무대 쇼를 열었다. 격식 있게 옷을 입은 그는 대포 방구의 천둥과 같은 소리로 등장했다. 여러 일상적인 것들이 뒤를 이었고, 가장 장엄한 것은 1906 San Francisco 지진의 모방이었다. 그는 15피트(4.5미터)의 거리로 직장으로 물을 발사할 수 있었고, 농장 주변에서 나는 선율을 노래했으며, 서로 다른 동물 소리처럼 들리는 방귀로 마침표를 찍었다.」

22 ⑤

reconstruct : 재구성하다   faithful : 충실한, 신뢰로운   charged : 강렬한   recollection : 회상

assassination : 암살   vivid : 생생한

「당신의 과거 생활 경험의 대부분에 있어, 당신은 아마 기억을 재구성할 필요가 있다는 것에 동의할 것이다. 예를 들어, 누군가가 3년 전에 생일 축하를 어떻게 했는지 묻는다면, 당신은 거꾸로 생각할 것이고 맥락을 재구성하려고 시도할 것이다. (A) 그러나, 사람들이 그들의 기억들이 원래 사건과 완전히 충실하게 남아있다고 믿는 몇몇 상황들이 있다. 플래시 벌브 추억 (flashbulb memories)이라고 불리는 이러한 종류의 추억은 사람들이 정서적으로 강렬한 사건을 경험할 때 생긴다: 사람들의 기억은 너무 생생하여 원래 사건의 사진처럼 보인다. 플래시 벌브 추억에 대한 최초의 연구는 사람들의 대중 행사에 대한 기억에 초점을 맞췄다. (B) 예를 들어, 연구자들은 참가자들에게 존 F. 케네디 대통령의 암살에 대해 처음으로 어떻게 배웠는지에 대한 구체적인 기억이 있는지 물었다. 80명의 참가자 중 한 명을 제외한 모든 참가자가 생생한 기억을 보고했다.」

23 ①

engagement : 교제 in terms of : ~라는 점에서 reflection : 심사숙고, 사고 slumber party : 파자마 파티 cement : 시멘트, 단단하게 만들다

「내 학생들 사이에서 사회적 교제를 촉진하기 위해, 나는 매트와 쿠션뿐 아니라 음식과 음료수를 학생들이 교실에 가져오도록 권장하기 시작했다. 이러한 항목을 통해, 교실이 사회적 측면을 얻음에 따라, 교실의 형태와 기능이라는 점에서 교실 공간은 (A) 변경된다. 사고연습을 하는 동안, 일부 학생들이 매트와 쿠션뿐만 아니라 베개와 장난감을 가져 와서 마치 잠자는 파티에 참석하는 것처럼 보였다. 매트와 쿠션이 사용되지 않을 때 학생들은 전략적으로 테이블 주위에 배열된 의자에 앉아 먹고 마시며, 그들의 초고를 토론하고 검토한다. 음식과 음료는 어떤 사회 문화적 담화에 있어서 중요하기 때문에, 사회적 분위기를 강화시키고 공동체 유대감을 (B) 단단하게 만들고, 학생들의 공유된 정체성을 강화시켜 준다.」

24 ④

armor : 갑옷 coincidence : 우연의 일치 deposit : 매장량, 매장지 feudal : 봉건의 annoyance : 성가심 sally forth : 힘차게 나아가다

☞ ④ 독일, 갑옷 기술의 중심지

「광업 및 갑옷 기술의 중심은 독일의 아우크스부르크(Augsburg)였으며 이는 우연이 아니었다. 아우크스부르크(Augsburg)는 유럽의 철광석 매장지 중 하나 근처에 있었고, 봉건(武裝) 기사단을 세운 봉건주의 국가의 금속에 대한 수요로 인해 곧 광업 산업이 번창하고 산업이 번성했다. 봉건 유럽 전역의 고객들의 성가심 때문에, 독일인들은 하늘 높은 가격을 부과했다. 그 고객에게는 대안이 없다는 것을 알고 있었다. 독일 갑옷은 세계에서 최고였고 만약 고객이 가격을 좋아하지 않는다면, 그는 막대기와 돌로 그의 다음 전쟁에 힘차게 나가야 했다. 이러한 풍성한 이익에 힘입어, 독일 건축가들은 광범위한 연구 개발 노력을 할 수 있었다. 예를 들어, 머리 전체를 감싸는 움직일 수 있는 바이저가 달린 철제 헬멧과 같은 더 강한 갑옷이 탄생했다.」

25 ①

haggle : 흥정하다 bargain : 협상하다 leave money on the table : 돈을 잃다. 버리다 can't hurt to ask : 물어봐서 손해 볼 건 없다.

☞ ① 물어봐서 손해 볼 건 없다.

「흥정하기 싫은가? 당신이 유일하진 않다. 전국 조사에 따르면 구매자들 중, 지난 3년 동안의 일상 용품 및 서비스에 대해 2007년 61%보다 낮아진, 단 48%만이 나은 거래를 위해 협상을 시도했다. 하지만 당신이 닭이라면, 당신은 진다. 흥정을 한 사람들의 89%는 적어도 한 번은 보상을 받았다. 건강 관련 비용에 의문을 제기한 사람들과 마찬가지로 성공적인 가구 흥정가들은 평균 300달러를 절약했다. 휴대 전화 요금제에 도전한 사람들은 80달러를 절약했다. 명백하게, 흥정하지 않는 사람들은 돈을 버리는 중이다.」

26 ③

Catholicism : 가톨릭 Protestant : 개신교도 fervor : 열렬, 열정 inevitably : 피할 수 없이 devotion : 헌신 ambition : 야망 inequality : 불평등

☞ ③ 경제적 이상주의에 대한 개신교의 영향

「가톨릭은 오직 신이 주신 직업은 사제직이라고 주장했으나 개신교는 사람들이 세속적인 공예품이나 무역품을 만드는 일을 하도록 부름을 받을 수 있다고 생각했다. 그들이 신에게 봉사했다는 믿음은 종교적 열렬한 노력으로 더 많은 물건을 생산하고 더 많은 돈을 별도록 유도했다. 웨버는 신교도들이 탐욕과 야망 같은 도덕적 의심 동기보다는 헌신의 증거로서 이윤 추구를 바라 볼 기회를 주었기 때문에 개신교 신앙은 필연적으로 자본주의 경제 사회로 이끌었다고 믿었다. 운명예정설의 개념은 또한 신자들이 물질적 부(富)가 영적 부의 표시였기 때문에 사회적 불평등과 빈곤에 대해 걱정할 필요가 없음을 의미했다.」

27 ③

polish : 광택을 내다　flatten : 평평하게 하다　coat : 코팅을 입히다　come up with : 떠올리다　compounds : 합성물　invert sugar 전화당　reducing agent : 환원제　evenly : 고르게, 평평하게

☞ ③ 상업 유리 거울 기술의 발달

「호기심, 허영심, 또는 아직 탐험되지 않은 동기이든 간에, 연령대의 사람들은 자신의 반사를 보고 싶어 했다. 일찍이 기원전 2500년경, 이집트인들은 매우 광택이 있는 금속, 대개는 청동, 때때로 은이나 금으로 만들어진 거울을 가지고 있었다. 최초의 상업용 유리 거울은 1564년 베니스에서 제작되었다. 이것들은 수은과 주석의 아말감으로 코팅되고 평평해진 바람에 말려진 유리로 만들어졌다. Venetians는 유럽에 수세기 동안 거울을 공급하기 시작했다. 1840년 전에 독일의 화학자인 Justus Liebig가 우리가 오늘날 사용하는 은화 방법을 생각해 냈다. 이 기술에 의해 은-암모니아 화합물은 전화당, Rochelle염 또는 포름알데히드와 같은 환원제의 화학적 작용을 받게 되고, 그 결과로 생성된 금속은은 매끄러운 판유리의 뒷면에 고르게 퍼진다.」

28 ②

curled up : 위로 말려진　engage in : ~에 참여하다　restful : 평화로운　therapeutic : 치료 목적의 impromptu : 즉각적인, 즉석의

☞ ② 특화된 애완용 가구를 홍보하기 위해

「당신의 개나 고양이가 말려진 채로 행복한 잠을 자는 것을 보는 것보다 더 위안이 되는 것이 무엇일 수 있을까? 두 종은 하루 중 거의 절반은 수면을 취하고 있다. 그러나 모든 동물들이 평화로운 것은 아니다. 나이든 동물, 근육 또는 관절 문제가 있는 동물, 또는 매우 활동적인 개는 종종 빈번하게 걸음을 옮기거나 위치를 자주 옮긴다. 귀하의 동반자가 이러한 범주 중 하나에 해당되면 그는 치료 침대의 혜택을 누릴 수 있다. 이러한 특별한 제품은 일반 침대 또는 즉석 수면 장소와 달리 지원 및 편의성을 제공한다. 나이와 건강에 상관없이, 좋은 침대는 근육 – 골격 건강을 촉진하고 추가로 젊어지고 치유의 혜택을 제공한다.」

29 ⑤

contentment : 만족　ill-fate : 나쁜 운　in need : 도움이 필요한

☞ ⑤ 당신 주변에 도움이 필요한 사람들을 도움으로써 행복을 발견해라

「행복을 살 수는 없다. 가장 가까운 식료품 가게에 가서 버터 한 파운드처럼 행복 한 파운드를 주문할 수는 없다. 그러나 행복은 내면에서 오는 것이므로 자신의 행동으로 행복의 척도를 확보 할 수 있다. 당신은 불행한 이웃을 도와줌으로써 만족감을 느낄 수 있다. 우리가 나쁜 운을 공유하지 않는 한, 운이 나쁜 운명 때문에, 행복한 크리스마스를 가지지 못할 사람들을 도울 수 있다. 평화와 선한 뜻의 이 기간 동안에, 도움이 필요한 사람들이 우리의 눈을 통해 행복을 보도록 강요하지 마라. 오히려 자신의 눈을 통해 행복을 보고 찾도록 도와줘라. 우리가 덜 운이 좋은 지역사회에 떨어지도록 만들지 마라.」

30 ②

sprint : 전력질주하다　stroke : 스트로크(수영할 때 젓기)　English Channel : 영국해협　summit : 산 정상

☞ ② 확고한 그리고 끈기 있는

「깊은 숨을 마시고, 나의 스트로크(수영할 때 손 젓기)를 세면서, 나 자신에게 내가 1000번의 스트로크를 할 때까지 다시 위를 올려다보지 않을 거라고 말하면서, 전속력으로 달렸다. 나는 발을 딛었고, 그때 거리는 1000야드 정도였다. 왜 나는 영국 해협이 수영의 에베레스트 산이었는지를 깨달았다. 모든 사람의 목표는 정상에 달하는 것이지만, 산 정상은 공기가 점점 더 희박해지고 모든 것이 어려워진다. 5백 번의 스트로크 동안 올려다보지 마라. 가능한 빠르게 나아가라. 밀어라. 당신이 가지고 있는 모든 힘으로 팔을 당겨라. 발을 차라. 그래. 다리를 뻗어라. 깊이 당기고, 더 빨리. 어서 당겨라.」

31 ③

altruistic : 이타적인   interests : 이익   discharge : 버리다, 포기하다   integrity : 순결, 고결성
therapeutic : 치료의   obligatory : 의무의

「원칙적으로 의사는 환자의 최선의 이익을 위해 행동할 때 이타적인 것으로 간주해서는 안 된다. 왜냐하면 그들은 우리가 일상적으로 이타주의와 관련짓고 행동하는 것을 선택할 수 없기 때문이다. 의사는 선택의 문제로 포기할 수 없는 전문적인 의무를 지니고 있다. 확실히, 의사가 되는 것과 환자와 전문적인 관계를 맺는 것은 선택 사항이다. ① 그러나, 의사가 이 관계에 들어가면, 그 또는 그녀는 의무들을 선택할 수 없다. ② 의사가 특정 상황에서 특정 환자를 치료하지 않는 선택을 할 수 있다면, 개인적 및 직업적 고결성을 손상시킬 수 있다. (③ 환자를 치료가 필요한 개인들로 보는 의사에게는 잠재적인 갈등이 발생한다.) ④ 그러나 의사는 환자의 진료가 다른 의사에게 전달되도록 해야 한다. ⑤ 일단 의사가 되면, 의사는 환자의 의학적 이익을 극대화할 것을 약속한다. 이것은 선택 사항이 아닌 의무 사항이다.」

32 ②

expand : 팽창하다   mercury : 수은   thermometer : 온도계   melt : 녹다   glacier : 빙하   ice sheet : 빙상

「다른 기후 문제와 달리 해수면 상승에 대한 과학은 매우 간단하다. ① 해수면 상승은, 모든 다양한 지역에서, 주로 열이 물에 미치는 영향으로 인해 발생한다. (② 해수면 상승을 막기 위해 물의 분자 구조를 이해하는 것이 가장 중요하다.) ③ 대기 온도가 상승함에 따라 대기 중 대부분의 추가 열(약 90%)이 대양에 가라앉는다. ④ 물이 따뜻해지면 온도계에 수은처럼 팽창한다. ⑤ 이 열 팽창은 해수면 상승의 3분의 1을 차지한다. 나머지 3분의 2는 그린란드와 남극의 산악 빙하와 빙상이 녹는 것에서 나온다.」

33 ①

ethical : 윤리의   be subjected : ~ 당하다   electrode implantation : 전극 착상   injection : 주사, 주입
conscience : 양심   polio : 소아마비   measle : 홍역   smallpox : 천연두   physiology : 생리학

「어떤 경우에는 연구자가 단순히 자연 속에서 동물을 하루 중 다른 시간, 계절의 변화, 식단의 변화 등의 기능으로 관찰한다. 이러한 절차는 윤리적인 문제를 제기하지 않는다. 그러나 다른 연구에서는 동물이 뇌 손상, 전극 착상, 약물이나 호르몬 주사, 그리고 분명히 그들 자신의 이익을 위한 것이 아닌 다른 절차를 겪어왔다. 양심에 걸린 사람(과학자 포함)은 이 사실에 괴로워한다. 그럼에도 불구하고, 동물 실험은 소아마비, 당뇨병, 홍역, 천연두, 다량 화상, 심장 질환 및 기타 심각한 상태의 예방 또는 치료 방법을 이끌어 내는 의학 연구에 중요하다. 생리학이나 의학 분야의 노벨상은 대부분 비인간 동물에 대한 연구로 수여되었다. AIDS, 알츠하이머 병, 뇌졸중 및 기타 여러 질환을 치료하거나 예방하는 방법을 찾는 희망은 주로 동물 연구에 달려있다. 의학 및 생물 심리학의 많은 영역에서 연구는 동물 없이는 천천히 진행되거나 전혀 진행되지 않는다.

비록 단순한 관찰연구와는 달리 동물들에게 수행되는 몇몇 (A) 실험적 연구들이 윤리적 문제를 일으키지만, 그러한 연구들은 다양한 의학 분야에서 진보를 만들어 내는 데 (B) 중요하다.」

34 ④

simplify : 단순화하다   constraint : 제약, 한계   tractability : 취급 용이성   abstract : 추상화하다   deem : 여기다   highlight : 강조하다   topology : 지세학, 풍토, 토폴로지

「일반적으로 모델은 목적을 달성하기 위해 만들어진 현실을 간략하게 표현한 것이다. (①) 그것은 특정 목적을 위해 중요하거나 중요하지 않은 것에 대한 일부 가정을 토대로 또는 간혹 정보 또는 취급 용이성에 대한 제약에 기초하여 단순화된다. (②) 예를 들어, 지도는 물리적 세계의 모델이다. (③) 지도는 지도 제작자가 그 목적과 관련이 없다고 생각한 엄청난 양의 정보를 추상화시킨다. (④ 그것은 관련된 정보를 보존하고 때때로 더욱 단순화한다.) 예를 들어, 도로지도는 도로, 기본 풍토, 이동하려는 장소와의 관계 및 기타 관련 정보를 유지하고 강조 표시한다. (⑤) 다양한 직업은 잘 알려진 모델 유형을 가지고 있다 : 건축 청사진, 엔지니어링 프로토타입 등. 이들 각각은 주요 목적과 관련이 없는 세부사항은 추상화하고, 관련 있는 내용은 유지한다.」

35 ②

case law : 판례법　precedent : 선례　interpret : 해석하다　referral letter : 요청서　termination : 낙태
conscientiously : 진심으로　abortion : 낙태　cover : 책임지다

「보통 법은 판례법(case law)과는 다르게 알려져 있고 판례법은 판사가 특정 경우에 대한 재판(또는 판결)을 위해 개발한 법이다. 판사는 선례 이론과 규칙에 따른다, 즉 "판례"는 선례를 설정한 이전 판결에 구속된다는 의미이다.
(B) 이것은 본질적으로 과거에 결정된 유사한 사건, 특히 최고 법원에서 결정된 사건을 고려해야 한다는 것을 의미한다. 의회가 법률을 제정하지 않은 상황이 있을 것이고 격차를 메우기 위해 판사에게 넘겨지기 때문에 판사가 만든 이 분야의 법은 중요하다.
(A) 마찬가지로 판사는 의회가 통과한 법을 해석해야 한다. 한 예가 낙태법(Abortion Act 1967)과 관련 있다. 한 비서는 낙태 참여에 진심으로 반대할 권리가 그녀의 (낙태 요청서 작성) 거절을 보호한다고 주장하면서, 낙태 요청서 작성을 거절했다.
(C) 판사는 "참여"라는 단어를 보고 그녀가 그 절차에 연루되지 않았기 때문에, 그 비서는 책임이 없다고 결정했다.」

36 ⑤

soulless : 영혼 없는　religion : 종교　animism : 애니미즘　differentiate : 다르게 만들다　not only A, but (also) B : A뿐만 아니라 B도

「로봇이 퍼지기 시작하면서 국가가 로봇 시대에서 성공할 수 있는 정도는 부분적으로 문화에 달려있다 – 얼마다 꾸준히 사람들이 로봇을 그들의 삶 속으로 받아들이는가.
(C) 서양과 동양 문화는 로봇을 보는 방식이 크게 다르다. 일본은 경제적 필요와 로봇에 대한 기술적 노하우를 보유하고 있을 뿐만 아니라 문화적 성향도 가지고 있다.
(B) 일본인의 80%가 수행하는 고대 신도(Shinto) 종교는 물체와 인간 모두 영혼을 가지고 있다고 믿는 애니미즘에 대한 믿음을 포함한다.
(A) 결과적으로, 일본 문화는 로봇을 영혼 없는 기계로 보는 서양 문화보다 실제 동행자로서 로봇 동반자를 더 많이 받아들이는 경향이 있다.」

37　38

sous chef : 부주방장　chop : 다지다　faucet : 수도꼭지　Britannica : 대영 백과사전　executive chef : 총괄 주방장
「우리는 미국으로 돌아 왔지만 줄리의 마음은 여전히 이탈리아에 있다. 그녀는 피자를 더 먹고 싶다. 그녀는 부주방장으로 나와 함께 직접 피자를 만들기로 결심한다.
나는 가지와 호박을 자른다. 우리 둘 다 조용하고 집안일에 집중한다. 다음은, 양파 깎기다. 나는 양파를 껍질을 벗기고 싱크대에 가져가며 수도꼭지를 켜고 흘러내리는 물 아래에서 썰기를 시작한다.
"뭐하고 있니?"
"나는 물 아래에서 양파를 자르고 있어."
"왜?"
"대영 백과사전에서 말하길, 그것은 눈물 흘리는 것을 막아 준데."
희귀한 유용한 힌트들 중 하나인 대영 백과사전의 Heloise 스타일의 힌트였다. 나는 이를 직접 실행해 보는데 꽤나 흥미로웠다.
"아니, 너무 위험해."
"그러나 그것은 대영 백과사전에 있는 거야."
"아니, 나는 총괄 주방장이고 너는 부주방장이야"
나는 대영 백과사전 대 내 아내라는 불행한 상황에 직면해 있다. 권위의 두 큰 근원. 어느 것을 선택할까? 음, 대영 백과사전은 꽤 신뢰할 만하다. 그러나, 내가 아는 한, 그 사전은 내 아이를 데리고 다니거나, 며칠 동안 나를 무시하거나, 그것이 싫어하는 티셔츠를 던져 버릴 수 없다.
그래서 나는 줄리를 선택하기로 결정한다. 양파는 물 없이 잘려질 것이고 나는 울 것이다.」

37 ④

④ 우리 집의 진정한 대장

38 ③

☞ 대영 백과사전에서 양파를 물 아래에서 자르면 눈물이 나는 것을 막아 준다고 했지만, 나는 줄리를 선택하였으므로 물 없이 양파를 자를 것이고 눈물을 흘리게 될 것이다.

③ 양파는 물 없이 잘려질 것이고 나는 울 것이다

39 40

raven : 까마귀 birdbrain : 멍청이 spot : 발견하다 deceive : 속이다 twist : 전환, 전개 replicate : 복제하다, 반복하다 distracter : 방해요소, 방해물 persist : 지속하다

「우리는 까마귀는 멍청이가 아니라고 오래 알아왔다. 그들은 나중을 위해 음식을 은닉하며, 끈을 모아 매달린 음식을 잡아당기고 심지어는 서로 속이려고 시도한다. Sience에 오늘 발표된 연구는 특히 인상적인 전개를 추가한다. 까마귀는 자연에서 결코 만나지 못하는 미래의 필요를 위해 준비할 수 있다.

이 새로운 연구는 스웨덴의 인지동물학자(cognitive zoologist)에 의해 주도되었으며, 이전에 유인원의 계획 능력을 (a) 시험하기 위해 사용 된 일련의 실험을 이번엔 까마귀를 사용하여 재현했다. 까마귀들은 먼저 돌을 사용하여 퍼즐 상자에서 음식 펠렛(작은 알)을 두드리는 법을 배웠다. 다음날, 상자가 없이, 새들은 돌 도구와 도구로 사용하기에 너무 가볍거나 부피가 큰 장난감인 "방해요소" 물체 사이에서 선택하도록 (b) 제안 받았다. 상자는 선택 15분 후에 다시 나타날 (c) 것이었다. 지연에도 불구하고, 까마귀는 올바른 도구를 거의 80% 선택하고 86%로 그들이 선택한 도구를 성공적으로 사용했다. 새들은 실험자에게 음식의 대가로 병마개를 주어야했을 때 (d) 마찬가지로 잘 수행했다. 비록 물물 교환을 하기 위해 15분을 (e) 기다려야 했을 지라도, 새는 방해요소가 아닌 병뚜껑을 선택했다. 까마귀가 도구나 물물 교환 토큰을 선호하여 작은 간식을 버려야 할 때와 17시간 지연 후에만 각 항목을 사용할 수 있는 경우에도 곧 유용해질 물품에 대한 선호가 계속 유지된다.」

39 ①

☞ '실험하기 위해 사용된' 이라는 의미로 used to v를 골라야 한다. used testing은 '실험하는 데 익숙한' 이라는 의미이다.

40 ⑤

⑤ 미래 필요를 위해 계획한다.

41 42

catch a fish in the air : 허공에 낚시하다, 헛수고하다 swamp mud : 진흙 ornery : 성질이 고약한 stubborn : 고집 센 be pulled onto : ~로 끌려가다. ~에 도착하다 chickabiddy : 삐악삐악 소리

「나는 가야만 했고, 갈 것이었다. 그리고 나는 나의 엄마의 생일에 그곳에 있어야 했다. 이것은 정말로 중요했다. 나는 엄마를 집으로 다시 데려올 기회가 있다면, 그것은 그녀의 생일날 일어날 것이라고 믿었다. 내가 만약 아빠나 조부모님께 이 사실을 말씀 드렸다면, 그들은 내가 또 허공에 낚시를 하려고 애쓴다고 말했을 것이었다. 그래서 나는 말하지 않았다. 그러나 나는 이를 믿고 있었다. (① 때때로 나는 늙은 당나귀만큼 성질이 고약하고 고집이 세었다.) 할아버지는 내가 부러진 갈대에 기대며, 언젠가는 진흙이 잔뜩 묻은 얼굴을 할 것이라고 말한다.

「내가 마침내 Hiddle 조부모님과 여행 첫날을 시작하면서 처음 30분 동안 관계가 견고하기를 기도했다. 나는 우리가 우연히 (나는 자동차와 버스가 두려웠다) 우발적 인 일이 없도록 기도했으며, 우리 어머니의 생일을 맞아 거기에 도착할 것이었다. 반복해서 나는 같은 것을 기도했다. 나는 나무들에게 기도했다. 이것은 하나님께 직접 기도하는 것보다 쉬웠다. 거의 항상 나무가 근처에 있었다. 우리가 오하이오 유료 고속도로에 도착 했을때, 그것은 신이 만든 창조물 중에 가장 평평하고 곧은 도로인데, Gram은 내가 기도하는 것을 중단시켰다. "Salamanca—"(②) 나는 나의 진짜 이름이 Salamanca Tree Hiddle이라고 설명해야 한다. 부모님이 생각한 Salamanca는 위대한 증조모가 속한 인디언 부족의 이름이었다. (③) 부모님들이 실수하셨다. 부족의 이름은 Seneca였지만, 부모님은 내가 태어난 후에 내 이름에 익숙해질 때까지 자신들의 실수를 발견하지 못했으므로 Salamanca로 남았다. 나의 중간 이름, Tree는 일반 나무에서 유래한 것인데, 나의 어머니에게 너무나 아름다운 것이어서 그녀는 내 이름의 일부분에 그것을 만들어 넣었다. 그녀는 더 구체적인 Sugar Maple Tree를 사용하고 싶어했다, 하지만 Salamanca Sugar Maple Tree Hiddle은 그녀에게도 역시나 너무 과했다. (⑤) 나의 엄마는 나를 Salamanca라고 부르곤 했지만, 그녀가 떠난 후, Hiddle 조부모님들만이 나를 Salamanca라고 불렀다. (그들이 나를 chickabiddy(삐약삐약)라고 부르지 않을 때). 대부분의 다른 사람들에게, 나는 Sal이었고, 특히 재미있다고 생각하는 몇몇 소년들에게 나는 Salamander였다.」

41 ⑤

☞ 마지막 문장으로 볼 때, 대부분의 사람들에게 나는 Sal이었고, 몇몇 소년들에게는 Salamander였다.
⑤ 대부분의 사람들은 나를 Salamanca 또는 Salamander이라고 불렀다.

42 ①

☞ 제시된 문장이 들어가기 적절한 곳은 ①이다.

43 45

disembark : 내리다 ceiling : 천장 illuminated : 조명이 달린, 밝게 빛나는 exotic : 이국적인 apt : 적절한, 적당한 subtitle : 자막, 번역 provoke : 유발하다 distinctive : 구별되는, 뚜렷한 nostalgic : 향수적인 elicit : 끌어내다 intensely : 강렬하게 congenial : 마음이 끌리는, 통하는 temperament : 성격, 기질, 성질

「암스테르담의 Schipol 공항에서 내릴 때, 나는 도착 홀, 출구 및 환승 데스크로 가는 길을 보여주는 천장에 매달려있는 표지판에서 몇 걸음 걷고 멈춰 선다. 그것은 세로 1미터 가로 2미터의 단순한 디자인인 케이블과 에어컨 덕트가 있는 천장에 붙은 철제 스트럿에 매달려 있는 조명이 달린 알루미늄 상자에 플라스틱 띠가 있는 밝은 노란색이다. 그것의 단순함, 심지어 세속적임에도 불구하고, 표지판은 나에게 즐거움을 준다. 이는 이국적인, 평범하지 않은, 그리고 적절한 것처럼 보이는 기쁨이다. 이국적이라는 것은 특정 장소에 놓여있다 ; Aankomst의 두 개의 a, Uitgang의 U와 i의 이웃, 영어 자막의 사용 속에서, "desk"를 위한 balies라는 단어의 사용, Frutiger 또는 Univers와 같은 실용적이고 현대적인 폰트 속에.

표지판이 나에게 진정한 즐거움을 불러일으키는 것은, 부분적으로는 내가 다른 곳에 도착한 첫 번째 결정적인 증거가 되기 때문이다. 그것은 해외에 있다는 상징이다. 비록 평범한 눈에는 띄지 않는 것처럼 보일지 모르지만, 그런 표지판은 내 나라에서 결코 정확히 이러한 형태로 존재하지 않는다. 거기에는 노란색이 적고 서체는 더 부드럽고 더 향수적 일 것이다. 그곳(자국의 표지판)에는 – 외국인들의 혼동에 대한 무관심 밖에서 – 자막이 없거나, 언어는 두 개의 A들을 포함하지 않고, 내가 느끼는 반복과 다른 역사와 사고방식을 포함하고 있을 것이다.

각기 다른 장소에서 기호가 다를 수 있다는 것은 간단하지만 즐거운 아이디어의 증거다 : 국가는 다양하고 관습들은 국경을 넘어서 다양하다. 그러나 차이만으로는 즐거움을 이끌어 내기에 충분하지 않거나 오래 가지 않을 것이다. 그 차이는 우리나라가 할 수 있는 것에 대한 개선인 것처럼 보인다. 만약 내가 Schipol 표지판을 이국적이라고 말한다면, 그것은 애매하지만 강렬하게 Uitgang이라는 표현을 넘어서 표지판을 만든 그 나라가 결정적인 방식들로 나의 성격과 걱정들보다도 훨씬 더 마음이 통한다는 것을 말해주는데 성공하고 있기 때문이다. 표지판은 행복의 약속이다.」

43 ③

① 이국적이면서 비현실적인
② 지나치게 난해한 표시는 호기심을 죽인다.
③ 달콤한 어리둥절함 : 내가 어디에 있는가?
④ 같은 플래터의 다양한 언어
⑤ 국경 넘어 : 선구자의 여행

44 ③

③ 혼란, 혼동

45 ③

① 길이가 높이의 두 배이다.
② 그것은 두 가지 언어로 쓰였다.
③ 그것의 단순함은 그것의 이국적임의 주된 이유이다.
④ 그것은 다른 나라에 도착했다는 증거가 된다.
⑤ 작가는 집에 돌아 온 것 같은 표지를 찾을 수 없었다.

01 ④

firm : 단호한, 확고한   tone : 어조   in spite of : ~에도 불구하고   pensive : 생각에 잠긴, 수심어린
☞ ④ thoughtful(사려 깊은, 생각에 잠긴)
① 공공연한   ② 과도한   ③ 만연하는   ④ 사려깊은, 생각에 잠긴   ⑤ 낙관적인
「그것의 수심이 담긴 온화함에도 불구하고, 그 어떤 것도 이 편지의 어조보다 더 단호한 어조는 없다.」

02 ⑤

assert : 주장하다   lifelong : 일생의   genome : 게놈(유전물질세트)   by no means : 결코~이 아닌
exhaustive 철저한, 고갈시키는
☞ ⑤ thorough(철저한)
① 보람이 있는   ② 혁명적인   ③ 관대한   ④ 독립적인   ⑤ 철저한
「그 의사는 인간 게놈에 관한 그의 평생의 연구가 결코 철저하게 행해지지 않았다고 주장하였다.」

03 ④

conundrum 수수께끼   face 직면하다
☞ ④ puzzle : (수수께끼, 퍼즐)
① 기구   ② 강도(질)   ③ 범죄자   ④ 수수께끼, 퍼즐   ⑤ 설명
「이 수수께끼는 그 경찰관들이 이전에 직면했던 다른 무엇과도 같지 않았다.」

04 ①

quarrel : 다툼, 불화   wound : 상처   just like : 마치 ~처럼   That's why : 그것이~한 이유이다
☞ ① 사과하기에 결코 늦지 않았어.
① 사과하기에 결코 늦지 않았어.
② 너는 모든 사람을 항상 기쁘게 해줄 수는 없어.
③ 가끔씩 불화는 팀에 유익이 돼.
④ 다른 것들처럼 시간이 모든 상처를 낫게 하지.
⑤ 그것이 말하기 전에 네가 생각을 해야만 하는 이유야.
「A : 어제 회의는 어땠어?
 B : 최악이었어
 A : 무슨 일이 있었어?
 B : 내가 해서는 안 될 말을 했어. 잭은 이제 나랑 말도 안 해.
 A : 사과하기에 결코 늦지 않았어.
 B : 그렇게 하기 위해 나는 모든 용기를 끌어모아야겠어.」

05 ②

print : 지문, 자국 arrest warrant : 구속영장 perpetrator : 가해자, 범인 ask for : 요구하다 statement : 진술 proof : 증거

☞ ② 우리는 느낌(직관)이 아니라 증거로 움직입니다.

① 저는 지금 즉시 구속영장을 요청하겠습니다.

② 우리는 느낌(직관)이 아니라 증거로 움직입니다.

③ 제 생각에는 우리는 이미 필요한 모든 증거들을 다 갖고 있는 것 같네요.

④ 우리 증인들의 진술에 집중하죠.

⑤ 우리의 주요 임무는 시민들의 안전을 보장하는 것입니다.

「A : Mills 형사님, 제 생각에는 이 사람이 저희가 찾고 있는 사내인 것 같아요.
B : 그의 지문을 범죄현장에서 나온 것과 대조해 봤나요? Flaherty 경관님.
A : 결과는 아직 나오지는 않았어요. 하지만 두 명의 증인이 그와 같은 인상착의를 지닌 사람을 봤다고 말했어요.
B : 구속영장을 발부받기에는 그것만으로 충분하지가 않아요.
A : 하지만, 이 사람이 그 범죄자라고 저는 확신해요.
B : 우리는 느낌(직관)이 아니라 증거로 움직입니다.
A : 알겠어요. 그렇다면 우리는 단지 실험실에서의 결과를 기다려야 하는군요.」

06 ④

recurrent : 되풀이되는 medical practitioner : 의사 be grounded in : ~에 근거하다 so-called : 소위, 이른바 therapeutic : 치료상의 privilege : 특권 preeminent : 탁월한, 우위의 withhold : (~을)주지 않다, 보류하다 deferential : 공경하는 adequacy : 적당함, 타당성 standpoint : 관점, 입장

☞ ④ those → that

of이하의 후치수식을 받는 대명사로서 단수인 standpoint를 받으므로 those가 아닌 that로 바꿔야 한다.

「법정에서 반복되는 이슈는 환자들의 의학적인 처치에 관해 얼마나 많은 것이 환자들에게 공개되어야 하는지를 결정함에 있어서 누구의 관점을 채택해야 하는 것인가이다. 대다수의 주(州)들은 전문가들을 선호하며, 같은 공동체와 같은 전공 분야 내의 "합리적인 의사"에 의해 합리적이라고 여겨지는 만큼만 의사들이 밝힐 책임이 있다는 입장을 주장한다. 이 접근법은 소위 치료적 특권에 근거하며, 이는 환자에게 해가 될 수 있는 어떤 정보를 주지 않을 수 있는 의사의 현저한 특권을 인정하는 것이다. (그 입장을) 덜 공경하는 소수자 규칙은 공개의 적절성은 "합리적인 의사"의 관점이 아니라 "합리적인 환자"의 관점에서 판단되어야 한다고 주장한다. 비록 이러한 일반적인 규칙들이 잘 정착된다 할지라도, 공개의 적절성에 관한 의문들은 여전히 제기된다.」

07 ⑤

chance : 우연한, 뜻밖의 crackle : 잔금무늬 glaze : 유약, 광택제 figurative : 화려한, 상징적인 infinite : 무한한 ceramist : 도예가

☞ ⑤ satisfied → satisfying

5형식의 목적격 보어 자리의 분사 형태를 묻는 문제이다. 라쿠의 관행이 만족스럽게 하는 것이므로 감정 동사인 satisfy의 분사 형태 중 현재분사인 satisfying이 오는 것이 적절하다.

「Raku는 세라믹 제품에 흥미롭고 우연한 표면 효과를 내는 저온에서 급속으로 굽는 인기 있는 공정이다. 소박한 하얀 잔금무늬 광택제에서부터 놀랄만한 스펙트럼 색깔에 이르기까지, 작은 찻잔에서부터 추상적이거나 화려한 조각의 형태에 이르기까지, 라쿠 관행에 존재하는 가능성과 혁신의 범위는 그것을 항상 참신하고 생기가 넘치게 해준다. 그것의 목적과 마찬가지로, 이 고대 공정의 현대적인 서구 관행은 그것의 동양의 뿌리와는 다르지만, 그들의 다양성, 에너지 그리고 미(美)에 있어서 라쿠의 결과는 여전히 무한하다. 일본과 서양 라쿠는 도예가에게 굽기의 최종 결과물을 비교적 짧은 시간 내에 경험할 기회를 제공해주며, 바로 이 특징이 라쿠 관행을 매우 만족스럽게 만들어준다.」

08 ③

manta ray : (어류)쥐가오리   sea horse : 해마   armor : 방호 기관, 갑옷/ compress : ~를 압축하다
resilience : 탄력, 회복력   rigidity : 경직   come from : ~에서 나오다, 비롯되다   square : 정사각형
segment : 마디   bony plate : 골판   vertebrae : 척추뼈, 등골   vulnerable : 취약한   build out of : ~로 만
들다   excursion : (짧은)여행   detonate : 폭발하다, 폭발시키다

☞ ③ (A)compressed(압축된) (B)resilience(회복력) (C)safe(안전한)

 (A) 꼬리가 평상시 크기의 절반까지 줄어든다는 문맥으로 보아 팽창(expanded)이 아닌, 압축된다는 의미
   인 compressed가 적절하다.

 (B) 바로 앞 문장에서 꼬리의 크기가 절반까지 압축된다는 내용에 근거하여 볼 때, 이는 움직이지 않는
   경직성(rigidity)이 아닌 탄력, 회복력을 뜻하는 resilience가 알맞다.

 (C) 지속적인 손상 없이 크기가 변화한다는 내용에 근거하여 볼 때, 꼬리의 구조물인 척추뼈 역시 안전함
   을 유지하면서 미끄러질 수 있다는 뜻의 safe가 적절하다.

「게, 새, 쥐가오리가 저녁거리로 해마를 주기적으로 찌그러뜨리려 하지만, 해마는 특이한 방호 기관을 가지고 있다. 그것의
꼬리는 지속적인 손상 없이 평상시 크기의 절반까지 압축될 수 있는 것으로 샌디에이고의 캘리포니아 대학 연구원들이 최근
밝혀내었다. 그 꼬리의 복원력은 각각이 4개의 골 판으로 만들어진 약 36개의 정사각형 마디인 그것의 구조에서 비롯된다.
그 판은 척추 기둥의 등뼈를 콜라겐과 연결하며, 척추를 안전한 상태로 두면서 서로를 지나 미끄러질 수 있다. 궁극적으로,
연구원들은 3-d 프린터로 해마의 유연하고 튼튼한 꼬리를 본뜬 로봇 팔을 만들고 싶어 하며, 수중여행을 위해 또는 폭탄을
폭파시키기 위해 그것을 사용하고 싶어 한다.」

09 ④

priming effect : 점화 효과   yield : (결과를) 내다   self-image : 자아상   autonomous : 자율적인
deliberate : 신중한   author : 창시자   think of A as B : A를 B라고 여기다   irrelevancy : 무관성   polling
station : 투표소   precinct : 선거구   proposition : 제안   separate : 별개의, 독립된   initiative : 주민 법안
발의

☞ ④ (A)threaten(위협하다) (B)irrelevancies(무관한 것) (C)increase(증가시키다)

 (A) 점화 효과가 가져온 결과에 대해 설명하면서 예시로 든 투표행위에서 이전의 선택이나 노출에 영향을
   받는다는 내용으로 보아 의식적인 창시자로서의 우리의 자아를 확인(confirm)하는 것이 아니라 위협
   (threaten)한다고 보는 것이 적절하다.

 (B) 투표가 무관한 것들에(irrelevancies) 의해 영향 받아서는 안 된다는 우리의 일반적인 생각에 대해
   서술하고 있으므로 합의(consensus)가 아닌, 무관한 것(irrelevancies)이 정답이다.

 (C) 학교 관련 이미지를 노출시켜 지지하는 경향을 증가(increase)시키는 점화 효과의 예시에 관한 내용
   이므로, increase가 오는 것이 문맥상 적절하다.

「점화 효과에 관한 연구는 우리의 판단 및 선택에 대한 의식적이고도 자율적인 창시자로서의 우리의 자아상을 위협하는 발견
을 가져왔다. 예를 들어, 우리 중 대부분은 투표를 정치에 대한 우리의 가치와 평가를 나타내며, 무관한 것에 의해 영향 받아
서는 안 되는 신중한 행위라고 생각한다. 예를 들어, 우리의 투표는 투표소의 위치에 의해 영향 받아서는 안 되지만, 그것은
영향을 받는다. 2000년도에 애리조나의 선거구에서의 투표 패턴에 관한 연구는 투표소가 (투표자들과) 가까운 곳에 있었을
때보다 투표소가 학교 안에 위치해 있을 때, 학교 지원금을 확대시키기 위한 제안에 대한 지지가 상당히 더 크다는 것을 보여
주었다. 한 가지 별개의 연구는 교실과 학교 로커의 이미지에 사람들을 노출시키는 것이 학교 법안 발의를 지지하는 참석자들
의 경향을 또한 증가시켰다는 것을 보여주었다. 그 이미지의 효과는 부모들과 (부모가 아닌) 다른 투표자들 간의 차이보다
더 컸다.」

10 ⑤

point in time : 때, 시점   elude : 회피하다   plausible : 그럴듯한, 타당한 것 같은   immensely : 엄청나게
put to use : 이용하다   deploy : 효율적으로 사용하다   theoretical : 이론상의   serve as : 역할을 하다
building block : 구성물

☞ 해결책이 그 이상의 이론화를 위한 구성물로서 역할을 하는 곳에서 그 이상의 작업이 중요하고 긴급한
경우에 남들보다 좀 더 일찍 획득한 정보를 가치 있게 쓸 수 있는 경우를 설명하고 있으므로, 문맥상
later가 아닌 earlier가 적절하다.

「발견을 더 나중의 시점에서 더 이른 시기로 정보의 도달을 옮기는 행위라고 생각해봐라. 발견의 가치는 알려진 정보의 가치와
동일한 것이 아니며, 오히려 그렇지 않았을 때보다 더 일찍 이용 가능한 정보를 가지게 되는 것의 가치와 동일하다. 과학자나
수학자는 많은 사람을 피해가는 해답을 찾는 데에 첫 번째가 됨으로써 엄청난 기술을 보여줄지도 모른다. 그러나 만약 그
문제가 어떤 식으로든지 빨리 풀리게 된다면, 그 일은 아마도 세상에 많이 도움이 되지 않을 것이다. 약간이라도 더 빠르게
해결책을 갖는 것이 대단히 가치가 있게 되는 경우가 있다. 그러나 이것은 해결책이 즉각 활용될 때 가장 그럴듯하며, 몇몇의
실용적인 목적을 위해 효율적으로 사용되거나 더 나아가 이론적인 작업에 대한 토대로서 역할을 한다. 그리고 후자의 경우
해결책이 더 많은 이론화를 위한 구성물로서 역할을 한다는 의미에서 즉시 사용되는 경우, 추가 작업이 그 자체로 중요하고
긴급한 경우에만, 해결책을 약간 일찍 얻는 것이 엄청난 가치가 있다.」

11 ③

be committed to : ~에 전념하다   persuade A of B : A에게 B를 확신시키다   tacitly : 무언으로   validity
타당성   theorem : 정리   be entitled to : ~할 권리가 있다   steadfast : 변함없는   dazzling : 현혹적인, 눈
부신   manipulate : 다루다, 조작하다   albeit : 비록 ~일지라도   probabilistic : 확률적인, 개연론의   seek
to : 추구하다   tentativeness : 실험적임, 망설임   cognizant of : ~을 인식하고 있는

☞ ③ 과학적 진보는 확률적(probabilistic)이고, 변경의 대상이 될 수(subject to revision) 있으며, 망설임
과 불확실성을 알고 있는 가치시스템이므로 ③번의 변함없는이라는 뜻을 가진 steadfast는 답이 될 수
없다. 이는 변경가능 changeable 하거나 가능성이 있는 possible 류의 단어로 바뀌는 것이 적절하다.

「우리는 이성에 전념한다. 만약 우리가 질문을 하고, 가능한 대답들을 평가하고, 그러한 대답들의 가치에 대해 다른 이들을
확신시키려 노력한다면, 그렇다면 우리는 (논리적 근거에 따라) 추론하게 되고 따라서 이성의 타당성에 대해 암묵적으로 동의
하게 된다. 우리는 수학과 논리의 정리처럼, 이성의 세심한 적용에서 나오는 결론은 무엇이든지 전념하게 된다. 비록 우리가
물리적인 세계에 관한 어떤 것을 논리적으로 정의할 수 없다 하더라도, 그것에 관한 특정한 믿음에 있어서 확신을 가질 권리
를 가지게 된다. 세상에 관한 가능성 있는(변함없는) 일반화를 발견하는 관찰과 이성의 작용은 우리가 과학이라 부르는 것이
다. 세상을 다루고 설명하는 데 있어 그것의 눈부신 성공을 이룬, 과학의 진보는 비록 항상 확률적이고 변경될 수는 있지만
우주에 관한 지식이 가능성 있는 것임을 보여준다. 과학은 사실 우리가 지식을 얻는 방법에 대한 패러다임이며, 이는 과학의
특정한 제도들이나 방법들이 아닌, 말하자면 세상을 설명하는 것을 추구하고, 후보 설명들을 객관적으로 평가하며, 언제라도
우리의 이해에 대한 망설임과 불확실성을 인식하고 있는 그것의 가치시스템이다.」

12 ⑤

plier : 집게, 펜치   nostril : 콧구멍   writhe in agony : 고통으로 몸부림치다   profusely : 풍부하게   tick
: 작동하다 째깍거리다   log : 기록하다, 기록을 달성하다   desperate : 필사적인   manage to : 겨우 ~해내
다   dislodge : 제거하다   refuse : 쓰레기   lay bare : 발가벗기다   toll on : (~에 끼치는) 대가, 피해
albatross : (조류) 신천옹   burst with : ~으로 터질 듯하다   unscathed : 상처가 없는   strain : 잡아당기다
snare : 올가미로 잡다

☞ ⑤ 야생동물에게 끼치는 플라스틱의 피해를 묘사한 예시 중의 하나이다. 억센 플라스틱에 당겨져 상처가 생기지 않은 것(unscathed)이 아니라 상처가 생긴(scathed or wounded) 즉, 문맥적으로 반대의 의미가 들어가야 적절하다.

「코스타리카에서 떨어진 보트 위에서, 한 생물학자가 바다거북의 콧구멍에서 플라스틱 빨대를 뽑아내기 위해 스위스 군용 칼의 집게를 사용한다. 그 거북이는 다량 출혈을 하며 고통으로 몸부림을 치고 있다. 고통스러운 8분 동안 유튜브 비디오가 작동하고, 시청하기에 매우 힘들다 할지라도 2천만 명 이상의 뷰라는 기록을 달성했다. 결국, 점점 더 필사적인 생물학자들이 그 동물의 코에서 4인치 길이의 빨대 한 개를 간신히 제거한다. 야생동물에게 끼치는 플라스틱의 피해를 발가벗기는 이와 같은 가공되지 않은 장면들이 흔해지고 있다 : 그것의 배가 쓰레기로 터질 듯한 죽은 신천옹. 수년 동안 억센 플라스틱에 당겨져 상처가 생긴 (상처가 없는) 껍데기가 여섯 개의 팩 고리에 끼인 거북이. 버려진 어망에 잡힌 바다표범. 누구에게 책임이 있는가? 거울을 잘 들여다보라!!」

13   ⑤

microbe : 미생물, 세균   with 명사 ing(독립분사구문) : 명사가 ing 하면서   team with : 풍부하다   cosmic : 우주의   rage : 고조에 달하다, 한창이 되다   exoplanet : 태양계 외 행성   exomoon : 외계 위성   suitable : 적절한   emerge from : ~에서 나오다   extraordinary : 놀라운   intergalactic : 은하계 사이의   hoax : 짓궂은 장난

☞ ⑤ 거기 밖에 누구 있나요?
지구의 유일성, 특별함에 관하여 초점을 맞춘 글이 아니라 지구 그 너머에 있는 생명체 내지는 서식지로서의 외계 행성의 존재에 대해 열린 가능성을 염두에 두고 쓴 글이므로, ⑤번이 글의 제목으로 적절하다.
①번은 오히려 글쓴이가 전달하고자 하는 바와 반대적인 의미이므로 적절한 답이 될 수 없다.
① 지구, 그 놀라운 서식지
② 은하계 사이의 초고속도로
③ 미생물이 진짜 우리의 조상인가?
④ 우주 동물원 : 거대한 속임수
⑤ 거기 밖에 누구 있나요?

「우리는 진귀한 지구에 살고 있는가? 너무 특별해서 다른 행성들이 기껏해야 미생물의 서식지가 될 때, 생명의 풍부한 다양성을 수용하는 거의 유일한 것인가? 또는 우리가 거대한 우주의 동물원의 일부로 존재하는 것을 의미하면서 여기에 존재하는 것들만큼이나 복잡한 생명체로 가득한 지구에 우리가 살고 있는 것인가? 이에 관한 논쟁이 한창이지만, 우리는 후자가 매우 가능성이 있다는 것을 받아들일 때가 되었다고 말한다. 지금까지 우리는 적어도 3,700개의 외계행성에 대해 알고 있으며, 잠재적으로 거주할 수 있는 무수한 외계 행성들과 외계 위성들이 우리 은하계 내에 그리고 그 너머에 있는 것 같다. 우리는 생물체들이 보통 그들 위에서 어떻게 생겨나는지 알지 못하지만, 많은 과학자들은 그것이 어떤 적합한 행성의 화학적이고 물리적인 특성에서 아마 생겨났을 것이라고 생각한다.」

14   ③

briefly : 잠시/ short story : 단편소설   establish : 수립하다, 자리 잡게 하다   declare : 공표하다   be to : ~하는 것이다(명사)   prolific : 다작의   manners : 관습

☞ ③ 그의 글쓰기 경력은 1930년대 초반에 미국에서 잡지를 발행하며 시작된 것이므로 본문의 내용과 일치한다.

「Frank O'Connor는 너무 가난하여 그에게 대학교육을 시켜줄 수 없었던 아일랜드 cork의 한 가정에서 태어났다. 아일랜드의 독립투쟁 동안에 그는 잠시 동안 아일랜드 공화국군의 멤버였다. 그러고 나서 cork와 dublin에서 도서관 사서로 일했으며, 그는 단편소설의 작가로 자리 잡기 전까지 애비 극장의 감독이었다. 1931년부터 그는 미국에서 잡지를 정기적으로 발행했으며, 몇 년 동안 하버드와 노스 웨스턴 대학에서 (학생들을) 가르쳤다. 그의 공공연한 목표는 그의 소재를 만들어 냄에 있어서 이야기꾼의 목소리에서 자연스러운 리듬과 강세를 찾는 것이었다. 그는 사실 아일랜드의 관습과 아일랜드 인물에 관한 (작품의) 다작의 역사가였다.」

15 ⑤

freshwater : 담수 formerly : 이전에 be confused with : ~과 혼동되다 drastically : 과감하게 급격하게
hydroelectricity : 수력전기 expedition : 탐험, 원정(대) reportedly : 소문에 따르면 call for : (공식적으
로) 요구하다 in case : ~할 경우를 대비하여 revive : 요청하다 부활하다

☞ ⑤ 세계 야생동물 기금은 그 종의 소생에 대한 모든 희망을 포기한 것이 아니라, 오히려 소생 가능성에
대비해 서식지의 보존을 요청하고 있으므로 본문의 내용과 일치하지 않는다.

「반지(banjji)는 예전에 중국의 양쯔강에서만 발견된 담수 돌고래의 기능적으로 멸종된 종이다. 그것은 또한 중국 강 돌고래라
고 불린다. 그것은 중국 흰색 돌고래와 혼동되지 않는다. 중국이 산업화가 진행되고, 그리고 어획, 운송, 수력전기를 위해
강을 과도하게 사용하게 됨에 따라 반지(banjji) 개체 수는 수십 년간 급격히 감소했다. 반지(banjji)는 인간이 멸종으로 몰아
붙인 첫 번째 돌고래 종이 될 수도 있었다. 그 종들의 보존하기 위한 노력이 이루어졌지만, 2006년 후반 탐험대는 그 강에서
어떠한 반지(banjji)도 찾지 못 했다. 2007년 8월에, 전해지는 바에 의하면 한 중국인 남성이 양쯔강에서 수영하고 있는, 반지
로 추정되는 커다란 하얀 동물을 촬영했다고 한다. 세계 야생동물 기금(WWF)에서는 그 종들이 발견되거나 소생될 경우를
대비하여 반지의 가능한 어떠한 서식지에 대해서든 보존을 요청하고 있다.」

16 ⑤

most likely : 아마, 필시 address as~ : (호칭으로) 부르다 turn down : (볼륨을) 줄이다. 낮추다 look
forward to ing : ~하는 것을 고대하다

☞ ⑤ 간단한 인사로 시작하여 이웃의 십 대 자녀의 커다란 음악 볼륨에 대해 이웃들의 항의를 전달하기
위해 쓰인 편지이므로 글의 목적은 ⑤번이 적절하다.

「이번 기회에 저를 소개하겠으며, 이웃으로 오신 것을 환영합니다. 당신의 새로운 집에서 도로 바로 위에 있는 19번지에서
저의 아내 모니카와 저는 살고 있습니다. 우리는 Meadow 스트리트에서 지난 20년간 살아왔습니다. 아마도 제가 이 주변에
있는 모든 사람들보다 나이가 더 많기 때문에, 마을의 비공식적인 시장으로 종종 불립니다. 저는 당신이 이사 온 이래 발생한
문제들에 관하여 우리의 이웃 중 몇몇으로부터 그들의 요청을 전달해달라고 요구받았습니다. 우리 모두는 음악을 사랑하고
우리 중 대부분은 10대 자녀가 있거나, 앞으로 생길 겁니다. 그렇지만 당신의 십 대 자녀에게 볼륨을 줄여줄 것을 당신이
요청해주시면 우리는 감사하겠습니다. 우리 모두 만나서 인사할 것을 고대합니다.」

17 ①

laughter : 웃음 compatibility : 양립 가능성 beware of : ~에 주의하라 seriousness : 진지함, 심각함
dour : 시무룩한, 음울한 turn against : ~로 하여금 ~에게서 등을 돌리게 하다.

☞ ① 진지함만을 기반으로 하는 관계에 대한 위험성을 언급하면서 웃음을 기반으로 하는 관계의 중요성에
대해 언급하고 있으므로 정답은 "건강의 관계에 대한 핵심은 서로 웃는 것이다"라는 ①번이 적절하다.

「웃음은 양립 가능성을 보여주는 하나의 실마리가 된다. 그것은 장기간에 걸쳐 서로와 함께 하는 것을 당신이 얼마나 많이
즐길 것인지를 당신에게 알려준다. 만약 당신의 함께 웃는 것이 다른 이들을 상하게 하지 않으면서, 즐겁고 건강하다면,
그렇다면 당신은 세상과 좋은 관계를 맺을 수 있다. 웃음은 놀라움의 소산이다. 만약 서로를 웃게 만들 수 있다면 당신은
항상 서로를 놀라게 할 수 있다. 만약 당신이 서로를 항상 놀라게 할 수 있다면, 당신은 당신 주변의 세계를 새롭게 할 수
있다. 웃음이 없는 관계를 조심하라. 단지 진지함을 기반으로 하는 가장 친밀한 관계조차도 뚱하게 되는 경향이 있다. 시간이
지남에 따라, 세상에 관한 공통의 진지한 관점을 공유하는 것은 당신으로 하여금 같은 관점을 공유하지 않는 사람들에게서
등을 돌리게 하는 경향이 있으며, 당신의 관계는 함께 비판적인 것에 기반할 수 있다.」

18 ②

reductionism : 환원주의 consist of : ~으로 이루어지다 unify : 통합하다 microscope : 현미경 geographer : 지리학자 fit into : ~에 꼭 들어맞다 landmass : 대륙, 광대한 땅 adjacent : 인접한 eologist : 지질학자 appeal to : ~에 호소하다 upwelling 용승 push apart : 떠밀다 as for : ~에 관해 말하자면 physicist : 물리학자 dispensable : 불필요한 meticulous : 꼼꼼한

☞ ② 아프리카의 해안선이 미국의 해안선과 들어맞게 되는 이유를 설명하며 지리학자로부터 시작하여 지질학자를 거쳐 물리학자에게까지 이어지게 되는 지식의 환원주의에 대해 설명한 글이다. 정답은 불필요한 과학자가 없다는 의미의 "dispensable"이 적절하다.

「좋은 환원주의란 한 분야의 지식을 또 다른 것으로 대체하는 것으로 이루어지는 것이 아니라 그들을 연결하거나 통합하는 것으로 이루어진다. 하나의 분야에 사용된 빌딩블록은 다른 분야에 의해 현미경 아래에 놓인다. 한 지리학자는 아프리카의 해안선이 미국의 해안선과 꼭 들어맞는 이유를 대륙이 한때 인접해있었으나 서로 떨어지게 된 다른 판에 안착했다고 말함으로써 설명할지도 모른다. 그 판들이 움직이게 된 연유에 관한 질문은 그것들을 떠미는 마그마의 용승에 호소하는 지질학자들을 지나쳐가게 된다. 마그마가 어떻게 그렇게 뜨거워졌는지에 관해 말하자면, 그들은 지구의 중심 핵과 맨틀에서의 반응을 설명하기 위해 물리학자들을 불러낸다. 과학자들 중 어느 누구도 불필요한 사람은 없다.」

19 ⑤

sustain : 지속하다 per capita : 1인당 fold 겹, 배 spectacularly : 극적으로 velocity : 속도 consistency : 지속성, 일관성 transparency : 투명도 liquidity : 유동성, 현금

☞ ⑤ 작은 차이의 성장률이 오랫동안 지속되어온 결과로 미국이 오늘날의 가장 부유한 경제국이 되었다는 내용으로 볼 때, 두 세기 동안이나 소득성장률을 유지한 지속성(consistency)에 그 핵심이 있다고 할 수 있으므로 ⑤번이 적절하다.

「연간 경제 성장률의 작은 차이조차도, 수십 년 또는 수 세기 동안 지속된다면 결국 경제적 웰빙의 수준에 있어 큰 차이로 이어진다. 예를 들어, 미국의 1인당 국민 총생산은 1820년에서 1998년의 기간 동안 해마다 연간 약 1.7%씩 성장했다. 이것은 생활수준에 있어서 25배의 성장을 초래했으며, 이는 1820년도에 1인당 약 1200불에서 오늘날 1990년 달러로 약 3만 불로 1인당 소득이 증가한 것이다. 미국이 세계에서 가장 부유한 경제국이 되는 핵심은 연간 8퍼센트의 성장을 보이는 중국의 최근 업적과 같은 극적으로 빠른 성장에 있지 않다. 그 핵심은 지속성이며, 이는 미국이 거의 두 세기 동안 소득성장률을 유지했다는 사실이다.」

20 ②

believing-for-a-reason : 믿기지 않는 이유 reasoning : 추론 explicit : 명백한, 노골적인 introspection : 자기반성 self-observation : 자기성찰 relevant : 적절한 conscious : 의식적인 review : 검토, 재고 manifest : 드러내 보이다 demonstration : 입증 contradiction : 반박, 모순

☞ ② 이유에 대한 믿음은 자기반성이나 자기 성찰 없이 이루어질 수 있으며, 이는 의식적인 검토를 할 때, 반드시 드러나는 것이 아니라는 내용으로 보아, "어떤 의식적인 과정의 결과가 될 필요가 전혀 없다"인 ②번이 적절하다.

「이유에 관한 믿음은 어떤 의식적인 과정의 결과일 필요가 전혀 없다. 나는 나의 이웃이 아무도 그를 방문한 적이 없다는 이유로, 친구가 거의 없다고 믿을지도 모른다. 나는 결코 이러한 추론을 나 자신이나, 그 밖의 다른 누구에게도 명백히 해본 적이 없을지도 모른다. "왜 당신은 그가 친구가 거의 없을 거라고 생각하나요?"라고 질문을 한다면, 여전히 나는 어떠한 자기반성이나 자기 성찰 없이 대답할 수 있다. "왜냐면 어떤 누구도 그를 방문한 적이 없으니까요"라고 말이다. 주제가 관련된 상황에 있다는 것이 반드시 추론의 의식적인 검토를 할 때, 반드시 그 자체로 드러나지는 않지만, 입증의 형태 그리고 풍부한 자기 설명의 형태로서, 즉, 사람이 해줄 수 있는 자기 자신의 믿음에 관한 이성적인 설명 같은 것, 그것을 표현하는 능력을 필연적으로 수반한다.」

21 ④

evolutionary : 진화적인 foresight : 선견 intelligent : 지적인 genetic : 유전적 not only A but(also) B : A뿐만 아니라 B 또한 capability : 능력, 역량 superior to : ~보다 뛰어난 indicate : 암시하다 disguise : 위장, 가장하다

☞ ④ 인간 공학이 진화보다 훨씬 우월하며, 진화가 했던 일이라면 인간공학 또한 해낼 수 있을 것이라는 의미의 ④번이 빈칸의 내용으로 적절하다.

「우리는 맹목적인 진화의 과정이 인간 수준의 일반적인 지능을 만들어 낼 수 있다는 것을 안다. 왜냐면 그들은 한때 적어도 그렇게 이미 해봤기 때문이다. 예지력이 있는 진화적 과정, 즉 지적인 인간 프로그래머에 의해 고안되고 유도된 유전적 프로그램은 훨씬 엄청난 효율성으로 비슷한 결과를 낼 수 있어야만 한다. 인간 수준의 인공지능이 이론적으로 가능할 뿐만 아니라 이번 세기 내로 실현 가능하다고 주장하는 몇몇의 철학자들과 과학자들에 의해 이러한 관찰은 이루어졌다. 그 아이디어는 우리가 진화와 지능을 만들어내는 인간 공학의 상대적인 역량을 추정할 수 있다는 생각이며, 인간공학이 몇몇의 분야에서는 이미 진화보다 훨씬 뛰어나며, 남은 영역에서도 머지않아 뛰어나게 될 것 같다는 것을 우리가 알아차릴 수 있다는 것이다. 진화가 지능을 만들어 냈다는 사실은 그러므로 인간공학이 곧 같은 일을 할 수 있을 것이라는 것을 암시한다.」

22 ①

Paris climate agreement : 파리기후협약 as few as : 겨우~, ~뿐 lithium-ion battery : 리튬이온전지 give off : 방출하다 toxic : 유독한 ingredient : 재료, 성분 cobalt : 코발트 finite : 유한의, 한정된 extraction : 뽑아냄, 발췌 depletion : 고갈, 감소 consequence : 결과, 중요성 ratify : (격식)승인하다

☞ ① 전기 자동차의 호황이 가져오는 문제점에 대해서 언급하고 있으며 빈칸 뒷부분에서 유독성 가스와 수질 오염 등의 구체적인 사례를 제시한 것으로 보아, 환경적인 비용이 든다는 내용은 ①번이 적절하다.

「세계에서 전기 자동차의 수는 작년에 2백만 선을 넘어섰으며 국제 에너지 기구는 만약 국가들이 파리 기후 협약 목표치를 충족시킨다면, 2030년까지 전 세계적으로 1억 4천만 대의 차량이 있을 것으로 추산한다. 이 전기 자동차 호황은 지금과 2030년 사이에 재활용이 필요한 소모된 리튬이온배터리 1100만 톤을 남길 수 있다. 그러나 EU에서는 겨우 5%의 리튬이온전지들만이 재활용된다. 이것은 환경적인 비용이 든다. 배터리가 만약 손상될 경우 유독한 가스를 방출하는 위험을 수반할 뿐만 아니라, 리튬이나 코발트와 같은 핵심 성분들은 유한하고, 추출은 수질 오염과 다른 환경적 결과들 사이에서의 고갈을 야기할 수 있다.」

23 ③

electromagnetic : 전자기의 electron : 전자 Interchange : 교환하다 quantum : 양자 macroscopic : 육안으로 보이는, 거시적인 gust : 돌풍 localize : 국한시키다. ~의 위치를 알아내다 mingle : 어울리다, 섞이다 vast : 어마어마한 entity : 실체, 본질 identity : 독자성, 주체성 vector : 벡터, 궤도 ripple : 잔물결, 파문

☞ ③ 거대한 대양 내의 한 방울의 물처럼, 바람 속의 하나의 돌풍과도 같다는 예시를 살펴볼 때, 거대한 실체 속으로 들어가게 되면 전자는 자신만의 독자성이나 주체성을 가지지 못한다는 내용의 ③번이 빈칸의 내용으로 적절하다.

「전자기의 분야는 어느 곳에나 있으며 우주에 존재하는 모든 단일 전자는 그것에 속할 뿐만 아니라 언제 어디서든 다른 어떤 전자와 정확히 동일하다. 그것들 중 두 개를 교환해봐라. 그러면 우주는 알아차리지 못할 것이다. 그것 때문에, 그들이 표현하는 양자 분야 때문에, 어떤 것을 거시적인 물체로 묘사하는 것처럼 전자는 묘사될 수 없다. 그들은 그 분야에 속해 있다. 그들은 거대한 대양의 한 방울의 물처럼, 밤공기의 돌풍처럼, 당신의 그 위치를 알아낼 수 없는 한 방울이나 하나의 돌풍처럼 그것의 일부이다. 하나가 보이지 않는 한, 방울들과 돌풍들은 바람처럼, 대양 그 자체와도 같다. 그들 자신보다 훨씬 더 어마어마한 실체로 섞여 들어간, 그들은 그들 자신의 독자성을 갖지 못한다.」

24 ②

comparison : 비교, 비유 given~ : ~을 고려해볼 때 appropriate : 적절한 reliance : 의존 inherent : 내재의 n the surface : 외견상으로 seem to ~ : 인 것 같다 relate to : ~이해하다 length-of-run : 실행기간 instrumental : 쓸모 있는 indices : 지수 assessment : 평가, 조사

☞ ② 생산비에만 의존하는 것은 전체 산업의 이해에 그렇게 유용하지는 않지만, 비경제학자들이 볼 때, 좀 더 이해하기 명백한 개념이기에 생산비는 한정된 분석적 능력을 가진 도구기라보다는 하나의 목표로 여겨지게 된다는 ②번의 내용이 빈칸에 들어가기 적절하다.

「생산비 개념은 농업경제학의 이해에 그다지 유용하지 않다. 마치 피자 생산 비용이 피자 산업을 이해하는데 매우 유용하지 않은 것처럼 말이다. 농업에 있어서 공동 생산의 본질을 고려해볼 때, 더 적합한 비유는 피자의 생산 비용과 레스토랑 산업의 구조적 이해에 대한 관계이다. 뒤따르는 분석의 내재적인 취약성 때문에 생산 비용에 대한 너무 큰 의존은 위험하다. 즉, 다른 곳에서 더 잘 사용될 수 있는 생산비에 전념하는 자원들, 그리고 그것의 강조로 인해 발생할 수 있는 문제들의 제한된 초점이 그것이다. 표면적으로 볼 때, 생산비는 경제학적 분석에 있어서 유용하고 기본적인 요소인 것 같다. 더욱이, 공급함수, 투입 수요함수, 실행 기간과 다른 중요한 사안들은 덜 명백한 개념인 반면에, 비경제학자들은 생산비의 개념을 잘 이해한다. 그 결과 생산비는 종종 한정된 분석적 능력을 가진 도구기라보다는 하나의 목표로 여겨지게 된다.」

25 ①

infant : 유아의, 초기의 wean : 젖을 떼다 in contrast 대조적으로 in contact with : ~과 접촉하는 hunter-gatherer : 수렵 채집인 nourish : 영양분을 공급하다 demographic : 인구 통계의

☞ ① 젖을 떼는 나이와 구할 수 있는 음식사이의 관계

「미국에서 어머니에 의해 조금이라도 양육된 유아의 비율과, 그러한 양육된 유아가 젖을 떼는 나이는 20세기의 상당 부분을 통해 감소했다. 예를 들어, 1970년대까지 미국 어린이의 5 %만이 6개월의 나이에 양육을 받았다. 대조적으로, 농부들과 접촉하지 않고 경작된 식품에 접근하지 않은 수렵 채집인 중에서의 유아는 6개월을 훨씬 넘게 양육을 받는다. 왜냐면 그들에게 이용 가능한 적절한 유아용 음식은 어머니의 우유뿐이기 때문이다. 그들은 젖소의 우유, 아기용 분유, 부드러운 음식 대체품에 접근할 수 없다. 7개 이상의 수렵채집인 집단에서 젖을 떼는 평균화된 나이는 약 3살이며, 이는 아이들이 충분히 단단한 음식을 씹어서 스스로 영양을 공급을 마침내 할 수 있게 되는 나이이다.」

26 ④

default : 부도, 불이행, 디폴트 shoot up : 급증하다 infrastructure : 사회기반시설 sacrosanct : 신성불가침의 backlog : 밀린 일, 잔고 accumulate : 축적하다 casualty : 피해자 rescue : 구조하다 pitfall : 위험 unwarranted : 부당한, 불필요한, 부적절한

☞ ④ 중국 채권시장에 관한 불필요한 걱정

「중국 채권시장이 이렇게 폭풍우가 몰아치는 봄을 맞이하기는 처음이었다. 이미 2분기에 디폴트 기록을 달성했다. 기업에 대한 신용 비용은 급증했다. 심지어 사회기반시설에 투자하는 국영 기업들, 이전에 신성불가침의 영역이던 회사들조차도 위험으로 간주된다. 무엇이 잘못되었을까? 질문에 대한 답은 전혀 없다.(잘못된 것이 없다) 디폴트는 중국에 있어서 발전이며, 이는 누적된 부채의 잔고를 정리할 필요가 있는 것이다. 올해 피해자는 채권시장의 0.1%에 불과하다. 하지만 투자자들이 정부가 어려움에 빠진 큰 회사를 구조할 것이라고 가정할 때 그것은 여전히 최근의 과거에 대한 향상(호전)이다.」

27 ②

deficiency : 부족   innate : 타고난   persistent : 지속하는   provided that : 만약 ~한다면, ~을 전제로
plasticity : 가소성   masterpieces : 걸작   assimilate : 동화하다   superiority : 우월, 우수   expeditious :
급속한, 신속한   qualitative : 질적인, 정성의   undertaking : 사업/ suppress : 억압하다, 공표하지 않다
quantity : 양, 수량, 양적인

☞ ② (A)creates (B)speed

「타고난 능력의 결점은 지속적인 노력과 집중을 통해 보완될 수 있다. 노력은 재능을 대신하는 것이거나, 더 좋게는, 그것이
재능을 만들어낸다고 누군가는 말할 수도 있다. 자신의 능력을 향상시키기로 확고하게 결심한 그는 그렇게 할 것이며, 이는
신경 세포의 가소성이 크게 감소하는 기간 동안 교육이 너무 늦게 시작되지 않는다는 것을 전제로 그렇게 할 것이다. 걸작을
읽고 생각하는 것이 그 작품을 창조한 많은 기술을 동화하게 해준다는 것을 잊지 마라. 물론 저자의 통찰력, 지도 원칙, 심지
어 스타일까지 결론 그 이상을 넘어 확장하게 된다면 말이다. 우리가 위대하고 특별한 재능이라고 부르는 것은 보통 질적인
것이라기보다는 신속한 우월성을 의미한다. 그러나 과학적 사업에서 예술가처럼 과학자들은 생산 속도가 아니라 그들이 생산
한 것의 품질에 의해 판단되기 때문에 느린 것이 빠른 속도만큼 유용하다는 것이 입증된다.」

28 ①

embody : 구현하다   expertise : 전문지식   prestige : 명성   autonomy : 자율   dignity : 존엄   incompatible
: 양립할 수 없는, 모순된   struggle : 분투하다   purge A of B : A에게서 B를 제거하다. 없애다   censor : 검열관,
검열하다   ideologue 몽상가, 특정이데올로기 신봉자   bureaucracy : 관료주의, 관료   impediment : 장애
bluntly : 직설적으로   resistance : 저항   congruence : 조화   antipathy : 반감   affinity : 친밀   aspiration :
열망

☞ ① (A)resistance (B) antipathy

「직업은 전문 지식, 명성, 자율성, 존엄성 및 정규 학습, 정치와 종종 양립할 수 없는 가치를 구현한다. 그들 자신에게서 정치를
근절하기 위한 공공 직업의 역사적 투쟁, 예를 들어 도시 관리자 대 정치꾼들; 사서 대 무지한 검열관; 환경 과학자들 대
정치적 몽상가들 ; 모두는 이러한 저항을 반영한다. 전문가들은 마찬가지로 관료주의를 좋아하지 않는데, 이는(관료주의는)
그들이(전문가들이) 종종 자신의 전문 분야의 자유로운 행사에 장애로 여기는 것이다. 연방 정부에서 일하는 과학자 및 엔지
니어와 같은 특정 종류의 전문화된 전문가들은 연방 행정관보다 업무에 대한 만족도가 훨씬 낮다. 솔직하게 말해서, 공공
서비스를 선택하는 전문가는 종종 그것의 두 가지 주요 특징: 정치와 관료주의라는 특징에 대한 반감을 극복해야 한다.」

29 ②

at best : 기껏해야, 잘해야   at worst : 최악의 경우에, 아무리 나빠도/ distraction : 주의 산만, 혼란/
corrosive : 부식하는, 좀먹는   unruly : 감당하기 어려운, 사나운   deviant : 벗어난, 비정상인/ attest : ~을
입증하다   above all : 무엇보다   provisional 임시의   laceration : 찢기, 괴롭히기   disdain : 경멸하다
diversion : 전환   enlightenment : 계몽   probing : 속을 캐 보는, 철저한   stamp : 짓밟다

☞ 호기심이 다루기 어려운 것임을 제시문에서 설명한 뒤 (B)가 그 내용을 이어받아 호기심의 특성에 대해서
설명하고 있다. 이러한 호기심의 특성을 예시를 들어 나열한 다음 (A)에서 이를 요약한 뒤, (C)에서 이러
한 호기심의 진가를 알게 된 사회가 이를 대응하는 방식을 보여 주고 있으므로, 글의 순서는 B-A-C 순으
로 오는 것이 적절하다.

「대부분의 서양 역사에서, 호기심은 기껏해야 주의 산만이며, 최악의 경우 영혼과 사회를 좀먹는 독약이다. 이것에 대한 이유가 있다. 호기심은 다루기 어려운 것이다.

(B) 그것은 규칙은 좋아하지 않는다. 적어도 모든 규칙은 잠정적이라고 가정하며, 아무도 아직 물어볼 생각을 하지 않은 현명한 질문을 상하게 할 수 있다. 그것은 승인된 경로를 경멸하고, 전환, 계획되지 않은 여행, 충동적인 좌회전을 선호한다.

(A) 요약하자면, 호기심은 일탈적이다. 그것을 추구하는 것은 어느 시점에 당신을 권위와 충돌하게 한다. 갈릴레오에서 찰스 다윈, 스티브 잡스까지 모든 이들이 입증했던 것처럼 말이다. 무엇보다 질서를 중시하는 사회는 호기심을 억누르려고 노력할 것이다.

(C) 그러나 진보, 혁신, 창의성을 믿는 사회는 사람들의 탐구하는 마음이 그것의 가장 가치 있는 자산을 구성함을 인정하면서 그것을 육성할 것이다. 계몽주의 시대까지 유럽 사회는 그들의 미래가 호기심에 놓여있다는 것을 알고 그들을 짓밟기 보다는 속을 캐는 질문들을 격려했다.」

30 ⑤

drone : 드론, 무인 비행기 maintenance : 유지, 관리 autonomously : 자율적인 operative : 정보원, 숙련자 preprogrammed : 미리 정해진, 미리 장치된 automatically : 자동적으로, 반드시 remotely : 멀리서, 간접적으로 aspire : 열망하다 implication : 의미, 영향

☞ ⑤ 제시문에서 드론에 필요한 것들을 나열하고 있으며 이를 (C)에서 이어받으며 말미에 새로운 용어인 "drone-in-a-box."이 제시된다. 이 용어를 정의하는 (B)가 바로 다음에 나오는 것이 적절하며, 이에 따른 드론의 역할을 (A)에서 설명하는 순서로 배치해야 한다. 따라서 글의 순서는 C-B-A 순으로 오는 것이 적절하다.

「대부분의 기존 드론은 숙련된 기사에 의해 비행될 필요가 있다. 사실, 법은 종종 이것을 요구한다. 또한 드론은 기술적인 지원과 유지 보수가 필요하다.

(C) 그리고 그들을 운영하는 사람들은 그들이 무엇을 하고 있는지에 대한 법적 및 안전성 함의를 이해하도록 권고된다. 이런 이유로 '무인상자'의 매력이 있다.

(B) 이것은 연관 걱정 없이 드론의 이점을 판매하기를 열망하는 여러 회사의 제공품에 적용되는 용어이다. 문제의 상자는 드론을 수용하고, 그것을 재충전하고, 그것이 수집한 데이터를 고객에게 전송하는 기지국이다.

(A) 드론은 미리 정해진 일정에 따라 자율적으로 비행할 수 있으며, 방문하도록 명령을 받은 지점까지 자동으로 그것의 경로를 찾거나, 행성의 어느 곳에서나 통제 센터에서 시스템을 공급하는 회사의 숙련자에 의해 원격으로 조종될 수 있다.」

31 ③

lender : 빌려주는 자, 은행 vampire : 흡혈귀, 함정 congregate : ~을 모으다 mammal : 포유류 incision : 절개, 벤 상처(자국) suck : 빨아먹다 cope with : 대처하다 loan : 대출하다 alleviate : 완화하다 regurgitate : 역류시키다, 게우다, 토하다 debtor : 채무자 reciprocate : ~에 보답하다, ~을 교환하다 favour : 호의, 친절

☞ ③ 흡혈박쥐의 피를 매개로 한 대출 관계에 관한 글이다. ③번은 앞뒤 문장에서 나오는 loan이라는 동일한 단어의 사용을 통해 오답을 유도했다. 하지만 전체적인 글은 진화적인 내용과 전혀 관계가 없으므로 ③번은 글의 전체 흐름에 맞지 않다.

「많은 동물들이 효과적으로 협력하고, 몇몇 동물들은 심지어 대출을 해주기도 한다. 자연에서 가장 유명한 대출 기관은 흡혈귀 박쥐이다. 이 박쥐들은 수천 개의 동굴 내부에 모여 매일 밤 먹이를 찾기 위해 날아다닌다. 잠자는 새나 부주의한 포유류를 발견하면, 그들은 그들에 피부에 작은 절개를 내고, 그것의 피를 빨아먹는다. ① 하지만 모든 흡혈귀 박쥐가 매일 밤 희생자를 찾는 것은 아니다. ② 그들의 삶의 불확실성에 대처하기 위해, 흡혈귀들은 피를 서로에게 빌려준다. ③ (그러나 흡혈귀들은 진화적인 압박을 완화하고자 대출을 하지 않는다.) ④ 먹이를 찾는 데 실패한 흡혈귀들은 집에 돌아와 좀 더 운 좋은 친구가 훔친 피를 게워내도록 요청할 것이다. ⑤ 흡혈귀들은 그들이 피를 빌려준 녀석을 매우 잘 기억하여, 그래서 훗날 친구가 배고 픈 채로 집에 돌아오면, 그는 그 호의를 보답할 빚진 녀석에게 다가갈 것이다.」

32 ④

A is no more B than C is D : A가 B 아닌 것은 C가 D 아닌 것과 같다   property : 특성   rustish : 녹물색의, 녹슨 느낌   the same is true of : ~도 마찬가지다   bounce off : 반사시키다   neuron : 뉴런, 신경 단위

☞ ④ 주어진 문장을 흐름에 맞게 적절한 위치에 삽입하는 문제이다. 주어진 문장에서 녹슨 것과 물의 관계에 대한 비유를 활용하여 풀과 녹색의 관계를 설명하고 있다. 따라서 인간의 인식도 마찬가지로 녹색을 풀의 속성이 아닌 것으로 봐야 한다는 ④번의 자리가 적절하다.

「당신이 철 한 조각이라고 상상해봐라. 그래서 물 한 방울이 생길 때 당신은 평소처럼 아무것도 하지 않고 앉아 있다. 물에 대한 당신의 인식은 어떠한가? 물론 철근은 뇌가 없고, 전혀 인식을 갖지 못할 것이다. 하지만 그 불편한 사실을 무시하고, 철근이 물을 감지할 수 있다면 어떤 기분이 들지 상상해보라. 한 조각의 철의 관점에서 볼 때, 물은 그 무엇보다 녹이 슬게 하는 것이다. 이제 인간으로서의 관점으로 돌아가라. 녹슨 것이 실제로 물 그 자체의 속성이 아니라 그것(물)이 철과 반응하는 방식의 속성임을 알고 있다. 인간의 인식도 마찬가지다. (당신이 풀을 녹색으로 볼 때, 녹슨 것이 물의 속성이 아니듯이 녹색은 풀의 속성이 아니다.) 녹색은 풀에서 튀어나오는 빛이 뇌의 뉴런과 반응할 때 생기는 경험이다. 녹이 철분 조각에 들어 있는 것처럼 녹색은 우리 안에 있다.」

33 ①

Brussels : 브뤼셀(벨기에의 수도)   distressing : 비참한, 비통한   Belgium : 벨기에   come on board : 탑승하다, 귀선하다   forewarn : 미리 주의하다   anxiety : 불안, 걱정   unbearable : 견딜 수 없는   undisturbed 방해받지 않은, 평온한/ relieved : 안도한   discouraged : 낙담한   outrage : 격분   irritated : 화난, 안달이 난   terrified : 오싹한, 겁먹은   disappointed : 실망한

☞ ① nervous → relieved

기차에서 숨긴 반지를 들킬까 긴장되고 불안해했지만(nervous), 무사히 검사가 끝나자 안도하며 (relieved) 한숨을 내쉬었다는 내용으로 보아 심경은 nervous → relieved로 바뀌었다.

「나는 1939년 4월에 기차로 브뤼셀을 향해 떠났다. 내가 단지 아홉 살 때, 부모님을 두고 떠나는 것은 몹시 괴로웠다. 내가 독일과 벨기에 사이의 국경에 다다랐을 때, 기차는 잠시 멈추었고 독일 세관원들이 승선했다. 그들은 내가 가진 보석이나 다른 귀중품을 보여 달라고 요구했다. 나는 나와 함께 여행하는 젊은 여자에 의해 이러한 요청에 대해 미리 경고를 받았다. 그래서 나는 주머니에 나의 이니셜이 적힌 작은 금반지를 숨겨두었으며, 그것은 일곱 번째 생일에 선물로 받은 것이었다. 그들이 기차에 올라섰을 때, 나치 장교들의 출현으로 불안은 거의 참을 수 없을 정도로 높아졌고, 나는 그들이 반지를 발견할까 두려웠다. 다행히도 그들은 내게 거의 관심을 기울이지 않았고, 내가 방해받지 않은 채로 가게 해주었다. 그들의 발소리가 점점 희미해짐에 따라, 조용한 한숨이 입에서 나왔다.」

34   35

extract : 추출하다   mastery : 숙달, 전문 기술   pitch : 던지다. 투구   instant : 즉각, 순간, 찰나   decipher : 판독하다, 해독하다, 판독   curveball : 커브, 속임수   changeup : 체인지업, 변화구   wind up : 투구의 예비동작   subtle : 미묘한   seam : 솔기, 이음매   winnow : 키질하다, 골라내다   extraneous : 관계없는   variation : 변화, 변형   stance : 자세/ distinct : 뚜렷한, 다른, 독특한   sacrifice : 희생하다   move ahead : 전진하다   cull out : 가려내다   all but : 거의, ~외에 모두   chance of ~ing : ~할 가능성   Split-Second : 순간의, 아주 찰나의

「새로운 자료에서 핵심 아이디어를 추출하여 정신적 모델로 구성하고 기존 지식에 이 모델을 연결하는 법을 배우는 사람들은 복잡한 숙달을 배우는 데 있어 장점이 있음을 보여준다. 정신적 모델은 어떤 외부적 현실의 정신적인 표현이다. 투구를 기다리는 야구 타자를 생각해 보아라. 그는 그것이 곡선 볼인지, 변화구인지, 아니면 그밖에 다른 것인지 아닌지를 해독하는데 찰나도 걸리지 않는다. 어떻게 그는 그럴 수 있는가? 투수가 예비동작을 하는 방식, 던지는 방식, 공의 솔기 회전 등 몇 가지 미묘한 신호가 도움이 된다. 훌륭한 타자는 모든 관계없는 지각적인 산만함을 골라내고, 투구에서의 이러한 변화만을 보고, 연습을 통해 각 종류의 투구에 대한 다른 신호

세트를 기반으로 뚜렷한 정신 모델을 형성한다. 그는 볼의 가장 위에 머물러 있기 위해서, 타격하는 자세, 스트라이크 존 및 스윙에 관해 그가 알고 있는 것과 이 모델을 연결한다. 이것들은 그가 선수 포지션에 따른 정신 모델과 연결하는 것이다. 그가 1위와 2위를 차지한 사람을 (주자로) 두었다면, 아마도 그는 주자를 전진시키기 위해 희생할 것이다. 그는 각 종류의 투구를 식별하고 응답하는 가장 중요한 요소를 제외한 모든 요소를 골라내고, 그 학습으로 정신적 모델을 구성하고, 이 복잡한 게임의 다른 필수 요소에 대한 숙달에 그러한 모델을 연결했기 때문에, 전문가 플레이어는 그가 플레이트에 올라갈 때마다 직면하는 거대하고 변화될 수 있는 정보를 이해할 수 없는 경험이 적은 선수보다 득점을 올릴 확률이 더 높다.」

34 ①

☞ ① Split-Second Decision Made Easy (찰나의 결정이 쉽게 만든다)

35 ③

☞ ③ previous knowledge (이전 지식)

주요한 아이디어를 바탕으로 정신적 모델을 만들고, 그가 알고 있는 것과 이 모델을 연결함으로써 우위를 지니게 된다는 글의 핵심 내용을 이해한다면 풀어낼 수 있는 문제이다. 정신적 모델과 연결하는 것은 바로 그가 이미 알고 있는 지식, 즉 ③ previous knowledge임을 알 수 있다.

36 37

scarcely : 거의, 겨우, 가까스로 vernacular : 사투리, 지방어, 자국어 naturally : 당연히, 본래 take exception to : ~에 반대하다 usage : 활용, 실태 relentlessly : 끈질기게 wage : 전쟁하다, 벌어지다 in full swing 한창 진행 중인 hundredth : 백 번째의/ strike : 치다. 때리다. 공격하다 reiterate : 되풀이하다 contentment : 만족 encapsulate : 요약 하다 neatly : 깔끔하게 collectively 전체적으로, 총괄하여 term : 칭하다, 일컫다 significantly : 크게 현저히

36 ④

☞ ④ Standard vs Non-standard English : Doesn't It Matter?

표준영어 대 비표준영어 : 그것이 중요한가요?

37. ③

☞ ③ 자신의 영어에 대해 지적하는 브렉부인의 말을 납득하지 못한 상태이므로 노먼은 만족(contentment)한 게 아니라 불만족(discontent)한 모습을 보였다. 따라서 ③번의 contentment는 discontent로 바꿔야한다.

「내가 자란 서부 뉴욕 주에서는, 사실 세계의 영어권 지역의 상당 부분에서 그렇듯이, 그 형태는 모국어에 거의 존재하지 않는 다. 내가 어디 출신인지는 거의 모든 사람이 중요하지 않으며, 그 사람은 그런 게 필요 없다고 말한다. 당연하게도, 고등학교 영어 선생님인 브렉 부인은 이러한 실태에 강하게 반대하였다. 그녀는 그것에 대한 자신의 작은 전쟁을 끊임없이 벌였다. 나는 그녀의 캠페인이 한창 진행 중인 어느 날 수업에 앉아 있었던 것이 잘 기억난다. 그날 나의 반 친구 노먼이 700번째로 "그는 그걸 몰라요(don't)"와 같은 어떤 것을 듣고 그녀는 공격하기로 결심했다. "노먼, 그는 그것을 몰라(doesn't) 란다" 노먼이 대답했다. "네, 맞아요." "그는..(don't)" 브렉 부인이 흥미로운 표정을 지으며 되풀이해서 말했다. "don't 가 아니란다, 노먼". "하 지만…… 하지만……." 노먼의 얼굴에 불만족한 모습이 나타났다. "하지만 그것은 올바르게 들리지 않아요(don't)!". 이 작은 에피소드는 우리가 표준 영어라고 부르는 특정 형태의 영어와 우리가 통틀어 비표준 영어라고 칭하는 것 들이 있는 모든 영어의 다른 종류 사이의 대조를 아주 깔끔하게 요약한다. 대다수의 영어 사용자는 표준 영어와 항상 상당히 다르고, 때때로 극적으로 다른 현지 모국어 형태의 영어를 배우고 말하면서 자란다.」

induce : 유발하다　selection : 선발, 선택된 것　soothing : 달래는, 진정하는　instill : 스며들게 하다　despondency 낙심　duration : 지속기간　musical recording : 음반　questionnaire : 설문지　dismiss : 해산시키다　specify : 명시하다　if so : 만일 그렇다면/ willingness : 의지　vary : 달라지다/ be the case : 사실이 그러하다　adverse : 부정적인

38　④

☞ ④ Types of music influenced people's willingness to help.
음악의 유형(장르)은 돕고자 하는 사람들의 의지에 영향을 끼친다.

39　②

☞ 음악의 유형에 따라 피실험자들의 도울 의지가 달라졌는지를 알아보려는 테스트였음을 밝힌 후 빈칸 부분에 들어갈 테스트의 효과를 추론하는 문제이다. 빈칸의 뒷부분에 나온 멘델스존과 콜트레인 음악을 들은 그룹이 각기 다른 반응을 보였음을 알 수 있으며, 이로 인해 그 실험이 실제 다른 결과를 가져왔음을 인정하는 ② proved to be the case(사실로 판명되었다)가 적절한 정답이다.

「그 음악은 좋은 기분을 유발함으로써 협력과 도움을 증가시킬 수 있다. Rona Fried와 Leonard Berkowitz는 위스콘신 대학교에서 학생들과 함께 연구에 착수했다. 그들은 그들을 4개의 그룹으로 나누고 그들 중 3그룹에 다양한 음악작품을 연주하여 다양한 분위기를 유도했다. 멘델스존의 'Songs Without Words'에서 두 가지 엄선된 모음이 한 그룹에 진정시키는 분위기를 심어주기 위해 선택되었다. 듀크 엘링턴의 'One O'Clock Jump'는 다른 그룹에서 흥분감을 불러일으키기 위해 연주되었다. 존 콜트레인의 'Meditations'은 세 번째 집단에서 슬픔과 낙담의 부정적인 감정을 주입하는 데 사용되었다. 네 번째 통제 그룹은 음반의(연주시간) 7분 내내 침묵 속에 앉아있었다. 학생들은 음악을 듣기 전후에 기분에 관한 설문지를 작성해야 했으며, 이것을 그들의 감정에 상당한 차이를 음악이 만들어 냈다는 것을 확인했다. 이로 인해 음악이 자신의 감정에 중요한 차이를 낳았다. 그들이 해산되기 직전에 실험자들은 자원봉사자들에게 15분에서 2시간 사이의 시간을 필요로 하는 전혀 무관한 다른 실험을 도와달라고 요청했다. 그들은 그들이 도울 준비가 되어있는지를 명시하기 위해 양식을 완성하도록 요청 받았다. 그리고 만약 그렇다면 (도울) 총 시간의 양도 함께 말이다. 물론 이것은 실험자가 그들이 들었던 음악의 유형에 따라 도움을 주려는 의지에 있어서 네 그룹이 달라졌는지를 알아내기를 원했던 도움에 관한 테스트였다. 이것은 사실로 판명되었다. 두 번째 실험을 도울 의지와, 그들이 제공할 준비가 되어 있는 시간의 길이를 측정했을 때, 멘델스존의 작품을 들은 사람들이 가장 도움이 되는 것으로 나타났다. 두 가지 측정 모두에서 부정적인 감정을 이끄는 콜트레인의 음악을 들은 학생들은 도움이 될 의사가 가장 적었다.」

toolmaker : 연장 제작자 insignificant : 미미한 surrounding : 둘러싸는 other than : ~외에 주변의 dominate : ~을 지배하다, 장악하다 elusive : 파악하기 어려운 correlation : 상관관계 aptitudes : 재능 no matter how : 아무리~해도 flunk : 낙제하다 numerous 수많은, 다양한 push up the daisies : 죽어서 묻혀있다 spear : 창, 작살 dexterous : 솜씨 좋은 conquest : 정복, 승리 nimble : 날렵한, 민첩한 chimp : 침팬지 crafty : 교활한 deft : 솜씨 좋은 dexterity : 재주 largescale : 대규모의, 광범한

「지능의 정의에 따르면, 100만 년 전 인류는 세계의 챔피언 도구 제작자였을 뿐만 아니라 이미 가장 지능이 높은 동물이었지만, 그러나 주변 생태계에 영향을 거의 미치지 못하는 하찮은 생명체인 채로 있었다. 그들은 지능과 도구 제작 이외의 핵심 기능이 분명히 부족했다. 아마도 인류는 결국은 지구를 지배하게 되었는데, 그것은 어떤 파악하기 어려운 세 번째 핵심 요소 때문이 아니라, 단지 훨씬 높은 지능과 훨씬 나은 도구 제작 능력의 진화 때문인가? 그것은 그런 것 같지 않은데, 왜냐면 우리가 역사적 기록을 검토할 때, 우리는 인간 개인의 지능 및 도구 제작 능력과 전체로서의 우리의 종의 능력 사이의 직접적인 상관관계를 보지 않기 때문이다. 2만 년 전, 평균적인 사피엔스는 오늘날의 평균적인 사피엔스보다 더 높은 지능과 더 나은 도구 제작 능력을 가졌다. 현대 학교와 고용주들은 때때로 우리의 재능을 테스트할 수 있지만, 아무리 안 좋더라도 복지국가는 항상 우리의 기본적인 필요를 보장한다. 석기시대에 자연 선택은 매일 매 순간마다 당신을 시험했고, 그리고 만약 당신의 그것의 무수한 시험에서 낙제하면, 당신은 즉시 데이지 꽃을 들어 올릴 것이다.(죽어서 묻혀있을 것이다) 그러나 우리의 석기시대 조상들의 뛰어난 도구 제작 능력과 날카로운 정신과 훨씬 더 예리한 감각에도 불구하고, 2만 년 전 인류는 오늘날보다 훨씬 약했다.

그 2만 년 동안 인류는 돌로 깎은 창으로 매머드를 사냥하는 것에서 우주선으로 태양계를 탐험하는 것으로 옮겨 갔으며 이는 좀 더 솜씨 좋은 손이나 더 큰 머리의 진화 덕분이 아니었다. 대신, 우리가 세상을 정복하는 데 중요한 요소는 많은 인간들 서로 연결하는 능력이었다. 오늘날 인간은 지구를 완전히 지배하고 있는데, 이는 개별 인간이 침팬지나 늑대보다 훨씬 영리하고 손재주가 있는 손가락을 가졌기 때문이 아니라, 호모 사피엔스가 지구상에서 수없이 유연하게 협력을 할 수 있는 유일한 종이기 때문이다. 지능과 도구 제작 또한 명백하게 매우 중요했다. 그러나 만약 인간이 수없이 유연하게 협력하는 법을 배우지 못했다면, 우리의 교활한 두뇌와 솜씨 좋은 손은 여전히 우라늄 원자가 아닌 부싯돌을 쪼개고 있을 것이다.

40 ②

☞ ② 밑줄 친 were pushing up the daisies in no time.(즉시 데이지 꽃을 밀어 올리다)라는 말은 문맥상 살아남지 못하고 죽었을 것이다라는 내용으로 추론이 가능하다. 죽어서 무덤 위에 핀 야생 꽃 중 하나인 데이지 꽃을 들어 올린다는 의미이다. 따라서 정답은 ②번인 would die soon이 정답이다.

41 ⑤

☞ ⑤ 유연하게 협력하는 법을 배우지 못했다면 2만년 전의 사피엔스보다 못한 도구제작능력과 손재주를 갖고 있는 우리는 그 당시에 머물러 있을것이라는 추론이 가능하므로 정답은 ⑤"splitting flint stones rather than uranium atoms 우라늄 원자가 아닌 부싯돌을 쪼개고 있을 것이다"라는 내용이 빈칸으로 오기에 적절하다

42 ①

☞ ① (C)dexterity (D)domination

It is not higher intelligence or better dexterity, but largescale, flexible cooperation abilities which played a key role in Homo sapiens' domination of the world.

호모 사피엔스의 세계 지배에서 핵심적인 역할을 한 것은 그것의 더 높은 지능이나 더 나은 재주가 아니라, 대대적인 유연한 협동 능력이다.

43 45

childlike : 어린애 같은 in perspective : 올바른 균형으로 be weighed down : 짓눌리다 relate: ~에 대해 이야기하다 instinctively : 본능적으로, 직관적으로 melt away : 차츰 사라지다 enthusiasm : 열정, 열광 celebration : 축하행사 restless : 불안한, 쉬지 않는 midst : 한가운데 commotion : 동요, 소란 insist on : 주장하다 charge down : 몸으로 막다 throw oneself : 몸을 던지다 flash across : 퍼뜩 떠오르다 include : 포함하다, 함유하다

「(A) 어린아이 같은 세계관은 자주 성인의 삶을 넓은 관점에서 보게 만들 수 있다는 것을 당신은 알고 있는가? 아이들의 순수한 관점은 어른들이 그들의 문제로 인해 그렇게 짓눌리지 않도록 도울 수 있다. 탁아소의 책임자인 낸시 크레이버는 아이의 관점이 어떻게 큰 문제를 작은 문제로 바꾸는 데 도움이 되었는지에 대한 다음 이야기를 들려준다. 그것은 센터의 연례 다문화 저녁 식사에서 있었던 일인데, 이는 부모, 자녀 및 직원이 그들의 다양성과 함께 잘 일할 수 있는 능력을 축하하는 기회로 마련된 것이었다.

(C) 지난해의 축하 행사는 그녀가 마치 새로운 책임자로 고용된 것처럼 낸시에게 매우 어려운 일이었다. 올해 그녀는 안심하고 저녁 식사에 참여할 수 있도록 일찌감치 계획을 세웠다. 처음에는 단지 사소한 일들이 잘못되었다. 그리고 나서 누군가가 저녁 식사 후 프레젠테이션에 사용될 예정이었던 슬라이드 프로젝터를 떨어뜨렸다. 바로 그 저녁 식사가 끝났을 때, 아이들을 다른 곳으로 데려가 놀게 하려고 고용된 여자가 나타나지 않았다. 아이들은 쉬지 않고 뛰어다니기 시작했다.

(D) 이러한 모든 소동이 벌어지는 가운데, 한 노인은 주차장에서 그의 차를 막고 있는 차를 옮기라고 어떤 이에게 주장했다. 체온과 함께 긴장감이 높아진, 낸시는 그가 주차장에서 빠져나가도록 돕기 위해 갔다. 그녀가 막 건물로 돌아가는 순간, 어린아이 하나가 계단을 몸으로 막고 그녀에게 몸을 던졌다. 아이가 공중을 날아가고 있을 때 낸시의 머릿속에 퍼뜩 떠오르는 이미지에는 다친 아이, 충격을 받은 부모, 그리고 "거봐. 그녀는 우리 아이들을 통제하거나 심지어 보호할 수도 없어!"라고 사람들이 말하는 것이 포함되어 있었다.

(B) 그녀가 본능적으로 팔을 뻗었을 때, 그녀는 그 어린아이를 잡았을 뿐만 아니라 웃음과 흥분 또한 붙잡았다. 그 즉시, 그러한 첫 번째 끔찍한 이미지들이 녹아내렸다. 그녀를 흔들면서, 아이의 열정으로 낸시는 이것이 축하 행사라는 것이 떠올랐다. 그녀의 웃음과 놀이는 상황을 고치지는 못했지만, 그러나 그것은 낸시의 관점을 바꾸었다. 그리고 그 저녁은 그녀와 주변 사람들을 위해 계속해서 더욱 잘 진행되었다.」

43 ③

③ C-D-B

44 ③

③ C

☞ (C)의 그녀는 낸시가 잡은 어린아이를 의미하며, 나머지는 모두 낸시를 지칭하므로 정답은 ③번이다.

45 ③

☞ ③ She became the director three years ago. (그녀는 3년 전에 책임자가 되었다)
그녀가 언제 책임자가 되었는지 이 글에서는 알 수 없다.

01 ②

procrastination : 지연 slipshod : 대충 하는 inadequate : 불충분한 properly : 적절하게 hastiness : 조급함 postponement : 지연, 연기 spontaneity : 자발성 concern : 염려, 걱정, 관심 exaggeration : 과장

☞ 지연은 일을 적절하게 완수하기 위한 시간이 충분치 않기 때문에 중요한 업무나 책임이 행해지지 않은채 남겨지거나 대충하는 방식으로 완성되면 당신의 직장 생활에 주요한 문제가 된다.

02 ⑤

currency : 통화 plummet : 수직으로 떨어지다 boom : 폭등하다 bounce : 튀다 get stuck : 꼼짝 못하다

☞ 전 세계적인 금융 위기는 1997년 후반기에 시작되었는데, 그때 여러 개의 아시아 경제의 통화 가치가 폭락했다.

03 ①

weave : (이야기 등을) 엮다 quotation : 인용 deftly : 솜씨 좋게 fabric : 직물, 구조 prose : 산문 abjure : 포기하다 paraphrase : 다른 말로 바꾸어 표현하다

☞ 만약 당신이 인용구를 솜씨 좋게 당신의 산문 구조에 엮을 수 없다면, 그것들을 완전히 포기하고 대신에 다른 말로 바꾸어 표현해라.

04 ①

rudimentary : 가장 기초적인 optimal : 최적의 abstract : 추상적인

「개인용 컴퓨터의 폭발적인 증가는 사용자에게 더 똑똑하고 더 반응적인 응용프로그램들을 개발하는 것을 가능하게 만들고 있다. 철자나 문법의 오류를 확인해주는 검색 프로그램을 사용하는 누구든지 이러한 종류의 응용프로그램을 아주 기초적인 수준에서 경험한다.」

05 ⑤

tenacious : 오래 지속되는 arbitrary : 임의로 reliable : 믿을만한 graphic : 생생한 persistent : 지속적인

「구어를 다소 익숙하게 생각하는 이유 중 하나는 지금까지 그것들이 매우 오래 지속된 것이 입증되었기 때문이다. 중국어 체계는 3000년 이상에 거의 바뀌지 않았고, 현대 그리스어는 오랫동안 사용되어온 알파벳으로 쓰여진다.」

06 ④

fall back : 후퇴하다 haphazardly : 되는대로 covertly : 은밀하게 explicitly : 명백하게 randomly : 임의로 precisely : 정확하게

「결정을 하는데 있어서 명확한 공식이 부족하기 때문에, 우리는 무엇을 할지 결정하기 위해 익숙하고, 편한 방식으로 후퇴한다. 결과적으로, 우리는 되는대로 우리의 목표들을 뒷받침하지 않는 접근을 선택한다.」

07 ④

☞ ① "at which"는 "전치사 + 관계대명사" 구조로서 뒤에 구조가 완전 구조가 나와야 한다. "European ~ archaeology"는 완전구조이므로 어법상 옳다.

② "became transformed"는 "be transformed"와 같은 형태로서 수동을 의미한다. 주어인 "the collecting"이 변형된 것이므로 어법상 옳다.

③ "result from"은 "~로부터 기인하다"라는 의미로 선행사인 "the multi-volume publication"이 "expedition"으로부터 기인한 것이기 때문에 어법상 옳다.

④ 문맥상 "they"는 "Description del' Egyptek"을 의미하기 때문에 단수를 의미하는 "it"이 되어야 한다.

⑤ 뒤에 목적어 "the first real assessment of ancient Egypt"가 있기 때문에 능동을 의미하는 "providing"은 어법상 옳다.

08 ⑤

☞ ① "ha"는 면적의 단위를 의미하는, 명사 hectare의 약어 이다. ha 앞에 오는 350 million은 "100만의"를 의미하는 형용사이다. 복수를 의미하는 "millions"의 형태가 올 수 없으며, "million"이 어법상 옳다.

② "about half the global total"은 "~중에 절반"을 의미하는 형태로서 half 뒤에 of가 생략되었다. 이때 half는 대명사로 쓰였으며, 앞에 있는 about은 대략이라는 의미이다. 어법상 옳다.

③ "worst"는 "bad"의 최상급 표현으로서 어법상 옳다.

④ "As"는 문맥상 이유를 나타내는 접속사로서 어법상 옳다.

⑤ 앞에 있는 "a worry"를 추가적으로 보충설명 해주는 동격의 that절이 나와야 한다. which는 관계대명사로서 뒤의 문장의 구조가 불완전구조여야 한다. 따라서 which가 that으로 바뀌어야 한다.

09 ③

☞ ① "주어 & 동사" 수일치도 어긋나지 않고, 뒤에 간접목적어(us)와 직접목적어(anything) 둘 다 나와 있기 때문에 능동을 의미하는 것도 올바르다.

② "일련의"라는 표현을 의미하는 "a succession of"는 올바른 표현이다. a series of와 바꾸어 쓸 수도 있다.

③ 가정법 과거를 나타내는 문장으로서 종속절의 동사가 "had been"인 것으로 보아 주절의 동사는 "조동사의 과거 + have + pp"의 형태인 would have been이 와야 한다.

④ "just"는 "(명사·부사·구·절을 수식하여) 바로, 틀림없이, 꼭"을 의미하는 부사로 쓰였다. 어법상 올바르다.

⑤ "even if"는 "비록 ~일지라도"라는 의미로 부사절 접속사로 쓰이며, even though, although, though 와 바꾸어 쓸수 있다. 문맥상 올바르다.

10 ④

fully fledged : 필요한 자격을 다 갖춘 eminence : 명성 irrelevant : 관련 없는 rigorously : 엄격히

「"Superforecasting : Arts and Science of Prediction"이라는 책은 1909년에 태어나서 마법으로부터 온 의약을 완전히 발달한 과학으로 바꾸기 위해 어느 누구보다 더 많은 것을 한 Archie Cochrane이라는 스코틀랜드 의사의 담론으로 시작된다. 반세기 전에는 매우 논란이 있었던 그의 통찰력은 의사의 자격, 명성, 신뢰는 관련성이 없고 치료의 효율성의 유일한 시금석이었다. 그것은 통계적으로, 엄격히 효과가 있는 것으로 보일 수 있느냐 였다. 그 책의 작가인, Tetlock은 사람들이 미래 예측을 분석하는 방법에 대해 비슷한 정확함을 얻기를 바랬다. 그것은 쉬운(→ 어려운) 투쟁이 될 것이었다. 20세기 초의 의학처럼, 예측은 여전히 대개 증거보다도 명성을 근거로 한다.」

11 ③

veracity : 진실성 shade : 가리다 overstate : 과장하다 integrity : 진실성 sort : 구분하다

「여론조사는 인터넷 만남과 같다. 제공된 정보의 진실성에 있어서 약간의 재량권만 있다. 우리는 사람들이 특히 제시된 질문이 당황스럽거나 민감할 때, 진실을 가린다는 것을 알고 있다. 응답자들은 그들의 수입을 과장할지도 모른다. 그들은 투표하지 않았다는 것을 부인(→ 인정)하지 않을지도 모른다. 그들은 대중적이지 않거나 사회적으로 받아들여질 수 없는 관점을 표현하기를 망설일지도 모른다. 이 모든 이유들로, 심지어 가장 세심하게 설계된 여론조사조차 응답자의 답변에 대한 진실성에 의존한다. 선거 여론조사는 선거 날에 투표할 사람들과 그렇지 않은 사람들을 구분하는 것에 결정적으로 의존한다. 개인들은 종종 그들이 투표할 것이라고 말하는데, 그들이 그것이(투표할 것이라고 말하는 것) 여론 조사자들이 듣기를 원하는 것이기 때문이다. 투표 행위에 대한 스스로 하는 보고를 선거 기록과 비교하는 연구들은 지속적으로 응답자의 4분의 1에서 3분의 1 정도가 그들이 사실 투표하지 않았을 때 투표했다고 말한다는 것을 발견한다.」

12 ③

give birth to : 낳다, 초래하다 fertile : 비옥한, 다산의 sterile : 불임의 offstpring : 자손 cross over to : ~로 넘어가다

「생물학자들은 유기체를 종으로 분류한다. 동물들은 만약 그들이 (A) 번식할 수 있는 자손을 낳으면서, 서로서로 짝짓는 경향이 있다면 같은 종에 속한다고 전해진다. 말과 당나귀는 최근의 공통의 조상을 가지고 있고 많은 물리적인 특징을 공유한다. 하지만 그들은 서로 거의 성적 관심을 보여주지 않는다. 그들은 만약 그렇게 유도되어 진다면 짝짓기를 하겠지만 그들의 자손은 (B) 불임이 된다. 그러므로 당나귀 DNA에서의 돌연변이가 결코 말에게 넘어가지 않고, 그 반대도 마찬가지 이다. 두 종류의 동물들은 별개의 진화적 경로를 따라 움직이면서, 결과적으로 두 개의 (C) 별개의 종으로 여겨진다. 대조적으로, 불독과 스페니얼(개의 한종)은 매우 달라 보일지도 모르지만, 그들은 같은 DNA 풀을 공유하는 같은 종의 구성원이다. 그들은 행복하게 짝짓기를 하고 그들의 새끼는 자라서 다른 개들과 짝짓기 해서 더 많은 새끼를 낳을 것이다.」

13 ①

drawback : 결점 overwhelm : 압도하다 maximize : 극대화 하다 methodology : 방법론 evolve : 진화하다 drown : 익사하다, 물에 빠지다 adequate : 적당한 profound : 심오한 deadly : 치명적인 harness : 이용하다 renounce : 포기하다

「빅 데이터는 결점을 가지고 있다. 정보의 홍수 – 일부는 유용하고 일부는 그렇지 않은 – 데이터를 빠르고 효율적으로 처리하고 적절한 액션을 취할 수 있는 능력은 (A) 압도할 수 있다. 만약 우리가 빅 데이터를 사용하면서 방법론을 만들어 내고 이용하는데 실패한다면, 우리는 그것에 계속 (B) 빠질 지도 모른다. 국가적 보안의 맥락에서, 적절한 빅 데이터 툴의 부족은 심오한, 심지어 치명적인 결과를 가져올 수 있다. 하지만 우리가 성공적으로 빅 데이터의 힘을 (C) 이용하는 것을 보장하기 위해서 지금 취해야할 단계들 – 이미 많은 경우에 있어서 취해지고 있는 – 이 있다.」

14 ③

constitutional : 헌법의 fundamental : 근본적인 guarantee : 보장하다 worship : 예배하다 geographical : 지리적인

☞ 미국은 다양성과 현실의 이점을 인식해왔다는 내용이 주제로서, 갈등이 단지 사람들 사이에서 발생한다는 내용의 ③번은 글의 흐름과 맞지 않는다.

「미국은 실제로 다른 배경의 사람들이 어쨌든 모두 같아 진다는 의미에서 "용광로"가 아니다. 미국은 항상 매우 다양한 생각과 태도 그리고 행동들을 포함해왔다. 예를 들어, 교회와 주, 미국에서 이른시기부터 존재해온 근본적인 원리의 헌법적 구분이 모든 종교의 사람들이 예배와 종교적 행위에 대한 같은 자유와 권리를 갖도록 보장한다. 다양한 종교적 배경의 사람들은 한 종교로 함께 녹아들어가도록 기대되지 않는다. 갈등은 그들이 같은 배경이든 다른 배경이든 상관없이 단지 사람들 사이에서 발생한다. 다른 법들은 피부색, 성, 나이에 상관없이 모든 사람들의 동일한 권리를 보장한다. 미국은 심지어 공식 모국어도 가지고 있지 않다. 그리고 많은 정부와 다양한 지리학적 지역에서 다른 출판물이 마찬가지로 다양한 언어로 제공된다. 간단히 말해서, 한 나라로서 미국은 항상 다양성의 현실과 이점을 인식해왔다.」

15 ④

in the short run : 단기적으로 obsolete : 더 이상 쓸모없는 fireman : 기관사 shovel : 삽질하다 locomotive : 기관차

☞ 글의 주제는 기계가 노동자에 대한 필요를 줄이게 되면 또 다른 형태의 노동자에 대한 수요가 생긴다는 글로서 ④번은 글의 주제와 맞지 않는다.

「어느 누구도 기계가 어떤 직업으로부터 개인 노동자들을 대체하는 것에 의문을 제기하지 않는다. 그리고 단기적으로 이것은 종종 어려운 문제들을 만들어 낸다. 예를 들어서, 디젤엔진의 사용과 철도에 의한 전기 동력은 기관사 – 기차의 스팀을 생산하기 위해 석탄을 기관차에 퍼나르는 직원 – 의 지위를 더 이상 쓸모없게 만들었지만 노동조합의 도움 때문에, 철로는 이 자리를 수년동안 이 자리를 채워야만 했다. 스팀 동력이 기차에 의해서 사용되는 것을 멈춘 후에. 하지만 그러한 문제들은 일시적이다. 결국, 기계 기술의 발전은 비용과 가격을 줄이거나 그것들을 억제하는 경향이 있고 사람들로 하여금 더 많은 상품을 구입하도록 하게 함으로서, 새로운 고용기회를 만들어 낸다. 기계들은 인간 기술에 대한 필요를 줄인다. 만약에 어떤 사업들이 더 적은 노동자를 고용하면 다른 산업들은 더 많은 노동자를 고용한다. 동시에, 새로운 상품들은 소개되고 새로운 산업이 확립된다.」

16 ②

alternative : 대안의 compulsory : 강제적인 adjunctive : 부속의 incremental : 증가하는 preventive : 예방의

☞ 빈칸 앞문장에서 처치를 거부하는 권리를 갖는다고 했으므로, 빈칸은 강제적인을 의미하는 ②번이 정답임을 알수 있다.

「유능한 어른이 어떤, 심지어 생명을 구하는 처치를 거부하는 권리를 갖는 것은 많은 법적 시스템에 있어서 원칙이다. 이 원칙은 신체적 질병의 치료에도 적용된다. 하지만 그것은 많은 나라에서 정신 질환을 가진 사람들에게는 적용되지 않는다. 정신 질환을 가진 환자의 강제적인 치료를 통제할 수 있는 정신 보건 법이 있는, 영국을 예로 들어보자.」

17 ④

inequality : 불평등 participation : 참여 well-to-do : 잘사는 bond : 유대감 need : 필요 trend : 경향 standing : 지위 preference : 선호

☞ 골프와 같은 운동은 부유한 사람들이, 축구 야구와 같은 운동은 적은 수입을 갖는 사람들도 접근 가능하다고 했으므로, 빈칸은 지위를 의미하는 ④번이다.

「사회적 갈등의 분석은 스포츠가 사회적인 불평등과 밀접하게 관련되어 있는 것을 지적함으로서 시작된다. 어떤 스포츠들은 －테니스, 수영, 골프, 스키를 포함하는－ 비용이 많이 든다, 그래서 참여가 주로 부유한 사람들로 제한된다. 하지만 축구, 야구는 모든 수입 수준의 사람들에게 접근 가능하다. 간단히 말해서, 사람들이 하는 게임은 선택의 문제일 뿐만 아니라 사회적 지위를 반영하기도 한다.」

18 ①

motivation : 동기부여 motivational : 동기의 arousal : 자극, 흥분 assumption : 가정 mobilize : 전시 동원하다 fluctuate : 변동하다 stabilize : 안정시키다 alternate : 교대로 하다
☞ 빈칸 문장 뒷 문장에서 불가능 하지 않은 일에 가장 열심히 노력한다고 했으므로, 성공률이 양 극단에 있을 때는 자극이 약해진다고 하는 ①번이 정답이다.

「동기부여에 미치는 성공의 영향은 무엇이어야 하나? 그것은 반드시 동기부여를 증가시켜야 하나? 일찍이 이 논쟁은 만약에 학습자가 어떤 활동의 성공적인 수행이 그들의 목표에 의해 주도된다는 것을 깨닫는다면 그때는 기대가 높아질 것이라고 제안한다. 이것은 성공이 동기를 증가시키는 경향이 있을 것이라고 말하기 쉬울 것 같지만, 문제는 그리 간단하지 않다. 이 논쟁은 잠재적인 동기는 고려하고 동기부여하는 자극은 무시한다. 동기부여하는 자극은 어떤 활동을 정확하게 수행하기 위해서 얼마나 많은 노력이 필요한 지에 대한 사람의 가정에 토대를 둔다. 연구는 동기부여하는 자극이 적당하게 어려운 것으로 추정되는 일에서 가장 크다는 것을 나타낸다. 만약 성공률이 매우 높거나 매우 낮은 것으로 여겨지면, 동기부여하는 자극은 약해진다. 다시 말해서, 우리는 도전적이지만 거의 불가능하지 않은 것이라고 여기는 일에 가장 열심히 노력한다.」

19 ⑤

identity : 정체성 tricky : 까다로운 intellectual : 지적인 compilation : 모음집, 편찬 impose : 강요하다, 부과하다 aftermath : 여파, 후유증 emigrate : 이민가다 reportedly : 들리는 바에 의하면 fiercely : 맹렬한, 사나운 ancestral : 조상의 multifaceted : 다 측면 적인 ethnic : 인종의, 민족의 indigenous : 토착의
☞ 빈칸 문장의 다측면과 같은 의미를 가지고 있는 것은 유동적이라는 것이다. 따라서 정답은 ⑤번이다.

「아프리카 역사가들에게 정체성은 까다로운 지적인 문제일 수 있다. 아프리카 인들은, 어느 곳의 사람들처럼, 수많은 정체성들의 집합체인데, 그것들 중 일부는 개인적으로 또는 집합적으로 주장되고, 또 다른 일부는 외부인에 의해서 강요된다. 만약에 사람들에게 가장 유명한 살아있는 아프리카 인이 누구인지를 묻는다면, 보통의 대답은 넬슨 만델라 이다. 하지만 우리가 2006년 월드컵의 여파 속에서 이것을 썼을 때, 가장 유명한 살아있는 아프리카인은 Zinédene Zidane 이라고 말하는 그럴만한 경우가 있다. 누구, 또는 뭐, 지단이라고? 그는 Marseilles에서 태어나고 자란 프랑스 인이다. 하지만 그는 부모가 Algeria에서 이민 온 북아프리카 인이고, 가족의 뿌리가 Kabyle 산맥에 있고 그의 조상의 마을을 격렬하게 자랑스러워 한다고 보고되는 베르베르인이기도 하다. 그는 역시 그 자신을 무슬림으로 묘사한다. 그리고 그는 물론 풋볼 선수이기도 하다. Zidane 그 자신이 이러한 레벨 중(여러 개의 지단 중) 어떤 것을 사용할지 선택하는 것이 그가 어디에 있는지 그리고 그가 그 당시 어떻게 생각하는지 둘 다에 달려있을 것이다. 다시 말해서 정체성은 그것이 다측면인 것처럼 유동적이다.」

20 ①

rug : 융단 tapestry : 태피스트리 garner : 모으다 recite : 암송하다 memoir : 회고록 autobiography : 자서전 relativity : 상대성 (원리)
☞ 피카소와 아인슈타인을 예로 들면서 그들이 독창적일 수 있는 이유가 다작을 통해서라고 말하고 있기 때문에 ①번이 가장 알맞다.

「피카소의 일생의 작품은 스케치, 판화, 융단, 태피스트리는 말할 것도 없고, 1800점 이상의 그림, 1200개의 조각, 2800개의 도자기 12000개의 스케치를 포함하는데, 오직 그 중 일부만 칭송을 받았다. 시에서, 우리가 Maya Angelou 의 고전 시인 "Still I Rise"를 암송할 때 우리는 그녀가 165개의 다른 작품을 썼다는 것을 잊는다, (다시 말해) 우리는 그녀의 감동적인 회고록인 I Know Why the Caged Bird Sings를 기억하고 그녀의 다른 6개의 자서전에는 관심을 주지 않는다. 과학에서, 아인슈타인은 물리학을 바꾼 일반 상대성 이론과 특수 상대성 이론에 관한 논문들을 썼지만, 그의 248개의 많은 출판물은 영향을 거의 주지 못했다. 만약 당신이 독창적이기를 원한다면, 당신이 할 수 있는 가장 중요한 가능한 것은 많은 작품을 만드는 것이다.」

21 ②

doctorate : 박사학위 discipline : 학문

☞ 빈칸 문장 앞문장에서 심리학은 학구적인 학문이며, 응용된 기능을 거의 갖고 있지 않다고 했으므로, 실천하지 않고 연구했다는 의미의 ②번이 정답이다.

「Lightner Witmer는 1892년에 독일에서 많은 사람들이 실험 심리학의 창시자라고 여기는 Wilhelm Wundt아래에서 심리학 박사학위를 받았다. 그는 또한 또 다른 실험 심리학의 선구자인 James Cattell Cattell아래에서 연구했다. Witmer가 그의 박사학위를 받았던 시기에, 심리학은 본질적으로 학구적인 학문이었다. 그것은 오늘날 그 분야를 특징지을 만한 응용된 기능들을 거의 가지고 있지 않았다. 간단히 말해서, 1800년대 후반에 심리학자들은 심리학을 실천하지 않고 그것을 연구했다.」

22 ③

pose : 배치하다 common sense : 상식 commodity : 생필품 enormous : 엄청난 availability : 유용성 necessity : 필수품

☞ 빈칸 문장 다음에 물에 대한 이야기가 전개되면서, 물은 매우 중요하지만 무료이거나 매우 낮은 가격에 팔린다고 했으므로, 상품의 효용성은 가격에 영향을 미치지 못한다는 의미인 ③이 가장 적절하다.

「Adam Smith가 1760년대에 Glasgow대학에서 강의했을 때, 그는 퍼즐을 배치함으로서 수요의 연구를 도입했다. 그는 상식은 생필품의 가격이 그 상품이 소비자에게 가치가 있는 정도, 즉 생필품이 제공하는 효용성의 양에 의존해야 한다고 말했다. 하지만, Smith는 몇몇의 경우는 상품의 효용성은 그것의 가격에 거의 영향을 미치지 못한다고 지적했다. 그는 물은 대부분의 소비자들에게 엄청난 가치가 있다는 것을 지적했다, 사실 그것의 유용성은 삶과 죽음의 문제일 수 있다. 하지만 물은 일반적으로 무료이거나 매우 낮은 가격에 팔린다. 반면에 다이아몬드는 비록 거의 그것을 필수품이라고 생각하는 사람이 없지만 매우 높은 가격에 팔린다.」

23 ②

to-do list : 해야할 목록 tyrannize : 압제하다 trivial : 사소한 obligated : 의무가 있는 priority : 우선순위 inbox : 받은 메일함 dictate : 지시하다 overflow : 넘쳐 흐르다 masquerade as : ~로 변장하다 tackle : 다루다 squeaky : 삐걱거리는 deserve : ~받을 만하다 grease : 기름 duly : 적절하게

☞ 빈칸 문장 앞문장에서 소리가 나는 삐걱거리는 바퀴에 대한 언급이 나오고 빈칸 문장에서 역접의 연결사가 사용됐기 때문에 가장 크게 소리를 지르지 않는다는 내용의 ②번이 가장 적절하다.

「해야 할 일의 목록은 우리의 가장 좋은 의도의 유용한 집합체로서 역할을 하지만, 그것들은 우리를 해야 한다고 느끼는 사소하고 덜 중요한 일들로 압제한다. 왜냐하면 우리의 리스트 위에 있기 때문이다. 그래서 우리 대부분이 우리의 해야 할 목록에 대해서 좋아함과 싫어함의 관계를 갖는 이유이다. 만약에 허락된다면, 그것들은 받은 메일함이 우리의 일과를 지시할 수 있는 것과 같은 방식으로 우리의 우선순위를 정한다. 대부분의 받은 서류함이 우선사항으로 변장한 중요하지 않은 이메일로 넘쳐난다. 우리가 그것들을 받은 순서로 다루는 것은 마치 삐걱거리는 바퀴에 즉시 기름칠해야 마땅하다고 행동하는 것이나 다름없다. 하지만, 호주 총리인 Bob Hawke 가 적절하게 지적했듯이, "가장 중요한 것은 가장 크게 소리를 지르지 않는다."」

24 ⑤

currency : 통화 ledger : 원장 transact : 거래하다 fraudulent : 사기치는 premise : 전제로 하다 immutability : 불변성 alter : 바꾸다 entry : 입장, 입력

☞ 마지막 문장에서 과거의 입력 내용을 바꿀수 없다는 내용을 통해서 빈칸에 들어갈 말이 불변성(immutalbility)임을 알 수 있다.

「블록체인은 이중 지출 문제를 방지하기 위해 비트코인에서 사용된다. 비트코인 이전에 디지털 통화의 문제는 누군가가 같은 단위의 디지털 통화를 여러 곳에서 동시에 사용할 수 있다는 것이었다. 블록체인은 공유 원장을 제공함으로써 이 문제를 해결한다. 그리고 그것은 모든 사람이 얼마나 많은 디지털 통화가 어느 시점에 사용자들 사이에서 거래되었는지를 알고 동의하도록 보장한다. 블록체인은 부패 또는 사기 행위를 탐지하고 방지하는데 있어서 효과적인 도구를 제공할 수 있다고 생각된다. 이러한 생각은 블록체인의 불변성에 전제를 두고 있다. 불변성은 과거의 입력내용을 바꿀 수 없도록 막는다. 종이나 디지털 기록으로 할 수 있을지도 모르는.」

25 ①

pinpoint : 지적하다 unprecedented : 전례없는

☞ (A) 앞문장의 내용과 뒷 문장의 내용은 원인과 결과의 내용이기 때문에 그러므로의 의미를 갖는 therefore가 알맞다. (B) 앞문장과 뒷 문장의 내용은 반대를 나타내기 때문에 역접의 연결사인 However 가 적절하다.

「패트리샤 슈뢰더 전 여성 하원의원은 여성이 이처럼 유례없이 많은 숫자로 일을 하는 주된 이유는 가족을 유지해야 하기 때문이라고 주장할 때, 여성들이 직장에 들어가는 가장 중요한 이유 중 하나를 지적했다. 많은 가정 여성들이 일을 해야 하기 때문에 일을 한다. 다른 사람들에게는, 비록 가정이 작아졌지만, 욕구는 더 커졌다. (A) 그러므로, 이러한 가정 여성들에게 있어, 일은 실제 필요한 것이 아니라 사회적 필요성이다. 그것은 가족이 자신의 욕구를 충족시킬 수 있는 유일한 방법이다. (B) 그러나 일은 백인 여성들보다 흑인과 다른 소수 여성들에게, 훨씬 더 오랫동안 필수적이었다. 전체 근로 연령 여성 중 여성 비율 노동력에 있어서 여성들이 1972년 32%에서 2000년대 초반 70% 이상으로 높아졌다. 이러한 추세를 연구하는 분석가들은 비록 일부 매우 고소득 여성들이 일하는 것을 그만두고 그들의 아이들과 집에 머무를 것을 선택할 지라도, 아이를 가진 일하는 여성들의 비율이 계속해서 증가할 것으로 예상된다고 말한다.」

26 ③

derive : 이끌어 내다 address : 다루다 judiciously : 신중하게 evocative : 환기 시키는 popularize : 대중화 하다 spinning wheel : 물레 ply : (능숙하게) 다루다 rebel : 반항하다 dignity : 존엄 denounce : 비난하다 emblem : 상징 manual : 육체 노동의 despise : 경멸하다 compassion : 연민 infinitely : 무한히 patronize : 후원하다

☞ 본문은 인도의 전통문화에 관해 존중하고 지킨다는 글이다. 따라서 인도의 농촌 생활 방식의 존엄성을 비난하는 것이 아닌 칭송(praise)하는 의미로 바꾸어야 한다.

「인간의 행동이 그들의 감정 에너지를 신중하게 선택된 기호들에 의해서만 다루어지고 활성화될 수 있는 '심장'으로부터 유래되었다고 확신한, 간디는 회전하는 바퀴, 소, 그리고 '간디캡(그에 의해 대중화된 하얀 면화 모자)을 포함하는 문화적으로 환기시키는 상징의 강력한 군집을 진화시켰다. 예를 들어, 간디가 모든 사람에게 능숙하게 다루라고 요구한, 물레는 여러 개의 상징적인 목적을 수행했다. 그것은 현대 기술 문명에 대해 부드럽게 반항하고 인도의 농촌 생활 방식의 존엄성을 (비난→칭송)하는 방법이었다. 그것은 도시와 마을, 서구화된 엘리트들과 대중들을 하나로 묶었고, '그들의 동료애의 상징'이었다. 회전하는 바퀴는 또한 육체 노동과 그것에 종사하는 사람들의 존엄성을 확립하고 양쪽 모두를 경멸하는 전통적인 인도 문화에 도전했다. 그것은 사회적 연민을 상징했는데, 그것은 그 상품의 수익이 필요하지 않은 사람들이 가난한 사람들에게 그 상품들을 나누어주도록 촉구되었기 때문에, 돈을 기부하는 것에 대해 무한히 우월한 도덕적 행위였다. 그리고 그것은 또한 개인을 자기 자신과 단둘이 있게 하고 적어도 얼마 동안은 침묵을 준수하도록 강요했다. 간디는 이런 종류의 수많은 상징들을 진화시켰을 뿐만 아니라 스스로도 하나가 되었다.」

27 ②

☞ (a), (c), (d), (e)는 물레를 의미하고, (b)는 육체노동을 의미한다.

28 ②

tense : 긴장한, 긴장하다 stroll : 산책하다, 거닐다 glance : 힐끗보다 probe : 조사하다 distort : 일그러뜨리다 stare : 응시하다 exclaim : 외치다 chatter : 수다떨다, 잡담하다 chirp : 재잘거리다 chuckle : 빙그레 웃다 gaze : 응시하다 blur : 흐릿해지다

☞ 안나 가족이 기차안에서 독일 병사들에게 검문을 받는 묘사한 글이다. 처음에 검문받기 전과 검문받으면서는 무섭고 긴장감이 흐르다가 무사히 검문을 마치고 안심하면서 글이 끝나는 것을 알수 있다.

「기차가 다시 출발했다. 그들의 객차 끝에 있는 문이 열리고 두 명의 독일군 병사가 나타났다. 안네마리는 긴장했다. 여기 말고, 기차에서도? 그들은 어디에나 있었다. 병사들은 함께 차 안을 거닐며 승객들을 노려보며, 여기저기 멈춰 서서 질문을 던졌다. 그들 가운데 한 사람은 이빨에 무엇인가가 박혀 있었다; 그는 혀로 더듬어 자신의 얼굴을 일그러뜨렸다. 안네마리는 두 사람이 다가오자 일종의 놀란 표정으로 지켜보았다. 병사들 중 한 명이 지루하다는 표정을 지으며 내려다보았다. "어디로 가십니까?" 그가 물었다. "길레제," 엄마가 침착하게 대답했다. "오빠가 거기 사는데. 우리는 그를 방문할 것이에요." 병사가 돌아서자 안네마리는 긴장을 풀었다. 그리고는 예고도 없이 뒤로 돌아섰다. "새해를 맞아 오빠를 찾아가는 거야?"라고 그가 갑자기 물었다. 엄마는 어리둥절한 표정으로 그를 응시했다. "새해?"라고 그녀가 물었다. "이제 겨우 10월이다." "그런데 그거 알아맞혀 봐" 커스티는 갑자기 큰 목소리로 병사를 바라보며 소리쳤다. 안네마리는 가슴이 철렁 내려앉으며 어머니를 바라보았다. 엄마의 눈은 겁에 질려 있었다. "쉬, 커스티," 엄마가 말했다. "그렇게 수다를 떨지 마." 그러나 커스티는 여느 때처럼 엄마에게 전혀 주의를 기울이지 않았다. 그녀는 쾌활하게 병사를 바라보았고, 안네마리는 그녀가 무슨 말을 하려는지 알고 있었다. 이건 우리의 친구 엘렌이고 그녀의 새해잖아! 그러나 그녀는 그렇게 하지 않았다. 대신 커스티가 그녀의 발을 가리켰다. "헨리크 아저씨를 만나러 갈 거야," "그리고 나는 내 새롭고 빛나는 검은 신발을 신었어!"라고 그녀는 재잘거렸다. 병사는 껄껄 웃으며 앞으로 나아갔다. 안네마리는 다시 창문으로 시선을 보냈다. 그들이 해안을 따라 북쪽으로 계속 가면서, 나무와 발트해, 흐린 10월의 하늘이 흐릿하게 지나갔다.」

29 ⑤

felid : 고양이과 동물 reproduction : 번식 ripe : 익은 unripe : 익지 않은 taste bud : 미뢰 come to light : 사람들에게 알려지다 captive : 포획 breeding : 사육 clouded leopard : 대만 표범

☞ 고양이는 단맛을 구별할 수가 없고 그 대신에 고기의 맛을 구분할 수 있는 능력이 발달됐다고 했다.

「수백만 년 전, 12개 정도의 유전적 변화가 오늘날의 모든 고양이과 동물의 조상에게 발생했는데, 그 이후로 그들을 고기를 먹도록 가두어 놓았다. 모든 고양이들은 식단에 많은 양의 동물성 단백질을 필요로 하는데, 식물로부터 온 타우린과 같은 단백질은 고양이에게 필요하지만 다른 포유류(우리 인간을 포함한)는 필요로 하지 않는 어떤 아미노산이 부족하다. 고양이들은 - 번식하는데 필수적인 호르몬인 - 프로스타글란딘을 직접 만들 수 없어서 이것을 고기로부터 얻을 필요가 있다. 다른 포유류에 비해, 모든 고양이들은 니아신, 티아민, 레티놀과 같은 많은 양의 비타민을 필요로 하는데, 이것은 식물보다 고기에서 더 쉽게 추출된다. 그리고 고양이들은 익은 과일과 익지 않은 과일의 차이를 구별할 필요가 없기 때문에, 그들은 설탕을 맛볼 수 있는 능력을 잃어버렸다. 그들은 육류에서 다른 맛들을 구별하기 위해 그들의 '달콤한' 미뢰를 적응시켰다, 그래서 애완 고양이들이 가끔 주인에게 괜찮아 보이는 음식에서 멀어지는 이유다. 이러한 지식은 지난 40년 동안 사람들에게 알려져, 애완 고양이뿐만 아니라 대만표범과 같은 멸종위기에 처한 고양이과 동물의 포획 사육에도 혜택을 주었다.」

30 ③

throne : 왕좌 lengthen : 길게 하다 spear : 창 hoplite : (그리스의) 장갑 보병 retain : 유지하다 cavalry : 기갑 부대 line : 전열 incorporate : 통합하다 systematically : 체계적으로 conquer : 정복하다 mainland : 본토 exception : 제외, 예외 defeat : 패배시키다 conquest : 정복 era : 시대 territory : 영토

☞ 글의 중반부에 스파르타를 제외하고 그리스 본토 전체를 체계적으로 정복했다는 걸로 봐서 ③번은 본문의 내용과 일치 하지 않는다.

「왕위에 오르자마자, 필립은 마케도니아 군을 테베에서 보았던 것보다 더 성공적인 이미지로 바꾸기 시작했다. 필립은 더 나아가 테반스가 사용하던 이미 더 긴 창을 길게 늘여, 길이가 약 18피트 정도 되는 창인 마케도니아 사리를 만들었는데, 이는 전통적인 그리스 호블라이트 창보다 두 배나 많은 것이다. 그는 테반 웨지 편성을 유지하면서도 또한 중무장 기병을 그 전열에 추가하여 마케도니아인의 가장 강한 요소를 팔랑크에 편입시켰다. 그 결과는 스스로 말해 주었는데, 20년 동안 필립은 혼자 떠나기로 선택한 스파르타를 제외하고 그리스 본토 전체를 체계적으로 정복했다. 필립의 마지막 대승은 차아로나 전투(338년)에서였는데, 이 전투에서 마케도니아군은 아테네와 테베의 연합군을 격파했다. 필립이 본토 전체를 정복한 것은 한 시대의 종말이었고, 처음으로 영토 전체가 왕의 지배 아래 하나로 뭉쳤다.」

31 ②

decree : 법령 inheritance : 상속 criminal offense : 범죄 severity : 엄격함 commoner : 평민 restitution : 손해 배상 ordeal : 시련 retaliatory : 보복성의 malicious : 악의적인 manifest : 나타내다 morality : 도덕

☞ 글의 중반부에 결혼, 상속, 재산권과 같은 민원 업무를 주로 다루었다고 하였다. 따라서 형법만 다루었다는 내용의 ②번은 내용과 일치 하지 않는다.

「약 기원전 1792년부터 1750년까지 메소포타미아를 통치했던 바빌로니아 황제 함무라비는 아직 발견된 가장 초기의 법전 중 하나인 자신의 이름이 새겨진 법전으로 가장 잘 알려져 있다. 그의 주된 관심사는 권위를 통해 자신의 제국의 질서를 유지하는 것이었는데, 이는 그의 백성들의 요구에 부응하는 것이었다. 이 효과를 위해, 그는 신하들에게 복잡한 법령을 내렸다. 집합적으로 함무라비 강령이라 불리는, 그것의 282개의 법령은 현판이나 기둥에 새겨졌고 많은 곳에 세워졌다. 하나는 19세기에 페르시아 수사에서 발견되었고 현재 파리의 루브르 박물관에 있다. 이 법규는 주로 결혼과 상속, 가족관계, 재산권, 사업관행과 같은 민원 업무를 다루었다. 범죄는 가해자와 피해자의 사회적 지위에 따라 다른 정도의 엄격함으로 처벌되었다. 상류층의 권리와 평민의 권리는 분명한 차이가 있었다. 지급이 일반적으로 귀족들에 의해 평민들에게 행해진 손해에 대한 배상금으로서 허용된다. 그러나, 귀족에게 피해를 입히는 평민이라면 머리로 돈을 지불해야 할지도 모른다. 시련에 의한 재판, 보복행위에 의한 보복, 사형은 일반적인 관행이었다. 그러나 판사들은 고의적인 부상과 의도하지 않은 상해로 구별하였고, 일반적으로 금전적 벌금은 악의적인 의도가 드러나지 않는 처벌로 사용되었다. 종종 함무라비 법령과 관련된 "눈의 눈" 도덕은 적용이 상대적으로 제한되었고, 사회적 평등에 의한 그리고 (거기에) 반해서 저질러지는 범죄에만 적용되었다.」

32 ①

bounce back and forth : 여러 모로 검토하다 repercussion : 영향 clear : 승인하다 toddler : 갓난아기 unattended : 지켜보는 사람이 없는

☞ ① 멀티테스킹의 오류
   ② 멀티테스킹의 기초
   ③ 멀티테스킹 : 왜 그리고 어떻게
   ④ 멀티테스킹을 위한 대처 전략
   ⑤ 훌륭한 결과 뒤의 단순한 사실 : 멀티테스킹

글의 후반부에서 한번에 두 가지 일을 하려고 할 때 결국 둘다 못하거나 잘 못한다는 내용으로 봐서 ①이 정답임을 알수 있다.

「사람들은 실제로 걷기와 말하기, 껌을 씹고 지도를 읽는 것과 같은 두 가지 이상의 일을 동시에 할 수 있다; 하지만 컴퓨터처럼 우리가 할 수 없는 것은 한번에 두 가지 일에 집중하는 것이다. 우리의 주의는 여러모로 검토하게 된다. 이것은 컴퓨터에게는 괜찮지만, 인간에게는 심각한 영향을 미친다. 두 대의 여객기가 같은 활주로에 착륙하도록 승인되었다. 환자에게 잘못된 약이 주어진다. 아기 한 명이 욕조에 방치되어 있다. 이 모든 잠재적 비극들이 공유하는 것은 사람들이 한꺼번에 너무 많은 일을 하려고 노력하고 그들이 해야 할 일을 하는 것을 잊어버린다는 것이다. 한꺼번에 두 가지 일을 하려 할 때, 두 개의 일을 할 수 없거나 두 개 중 어떤것도 잘 하지 못할 것이다. 만약 당신이 멀티태스킹이 더 많은 일을 할 수 있는 효과적인 방법이라고 생각한다면, 당신은 그것을 거꾸로 하는 것이다. 그것은 덜 하는 효과적인 방법이다.」

33 ④

statistics : 통계 measure : 척도 disorganization : 붕괴 cite : 인용하다 ostracism : 외면

☞ ① 이혼통계의 사용

② 이혼 통계의 수집

③ 사람들이 이혼하는 이유

④ 이혼 통계의 조심스런 해석

⑤ 이혼과 가족 붕괴에 대처하기

　두 번째 문장에서 이혼이 가족의 불행 때문만은 아니라는 내용을 통해서 정답이 ④번임을 알 수 있다.

「이혼 통계는 가족 분열의 척도로 자주 쓰이고 있으며, 현재의 높은 이혼율은 미국 가정이 심각한 문제에 처해 있다는 증거로 인용되고 있다. 그러나 오늘날 과거보다 높아진 이혼율이 전적으로 더 많은 가족의 불행의 결과만은 아니다. 초기 세대에는 결혼 생활이 불행했음에도 불구하고 많은 부부들이 이혼을 피했다. 그들은 그것이(이혼이) 사회적 배척이나 여성의 경우, 잘 살 수 있는 기회가 거의 없고 빈곤을 의미하기 때문에 피한 것이다. 이혼한 사람들의 가능성이 높아지고 이혼을 하는 것이 쉬워지면서, 더 많은 불행한 커플들이 이 길을 택했다.」

34 ①

mortality : 사망자수 sustained : 지속된 precede : ~에 앞서다 distinction : 구분 demographically : 인구 통계학의 rehydration : 재수화 작용 immunization : 예방주사 communicable : 전염성의

☞ ① 유아 사망률은 출생률에 영향을 미친다

② 전 세계의 유아 사망률은 매우 빠르게 감소하고 있다

③ 부의 불균형은 유아 사망률에 반영된다

④ 유아 사망의 주된 원인은 형편없는 수질이다

　첫 번째 문장에서 태어난 아이들이 성인기까지 살아남게 하기 위해서 많은 아이를 낳는다고 했으므로, ①번이 정답이다.

「개발도상국의 대부분에서 그렇듯이, 유아 사망률이 높을 때, 부모들은 몇몇 아이들이 성인기까지 살아남을 수 있도록 하기 위해 아이를 많이 갖는 경향이 있다. 유아 사망률의 지속적인 하락이 먼저 선행되지 않는 한 유아 출생률의 지속적인 하락은 없다. 우리 인구 통계학적으로 분단된 세계에서 가장 중요한 차이 중 하나는 저개발 국가의 높은 영아 사망률. 더 나은 영양, 발전된 의료 서비스, 간단한 구강 수분 보충 치료, 그리고 전염성 질병에 대한 예방 접종이 유아 사망률에 있어서 극적인 감소량을 가져다 주었는데, 그것은 출생률이 떨어지는 대부분의 지역에서 성취되었다. 500만의 아이들을 쉽게 예방할 수 있는 전염성 질병들로부터 구하는 것이 2천만~3천만의 추가적인 출생을 피할 것으로 추정된다.」

35 ④

measurable : 측정할수 있는 infer : 추론하다 gravitational : 중력의 distribution : 분배 cluster : 무리 ubiquity : 편재 constitute : 구성하다 neutrino : 중성미자 hypothetical : 가설의 axion : 악시온 elude : 피하다 detection : 발견, 탐지 electromagnetic : 전자석의 radiation : 방사선 conventional : 전통적인

☞ (4)번 앞의 내용은 암흑 물질이 80% 우주에 있다는 내용은 주어진 내용의 편재성(어디에나 있음)과 연결된다.

「하지만, 그것의 편재성에도 불구하고, 천문학자들은 무엇이 암흑 물질을 구성하는지에 대해 실제적인 생각을 가지고 있지 않다.」

「암흑 물질은 측정할 수 있다. 단지 보이지 않을 뿐이다. (1)그것은 '어두워서' 보이지 않는다. (2)천문학자들은 암흑 물질의 존재를 추론할 수 있는데 그 이유는 은하가 어떻게 스스로를 지탱하고 있는지, 중력 렌즈가 어떻게 작동하는지, 은하 군단에서 보이는 고온 가스의 관측들을 설명할 수 있기 때문이다. (3)결론은 우주 질량의 80% 이상이 우리가 볼 수 없는 형태로 존재한다는 것이다. (4)그것은 무거운 중성미자와 같은 아원자 입자나 악시온과 같은 다른 가상 입자를 포함할 수 있다. (5) 그것의 일부는 단순히 탐지를 회피하는 물체에 갇혀 있을 수도 있다. 현재 천문학자들은 대부분의 암흑 물질이 전자기 방사선이나 원자와 상호작용하지 않는 것으로 보이는 약한 상호작용을 하는 거대한 입자(WIMP)라고 불리는 새로운 기초 입자로 구성되어 있다고 믿고 있다. 그러므로 그것들은 전통적인 탐지 수단에 보이지 않는다.」

36 ④

depersonalize : 비개인화 하다   burnout : 완전히 지침   afflict : 가하다   depersonalization : 비개인화
desperate : 필사적인

☞ 번 아웃된 노동자들은 그들이 도와줄필요가 있는 사람들을 비인격한다는 내용 이후에 구체적인 사례가
　　나오는 (4)에 들어가는 것이 가장 적절하다.

「번아웃 노동자들은 때때로 그들이 도와줄 필요가 있는 사람들을 인간으로 느끼기보다는 물건이나 사물로 생각하면서, 그들을
비인격화 한다.」

「번아웃은 날마다 장시간 근무 중 높은 수준의 업무 스트레스를 경험하는 일부 직원들을 괴롭히는 스트레스의 특별한 종류의
심리적 결과이다. 그것은 특히 직원들이 다른 사람들을 도와주고, 보호하고, 돌보는데 책임이 있는 있을 때 일어나는 것 같다.
간호사, 의사, 사회복지사, 교사, 변호사, 경찰관들이 그들의 직업의 특성때문에 번아웃을 키울 위험에 처해있다. (1)번아웃의
세 가지 주요 징후는 낮은 개인적 성취감, 정서적 피로감, 그리고 몰개성화이다. (2)번아웃 노동자들은 종종 그들이 남을 돕거
나 해야 할 만큼 성취하지 못하고 있다고 느낀다. (3)감정적으로 그들은 때로는 도움이 절실한 사람들을 대해야 하는 끊임없
는 스트레스로 지쳐버린다. (4)예를 들어, 한 번 아웃된 사회 복지사는 매우 겁먹은 12세가 아니라 사건 번호로서 새로운
상황의 필요에 있는 수양 자녀에 대해서 생각할지도 모른다. (5)이러한 심리적 결과는 그 번아웃된 사회 복지사가 차갑고
거리를 두는 태도로 그 아이를 다룰때, 행동적 결과로 이어질 수 있다.」

37 ③

intuition : 직관 versus : ~대, ~에 비해 trade-off : 균형 yield : 생산하다 at hand : 당면한, 가까이에
있는 put simply : 간단히 말해서 prime : 준비시키다 subdivide : 세분화 하다 chunk : 덩어리 aesthetic
: 미적인 holistic : 전체적인

☞ 주어진 글에서 합리적인 분석적 접근방식의 장점에 대해서 서술하고 있고, 하지만 직관적 결정의 장점에
　　대한 글이 (B)에서 언급되면서 글의 내용이 반대로 전개가 되고 (C)와 (A)에서 구체적인 예가 전개되고
　　있다.

「역사적으로, 합리적인 분석적 접근방식은, 비록 이러한 의사결정 과정이 훨씬 더 느리지만, 종종 직관에 비해 우수한 결과를
제공하는 것으로 보여진다. (B) 따라서, 일부의 사람들은 의사결정에서 속도 대 효과의 균형에 대해 말한다. 하지만, 직관은
의사결정자의 경험의 수준과 당면한 업무의 특징에 따라서 이성적인 모델보다 더 나은 결과 만들어 낼 수 있습니다. (C)
간단히 말해, 경험이 많은 개인 (즉, 전문가와 같은) 특정 분야에서 많은 경험을 가지고 있는 개인들은 그들이 직면하는 업무
의 유형에 따라 합리적인 의사결정을 하는 것보다 직관으로 더 효과적이 되도록 준비된다. 전문가들은 일반적으로 당면한
과제가 하나 이상의 정답이 있거나 과제가 쉽게 더 작은 덩어리로 세분화 될 수 없는 일일때 직관적인 의사결정의 사용은
가장 효과적이다. (A) 이런 유형의 업무는 인적자원 관리, 전략, 미학, 투자 결정 등에서 흔히 볼 수 있다. 요컨대, 직관은
전문가가 판단 및 전체론적 작업을 수행할 때 가장 효과적이다.」

38 ⑤

copilot : 부조종사 assertiveness : 자기 주장 mandatory : 의무적인, 강제적인

☞ 주어진 문장에서 비행기 내에서 의사소통의 중요성을 이야기 하고 있고, 그것에 관한 예를 (C)를 통해 처음 소개하고, (B)에서 비행기의 추락의 이유가 효과적인 의사소통의 부재로 인해 발생했다는 내용이 전개되고, (A)에서 그러한 문제의 해결책에 대해서 설명하면서 글이 마무리 되고 있다.

「오늘날, 우리 모두는 항공사 기내 승무원, 조종사, 비행 승무원 등의 서로 서로의 그리고 승객들과 효과적으로 의사소통할 수 있는 능력이 위기를 예방하는데 필수적이라는 것을 알고 있다. (C) 효과적인 의사소통이 여객기에서 중요하다는 방식을 보여주는 비극적인 예가 에어 플로리다 737기가 워싱턴 D.C.에 있는 국립 공항을 이륙한 후 포토맥 강 위의 다리와 충돌했을 때이다. (B) 미연방 항공국 조사자들은 부조종사가 엔진 센서의 얼음으로 인해 발생한 엔진 출력 측정값에 대한 문제를 조종사에게 알리지 않았기 때문에 추락이 일부 발생했다고 판단했다. (A) 이것과 의사소통이 원활하지 못한 다른 위험한 사건들 때문에, 미연방 항공국은 그들이 효과적으로 의사소통 할 수 있는 능력을 갖도록 하기 위해서 모든 항공사 승무원들을 대상으로 한 주장과 민감도 훈련을 의무적으로 만들었다.」

39 40

facilitate : 용이하게 하다 festivity : 축제(분위기) conditioning : 조건부 estimation : 평가 facilitation : 용이함 internalize : 내면화 하다 property : 특징

「어린 시절부터, 가족 내에서든 다른 집단과 함께이든, 사회적 상호 작용은 대부분의 음식 경험이 발생하는 맥락을 제공하고, 따라서 그로 인해 음식의 선호에 대한 학습이 촉진된다. 그러한 상호작용과 관련된 즐거움—예를 들어, 친구들과 나누는 식사의 축제—은 달콤함과 같은 새로운 음식 맛에 대한 긍정적인 조건부 자극을 나타낼 수 있다. 그래서, 그것은 어떤 식당에서의 음식에 대한 평가가 그 요리사의 기술과 관련이 있는것 만큼 사회적 환경과 많은 관련이 있을 수 있다. 아이들의 경우, 음식을 친구들, 좋아하는 유명인 또는 어른들의 의한 관심과 짝짓는 것은 이런 음식에 대한 선호를 증가시킨다, (그리고) 의심할 여지도 없이, 아이들에게 각각의 이러한 그룹들의 긍정적인 가치를 반영한다. 이러한 과정은 다른 사회적 상호작용이 아이들의 음식 선호에 미치는 상대적인 영향에서 강하게 나타난다. 놀랍게도, 부모들이 먹는 음식에 아이들을 노출시킬 수 있는 가정에서 엄청난 기회에도 불구하고, 부모의 선호도는 어린이 음식 선호도의 강력한(→ 형편없는 poor) 예측 변수다; 사실, 그들은 다른 어른들의 선호보다 더 나은 예측 변수가 아니다. 이것은 이러한 일련의 선호가 관련되어 있는 범위가 가족 내의 특정한 음식 습관보다 더 넓은 문화와 관련이 있음을 시사한다. 어린이의 음식에 대한 호불호는 음식은 부모의 음식에 대한 호불호 보다 또래, 특히 특정한 친구의 호불호와 훨씬 더 연관될 가능성이 높다. 음식 선택의 사회적 촉진에 대한 궁극적인 영향은 그 취향은 결국 내면화 된다는 것이다. 즉, 다른 사람들이 그렇게 하기 때문에 선택된 음식들은 그들 자신의 감각적 특성으로 호감을 갖게 된다.」

39 ⑤

☞ ① 달콤함에 대한 갈망
② 맛있다!: 음식에 대한 타고난 반응
③ 새로운 맛에 대한 조건부 자극
④ 아이들 양육을 위한 현명한 음식 선택
⑤ 어떻게 음식 선호는 사회적으로 형성되나?

40 ④

☞ 아이들의 대한 음식 선호는 부모에 의해서 보다는 친구들이나 좋아하는 유명인사에 의해서 형성된다고 했으므로 부모들의 선호는 아이들에게 강한 영향을 미치는 것이 아닌 형편없는 영향을 미친다고 볼 수 있다.

41 42

boast : 자랑하다 formidable : 가공할만한 play host to : …의 개최 장소[수용처]가 되다, …을 주최[개최]하다
subterranean : 지하의 communally : 공동의 be equipped with : ~을 갖추다 claw : 발톱 acute : 잘 발달된
come in handy : 유용하다 venture : 모험하다 burrow : 굴 stand sentry : 보초를 서다 bird of prey : 맹금류
lookout : 망보는 사람 shrill : 날카로운 make a dash for : ~을 향해 돌진하다 bolthole : 도피처 territorial
: 영토의, 세력권을 주장하는 pitch into : ~에 열을 올리기 시작하다 pup : 새끼

「(A) 미어캣은 아프리카 평원에서 가장 큰 동물이 아닐지도 모르거나, 코뿔소의 뿔처럼 어떤 특별한 가공할만한 무기나, 치타의 스피드처럼 인상적인 기술들을 자랑할 만한 것 같지 않다.

(D) 그럼에도 불구하고, 강인한 생물학의 조합, 영리한 속임수와 독특한 공동체 정신을 통해, 이 포유류들은 그들의 거친 환경에 완벽하게 적응했다. 그들은 지하 굴에 살면서 남아프리카 공화국의 가장 극심한 온도 – 미어캣을 먹이로 하고 싶어 하는 많은 포식자 뿐만 아니라 – 에서 탈출한다.

(B) 일부 지하 네트워크는 50마리 정도의 개체를 수용할 수 있다. 비록 평균적인 집단이 이것의 절반 사이즈로서 2–3가구가 함께 살지만. 몽구스의 일종으로, 그들은 위험을 발견하는데 매우 편리한 잘 발달된 시력 뿐만 아니라, 땅을 파거나 자기 방어에 사용되는 날카롭고 구부러진 발톱을 갖추고 있다. 사실, 그들이 먹이를 찾기 위해 굴 밖으로 모험을 할 때, 적어도 보초를 서고 있는 – 종종 바위 위나 수풀안에서 – 한 마리의 미어캣이 그들의 가장 중요한 적인 맹금류 때문에 하늘을 바라 보면서 있을 것이다.

(C) 어떠한 위협도 감지되자마자, 망을 보는 미어캣은 날카로운 경고음을 짖으면 다른 미어캣들은 즉시 가까운 도피처나 다른 피할곳으로 돌진할 것이다. 미어캣은 다양한 범위의 위협을 나타내기 위해서 수십개의 다른 울음소리들을 가지고 있다고 생각된다. (그들의) 영역 범위에서 사냥하는것 뿐만 아니라, 미어캣은 역시 미어캣은 새끼들을 보살피는 일도 함께한다. 보통은, 군집의 우두머리 쌍만이 짝짓기를 할 것이다. 하지만 다른 모든 미어캣들은 먹이를 찾는 방법, 싸움 놀이, 전갈의 어떤 부분을 물어야 되는지와 같은 소중한 삶의 기술들을 설명하는것 뿐만 아니라, 새끼를 재우고 먹이를 주면서, 새끼들을 돌보는 일에 열심이다.」

41 ⑤

☞ (A)의 열악한 미어캣의 신체적 조건에도 불구하고, 다른 환경에 유리한 미어캣의 특징을 가지고 있다는 내용이 나오는 (D)가 이어지며, (B)와 (C)의 공동체 생활의 특징이 뒤에 이어진다.

42 ②

☞ (B)의 첫 번째 문장에서 대략 50마리정도의 미어캣이 무리로 생활한다는 내용으로 보아 보기 ②번의 미어캣이 독립적인 생활을 한다는 내용은 본문의 내용과 일치하지 않는다.

spatial : 공간의 reasoning : 추론 make the news : 뉴스거리가 되다 doting : 맹목적인 suspicious : 의심스러운 around the clock : 24시간 내내 disconfirm : ~의 부당성을 입증하다 narrate : 이야기 하다 alert : 기민한, 경계하는

「[가] 두 연구자들은 대학생들이 모차르트 피아노 소나타를 들은 이후 그들이 특별한 추론 시험에서 높은 점수를 올렸다고 보고했다. 이 관찰이 뉴스거리가 되고 나서 바로 맹목적인 부모는 하루종일 그들의 아기를 위해서 모차르트를 틀어주었다. 분명히, 그들은 대학생들처럼 그들의 아이들이 더 똑똑해 질 것을 희망했다. 하지만, 부모들은 그러한 마법적인 효과를 준다고 주장하는 어떠한 관행도 의심해야 한다.

[다] "모짜르트 효과"의 주된 (B)문제는 최초의 실험이 어른에게 행해졌다는 것이다; 즉 그것은 우리에게 유아에 대한 어떠한 것도 말해주지 않는다는 것이다. 역시, 그 연구는 다른 형식의 음악은 시험하지 않았다. 그 문제에 대해서 왜 바흐나 슈베르트는 사용하지 않는가? 훨씬 더 중요한 문제는, 모차르트 효과는 실제로 존재하는가? 이다.

[라] 왜 몇몇 연구들은 그 효과를 지지하고 다른 연구들은 부당성을 입증하는가? 대부분의 연구들은 음악을 듣는 학생들을 조용히 쉬는 학생들과 비교해 왔다. 하지만 두 명의 심리학자들은 구현된 이야기를 듣는 것이 역시 테스트 점수를 향상시킨다는 것을 밝혀냈다. 이것은 특히 이야기를 듣는 것을 좋아하는 학생들에게 그렇다. 그래서 모차르트 음악을 들은 후에 높은 점수를 받았다는 학생들은 단지 더 기민해 있거나 더 기분 좋은 분위기에 있었다.

[나] 그 증거는 무엇을 암시하나? 몇몇 연구는 모차르트 음악에 노출 되고 나서 공간적인 지능에 있어서 작은 변화를 발견했다. 하지만 대부분의 연구자들은 그 효과의 (A)부당성을 증명할 수 없었다.」

43 ②

☞ [가]글 마지막에서 모차르트 효과의 의심해야 한다는 내용에 이어서, 구체적인 근거가 [다]에서 이어지고, 심리학자에 의해서 행해진 또 다른 연구가 있다는 내용과 함께 내용이 [라]에서 이어지며, [나]에서 글이 마무리 된다.

44 ①

☞ ① 모짜르트 효과 : 마법적인 어떠한 것도 아니다
② 모짜르트 : 천재의 탄생
③ 왜 클레식 음악은 아이에게 좋은가?
④ 모짜르트의 소나타 : 가장 높은 음악적 정확함
⑤ 모차르트의 음악과 그것의 교육학적인 암시

45 ③

☞ ① 지지하다   …   염려
② 복사하다   …   이익
③ 복사하다   …   문제
④ 부당함을 입증하다 … 이익
⑤ 부당함을 입증하다 … 문제

서원각이 취업을 찢었다!

봉투모의고사 **찐!5회** 횟수로 플렉스해 버렸지 뭐야 ~

국민건강보험공단 봉투모의고사(행정직/기술직)

국민건강보험공단 봉투모의고사(요양직)

합격을 위한 준비
서원각 온라인강의

요점만 담은
알짜이론

믿고보는
교수진

www.sojungedu.co.kr

공 무 원	자 격 증	취 업	부사관/장교
9급공무원	건강운동관리사	NCS코레일	육군부사관
9급기술직	관광통역안내사	공사공단 전기일반	육해공군 국사(근현대사)
사회복지직	사회복지사 1급		공군장교 필기시험
운전직	사회조사분석사		
계리직	임상심리사 2급		
	텔레마케팅관리사		
	소방설비기사		